PAUL MARTIN

THE LONDON DIARIES 1975-1979

The High Commissioner for Canada, 1975-79.

(National Archives of Canada/PA-164936)

PAUL MARTIN

THE LONDON DIARIES 1975-1979

Edited and with an introduction by William R. Young

For André
with the best wishes
of Paul Martin
Christmas '88

University of Ottawa Press

Printed and bound in Canada
ISBN 0-7766-0225-X

Canadian Cataloguing in Publication Data

Martin, Paul, 1903-
Paul Martin: The London diaries, 1975-1979

Includes index.
ISBN 0-7766-0225-X

1. Martin, Paul, 1903- . 2. Diplomats — Canada — Biography. 3. Canada — Foreign relations — Great Britain. 4. Great Britain — Foreign relations — Canada. 5. Canada — Politics and government — 1968-1979. 6. Great Britain — Politics and government — 1964-1979. I. Young, William Robert, 1947- II. Title.

FC621.M37A3 1988 327.2′092′4 C88-090390-2
F1034.3.M37A3 1988

Typeset by Reprographic Services, University of Ottawa.
Printed and bound by Friesen Printers, Altona, Manitoba.

UNIVERSITÉ D'OTTAWA
UNIVERSITY OF OTTAWA

Many of the photographs are from the Martin family's collections. The sources of the others are credited in the captions.

To my mother and father,
my brother and sisters, and our grandchildren

Quis est Homo?
Mancipium mortis, transiens viator,
loci hospes.

Alcuin of York

What is man?
The slave of death, the guest of an inn,
a wayfarer passing.

Helen Waddell

Contents

Preface

From New Year's Day 1975 until the end of October 1979, I served as Canada's high commissioner to the United Kingdom. For me, at the age of seventy-two, it was the start of a new career. To be sure, I had maintained an active interest in international affairs throughout my life and have since written about them in my memoirs, *A Very Public Life*. During my student days in the 1920s I sat in the gallery observing the delegates to the League of Nations at their debates. Then, in 1938, during my first term as a member of Parliament, Prime Minister Mackenzie King asked me to serve on the Canadian delegation to the League. In 1945 he appointed me as a delegate to the first assembly of the United Nations and, during the 1950s, I attended the UN several times with Mike Pearson or on my own as chairman of the Canadian delegation. When Pearson became prime minister in 1963, he chose me as his minister of external affairs, and I served in that portfolio until Pierre Trudeau became leader of the Liberal party in 1968. I served in Trudeau's cabinet as leader of the government in the Senate. Late in 1974, Trudeau asked me to see the world from the other end of the telescope and to try my hand at diplomacy as a public servant.

My London odyssey began several months before I arrived in the United Kingdom. On July 8, 1974, Pierre Trudeau won a majority in the general elections and shortly thereafter decided to shuffle his cabinet. On election night, when I spoke to the prime minister over the telephone, I reminded him that, as the Senate leader and the third minister from Essex County, I should not be regarded in the same manner as the other ministers if he wanted to change the regional representation in his cabinet. About a week after the vote, I knew that I would not be returning to Ottawa as a minister. Trudeau asked me if I wanted to become a roving ambassador. When I demurred, knowing full well the limitations of such a role, there was some discussion of my going to Washington. I preferred London.

With great resolve, I set about marking the London appointment as a new phase in my life. As a neophyte ambassador entering uncharted diplomatic seas, I decided to set the time apart by another departure and to begin, systematically, to maintain a daily record. My only other similar attempt to keep a diary had taken place in 1928 as a twenty-five-year-old candidate in a provincial by-election. That diary did not outlast the campaign. But this time would be different and, for nearly five years, I used some of that most scarce of commodities—free time—to record activities, personalities, and issues as I saw them from my new vantage point.

Paul Martin
Windsor

Acknowledgements

The saying that runs "of making many books there is no end" can be proven wrong with the help of friends and associates. The preparation of these diaries for publication is a case in point.

Thanks must begin with the secretaries in London who transcribed the original handwritten notes into typescript. When the time came to prepare this book, Solange Fortin helped with the first draft. From then on, Kevin James was indispensable. He carefully looked after the various editions, performed additional research, and helped to select photographs.

As in the case of my volumes of memoirs, *A Very Public Life*, I am greatly indebted to my editor, Bill Young, without whom it would not have been possible to complete the examination of my diaries from which this publication ensues.

And then there is "the team." This amiable group, which prepared *A Very Public Life* for publication, took on the same task for this book. Pauline Johnston, ostensibly a production manager but also a skilled mixture of martinet and mother, applied the whip and offered the carrot as required. Editorial consultants Mary McDougall Maude and Rosemary Shipton found the solution to cutting what appeared to be uncuttable. In addition, Mary Maude capably shepherded the final manuscript through its various transmogrifications.

Friends provided advice, sympathy, and tea, as well as an occasional stronger beverage. I would like to thank John English, Robert Bothwell, and Jack Granatstein.

Finally, I am grateful to Toivo Roht and the staff of the University of Ottawa Press for making the whole process of publishing this book as painless and efficient as possible.

P.M.

Introduction

When I first met the Honourable Paul Martin, he was the high commissioner to the United Kingdom and I was looking for a job. As it turned out, I took charge of the research for his memoirs, *A Very Public Life*. Because I began this task not long before his retirement from the London post, I was able to visit him there and to witness some of the events that he describes in his diary. At one of the lunches in the imposing house at 12 Upper Brook Street, I sat — below the salt — and listened to the banter among some political and literary figures from Canada and Britain. The guests included the Duke of Westminster, the editor of *The Times*, Lord Amory, Eric Varley, the former minister of energy, and Premier William Davis of Ontario. On another occasion, I visited Canada House and its magnificent high commissioner's office during Mr Martin's regular Thursday "at home" for Canadians in London. In retrospect, this visit was a useful preparation for editing the diary he kept.

As a professional historian and someone privileged to know the author, I found preparing the diaries for publication both a fascinating and a taxing exercise. During the five years that he spent in London, Mr Martin meticulously recorded approximately 150 typed pages every month to provide an incredibly rich tapestry detailing his life and times. The complete diary is now held by the National Archives of Canada and those who have been given access to it know that it will become an invaluable source for the years 1975-79.

The beginning of the diary, both the manuscript and the published version, reflects the uncertainty of a person entering a new career as a diplomat and as a diarist. He was well aware, as he put it, that he "would not be surprised if they wondered about me." This statement reflects not only that he was a "new boy" in London but that he was also a former politician who had moved into a foreign service where career diplomats jealously guard the top spots. But he was moving into the high commissionership in London, the oldest Canadian diplomatic post, where diplomacy and politics have historically shared a place since the first high commissioner, Sir Alexander Galt, was appointed in 1880. Before and after the establishment of a professional diplomatic service, the London post has often been filled by political figures — some serving concurrently in the Canadian cabinet.

Among Canadian high commissioners in recent years, Mr Martin undoubtedly had the longest association with international affairs and the broadest acquaintanceship with its political and bureaucratic practitioners throughout the world. The diary is full of such phrases as "I had last met him when. . .," and the years stretch back to Mr Martin's first sojourn in Britain in 1929-30, as a student at Cambridge University. That year, he and Harold Wilson (prime minister of Britain in 1975) had briefly shared the apartment of a mutual friend in Geneva. During the years prior to the election of Margaret Thatcher, the diary conveys a sense of this "old boys' network" with shared experiences, assumptions, and friendships.

The diary provides some insights into the nature of this group of friends and acquaintances which was slowly disappearing. In 1978, Mr Martin joined former British prime ministers Harold Wilson and Lord Home, as well as Lord Carrington, then Conservative leader in the House of Lords, in a jet taking the Prince of Wales to Australia. The occasion was the funeral of a common acquaintance, Sir Robert Menzies, the wartime and post-war prime minister of that country. They reminisced comfortably on the airplane and the diary gives a sense of long-shared memories and experiences. This camaraderie and common outlook is absent in the accounts of the "new faces" in the British political scene at the time, with foreign secretary David Owen, for example. It hits the reader directly when, during Mr Martin's farewell call, Prime Minister Margaret Thatcher was clearly unaware of his long career.

Despite the bumps and blips and peregrinations common to all such daily accounts, in one sense this diary is a complete entity. Mr Martin arrived in London following the re-election of the Trudeau government in 1974 and stayed until after Joe Clark and the Conservatives gained power in Ottawa in

1979. These years coincided with the final term of the Labour government under the leadership of Harold Wilson and then James Callaghan, who was bested by Margaret Thatcher at the polls. The high commissioner's residence in London seems to have been almost like a hotel for visiting Canadian cabinet ministers and a good restaurant for their British counterparts. Through his frequent contact with Canadian visitors, Mr Martin kept in touch with Canadian political gossip and events. He took his new position as a diplomat at face value and dealt with his former opponents in Parliament in an open and non-partisan way.

At the same time, one salient feature which emerges in the diary is the comfortable nature of the relationship between the Liberal government in Canada and the Labour government in Britain. Although there were doubts about what Britain's ultimate port might be, given the decision in 1975 to continue as a member of the European Community, the relationship between the political and bureaucratic leadership in the two countries is depicted as an easy one based on personal contact and familiarity. Given this, it is hardly surprising that the diaries analyze events and draw continuous parallels. In the economic area there were the problems of inflation and labour troubles which contributed to the defeat of the Liberal and the Labour administrations. In the political arena were the questions of regional autonomy — the devolution of power to Scotland and Wales is compared with the election of the separatist government in Quebec in 1976. Because of the good personal relations which prevailed during the Labour régime, Pierre Trudeau's efforts to patriate the Canadian constitution were much smoother, from the London perspective, than they appeared to be four years later when Margaret Thatcher held a firm grasp on the governance of Britain.

Despite the prevailing good will between the two governments, occasional disputes did flare up. When the British government wanted to move Air Canada from the more central airport, Heathrow, to the more remote, Gatwick, Martin used every possible ploy to fight for the Canadian airline. For him, the battle to stay at Heathrow reflected his overriding concern that Canada not be overlooked in Britain's reorientation towards Europe.

While the diaries convey a sense of completeness in dealing with the life of the political regimes in the two countries, they also show Mr Martin very much thrust *in media res* on various international issues. He went to London during a time when it appeared that the world economy could slide into damaging protectionism. Deep divisions had appeared among western nations as well as between them and the developing countries. Commercial diplomacy was (and is) more than a matter of economics. The protracted economic negotiations that were underway among sovereign states were intensely political and involved domestic interests and issues to an unprecedented degree. In the foreground, the major powers were jockeying for position in a reshaped global economy. Behind the scenes, the explosion of non-tariff barriers meant that a huge number of government policies in almost one hundred countries might be up for negotiation.

No one involved in diplomacy or international politics during the late 1970s could have avoided these issues and, as high commissioner to the United Kingdom, Mr Martin was at the centre of some and connected to them all. Throughout, his aim was to advance Canada's interests in the forum available to him. He picked up the reins in London when Canada had begun to negotiate a formal connection with the European Community, the "contractual link." This was the Trudeau government's response to the formation of international trading blocs and was designed to avoid isolation and to encourage diversification so that Canada would not remain as dependent on the United States. Mr Martin contributed to the achievement of the contractual link by lobbying the British government. But he left London before this effort had failed as a vehicle for significant change in Canadian relations with the European Community.

During those confusing years, the diaries constantly assess Canada's position in the context of the relations between the rich nations of the west and the poorer countries struggling to raise the living standards of their people. The oil crisis of October 1973, when oil prices quadrupled, had startled the developed nations which, for the first time, experienced a situation where decisions, vital to their welfare, were being taken by countries which had been perceived as economic vassals.

The major western industrialized countries reacted by organizing the first economic summit in 1975 to co-ordinate a response to economic problems, particularly inflation. President Giscard d'Estaing of France excluded Trudeau from the invitation to six other western leaders to attend this initial meeting at Rambouillet. Mr Martin took Canada's exclusion very personally and presents it in his diaries as an extension of the Gaullists' disdain for Canada which caused him so much trouble in the late 1960s, when he was minister of external affairs. Zealously, he tried to convince the British government to do a little arm-twisting to reverse the French decision.

Although the economic summits are the most dramatic of events, Mr Martin also played a quiet role, as head of a diplomatic mission, in promoting Canada's position in the multilateral trade negotiations. These talks, known as the Tokyo Round, began in 1978 when ministers representing the member nations of the General Agreement on Tariffs and Trade (GATT) decided to discuss reforms to the international trading system. When Mr Martin left London, the process of consultations among the various competing economic interests throughout the world continued, as they still continue.

The conundrums of economic change also affected the nature of the Commonwealth organization and its place in the political and economic scene. As the seat of the Commonwealth, London provided a unique listening post and liaison station of international importance. The diaries constantly reflect the assessment of Canada's position in the organization and the multilateral nature of relations among the members, particularly the developed countries or "old Commonwealth" and the economically underdeveloped members. To express their dissatisfaction with the development policies of the industrialized countries, the latter group had supported the call for a special session of the United Nations General Assembly in 1974. The program adopted at this session, the New International Economic Order, was designed to eradicate international inequalities. A series of international conferences took place during the late 1970s which attempted to work out solutions to development problems. One of these, to set up a common fund to stabilize prices of commodities produced by the lesser developed members of the Commonwealth, took place in London in 1979, with Paul Martin as the Canadian representative. For him, this was a prickly meeting; he was all too aware of the gap between the rhetoric and the actions of the Trudeau administration. While the Canadian government publicly supported reforms that would benefit lesser developed countries, Martin received instructions — which he disapproved — to delay.

The most intractable problem which faced the Commonwealth during Paul Martin's high commissionership was the future of southern African states, Angola, South Africa, and, in particular, Zimbabwe-Rhodesia. The struggle of the blacks to gain majority rule and the stubborn efforts of the white government led by Ian Smith to torpedo progress remain a constant subject for discussion in the diaries. In many ways, the book treats this issue as a case study of events and negotiations.

Paul Martin was involved in the constitutional negotiations in London in 1979 which led to black majority rule and internationally recognized independence in 1980. This agreement concluded the long armed struggle against the white minority regime of Ian Smith which had unilaterally declared independence (UDI) from Britain in 1965. For the next fifteen years, the Commonwealth teetered on the verge of an irreconcilable split as the various member states sought to resolve the differences among the white Rhodesians, the black nationalists, and the British government. Despite pressure from the black states of the Commonwealth, Britain refused to use force against Rhodesia. Instead, after UDI, the British persuaded the United Nations to impose voluntary, later compulsory, economic sanctions. Although the British, aided by the Americans, attempted to negotiate a settlement, it was the revived and united guerrilla operations based in Zambia and newly independent Mozambique which turned the balance.

The fierce fighting in an unwinnable war led South Africa to press Smith to reach a settlement. The black nationalist leaders, Joshua Nkomo and Robert Mugabe, in turn, were urged to the bargaining table by the leaders of the surrounding black governments — the front-line states — which also suffered economic hardships as a result of the conflict. In his final effort to avoid turning the government over to the guerrilla leaders, Smith agreed to an "internal settlement" in

1979 with the moderate blacks, led by Bishop Abel Muzorewa. Although elections were held on the basis of this agreement, it left the foundations of white rule untouched, and the guerrilla struggle continued. Finally, in September 1979, at the Lancaster House Conference observed by Paul Martin, Ian Smith agreed to a new constitution which led to the triumph of Robert Mugabe in elections the following year.

The manner in which the diary recounts the ebb and flow of international events demonstrates Mr Martin's great interest in the world around him and reflects his long determination to be a world statesman. Where other diplomats might stick to their task of promoting bilateral relations between countries, Mr Martin always took a larger interest, which was aided and abetted by his vast range of contacts. On the problems in Cyprus, for example, he could call upon an acquaintanceship with the island's president, Spyros Kyprianou, dating from 1964 when Martin had arranged for Canadians to go to Cyprus as UN peace-keepers.

Characteristically, Mr Martin directed all his energies to his new assignment. He presided over the largest Canadian mission, with a staff of more than 500 drawn from many Ottawa departments and scattered in offices and consulates across the United Kingdom. In his first days on the job, he proceeded, as he had as a cabinet minister, to make the rounds and to greet those who would fall under his authority. He then moved on, in ever-widening circles, to "show the flag" in the offices of British ministers and bureaucrats, in towns, in universities, and in every conceivable organization throughout Britain. For Mr Martin, the high commissioner's task is not only to meet with the "movers and shakers" and to report to Canada on current political developments which affect bilateral relations. It is also to find out what "makes a nation tick" and to serve as a conduit, in both directions, for any information that might promote understanding.

The diary tells much about the fabric of British society—from the point of view of a person greatly appreciative of the legacy of British institutions. Throughout his five years in London, he was wined and dined by royalty, aristocrats, ecclesiastics, and politicians. But his own lunches and dinners were not just with political figures but with anyone he thought might be an interesting dinner companion: authors C.P. Snow and Iris Murdoch, trade unionist Jack Jones, and astronomer Bernard Lovell. And then there were the daily swims in the neighbour's pool, the regular walks and chats with whoever happened by—schoolboys, cleaners, butlers, businessmen, and cooks. A weekly entry detailed the various trips to the bookstores—Hatchard's or Foyle's on Saturday, and the Westminster Cathedral shop after mass. The resulting purchases were not mere decorations for a bookshelf, for the diary chronicles the almost daily analysis of a book of current interest, usually philosophy, biography, or international affairs. British academics and universities continue to fascinate Mr Martin, and Cambridge remains a touchstone for all he values in academic life. One of his greatest pleasures is his achievement in promoting the establishment of the Canadian Institute for Advanced Legal Studies. This symposium brings judges, legal scholars, and lawyers to Cambridge for a period of lectures and reflection.

Finally, and perhaps more importantly, the diaries show something of the personal life and feelings of a very complex individual. They reveal the pride of accomplishment, the insecurity about the past and for the future, the desire to be known as a person who has performed well. And the diaries are the story of a family and a marriage that provided Paul Martin with the private support he needed to live his public life. His wife Nell was always there to keep life on track and his feet on the ground. With the vivacious and direct style for which she is known, Mrs Martin set about putting her own independent stamp on her life in London.

In preparing the diaries for publication, I have tried to retain the flavour of the original 9000 pages. The editing aimed to keep enough background so that events could be understood as they occurred. Naturally, there is an emphasis on entries which would be of interest to a Canadian reader. Purely British events have been pruned back, as have international issues which are tangential to the main themes of the book. Although many routine activities, social occasions, and discussions of reading have been edited out of the published book, enough remains to demonstrate the broad range of interests and contacts which Paul Martin maintained during his years in London.

I have tried to avoid undue interference with the text, while ensuring that references are adequately explained. In order not to disturb the flow of events, introductions to the chapters have been prepared in the first person. Punctuation and spelling have been tidied up and a list of characters has been prepared to help readers cope with the hundreds of people whose names appear. Individuals identified by an asterisk are included in this list, which is found at the end of the diaries. Annotations have been kept to a minimum and are found either as interjections in square brackets or as footnotes.

William R. Young
Ottawa

I

January – February 1975

When I arrived in London, the British political situation rested in a precarious balance. The country had given Harold Wilson and the Labour party a majority of three on October 10, 1974. But that party had split over the question of continuing British membership in the Common Market and Wilson's hold on power was teetering. Although the country had only joined the European Community in 1973, the Labour party platform was committed to a renegotiation of the terms of entry. In the October election campaign, Labour had promised a referendum to decide the question of British membership and until that vote, the first referendum in Britain's history, which took place on June 5, 1975, the subject formed a major element in my discussions with British officials.

Thursday, January 2, 1975

I made my first calls today on the Permanent Under-Secretary of State and head of the diplomatic service, Sir Thomas Brimelow.* Our talk was pretty general, more social in character than anything else. It was otherwise with John Killick, the Deputy Under-Secretary of State, who had with him Lord Nicholas Gordon Lennox, Head of the North American Department. We talked about what the government will do about the Common Market. . . . What will be the timetable? Am I going to see Harold Wilson?* I will likely know more than they [the bureaucrats] know of what ministers' intentions are. Anthony Wedgwood Benn* only this morning in a letter to his constituents blasted British participation. Killick said something like this — "If you could find out what various ministers really think, this would be most helpful." . . . Of course, it would be highly improper for me, if I do obtain this information, to report it to anyone other than the Canadian government. Sir John perhaps, as he made the request, had his tongue in his cheek and a glow in his eyes. . . .

It was great seeing Burgon Bickersteth,[1] but I found him much changed even though still active. He is very bent but at eighty-seven his memory is colossal. . . .

I mentioned to Burgon that the retiring Archbishop of Canterbury[2] was a contemporary of mine at Trinity College, but he looked so much older, and in fact was older than I [if by only a year]. Burgon then told me something very interesting. Most of those who were making private recommendations from the Anglican Church had recommended another personality other than the new Archbishop.[3] It was the Queen herself who made the decision that Coggan should be appointed. He [Bickersteth] told me this, of course, in the strictest confidence, observing that perhaps there might have been a constitutional breach by the Queen. I don't see how this could be the case unless the advice of the Prime Minister in such a matter is to be taken.

This recalls my talk with George VI [in 1945] during the early days of the United Nations meetings here in London when the monarch asked me what I thought of Ernest Bevin's performance in the Security Council in his debates with Vishynsky.[4] In reply, I said that Bevin was proving to be quite an adversary. The King then said, "and to think that they wanted him to be Chancellor of the Exchequer. Good as he would be at that job, I insisted that he should become Foreign Minister." Somewhere I have read that Attlee[5] acknowledged the King having suggested Bevin's name for the Foreign Office. The King, however, in his talk with me went further

1. My friend from student days and the former warden of Hart House at the University of Toronto.
2. Michael Ramsey, archbishop from 1961 to 1974.
3. Donald Coggan, who succeeded Ramsey.
4. Bevin was British foreign secretary and Andrei Vishynsky, sometime Soviet foreign minister, was head of the USSR delegation to the United Nations.
5. Clement Attlee, the Labour prime minister in the immediate post-war years.

and said that he had insisted. I have often thought that here was a constitutional breach. . . .

Tuesday, January 7, 1975

I called on . . . Roy Hattersley* [who] is in charge of economic matters at the Foreign Office. I was very impressed with him. It is understandable why he should be marked for promotion. I took advantage of my initial fifteen-minute talk to put a query or two on Common Market problems. "How did he see the timetable from now on?" In reply, he said the government was anxious to have the whole matter out of the way by summer. The aim would be proceeded with almost at once with legislation providing for the referendum. This would be even before the discussions in the Community terminated and before the government had taken any formal decision [about continued British membership]. I queried him about this—"How could the government introduce legislation when it had not committed itself to the principle of the proposed enactment?" The government had committed itself to the principle of a referendum, he said. What the government had not done was to state publicly whether or not it would recommend acceptance of the results of the Common Market renegotiations. He implied, of course, that he fully expected the renegotiations to be accepted by the government and that to proceed with legislation on the referendum forthwith meant a saving of time in order to get the whole matter out of the way by summer. . . . His only caveat was that this whole programme of action would be decided by the Prime Minister, the Foreign Minister, Jim Callaghan* and Roy Jenkins.* . . .

At 5:00 p.m. I paid my first call on the Prime Minister who was very warm in his welcome. I thanked him for seeing me so early and for passing on his approval of my designation last August so quickly. "How could I do anything else; we have known each other so long and so well. . . ."

Wilson made it clear he wanted the Common Market matter to be settled by the end of June or thereabouts. I then asked him, that being the case, would it not be necessary to seek some short-cuts or resort to parliamentary procedures to avoid the delays that undoubtedly would result from an extended debate in Parliament, both in the House of Commons and in the House of Lords. For instance, did he have in mind presenting any legislation at once to establish the right of referendum? He said "Well, this is a matter which I will be taking up with some of my colleagues at the beginning of next week, as soon as Jim [Callaghan] returns from Africa." . . .

I then mentioned the letter which Wedgwood Benn had sent to his constituents, [which] . . . vigorously opposed acceptance of any proposal following renegotiation that would keep Britain in the Common Market. Wedgwood Benn's letter was to be contrasted with the condemnation of the letter by Hattersley. "Was this not a serious matter?" I asked—two ministers taking a different position publicly on matters of government policy. The Prime Minister recognized that, of course, this was a problem. "Maybe this situation is more unique. Remember, this is a matter on which some of the cabinet members feel very strongly and have so felt for a long time. . . ." He was toying with the idea, he said, of allowing this kind of freedom of discussion among cabinet members. "I am on a difficult wicket; the party is very much divided on this question and I have to do a lot of manoeuvring." One thing in all this is clear in my mind—he will want to stay in the Market and he will recommend a favourable vote on the referendum. . . .

The first interview lasted forty minutes and I was pleased with it. . . .

Thursday, January 9, 1975

When I first knew the High Commission in London, as a student[6] and much later as minister, the operation was centred entirely in Canada House at Trafalgar Square, almost the centre of the world! To accommodate the larger personnel, a new building had to be found and the staff for the most part are now lodged in the Sir John A. Macdonald building in Grosvenor Square, not far from the American Embassy.

Today, I spent the full day in the office at Canada House. I have decided to come here every Thursday and . . . use part of the morning to circulate among visitors who come to

6. I went to Cambridge in 1929-30.

Canada House. . . . This must not interfere with my main job which, as I see it, is essentially contribution to policy. . . .

Sunday, January 12, 1975

Mitch[7] is here as head of the Canadian parliamentary delegation looking into British parliamentary practice and procedures. . . . I was a little surprised that Mitchell expressed some doubt as to his successor's role. I had always felt that Mitch was a great admirer of Allan.[8] I think Allan will do well because he is able. . . . I am not particularly impressed by those who say he has had no experience in foreign affairs. . . .

The fact is that whoever is appointed to any job will always have his detractors. Allan became Secretary of State for External Affairs in succession to Mitchell Sharp because he wanted the job. He came into my office one day and he said, "What are you going to do?—I know damn well what I am going to do, I am going to demand that I become foreign minister." Allan's record as Leader of the House during the period of minority government [from 1972 to 1974] was brilliant. Trudeau* owed him a great deal and so did the Liberal party. He had a strong claim for services rendered and he was firm in his demand. This does not mean to say that he went ahead without considering Sharp. He was going to be moved in any event, not because Trudeau thought he didn't do well, but because he was confirmed in the view that those ministers who had been in posts for five or six years ought for the most part to be transferred to other departments. . . .

Tuesday, January 14, 1975

My day concluded with attendance at the House of Commons Speaker's reception. I had not seen Selwyn Lloyd* for fifteen years, as he reminded me. We first met at the United Nations twenty-three years ago. I am told he is a good Speaker. It is something unique for one who has been a Minister of State, Chancellor of the Exchequer and Foreign Secretary to end

7. Mitchell Sharp*
8. Allan MacEachen*

up as Speaker of the House. I am not so sure that I would have wanted to do this. Trudeau twice wanted me to take on the speakership of the Senate. I just could not see myself in this role. . . .

Wednesday, January 15, 1975

My first call on the Foreign Secretary, Jim Callaghan, was pleasant and substantial. As I would have expected, his welcome was very warm indeed. . . .[9] He had seen me in the gallery — had I got his wave? . . . He told me in the strictest confidence that Muller,[10] the South African Foreign Minister, was coming to London next week [on] his first visit since the withdrawal of South Africa from the Commonwealth, and it reflects Vorster's[11] determination to find a solution to the Rhodesian question, but as Jim said, "How can he urge [black] majority rule in Rhodesia and not get it in South Africa?" The foreign minister thought the settlement would take some time to achieve, but there was no denying the unfolding of clear-cut and obvious results in Africa with consequences for Rhodesia and South Africa itself. . . .

I told Callaghan that . . . from his reference in the House of Commons statement . . . I greatly appreciated he had disclosed his real view about British participation in the Common Market. "There really can be no doubt about this," he said. . . . He went further than the Prime Minister in the matter of legislation being introduced early on . . . for the holding of the referendum. Time had to be saved, the matter had to be totally resolved before the middle of the summer.

On the divisions in the cabinet, he acknowledged that this was a problem, but perhaps the question itself was unique and permitted an extraordinary procedure. The real fact is that the question of cabinet solidarity is not a matter of law, but of custom and tradition. If cabinet freedom of expression outside were to become the rule, the cabinet would not last very [long]. . . . I am quite satisfied from my talks with Hattersley, the Prime Minister, and now Jim Callaghan, that the

9. We had last met at NATO meetings in June 1974.
10. Hilgard Muller
11. Johannes Vorster,* the prime minister of South Africa.

dominant and leadership element in the cabinet have made up their mind that Britain will stay in. I find it hard to conceive that the public would not accept the government's recommendation to vote "yes."

Thursday, January 16, 1975

A call from Mrs. Belle Shenkman who is engaged in some useful activities here on behalf of Canada revealed that I would have further obligations in connection with the visit of the National Ballet of Canada. I do not want to get overly involved in this but I cannot discourage her Herculean efforts. The immediate problem is to get a Royal Patron or Patroness, the Queen Mother, the Prince of Wales, the Princess Anne all being engaged on the concerned dates. I have written to the Princess Margaret asking her to lend her patronage. If she cannot come, we will try the Duchess of Gloucester and so on. . . .

Martin O'Connell came to lunch. . . . He told Nell and me he was quite disappointed that he was not brought back into the cabinet.[12] I think he was hurt that the Prime Minister had not at least called him to explain why, or to point out his difficulties in cabinet-making. Martin has no animus in the matter but an understandable feeling such as I often have. I remember telling Trudeau on one occasion how important it was to recognize human reactions. The Prime Minister is a kind man. He has not had the opportunity of fully knowing what want means nor, I suspect, has he had many disappointments. His political advancement has been quick and easy. . . .

Sunday, January 19, 1975

We went to 9:00 o'clock Mass at Westminster Cathedral. This byzantine structure has not been a favourite of mine. However, its more finished state, particularly of marble throughout, makes it more cheerful and better. . . .

12. He had served as minister of state from August 12, 1971, to January 12, 1972, and then minister of labour until his defeat in the 1972 general election. He was re-elected to the House on July 8, 1974.

Tuesday, January 21, 1975

We called on Her Majesty, the Queen, at 11:40 this a.m. Nell was a little nervous on our way there but I was bolder. However, as it turned out, Nell seemed during the interview to be more composed than I. . . .

The Queen greeted us with a warm smile and at once made us feel very much at home. Several times, however, I was tongue-tied. Nell was eloquent and fluent throughout. The Queen asked us how long we had been here and then said almost at once: "You have a very nice house" (on Upper Brook Street). Nell told her of our plans for new paintings, prints and rugs. This seemed to greatly interest the Queen who said that, after all, every new occupant of a Commission should seek to have things as they wished and also to reflect their interests and personality. . . .

The Queen mentioned that shortly she would be going to Jamaica to open the Commonwealth Prime Ministers' Conference. . . . From Jamaica she and the Duke of Edinburgh would be going to Japan for their first official visit and their first sight of Hong Kong. . . . Of course, she would be seeing Emperor [Hirohito]. This would be a return visit for his visit to England a year ago. One felt that the Queen might echo what more than one person has said, that the Emperor, poor man, was "very hard to talk to. . . ." It has been said: "You cannot be God one moment and an agreeable, approachable person the next. . . ."

It was a pleasant visit. I was very proud at the way my wife handled the situation. I have a feeling that queens judge husbands by their wives. I am sure that I have been well judged.

I got a kick out of the fact that my morning coat and my silk hat had constituted my wedding apparel some thirty-eight years ago. . . . I must, nevertheless, lose ten pounds . . . .

Wednesday, January 22, 1975

My views of the monarchy are moderate. I would have difficulty perhaps in an expression of full support if the monarch were not in my judgment a good person. . . . I laugh when I recall what I told her on Tuesday to the effect that the first time I met her at the Palace in 1946 she was a young girl of seventeen [and] she said to me when we were introduced—"Now don't tell us anything about the Mounted Police, we know all about them." . . .

Thursday, January 23, 1975

It is better, I think, when one has time, to go to the House of Commons and listen to important statements rather than to rely merely on the text of what is said. So this afternoon, I went . . . to hear the Prime Minister's report on the procedures to be taken in connection with British participation or non-participation in the [Common] Market. . . .

I think there was a little ambiguity in Wilson's statement. . . . He is hemmed in, he has a difficult cabinet and, if he is going to achieve the objective of keeping Britain in the Market, he has got to do a lot of mountain skipping. . . .

Monday, January 27, 1975

On Friday, I met with Denis Healey and then followed this on Monday by a meeting with Michael Foot.* At first Foot did not remember our earlier meeting in the mid 1950s.*[13]

I found him a little tense. Perhaps this is due to his dedication and great industry but once he got going, his resonant voice took on the eloquence for which he is noted. "What was the state of the social contract?[14] What changes did he contemplate?" With these questions I introduced the subject primarily on my mind for on him reposed the responsibility for the smooth operation of the social contract. Of course, he said, the social contract was not statutory. . . . I told Michael Foot that I thought the concept of social contract was good, particularly if it were left on the basis of consensus. There is no such arrangement in Canada. It is a matter of dog eat dog. . . . I must send something to Ottawa about this. The idea would appeal to Trudeau, I think . . . .

13. This is described in the entry for March 28, 1976.
14. The social contract was the phrase that was used to describe the relationship between the unions and the Labour government. Although it was never defined, it came to mean the informal agreement between the government and the union movement to regulate prices and incomes.

Michael Foot . . . dedicated and able as he is . . . does not seem to have the tranquillity of mind of the Prime Minister, Jim Callaghan or Denis Healey. . . .

On the Common Market, he clearly indicated his opposition to it—certainly [to] British participation. What really disturbs Foot and some others is the loss of sovereignty and he brushed aside my suggestion that the veto given to ministers in the council really took care of this theoretical objection. . . .

Before lunch, André and I went to see Madame Tussaud's.[15] This was certainly not a visit of curiosity. It was in pursuance of duty. When I saw the Trudeau figure, I agreed with Ivan Head* that it was not a good likeness, but as I later told Ivan on the telephone, there are not very many good likenesses outside of Henry Moore, Picasso and perhaps Tubman of Liberia. . . . So my judgment, as reported to Ottawa, was that Trudeau would be unwise to sit [for a replacement]. . . . Both Diefenbaker* and Mike,[16] I found, are no longer on public showing. They have been put into the barn along with other greats of the past. . . .

Tuesday, January 28, 1975

I had a good meeting with Ted Heath* this morning. Although deeply engaged in battle for continued leadership of the Opposition and his party, Heath generously received me in his inadequate facilities. . . . The Leader of the Opposition himself has no office and uses that designated for the shadow cabinet in the Opposition. His personal staff clutter about, seemingly always in a standing position in a small outer office. He is confident, but Mrs. Thatcher* is making quite a bid [to dislodge him as Conservative leader]. He, himself, was the first leader of the Conservative party to be elected [by the MPs]. Alec Home* had been called on by the Queen after Harold Macmillan* had summarized for her what he regarded as party opinion. Rab Butler,* of course, was not very pleased as he has several times told me. . . .

15. André Bissonnette,* the deputy high commissioner, and I had to visit the famous wax museum.
16. Lester B. Pearson*

The Leader of the Opposition thinks that the electorate's verdict on the [Common Market] referendum will be favourable and he will certainly work hard towards that end. He will point out the consequences of rejection . . . [and] the confusion that would result. If Prime Minister Wilson had faced up to the matter in the first instance, he would not have had the trouble he is facing with dissident ministers and there would be no occasion for the tactic of referendum. . . .

I was amazed at the frank way in which Ronald Spiers, the U.S. Counsellor, discussed Kissinger* with me. Kissinger will not last, he said. He has proceeded seemingly relaxed in his solo performance but my American friend said this he cannot do for very long. The State Department is disorganized and unhappy—it needs someone at the helm and direction is not being given by the man whose forays in the Middle East . . . China and the Soviet Union have taken him away. . . .

Thursday, January 30, 1975

Nell and I went to a ballet reception, the forerunner of the big event in a month's time, to meet the guest of honour, Dame Margot Fonteyn.[17] The reception was at the home of W. G. Buchanan, the representative of the CNR. On our way up in the lift, a very pleasant woman of about forty-five years of age joined us. I introduced my wife and myself and . . . I said, "and who are you?" Nell, of course, informed me, as I should have known, that this was Dame Margot Fonteyn herself. I am afraid, while I was not rude, I may have seemed abrupt. . . . When I got home my wife expressed her opinion quite strongly. . . .

Monday, February 3, 1975

As I was going in to see the minister of energy, Eric Varley . . .

a young, bright Englishman came up and shook hands with me. I did not know exactly who he was at first. "We have met several times in Canada and I know you," he said. He fully expected that I would say in return "and I know you." It was James Cross who is now on the Coal Board. He had been

17. The famous ballerina.

kidnapped by the FLQ in 1970. . . . We talked about it. I asked him jocularly, "Do you ever see your friends who are now in France having tired of Cuba?" "The matter is up to you," said Cross, to which I replied that they apparently could not be extradited from France. . . .

As we sat in Varley's outer office waiting to see the minister, Cross said if we had not acted in Canada there is no doubt what would have happened to him. They would have dumped him into the St. Lawrence. They really wanted to kidnap the American consul but he was out of town. . . .

Tuesday, February 4, 1975

The thing that stands out in all of these ministerial calls is how generous the ministers are with their time and their prompt acceptances of an offer to see them. This is in contrast with the situation at home, where most Canadian ministers take a long time before they see an ambassador and act as though it was a favour that they were granting. . . .

I learned that Ted Heath was second to Mrs. Thatcher in the race for the Conservative leadership. She has eleven votes ahead of him. He will have a hard time catching up—I feel sorry for him. I cannot help but recall my own disappointments in the leadership races, but that is life and some would say, all for the best. Pearson was a good Prime Minister and I had the greatest love for him, but I am still not convinced that I could not have done a better job. . . .

Wednesday, February 5, 1975

Today was the first Canada/United Kingdom Chamber of Commerce luncheon since I arrived. It was held at the Dorchester Hotel [and] . . . I was duly welcomed as the new Honorary President of the Club and as the new Canadian High Commissioner in London. Everyone was kind. I haven't quite got used to the title "Your Excellency" and I don't altogether sit comfortably when it is pronounced.

Wedgwood Benn, the Minister of Industry . . . spoke of the need for a growing participation between industry and the state in the ownership and operation of industry. Such a partnership was inevitable when the confrontation between labour and management had reached a stand-still. . . . It must involve knowledge of and participation in the planning process. . . . It was a very effective performance and philosophically one to which I am not altogether opposed. . . .

He was thanked by the European Manager of the Bank of Montreal. Normally a vote of thanks is perfunctory and formal in character. Not so this time. The bank official, with free enterprise oozing out of his ears and nostrils and eyes, spoke almost as long as Benn, attacking the latter's thesis. Undoubtedly, his ideas were those of the audience. . . .

Malcolm MacDonald* called on me just before tea-time. We are old friends. . . . Malcolm [son of Ramsay MacDonald, first Labour Prime Minister] was an active member of the Chamberlain and . . . the Churchill governments. . . . Later, he became High Commissioner in Canada during the war when, I think, Winston tired of him. Unjustly so. Malcolm was a first-rate High Commissioner, alive and full of vigour. . . . [Mackenzie] King* once told me that he deliberately went out of his way to speak highly of Malcolm in Churchill's presence so as to let the great war leader know what a valuable asset he had in Canada. . . . I regard . . . Malcolm MacDonald as among Britain's best ambassadors. . . . I may be wrong, but I thought he looked older this time than ever and shorter too. . . .

I went to bed a little tired but happy, wondering what the people back home thought. I am now away from the centre of power—no longer part of it, and yet, when I look back on my talks with the Prime Minister here and others, perhaps I can do as much, if not more, than I think for Canada and for the international community.

Thursday, February 6, 1975

Jeremy Thorpe,* the Liberal Leader, is always a pleasant and agreeable man to visit. When I called on him this morning at his office, he was in good form and, although a delegation from the Western European Union was outside his office in the corridor waiting for him even before I arrived, he kept me almost three-quarters of an hour. . . .

We attended our first Maple Leaf Ball in our present capacity and welcomed some five hundred guests with whom we sat down at dinner. However, we did not stay for the dance. I was going to have a heavy day tomorrow and thought I had better get to bed early. . . .

Friday, February 7, 1975

At noon I made my first call on the French Ambassador whom I knew well during my time as External Affairs Minister. Jacques de la Rue, Baron de Beaumarchais, is the descendant of the nineteenth-century playwright. After a period in Moscow, he returned to Paris where he was Couve de Murville*'s director of cabinet. "For me, you will always be Monsieur le Ministre," he said in greeting me, "and I am so happy to see you here."

I asked him point-blank if France wants the United Kingdom in the [European] Community. His answer was "Yes." He agreed, without saying so, with what Heath told me: that it would be a heavy responsibility for the British people . . . to refuse to continue in the Market. Now that the United Kingdom was in, the consequences for Europe would be bad if the British did not stay in. [It] would depend on whether or not the cabinet under Wilson recommended staying in. . . .

"What about you?" de Beaumarchais asked, "does Canada really want Britain in?" My answer was "Yes." We think it will be good for Britain and it will be good for the Common Market, good for Europe and good for international collaboration. I said I thought it was really difficult to assess in a mathematical way the economic advantages one way or the other. The political argument was an overwhelming one. . . . In the short term there are disadvantages, but there are great advantages, particularly for a country like Canada who wishes to diversify its trade interests and patterns. The United States is our main market but we don't want to rely only on that market. . . .

The preparatory meeting that the French would call shortly regarding oil and gas would be confined to two items, the agenda and who should be invited to the full conference later on.[18] It was, therefore, desirable that [attendance at] the preparatory meeting be limited. I told him what we had been saying elsewhere. Canada thought it might be helpful if she were to be at the preparatory meeting. He recognized that Canada had strong claims and I was reminded, as he men-

18. This meeting prepared the way for the first Economic Summit held at Rambouillet, November 15-17, 1975.

tioned other countries too, of Mackenzie King's story involving the bride who told her bridegroom that the latter's parents were not to be invited to the wedding ceremony because the line had to be drawn somewhere. There is no doubt that the French think the responsibility of acting as hosts and conveners of the preparatory meeting is theirs. . . .

Monday, February 10, 1975

My 11:00 o'clock appointment with the Minister of Industry, Anthony Wedgwood Benn, warranted careful preparation. . . . I had been greatly impressed by Benn's capacity when he spoke to the Canada/United Kingdom Association on Friday last. Benn could easily emerge as the leader of the social revolution in modern England. . . . Wedgwood Benn greeted me warmly and made me feel instantly at home. . . . [His] main objection to continuation in the Market is on the ground of sovereignty. To stay in the Market means that Britain and her parliamentary democracy will be seriously eroded. . . . All the way through our talk I was very impressed with his logical and brilliant mind and his tremendous capacity for articulation, but there was not much in the Market that satisfied him. . . .

The main feature of my discussion with the Minister of Industry had to do with the participation of government in industry as demonstrated in [his own] Industry Bill. Of course, the Labour party has for many years been committed to public ownership of industry. Since the election, they have been committed to joint planning with individual large companies. . . . There is to be a national enterprise board capable of buying into private companies. . . . When I asked him if he intended to use the board to acquire a state interest in a wide range of companies or merely help companies in trouble, he reminded me of the overall plan of the government towards nationalization. While the approach may be pragmatic, Benn clearly intends that this measure will be the basis for the establishment of the socialist state. . . .

He said to me, "You know, you are the only High Commissioner who has ever come to discuss these problems with me and I am greatly pleased and flattered." He walked with me down four flights of stairs to my car on the street, obviously pleased with his interview. I was certainly impressed with him. . . .

Wednesday, February 12, 1975

I had lunch with the owners of The Times, *Roy Thomson (Lord Thomson of Fleet) and his son Ken.*

Roy and I joshed one another about the government, which I serve, and its Prime Minister. I defended Trudeau to the hilt. Roy, like so many English-speaking Canadians, does not understand the full nature of the Canadian family. The French factor is not as pleasing to them as it should be. I suspect some of his criticisms of the Prime Minister arose over the legitimate drive to establish bilingualism in Canada. . . . There is another reason for his dislike of the Liberal administration and that is, he is a Tory, having run at one time as a Tory candidate. He recalled how I had sought to dissuade him from making a venture which he now admits was unwise, but he did hold it against Pearson that he had lost his citizenship when he became a member of the House of Lords. Several times I had told him that this criticism of Mike was unjust. "Criticize me if you will," I said. "The reason you have lost your citizenship [if you did] is because of a provision in the Citizenship Act which I introduced when I was Secretary of State."[19] Nevertheless, Roy never seemed to hold this against me as much as he did against Mike. . . .

Tuesday, February 18, 1975

Allen Lambert . . . of the Toronto-Dominion Bank[20] invited me to luncheon in the city at their London offices. . . . This was a pretty high-powered group. What its members had to say about Prime Minister Wilson, Wedgwood Benn and the government generally revealed the lack of respect for and confidence in the government. In Canada, businessmen very frequently take issue with the government but the hostility at home is nothing compared with the hostility here. . . .

19. This act was passed in 1946; see my *A Very Public Life*, I, pp. 445-53.
20. He was chairman of the board.

Wednesday, February 19, 1975

I had a good chat with [Merlyn Rees*] the Secretary of State for Northern Ireland. The Secretary believes that there is a long way to go yet before there will be a final settlement and peace. The strong Orange extremist groups are at the core of the problem, and are largely responsible for it, he seemed to suggest. To my surprise, he told me that the South, while it may talk against partition, would not have Ulster as part of its State at the present time. . . .

Saturday, February 22, 1975

Nell and I met Otto and Adrian Lang* at Gatwick on their return from a law conference in Lagos. . . . The Langs are staying with us. Adrian thinks that Donald Macdonald* should be the next leader [of the Liberal party]. Certainly, I have a very high regard for Donald. Otto would like to be minister of finance and he would make a good one. Apparently there is some talk in Ottawa that John Turner* may seek to follow Bob McNamara[21] at the World Bank. This I doubt. The Americans are not likely ever to agree, certainly in the present circumstances, that the head of the bank should be anyone other than an American.

Thursday, February 27, 1975

The afternoon was spent at the residence where I worked quietly and had a good snooze prior to our dinner for Charles and Sylvia Ritchie.* The Smiths,* the Bissonnettes and the Buchanans were others who kindly accepted our invitation. The whole idea was Nell's—it was a great success and she deserves the credit. We had a lot of fun, particularly at dinner. I had found a photograph in one of the drawers of a cabinet in the main drawing room. Herein are memorialized Vincent Massey,* Charles Ritchie, George Ignatieff* and others of the Commission staff in Vincent Massey's day [in the 1930s]. Charles and Vincent are looking intently at one another. Their

21. Robert McNamara, former secretary of defence during John Kennedy and Lyndon Johnson's administrations, was president of the World Bank.

confrontation of each other was not allowed to go unrelated to comments that were being made in a jocular way about Charles' interesting diary entitled *The Siren Years*. Ritchie is really good fun and he talks a good deal of keeping so well. . . .

II

March – April 1975

ALLAN MACEACHEN AND PIERRE TRUDEAU both came to London to pursue Canada's objective of a connection with the European Community — the so-called "contractual link." The government wanted to diversify its relations and to establish alternative connections to our American ties. It was part of Trudeau's prime ministerial diplomacy initiative. Such visits inevitably take their toll on the head of a diplomatic mission who must wine and dine — as well as make arrangements and attend the meetings.

Once Trudeau had left, our social activities and work took on a more "normal" aspect — if a night at Windsor Castle can fit into this category.

Sunday, March 2, 1975

Allan MacEachen, my minister and colleague of many years in the House of Commons . . . arrived on time at Heathrow Airport tonight. He was . . . in a high mood, prompted, I have no doubt, by the generous flow of the sacred liquor. . . . Allan spent an hour or so with me at the residence, bringing me up to date on the state of things in Canada, the goings on in Parliament and, more particularly, the troubles of the cabinet. The long absence of the Prime Minister on his present European tour does create some political problems at home.[1] This, I suppose, is always the case. My view is that the overall result of visits to Holland, Germany, Italy, the United Kingdom and Ireland will inure to the benefit of Canada and

1. In late February, Trudeau had come to Europe to pursue Canada's desire for a contractual link with the Common Market.

its image and consequent influence in the international community. . . .

Monday, March 3, 1975

MacEachen and I called on Margaret Thatcher, the new leader of the opposition, who had been elected on February 11.

This was my first meeting with her. Indeed, she is quite an impressive young woman of between forty-five and fifty, good-looking, primly and well-dressed and most articulate. It is too early to say how well she will do, but her present prospects look good. She has certainly created a chain reaction and I would not, as a result, be surprised to see Flora MacDonald* become the Leader of the Conservative party in Canada. . . .

Tuesday, March 4, 1975

Now I know how much trouble I caused when, as a minister, I would visit particular missions. This, of course is inevitable and the experienced public official understands. Allan's visit, welcome as it is, nevertheless has brought home to me the changes in programme occasioned by a ministerial visit and particularly when the minister happens to be the foreign minister. . . .

My membership in the Reform Club has not been finally processed so I asked André Bissonnette to take Allan and me to lunch at the Club.[2] This he kindly did. . . . One can visualize in the library Mr. Asquith or Mr. Gladstone seeking a quiet corner in the late afternoon to read, think, and get away from the parliamentary jungle. This pleasant retreat I am beginning to appreciate in the busy and hectic life I lead here in London. . . .

Allan and I called on the Foreign Secretary, Jim Callaghan, at the House of Commons. Our foreign minister had really little to discuss and thought that our visit would not be for more than a few moments and perhaps more of a formal call than substantive. It turned out to be otherwise. We were there

2. London's Reform Club was founded in 1832 for political (Liberal) membership and it opened its own club house in 1841. Most leading nineteenth-century Liberal figures were members. Today, membership is more social than political and, since 1981, includes women.

for some forty-five minutes and kept the Australian foreign minister waiting way beyond the hour scheduled for his appointment.

Jim Callaghan began by saying that, much as he would have liked to have Canada at the preparatory meeting of oil-consumer and oil-producing nations, he had not been able to convince the French, who are convening the preparatory meeting. We, of course, will attend the full conference. . . .[3] The French and, I suspect, perhaps even the British, in spite of what Jim Callaghan said, are inclined to limit the number of states attending this preparatory meeting. . . . Allan put in a pitch for our claim to be at the preparatory meeting but, after several further statements of our position, acknowledged to Jim Callaghan that he could regard the matter as closed as far as we were concerned. We will not be prejudiced if the preparatory meeting confines itself to what is to be on the agenda.

Callaghan then raised the Jamaican Prime Minister's[4] proposal for a new world economic order that would lead to stabilization of prices for the products of the Third World. Callaghan is anxious that there be some time given to think out this whole matter. He would regard the discussion of the matter at the Prime Ministers' Conference in Jamaica[5] and even at the General Assembly of the United Nations next fall, as trial runs. There should not be a confrontation between the less developed countries and ourselves. . . . Some interest has arisen in this matter because, as far as I can see, it was Trudeau who raised it with Wilson in Ottawa a few weeks ago. We were all surprised when the British Prime Minister publicly spoke about the desirability of action in this field, not knowing, we hinted, that he was taking away someone else's thunder. I felt like telling Callaghan that it would be difficult to reconcile Wilson's speech with Callaghan's desire not to have any finality reached at the Commonwealth prime min-

3. The meeting became the November Economic Summit at Rambouillet which was itself held in preparation for the conference on international economic co-operation between oil-producing and oil-consuming countries held in mid-December 1975.
4. Michael Manley
5. Scheduled for April 26 to May 6.

isters' meeting in Jamaica and then later in the General Assembly. . . .

Somehow or another I have an idea that Jim Callaghan is not unlike many foreign ministers—so overburdened with work that he doesn't really fully grasp some of the problems with which he has to deal. . . .

Wednesday, March 5, 1975

Allan MacEachen came to Canada House and I introduced him to some of the Canadian visitors who were in the building. Ministers have their different approaches and ways of doing things. When I was Secretary of State for External Affairs, I made it a point almost at the outset of each visit whenever I was in a Canadian mission to meet the personnel. I wanted to know the people who worked under my direction. This is not Allan's method. I have confidence in my approach to this, but perhaps others think Allan is right. . . .

Thursday, March 6, 1975

The big event today, of course, has been the dinner which Nell and I gave for the Prince of Wales. . . . The preparation for an event of this kind is something long to be remembered. Not the least of the concerns has to do with the question of security. A problem in this area developed but was very well handled by Lorne Green,* Price,* and the security agents who follow the Prince at all times. Several days before the dinner, Price had hired a middle-aged Irish kitchen maid. Price said she was a very good worker and a good talker. She began complaining about the fact that so much effort and preparation was expected for royalty, in this instance the heir to the throne; [yet] there was such poverty, why should people provide such a sumptuous feast for a member of the royal family? She carried on in this vein and added she approved the killing of a policeman a few days before who had sought to stand in the way of an I.R.A. thug. Price reported this to Lorne Green. We both agreed that this lady should be dismissed forthwith. Scotland Yard was informed about the situation and we had further conversation at the residence with the Prince's security officers. Nothing more has been heard of the incident. It may be that the woman in question was a hard-working garrulous Irish personality who meant no harm— the fact is we cannot take a chance. . . .

The staff had provided a wonderful table and everyone commented on this. Everyone seemed relaxed and I was particularly proud of the way Nell took hold of things. She and the Prince began discussion of oriental religions. . . . The Prince, recently returned from Nepal, was able to speak knowledgeably about Asian buddhists, a subject quite obviously of great interest to him over a long time. He and I had an animated, across-the-table, exchange on Trinity College and more particularly its academic personalities. . . .

Monday, March 10, 1975

Nell and I and others from the High Commission met Trudeau on his arrival from Venice tonight. Roy Hattersley, Minister of State for Foreign and Commonwealth Affairs, was on hand to welcome the Prime Minister on behalf of the British government. I had arranged to have Roy ride in with Trudeau. The latter, however, persuaded Hattersley not to inconvenience himself and this gave our boss an opportunity to talk things over on the way in with André Bissonnette and myself. . . .

Tuesday, March 11, 1975

Before joining the Prime Minister at the Savoy, I had a quick swim just before the lunch-hour and at a few minutes to three we departed for the House of Commons. . . . We walked in the drizzly rain, with hundreds of cameramen pursuing us, through St. James's Park for a meeting with the Secretary General of the Commonwealth Organization, Arnold Smith. . . .

Wednesday, March 12, 1975

[Today, Trudeau and I] went to Canada House where hundreds of people were awaiting the Prime Minister, upstairs and downstairs. He was very moved by this reception and I was surprised [at] how many people I could present by name. After all, I have been here little more than two months. . . .

Our talks at No. 10 Downing Street were delayed fifteen minutes. . . . Our big pitch . . . concerned our desire for a contractual relationship with the Common Market. In Holland, Germany, and Italy we have had fairly good assurances for support. . . . We made it clear in our discussions this afternoon that we would like to have equally strong support by the British. It was clear that from what Wilson and Jim Callaghan said . . . [that] the British are more interested in having a declaration of both the Common Market and Canada instead of a contractual document. Basically, our position is to get our foot in the door of the largest market.

[Trudeau] . . . emphasized that our policy of diversification was not anti-American. It was designed to reduce dependency on the United States by supplementing rather than supplanting relations with that country. . . . Trudeau made it clear that we wanted the active support of the British government and not just its willingness to interpret Canadian policy to the E.E.C. As to the exact form and content of this link, it would become clearer in the exploratory talks. . . . Originally our proposal was to concentrate on trade. Now we are looking with the Community at other possibilities for economic cooperation.

On the question of Britain's continued presence in the Market, our discussions this afternoon emphasized Canada's view that this was a matter for Britain herself to decide. When the United Kingdom had joined the Market, we reminded Wilson, we had told the British government how pleased we were with this decision, even though in the short run it occasioned some disadvantages for us. . . .

Thursday, March 13, 1975

I joined the Prime Minister at the Savoy Hotel for Mrs. Thatcher's call on him. She talked quite assuredly about the high cost of living and its main cause, the undue increase in wages. Nevertheless, she is not in favour of controls, certainly not of the type envisaged by Robert Stanfield* during the last general election in Canada. She felt, however, that if the present situation continued in Britain, the present government would be driven to a new incomes policy. . . .

We returned for our talks with . . . Wilson at No. 10. Our Prime Minister returned to our objective of a contractual link with the Market. . . . I whispered to Trudeau that unless we could get the British to agree to particular words, we would find that they would continue to be vague. . . . Trudeau, I think, feels that with the two talks that have taken place already with Community officials, we are making progress. Nevertheless, I could not help but observe that if we could have tied them down more, as he apparently succeeded [in doing] . . . with the Germans and Italians, it would have been better. I think the British are a little concerned that if they do not stay in the Market, they will be prejudiced in their trading relations with us if we do acquire a contractual relationship. . . .

The final event of the day was, of course, the dinner at 12 Upper Brook Street. My darling wife never looked so beautiful and never did she preside so effectively over events. . . .

Friday, March 14, 1975

There is no doubt that Ivan Head serves the Prime Minister well. . . . His role and that of the Secretary of State for External Affairs are not necessarily compatible under our system. Mitchell Sharp was forbearing and this helped. I hope Allan will be too. Increasingly, our Prime Minister shows that he wishes to have a hand in foreign policy, even though at the beginning he eschewed this. Ivan, I think, performs a . . . valuable service notwithstanding the constructural anomaly—in fact he helps the Prime Minister and External Affairs as well. Would this have worked if I had been Secretary of State for External Affairs? I doubt it. . . .

[During the chat I had with him] Ivan wanted me to know that the most important objective of the trip was not only the contractual link with the Common Market but getting support for the ratification of the Nuclear Partial Test Ban Treaty and clarification of the New Economic Order programme. The contractual link concept was John Halstead's idea, he explained.[6] It seemed best to work with it. The Prime Minister told me on the way out to the airport that at first he wasn't very strong on the contractual link policy but gradually he

6. John Halstead was a career diplomat and deputy under-secretary in the Department of External Affairs.

had come to buy it and now was pushing it. It was important to get one's foot inside the door. . . .

This was a successful visit to London for Trudeau. . . . Canadians usually complain about attention paid to them in the news media in the United Kingdom. There could be no legitimate complaint this time. Trudeau, of course, is not only charismatic but he is newsworthy. The newspapers, radio and particularly television follow him throughout. While he was here it certainly was Canada's week.

Why should I hesitate to acknowledge the extraordinary qualities of this man? [Certainly] not because he, more than anyone else, took away from me the prime ministership. That would be no reason — that battle is over and lost.

The ceremony at the Guildhall and the speech at the Mansion House[7] and part of the award of the Freedom of the City was a memorable one. As Trudeau walked down the aisle at the Guildhall, preceded by the Aldermen in their robes, to be welcomed by the Lord Mayor, I could not help but think of [my] reaction as a young boy of nine when my father read out the account in *The Ottawa Journal* describing the awarding of the Freedom of the City of London to Sir Wilfrid Laurier — Laurier my hero, Laurier my ideal. Now I was witnessing many years later a ceremony marking a similar bestowal of honour on a Canadian Prime Minister and, like Laurier, one who hailed from Quebec. The liturgy of the ceremony touched me as it did when I read about it many years ago. Trudeau looked a little like Laurier as I have found him to . . . at other times. He argued our case well before members of the British government, headed by Prime Minister Wilson. He carried himself well wherever he went and I felt proud of him and of Canada.

When I got back to the residence [after seeing Trudeau to the airport], I felt a great burden lifted from my shoulders. . . .

Monday, March 17, 1975

This is the day of the ubiquitous Canadian member of Parliament. . . . In the three months that I have been here, I believe, I have seen now over thirty Canadian members of the House

7. Mansion House is the official residence of the Lord Mayor of London during his year of office.

of Commons. Certainly the privileges of foreign travel are more open to them than they were to our group in the House of Commons during my thirty-three years. . . .

Wednesday, March 19, 1975

As Leader of the House, [Edward] Short* has the responsibility for legislation dealing with the devolution of powers to Wales and Scotland. He was interested in my views as one [with] . . . some experience in federal-provincial legislation in Canada. I took the opportunity of saying to Short that the government should be careful . . . how far it went in this devolution process. In our case, the intention of the British North America Act had been undermined by the judicial law-making processes, particularly by the Judicial Committee of the Privy Council. The Fathers of Confederation and the British Parliament had intended that there would result an emphasis of greater power at the centre in Canada. [The law lords] . . . had eroded the central power by giving more authority to the provinces. The consequences in later years for Canada were burdensome.

In the Pearson and Trudeau period, the emergence of chauvinistic Quebec made it necessary to extend this erosion. I pointed out to Short that during my time as Minister of National Health and Welfare,[8] we had taken initiative in the field of social welfare and health, forcing the pace with the provinces and establishing national criteria for social and health standards. Now, we were driven into the position of preserving Canadian unity by a process of opting out, giving more and more power to the provinces. There was no other way open if we wanted to avoid fragmentation. The lesson of all this, I suggested to Short, was clear for the United Kingdom.

Thursday, March 20, 1975

Over the years, like others who have had to do a lot of speaking, I have been amazed to find in the largest hotels where one would have thought the demand was great, that

8. From 1947 to 1957.

they do not have practical lecterns. . . . The speech I was making tonight at the Savoy Hotel to the Canada Club required that my words be chosen carefully in what was to be my first speech. And so, accompanied by Lorne Green, we went to the Savoy Hotel, examined their lectern situation, finding it as inadequate as in other [cases]. . . . Lorne had a lectern made . . . and it was in place when I spoke. . . .

Although I have given a lot of speeches in my life, this one troubled me. It was to be my first major speech as a diplomat. In this capacity one has less freedom than a minister or a member of Parliament. . . . I decided that the best thing to do was to have a careful text, giving a picture of what Canada is and what her intentions are. . . . All nations today had to come to terms with the realities of the 1970s. . . . I ended my speech by quoting from Trudeau's Mansion House address: "Let us begin to search, and let us do so with boldness and with excitement, not with hesitancy and uncertainty. . . ."

Monday, March 24, 1975

We had a good briefing at the economic consultative group meeting this morning, paying particular attention to the Canadian objective of developing a contractual link with the Common Market. . . . I emphasized that it was clear we did not have the full-hearted support of the British in our objective. They would agree to push our claim, but more as an interlocutor than as a supporter. Of course, the whole question is somewhat ambivalent as the Prime Minister said in his press conference—"we seek a contractual link, we want support for this by the nine countries in the Market, but we cannot expect any country at this stage to sign a written document when the provisions have not been articulated." I urged the members of the committee to remember that the Foreign Secretary had asked would we not be satisfied with a declaration [by member countries] . . . of a promise to consult with Canada. It was not to be forgotten that the Prime Minister had rejected this. What he wanted was some guarantee, some compulsion that there would be consultation. . . .

Tuesday, March 25, 1975

I am no lover of the ballet, nor is Nell. Perhaps I should put it this way—we have not exposed ourselves to the ballet and, therefore, have not learned to appreciate it. I have seen only one performance of the ballet and I must admit it was an unforgettable experience. This was in Moscow when, on our official visit, Andrei Gromyko* took us to the Bolshoi. There we sat in the Tsar's box now reserved for the secretary of the party. . . . Mrs. Shenkman, formerly of Ottawa, devotes so much of her time to bringing the Canadian ballet to London; the proceeds from the performance go to assist ballet dancing in Britain. . . . Mrs. Shenkman, perfectionist that she properly is, insists on a rehearsal this morning [and] we all foregathered at the Coliseum to learn our positions and our roles on opening night when Princess Margaret attends. . . .

Tuesday, April 1, 1975

My first meeting with Elliot Richardson went off very well.[9] I lunched with him . . . at the embassy on the other side of Grosvenor Square. . . .

It is obvious that Elliot has not practised law for a protracted period. It is further obvious that he has a political career still in mind. . . . It is conceivable that Richardson could even be the next Republican candidate for the presidency, but only if Ford[10] should not persist. It is very much in the cards, I am sure, that Richardson could be a Republican candidate . . . in the presidential elections five and a half years from now.

I think he and I approach our respective assignments here a little differently. Within a week of his arrival, he had gone for a week's skiing in Austria. I haven't ventured away from the office since I came. . . . He told me yesterday that he will be going to the United States in two or three weeks' time for a fairly extended period. I mentioned all this to André who replied, "Well, this is what a big power can do. . . ."

Wednesday, April 2, 1975

The gala opening at the Coliseum tonight by the National Ballet of Canada was a brilliant affair. I greeted Princess Margaret. . . . I thought the Princess was in a very happy

9. He had served as the U.S. secretary of health, education and welfare, 1970-72, of defence, 1972-73, and attorney general, 1973. He resigned over the Watergate coverup by Richard Nixon.
10. Gerald Ford,* the U.S. president who took over when Richard Nixon resigned.

mood and the impression she created on meeting was much better than when I saw her ten years ago at the Maple Leaf Ball. . . .

Monday, April 7, 1975

My head cold persists and it makes me cranky and isn't too good for one's perspective. However, when George Hees* and his wife called on me today, I hope I did not show the effects. They are old friends and George is a long-time political adversary. He and I used to spend half an hour or so every day in the Chateau Laurier pool. This daily meeting put our political confrontations in the right place. . . .

I gave my second press luncheon today for eight press men. . . . Miss [Elizabeth] Armstong of *The Toronto Star* told me that this was the first time she had been at the residence for lunch and thought that the idea of having journalists together was an excellent one. Certainly it gives me a chance to know some of the leading political writers of Britain and at least three of them were present today.

Tuesday, April 8, 1975

In many ways, tonight's visit to Windsor Castle to dine and to stay with the Queen and the Duke of Edinburgh was the highlight of our stay here in the first three months. We arrived at Windsor Castle sharp at 7:00 p.m. and our suite—one of the most magnificent suite of rooms Nell and I have ever laid our eyes on—[is] reserved on state visits for heads of state. Within ten minutes of our arrival, we were escorted to a large reception room where a number of guests had already assembled. . . . I did not notice the Duke of Edinburgh, tall as he is, standing behind someone. I went over and shook hands with Mrs. Wilson, only at that particular moment realizing that . . . Edinburgh was present. He understood the situation and gave me a warm welcome as he did Nell, whom he had already greeted. The Queen entered shortly after, accompanied by her five dogs . . . who are obviously very much part of the impedimenta of the royal household. The Queen talked to Nell and me for about three-quarters of an hour and it was so noticeable that she relaxed in her own house; friendly and charming are the right adjectives. She spoke of her forthcoming visit to the [Commonwealth] heads of government meeting in Kingston [Jamaica]. . . .

After dinner we were taken on a tour of the reception rooms of Windsor Castle. . . . Historical paintings, objets d'art, memorabilia — part of the history of a long period — were everywhere. . . . It was well after midnight when we went to bed, our lights being put out by a gentleman servant who had been in the service of the royal family for some thirty-five years. I slept hardly a wink. Nell did a lot better than I, who wondered would we see a Windsor Castle ghost? . . .

Wednesday, April 9, 1975

The presence of the Prime Minister . . . last night enabled me to have several good chats with him. Wilson had a difficult day in the House of Commons. Threatened with substantial opposition in his own party to continuance in the Market requires a dexterity on his part which only a Mackenzie King could meet. The opposition in the back benches will be greater than anticipated, he told me, and this applies as well to ministers who are not in the cabinet. Wilson intimated that he would not stand for a violation of the rules of the game which he and the cabinet have laid down and, quite bluntly, he said that if Heffer[11] tomorrow defies these criteria he will be out of the cabinet. . . .

Friday, April 11, 1975

With three ministers to stay [at the residence] in three days, I knew I was to have a hectic [time] . . . but it gives me a chance to get caught up with the Canadian scene. Particularly with the visit of Allan MacEachen, I can exchange directly views on foreign policy matters. This is very helpful in enabling me to discharge more efficiently my job here. Today my concern was Barney Danson* whom I accompanied on his call on the Secretary of State for the Environment, Anthony Crosland.* Crosland is a nice man and a moderate in the

11. Eric Heffer, a left-wing Labour MP, served as minister of state for industry since 1974.

cabinet. . . . Barney, of course, was concerned with housing problems and these he discussed with considerable ability, I thought. There is no doubt that our housing in Canada, while very expensive, is better than here in England. . . .

Saturday, April 12, 1975

Allan's plane was on time and almost from the time of arrival until lunch time we reviewed problems that concern us both. . . . Allan told me of his luncheon meeting with Kissinger about ten days ago in Washington. No doubt the Secretary of State was very disappointed with his recent Middle East effort and thought Israel unreasonable. . . .

Sunday, April 13, 1975

I longed for a weekend when I could read and write but, alas, Allan is here, Barney is about to go, and the Leader of the Government in the Senate[12] is about to arrive. I don't complain about this, I just state my mood as I woke up. I must confess though that because Barney's plane was late, my library became a public station and this irritated me a little bit, but things settled down. . . .

Monday, April 14, 1975

Senator Perrault, who will be leaving around noon, called on me at Macdonald House. . . . He has his problems in the Senate as I had. . . . Being a member of the cabinet and Leader of the Government in the Senate creates an inevitable confrontation. Some senators, because of the certainty of tenure, act as sovereigns in themselves. On the other hand, the government doesn't always understand the problems of the upper house. . . .

I went to the House of Commons to hear Denis Healey pronounce his budget. . . . There is no doubt about [his] ability [but] . . . I did not remain for the whole budget, departing just at the time the proposals for taxation or relief therefrom were being litanized. Budgets, I have always found, are very dull to listen to and hard to follow. . . .

12. Raymond Perrault

On my way out I ran into Arthur Bottomley,* an old friend of Wilson's and his former Secretary of State for Commonwealth Affairs. I told Arthur that I thought Wilson was handling the question of the Market, in the light of party and parliamentary division, in an able way. Politics is the art of the possible. A political leader has to deal with the material at hand. Wilson wants to stay in the Market and his government has now decided to do so, subject to the will of the electorate expressed in the proposed referendum. He faces a party against him on this, even though Parliament has given him an affirmative vote. He has had to move carefully and even illogically to achieve the desired objective and not destroy the unity of both party and country. His critics do not understand [this]. . . . "Would I mind if he told Harold all of this?" I said, "Of course not. . . ."

Within less than a week I made my fourth visit to Heathrow to welcome John Turner on his way to the Middle East. His plane was late and I went to bed very late, trying to put myself to sleep by reading a few pages of Trevelyan on *Garibaldi*. . . .

Tuesday, April 22, 1975

When the NATO summit meeting was first proposed, Jim Callaghan had told me that he was anxious to have it before the CSCE meeting.[13] Allan MacEachen and the government preferred having the meeting take place after the larger [CSCE] summit gathering. Subsequently, the failure of Kissinger's latest Middle East talks and the criticism against the United States in Vietnam made it useful for President Ford and Kissinger to receive collective support in a common cause with their NATO partners. However, when one considers that there was a NATO meeting in Ottawa last May and a summit meeting in the same month in Brussels with President Nixon in attendance, it is not difficult to look at the synthetic reasons for the NATO summit meeting. As a matter of fact, surveying the number of international conferences that will take place between now and the end of June causes one to wonder. . . .

13. The NATO summit was held on May 29-30; the Conference on Security and Co-operation in Europe took place in Helsinki on July 31 and August 1.

Thursday, April 24, 1975

We had our dinner tonight for the Archbishop of Canterbury and Mrs. Coggan. They are going to Canada next week. . . . The Archbishop is a fine and impressive man who taught for some nine years . . . at Wycliffe College in Toronto. Nell and I had decided to make this dinner an ecumenical one . . . attested by the presence of the Duke of Norfolk, Father Corbishley, S.J., Christopher Hollis and, of course, the Apostolic Delegate. . . . The Archbishop referred to his friendship with Burgon Bickersteth, C.M., [another guest] and stated how he had known of me over the years through Burgon. . . .[14]

Friday, April 25, 1975

The Swedish Ambassador, Mr. Ole Jödahl, told me today that he was certain the CSCE summit meeting would not take place until the fall. It is odd that he should have this information and that I should not have been aware of it, because our sources are really better than anyone else's except the Soviet Union, the United States and Great Britain. . . . The postponement of the bigger summit meeting is wise because such meetings should not take place unless there has been the fullest preparation. . . .

Monday, April 28, 1975

The Turkish Ambassador whom I called on this morning, Turgut Menemencioglu, I had known at the United Nations and at NATO. . . . Like the Italian Ambassador,[15] Menemencioglu doesn't altogether like the principles that operate in Kissinger's mind. There must not be a compete abandonment of moral principle. To argue and act on the basis of historic model, I agree is not the only way to act in foreign policy. There is room for idealism and perhaps this is where Kissinger is falling down. Perhaps there is too much Metternich in him. . . .

14. Bickersteth lived within the precincts of Canterbury Cathedral.
15. Raimondo Mancini

Tuesday, April 29, 1975

This has been a day of history. The war in Vietnam is over —twenty years of American combat action have come to an end—thirty years of war in Indo-China has come to a stop . . . the whole thing a tragedy and a wasteful expenditure of human life. History may argue that the advance of Communism might have been stopped if the Indo-China wars had ended in American victory. This doesn't take into account the loss of human life during these last thirty years. My conscience is clear. As Canadian foreign minister I know that we did everything during the Pearson administration to help bring about a cease-fire. . . . Sometimes, I believe the war in Vietnam, now so universally condemned, may help to bring an end to the wasteful use of force by nations—never again will the United States, I am sure, make such rash judgments with such fateful consequences involving the waste of human life —war is an anachronism. . . .

III

May – July 1975

AS WAS POINTED OUT in the introduction to this book, the western countries were responding to the demands of the Third World for ways to move beyond the accepted means of equalizing economic opportunities. This became known as the New Economic Order. Most of the activities in this area involved conferences which were designed to increase awareness of the problem. The Commonwealth Conference and other international meetings scheduled for later in the year drew closer, and I spent considerable time studying the question.

British political figures were absorbed by the referendum campaign on whether the U.K. should stay in the Common Market. In the vote on June 5, the majority voted to remain in the Market. Following the referendum, Harold Wilson had to cope with an economic crisis and a rapidly rising inflation rate.

Late in the month of July, just before leaving on holiday, I had to see Jim Callaghan to ask him for British support for our request to postpone a conference on crime scheduled for Toronto. An outcry in Canada over the participation of the Palestine Liberation Organization prompted our government to make the request.

Thursday, May 1, 1975

Wilson has made it look as though he has put forward a very important new initiative on the so-called New Economic Order (prior to the Commonwealth meeting in Kingston). Jim Callaghan told MacEachen and me six weeks ago that he wanted to play this whole question in low key—certainly he wished to avoid confrontation in Kingston. This low key posture, however, has not been maintained by Wilson who has done nothing more than table a lot of information about the proposals for a New Economic Order. The story in *The Times* portrays the British Prime Minister as having brought forward a bold new initiative. The . . . matter in any event will be discussed at the next United Nations General Assembly. I am sure there will be a confrontation there. The problem is not an easy one. The difficulties of the under-developed world cannot be resolved by grants in aid—bilateral or multilateral—alone. More fundamental injections [of capital] have to be provided. The economics of the under-developed nations have got to be livened up. The establishment of cartels would result in world chaos, but they [the lesser developed countries] will not be content with commodity agreements [to protect the prices of their exported raw materials]. . . .

Saturday, May 3, 1975

Ed Ritchie* and I had a good chat this morning before lunch. We talked about Gordon Robertson* who has moved over from being Clerk of the Privy Council to responsibilities for federal-provincial relations. We both agreed that there is not likely to be much action in this field. . . . As a consequence, will Gordon's great talents not be unused—would it not be better for him to be more productively engaged? In the transfer of responsibilities, was the Prime Minister largely influenced by his desire to have Michael Pitfield nearer to him[1] or did Gordon himself think that the time had come to move on? This I doubt. . . .

Before retiring tonight, Ed and Jim Grandy[2] joined me as we surveyed the problems of the world. Ed recently had been at the Prime Minister's residence where there was a discussion on the current cabinet committee system which Trudeau prefers and likes. . . . Ed laughed when I suggested that he, Jim Grandy and others really ran the country. Jim Grandy fully agreed and thought that at cabinet committees it was a mistake for ministers and leading civil servants to vie with one another. How can a minister know his department?

1. He became clerk of the Privy Council.
2. Grandy had recently resigned as deputy minister of industry, trade and commerce.

How can he get to know the people in it unless he spends a good bit of time in the department and with those who work with him? . . .

Sunday, May 4, 1975

On the way home I stopped off at Hyde Park and listened to the Sunday orators. I have heard very few of these chaps who are really good; most of them seem to be cranks, and even some humorists. Today there was one serious man speaking on behalf of the Catholic Evidence Guild. He was not very effective in his presentation and for a moment the doctrine seemed to be in doubt. Another man was a world federalist, explaining the programme and not doing any better than the Catholic speaker. The spokesman for world socialism was articulate but the crowd had a lot of fun heckling him. . . .

Tuesday, May 6, 1975

News came in today that the government has renewed NORAD for five years. I well remember in 1967 and in 1968 how some of my cabinet colleagues were opposed to our renewing the agreement at that time. Jean Marchand,* Gérard Pelletier,* Walter Gordon,* and Trudeau were opposed. The committee in recommending the five-year agreement this time said that it was impressed by the argument that a Canadian decision to withdraw from NORAD would be interpreted at home and abroad as evidence of a possible major change in the orientation of Canadian foreign policy. This is what I argued when I was foreign minister against my cabinet critics. This is a further illustration that foreign policy cannot be turned off and on like a tap. Our relations with the United States do mean something to us. These same critics wanted us to get out of NATO. We wouldn't have much chance of developing a contractual link with the Common Market if we had left NATO, as some proposed in 1967 and 1968. . . .

Wednesday, May 7, 1975

I was glad to get back to the residence to greet Nell who had returned from a five-day jaunt in Canada. She had gone to christen a ship built by the Davis Building Company for the

Cunard Line. The ship was named *Lucellum* by her. She pronounced the name and broke a bottle of champagne on its bow to mark the occasion. Apparently, Paul's speech of introduction of his mother was classic and full of good humour. Nell's reply, together with her interjections, apparently were good. In a column in *The Montreal Gazette* a sentence of hers was taken as the "quote of the week." She thanked Canada Steamship Lines for giving her son a job. [He is the company president.] This apparently brought the house down. . . .

Thursday, May 8, 1975

After my very good swim this morning at 6:30 a.m. I was almost frustrated to note that I have put on two pounds. The new cook perhaps is too good. Knowing that I like fish, he insists on serving fish as well as meat—hereafter I must cut down. I had taken off seven pounds from the 1st January—how did I get back into the old groove? . . .

Friday, May 9, 1975

When I was Canadian foreign minister, two men who were Ministers of State in the Foreign Office impressed me greatly—one was Fred Mulley and the other was George Thomson. The latter is now one of the British Commissioners in the Common Market and Fred Mulley is Minister of Transport. We had a chat in his office this morning. [Mulley] is president of the Labour party and, in view of the Common Market decision to be taken on June 5th, a very important person indeed. When the Referendum Bill came up in the Commons he abstained from voting. Harold Wilson was irritated, but then Fred explained he could do more good by adopting a neutral position as president of the party conference than he could by a positive vote which might have alienated him from many of the Labour party members, particularly in the trade unions. . . . He is afraid that there might be a small vote on June 5th—otherwise he feels that it will carry triumphantly.

In Mulley's view, the post-referendum crisis will be more severe than the Common Market problem. Britain's balance-of-payments problem will reach a critical stage unless some halt is brought to the inflationary spiral and unless there is a recognition of the need for national co-operation by political parties, labour and industrial management. . . .

Saturday, May 10, 1975

After a relaxing morning, Nell and I went on our way to Cambridge, arriving an hour and a half before luncheon with the Master, Rab Butler, and Lady Butler at Trinity.

I arrived early so that I could take a relaxed look at Cambridge again. The chauffeur, John Rowan,* had not been to Cambridge too many times and, consequently, I acted as a guide in showing him Trinity College, St. John's, and King's College Chapel which has been cleaned inside. What an impressive chapel it is. The organist was at work getting ready for tomorrow's service. As the organ pealed through this great and beautiful Norman structure, one thought of the tremendous history represented in this place since the eleventh century. I get a tremendous amount of pleasure out of the memories of my year at Trinity and Cambridge. . . .

Monday, May 12, 1975

Prime Minister Wilson's television interview yesterday has opened the flood gates. Labour is dissatisfied and so is big business. I think he handled himself cleverly. The financial and economic picture in Britain, however, is serious. The Prime Minister is betting on having the referendum vote over before any serious development in the financial situation emerges. Can this be avoided? The pound is tottering; some bolstering is obviously taking place. The kind of talk I heard at the Danish Ambassador's from Alec Home and Harold Caccia[3] is now surfacing. Some are urging the formation of a coalition government but yesterday Wilson said he was against this. I propose sending a good analysis of this situation to Ottawa before the end of the week. . . .

Wednesday, May 14, 1975

The . . . United Nations Association had its annual party in the gardens at No. 10 Downing Street where I went in the late afternoon. . . . I had a chat with Prime Minister Wilson

3. Harold, Lord Caccia, was a former U.K. ambassador to the United States.

who asked me if I had noted that he had changed the United Kingdom's sitting place at the Prime Ministers' Conference, bringing him side by side with Trudeau. Wilson explained that he had arranged this because he did not want to sit next to Uganda (I suppose in the event that Amin[4] was present). . . .

Sunday, May 18, 1975

The [Marc] Lalondes* joined us at Farm Street Church this Pentecost day. After Mass, I introduced them to a French Jesuit priest, whom I had met a few months ago. On the way home Marc told me that Jean Marchand will be leaving the government soon. It is too bad that his health makes this necessary. My impression ten years ago was that he would not last. Walter Gordon[5] suggested Jean to succeed Pearson [in 1968]. I was not the only one then who thought Marchand to be too temperamental. This was another case of Walter Gordon's bad judgment. Marc thinks that Gordon Roberston is happy in his new responsibility but I doubt this. . . .

Monday, May 19, 1975

Darcy McKeough, the Provincial Treasurer in Ontario, came to see me at the residence with the Agent General.[6] He is on his way to Zurich to arrange for some Ontario financing. He thought that Turner might be forced to bring in some statutory [wage and price] controls. I scotched this idea. It is interesting to note that Canadians are disturbed about their economic situation and express views not unlike many that we hear in the United Kingdom. Our situation, however, is not to be compared with the plight of Britain. McKeough points out that our abnormally high wage increases, above those in the United States, will cause us great trouble in a year or so. Our capacity for meeting world competition will be reduced because of the higher costs of production. . . .

4. Idi Amin* seized power in Uganda in 1971 and inaugurated a reign of terror.
5. Walter Gordon was president of the Privy Council at the time.
6. Ward Cornell

Tuesday, May 20, 1975

I have been calling on many ministers, ambassadors and high commissioners . . . [and] I am discovering that even in a courtesy call one picks up good information and one is more likely to establish a friendship than in a collective gathering. . . . The American Ambassador, Elliot Richardson, is following a different procedure. Today at noon, he had a reception at his beautiful residence in Regent's Park, where he received the entire Diplomatic Corps. He certainly saved himself a lot of time and effort, but I doubt if he got anything like the kind of information that I have been gathering during the past five months. It is easier, of course, for the world's largest power to adopt this course, but is it a good and wise course even for the United States? I have my doubts. . . .

On May 22, I went on my first return trip to Canada to preside at the convocation at Wilfrid Laurier University where I was chancellor. It was strange for me to be home and not be part of the "scene" but I went through the rounds of dinners and receptions associated with university graduations. On May 26, I returned to London and my work there.

Tuesday, May 27, 1975

When the Earl of Athlone[7] and Princess Alice, his wife, were in Rideau Hall, Canadians learned to appreciate them. In particular they developed a strong affection for Princess Alice, the last remaining grand-daughter of Queen Victoria. Nell and I had tea with her today. At the age of ninety-two she is handsome, humorous, and surprisingly alert and full of vigour. Above all, her sense of humour is something to behold. We talked of Mackenzie King—had she known of his spiritualism? Yes, of course, she did and this surprised me. I know of no one who did. On one occasion Mr. King had told this grand-daughter of Victoria what his dead dog had just said to him and what his mother had revealed to him in their most recent contact. . . .

At the reception given for African heads of missions by the Ambassador for Egypt, Sadat's former chief-of-staff, I saw

7. The Earl of Athlone served as governor general of Canada from 1940 to 1946.

very few white people and I could tell from the greeting given us on our arrival how pleased they were to see the Canadian High Commissioner. I just don't understand why certain heads of missions do not show their friendship for the emerging African countries. . . .

Wednesday, May 28, 1975

The Minister of Overseas Development, Judith Hart, was a member of the inner cabinet in the previous Wilson government. She is on the outer rim now. I am not so sure what this means. That she is bright I have no doubt but I have some question marks in my mind about her. . . . I called on her this morning. . . . Recently she went to Southern Africa to meet with Mozambique leaders to ascertain their financial requirements in the event that an independent Mozambique decides to apply U.N. sanctions against Rhodesia. . . . If and when these are applied, Rhodesia's rail access will be cut off. The other countries will have to assist Mozambique financially. She called me "Paul" throughout and I called her "Mrs. Hart." . . .

Thursday, May 29, 1975

The previous day, I had gone to Birmingham on one of my periodic trips around Britain.

I was full of beans when I woke up this morning. Everything was so nicely English, the kind of Englishness that J. B. Priestley writes in his book on the English people.[8] I was excited once again to see Birmingham, where I had not been since my motorcycle visit in my Cambridge days in 1929. . . .

Saturday, May 31, 1975

Nell and I motored to Sevenoaks for our weekend visit with Malcolm MacDonald. . . . It was inevitable that we should talk about the current situation in Britain. Malcolm is strong for coalition, and thinks that Jim Callaghan could head a government in such circumstances. My view of this, I emphasized, is that Harold Wilson is the strongest political leader at the

8. J. B. Priestley, *The English* (London 1973).

moment. Labour would not join a coalition and Harold Wilson has already intimated his opposition. Would Mrs. Thatcher rise to the bait? I think not. Politically she would have more to gain by waiting. The question is should she put the country's interests first, assuming that this question involves that kind of approach. . . . I am a little prejudiced in this matter of coalition government. It is a sort of abdication of the parliamentary system as we know it. It is an admission that [the] parliamentary form of government in moments of crisis cannot be effective. . . .

Thursday, June 5, 1975

Today is the day when the British will decide whether or not to continue in the Community. It would be interesting to estimate the influence of last night's debate at the Oxford Union Society when the visiting participants were Ted Heath, Jeremy Thorpe, Barbara Castle* and Edward Shore. Shades of my days at Cambridge and the Union Society there . . . . In any event, the Society voted overwhelmingly that Britain should stay in the Community and this, I suspect, is what they will do tomorrow in their great numbers.

After the dust settled on the referendum question, the British electorate expressed its opinion in no uncertain terms (67.2 per cent of the voters favoured membership and 32.8 per cent were opposed).

In light of my determination to show the flag throughout the United Kingdom, I continued my periodic trips throughout the country. On Sunday, June 8, I went to Glasgow for a visit and then went on to Edinburgh the following day to continue my visit in Scotland.

Monday, June 9, 1975

When I met the press, I expressed satisfaction over the Common Market referendum decision. I recognized that in the short term there were problems for Canada in British membership in the Market. The long-term value was positive for Britain, and for Canada. Our desire for a contractual link with the Market was the logical outcome of our desire to diversify our trade and economic patterns. . . .

Saturday, June 14, 1975

Nell and I were the Prime Minister's guests at the Trooping the Colour on the Horse Guards' Parade in celebration of the Queen's birthday. When the Prime Minister greeted us at No. 10 Downing Street, I congratulated him on the Common Market referendum result. He was all smiles, recalling what he had told me early in January about his hopes, plans and the time-table relating to the great event of June 5th when the Common Market proposal received such a tremendous national endorsement. Now he is faced with economic and financial problems and labour strikes. . . .

Monday, June 16, 1975

This afternoon Nell and I went to Windsor Castle to observe the procession of the Most Noble Order of the Garter. The Queen's secretary, Martin Charteris, had kindly invited us to join a number of guests on the roof top of the Castle where we had a perfect picture. . . . There were the Prince and Princess Mikasa, the youngest brother of the Japanese Emperor and an interesting man. He is pursuing some researches in Near East history, with special emphasis on the Old Testament, at King's College in the University of London. . . . The Apostolic Delegate, Archbishop Heim, was at the Castle. I don't find him the easiest person in the world to talk to but I did like Dr. Alan Glyn, the MP for Windsor, and his wife, Lady Rosula. . . .

On my way home Nell and I dropped in to see Margaret Alexander[9] whom we had known when she and the Field Marshal were at Rideau Hall. . . . She quite obviously was particularly glad to see Nell, whom everyone really loves and rightly so. . . . Margaret told us that several years ago she had gone to the Garter luncheon with Field Marshal Montgomery, Alex's great rival. The attendant at the Castle enquired if the lady he was accompanying (Lady Alexander) was his wife. Scornfully Montgomery said "No," to which Margaret observed "As for *me*, one Field Marshal is enough. . . ."

9. She was the widow of Field Marshal Earl Alexander of Tunis who had been our governor general from 1946 to 1951.

Wednesday, June 18, 1975

Another provincial premier has crossed the ocean and so I met Premier Barrett of British Columbia at the airport with Micky Sterling, British Columbia's retiring Agent General. Barrett seemed to be surprised but pleased with the fact that I was there to welcome him. On the way in from Heathrow, we talked of the developing political scene. He does not think Lougheed* has a strong enough base in Ontario to succeed as national Conservative leader. I will accompany him, of course, on Monday next when he sees Prime Minister Wilson. This is a responsibility of the High Commissioner when a provincial premier calls on the head of a "foreign" government. This is the constitutional position—not observed by General de Gaulle and Jean Lesage,* both of whom should have known better. . . .

Thursday, June 19, 1975

I noticed today at Ascot the women ticket sellers . . . are hidden from a view of the track itself, their stalls being under the stands. The men wore grey toppers and many women were lavishly dressed, some extravagantly and, by design, ridiculously so. A holiday spirit prevailed. It was fun. . . . I made a few bets and lost. In the race for the Gold Cup I put a pound on one of Lady Beaverbrook's horses. In doing so, I thought Lord Beaverbrook [from the great beyond] might put in a good word. Nell had more success. She acted on advice given her by Price [our butler]. . . .

I had an excellent chat with Jack Jones,* secretary-general of the Transport Workers. . . . There are three or four powerful trade union leaders in the United Kingdom at this time and Jones heads the largest group. He has a great admiration for Denis Healey whom he thinks would succeed Harold Wilson in the leadership if this became open. Curiously enough, he has reservations about the contemporary trade union idol Wedgwood Benn. The fact that the latter . . . was at one time in the House of Lords seemed to be an obstacle for Jones. The support of the academics and of the upper classes is welcome to Labour, but the rank and file of the working people is what counts. Next to Denis Healey, Michael Foot stands high and not because of the biography of Aneurin Bevan.[10] Jones assured me that Labour people do not read books. I doubt this. . . .

Monday, June 23, 1975

Nell and I had invited a representative group to dine with us [at the residence] in saying farewell to Arnold and Eve Smith. . . . I must say that Nell does handle these situations admirably. I have never seen anyone make their guests so comfortable and contented. Any party she has anything to do with is not stilted. This dinner arrangement was the best ever.

After the ladies had gone upstairs, we had good discussions on the post-referendum period among other things. Alec Home, shifted the emphasis he made when I discussed this matter with him just before the referendum. . . . Now Alec was happy, the referendum was strongly supported, the nation had acted in one strong voice . . . [but] there would be a demand for referenda to cover the Ulster problem and the separatist demands of Scotland and Wales. I countered by saying that I did not think that this followed if the government showed strongly that it did not believe in referenda as a normal practice. There was no disposition in Canada, for instance, to hold further plebiscites. Recently, Trudeau had said that a referendum on separation in Quebec would not be recognized by Ottawa, and that this procedure would not be used at any time by the federal government to meet the wishes of René Lévesque* and company. Alec emphasized that there was a strong disposition for devolution in Scotland. He, however, agreed with me when I said that on my recent visit to the cities of Scotland I did not find among the leaders I met any disposition for Scottish independence and separation. That a free Assembly for Scotland would likely be established, I added, did not mean that this would be followed by separation from the rest of the United Kingdom. . . . The leaders of Britain, I told Alec . . . had to give some lead themselves and must not play into the hands of emotional separatists.

10. Michael Foot, *Aneurin Bevan: A Biography*, 2 vols (London 1962-73). Bevan was a Welshman who became Attlee's minister of health (1945-51) and introduced the National Health Service.

Tuesday, June 24, 1975

John and I motored directly . . . to Cambridge for the Master's dinner for Trinity College students of the years 1929, 1930, and 1931. . . .

Rab [Butler] and I talked about many things at dinner. I asked him if he ever saw Selwyn Lloyd, the Speaker. After all, they had been colleagues together in Harold Macmillan's government. He replied in the affirmative, saying that Selwyn had been down to Trinity on two occasions at least. He then observed, "Perhaps no one (adding, 'I am sure, no one') knows as much about Suez as Selwyn. He was a party to the whole shoddy business. . . ."

Wednesday, June 25, 1975

Merlyn Rees, Secretary of State for Northern Ireland, strikes me as very well fitted for the tough job that is his. This was my first impression when I first met him . . . several months ago and this is my reaction after seeing him again today. He expressed appreciation for the complete manner in which the Canadian authorities have clamped down on the export of arms for use in Northern Ireland. The more serious problem in this connection, of course, exists in the United States. . . .

Thursday, June 26, 1975

In many ways Nehru[11] was for me the conscience of mankind. . . . I have never regarded Indira,[12] his daughter, as of the same calibre. Indeed, I was surprised when she succeeded her father as Prime Minister [in 1966]. Nevertheless, it came as a shock when we all learned within the last few hours that some seven hundred right-wing opposition leaders had been arrested and that a state of emergency had been imposed because of "internal disturbances." Among those apprehended was Morarji Desai, the former Deputy Prime Minister. Nell and I had got to know him well when we were in India in 1956 and '57. One of India's great achievements since independence has been its ability to maintain the free parliamen-

11. Pandit Nehru, prime minister of India, 1947-64.
12. Indira Gandhi

tary system and for this thanks are due to Nehru. Has Indira undone all this by her present dictatorial policy? Mrs. Pandit[13] was in town last week. I regret that I did not seek her out. . . . When I last saw here she was very critical of her niece.

Friday, June 27, 1975

I had a useful and important meeting in mid-morning with Sheikh Abdulrahman Al-Helaissi, the Ambassador of Saudi Arabia, who received me at his residence. . . . [He said,] "My country takes a sensible position on the Middle East problem. . . . Jerusalem must not remain the exclusive property of Israel. The *status quo ante* must be restored so that all religious sites, be they Moslem, Christian or Jewish, remain the property of each religion respectively." I suspect this will be one of the very difficult points for the Israelis now that they have taken over Jerusalem. The Ambassador thought Syria's claims for the Golan Heights were excessive. Here Israel had a case. Some guarantee of security to both sides was understandable and necessary. De-militarization was a way out. . . .

I tried to get an acknowledgment of Sadat*'s statesmanship. [The Ambassador] was not prepared to be that generous. The Egyptians' horizon, he said, stops at the Nile. . . . Kissinger, however, the Sheikh readily affirmed, was a different matter. He is a wise foreign minister, but he has lost the confidence of Israel. When I expressed some doubt about this, he said, "I hope you are right. Israel will make a big mistake if it does not agree to a solution before Kissinger disappears from the scene. After all, he is a Jew, but one with vision and a sense of collaboration. . . ."

Sunday, June 29, 1975

I had a nice day in the country. First I went to Bramshott for the memorial service. In the cemetery are the graves of a number of Canadian soldiers and once a year the Canadian veterans in Britain come here for a memorial service. . . .

The Brookwood memorial service, the chief event of the day, was something I will always remember. . . . In this Brook-

13. Vijaya Pandit, Nehru's sister.

wood cemetery are buried some . . . twenty-five hundred Canadians [and] the Canadian war veterans in Britain were there in great force. I reviewed them and placed a wreath at the foot of the concrete cross that dominates the Canadian section. . . . There was a quiet peace as we surveyed the well-kept graves and observed the uniform stones—the kind of peace that these brave lads fought for.

When I went back to reading [of] F. D. R. and Yalta, with Brookwood in my mind, I could not help but reflect on how quickly the big three had carved up the world.[14] Why were the Canadian and other participating governments in the Second World War not at Yalta? What right had the United States, Britain, and the Soviet Union to make fundamental decisions without us and the others? We, too, had made our sacrifice for the preservation of freedom in the common struggle against Hitler. Why weren't we?

Tuesday, July 1, 1975

I awoke this morning anticipating . . . a long and interesting day—July 1st, our national birthday. I received the Diplomatic Corps at noontime in my office at Canada House and we toasted Canada. I had hoped to receive as well Prime Minister Wilson [to] . . . celebrate the 50th anniversary of Canadian occupancy of Canada House in Trafalgar Square. The crisis of the pound, a reflection of growing inflation, made it necessary for the Prime Minister regretfully to stay at his post, which meant continuing with a cabinet meeting which was under way at the noon hour. . . .

The High Commissioner is not only the honorary president of the historic Canada Club which meets at the Savoy three times a year, but he also becomes the presiding officer at the club's dinners. Tonight, I wore my chain of office for the first time, one that has been worn by the presiding officers since 1832, when the chain was presented by some generous

14. Jim Bishop, *F.D.R.'s Last Year, April 1944-April 1945* (New York 1974). Yalta in the U.S.S.R. was the site of a wartime meeting in February 1945 of Stalin, Churchill, and Roosevelt. Later the agreement reached there was criticized for handing eastern Europe to the Russians and inviting them into the Far East.

benefactor. The club actually is older than Canada itself, having been established in 1810 by Englishmen whose forebears had connections in British North America. . . . Denis Healey, the Chancellor of the Exchequer, had weeks ago agreed to be the speaker. He too, like his Prime Minister, could not come. Instead we had [Edmund] Dell, the Paymaster-General, [whose] speech covered the ground traversed by the Chancellor himself a few hours earlier in the House of Commons. At that time, Healey announced that the government would seek to reduce inflation to ten per cent by the end of the next wage round. If this did not succeed, it would have to bring in statutory controls. . . .

Wednesday, July 2, 1975

Jim Callaghan's dinner at Hampton Court Palace was quite an affair. The Attorney-General, Silkin,* and I had a good talk about the *Crossman Diaries* and the extent to which there has been an infringement of the thirty-year [closure] rule by their publication.[15] When the issue is tried shortly, the Attorney-General will take the case himself. He reminded me that the issue is now being considered by a parliamentary commission. I suspect that in future an effort will be made to take into account the wish for more open government, without violating the necessity of non-disclosure in clear situations. I remember Trudeau thinking that Pearson and I were too secretive. Not long after he became Prime Minister he said, "Paul, how right you were. . . ." The fact is, it is just not possible to govern well unless confidentiality of discussion at cabinet level is observed. . . .

Thursday, July 10, 1975

Before leaving the office tonight, I impressed on Mr. Eastham, the next ranking officer in the High Commission at the moment, the importance of a good report to Ottawa on the details of the British government's income policy which will be announced in the House of Commons by the Prime Min-

15. Richard Crossman had been a minister in Harold Wilson's first government. While in office, he had kept quite extensive diaries based in part on discussions in cabinet which were supposed to be protected for thirty years as official secrets.

ister tomorrow. . . . In effect, what is announced as a policy of voluntary restraint will be a compulsory arrangement. Most people now, in the government, business and the unions, recognize the importance to Britain at this critical time of a programme which will restrain the up-scale rate of inflation. . . .

Monday, July 14, 1975

Carel de Wet, the South African Ambassador, received me warmly. . . . [He] . . . has great confidence in Vorster. He is more pragmatic and is trying to reduce South Africa's liabilities. Vorster had established a good relationship with Kaunda.* They have not met—discussions are being carried on vicariously. These could lead to a settlement in Rhodesia and to an improvement in South African relations generally. . . . De Wet told me that Vorster was not telling Rhodesia what do to, but urging that she should negotiate. . . . (As the Liberian Ambassador was to remind me, in this way South Africa was at least buying time for herself. . . .)

Tuesday, July 15, 1975

The Laskins had lunch with me at the residence. Bora said that his appointment as Chief Justice came as a complete surprise. His first intimation was a telephone call from Otto Lang who wanted answers to some questions: How did he get along with his brothers on the bench? Would he accept to become Chief Justice?—and so on. Mr. Justice Martland,[16] who might have expected to be appointed, was very generous in his attitude. Martland is a fine man and I know from personal experience how disappointed he was not to have been appointed. Bora Laskin will make a great Chief Justice. . . .

The garden party at Buckingham Palace was a fine affair, even though late in the afternoon the downpour of rain was heavy. I had the honour of presenting to Her Majesty and Prince Philip, Chief Justice and Mrs. Bora Laskin, Mrs. Ward Cornell (the Ontario Agent General's mother) and Professor and Mrs. Schurman . . . [who has] received a grant from the

16. Ronald Martland was the senior justice of the Supreme Court.

Canada Council to examine and catalogue the fifteen thousand letters which Disraeli wrote during his lifetime. Like the Queen, I found it incredible to believe that one person could have written so many letters but this apparently is the fact. As the Duke of Edinburgh remarked, we do not write letters, telephone, write memoranda but, as a "distinguished citizen" of another country recently did, we put "it" on tapes. . . .

Friday, July 18, 1975

Ma'an Abu Nowar[17] and I had an animated and useful talk. He said, there will be no difficulty in establishing a Palestinian state on the West Bank. It could be in the form of a confederacy under the king[18] or an independent state. In such an event, I suspect, it is believed that, since it would be difficult for the state to surmount its problems, it would, sooner or later, want in some way to be related to the Hashemite Kingdom.

Surely the decision of all the Moslem countries urging the expulsion of Israel [from the United Nations] will be prejudicial to the integrity of the United Nations itself, I asked the Ambassador. He said, "of course, such a proposal in the Assembly would end in a Security Council veto as was the case of South Africa last year." "Furthermore, it must not be forgotten that resolution after resolution has been ignored by Israel," he argued. Can the United Nations stand by and ignore this disregard of its authority?

If the opportunity for settlement is not seized upon by Israel, there will be hostility and dangerous strife. At the moment, no one wants war. "Will this last?" Nowar, looking at me intently, asked. "Israel will make a mistake to overlook that Sadat is not Nasser and that Kissinger and Assad[19] are important personalities, whose presence should be utilized. When these men are no longer on the scene, Israel should ask herself what kind of men will be in authority." The Ambassador recognized that there were faults on all sides and

17. The ambassador of Jordan.
18. King Hussein.
19. Gamal Abdul Nasser, former president of Egypt, and President Hafez al Assad* of Syria.

he implied that Nasser had gone too far. If peace comes to the Middle East, this will be to the West's advantage and to the world also. The Moslem world can never accept communism and will not. Jerusalem is really the key point. Jerusalem, as of the Six-Day War, must be returned to its rightful owner. Internationalization of Jerusalem [and the Holy Places] will not be enough. . . .

Monday, July 21, 1975

Ivan Head told me today on the telephone that the Prime Minister would fly directly to Helsinki to the CSCE summit and return without stopping elsewhere in Europe. I wanted to make sure that I could take a few days' holiday and not be away if he should come to London. It is always well to be on the job when the boss is around. At least that is what I would have expected if fate had put me where Trudeau now is. We talked of the French change of attitude towards Canada's desired connection with the Common Market. As Ivan said, since 1968, our policy toward France has paid off. It would be interesting to know, however, why the French have now agreed that Canada should have a contractual relationship with the E.E.C. The more I think about the matter, the more convinced I am that access to our natural resources could be foremost among the reasons. . . .

I was not through with receptions. At Marlborough House, Jim Callaghan and the High Commissioners had assembled to welcome the new Commonwealth Secretary General, Sonny Ramphal,* whom I have known for over ten years. . . .

Jim Callaghan and I had a ten-minute chat. He told me of his visit to Mobotu in the Congo (Zaire)[20] and, of course, later in Uganda with Field Marshal (self-named) Amin [who] . . . is not a normal person. Not only is he odd, but Jim insists that he is a somewhat dangerous fellow. . . .

Tuesday, July 22, 1975

At the 30th anniversary dinner of the United Nations Association at Plaisterers Hall, larger than such an event would be in Canada, I had the impression that it was just a little more

20. President Mobuto Sese Seko, president of Zaire.

successful than such a gathering would be in Canada or, in the present circumstances, in the United States. Shirley Williams* proposed a toast to the United Nations and my friend, Maurice Strong,* replied. . . . Shirley, one of the most impressive members of the government, is steady, moderate, progressive and intelligent. She speaks extremely well, making out as good a case for the United Nations as I have heard in a long time. . . .

Friday, July 25, 1975

At noon I saw Jim Callaghan, the Foreign Secretary. He had returned from a meeting with the German Chancellor[21] reaching London at 3:00 a.m. MacEachen had cabled, on an urgent basis, with instructions to enlist British support for the Canadian position at a meeting in New York later in the day, when a Canadian proposal for a postponement of the Toronto United Nations Crime Conference would be considered. Allan telephoned Kissinger last night, asking for United States support as I was asking Jim Callaghan for United Kingdom support. In Canada, public opinion has been aroused over this United Nations meeting, which is to be attended by the P.L.O. as observers. . . . Jim agreed to help us at today's committee of the United Nations. MacEachen will ask that the meeting be postponed and held in Canada at a new site in 1976. Callaghan asked why we wanted to have the meeting at all. Having agreed in 1974 to have the conference in Canada, I pointed out it is not easy for Canada, a good United Nations member, to resist what after all is a United Nations General Assembly decision. Today's meeting in New York will likely pass the problem over to the 1975 General Assembly. Because of the P.L.O. Canada would not likely cry over such a decision. . . .

Sunday, July 27, 1975

This morning I left for home and a holiday. Not since 1929-30, when at Cambridge, have I been out of Canada so long. The flight (Air Canada) was smooth and uneventful—a cocktail, browsing, reading some Canadian papers and good sleep. . . .

21. Helmut Schmidt*

IV

August – October 1975

AT THE END OF JULY, Nell and I went back to Canada for a month's holiday. After this pleasant interlude, when we returned to London, the threat of IRA terrorism forced us to vacate the residence as the result of a bomb scare.

I became involved in manoeuvring to make certain that Canada was included as an equal partner with the other leading industrial nations in economic discussions. What I was protesting to the British was that the country which proposed an international meeting on a certain subject was unilaterally selecting the participants at the gathering. The French who were initiating the first Economic Summit refused to include Canada. As the discussions on this subject proceeded, I began to have doubts whether the British were doing their utmost to promote Canada's attendance at the meeting, just as I wondered about their zeal in pushing our desire to establish a contractual link with the European Community.

Towards the end of October, I spent most of a week in Scotland with Allan MacEachen where he held a party that lasted until the wee hours at Edinburgh Castle.

July – August, 1975

During our holiday time in Windsor, I spent some time with my daughter Mary Anne, her husband Michael and my first granddaughter Catherine. Generally an early riser, I caught up on my reading although business intruded from time to time, as I noted on July 31:

The United Nations Crime Conference will take place on schedule on September 1st in Geneva. Our plea for a postponement until 1976, at a new site in Canada, was turned down this p.m. by the United Nations Committee. Our United Nations delegate indignantly rejected what he termed "the questioning of Canada's motives." He said it was difficult to remember a time when Canada had turned down a request from the United Nations. . . .

Trudeau said some wise things at the Helsinki Conference.[1] . . . The security of Europe is important for Canada. . . . Helsinki is a reaffirmation of the United Nations charter. . . . Present boundaries can be changed by peaceful means. It is agreed that they will not be changed by force. Trudeau is right in saying "the breakdown of barriers between the NATO and Warsaw Pact countries is an important achievement." The Russians did not get approved control over Eastern Europe. The Canadian Prime Minister observed: "The principle of self-determination might at some future point work peacefully to change boundaries in the Baltic countries absorbed by the U.S.S.R."

The reactions to Helsinki will be varied. For five years Pearson and I worked hard for Canadian participation in this European Conference. Good progress toward a peaceful régime has been made. We must drive on in this direction. . . .

Until August 22, I spent my time in Windsor and at our cottage in Colchester. I went fishing with friends and former workers in my election campaigns and got caught up on the political gossip. Both Mark MacGuigan and Herb Gray came to talk about their political futures. Both were considering running in the provincial election which was called that month. While I examined their concerns with them, I noted in my diary that, "It is somewhat ironic that all this interests me less and less! . . ." On August 22, Nell and I left for Montreal and then on to a fishing camp on the Saguenay with my son and his boys.*

Just before I was to return to London, Trudeau shuffled his cabinet on August 30. Gérard Pelletier resigned from the cabinet to go to Paris as the new ambassador to France and Jean Marchand gave up the Department of Transport to become a minister without portfolio.

1. The Helsinki Conference was the Summit meeting of the Conference on Security and Co-operation in Europe.

We returned to London on August 30.

Monday, September 1, 1975

The High Commission was only at half-strength today . . . respecting the statutory holiday in Canada, Labour Day. No Labour Day holiday here, but much labour, that is trade union news. Jack Jones of the Transport Workers made the headlines with his proposal for an investment fund programme to improve employment. . . .

Certainly, we are heading into rough weather — not only here, but in Canada and elsewhere. . . . The serious question is not whether the recession will recede, but whether inflation will get seriously worse. . . .

Tuesday, September 2, 1975

Franca and Herb Moran are staying with us en route to Turkey, where Herb had been Ambassador. . . . Herb had at one time been in charge of personnel in External Affairs. He believed strongly that ability should be the first and determining factor in an assignment of a person to a job in the government service. Because of this ideal, which is not always observed, he finds fault with many recent appointments . . . particularly at the deputy minister level. . . . Nor was he pleased with Jake's[2] appointment in Washington. Jake is an able trade negotiator [and Moran believed that] the place for a man like Jake is at GATT in Geneva,[3] where he could utilize his experience and skills in trade negotiation. What Washington needs, Herb thinks, is someone of political stature who could easily contact the political authority in Washington. This is where he thought I should have gone.

I told him at once that there had been a suggestion that that was where I should go but that I had given it the cold shoulder. Washington was a frustrating place. Access to the Secretary of State and the President in normal circumstances

2. Jake Warren* had just been appointed the Canadian ambassador to the United States.
3. GATT [the General Agreement on Tariffs and Trade] is a specialized agency of the U.N. to work for liberalization of trade established in 1948.

is not easy. Under Nixon and Kissinger, access was impossible. Access now to Kissinger continues to be wellnigh impossible. No sir—not for me.

London is different and that is why I accepted to come. Accessibility is the rule in this capital and particularly in my case because of my acquaintance with the Prime Minister and certain members of the government with whom, as a minister, I served on an equal footing. London may not be the most important political capital in the world. It is, however, the forum for good and useful dialogue in matters intimately relating to the great decisions. . . .

I detect a slow change in some of Kissinger's basic attitudes. These attitudes have been greatly influenced by his study of the power politics of the last century. He is being forced, however, to recognize the importance of world economics. Oil, copper and wheat *et al.* are now no less important than army divisions and rockets. . . . The cold war division into two blocs has broken down. Important changes are taking place in the international economy. We now have to go beyond the left-over doctrines of the nineteenth century. Kissinger is now talking less of confrontation and more of dialogue. This does not mean that he is accepting many of the statements from the poorer countries but he is recognizing increasingly the importance of something being done to meet their situation. He would avoid wide fluctuations in the earnings of the poor countries and the costs of the richer ones. He has not yet provided an answer to the problems facing the poorer countries of freer access of their manufactured goods in the markets of the developed countries. It is in this area that the greatest challenge to present ways of life exists. The products of the under-developed world will simply have to find an opportunity for access to wider markets, but it is important that this at least be recognized and, while Kissinger does not offer a solution, he now acknowledges the problem. . . . Gifts will not provide the answer. Conventional commodity agreements will not provide a solution. Certainly a wide-ranging co-operative effort will be needed. . . .

Monday, September 8, 1975

The Saudi Arabian Ambassador called on me this morning. This was our third meeting. He is of the view that the recent Egyptian/Israeli settlement does not represent a real basis for lasting peace because it has not dealt with the main issue, the Palestinians, and has caused great dissension in Arab ranks. The agreement has isolated Syria. On the other hand, Assad could not go to war alone. Nevertheless, there have been imposed strains and other problems on the Arab world. Obviously, Sadat was seeking to make a name for himself. He wanted his place in history. Sadat's wife was an important factor in pushing him towards a peace settlement.

Pat Lavelle, secretary of the Automobile Parts Association in Canada, called to emphasize the deficit the Canadian industry is suffering vis-à-vis the United States. He states that the time has arrived when there should be a revision of the United States/Canada Auto Pact.[4] There is, of course, danger in doing this when the Americans, including Senator Hartke,[5] are complaining about what they call the one-sided factor of the pact, but a whopping deficit such as Lavelle points out is disturbing. He does not think that Alastair Gillespie* is on top of the situation. My own impression is that the latter is a good minister. . . .

Wednesday, September 10, 1975

The Secretary of State, Hugh Faulkner . . . is the fourteenth Canadian minister I will have welcomed to London. Hugh was interested in the rumour that John Turner may leave the government to join the International Bank. All rumour so far. Hugh said that it may be true. John has wanted to get out for some time. We may know more tomorrow. . . .

On Thursday, Nell and I flew to Edinburgh where I was to participate in the military tattoo held there annually.

Friday, September 12, 1975

Now it is definite. John Turner has resigned as Minister of Finance and from the cabinet, and the telex from Ottawa indicates he will resign his seat at the end of the year. Why? He has let it be known that he will not be taking a post, as

4. This agreement, which allowed for freer trade in automobiles, was signed in 1965 while I was secretary of state for external affairs.
5. Senator Vance Hartke of Indiana.

rumoured, with . . . the bank. Is it because he has not been able to get agreement on financial and anti-inflation policy? For the full story we will have to wait. The London *Financial Times* in today's issue says "inter alia," "Turner did not want to spend as long a time waiting around as did Anthony Eden and Paul Martin." Amusing! . . .

The Edinburgh Tattoo was outstanding in conception and execution. I took the salute at five different periods during the performance. Some ten thousand people from all the countries sat in the stands during the coolish night. I was perched on a throne-like seat, the spotlight on me, as I returned the salute by standing. . . .

Sunday evening, Nell and I returned to London.

Monday, September 15, 1975

I am doing today's diary notes the day after, and it has been a "day after." After returning from a small dinner party at the Lord Mayor's, we retired immediately, only to be awakened by Price who told us that we had a bomb scare. . . . The police were in the residence and were actually inspecting the premises. What a surprise! I woke Nell at once and she took it quite philosophically and almost humorously. . . . Discussing the matter with the police inspector, we were told that an English voice had called police headquarters to say that the Canadian embassy would be bombed tonight. Moreover, this information had been telephoned to *The Daily Mirror* and *The Sun*. . . .

What should we do—should we act defiantly and stay in the residence or should we leave? My own disposition was to stay. The police, however, advised that we should go to friends and spend the night. This advice having been given, it would have been difficult not to act on it, so we arranged . . . to spend the rest of the "morning" with André and Pierrette Bissonnette. I hesitated leaving the staff in the residence and told Price that he and the others should go to the Britannia Hotel for the night. Price believes that the danger is not as great as might be thought. Bombing from the exterior would not be so easy to accomplish and so he decided, as did the others, to stay at 12 Upper Brook Street. . . .

Tuesday, September 16, 1975

The day has been an eventful one because of an absolute inundation of visitors—Ministers, Members of Parliament, Senators—Canadians all. September is a popular time to come to London and the High Commissioner is a target. Normally, I take this kind of thing in my stride. I must say I did not do so today—nor was it easy to work. The interruptions were constant and everything just seemed to go wrong. . . .

Maggie[6] led us through a discussion, in preparation for the Canada-United Kingdom Economic Committee meeting in October in Ottawa, on the proposed New World Economic Order. The meeting in Guyana [of Commonwealth finance ministers] was much better than one could have anticipated. . . . John Turner was unhappy at *not* being chairman of our delegation in Guyana. He was further chagrined, I believe, at the extent of our approval for the objectives of the under-developed countries and the proposal for a New Economic Order. The problem was not easy. Trudeau, on the one hand, wishes to be pragmatic and realistic. As a political leader, he realizes it is wise to let the Third World know at least where our long-term sympathies lie. Turner's method would be to say "No—your proposals are not sound and not immediately realizable, if ever." To all this the response must be, that the world has to move . . . and to take a firm . . . position means no progress. . . . Negotiation is, therefore, inevitable. . . .

Wednesday, September 17, 1975

The International Commission on Northwest Atlantic Fisheries meets in Ottawa on the 22nd September to consider a Canadian request for a forty per cent reduction in fishing by foreign fleets and for the need to maintain Canadian fishing at the same level in Atlantic waters. The British seem to have some difficulty in accepting our position, and I was, therefore, instructed by Ottawa to discuss the matter at the highest appropriate level. . . .

6. Margaret Catley-Carlson, one of the High Commission's senior officers who specialized in economic affairs.

I called on the Minister of State for Foreign Affairs . . . , Lord Goronwy-Roberts,* who kindly received me. There is no question what the situation will be when the 200 mile zone is established, insofar as the special status of coastal states is concerned. The British and other countries are anxious that Canada should hold the line on unilateral action. . . . They would prefer to see the 200 mile zone become international law as the result of a collective and orderly international decision — so would we. Trudeau said this the other day. But the pressure on the [Canadian] government to declare unilateral jurisdiction over a 200 mile zone is great. We are now asking for a forty per cent reduction in fishing effort. We say that, if this were accepted, it would enable us to hold the line on unilateral action. . . .

Friday, September 19, 1975

Eddie Rubin is a friend of Trudeau and has become a good friend of [my son] Paul. He is in London on his way to Indonesia and Hong Kong. . . . What did he think of Turner's resignation? Was it over a matter of policy? — No, he says it was not. John wanted to be coaxed, cajoled and perhaps even praised. These are things that Pierre Elliott Trudeau does not do. Rubin thinks that John's resignation amounts to no more than pique. . . .

Sunday, September 21, 1975

Bud Drury,*[7] on his way to Moscow, was met at Heathrow by Nell (a close friend), while I went to Westminster Abbey to attend the "Service of Thanksgiving for Victory granted in the Battle of Britain in 1940." I was surprised that the Queen was not present. Baroness Spencer Churchill, in a wheelchair and looking so much older, was there. The last time (May 1958) I saw her was with her famous husband, Winston, at Lord Beaverbrook's place in Leatherhead (Stornaway) in Surrey. The occasion was Lord Beaverbrook's annual birthday dinner. . . .

7. Minister of public works.

Tuesday, September 23, 1975

No bombs tonight!

Wednesday, September 24, 1975

I paid a courtesy call this morning on Rear-Admiral Kaare Olsen, the Ambassador of Chile. He was interested in my visit to Salvador Allende on the occasion of the UNCTAD Conference in Santiago three years ago.[8] . . . [The ambassador told me that prior to the military revolt against him] Allende had made arrangements for Soviet submarine activities and for the establishment of a Soviet submarine base. Had he been allowed to continue, there is no doubt that "Chile would have become a second Cuba." This story I had not heard before. I must check on it. Allende had been given an opportunity, together with his colleagues, to flee in a special plane provided for that purpose, several hours before he took his own life. [Actually, he was murdered.] The Cardinal of Santiago was a friend of Allende's. Many of his fellow bishops find themselves in a difficult and unusual position. I was told that the Cardinal is a thorn in the flesh of the present administration. . . .

Friday, September 26, 1975

Miss Gadd[9] was in to see me early this a.m. It is clear from the way engagements are piling up I am going to have a busy autumn and, in the midst of it all, I will have to be in Ottawa in two weeks' time for the annual Canada-United Kingdom Consultative Committee meetings. Oh well—I can do no more than one thing at a time. . . .

Saturday, September 27, 1975

Mrs. Thatcher has returned from Canada and the United States. In an unusual statement of personal praise, she spoke of her visit as demonstrating that she was now an acknowl-

8. Salvador Allende, a Marxist, was elected president of Chile in 1970 but was overthrown and killed by a military junta in 1973. The occasion was the United Nations Conference on Trade and Development.
9. My social secretary.

edged international leader. Harold Wilson is going to have much enjoyment over this statement. It reminds me of the day in Parliament when Donald Fleming,* then Minister of Finance, told us how many hours a day he worked.

The OPEC[10] countries decided today to freeze oil prices at a ten per cent higher level. I reported that this would be the likely decision ten days ago, when the Saudi Arabian Ambassador came to see me at Macdonald House. This, I suppose, is what is called a diplomatic scoop. No one seems to have noted it in Ottawa. Did I notice these incidents when I was in the East Block? . . .

Sunday, September 28, 1975

Word has just come to me of cabinet changes in Ottawa. Don Macdonald has taken over Finance. Good. If he watches his temper, he will do well. Bud Cullen from Sarnia has been given a cabinet post.[11] I am so sorry for Mark [MacGuigan]. He wanted so much to get in. He would have done well. I doubt that he will stay in Parliament now. Maybe he will try for the Ontario leadership, or will he go back to academic life? Don Jamieson*[12] now goes to Trade and Commerce. He will do well there. It was a mistake to take him out of Transport and replace him by Marchand. The latter becomes Minister without Portfolio. I, of course, feel for Jean, but I never thought him strong. And to think that Pearson thought of him as his successor! . . .

Monday, September 29, 1975

Although it was late when I met Allan MacEachen, our Minister of External Affairs, and Premier Lougheed of Alberta as they disembarked at Heathrow last night, it was early this morning when Allan left 12 Upper Brook Street. My officers suggested that, as the Premier was on official business in London, I should drive him in to the city in the official car,

10. OPEC was formed in 1960 to check over-development of oil companies, but in the early 1970s became a cartel which set oil prices.
11. Minister of national revenue.
12. Formerly minister of regional and economic expansion.

flag flying, etc. MacEachen thought otherwise. I should accompany him. I had to think fast. I told the Premier, who had been advised he would be with me, that I had pressing matters to discuss with the foreign minister, etc. Lougheed got the point and was generous in his reaction. Allan was a little difficult. We must have the point of protocol settled once and for all. . . .

[Allan and I] had a good and long chat at the residence. MacEachen had been very unhappy over the cabinet's decision on the United Nations Conference on Crime. He thought there should not have been a postponement. He was right. The Prime Minister didn't agree and, without due consultation, told the cabinet what its decision was to be. Allan is anxious that I should attend the dinner for Kissinger in Ottawa on October 14th. I have agreed to go. . . .

Tuesday, September 30, 1975

Premier Lougheed spoke on Alberta and Canadian problems, at Chatham House at noon. He did well. His speech and responses to questions were responsible and in the spirit of good federal-provincial relations. The provinces own the resources, but the central government must protect Canadian trade and economic interests as a whole. Where there is conflict in this area, the "Canadian way," as he called it, must be called into play. This involves not judicial determination, but compromise and accommodation between the governments. . . .

Thursday, October 2, 1975

As I listened to the news last night on the radio, Portugal, Spain, Amin, the fifth day of imprisonment of Italian hostages by three gunmen in London, the bombings in Ulster, the security precautions for Hirohito in Washington and the President, the rumblings at the Labour party meeting in Blackpool etc., etc., I thought that perhaps this was one of the silliest periods in many a year. It must stop somewhere . . . .

Friday, October 3, 1975

A busy work week ended with an extremely busy Friday. Early morning instructions from the highest Ottawa level directed that the British, at the highest level, be urged to see that

Canada be included in important discussions on monetary questions in New York on the 5th and 6th October. This meeting has been called by France and was to include the "Big Five"—the United States, Britain, France, West Germany and Japan. Italy was added, allegedly because of her domestic political problems. We have protested. In Nairobi, however, a few months ago, Turner, objecting to a meeting of the five, said we would expect, if a sixth county were invited, to be that guest. Several months ago, when the producer and consumer oil countries met for planning purposes, we were not included because "to admit Canada would be difficult for other similarly placed nations. . . ."

At noontime, when I was at the doctor's getting an X-ray of my back, I spoke to Denis Healey, the Chancellor of the Exchequer, on the telephone about this. He promised to help; as I learned at 5:15 p.m. from the Permanent Under-Secretary,[13] he carried out his assurances. Denis had recalled the Turner conversation of some months ago. The British response was formally conveyed to me in Sir Thomas Brimelow's office: ". . . our first reaction to that is it may be too late to change the arrangements for the New York meeting. . . ."

I told Sir Thomas that Washington, Bonn and Tokyo were supporting our attendance. He then interjected, "We are supporting your inclusion, likewise." I then asked him how the matter of our participation could be raised. We would expect our friends to present our request. He then said that this was a new and crucial question, which would now have to be put to the Prime Minister and the Foreign Secretary. . . .

Before taking my leave of Sir Thomas, I observed that an unusual and undesirable pattern appeared to be emerging whereby, on vital world issues, a particular nation can take the initiative in calling a meeting and, because of this initiative, it can set the pattern of attendance. I added that this practice was one which many countries would find difficult to accept. Sir Thomas said he would not dissent from this view. "The matter of the [oil] producers/consumers meeting still sticks in Callaghan's throat," he said. . . .

13. Sir Thomas Brimelow

Saturday, October 4, 1975

As of tea-time, no word has come from Chequers or the secretary to the cabinet concerning our démarche on the New York meeting tomorrow on monetary matters. A message from Tokyo suggests support for our position, with the suggestion that we raised the matter too late. The decision was taken by the Five hastily and without proper notice. I note that Ross Campbell[14] raised the same question I had put to Tom Brimelow. It is all very well to say that country "A" supports our request, but which country will raise the matter on our behalf? I still have not quite given up hope, but the hour is late. . . .

Tuesday, October 7, 1975

Good news. Sir Thomas Brimelow . . . told me that our participation in the preparatory meeting in New York had been discussed, with only the French standing out against Canada. President Giscard* . . . has not changed his position. . . . Jim Callaghan, the British Foreign Secretary, spoke to his French opposite number in Luxembourg, asking the latter to contact Giscard, who refused to budge. . . . The French position is, of course, tactical but, nevertheless, an important . . . issue on international collaboration arises and cannot be ignored. I am grateful to the British for their help. . . .

At the reception tonight which Nell and I gave for André and Pierrette Bissonnette, Sir Thomas Brimelow, taking me aside, said that [the Americans] had intimated at the end of the . . . monetary meeting in New York, that . . . President Ford might refuse to go to the proposed summit meeting in Paris in December unless Canada were included among the participating countries. . . . It shows that the steps we took here and in other capitals on Friday and Saturday were not wasted. I appreciate that the United States strongly support us because in the monetary discussions we would likely be on their side. The French, for tactical reasons at least, would prefer to minimize opposition to their monetary views. . . .

14. Canadian ambassador to Japan.

Wednesday, October 8, 1975

The new No. 2 man in the Foreign Office, Richard Sykes, gave a farewell luncheon for André at Brown's Hotel. . . . I had not been there since the early winter of 1946 [when] Campbell Stuart, a man-about-town in those days in this great city, hosted a lunch for the new Governor-General-designate of Canada, Field Marshal Alexander. It was an unique luncheon, for in attendance were the living next-of-kin of all Governors-General of Canada. My impression at that time was that I was lunching with ghosts. . . .

Thursday, October 9, 1975

When, in accordance with instructions, I called on the Secretary of State for Employment, Michael Foot, I found a sympathetic acceptance of my representations that the United States should be urged not to serve notice of intention to withdraw from the International Labour Organization. . . .

Michael Foot is a great orator—a man of great passions and sympathies. Somehow or another, he strikes me as a sad man. I am sure that he is good in the labour portfolio. He does not seem to be overly interested in foreign and world problems. If he were, he would be an eloquent champion of the changing world system and this is what is implied in the New World Economic Order. No doubt about it, the international system is changing from a system designed to promote peace between nations to a system designed to promote progress on many fronts between states. . . .

Friday, October 10, 1975

Tom Brimelow called to give me some news. There would be an announcement at 4:00 p.m. of the meeting of the five with Italy on monetary questions. Another preparatory meeting will take place sometime in November. The French have not moved. . . . Kissinger will discuss the matter with us in Ottawa on Tuesday. I don't like the look of the situation. French intransigence is annoying beyond words and, at this point in time, so is the weak resistance of some of our friends. We will see how far Kissinger will go. Our man in Tokyo may be right. What strong representations have been made in Paris by our four friends, the United Kingdom, Japan, the United States and Germany? . . . The whole procedure is fantastically ridiculous. How can France be permitted to stand in the way of the wishes of the other countries? How far will Trudeau wish to go? I recognize that our Common Market contractual link has to be borne in mind. . . . I suppose we can do no more now than wait for developments. . . .

Tuesday, October 14, 1975

I went to Canada for the joint ministerial meetings between Canada and the U.K.

I must confess I feel a little strange in Ottawa at the moment. So much is happening on the Hill—and I am not part of it. When our meetings with the British begin, the mood will change. There, I will be active in the infrastructure of the public service.

The government has announced strong measures to curb prices and incomes. Pay increases will be kept to ten per cent and costs will determine mark-ups. . . . Joe Morris, head of the Labour Congress, however, is against the programme. So is the N.D.P. Wilson and Denis in the United Kingdom have carried the labour leaders with them [and] Trudeau will have his problems, if labour will not go along. Stanfield must get some satisfaction out of all this. This is what he had urged in the elections of 1974. Trudeau has taken the right course, and almost at the right time. . . .

Kissinger is here on an official visit. MacEachen had me to a dinner for him. I had not seen or talked to him since the NATO Summit in 1974. Kissinger is sticking to the United States' view, that Canada should be among the six countries at the summit on monetary questions, in a month's time. . . . This statement will strongly supplement the letter President Ford has written to the French President. I find it ridiculous, however, that we should have to go hat in hand to France. . . .

At the Country Club last night, where I had gone to the dinner for the two delegations of the United Kingdom/Canada Committee, in a useful exchange with Jack Johnston,[15] I

15. The British high commissioner to Canada.

stressed the importance of our two countries helping one another. Some in Ottawa wonder if the United Kingdom had pushed strongly for our participation in the Economic Summit. Had the United Kingdom really gone to bat for us when, in September, we asked the United Nations for a postponement of the Conference on Crime? I had gone to see Jim Callaghan over this. He promised strong support, but MacEachen told me the British did not deliver. Is the United Kingdom about to create difficulties for us in our objective for a contractual link with the Common Market? . . . We will hear more of this at our meeting with the British this morning. It is important that the United Kingdom and Canada have the fullest confidence in the other. It is my job to see that this is so. . . .

Thursday, October 16, 1975

The British have all along assured me of their support for our objective to have a "contractual link" with the Common Market. The British are now taking the position in Brussels that an agreement with us should not be concluded with the Commission but with the nine countries and the Commission. Tactically, we would prefer that the agreement between the E.E.C. and Canada should be with the Commission only. It was always clear that the Council on Ministers would approve or disapprove any Commission judgment. At our meeting with the British today, we raised the matter obliquely. They replied by saying, whatever the constitutional position, the United Kingdom was in support of the Canadian objective. It may not be realistic [for us] to assume that the Council of Ministers in the E.E.C. would forego their sovereign powers to allow the Commission alone to take decisions affecting the trading interest of member countries. . . .

Monday, October 20, 1975

After an all-night flight to London two days earlier, I just managed to recuperate in time to meet the external affairs minister.

Allan MacEachen was anxious to discuss the state of play on our contractual link objective before his meeting with the Foreign Secretary. . . . I reviewed the matter with some of my officials. . . . The British suggestion of concurrence by the

E.E.C. Commission and the nine could have a delaying effect. . . . A simultaneous negotiation between the Commission and the nine could become complicated. The suggestion of a "mixed" arrangement has come from the British, the French apparently having withdrawn their support for the formula. Allan MacEachen will urge the British to facilitate an early agreement with us.

Now in Edinburgh. We left London about 5:30 p.m., checking in at the North British Hotel. . . . It has been a long day. This should be a good week for Canada in Edinburgh and Scotland. MacEachen is in his glory, even if he has not yet donned the kilt. . . .

Tuesday, October 21, 1975

After lunch, we inspected the future home of the Centre for Canadian Studies at 21 George Square on the University grounds. This is an elegant old house designated by the University for the Centre's purpose. Following this visit, we joined MacEachen, who presided at the opening of the "Canadian Exhibition" in the university library.

Later, the Chair of the Centre of Canadian Studies was formally inaugurated in the New Senate Room at the University in Old College, South Bridge. . . . Professor [Ian] Drummond gave the inaugural lecture, entitled "Movement of People and Movement of Ideas." . . . It might have been better, however, if his talk had been of a more general character, having in mind the nature of the inaugural ceremony. . . .

Wednesday, October 22, 1975

I went with [MacEachen] to [Edinburgh] Castle this afternoon to discuss the arrangements for his *ceilidh* tomorrow night. . . . I doubt if he is fully aware of the problems I had in getting the Secretary of [State for] Scotland to agree to our use of the castle. The secretary, and indeed the governor of the castle, had taken the position that use of any of the rooms in the castle could only be by ministers of the government in the United Kingdom. I was able to persuade Jim Callaghan that an exception ought to be made or a formula devised that would permit MacEachen to have his *ceilidh* in the castle. After much correspondence and negotiation, it was finally agreed that invitations to the *ceilidh* would be in the name of the Secretary of State for Scotland and the Secretary of State for External Affairs for Canada. Allan's love of the Scottish is something to behold! . . .

Thursday, October 23, 1975

I joined Father Macdonnell, President of St. Francis Xavier University, and Allan MacEachen at the School of Gaelic Studies at Edinburgh University this morning. . . . We had a revealing discussion on Scottish nationalism. Our hosts not only want to strengthen the fact of language, they wish to bring about a fully independent Scotland. . . . Tactfully, I suggested cultural independence need not involve so drastic a step. The drift in the world should be towards internationalism. . . . At lunch with Lady Rodney and Sir Andrew Miller, a former Lord Provost of Edinburgh, Allan and I were given the other side of the coin. The separatists in Scotland are a noisy minority, whose programme is not supportable. The North Sea oil development, it was admitted, helped the nationalists in their campaign. The United Kingdom government's policy on devolution will provide for a Scottish Assembly, but its powers will be delegated — and remain the creature of Parliament at Westminster. . . .

More manifestations of the Gaelic embrace were given at Allan's *ceilidh* in the Great Hall in Edinburgh Castle, which lasted into the early hours. . . .

Friday, October 24, 1975

Not much sleep last night. Early this morning, with my foreign minister sound asleep at the North British Hotel, I set out for the Edinburgh Airport en route to London. . . .

Monday, October 27, 1975

After being away from London for almost a week, there was much to do. So many things to catch up with. I do not make a practice of taking telegrams away from the office, and so, absence for a few days means that matters pile up. No head of mission can do his job well if he does not keep up with the telegrams. There was one that captured my interest and gave me temporary satisfaction. *Agence France-Presse* had reported on Friday that Canada was going to be invited to attend the Economic Summit. . . . It now seems that the story was premature and, I am afraid, inaccurate.

Tom Brimelow, the Permanent Under-Secretary, received my Deputy High Commissioner[16] . . . today. He was shown, "à la vitesse," President Ford's letter to Harold Wilson and what a letter it is. Earlier, the suggestion had been made by the President of France that the common features of the United States and Canadian economies did not warrant Canada's participation [in the economic summit]. President Ford took strong exception to this and rightly so. . . . President Ford argued strongly for our inclusion, saying in substance what Kissinger had said in Ottawa, that it was essential that we should be invited. . . . What right has France to limit the participants at an international conference? It is about time that someone made this point in a forceful way since the British have not been prepared to make it themselves. . . . The Foreign Secretary has instructed his Ambassador in Paris to make further representations at the highest level. Jim Callaghan in his instruction has reiterated some of the arguments in President Ford's communication . . . but a well-placed informant has suggested that Giscard is not likely to change his mind. Callaghan . . . told MacEachen a week ago today, that he did not stir up more trouble for us because he himself was engaged in a controversy with the French and others in the Community over British insistence for separate British representation at the energy conference.

All along it has been evident to me that this was the reason why the British did not raise the matter in the first instance on behalf of Canada at the New York meeting two weeks ago. I asked myself, as undoubtedly will the Canadian government: Is this good enough? How will the British be prejudiced by fighting for our participation at the Economic Summit Meeting? . . . Countries, no matter how friendly, have differences which often are unrelated to other matters, and who is the President of France that he should be able to take umbrage at British championship of our cause. . . .

16. André Bissonnette was replaced by Christian Hardy.*

And so, what looked like promising news this morning now looks like a turn-down by nightfall. All this information, of course, we are sending to Ottawa. The question now in my mind is of what value would it be now for me to see Jim Callaghan, the Prime Minister or Tom Brimelow on this matter. . . .

Tuesday, October 28, 1975

The Ambassador for Luxembourg and I were the only heads of mission at the South Africa Club Dinner at the Savoy tonight. I went, not because I approve of apartheid — few have been more outspoken than I — but because the present Prime Minister of that country has embarked on a liberalization programme and, from all that I can see, wants to pursue it much further. . . . Moreover, I like the South African Ambassador here, with whom I have had a number of talks. To have refused his invitation would have been a snub and that I did not propose to give. The dinner was in honour of Sir Arthur Snelling and J. Donald McCall. Sir Arthur, a former British Ambassador, spent most of the time in outlining what Britain had done for South Africa and by clever sideway snipes at apartheid. . . . That of Donald McCall, an Englishman who has gold-mining interests in South Africa, was reactionary, condescending and I almost felt like leaving. . . .

Valéry Giscard d'Estaing made a speech tonight calling for "a new world economic order capable of preventing the brutal shocks of the past few years." The new arrangement would include various ways of assisting the developing world, a new monetary structure with "stabilized parties" and "equal rights" between the United States and nations in the European float.[17] Because Canada supports the United States position on the float, Giscard does not want us to participate in the Conference which is to take place over a period of three days, from November 15th to 17th. . . . It makes me boil to think that we are not to be included in this group to discuss these momentous issues. I should like to see the letter Giscard sends to Trudeau. It will have to be a very strong one to justify our exclusion. The French are just too damn arrogant. . . .

17. The European currency system.

Wednesday, October 29, 1975

Tired after an interesting and long day, we went to bed at once. Half an hour later Price woke us up, saying that McCracken of Macdonald House strongly urged that we should sleep at the back of the residence. A bad bombing had taken place on South Audley Street. Some eighteen people had been injured. . . . I was too sleepy, however, to do anything more than to move down to the guest room, where I continued my imperfect sleep. This bombing, [together with] that last week at the residence of Hugh Fraser, MP, and other repeated acts of terror is certainly putting this community in a continuous state of apprehension. This is the second time we have had to move at night. . . . We continue to have a ridiculous glass door at the front of the residence, which no one but me wishes to change. This is symptomatic only of the much wider problem which we face and about which, I suppose, Ottawa has little but passing interest. . . .

V

November – December 1975

As November 15, the date for the Economic Summit at Rambouillet, France, drew near, Canada's resentment of President Giscard d'Estaing's high-handed exclusion of our country increased. I made continuous representations to Harold Wilson's government in an effort to get Trudeau to Rambouillet. The French remained adamant.

After the meeting, I tried to find out how its decisions might affect Canada. The year wound down with a flurry of Christmas entertaining.

Saturday, November 1, 1975

Shortly, I expect, the British will announce their acceptance of a single E.E.C. agreement with Canada, provided they are given undertakings about the limited competence of the Community to negotiate co-operation in certain economic and industrial spheres, without the prior approval of national governments. Accordingly, I expect the Council of Ministers of the E.E.C. to sanction the formal opening of negotiations with Canada early in the New Year.

Michel Gauvin*[1] saw Bourassa,* the Quebec Prime Minister, in Athens a few days ago. The Premier has no objection to welcoming the Queen when she comes to Quebec in 1976 and, moreover, he told Michel it would be better for *Britannia* to dock at the harbour in Quebec City and not at Three Rivers. . . . He does not think, however, it would be wise to have a large and public welcoming ceremony in Quebec City. . . .

1. Gauvin had just taken charge of organizing royal visits.

Wednesday, November 5, 1975

Mike Berry, who was one of our top economic men here when I first came to the High Commission . . . dropped in this morning. . . . I discussed with him a telegram we received from Washington yesterday. Sonnenfeldt[2] told Jake [Warren] that the French President has replied to President Ford regarding Canadian participation in the Economic Summit. . . . The reply continues to be in the negative. The pressure is still on nevertheless. Ford had gone back to Giscard over the weekend. Washington understands that Prime Minister Wilson has made, or was considering making, a direct approach to the French President. It is suggested that we should check on this. . . .

Giscard, in his reply, noted that Canadian participation meant further enlargement since other countries were concerned over their exclusion. Another argument given by the French President was that Canada, a major raw material producer, was not in the same situation as the six who were important manufacturing countries and importers of raw materials. These are specious arguments. A suggestion is made that Giscard may not have forgiven our Prime Minister for isolating France at the NATO Summit Meeting, when Trudeau proposed more frequent heads of government sessions. I doubt that this is a reason for France's attitude. I think the real reason is that the French President does not think it necessary for North American interests to be represented by a second voice. . . .

I asked R. H. G. Edmonds, Assistant Under-Secretary in the Foreign and Commonwealth Office, to join us at the luncheon I was having for Dr. François Cloutier, the Quebec Minister of Intergovernmental Affairs. Fortunately, Edmonds was the first to arrive. I put to him the question "Was it a fact that Washington had asked Prime Minister Wilson to communicate again with the President of France, urging Canadian participation in the Economic Summit Conference?" He replied at once by saying in a non-attributable way, that Wilson had either sent or was about to send such a letter to the French President. I sent on this word to Ottawa at once. I cannot believe that it will change the situation. . . .

2. Helmut Sonnenfeldt, a counsellor in the U.S. State Department.

Cloutier made a good statement outlining his own strong attitude for the preservation of Confederation in Canada. He is satisfied that his famous education Bill 22, in the long run, will be fully understood as a necessary measure.[3] I said I agreed with the principle of the bill. The French fact in Canada has to be preserved, otherwise the country would break up. There were one or two points in the bill which I thought did not meet the requirements of the constitution and he agreed. . . .

Elliot Richardson called on his return from Cambridge. I congratulated him on his appointment as Secretary of Commerce [in Gerald Ford's cabinet]. . . .

Thursday, November 6, 1975

I was talking to Ivan Head at NATO headquarters in Brussels this morning. . . . Ivan and I are agreed that it would be wrong for Trudeau to write to Giscard now [about the Economic Summit]. I suggested, however, that it would be appropriate for the Prime Minister to write a note of appreciation to the Prime Ministers of the United Kingdom and Japan and the Chancellor of Germany for their loyalty [to] and support of Canada. Ivan made the important point that we should realize the support we had received in this instance from Washington was because they would have in us an ally at the Monetary Summit Meeting. . . . Ivan wanted me to know as well that Trudeau and Ford had been talking on the telephone a few days ago. Their relations are good and must be kept that way. . . .

At 11:00 o'clock I accompanied Dr. Cloutier . . . and the Quebec Agent General, Jean Fournier, to the Foreign Office for a three-quarter hour meeting with Lord Goronwyn-Roberts, Minister of State for Foreign Affairs. In a sense this was an historic meeting. When the Cloutier visit was first broached,

3. Bill 22 was introduced by the Bourassa government on May 21, 1974. It made French the official language of the province and tried to enforce the use of French in business. It also required that French be the normal language of instruction in the schools unless by permission and that the children of immigrants be educated in French. Needless to say, the bill was attacked both by separatists for not going far enough and by the Quebec anglophone population for going too far.

I had expressed some doubt about the practice of a provincial minister calling on the Foreign Office. . . . When I was Secretary of State for External Affairs, I did everything I could to stop the precedent in Paris from developing. I was, therefore, not anxious to see it extended in other capitals. . . . [When] I discussed the matter with Allan MacEachen about five weeks ago . . . he saw no problem. This, at the time, surprised me. He could not have been aware of the situation as it unfolded some ten years ago. I fully realize that once Quebec put forward its claim to the Foreign Office in London, there was no logical way it would be denied. Heretofore provincial ministers have called on British ministers but not on the Foreign Office. . . .

Goronwy-Roberts obviously had been well briefed [about] what our sensitivities had been and what mine likely were. . . . [He] wanted to know about Quebec House in Paris. Cloutier replied: "that is a special situation where the Quebec Agent General possesses pretty wide diplomatic authority, just short of that exercised by the sovereign arm in Canada. . . ." The visit passed off as well as it could, but not as it should.

At the Soviet Ambassador's reception at his residence, the Italian Ambassador[4] told me that the inclusion of Italy in the countries to participate in the Economic Summit was achieved only after the greatest effort on the part of Italy and "some friends." As far as Italy was concerned, to add Canada would not create a problem. What is the difference between six and seven or five and six? Obviously there is more to this than we presently know. I mean to find out. . . .

Friday, November 7, 1975

A surprising bit of information reached us this morning that the Americans urged on the French the inclusion of the Italians . . . in the Economic Summit Meeting. I later learned from an impeccable source[5] that at the Helsinki meeting,[6] there was some restricted discussion about an economic summit, the United States had suggested to the French the inclu-

4. Roberto Ducci
5. Ronald Spiers, the counsellor at the United States Embassy in London.
6. The CSCE meeting.

sion of the Italians. . . . There would [consequently] be some defusing of a consensus . . . prejudicial to the position the United States takes on monetary matters. If these two reports are correct, then the reason for the United States' support [of Canada] is now clear. One wonders why the United States would not have proposed us at the outset. Perhaps it was only after we had hollered, that [the U.S.] saw how difficult it would be for them not to support us, particularly if the suggestion about Italian participation had originated with them. . . .

Sunday, November 9, 1975

The ceremony at the cenotaph in London is part of the institutional arrangements of my adult days. Today I was part of it. At the cenotaph in Whitehall, in front of the Home Office, the Queen, members of the royal family, and government laid wreaths. I led the heads of missions from the Commonwealth in doing the same. The Bishop of London pronounced the benediction. The ceremony, timed to the minute, was not protracted and was impressive. . . . It is the first time I have seen Elizabeth II in the lead at this ceremony. I had seen George VI lay the first wreath in the summer of 1939 at the war memorial in Ottawa, several months before the Second World War.

After the ceremony, we joined the Prime Minister and Jim Callaghan for some refreshments at the Foreign Office. . . . Ted Heath . . . told me about last night's bombing incident in front of his house. A bomb, underpinned in a car, was defused just in time to avoid an explosion. He himself was driving in from the country at the time. He is confident that the bomb was intended for him. . . . Mrs. Thatcher told me . . . she was impressed with Toronto, but not so much with some of our newspaper fellows. Like so many in the United Kingdom, she wondered at their lack of knowledge. I suggested that our journalists were not that bad. . . .

Tuesday, November 11, 1975

Sir Martin Charteris, the Queen's private secretary, lunched with me at 12 Upper Brook Street. Martin has served the Queen in this capacity for twenty-four years. I have known him most of this time. He is a knowledgeable and wise man. . . . Martin was pleased that [Harold] Macmillan was lunching at the residence tomorrow. He greatly admires the former Prime Minister as does the Queen. The other Harold and the present Prime Minister are liked "at the top." Wilson's imperturbability carries him through at meetings with the palace staff and "beyond." Ted Heath was rigid and, like Anthony Eden, was not free of tension during weekly audiences. Shades of Melbourne, Disraeli and Gladstone! . . .

Who did I think would succeed Wilson, I was asked. In the short term, Callaghan — in the longer run, Crosland. This seemed to surprise Martin, who does not know this long shot. This is Selwyn Lloyd's view. Did I know Wedgwood Benn? Yes, I did and I like him. Agreed, replied the Queen's secretary, and he is such a good speaker. . . .

Wednesday, November 12, 1975

I called on Signor Roberto Ducci, the Italian Ambassador. We met in his fine study. I was anxious to ascertain if he knew what was going on at the official meeting preparatory to the Economic Summit. He did not know, but he would call me tomorrow and perhaps would have some information. The information I wanted I did get later in the afternoon from Sir John Hunt.* The United States and the United Kingdom, at the meeting of officials, expressed again the view that Canada should be at the Summit and they expected that Canada would be. The note of expectancy was put in a rhetorical way. These two interventions did not draw any reaction whatsoever from France. This I reported to Ottawa. . . .

Our luncheon guest, the Rt. Hon. Harold Macmillan, the former Prime Minister, is one of the most accomplished speakers of the day anywhere. . . . He spoke of Diefenbaker and the circumstances of their meeting with Jack Kennedy in Nassau. Diefenbaker apparently imposed himself on that meeting. Jack Kennedy was unruly, in my judgment, in speaking so disparagingly of John to Macmillan. . . .[7] I told the

7. Diefenbaker, claiming an invitation from Harold Macmillan, went to Nassau, the Bahamas, on December 21, 1962. The meeting was part of the debate over Canada's acquisition of nuclear weapons which ultimately forced Diefenbaker out of office the following year.

former P.M. I did not have the same high opinion of Kennedy which he had. . . . His [Kennedy's] youth was, of course, to his great advantage, but was he comparable to Adlai Stevenson?[8] Certainly not in my judgment. He gave to the younger generation an opportunity for political leadership which it is entitled to, but not monopolistically. Why should the young necessarily govern? I suspect Harold Macmillan knew what I was saying — that I was showing a little bitterness — that, because Kennedy had been elected President, this had reinforced the argument that political leadership in Canada should not go to men over sixty. . . .

Yes, [Macmillan believed] Harold Wilson is doing well at the moment. There is no rival in any party to his political leadership. He is at the height of his power. "Wilson has been kind to me," said Macmillan. I have always noticed how those in power do extend acts of consideration and kindness to former political opponents. . . .

Sunday, November 16, 1975

The five countries have been meeting all day at Rambouillet in France.[9] They will not confine themselves to monetary questions. . . . The British Prime Minister, it is rumoured, will raise energy questions as well as economic issues. This makes Canada's exclusion all the more ridiculous. We are more important in the field of energy than France or Britain. But we are not there. . . .

Monday, November 17, 1975

Last week I reported to Ottawa [that] I had learned from a good source, that the President of France would not be writing to our Prime Minister until the eve of the conference. This is exactly what has happened. I said as well that Giscard wrote a somewhat similar letter to the other heads of state who supported Canadian participation. I think this is an unsatis-

8. The Democratic presidential candidate in 1952 and 1956.
9. The participants were Prime Minister Takeo Miki of Japan, Prime Minister Harold Wilson of Britain, President Valéry Giscard d'Estaing of France, President Gerald Ford of the U.S., and Prime Minister Aldo Moro of Italy.

factory letter. First of all, it was sent at the last moment, just [as] the meeting was about to convene. Only France took exception to our participation. Our economic position in the world is such that we should have been included. I hope Trudeau will say so, if and when he replies to the President of France. . . .

Further news about the Economic Summit—it is over and seems to have gone off well. The main achievement lies in the agreement between the United States and France to resolve their differences on floating exchange rates. The agreement is part of a broader consensus between the heads of the six . . . industrial nations on co-ordinating their economic recovery policies. . . . The British did not rule out protective measures for particular British industries "suffering or threatened with serious injury as a result of increased imports." The main agreement was on exchange rates. The United States and France particularly would move towards "more stable structures" and in particular towards reducing "erratic" fluctuations in exchange rates, making them more "viscous." . . .

There was no vacant chair for Canada at the conference. Maybe some unknown American had rightly interpreted the mood of the participants when he said: "Canada would not have had much to offer anyhow," to which I take the strongest exception.

Tuesday, November 18, 1975

President Nyerere* was guest of honour tonight at a state banquet at Buckingham Palace. Only ten heads of mission had been invited. I suppose high commissioners and ambassadors are taken in turn. . . . After shaking hands with the Queen, I got a warm greeting from Nyerere . . . whom I have known since 1963. I could not help but think, seeing and hearing him speak in Buckingham Palace, of the time around 1964 or 1965 when he withdrew his High Commissioner from London in protest against Britain's policy in Rhodesia. I had urged Nyerere not to take this step, believing that it was not going to really help provide a solution. I think he would now agree that this was the correct view. . . .

Wednesday, November 19, 1975

In my public life, I have attended about thirty-eight or -nine formal openings of Parliament. On thirty-three of these occasions I was in the Commons and the remaining openings were when I was Leader of the Government in the Senate. . . . This morning I attended the opening of Parliament by the Queen, when she read the address. . . . The Speaker's reception reminded me [that] after a while, I used to dodge these receptions in Ottawa. I found them time-consuming and something of a bore. Here, today, the climate was different and I was somewhat like a new boy. Selwyn Lloyd welcomed me with open arms. . . .

Thursday, November 20, 1975

As I drove from the Temple [after dinner with barristers], I sighed with relief. What a tense eight or nine days I have had. A state banquet, seven lunches and three dinners at Gray's Inn, Lincoln's Inn and the Middle Temple. My digestive powers must be good. . . .

Saturday, November 22, 1975

Leaving London in CAN-1,[10] the efficient John at the wheel, we reached Salisbury to visit the Cathedral, spent the night at the King's Arms Hotel, and on about nine miles away to Alvediston for lunch with Anthony Eden. The inn where Charles II was once lodged is replete with seventeenth-century charm.

After we had checked in, we drove to Stonehenge — that ancient monument, where we were greeted by the chief custodian, Tom Woodhouse. . . . He complained that yesterday a Canadian athletic group had visited this historical region. They had acted rudely and in [a] ruffian fashion. I promised to look into the matter and expressed my apologies. . . .

Sunday, November 23, 1975

At one point, we had to make enquiries as to which direction to take. A young lady, who turned out to be Eden's secretary, pointed the way and told us that Lord and Lady Avon were

10. My name for the High Commissioner's car, given because of the licence number. The driver, John Rowan, became a valued friend.

awaiting us. In no time we received a warm greeting from both. . . .

He was interested that we had lunched with Harold Macmillan at 12 Upper Brook this week. He knew Rab Butler had thought that he [Eden] had picked Macmillan as his successor. That was not true. He did not believe that a leader should pick his successor. . . . Eden [had in fact] suggested to the Queen that she should seek the advice of a reputable and respected peer, like Lord Salisbury, the former Viscount Cranborne, and the man who was persistently a loyal colleague of Eden from the thirties at the League of Nations. It was Salisbury, for one, who offered advice that Macmillan should be called on to form a government. . . .

We did touch on Suez, but not as deeply as I would have liked. Somewhat wistfully, I thought, Anthony said "I made one mistake." "I counted too strongly on the strength of our military forces." . . . "It was wrong of Rab to infer in his autobiography that he was not a party to Suez." I recall Rab telling me at the Master's table at Trinity, when I was his guest last May, "Only Anthony and Selwyn have the Suez secret."[11] Like Selwyn, Eden stated all the cabinet were in on the Suez decision, and this included Rab. Clarissa added that the cabinet discussions on the question were actually held up, until Rab came into the cabinet room, inferring that, perhaps, he had deliberately delayed his entrance in the hope of avoiding participation in the discussion and decision. . . .

Monday, November 24, 1975

An unexpected visitor today was Doug Fisher.[12] We had a long chat. . . . He says Trudeau is in trouble. I reminded him that political leaders had their ups and downs. The government has great problems. Trudeau will survive these. . . .

11. The Suez crisis began after President Nasser of Egypt nationalized the Suez Canal Company, owned by the British government and French investors. Israel attacked Egypt on October 29 and Nasser rejected a British and French ultimatum that he halt military operations. The British and French attacked Egyptian bases on October 31 and landed forces. This invasion was condemned by the United Nations, the United States, and Canada. In response, the Anglo-French operations halted on November 7 and at Mike Pearson's instigation the United Nations sent an emergency force to keep the peace. The crisis weakened Anthony Eden's reputation for statesmanship, and he resigned two months later.
12. Former NDP member of Parliament (1957-65) and then a journalist.

The head of Reuters, Lord Barnetson, lunched with me at the residence. . . . I hope to enlist his co-operation in promoting more Canadian news in the United Kingdom, likewise helping getting more news to Canada of the work of this mission, and our other posts. . . . He is in close contact with Prime Minister Wilson and, only a few months ago, went to the House of Lords . . . but he preferred not to be known as a "Press Lord." . . .

I have been trying to get Nell to come to the House of Commons ever since we came here. I have had thirty-nine years of Parliament, she would say: "I have seen you go through the [grilling in] the pit of the Commons and in the Senate at home. I don't want to see or hear of those places again." When she saw the House of Commons last night, however, with its box-like dimension and the intimacy thus created, her interest was awakened. The Minister of State for Education who was speaking, was so impressive that Nell was enthralled with the visit. She was amused [at] how the front bench put their feet on the clerk's table. I explained to her that this was not rudeness, but the observance of a tradition, although, when I first saw it I was somewhat appalled. I think it was Anthony Eden whose feet adorned the table when I first noticed the practice. When Nell registered this chuminess, I thought of the visit Alec Home as Prime Minister and Rab Butler as foreign minister, paid to us in 1965. They had come to our cabinet. Alec sat next to the Prime Minister and Rab on Home's left. All of a sudden, Rab put his feet on the cabinet table. We were all shocked. I believe Rab did this as a matter of habit, so used was he to doing the same thing in the House of Commons. . . .

Tuesday, November 25, 1975

Doug Fisher called me at Macdonald House. I suggested that he come over to the residence for a drink. There he and I and Nell had a good hour or so of conversation. . . . Doug thinks there is an impression developing in Canada now that the provincial arena is more important than the federal— they deal with matters more directly related to the people. Perhaps he has gained this impression because he has just concluded service on a commission in Ontario looking into the structure of government and conditions in the legislative process. He has no great love for Trudeau. I told him he was wrong. . . . The latter is able and has strong intellectual interests, which should appeal to Fisher. No prime minister has ever captured the continuing admiration of the press. Their relationship is an adversary one by its very nature. The newspaper man cannot see this. . . .

Wednesday, November 26, 1975

At our executive committee meeting this morning, I disclosed that I was anxious to give every person in the employ of the High Commission an opportunity, at some time in the year, to attend a reception in the High Commissioner's residence. We had much discussion about this. I proposed [this], nothwithstanding the view that this could be a difficult precedent. . . .

Nell and I ended the day with the Queen's evening reception for the diplomatic corps at Buckingham Palace. . . . Prince Charles, with his garter on the left leg, was in a particularly happy mood. Nell said to him how much she had enjoyed his television appearance—how good he was on television! With a smile he said, "Mrs. Martin, flattery will get you everywhere." . . .

Thursday, November 27, 1975

Brian Flemming, vice-president of the Canada Council and an active Nova Scotian lawyer, brought me up to date on the Liberal party convention in November. His report was not as critical as some others [that] I have received. Donald Macdonald apparently did well at the convention, and Trudeau's emotional introduction of Mackasey* provoked a sustained ovation. Brian thinks that Brian Mulrooney* [sic] has a good chance to become Tory leader. . . .

Friday, November 28, 1975

Edward Short, the Lord President of the Council, tabled his white paper on devolution. At first glance it doesn't contain anything that he had not told me about when I called on him some weeks ago. It is the big news, however, this morning. A form of miniature cabinet is proposed for Scotland. The paper proposed elected, single-chamber Assemblies in Scotland and Wales. That in Wales will have no legislative powers. The Scottish Assembly, however, will be given full powers to pass bills on a range of domestic subjects. . . .

I am inclined to believe that the wisest course would have been to resist this form of devolution, so dangerous potentially to United Kingdom unity and integrity. The need for decentralization is obvious. This could have been provided by a programme of regionalism bringing government closer to the people, but in a way that would minimize the danger of fragmentation. All of this gives Canada some comfort. We have been through it. Our Gethsemene is not over. It is regrettable to see that Britain may be beginning to have hers. . . .

[When] the foreign services officers met with me and the deputy high commissioner . . . I made the point that oftentimes, when we discussed relations between one country and another, what we were really underlining was the attitude of the leaders at a particular time in history. Relations between Canada and the United States in the days of Roosevelt were happy and good, largely because relations between Roosevelt and King were good. Some of our troubles in the Johnson period arose over the deterioration in relations between Pearson and Johnson, and likewise in the Nixon period, between Trudeau and Nixon. . . .

Wednesday, December 3, 1975

I drove from London for a trip to Manchester and then a conference at Ditchley Park.[13] I had read about Jodrell Bank and Sir Bernard Lovell.[14] Now I was to see both. . . .

I knew I was with an extraordinary man, who communicated an important fundamental point in man's relationship to infinity. . . . He asked: Has Man arrived at a fundamental obstacle in his effort to understand the universe "in a physical sense"? How long can Man endure the consequences of the

13. Ditchley was a meeting place of Winston Churchill's cabinet during the war and more particularly where he often spent the night.
14. Sir Bernard Lovell was professor of radio astronomy at the University of Manchester, and Jodrell Bank (Cheshire) was the site of the radio telescope that he used to make some of the principal advances in radio astronomy.

scientists' researches to "break through this barrier"? His work at Jodrell Bank causes Lovell to examine if "our life on earth is unique in the whole universe." . . . [Lovell] moved me as I have rarely been, when I noted his considered word—"Human existence is itself entwined with the primeval state of the universe and the pursuit of understanding is a transcendent value in man's life and purpose."[15] . . .

[In Manchester] we spent an interesting hour with the editors of *The Guardian*. . . . They agreed with me that Canada did not get the attention it deserved in Britain. I am sure this is because (1) the High Commission information division has not gone at the problem in the right way, (2) the Canadian Press is not active enough in London and in other European capitals, and (3) because the Canadian news is carried by the C.P. through Reuters or otherwise in London and other centres in Europe. . . .

Thursday, December 4, 1975

A quick lunch in the King's Arms—then to Bladon and the Anglican cemetery, where lies Churchill in his simple grave, surrounded by Jenny, his father Randolph, and others in the family. Young boys were making noise at play in a natural manner and oblivious. To three of them I gave our little brass maple leaf pins. . . . I asked the boys, did they know whose grave we had come to see? . . . One of the three replied: "He won the war." . . .

[At Ditchley] we had about an hour and a half's discussion on relations between Australia and New Zealand with the United Kingdom and the United States. Prince Philip was an active participant and chairman. He made the point that . . . the Crown . . . did not, when "down under," seek to represent anything but Australian and New Zealand interests, even though the High Commissioner for the United Kingdom (Charles Johnston) had wanted the Crown to take part in essentially United Kingdom organisms in Australia. The changes which have taken place between Australia, New Zealand and the United Kingdom are more in the sense of development than conscious change, said Philip. . . .

15. In his presidential address to the 137th meeting of the British Association for the Advancement of Science.

Friday, December 5, 1975

I stated my views in today's morning session. The option before us is to build stronger bridges from Canada to Europe, and from Canada to Japan for both political and economic reasons. Essentially Canada, Australia and New Zealand are in similar positions as regards their relationships with the two Atlantic power centres. In the economic sphere, however, this is not the case. Canada is trying to diversify. We don't wish to be over-dependent on the United States. . . . Australia and New Zealand are seeking to develop and assert new ties in their own regions, because of decreasing economic contact with Europe, primarily . . . the United Kingdom. The pivotal event in both of these shifts was the United Kingdom's entry into the E.E.C. In the light of our loss of trade preferences in the United Kingdom market . . . United Kingdom entry forces Australia and New Zealand to even more profound and soul-searching about their economic futures. The main dilemma for each is how to replace the European position in their own economies without being totally tied to Japan. . . . Sir Michael Palliser* . . . mentioned that the present accessibility we enjoyed with the government and public service in the United Kingdom could become less a fact as Britain's participation in th E.E.C. became more absorbing. . . .

Monday, December 8, 1975

Ottawa wishes us to urge the British to support Canada as a member of the Commission on Energy [CIEC] at the Conference of Producers and Consumers in France next week. We would also like to be on the resources and finance committee. . . . Giscard d'Estaing told Don Jamieson last week that France would be happy if we did take on the co-chairmanship. My view is that we should not. France has suggested us for this role now because of our dissatisfacion over having been excluded from participation in the Economic Summit meeting a few weeks ago at Rambouillet in France. We are showing a lack of sophistication in agreeing to be a co-chairman of this conference. . . . Ottawa is the master. My duty is to follow instructions. . . .

Tuesday, December 9, 1975

It now seems it is agreed that Allan will be one of the co-chairmen at the CIEC. . . . If this eventuates and we actually do get on the Energy Commission, Ottawa should be pleased. Allan, however, will have his hands full. . . .

Wednesday, December 10, 1975

Rumblings from the Economic Summit at Rambouillet continue. Chancellor Schmidt seemed pleased with the letter Trudeau sent him, thanking the Chancellor for his support for Canada's inclusion at the summit meeting. The Chancellor has reiterated that Canada should have been at Rambouillet and must be at future meetings. . . . Not only did he speak to Giscard d'Estaing in person, but later on the phone, urging Canadian participation. . . . It is not likely that there will be any meetings of this kind in the near future. . . .

Thursday, December 11, 1975

I made my first call on Sir Michael Palliser, Tom Brimelow's successor as Permanent Under-Secretary and head of the diplomatic service at the Foreign Office. . . . I thanked him for his quick action in getting British support for Canada on the Energy Commission at the Conference of Producers and Consumers, in Paris on Tuesday. "May I now ask for something from you?" said he. It was agreed at the Rome meeting of the nine Common Market ministers the other day that there would be but one E.E.C. spokesman at next Tuesday's meeting. Jim Callaghan had been arguing for separate British representation as the only oil-producing country in the Community. The other eight countries did not agree, but apparently a compromise was reached. It is always desirable in these matters to provide a self-saving device. . . . It will be possible for Callaghan to speak with special reference to Britain's oil interests in the North Sea. . . . Callaghan is anxious to be one of the occupants at the table along with the President of the E.E.C. It now appears that the French object to this arrangement. Michael wanted me to do all I could with Allan to see that Callaghan's wishes are met. . . .

On three occasions within the past three months, on behalf of Canada, I had asked for British support. I did not want to fail the latter now on their first request to me. . . .

My last engagement tonight was at the Law Society, where I was the guest of honour. The Law Society represents the organization of some thirty-three thousand solicitors in this country. . . . As I expected, interesting as the dinner was, it lacked the sophistication and liturgical richness, which I observed a few weeks ago at [the dinners of the barristers at] Gray's Inn, the Middle Temple, and Lincoln's Inn. . . .

Saturday, December 13, 1975

The day before, I had gone to Brussels to attend a meeting of heads of Canadian missions in Europe.

We met for four hours this morning at our heads of post meeting. I raised the question of our contractual link with the Market. We have been saying, all of us, that we wished to improve our consultative arrangements with the Community and develop more industrial co-operation. The time had come, therefore, for all heads of mission to be able to say that the contractual link meant much more. Businessmen were becoming dissatisfied with our responses as well as those of the government. . . . Unless we put some meat on the skeleton, the government and heads of mission could be in trouble. . . . John Halstead, our Ambassador in Bonn, one of the architects of the contractual link objective, agreed with what I said. He believes that the reason for little progress in identifying what we precisely have in mind lies with [the Department of] Industry, Trade and Commerce. At almost the top level in that department, there was a lack of interest in the contractual link. . . .

I took strong exception to the [Canadian] Economic Council suggestion for a free trade zone with the United States. This had been raised by Gérard Pelletier, who may be in favour of the idea. Free trade between Canada and the United States alone would be disastrous for us. We would be gobbled up. A freer trade arrangement with the United States, Japan and others makes more sense. . . .

We had a good discussion on Spain. Our Ambassador, Georges Blouin, made a good presentation. Franco is dead. Spain starts all over again. The King is accepted. . . . Understandably, however, in many European countries (and I venture to suggest this is also true in Canada) there is a sensitivity about the lengths to which we should go at once with Spain. I cannot forget the Spanish war. It caused great divisions in my generation and many of us are still about. . . .

At his lunch today at L'Hotel Amigo, Allan reported on the NATO Foreign Ministers' meeting of the last two days. An offer was made to the Warsaw Pact countries, designed to break the negotiation deadlock on East-West force reduction in Central Europe. The West can afford this concession. They maintain a superiority in tactical nuclear weapons. The offer means the withdrawal of 1,000 out of 7,000 tactical nuclear weapons, in addition to the long-standing offer of the 1,900 United States troops. . . .

Monday, December 15, 1975

The elections [last week] in British Columbia where the N.D.P. went down and in Australia where Labour lost are taken as reactions against the Left. Mrs. Thatcher seemed to jump the gun in her congratulatory message to the new Prime Minister, Malcolm Fraser. She said Australia's rejection of socialism in favour of personal freedom and private enterprise was "a shot in the arm" for British Conservatism. "We in Britain confidently intend to follow your good example."

There are many candidates for the Conservative leadership in Ottawa. [Peter] Lougheed may not run after all. There is a strong suggestion that he is not well. If he does not take the Tory leadership—who is there? Pierre will be top man for a long time. Laurier was Prime Minister for sixteen years. . . .

Tuesday, December 16, 1975

[Gough] Whitlam in Australia is now leader of the Opposition, and . . . Malcolm Fraser, a relatively young Australian and affluent, takes over the reins of government today and so the process goes on. How important it is to keep one's perspective. . . . The whole business is a matter of musical chairs. . . .

Wednesday, December 17, 1975

We have boosted our defence commitments to NATO. Several people at my reception in Canada House yesterday commended us for firming up our military presence in NATO. The significant increases in our defence commitment fulfil the pledge given by Trudeau, when he appeared at the NATO Council last spring. . . . Our further commitment to NATO is justified but I cannot help but be amused a the change of heart in high places. At the Liberal convention in 1968, I was attacked because of my continuing support for NATO and, after the convention, the boys [in the cabinet] continued their strong opposition to NATO. One learns only by experience. I had to tell a number of them in the cabinet, when the foreign policy review was under way, that foreign policy was an evolutionary programme. . . .

At the children's Christmas party this afternoon at Macdonald House, I assumed the role of Santa Claus and distributed gifts to the children of our personnel. . . . The very little ones seemed to be frightened by Santa. The three- and four-year-olds were blind in their faith in Santa but, from six on, their scepticism was just as profound as that of David Hume.[16] I had a lot of fun. . . .

At a dinner party at Peter and Franca Winkworth's I had a chat with Peter Thorneycroft, the president of the British Conservative party.*

He liked Heath but thought he was too rigid and not willing enough to heed advice. Had Heath listened to his friends and colleagues during the miners' strike, Thorneycroft said, he would still be Prime Minister. He believes Margaret Thatcher has a good chance of becoming Prime Minister, if the election is held off for a while. The central office does research on many of her speeches, but most of them are her own. She works laboriously on their preparation. . . . I suggested that Margaret had a strong rival in the Prime Minister. On that, he agreed there could be no doubt. Harold is the undisputed political master at the moment. One thing was clear, "Ted Heath could not have made it at the present time. Ted was a sincere good man who suddenly realized that everyone did not like him." This realization caused him much pain after he lost the leadership. A reconciliation has not yet taken place. . . .

Thursday, December 18, 1975

A message from [our] Prime Minister to Harold Wilson about John Diefenbaker was on my desk when I reached the office this morning. Someone in Ottawa apparently had been trying

16. David Hume, the eighteenth-century Scottish philosopher and empiricist, set out to establish a science of the human faculties.

late last night to get me. John Diefenbaker is to be recommended for the Companion of Honour. Trudeau asked me to ask Wilson to make this recommendation to the Queen. Harold Wilson will act on Trudeau's recommendation. As a precaution, I spoke to Martin Charteris at Buckingham Palace first thing this morning. . . .

Friday, December 19, 1975

The big event today was word of the [Canadian] government's new programme of retrenchment. It will affect all departments. Many programmes will be eliminated. Marc Lalonde will certainly not be happy with the removal of the indexing of family allowances next year. This alone will save two hundred and fifty million dollars. . . . It is going to be tough. A preview of the cuts was given us in Brussels last weekend by MacEachen. . . .

Tuesday, December 23, 1975

I felt a little groggy this morning after our party for the staff on the third floor of Macdonald House. I had taken, I think, a little too much vodka. . . .

Nell and I spent a quiet Christmas and then went to Cambridge for a few days.

Wednesday, December 31, 1975

Tomorrow we start a clean sheet. . . . A friend of mine suggested that 1975 was the year of poor theatre. It certainly was a year of terror, instability, wild nationalism, and confrontation. It was a year in which human life was held in such poor regard by minority groups who took out their vengeance on so many innocent people in Ulster, in Lebanon, in the restaurants of London, and in the airports of several countries. And yet, while all this was happening, I had a feeling that there is some resurgence towards transcendentalism, if not fully toward religious belief. . . .

VI

January – February 1976

AS THE NEW YEAR BEGAN, I found it hard to believe that I had been in London for a year. Between social and business responsibilities, I had worked flat out for the previous twelve months.

In February, I was involved in the "to-ing and fro-ing" regarding Trudeau's visit to Fidel Castro as part of his official visit to Mexico, Cuba and Venezuela from January 23 to February 2. The Cuban visit had raised controversy because it took place while Cuba was intervening in the Angolan civil war. The opposition in Canada claimed that Trudeau's visit was a triumph for Castro and my job abroad was to demonstrate the constructive results of Canada's foreign policy.*

Friday, January 2, 1976

I had made arrangements . . . to go to Canterbury [today] to see Burgon Bickersteth, now in his eighty-eighth year. The Governor-General had asked me to invest him with the insignia of a Member of the Order of Canada. . . . The Archbishop of Canterbury standing at his side, Burgon, quite moved by the whole affair, listened as I outlined the highlights of his long career. [As] Warden of Hart House 1921-47, . . . he had a great effect on several generations of young Canadians. Many of his undergraduates have since become moulders of Canada's destiny: leaders of its administrative, diplomatic, academic, cultural, scientific, and religious life. . . . He revived Canadian drama at a period of its lowest ebb and Hart House's chapel and inter-faith activities broke ecumenical ground forty years ahead of its time. . . .

I then pinned on his lapel the insignia of a Member of the Order of Canada. . . . Burgon is old but his mind is young. He will remember this day as will many in Canada who recall the good he did.

Sunday, January 4, 1976

The last few days of the holiday season are generally a bore. . . . I don't like this absence from work to last too long. I get tired of being a "house prisoner." That is my present mood. Tomorrow I begin again the active round. . . .

Wednesday, January 7, 1976

At our political consultative group[1] this morning . . . reference was made by several participants to the high degree of accessibility which I enjoy with top ministers and public servants. Similar accessibility was experienced by the members of the group with their opposite numbers in the British public service. In view of Britain's commitments to the Community, the question was asked, would our present opportunity for ready consultation continue? . . . I think too much could be made of this [and] there will [not] be much change. . . . The more important question in many ways is what will be Britain's commitment to the Commonwealth? . . .

I had to miss the executive committee meeting because of my appointment with Elliot Richardson.[2] . . . His knowledge of Canada, as he himself said, is mostly recreational, having spent holidays in New Brunswick, Quebec and British Columbia. . . . I emphasized that Canada was, as Kissinger said, one of the important economic powers in the world today. . . . Canada will be a more important country than Britain and France within the next two decades . . . [and] a country of our dimension would have objectives of its own. These objectives were bound to create different interests and de-

1. It was my idea to form the consultative group with all the political officers on the High Commission's staff to meet on a regular basis. This would parallel the existing regular meeting of the High Commission's economic officers.
2. Richardson was leaving his post to become Gerald Ford's secretary of commerce.

mands. . . . These differences should not discolour the true nature of Canadian-American relations. He readily agreed. No one could quarrel with Canada because it exercises the right of national independence. Most Americans understood this. . . . He thought it would be a good idea, if I could arrange for his going to Canada soon after he became Secretary of Commerce. . . . Above all, he would like to meet the Prime Minister. . . .

Friday, January 9, 1976

In talking about his appointment as a Companion of Honour, John Diefenbaker made an unusual statement when he said "It is a designation by the Queen herself and not based on a recommendation by the Prime Minister." Why he should have said this I find it difficult to understand, unless he did not wish in any way to be beholden to Trudeau. . . .

Saturday, January 10, 1976

Paul Hellyer,* I have just learned, has announced that he will be a candidate for the leadership of the Conservative party. This comes as a shock. We had been colleagues in both the St. Laurent and Pearson governments. Like me, he sought the leadership of the Liberal party in 1968. . . . If Paul becomes Tory leader, "Dame Irony" will have become enthroned in a surprising manner. . . .

Monday, January 12, 1976

I dropped into Lowndes Lodge Gallery today to see a painting of Margaret Thatcher. André de Moller, the owner of the gallery, kindly told me about the painter, a barrister-at-law, who hopes to devote his entire time to painting. It is a good painting of the Conservative leader but, as is so often the case, first impressions seldom last. . . . The owner of Lowndes Lodge Gallery told me that Lord Tweedsmuir had been in to see the painting to ascertain if it should be purchased by the Carlton Club. It is not as well-endowed as one might think and, therefore, there is some hesitation as to whether the portrait should be purchased at £2,000.00 for the Club. Even the Tories are broke. . . .

Wednesday, January 14, 1976

The Times has a headline asserting "Queen to ignore Quebec's 'stay away' warning." Apparently Victor Goldbloom, the minister responsible for the installations at the [Montreal Olympic] Games, said in a French-language broadcast that "he did not believe it was necessary to import foreign personalities to open our Olympics." Buckingham Palace . . . pointed out that the invitation to the Queen to open the Games had come from the International Olympic Committee on the advice of Prime Minister Trudeau. The Queen is going to the Games and rightly so. Why muddy the waters? What Goldbloom has said will make problems for Bourassa and others. . . .

Thursday, January 15, 1976

Jim Callaghan is a good politician who moves with the winds. His style is good, his despatch, however, I don't think is comparable to Kissinger's. He is undertaking an examination of British foreign policy requirements at home and abroad. . . . Jim is reacting to letters in *The Times*' letter-box — hardly a reason in itself for doing something which perhaps should be done, but for an altogether different provocation. As I say, Jim's style is good, so is Kissinger's and so is Trudeau's. Statesmanship, however, requires more than style. It must involve substance and meaningful action. . . .

Bruce Hutchison[3] made a blistering attack on Trudeau for his New Year's statement on controls in a free society. Bruce should recall that forty years ago some of his friends talked about the necessity for controls to meet the dilapidated state which confronted Canadians during the depression. Moreover, one should not forget that Bruce himself had such high praise for Trudeau when he assumed leadership. The boy from Victoria is now jumping ship. I continue to believe that what Trudeau said on New Year's Day was common sense. I

3. A long-time Liberal journalist and the editorial director of the *Vancouver Sun* and former editor of the Victoria *Daily Times*. In his New Year's message, Trudeau had spoken about greater government intervention in the economy and had given a general critique of the free market system.

had said these things in my first election and said them many times later. We must maintain as much free enterprise as we can, but the man is blind who thinks that society in 1976 in Canada or in the western world is what it was in 1968 or 1945 or 1930. . . .

Saturday, January 17, 1976

Word has just come to me that Bourassa reaffirmed yesterday the Queen would preside at the opening of the Olympics. . . . The St. Jean Baptiste Society sent a telegram to the Queen warning her of trouble "if she opens the games. The Queen's visit would threaten the social and political peace of the province. . . ." Goldbloom's comment that he was "a bit uneasy" about the visit was certainly ill-timed. . . .

Monday, January 19, 1976

The socialist leaders of Western Europe are meeting in Denmark. Most of them are not socialist in fact, but only in name. These socialist leaders are liberals. They have dropped the idea of the ownership of the instruments of production by the state. Some are not such defenders of oppression and aggression as they make out. This I learned in the NATO Council, particularly when they would not agree to discuss Vietnam in a restricted session [in June 1967]. . . . In my student days, the socialist leaders pioneered in international affairs and the development of international organization. Are they pioneers now? . . .

Tuesday, January 20, 1976

When I reached the office this morning, there were some telegrams of congratulation on my being made a Companion of the Order of Canada. . . . No longer will I be able to say when I wear [a] white tie that I have nothing to put around my neck. Nell thinks it is a great idea. . . .

At our consultative economic committee meeting this morning, we had a good discussion on the economic climate of the United Kingdom. All indications show that the country has been declining over the past ten years. There is no doubt that the Wilson government is giving effective and responsible leadership at the moment, but there is the fact of inflation and poor investment prospects. The economic climate was not assisted by uncertainty about Britain's membership in the Community, which was resolved only by the 1975 July referendum. During 1975, the cost-of-living rose by 25.9 per cent, alongside negative growth. Unemployment is at least now 1.2 million and could rise to one and a half million. Capital investment has been chronically low and has contributed to British industry's low productivity and is expected to be less this year than last. The private sector has encountered serious financial problems stemming from inflation and recession. . . . The fact that oil-producers have been willing to place funds in London explains the fact that Britain has encountered little difficulty in financing this large deficit. . . .

Wednesday, January 21, 1976

I read in *The Times* that Trudeau said last night "a new society" was needed in Canada to deal with inflation, unemployment, pollution, and resources waste. On television, the Prime Minister said "the economy was out of joint. It required strong medicine. The government was prepared to step in if business, organized labour, and individual Canadians did not act to reform the system." This is the answer Trudeau gives to those who have been criticizing his New Year's Day talk. He said the government did not want to impose more regulation on small businesses and "truly competitive sectors." . . . All [hell] has broken loose. The N.D.P. and the Tories are on the rampage. What Trudeau has said, of course, is sound. Is now the moment to say these things? . . .

Late Wednesday night, I went to address the Canadian Club at the NATO base in Lahr, West Germany.

Thursday, January 22, 1976

I was sorry to miss Allan MacEachen in London. We talked on the phone before I left Lahr. His visit to the Middle East was useful. . . . As he said, he is the first Canadian minister to go to this area. . . . Allan . . . is wise to make these visits. It is well that he went to Israel and Egypt. His talks in Israel would give him a picture which lack of earlier contacts would have denied him. . . .

Saturday, January 24, 1976

After my quick trip to Germany, I was back in London.

Reviewing the papers on MacEachen's visit to the Middle East, I am impressed with his exchanges and the visit itself. . . . Saudi Arabia stated flatly that Canada was the kind of country it wanted to deal with. We could be helpful with our experience in telecommunications, long distance transmission of electricity, integration of foreigners into our work force, development of high level public services, and our objective approach on economic matters. . . . The Saudis are sceptical about Israel's desire for peace negotiations. The creation of Israel was at the expense of Palestinians they contend.

The Canadian position, well-stated by Allan in his talks, emphasized a general positive attitude towards Israel . . . and that Palestinians had to be involved in peace negotiations. [He also pointed out that] we readily accepted the view that there had to be a Palestinian political entity [but] it was not for us to say who should speak for Palestinians in negotiations. This was a matter to be settled by the parties concerned. . . .

The Israeli position is: (1) It has not been possible to achieve a pact with any Arab country separately. Egypt would not agree to a formal treaty if Israel withdrew from all Egyptian territory. This means there could at present be no freedom of movement, except the exchange of diplomatic missions. (2) The Arabs demand complete withdrawal from occupied territories. Israel does not agree to the principle of total withdrawal. (3) Israel will not agree to the creation of an additional state between Israel and Jordan. This would only give rise to future trouble. . . .

Sunday, January 25, 1976

This afternoon I went to St. Paul's Cathedral for evensong and a sermon by His Eminence Cardinal L. J. Suenens, the Archbishop of Malines-Brussels. . . . I was given a seat in the stalls, across from the Cardinal. It is the feast of St. Paul, the third Sunday after the Epiphany. . . . The [ecumenical] dialogue must go on said Mercier's successor.[4] . . . Rome must talk to Canterbury and to Istanbul, Canterbury to Rome, and Istanbul to Canterbury and Rome. . . . As I got into my car, a man was carrying some signs: "Go back to Rome, no priests here."

Monday, January 26, 1976

The Minister of Defence, Roy Mason, attacked Mrs. Thatcher last night for her criticism of the Soviet Union.[5] She was "screeching from her pantry door, harking back to the days of Britain's imperialistic grandeur as if Britain alone could force Soviet communism back to its own shores." The Minister of Defence says we are anxious to enter an era of détente. A good start has been made. Mrs. Thatcher's speech is ill-timed and provocative. Reginald Maudling, the shadow Foreign Secretary, said in reply to Mr. Mason, "Poppycock." I think, if I had been Mason, I would have left the attack to someone else. . . .

Wednesday, January 28, 1976

I talked to Ken Thomson yesterday. His father has been in hospital in Canada — doing too much. Lord Thomson of Fleet said, a few days ago, that Trudeau and growing socialism are discouraging private enterprise: "Trudeau and his men in Ottawa are holding back development in this country." Roy's views got wide circulation. He is the proprietor of thirty-four daily Canadian newspapers and one hundred-and-fifty around the world, including *The Times*. Roy is a good businessman. This does not make him infallible on the nature of Canadian society. When he returns to London, I must have a good chat with him, particularly on the question of bilingualism. He is

4. Désiré, Cardinal Mercier, founded the Institut supérieur de philosophie at Louvin in 1889 and had become Cardinal of Malines (1907-26). He presided over the Malines Conversations (1921-26) which studied the conditions for union between Catholics and Anglicans.
5. She had made a speech the week before accusing the Wilson government of being soft on Communism and she restored the defence issue to a central position in her programme.

reported as having said: "I think there is more animosity in this country than ever before because of forcing bilingualism on people which keeps the country divided. . . ." Roy, my friend, does not fully understand the nature of the Canadian scene. Bilingualism is difficult to attain but much progress has been made. He is quite wrong in saying that bilingualism means forcing a language on people. It means no such thing. No one is being compelled to speak French. Moreover, Canada is not only an English-speaking country!

Thursday, January 29, 1976

The shadow foreign minister in the Conservative party, the former Chancellor of the Exchequer, Reginald Maudling, came to see me this morning at Canada House. . . .

I asked Maudling, if it is not a fact that there are now less foreign affairs debates in the House of Commons than previously. This is true, he replied. The fact is that the Opposition does not have much disagreement with foreign policy as pursued by Callaghan. Callaghan's opposition comes from his own ranks. When the Conservatives were in office, the situation was the same. He [Maudling] likes Callaghan. They had much private conversation and he, as shadow foreign minister, was not out to embarrass the Secretary of State for Foreign Affairs. Regrettably, this is not the situation in Canada. . . .

Friday, January 30, 1976

Yesterday in the House of Commons, the Chancellor of the Exchequer[6] indicated that he had in mind a wide-ranging programme to reduce unemployment. There is a real split in the ranks of the Labour party over the increase in the number of unemployed. . . . The Chancellor of the Exchequer urged the nation not to lose its nerve at the moment when economic recovery was in the offing. Denis ruled out reflation or an extensive import control programme. . . . What he likely has in mind is a scheme of subsidies to avoid lay-offs in industry. . . .

6. Denis Healey

Sunday, February 1, 1976

We have a heavy week ahead: three speeches, lunches, and dinners with the Lord Mayors of Leeds, Lincoln, and York. A visit to Lincoln and York Cathedrals and a call on the Archbishop of York, who is going to Canada in March . . . . A good High Commissioner must get around the country . . . .

I am pleased to see that no one believes Norman Scott's charge about his past [sexual] relations with the Liberal leader, Jeremy Thorpe. . . . Jeremy has denied the mentally-deranged Scott's story. *The Times* agrees that the accusation "should not be held against Mr. Thorpe as the Leader of a political party. . . ." The Liberal leader has had a tough week. He will not resign now, nor will he be expected to do so. It may be more difficult to carry on as leader in the long term. . . .

Thursday, February 5, 1976

After my return to London,

I found that Ivan Head called yesterday to say that he may come and see me next week. . . . The British should . . . be informed that [Trudeau] . . . spent three hours on Angola with Castro, urging the latter to reconsider his policy of intervention in Africa. The United States will not be so easy to placate.

The press has been hard on the Prime Minister and his wife. Margaret obviously is not well. Nell and I would so much like to help both if we could. It is to be hoped that the whole "mess" will dissolve into thin air. . . .

Friday, February 6, 1976

Ottawa takes the view that . . . we should only report on those matters involving the labour leaders which touch on matters directly relevant to a comparable situation in Canada. This is a doubtful proposition. The job of an ambassador is to report on what is transpiring in the nation where he is accredited, whether or not it has a relevance at home. What Labour is doing in Britain about the anti-inflation programme and the Common Market are matters of interest to Canada. I have told Ottawa very firmly that this is my view. . . .

At the Foreign Affairs Club dinner at the Savoy, I listened to a good tour d'horizon by Herr Helmut Schmidt, the Chancellor of the Federal Republic of Germany. . . . A strong anglophile, he is credited with having brought strong pressure on Wilson to stay in the E.E.C. Germany regards Britain as part of Europe. He thinks the global economic system is on the way up. . . . And the conviction is growing that "the advantage for all in the Community is greater than for the British alone, the Germans alone, the French or the Italians alone which makes us carry on." Good stuff. The British government does not embrace this with much enthusiasm. Wilson and Callaghan are wrong in their hesitancy. . . .

Saturday, February 7, 1976

Mary Anne and Mike Bellamy will be pleased to learn about our luncheon for Iris Murdoch. . . .[7] The build-up has been so great we were a little nervous. She is a pleasant, mild mannered, kind woman, who is anything but the obvious pessimist. This I had inferred her to be after learning that she was a sort of disciple of Schopenhauer.[8] Certainly the deduction one makes after reading her books is that the author is a person of profound pessimism. . . .

After lunch, Ivan Head and I adjourned into my library for an exposition on Prime Minister Trudeau's trip to Cuba, Mexico and Venezuela. Long before the decision to go to these places . . . Ivan himself had discussed the Cuban visit at the NATO Summit meeting with Kissinger. It was natural that so sensitive an area as Cuba should be mentioned in this way. Canada would expect to be treated likewise. . . . After the visit, the State Department, on Trudeau's suggestion, sent someone to Ottawa to learn of the Castro-Trudeau conversations. . . .

7. Mike Bellamy, my son-in-law, had written his doctoral dissertation on her novels. She began writing in 1954 with *Under the Net.*
8. Arthur Schopenhauer (1788-1860) was a German metaphysicist known for his idea that will is the reality of the universe. His philosophical writing emphasized reality and suffering and he is called the philosopher of pessimism.

Ivan told me that Trudeau had recently written to Whitlam,[9] as he had done following Ted Heath's loss of the Conservative party leadership last winter. Trudeau was of the view, and I think rightly, that he should keep his contacts with those who have been in but who are now out. After all, in the parliamentary system it is a matter of musical chairs. A man may be leader of the opposition now and prime minister tomorrow. . . .

Before dinner, I opened an Exhibition of Canadian Books at Canada House. . . . It is hoped that we can display the books of Canadian writers, who are emerging all the time. . . . I thought I had made a rather indifferent speech, but one Canadian press representative who was there, and whose manner always puzzles me said: "Well, that was a good speech. I didn't think you knew so much about authors and particularly Canadian poets." Of the latter I know so little. This I readily acknowledged but my reporter friend did not seem convinced. . . .

Tuesday, February 10, 1976

Ivan and I called on the Minister of State for Foreign Affairs, David Ennals.* Once again, Ivan ably repeated the story on Angola. . . . Ennals gave the impression that much of the information conveyed had already been passed on by the United Kingdom Ambassador in Havana. I am sure this is not fully the case. . . . Obviously, Castro has confidence in Trudeau. This is all to the good. Castro listened carefully, when Trudeau told him why Cuban intervention in Angola was unwise. It could be that Cuba's stay there will not be of long duration. This might enable another large African country to take over paramilitary or police duties. Cuba will not want to be mired in Angola for a long period. Kaunda and Nyerere must not be separated from one another. Cuban intervention has assisted in setting them apart. They are two such balanced African leaders. Their constructive collaboration must not be lost. Castro was inclined to look upon Kaunda as idly idealistic, old-fashioned and clumsy. Certainly, this is a wrong picture of a dedicated and troubled man. . . .

9. Gough Whitlam had resigned as prime minister of Australia after losing the election.

At tea-time . . . we were given the drill for the ball on Thursday night, when I am to dance with Princess Anne and lead off, an event which causes me more trepidation than if I were to have an audience with Amin. . . .

Wednesday, February 11, 1976

In the House of Commons yesterday, Prime Minister [Wilson] mentioned what he called the "nauseating" press campaign of innuendo against the Leader of the Liberal party. . . . When Ivan Head and I had seen Thorpe yesterday morning in his office at the House of Commons, he mentioned that he would be speaking tonight to the London press club. His theme would be the freedom of the press. I wondered how wise Jeremy was to get into this theme, in view of his own predicament. Apparently, from the press account he discussed the subject without involving himself unduly. . . . Jeremy said: "We have got to get our law of defamation, privacy, privilege, and official secrets right." Many people will say, "hear, hear." The cleavage on this point between the press and Parliament is greater than one may think. . . .

As a result of Ivan Head's visit and our meetings with British ministers and officials, I reflected again on the role of the Prime Minister's Office in the formulation and execution of Canada's foreign policy.

As long as the Prime Minister [Trudeau] played an active role in diplomacy, he would require someone in his office who knew what it was all about. Ivan has a combination of knowledge, with a strong and effective personality. His situation was somewhat unique in our system. There were problems of competing authority. The Secretary of State for External Affairs was over-shadowed in some ways. The latter would be wise, however, to recognize the facts and to play along. Ivan said this is what Mitchell Sharp did. He did not find it easy to carry out his present role with MacEachen looking over the fence in envy, perhaps with understandable jealousy. I suggested to Ivan that he should stay on. . . .

Thursday, February 12, 1976

The Maple Leaf Ball tonight was a great success. Princess Anne had created much interest. . . . Anne has the popular misconception of Parliament. I sought to correct her. Her estimate of Harold Wilson would not please the Prime Minister. I didn't expect that she would be so frank in disclosing her views. Why didn't Trudeau take hold of the Olympics from the beginning? I explained that the Olympics in Canada began as a Montreal affair. The Games had been taken over by the provincial government because of financial difficulties. It was clearly not a matter for which the federal government had any responsibility. From the outset, it proclaimed its intention not to provide financial assistance. The Princess observed that Canada, as a whole, would be held responsible by public opinion if things did not go well. The present unsatisfactory state of readiness at the Games site was a reflection on Canada, she said. This I did not deny. I assured her, however, that the Olympic Games would go on. They would be successful. We both agreed, however, that they had become too expensive and too mammoth-like. . . .

I had heard all sorts of stories about the lugubriousness of Princess Anne. I found her pleasant, approachable and good in her conversation. . . . Nell thought everything had gone off well, even in the opening dance with the Princess, when we faced the music. Captain Mark Phillips is a nice young chap, very pleasant indeed, but I should think Anne could hold her place with him any time. . . .

The security arrangements at the hotel were extraordinary. The death of a Provisional I.R.A. staff officer, after a sixty-one-day hunger strike in a British prison, caused a nation-wide police alert to be set up. No chances were taken at the public appearance of Princess Anne. Everyone was searched coming into the hotel. Plain-clothes men were all over. . . .

Friday, February 13, 1976

Ivan Head attaches great importance to the Secretary General of the Commonwealth Organization, Sonny Ramphal. I share his view. He briefed Sonny on the Prime Ministers' conference on Angola. I am beginning to wonder if the Soviet Union gave guarantees to Cuba if there were Cuban casualties in Angola? Ramphal believes there is some unrest in Cuba over Cuban participation. . . .

The Secretary General is concerned about the effect of developments in Angola on Rhodesia. . . . Now South Africa feared the Soviet Union and its influence in Africa. Would this cause Vorster to help Smith* and resist agreement? Would Nigeria send in troops if South Africa and Cubans openly clashed [in Angola]? The situation is . . . very grave. . . . The Secretary General has impressed on the British the importance of using whatever influence they have left to bring about a settlement in Rhodesia while there is still time. If negotiations with Nkomo* break down, there is no one else to carry them on. Kissinger has been advised of this. Cubans must be taken out of Africa. . . . Head has shown Ramphal how Trudeau had sought to convince Castro of the gravity of the situation, and how wrong he had been to intervene. Castro doesn't fully appreciate the position in Africa in spite of his confidence of knowing the African mood. He was unaware that South Africa is not in the Commonwealth and is not in the O.A.U [with most African countries]. . . .

Angola is a worrying situation. It is interesting to note that, while many at home are criticizing Trudeau for his Cuban visit, Joseph Luns* adds that Trudeau has done a service in the advice he has been giving to Castro. I was amused to see that the Secretary General suggested, with some subtlety, that Trudeau may have been a bit naive in his discussions with Castro. Another example of Luns' ineptness. . . .

Tuesday, February 17, 1976

The Conservative leadership convention takes place this weekend. Unfortunately absence does not make the heart grow fonder. I feel very remote from Canada and things political than I could possibly have imagined. Brian Mulroney (Paul's friend), is getting a lot of ink. Is Paul Hellyer linking up with Wagner* to stop Mulroney? It looks that way. Mulroney, on the other hand, is avoiding a public linking with Dalton Camp.* It has always puzzled me how Camp persists in being a political public figure. After all, he has been little more than a party organizer. He was never elected to Parliament, and has not made a substantial contribution to the great questions. Moreover, he did his party irreparable harm when he sabotaged John Diefenbaker. . . .[10]

10. John Diefenbaker lost the Conservative leadership in 1967 largely as a result of Camp's manoeuvring.

Friday, February 20, 1976

Nell and I finished the day at the Garrick theatre, where Richard Briers is starring in "Absent Friends." Not particularly good. Humorous in spots. A little boring on the whole. It was good, however, to see this old Victorian house. One can hear the rumble of the tube trains from time to time. A stray cat came on stage, in front of the curtain, at the end of the first act. Its antics pleased everyone. Really the star of the show. . . .

Monday, February 23, 1976

We arrived at the University of Warwick around 11:00 a.m., and were greeted by Professor Alistair Hennessy, one of the original members of the provisional executive council of the British Association for Canadian Studies. . . .

I had known that the former President of Nigeria[11] was *in statu pupilari* at Warwick. I took no steps, however, to see him. I felt he might want to be alone. I was overjoyed, therefore, when he turned up at the reception. We had a good three-quarter hour chat. . . . He would have liked to have gone to Cambridge as a student, but it did not seem appropriate for him to become an undergraduate in the university where he had just received an honorary degree. This also precluded his going to Oxford, so he settled on Warwick, where he is happy and well settled in. He told me that he is doing a course in political science, leading to a B.A. degree. As a graduate of Sandhurst, of course, he has the equivalent now. As he said to one of the students later in the afternoon, "there is quite a difference between a course in political science and governing a country." Gowon is not yet forty. It is hard to believe that for over eight or nine years he was President of the largest African country, with a population of close to sixty-five million people. . . .

Before he had gone to the O.A.U. meeting in Uganda, he had called in General Murtala Muhammed for a three-hour

11. A Nigerian military officer, General Yakubu Gowon served with the United Nations peacekeeping forces in the Congo and then became chief of staff of the Nigerian military in 1966. He took over the government of Nigeria that same year and was deposed in a coup in 1975.

chat. There had been rumours that General Muhammed was out to replace him, although they had been comrades-in-arms for a long time. General Muhammed denied the rumours, assuring Gowon of his loyalty and fidelity. With these assurances, Gowon left for Kampala, believing that all was well. Lurking in his mind may have been a doubt, but not a substantial one. When he was handed a note informing him what had happened in his absence, his pain was great, not only because he had been deposed, but because he had been betrayed by someone whom he had supposed to be a loyal friend. . . . He was sorry about the assassination and coup. As he said publicly, that "wasn't the way to further the progress and unity of the nation." A coup is anything but stabilizing. He was opposed to the coup. He was not in any way involved in it—"So help me God and I say this to you, Mr. Martin, in full conscience and tell this to Trudeau." . . .

Tuesday, February 24, 1976

The E.E.C. took a forward step last night, when it announced support for the self-determination and independence of Rhodesia and South-West Africa (Namibia).[12] The Nine in Luxembourg condemned apartheid in South Africa and external military intervention in Angola and surrounding African countries. . . . The E.E.C. is developing a common foreign policy technique, slowly but inevitably.

There was a small reference to Joe Clark*'s election as Conservative Leader in *The Times* this morning. Tucked away down at the bottom of page six is an unexciting story about "Professor of thirty-six is Opposition chief in Canada." I am anxious to see the press accounts of the convention. Joe Clark

12. Namibia or South-West Africa was a former German colony administered by South Africa since 1915. From 1948, South Africa had tried to integrate this territory despite the United Nations mandate. The South-West African People's Organization (SWAPO) began a guerrilla war against South Africa in 1966 and the United Nations recognized SWAPO in 1971. On January 30, 1976, the United Nations Security Council accepted a proposal for supervised elections to an assembly that would set up an independent Namibia. The sponsors of the resolution were Canada, Britain, the United States, and West Germany.

will really do well. He is bilingual, young and intelligent. I do not know him well but, when I did meet him last year, I was impressed. . . .

Our dinner at 12 Upper Brook Street for Denis Healey went off happily and well, in spite of the fact that one of the imported waiters misjudged Denis' left shoulder and poured some good red wine down Denis' shirt. The Chancellor of the Exchequer looks none the worse for the tough trial which he is going through. He is being knocked about not only by waiters but by teachers, students, capitalists, socialists, pensioners, etc. . . .

Wednesday, February 25, 1976

I learn that Hugh Watt, the New Zealand High Commissioner in London, is going to resign. It is suggested that the pressure on him from the new government in Wellington has been very strong. . . . On the whole, I believe that a government is justified in giving a prime minister some leeway in particular foreign assignments. London certainly is one of these, if not perhaps the foremost one. Most of my predecessors have been men who have held high political office in Canada and most of them have been prominent public figures. . . . From my vantage point as Secretary of State for External Affairs, I thought these kind of appointments were every bit as good and, in some cases, perhaps better than heads of mission who had spent their whole career in external affairs. . . .

Friday, February 27, 1976

For the third time in fourteen months, Nell and I were invited to ceremonies at the Guildhall of the "Admission to Freedom of the City of London"—first for Trudeau, then for Wilson and now for Princess Anne. . . .

I sat directly in front of the Prime Minister. We had a useful exchange. Wilson said that Trudeau's visit to Castro would turn out to have been helpful. Castro obviously has confidence in our man. What our Prime Minister had to say on Cuban intervention in Angola had to be said. As Ennals had insisted, when Head and I had seen him at the Foreign Office, the British were pursuing an identical policy with Cuba. She must not be further isolated. When the time comes,

Trudeau may be able to help in composing differences between Cuba and the United States. Every effort must be made to persuade Cuba of the dangers of further involvement in Africa. Wilson is greatly concerned about developments in Rhodesia and Southern Africa generally.

At this point Mrs. Wilson spoke up, deploring the way the press were treating Margaret Trudeau. She said Mrs. Thorn, the wife of Luxembourg's Prime Minister, and she had written to Margaret. . . .

I said to Wilson that I thought Denis was doing well as Chancellor. He surprised me by his hesitation to fully agree. The trouble with Denis was that he still reasoned as a Marxist, but not as a communist, the Marxists were like the Schoolmen.[13] There was a set pattern in analysis, formulation and conclusion. Wilson prefers a more flexible methodology. . . .

13. Mediaeval philosophers, including Thomas Aquinas.

VII

March – April 1976

ONE OF THE MORE TRYING QUESTIONS during my time in London was the constant need to explain Trudeau's attitude to the monarchy. During these months, Trudeau's plan unilaterally to patriate the constitution raised the issue yet again as did Trudeau's unfortunate comment that "we don't need the Queen to run Canada."

The British political scene took an unexpected turn in mid-March when Harold Wilson announced his resignation as prime minister. The Labour party began the process of choosing a new leader, and, on April 5, Jim Callaghan emerged from the fray as prime minister.

In the midst of the voting, I had the unpredictable former prime minister, John Diefenbaker, as a houseguest. Although he was in Britain to be made a Companion of Honour by the Queen, Diefenbaker used this visit as a rostrum to attack Pierre Trudeau.

I too received a decoration, the first honour I allowed myself to accept, when I was invested as a Companion of the Order of Canada in April. Then it was back to London to deal again with the contentious issue of patriation of the constitution as well as the role of the Commonwealth in achieving a settlement in Rhodesia and South Africa.

Monday, March 1, 1976

I talked to David Ennals tonight at Lancaster House. . . . Jim Callaghan will take a week or so before making up his mind on the report. There apparently was little movement on Smith's part in his official talks[1] but, from private observations

1. The British government had sent Denis Greenhill, a former head of the diplomatic service, to see Ian Smith in Rhodesia.

which he has made, it would appear he recognizes that this may be the last chance. One of Nyerere's closest advisers, Jamal,[2] discussed developments in Rhodesia with . . . me. I had wondered why Nyerere kept insisting that there was only one alternative left to bring the Rhodesian problem to a conclusion, the use of force. I said that this surprised me. Jamal explained that this statement by Nyerere did not mean that he would use force, but that the parties concerned in Rhodesia and in Mozambique had decided on the application of force. It could be that Nyerere was warning Britain when he spoke this way last fall in Britain and more recently in Africa. I suspect that between now and the middle of next week, we are likely to see some developments on the Rhodesian question. . . .

Wednesday, March 3, 1976

[Lord] George-Brown made the headlines this morning. I listened to him on the radio while shaving. He seemed to be in rare form, although I suspect he had had a refresher or two. What has he done now? He has resigned the Labour Whip in the House of Lords. . . . George-Brown was Foreign Secretary, during the last two years when I was Secretary of State for External Affairs. There were occasions where he was kind and generous and sometimes brilliant, but there were other occasions when he was unruly, boisterous, insulting and downright drunk. An interesting character but I wouldn't want to trust the reins of government to him. . . .

Thursday, March 4, 1976

Mozambique has placed itself on a war footing and set up blockades against Rhodesia. The border has been closed. President Samora Machel* of Mozambique said that sanctions would be rigidly applied against Rhodesia. This, of course, is a requirement of the Security Council and has been so now for almost six or seven years. Canada was one of the countries to apply sanctions right from the beginning. . . .

2. Amir Habib Jamal, minister of finance of Tanzania.

Friday, March 5, 1976

Martin [Charteris] seemed pleased with my assurances that the Queen's visit to Canada would go well. In any event, she has to go. If, because of Quebec opinion, she were to cancel out, the outcry in the rest of Canada would be great. The Queen, I am sure, has never wavered in her decision to accept Trudeau's invitation to open the Olympic Games. . . .

Saturday, March 6, 1976

It is now revealed in today's morning papers that money was paid to Scott . . . on Jeremy Thorpe's behalf, but without his knowledge. The press is merciless. The [Liberal party's] loss of the by-election in Coventry and this outburst in the Scott-Thorpe affair will make it difficult for Jeremy to stay on as Liberal leader much longer. Privacy is difficult to maintain in this so-called open society. Curiously enough, the Prime Minister talked about the need for a voluntary pact between the news media and government to protect legitimate privacy of "public" persons. Responsible news leaders recognize the need for such an arrangement. . . .

Monday, March 8, 1976

At one point I had suggested to Trudeau that we might give consideration to patriation of the constitution without reference to the provinces. . . . A move, based on consultation and approval with less than the ten, might be desirable, but only if they would agree to patriation without conditions. Quebec is the main province to stand in the way. If we proceeded with the consent of most of the others, we would present Quebec with additional argument. It might be best, therefore, failing agreement with all the provinces, to proceed with patriation, as St. Laurent did in respect of those sections of the constitution which were exclusively federal.[3] I was not

3. In 1949-50, Prime Minister Louis St Laurent discussed the patriation of the British North America Act. He proceeded to enact amendments which would allow the federal government to amend the act, without British consent, for matters that lay within federal competence as defined by the act.

surprised to see in the *Herald Tribune* today a suggestion that Trudeau was contemplating action. . . .

I had a useful exchange with the Minister of State in the Northern Ireland Office, Stanley Orme. . . . Eventually, Britain aims to have some form of devolved government, based on partnership between Protestant and Catholic communities. . . .

Rees and now Orme centre the blame [for delay] on Paisley.[4] I think that I should see Paisley and have a talk with him, just to see what makes him tick. Orme says that eighty-five per cent of the weapons captured in Ulster were of United States origin. Canadians were less inclined to contribute to extremists in either community than Americans, but he urged us to be aware of the situation. The British government receives full support from the Republic of Ireland. Most Southern Irish hope for unification as some future goal, but the Irish government does not want the reluctant Ulster at present. . . .

Tuesday, March 9, 1976

A letter received today from Paul revives his desire to get into public life and politics. I have suggested to him that he should wait until he has reached forty-five. He is doing so well in business. Few young men in Canada have made such progress. My view would be that he should go into politics, if he wishes, after he has established himself firmly. I entered Parliament at thirty-three years. I was doing well at the bar but I had not reached the pinnacle, as Paul will certainly do in business if he bides his time. . . . I called him and repeated my views once again. . . . Nell and I are both agreed. . . .

The *Daily Telegraph* in its issue of yesterday has a heading "We don't need the Queen to run Canada, says Trudeau." What an unfortunate headline. I have sent for the text of what the Prime Minister said in Quebec. I am sure he didn't put it this way. . . . First of all, the Prime Minister reiterated that, as head of state, the Queen would come to open the Olympic Games. He then spoke of patriating the Canadian constitution. I can imagine that, having stated this objective,

4. The Reverend Ian Paisley, extremist Protestant leader in Northern Ireland.

he would want to graphically explain what it meant. He is quoted as saying, "We don't need the Queen or Harold Wilson or the Pope either. Let's get together and tell England to stop making our laws for us." This is the language which people understand. A strict examination of the words, however, offends. The Queen doesn't interfere in our affairs. Nothing would please Harold Wilson and the British Parliament more than to give Canada full statutory right to amend its own constitution without reference to Britain. If Westminster has to pass an act in respect of an amendment to the Canadian constitution, it is only because Canada wills it. All we have to do is to say that we want to do it ourselves and the British Parliament will act accordingly. . . . I am afraid that, in this instance, the Prime Minister has done himself an injustice and the country too. John Diefenbaker and others will take advantage of this apparent, but not genuine, attack on the Queen. Nevertheless, I am worried about the matter. It is an unnecessary diversion.

Wednesday, March 10, 1976

I had lunch today with the Ambassador for Israel.[5] Abba Eban, the former foreign secretary,[6] was present. It was nice to see him again after a long interval. . . . It was agreed in our discussion that the pivotal issue now in the Middle East is the matter of a Palestinian state on the West Bank. I mentioned that in my talks with Arab ambassadors in London, it was emphasized that, if Israel would agree to the establishment of a Palestinian state on the West Bank, peace would come to the region. For the first time, I detected an acknowledgment by Eban that there would have to be territorial concessions. This would be part of the ultimate settlement. . . .

Monday, March 15, 1976

The parliamentary Liberal party seems to be closing in on its leader, Jeremy Thorpe. Most Liberal MPs are saying that Jeremy should resign and that there should be a leadership

5. Gideon Rafael
6. From 1966 to 1974.

election. . . . It was interesting to note on television yesterday that party supporters did not share the same readiness to dismiss Thorpe, as his parliamentary colleagues seem disposed now to do. Jeremy has my sympathy. I wish I could help him. A lot of other people feel the same way, because of the crushing manner in which he has been dealt with by the news media. . . .

Harold Wilson's sixtieth birthday marks his ascendency as a strong political leader. He has been Prime Minister in peacetime longer than anyone in this century. . . .

Wednesday, March 17, 1976

The dominant news today, of course, has to do with Wilson's announcement that he is resigning. . . . At this stage, I think that the Foreign and Commonwealth Secretary, Jim Callaghan, will succeed him. The choice will be made by the parliamentary Labour party. When I saw Jim Callaghan a year and a half ago, on my first call, he expressed satisfaction at being Foreign Secretary. He said that he no longer had any ambition to become leader of the Labour party. Present events, of course, have changed the picture. . . .

Wilson's announcement astonished his colleagues who met with him at 10 Downing Street yesterday morning. . . . Wilson's announcement in the House of Commons yesterday brought tributes to him from all sides. Mrs. Thatcher, who had referred to Wilson a week ago as a man without principle, praised his contribution to public life and to the government of this country. . . .

Unlike some other Labour leaders, he understood Canada and wanted to work with us. Certainly, during the time I have been High Commissioner, he has shown nothing but friendship. I have refrained from pursuing him needlessly but, whenever I have, the welcome mat was always out. My last talk with him at the Guildhall ceremony prompted him to say that it might be desirable for me to drop in and see him soon. . . .

A message from the Prime Minister came in early this morning, asking that I deliver a letter to Prime Minister Wilson following yesterday's announcement. . . . Trudeau acknowledged the contribution Wilson had made to Britain, the

Commonwealth and the world community. The Prime Minister received me at 3:00 o'clock. A number of other ambassadors were waiting when I came in. For some reason, I was not kept waiting and was taken directly to see him. . . .

When the Prime Minister received me, he said: "You know, Paul, we have known one another for a long time. I have known you over a longer period than most men with whom I deal and I greatly appreciate that you are the person selected to come and say goodbye to me on behalf of Canada." . . . I said that it was not my function to make political judgments in this country but, as one who had participated in public life over a long period, in fact longer than Wilson himself, I could not refrain from noting the great skill displayed by him in presiding over the affairs of Britain at a critical time. He said he had made up his mind two years ago to retire about this time, and had intimated to the Queen last December his intention to hand over the reins of office, not later than at the end of March. . . . I have the clear judgment that his preference is for Jim Callaghan, because he said "to retire now will give people like Jim (and he quickly added other names) an opportunity to experience the burdens of the office of Prime Minister." . . .

Thursday, March 18, 1976

André Ouellet, Canada's Minister for Consumer Affairs, has resigned. I always regarded him as a man of the future. On the Quebec side, he and Jean Chrétien* struck me as strong and potential soldiers of political fortune. André has been found guilty of contempt of court. As Minister of Consumer Affairs, he had complained [to the judges] of a judgment against the [Montreal] sugar companies. Several of his colleagues, Bud Drury in particular, and in the best of faith, I am sure, had sought to intervene. This was an imprudent thing to have done, no matter how well intentioned, and it looked, up until yesterday at any rate, that Bud would have to resign. . . .

I sent a telegram to Ottawa today conjecturing that Jim Callaghan would get the leadership and prime ministership in succession to Wilson. The next strongest candidate, I should think is Roy Jenkins. Some think that Michael Foot will give

Callaghan the best run—some think he may even win. This would greatly surprise me. Tony Benn will not get formidable support, perhaps half of the now divided Tribune group.[7] Denis Healey will not gather the support which his great abilities warrant. Crosland, whom some speak of as a long-term leader, may get about the same number as Tony Benn. . . .

Friday, March 19, 1976

The problem of security in public and other buildings receives much attention these days in bomb-weary London. I don't think we have gone overboard at Macdonald House or Canada House. I would be unhappy if these Canadian buildings became less warm and inviting than they have been, because of police requirements. It would be so easy in these days to take advantage of the openness of the ground floor at Canada House. . . .

Saturday, March 20, 1976

Prime Minister Trudeau said the other night in Quebec City that the government was considering moving to patriate the constitution, hopefully with provincial concurrence, if forthcoming; otherwise unilaterally. Why not? The federal government's request would be by addresses of the Senate and House of Commons passed by resolution of both houses. The address embodied in the resolution would be in the form of a petition to the sovereign. I would presume, as on other occasions, a model bill, embracing the amendment sought, would be included in the address. This would facilitate passage by the Westminster Parliament, as I recall when we moved for concurrent federal-provincial jurisdiction for old age pensions. There are, therefore, good precedents for this procedure. No legal or constitutional problem is likely to arise, even if the provinces do not give consent. The provinces in the past have taken exception to unilateral action by Ottawa in constitutional amendment applications. . . .

7. A group of left-wing Labour MPs.

Monday, March 22, 1976

I went to the House of Commons to hear Jim Callaghan make a statement of Rhodesia. . . .

Callaghan was the star of the show. He had a good opportunity today to gain advantage in the leadership race. As he said at one point, in answer to a question, he "did not come into the House this afternoon to make enemies." The House roared as he did himself. This made him appear as a good-natured, practical and dominant person. . . .

Tuesday, March 23, 1976

A strict examination of Callaghan's speech reveals in it nothing that is new. It must always have been understood that there would have to be a time limit to enable majority rule to be implemented. What really is new is that events in Rhodesia are coming to a head. The options are all closed, but one. If Smith cannot make up his mind to accept these pre-conditions, Callaghan bluntly suggested that the European community in Salisbury should see that a new head of government takes over. The apprehensions of the white population in Rhodesia are understandable. Callaghan said that there would be financial help, once the pre-conditions were met. . . .

We were guests of honour at the Carlton Club tonight at a delightful dinner given by Lord Derick Amory.* This was my first visit to the Carlton Club, with its not too prepossessing entrance, but with a very fine and well-conceived grand stairway with much wall-space, on which hang paintings of the great political figures of England's Tory past. In the dining room is a mammoth painting of Arthur Balfour[8] as he stands wearing his long black, silk-lapelled, coat. . . . We talked of the way political leaders are selected in this country, by the parliamentary party meeting at the Carlton Club or somewhere else in London. Not in many years has a Canadian political leader been selected by anything less than a national convention, duly representative of constituencies in every part of Canada.

8. Prime minister from 1902 to 1906.

Wednesday, March 24, 1976

I was amused when the representative of *La Presse* called on Christian Hardy and me the day before yesterday, to discuss the patriation of the constitution. This lad hadn't the slightest idea what was involved. His concept of bringing the constitution back home is that there will be a physical act of transporting "something" back to Canada literally. He does not realize that what is in question is an amendment to a bill of the British Parliament. Sometimes it is inconceivable how some contemporary journalists just do not have any idea about the most elementary problems, about which they write so knowingly and with such authority. . . . Senator Eugene Forsey thinks that most English Canadians don't lose much sleep over patriation of the constitution. I think he under-estimates the interest which Canadians have in this matter. . . .

Friday, March 26, 1976

As was expected, Michael Foot leads in the first ballot in the Labour leadership race but, only six votes behind was Jim Callaghan. The Home Secretary, Jenkins, who came third, withdrew from the contest as did Wedgwood Benn. The latter said that he would support Michael Foot. Roy Jenkins did not indicate who he would support, but it is expected that many of his votes will go to Callaghan. Crosland, who I think will be heard of on a future occasion, only got sixteen votes. It is not clear where his support will go. Anything can happen but I suspect Jim will come out on top. . . .

Sunday, March 28, 1976

What would Max[9] say if he were alive, about Michael Foot's candidacy for the leadership of the Labour party? They were close friends, at Suez and long before that, in the Second World War. Ideologically, they were poles apart. Certainly he and Max had little in common, except that each seemed to interest the other. Michael Foot worked for Beaverbrook, as editor of *The Evening Standard*. Max was a devastating enemy

9. Lord Beaverbrook, who was a Tory mentor of Labour MP Michael Foot.

of the Left; Foot a protagonist of the Left. Foot for a long time lived at Leatherhead, in Beaverbrook's side house and on his property. Once at a birthday party Max gave, with Churchill present along with Lord Rosebery, Foot and others, I witnessed an unusual spectacle. After Churchill had toasted his friend and the dinner was over, Max and the older guests retired. The rest of us, including Michael Foot, went into Beaverbrook's spacious library. Sir Patrick Hennessy, president of the Ford Motor Company, took over. Standing in the centre of the room and looking down at Michael Foot, deeply embedded in a comfortable armchair, Hennessy poured forth a torrent of abuse at Foot, the "Leftist and bloody revolutionary." Said Hennessy, "I have waited for this opportunity to tell you what I think of your perennial criticisms of the society I want to see preserved. You damn communist" and so on—only much worse, and seemingly without end. We were all embarrassed. One could not help but admire Michael Foot's forbearance at a man obviously influenced by too much port. One of the Duke of Edinburgh's friends was present. He too had had his share of Hennessy and port. The tirade must stop and so, gulping another glass of port, he approached Pat Hennessy asserting, "enough of this abuse," and struck him cold. Hennessy was out. Michael Foot looked on helplessly. . . .

John Diefenbaker and Joel Aldred[10] have arrived. I welcomed them at Heathrow. John has had the flu. No wonder he looked pale. He had travelled all night. At his press conference, he [said that] he was honoured to receive the C.H. which had come from the Queen, the message being conveyed via Wilson and Trudeau. Not true. It was Trudeau who first made the recommendation and then asked John if he would accept. Wilson had to advise the Queen following Trudeau's initiative as it is a British decoration. In any event, it is naughty of John to relegate Trudeau to the background. . . . At lunch [John] said he lost the 1965 election because John Robarts* did not do his share [to help the Tories]. As a matter of fact, Diefenbaker came close. . . . He is glad that he has continued to sit in the House of Commons. It is apparent, of course, that no love exists between Diefen-

10. A broadcaster and a prominent Conservative.

baker and Stanfield, who John says will now go to the Senate. . . .

Wednesday, March 31, 1976

The second round of the ballot for the Labour party leadership is over. Callaghan is now ahead by eight votes. Denis Healey has been eliminated. There will have to be another ballot but the question is, where will his thirty-eight votes go. . . .

John Diefenbaker had a sell-out audience at the Canada/United Kingdom Chamber of Commerce luncheon. I was on his right with Lord Thorneycroft, president of the Conservative party, on my right. John was a little nervous before his speech. Frankly, so was I a little apprehensive that he might touch again on the role of prime ministers in British awards. . . . As it turned out, his speech did not touch what I would regard as some of the politically sensitive issues. If he had, there would have been nothing I could do. . . . His speech took on another turn altogether, at the outset a lot of jokes. Then he gave his view of the problems in Rhodesia and South Africa. In thanking him, I pointed out that we had not spoken too often on the same platform in the past. . . .

Thursday, April 1, 1976

Along with General Dextraze, Chief of Staff, and the [Canadian] veterans, I represented Canada at the funeral in St. George's Chapel of Field Marshal The Viscount Montgomery of Alamein. The Duke of Devonshire represented the Queen. Top military men from most of the United Nations countries were in attendance. It was interesting to see the Field Marshals of Britain, members of the Garter, the Military Knights and others who paid their last tribute to Monty. His black beret on top of the coffin and his medals on three cushions, carried by officers, reminded one of his military achievements and victories. . . .

Friday, April 2, 1976

When I returned to the residence just before six o'clock, John D. was declaiming once again to the press. God knows what he dogmatized about today. Nothing I can do — being a mere public servant. Certainly I cannot contradict him openly. That responsibility rests with another group of my "political masters." . . .

Monday, April 5, 1976

Considerable attention is focussed on Jim Callaghan today. He is certain to poll more votes than Michael Foot. . . . I wish him luck. MacEachen has been in touch with me about the likely change at the Foreign Office. . . . It is now definite. Jim Callaghan is Prime Minister. On television he has repeated Wilson's assurance that "tough times lie ahead."

Tuesday, April 6, 1976

I flew to Ottawa and remained until April 11 to be invested as a Companion of the Order of Canada.

For one brief moment I suffered nostalgia, brought on by a look at the tower on Parliament Hill. It brought back, almost in a single picture, so much to me—achievement, noble purpose and failure in some plans, hopes and effort. But, today is today. There is so much to do. . . .

Wednesday, April 7, 1976

Denis Healey, brought down his long-awaited budget in London. . . . He wants to reduce personal income taxes if the unions agree to restrain their wage increases next year to an average three per cent. . . . Mrs. Thatcher . . . argues that the Chancellor has given in to the unions, representing a minority in the nation, the decision about tax levels. This smacked of "taxation without representation." Denis is obviously going to have much difficulty. He is trying hard in an almost impossible political climate. . . .

Paul and Sheila were here for the investiture. I was made a Companion of the Order of Canada. It was a simple and dignified ceremony at Rideau Hall, presided over by Jules Léger, the Governor-General. Nell and I were seated at Gaby Léger's table with Bora Laskin, the Chief Justice. Nell had everyone laughing when she asked Bora "if he had had any telephone calls recently." This, of course, was a play on the

"Judges Affair" involving Bud Drury and André Ouellet's resignation from the cabinet.

Thursday, April 8, 1976

Prime Minister [Trudeau] and I met before dinner. He is determined to proceed with patriation of the constitution, and will be tabling recent correspondence with the provinces. . . . He will act unilaterally if they do not agree. In this event, I will have to follow the matter through in London where, of course, there will be no problem. The constitution patriated will include the formula for amendment, the language guarantees and the existing provisions of the B.N.A. Act. Ontario and Quebec will have a veto over future proposed changes. A combination of other provinces, however, could block suggested alterations. Trudeau was very generous in his comments on my work in London. . . .

Friday, April 9, 1976

Callaghan has picked Anthony Crosland as Foreign Secretary. This is a surprise. I thought it would be Roy Jenkins, who will continue as Home Secretary. It may be that Michael Foot's new-found power enabled him to regard Jenkins as too committed to Europe, and that he said so to Callaghan. Michael Foot has now become Leader of the House of Commons. Denis Healey will stay on as Chancellor of the Exchequer. . . .

Yesterday, Trudeau gave Bryce Mackasey the Consumer Affairs portfolio. He will stay on as Postmaster-General until the summer. Bryce has made a good comeback. He went out of the cabinet before the elections in 1974, over criticisms of the unemployment insurance administration. Trudeau then wanted him to take another portfolio. Bryce contended that Trudeau was easing him out. Their friendship always had been close. When in pasture, Bryce sulked and became critical of his friend. All is well now and has been for a year. . . .

Sunday, April 11, 1976

The week's end brings support for Trudeau's determination to establish the constitution at home. The Conservative leader[11] offered "sincere support." He warned that a confrontation

11. Joe Clark

with the provinces could be divisive. . . . I discussed the matter with Gordon Robertson last week. He is Trudeau's chief adviser on this question. Bourassa will stand in the way. He will not be satisfied with the entrenchment of some guarantees for the French language. He wants a new division of federal-provincial powers. The division of powers can always be discussed. It can be taken up after patriation [and] . . . should not be allowed to stand in the way of domiciling the constitution in Canada. There are three ways to do this:
1. Bring the B.N.A. Act home, leaving the amendment procedure to be settled after patriation. . . . 2. Ask Parliament at Westminster to include in its act the amendment formula proposed at Victoria in 1971. The law would stipulate that the amendment formula would lie dormant until all governments agreed to its implementation. The formula, which we worked out in Victoria, provides for an amendment with the consent of Parliament and a majority of the provinces. This means Quebec and Ontario, who would be given veto powers, at least two Atlantic provinces and at least two Western provinces having at least fifty per cent of the population of Western Canada. I prefer this method. 3. This option would include language protection, which would be dormant until an overall agreement had been reached, after patriation. . . .

Monday, April 12, 1976

Nell and I attended, in the Housman Room at University College, a reception in honour of Chief Justice and Mrs. Bora Laskin. In this room, in a glass case, is the skeleton, without head, of Jeremy Bentham. . . . Bentham is wearing the clothes he had on at the time of death. . . .[12] Laskin gave the . . . formal address: "Mr. Bentham, My lords, ladies and gentlemen." In this way, members of the Bentham Society pay tribute to the leader of English Utilitarianism. . . .

12. Jeremy Bentham (1748-1832) was an English utilitarian philosopher who set out that all laws should work for the greatest happiness of the greatest number. Utilitarianism became the impetus for much social reform in the nineteenth century.

Sunday, April 18, 1976

Easter Sunday did not seem an appropriate day to study the opening statements of Michel Dupuy* and the Commission in the Canada-E.C. negotiations [on the contractual link]. I spent some time, however, on them tonight. Frankly, I was disappointed. There is not much meat on either side in these statements. The value of the agreement from our point of view will be the setting up of a body to promote the objectives, vague as these are declared to be. We hope that a joint committee, composed of senior level people, including ministers, will develop programmes of action. Out of this, there will be continuing consultation and perhaps some useful trade consequences. Much will depend on the follow-up by the private sector. The agreement will establish a framework for future co-operation. It will not create new rights or obligations on access to resources or markets. . . .

Wednesday, April 21, 1976

At the end of last week John Hay of the Canadian Press told me that an unknown official in the Foreign Office had intimated that it would be difficult, without provincial consent, to accede to a unilateral request by the government of Canada to patriate the constitution. . . . Today in *The Times* part of what John Hay has reported is repeated. The story goes on to observe that this opinion of a British government official is not likely to give comfort to Trudeau. I must decide today whether, without instruction, I should go over and do some missionary work. It may be that some young lawyer in the Foreign Office has spoken unwisely and incorrectly . . . but there isn't any question of the right of the federal government to proceed on its own. There is no constitutional bar to such action. . . .

The Commons, or more likely the Senate, is a possible obstacle to patriation of the constitution. The Senate could very well balk. It would have to join in the request to Westminster for patriation. If the constitution is domiciled in Canada, the subsequent amending formula will have to provide that the Senate will not have power to disagree with the House of Commons on a constitutional amendment, supported by the Commons and Ontario and Quebec and a majority of the provinces as provided in the Victoria conference arrangement. . . . The Senate's concern lies in the situation which could result in action to abolish the Senate. Even so, the Senate could not stand in the way of a popular wish, expressed through constitutional legislative bodies expressing a majority judgment. . . .

Thursday, April 22, 1976

There is some speculation that there may be an early British election. . . . I think Callaghan would make a mistake to have an election now. He wouldn't win it. He may do so later. Harold Macmillan took on the prime ministership after Eden during a mid-parliament.[13] He became stronger in the two and a half years of prime ministership before he held an election. After that interval, he did win the election sweepingly. The office of Prime Minister makes a man stronger, particularly if he has revealed that he knows how to use the office. I doubt that Jim will have any election before the autumn of 1978. Will Mrs. Thatcher give him that trial period? If she does, then I think it is in Callaghan's interest and the national interest to wait. . . .

Further enquiries at the Foreign Office do not confirm the newspaper stories about reluctance to proceed with patriation of the constitution in the absence of provincial concurrence. Talking to some Canadian newspaper men I find that, for the most part, the source seems to reside with a member of Parliament, who thought that the course would not be as easy as I have postulated. . . . Further examination of the problem clearly reveals that, if unilateral application for patriation is made by Trudeau, there will be no . . . obstacle on the part of Westminster. . . .

Sunday, April 25, 1976

What is now to be the position of the liberal democracies regarding South Africa? They cannot be for the whites or the blacks. This "either/or" policy will be hard to achieve or maintain. Another option would be to say that the West is unable

13. In 1957.

to make up its mind. The result of this would be to wait and see which — the black or the whites — will come out on top. This would be the easiest course to follow. This would mean not following a positive policy. It would amount to having no influence on the future of South Africa — black or white. Perhaps this course would mean leaving South Africa to an imperialist Soviet Union. The West must . . . show South Africa the desirability of a change in policy to avoid a deadly racial conflict. Only in this way can the West avoid making a choice between blacks and whites. . . . The whites in South Africa have a rightful claim to a place in Africa, but that place has to be fairly designated. . . . If the white South African was faced with obliteration, the consequences in the United States and Western Europe would be serious. Moreover, the blacks and whites will want the continuance of an efficient economy. This the whites can guarantee — at least "for the next generation" . . . . Conditional on a South African change of policy, the black nations agreed to leave the "pace and method" to South Africa. Vorster, during the last twelve months, has been moving in this direction. He will have to move faster. Under Vorster's scheme, [the] black four-fifths of South Africa will only get one-eighth of the country's territory, in which to parade their independence. The proportion has to be changed. Otherwise a substantial part of black South Africans, living in white territory, will for all time be without a "home" and will remain disenfranchised. The whites will have to agree to sovereignty over less territory. The whites will have to accept "a minority role" in a flexible confederation arrangement, which will apply to the entire area, known as South Africa. . . .

Monday, April 26, 1976

The secretary to the cabinet in Manitoba, Derek Bedson, called on me at noon. He is strongly of the view that a unilateral petition to patriate the constitution, without provincial consent, will provoke a protracted debate and much dissatisfaction. Undoubtedly he reflects the opinion of his Premier, Ed Schreyer. I mentioned that I had no instructions in the matter. Nevertheless, I was strongly of the view that, in the absence of provincial agreement, the federal government would be wise to proceed with a unilateral petition. . . .

Wednesday, April 28, 1976

Kissinger made an important speech in Lusaka ... [and] called for co-operation to achieve the goals of national independence, economic development and racial justice for black Africa. Africa, however, must work out its own destiny. . . . The Smith régime will not be given diplomatic recognition or material from the United States at any stage in its conflict with African states or liberation movements. . . . The United States will take steps to uphold full sanctions against Rhodesia, and will urge the Congress to repeal authorized Rhodesian chrome imports. . . . The United States will aid Mozambique in the amount of twelve and a half million dollars to help compensate it from the closure of its border with Rhodesia. . . .

Thursday, April 29, 1976

I was looking at *The Guardian* in between appointments this morning. What struck my fancy were two pictures; one of Callaghan and Harold Wilson. Both are smiling and showing their teeth. On the back page is another photograph of Ted Heath and he is showing his teeth, smiling famously, as are the other two. These photographs tell a tale. Modern politicians or statesmen are always photographed now as happy, smiling, teeth-showing individuals. The same is true at home. . . . If one looks at photographs of Canadian, American and British statesmen forty years ago, the practice of smiling and showing one's teeth was not normal. . . . There is something synthetic in the photographs of the average politician today. This is not confined to political people. It is true of actors, university presidents and even trade union leaders. One never sees a painting, even now, of a smiling prime minister, whose teeth in their absolute whiteness dominate the canvas. . . . Ted Heath, who was regarded as an inflexible person but an interesting and nice one by those who know him, is not any more interesting because he shows teeth in good order.

VIII

May – June 1976

THE MONTH OF MAY was relatively quiet for Nell and me. Allan MacEachen came to London and we discussed the state of political leadership in Canada. Rumours that Pierre Trudeau might follow Harold Wilson's example were rife — if not accurate. It was a pleasant time of year for me to continue my series of visits around the United Kingdom and I went to Wales. During my week there from May 11 to 14, I toured around and was particularly impressed by Portmeirion and my meeting with architect Sir Clough Williams-Ellis.[1] *Towards the end of the month my daughter Mary Anne and her family arrived for a visit. My granddaughter, Catherine, quickly became a star at 12 Upper Brook.*

In early June, I had some dealings with the Northern Irish Protestant extremist, Ian Paisley. A more pleasant task was getting organized for a dinner on June 29 for the Queen prior to her trip to Montreal to open the Olympic Games. The mission was also involved in providing advice to the government regarding the Economic Summit in Puerto Rico on June 26.

Monday, May 3, 1976

I sat up with Allan MacEachen until well after 2:30 a.m. Most heads of mission would welcome an opportunity to discuss their problems and issues generally with their foreign minister. . . . The penalty, however, for keeping such a late hour is great. . . . He agrees that Turner should not have left the cabinet and that he will not find it easy to return. Certainly

1. Sir Clough Williams-Ellis, the Welsh architect and environmentalist, created Portmeirion, North Wales, as a model resort village.

the directorates, which he is taking on bit-by-bit and hour-by-hour, will not make him a more valuable figure insofar as the general public is concerned. Allan regretted Turner's departure from the government. There are several versions of what actually went on between Trudeau and Turner. The Prime Minister said that he had offered him other portfolios [than the Department of Finance]. This version is not accepted by Turner. Allan is worried about developments in Parliament and the reaction of the country to the government. Trudeau, however, is a strong leader and will be able to withstand the opposition. He does not believe that Joe Clark is as good as earlier prognostications suggested. Allan believes that the next Governor-General will be Stanfield. I had not thought of this, but it strikes me as quite possible. . . .

Tuesday, May 4, 1976

The long chat we had the night before last, way into the hours of the early morning, enabled me to form the impression that MacEachen is taking hold of his job, particularly on the policy side. His methods of work appear disorganized and cause a good deal of frustration. I despair that there will be any improvement in this side of his operation. . . .

The Queen had invited us, along with about ten other heads of mission, to a state banquet in honour of the President of Brazil. . . . This was an impressive event, with all members of the royal family in attendance, a large suite accompanying the President, members of the cabinet and specially invited guests. I suppose there is no royal household — or head-of-state household — where the ceremony of a state banquet is as well observed as in this country. Tonight's affair was no exception. . . .

Wednesday, May 12, 1976

It now appears likely that the former Liberal leader, Joe Grimond, will succeed the unfortunate Jeremy Thorpe. . . .[2] The party of Gladstone and Asquith is in a sad state. In Britain's political climate there is no room for a strong Labour

2. Jeremy Thorpe had resigned the day before.

The high commissioner's office at Canada House.

"Allan's visit, welcome as it is, nevertheless has brought home to me the changes in programme occasioned by a ministerial visit. . . ." *March 4, 1975.* Allan MacEachen with me, my driver John Rowan, and CAN-1 outside Macdonald House.

"Nell and I . . . met Trudeau on his arrival from Venice tonight." *March 10, 1975.*

"We walked in the drizzly rain, with hundreds of cameramen pursuing us through St. James's Park. . . ." *March 11, 1975.* With Pierre Trudeau and Jean-Jacques Blais, the minister of national defence.

"The final event of the day was, of course, the dinner at 12 Upper Brook Street. . . ." *March 14, 1975. Left to right:* Nell Martin, Harold Wilson, Mary Wilson, Price (the butler), Paul Martin, Pierre Trudeau.
(Fox Photos Ltd/National Archives of Canada/PA-164946)

"He and I had an animated . . . exchange on Trinity College and more particularly its academic personalities. . . ." *March 13, 1975.* Prince Charles at a dinner at the residence.
(Sidney Harris/National Archives of Canada/PA-164974)

"The Archbishop is a fine and impressive man who taught for some nine years at Wycliffe College in Toronto." *April 24, 1975*. Donald Coggan, Archbishop of Canterbury, signing our guest book.
(Sidney Harris/National Archives of Canada/PA-164947)

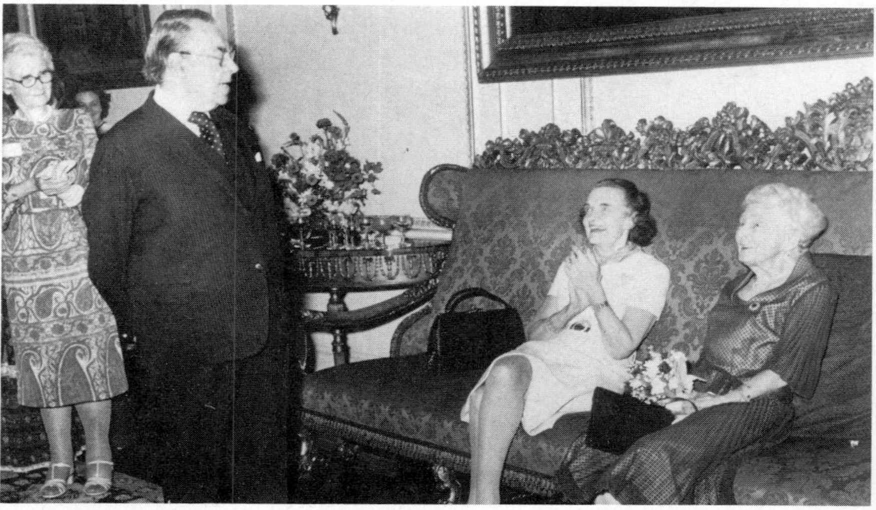

"At the age of ninety-two she is handsome. . . . Above all, her sense of humour is something to behold." *May 27, 1975*. Nell and I with Princess Alice at a tea in her honour.

"There was a quiet peace as we surveyed the well-kept graves . . . the kind of peace that these brave lads fought for. . . ." *June 29, 1975.* With Canadian veterans, to lay a wreath at the annual ceremony at Brookwood cemetery.

Unveiling a plaque commemorating the Dieppe Raid.

"July 1st, our national birthday. I received the Diplomatic Corps at noontime to celebrate the fiftieth anniversary of Canada House in Trafalgar Square." *July 1, 1975.* Cutting the cake with Lord Elwyn-Jones and Peter Shore.

". . . The High Commissioners had assembled to welcome the new Commonwealth Secretary General, Sonny Ramphal, whom I have known for over ten years. . . ." *July 21, 1975.*

Arriving at the Canada Steamship Lines' fishing camp, August 1975. Our grandsons David and Jamie are in front, and on my right my son Paul peeks over Nell's shoulder.

"More manifestations of the Gaelic embrace were given at Allan's *ceilidh* in the Great Hall at Edinburgh Castle. . . ." *October 23, 1975.* Allan MacEachen (centre). (Capital Press/National Archives of Canada/PA-164926)

"The three- and four-year-olds were blind in their faith in Santa but, from six on, their scepticism was just as profound as that of David Hume." *December 17, 1975*. Our High Commission Christmas party.

"Poppa and his boys." Our grandsons David, Jamie, and Paul.

"The Maple Leaf Ball tonight was a great success." *February 12, 1976.* Lady Margaret Alexander sits two places from Nell.

"Nell thought everything had gone off well, even in the opening dance with the Princess, when we faced the music." *February 12, 1976.* Princess Anne at the Maple Leaf Ball.

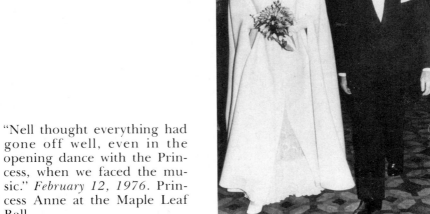

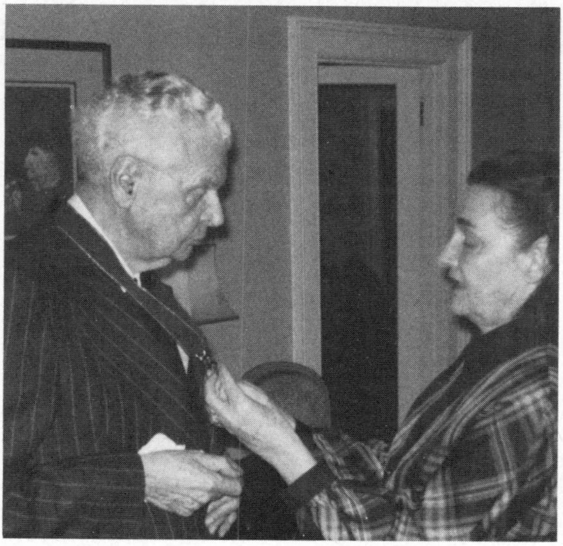

"When I returned to the residence . . . John D. was declaiming once again." *April 2, 1976*. John Diefenbaker with Nell.

"The television boys had a field day with the Indian chiefs. . . . As they sauntered about Trafalgar Square, even the pigeons looked on in awe. . . ." *June 29, 1976*.

(Keystone Press Agency Ltd/National Archives of Canada/PA164970)

"Price . . . had the residence looking at its best." *June 29, 1976.* Our dining room when the Queen and Prince Philip came for dinner.

"From the time of arrival the Queen was in good humour . . . making everyone feel . . . equally happy." *June 29, 1976.* Dinner at the residence.

On holidays, August 1976, in Colchester, Ontario.
(National Archives of Canada/PA-164958)

"He is most considerate and generous and, I suspect, will be a formidable political opponent." *September 21, 1976.* Greeting Joe Clark at Heathrow. (Keystone Press Agency Ltd/National Archives of Canada/PA-164924)

". . . this gracious woman, who would have been impressive under any circumstances, queen or no queen. . . ." *February 9, 1977*. The Queen Mother signing the guestbook prior to dinner at the residence.
(National Archives of Canada/PA-164937)

"I thought Harold was in good form, in spite of his innocuous speech."
February 10, 1977. Harold Wilson at Canada House.
(Keystone Press Agency Ltd/National Archives of Canada/PA-164935)

"... to my surprise and pleasure, I was given a helmet, No. 99, worn by the London city police." *March 29, 1977.* After being given the Freedom of the City of London.

(James Johnson/National Archives of Canada/PA-164939)

"Today we had a procession from Canada House to the Mansion House ... conveyed in a landau at the centre of the R.C.M.P. escort." *May 10, 1977. Left to right:* Commodore Noel Cogden, R.C.M.P., myself, Commissioner M.J. Nadon, and Lord Mayor Sir Robin Bullitt inspect the escort.

"We spent the day at Windsor Castle. . . . The Queen was full of gaiety." *May 15, 1977*. With the Queen and Commissioner M.J. Nadon of the R.C.M.P.

"Commissioner Nadon presented the Queen with the fine horse, Centennial. . . . That she appreciated the gift was apparent today." *May 15, 1977*. At Windsor Castle.

and Liberal party, just as in Canada there is no room for a strong Liberal and N.D.P. Jeremy is not the whole reason for the situation. . . .

Sunday, May 16, 1976

After lunch I drafted a telegram to Allan MacEachen about the dinner for the Queen which Nell and I will be giving on June 29th. From every point of view, it is desirable that he should not be present. He will be in the welcoming party in Ottawa and in Nova Scotia. It would be unusual for him to attend the High Commissioner's dinner wishing the Queen bon voyage when, in a few days, he will be occupying the reverse role. . . . It really is our show and I think that is the way it should be. Allan never sought to intervene; it was my suggestion in the first place, made without the consideration which I usually give to matters of importance. . . .

The High Commissioners for Australia, Canada and New Zealand gave a reception tonight at Australia House for the members of the Royal Life Saving Society. . . . The guest of honour and Patron was H.R.H. Princess Alexandra, whom I had last met in Windsor sometime between 1957 and 1963. . . . When she arrived this evening, she asked when had we last met. Would it have been naughty of me to have said to her "Well, when did we?" She is very popular, certainly with my wife. I don't dislike her, but she has not been popular with me for some reason or another which, I suppose, is not too rational. That she is friendly goes without saying but perhaps a little too smart. . . . But she is a good sport and stayed for a long time, giving the folks their money's worth.

A more interesting guest for me was Lord Louis Mountbatten, with whom I had three good chats. In the first of them he said that if Canada didn't put up the £500 for membership in the Royal Life Saving Society, he would send me a cheque for this amount. This was a very clever way of saying "Pay up, boys," but Mountbatten is a man. . . .

Thursday, May 20, 1976

When Allan MacEachen was here, he discussed with me what position he should take at the United Nations Economic and Social Council on a resolution which condemned Zionism as a form of racism. This aspect of the resolution was almost hidden in a series of resolutions covering many subjects. It would have been possible to abstain. Given a good explanation for an abstention, that vote would have been logical, but abstentions are not easily understood in Canada. It seemed better, therefore, that we should take a positive position and vote against the resolution. This MacEachen instructed Saul Rae to do. . . . As Saul later said, "Canada cannot and will not accept any attempts to force a link between racism and Zionism. . . ."

Yesterday, in the British House of Commons, a select committee on Cyprus made a report in what can only be described as a remarkable document. It would be interesting to know whether there is any constitutional precedent for it. This committee was set up to look into the government's foreign policy on the administration of overseas territories. In this instance, the committee looked into British policy on Cyprus, during and since the crisis there of July-August 1974. It found British policy to be wanting and defective. . . . It is clear that the actions of the American Congress have influenced this Cyprus committee. It is a dangerous thing to take away the control of foreign policy from the executive. This does not mean that the Congress or Parliament has no responsibility or ultimate authority in foreign policy, but it is foolhardy to overlook the dangers involved in an attempt to give to a parliamentary committee the conduct of foreign policy. The day-to-day executive decisions which have to be taken in foreign policy cannot be embraced by a parliamentary assembly. . . .

Friday, May 21, 1976

I called on the Chancellor of the Exchequer at 3:00 o'clock this afternoon. . . . Denis was obviously pleased with having reached an agreement with the trade unions for the second phase of the incomes policy. . . . Denis said that labour unions have bargaining power. The important question is to convince them to abandon part of it for the time being in the national interest. Heath had tried this but failed. . . . [But Healey] hopes to cut the rate of inflation by half—to six per cent by the end of next year.

Denis is concerned, nevertheless, about world recovery. . . . He pooh-poohed my suggestion for important cuts in public expenditure. Nevertheless, he would not want his colleagues to exceed present expenditure ceilings. . . . He agreed with me that new investments were essential to the new industry strategy, but he did not believe that he would induce new investment through tax concession. . . .

Monday, May 24, 1976

Tom Jackson, the president of the Union of Postal Workers, had invited me to their conference at Bournemouth on Sunday. Thanks to John Noble [one of the officers at the High Commission], I seem to have an "in" with some of the Labour leaders. . . .

I reviewed . . . the aide mémoire, which I am to present at the highest appropriate level, perhaps on Thursday. This aide mémoire points out that the government of Canada remains firmly dedicated to a multi-lateral solution of the question of fisheries jurisdiction in 1976. We will do all we can to bring the Law-of-the-Sea Conference to a successful conclusion at the summer session this year. In any event, 1976 must be the year of decision for Canada in the extension of fisheries jurisdiction. In taking, if necessary, a unilateral position later, Canada will respect bilateral agreements with countries who do not have bilateral agreements with us. Canada is prepared to co-operate but we will expect cooperation in return to meet Canadian objectives. . . .

Tuesday, May 25, 1976

Our butler, Price . . . gave a month's notice. He and the cook, Howard, do not get along. It is hard to know who is responsible. . . . Whether one lives upstairs or downstairs, human frailty manifests itself in tragic and amusing circumstances. . . . The only disturbing aspect is that, with the Queen's dinner in the offing, everything must run smoothly. . . .

Lord Barnetson was kind enough to ask me to his annual luncheon. . . . In addition to Barnetson himself, Harold Wilson . . . Mrs. Armstrong,[3] the Italian Ambassador, Max Aitken,

3. The new United States ambassador to Britain.

Roy Thomson and Lord Goodman were [my] table-mates. Wilson told me that he has practically completed his new autobiography, based on his years since his first defeat. . . . I don't know how he can write a book so quickly, since his retirement. He must have begun its preparation before he left the office of Prime Minister. I greatly suspect that, while he was there it was being written, undoubtedly with a lot of outside help, otherwise it could not be ready. . . .

Roy Thomson . . . told me that Diefenbaker had offered him the post of Governor-General at one time. If he had accepted, he would not have become proprietor of *The Times*. His life would not have been as complete as it has proved to be. . . . Roy is not without a good sense of humour which, when displayed sometimes, is revealing. He said: "No, I would not have wanted to be Governor-General, I would have preferred a higher job." . . .

Wednesday, May 26, 1976

Mrs. Thatcher received a great ovation in Germany yesterday, when she spoke to the Christian Democrats. She indicted socialism, calling for a return to "safer and saner political ideas." Mrs. Thatcher doesn't recognize national frontiers. . . . In the United States she had no hesitation in attacking the government of the United Kingdom. A few years ago, no political leader would have attacked his or her country or government, when abroad. This is partly, I suppose, because questions are now of such international implication that the practice of non-interference is being eroded. . . .

Tuesday, June 1, 1976

When Governor-General Roland Michener paid an official visit to Trinidad, decked out in plumes and all, I objected. Pearson, however, had agreed with the proposed visit. It seemed to me that such a visit belied the character of Canada. It was not a question as to who really represented the head of state. I thought such a visit should have been made by the Prime Minister. Certainly in a Commonwealth country, where the Queen is head of state, it looked like an odd arrangement. Then later, when under Trudeau, Roly Michener and Norah crossed from Britain to Holland in a Canadian warship on a state visit, that too seemed ridiculous. Mitchell Sharp, my successor in External Affairs, agreed with me but Trudeau had agreed to the visit. No wonder Queen Juliana observed privately that "it was odd for Canada's Governor-General to be travelling about in this way." Was this the image Canada wanted? . . . Now comes a suggestion from the present Governor-General, Jules Léger. It is suggested that he would like to "Canadianize" his office by making more official visits abroad. I have my doubts about the wisdom of this plan. Jules Léger's visit to the Canadian Arctic was more to the point. More visits within Canada are what is needed. . . .

After going through the accumulation of telegrams of the last four days, I went over to Quebec House to see the Agent General, Jean Fournier. It was an amusing visit. When I arrived a lot of people were holding placards in front of Quebec House. They were members of the English Teachers' Union, who were complaining . . . [about] legislation barring strike action by the teachers in Quebec. When I saw Jean, I told him that I had come as a spokesman for the teachers. For a moment he took me seriously and the occasion was one for a good laugh. . . . On the way out I spoke to some of the protesters. I thought Jean handled them well. He asked them if, when they were through protesting, they would let him have their signs. With these he would be in a better position to impress his principals in Quebec with the nature of the protest. The police by this time had assembled to give some semblance of security protection. In the circumstances, however, this was not needed. . . .

Wednesday, June 2, 1976

The news that Canada is to be the seventh nation in the follow-up to the Rambouillet Summit pleases me. I had assumed that we would have known about this. Word which I have from Washington, however, indicates that our embassy [there] has no information other than what has appeared in the public press. The statement of a White House spokesman indicates "tentative plans for a seven nation (including Canada) follow-up of the Rambouillet summit this summer." To date, Washington has said nothing to our people in Ottawa about the plans. We should hear any time now one way or the other. Kissinger may have mentioned it to MacEachen at the NATO meeting. . . .

I received a letter from Trudeau today, acknowledging what he calls my "fascinating assessment" of the issues which led to Harold Wilson's resignation. He believes the state of the British economy is a matter of intense concern to all in the industrialized world. He says, "While we are fortunate in Canada to have enjoyed much greater success in most of our economic endeavours, the lessons remain applicable to us and to all industrialized countries, that productivity and continued investment in modern plants is absolutely necessary if we are to maintain any semblance of growth and economic stability." . . .

[Trudeau] thinks highly of Jim Callaghan [and] . . . is anxious that he should visit Canada in September. . . . It will not be too convenient for me. I will, however, have to cross that bridge when the time comes.

Monday, June 7, 1976

The Reverend Ian Paisley has been calling me on the telephone from Belfast. . . . One of his ministers, a Rev. Frank McLelland . . . has gone to open a branch of the Free Presbyterian Church of Ulster in Toronto. Apparently he had hoped to be able to purchase a church property. The [Toronto] school board has now decided to turn it into a parking lot. The suggestion is that religious bigotry stands in the way of his getting the property. . . . I will, of course, see Dr. Paisley, if he wishes to come, as he had told a Belfast newspaper he wants to do. . . .

Tuesday, June 8, 1976

Ottawa has not dropped the plan for patriation of the constitution. I wouldn't be surprised if a question were to be put in the House of Commons here soon, asking what would be the attitude of H.M. government in the United Kingdom to a request by the government of Canada. . . . The question would elicit the response that the government at Westminster would act on the petition forthwith. Such a reply at this stage would have a quieting effect in some quarters at home. . . .

At the post management meeting at Canada House, I . . . raised the matter of the telephone call and proposed visit by the Reverend Ian Paisley. Our consul in Dublin reviewed the matter from his point of view. He says that Paisley is a demagogue and that this is widely recognized in Belfast by all of the religious leaders and most public people. He could do so much, if he only would, to ease the fires of hate. I am rather anxious to meet Paisley and see what makes him tick. It has now been arranged that he is coming to see me on Thursday morning. He will complain that in Canada there is religious bigotry. I will remind him that the attorney-general who complained about him is not a Catholic. I will point out that there is no denial of religious liberty in Canada. I hope he will get the message. . . .

Wednesday, June 9, 1976

There is a story current here that Trudeau is getting tired of the job and that he may step aside before the next election in 1978. This I doubt. Some say Trudeau is depressed and frustrated. . . . They also say that he has lost his spark. This, again, I don't believe. . . . It is a fact, however, that Trudeau is having his ups and downs—with the business community, with some of his own colleagues and some of their mistakes. It is fashionable to say that the cabinet needs revitalization. Trudeau himself said that, if the party lost confidence in him, then he would think of retirement. The party will not lose confidence in him. He would be wise, however, to be a little less daring. Alas, to endure in politics one must be cautious. People like bold initiatives only for a while. One can always come back to a good initiative. Somehow or another, people prefer the hard collar to the soft collar, in spite of what they say. . . .

Our immigration division [at the High Commission has] . . . advised Ottawa of Paisley's desire to see me. Apparently, Bob Andras* will say in the House today that the question of Paisley's admission to Canada is one which he will look into. I am strongly of the view that he should say forthwith that there is no reason why Paisley will not be admitted to Canada. He is a member of the British Parliament. . . . I had a chat on the telephone with the Secretary for Ireland, Merlyn Rees.

He already knew that Paisley wanted to see me. The Ulster papers have been talking to him. I told Rees that I could not refuse to see Paisley. He fully agreed. He thought it would be wise to say to Paisley—"Well, I cannot see you tomorrow but how about next week?" Rees has had a lot of experience with this gentleman, for whom he has no admiration. . . . I had no sooner made this notation, when I learned that Paisley would like to see me this afternoon. This is impossible because of my other engagements. We have so informed him. . . .

Sir Martin Charteris, the Queen's private secretary, lunched with me [to discuss our dinner for the Queen on June 29]. . . . The Queen sometimes likes a dry sherry before dinner, oftentimes a gin-and-tonic and sometimes a good martini in the American and Canadian style. At dinner, a good French red wine always does the trick. The same apparently applies to Philip. He repeated the Queen's liking for Harold Wilson, obviously an easy man with whom to converse. . . . This quality in Wilson I have noticed, a capacity to accommodate himself to anyone with whom he had to do business or talk. . . .

We talked about patriation of the constitution. He wanted to know what I thought about it, what the procedure would be and what would be the net result. . . . I emphasized that once the Parliament of Westminster had acted, there would be no legal consequences in Canada. In any event, that was our problem and not that of Westminster. . . .

When I went to see the Minister of Employment, [Albert] Booth, around four o'clock in the afternoon, I ran into Paisley in the House of Commons lobby. I introduced myself. He seemed to be astonished and surprised to meet me in these circumstances. He looks much like his pictures and seemed a lonely and aloof man. He would let me know next week when he would call. . . . It may be that he will not come at all now. Perhaps his purpose has been served and there is nothing more for him to gain by criticizing Canada. . . . I proceeded on my way, only to run into the . . . affable and co-operative Rees. . . . From what the Secretary of State said under his breath, but audibly enough for me to hear, Paisley is no bosom friend of the Secretary of State. . . .

Friday, June 11, 1976

Last year I had gone to St. Giles Cathedral in Edinburgh for the first Commonwealth Day service there. That was a memorable experience as was today [in Westminster Abbey]. Sitting in the stall, reserved for the High Commissioner for Canada in the choir, I was about eight places from the Queen and on the same level in the wall stall seats. An impressive ecumenical service indeed! . . .

Saturday, June 12, 1976

[At] the "Trooping the Colour" ceremony on the House Guards Parade, in celebration of the birthday of the Queen, this morning . . . His Honour and Mrs. Steinhauer, the Lieutenant-Governor of Alberta and his wife, sat between Nell and me, directly behind Jim Callaghan. After the ceremony, we had refreshments in the garden at No. 10 Downing Street, where I presented Canada's first Indian Lieutenant-Governor.[4] I told the Prime Minister that I hoped, when he went to Canada in September, he would take a few days holiday in Alberta. This, he said, he wanted to do. Trudeau and I, however, seemed anxious to keep him working. . . . This Canadian visit is more important to Jim than he may think. He doesn't know Canada too well. Apart from Harold Wilson and perhaps Ramsay MacDonald,[5] Labour leaders have underestimated the importance of Canada. . . .

Tuesday, June 15, 1976

For the next few days, the forthcoming Economic Summit in Puerto Rico preoccupied me. France was pushing for a conference communiqué that stated that the six other participants had met with the head of the Canadian government, who was specially invited by Gerald Ford. I had no doubt that the French intended this proposal to cast doubt on Canadian participation in subsequent summit meetings.

We cannot accept such a proposition. . . . I understand that someone in External Affairs has registered our protest to the French Consul over the action taken by the French. Giscard gives me a pain, as I am sure he does many others. . . .

4. Ralph Steinhauer had been a councillor and chief of the Saddle Lake Indian Band in Alberta.
5. Ramsay MacDonald was prime minister in 1924 and again from 1929 to 1935.

Wednesday, June 16, 1976

About ten o'clock this morning, I learned that Allan MacEachen at the last minute, because of engine trouble, was flying to London on his way to Paris. . . . Allan was kind enough to call this morning. We discussed the Puerto Rico meeting. . . . He thinks that the P.M.O. is responsible for the French recommendation that the communiqué should explain why Canada was included as a participating member at Puerto Rico. . . . He thought the matter had better be allowed to rest at this point. . . . Later, in some speech, he would make a general reference to the French reservation. I agree with him that now is not the time to raise the issue. . . .

Thursday, June 17, 1976

I called on Sir John Hunt. He had just returned from the preparatory meeting of the second Economic Summit. . . . The meeting in Puerto Rico will begin in the morning of one day and finish next day at noon. It is hard to see how a comprehensive discussion of a comprehensive agenda can ensue. There is no doubt in John's mind that the meeting was scheduled for political reasons, notably the United States elections.[6] On the other hand, it was thought that the Rambouillet meeting last November had a political undertone, and yet, from that meeting emerged an important agreement on fixed rates of exchange. The British, therefore, would assess the Puerto Rico meeting in the light of political reality and unexpected result. . . . It is thought that the President, as the host, will likely open the discussion. The British have no particular subject which they wished to suggest for the agenda, nor did they have any special concern which they would like the Summit to take up at this point. . . .

Friday, June 18, 1976

The rioting in Soweto [South Africa] carried on into a second day, with over forty-one people killed. The police shooting of black students, who protested the use of Africaans in their lessons, is an event of stupendous proportions. It will likely

6. Scheduled for the following November.

weaken Vorster's position when he talks to Kisssinger in a day or two. It may push back progress in Vorster's dealings with African leaders, like Kaunda and Nyerere. It may force him into further unco-operative action with Smith. It projects apartheid into the forefront.

Cabinet leaks take place in the United Kingdom as well as at home. The day before yesterday there was a leak of a complete set of cabinet papers on business relating to the government's incomes policy. . . . In the days of King and St. Laurent in Ottawa, this kind of leak was unknown. It developed in Pearson's time and [has] bloomed in Trudeau's régime. It seems to me that there is an odd quirk in modern society which permits responsible and patriotic institutions to encourage this sort of thing and to participate in it. After all, the cabinet is at the centre of government. If confidentiality is not observed regarding its operations, the principle of collective responsibility would be impaired and cabinet discussions would be less frank. What this does to the freedom of public servants' participation leading to government decisions and discussions must be obvious. In some cases, it may be argued successfully that some good comes from such disclosures or leaks. Nevertheless, to condone the practice is dangerous, irresponsible and uncivilized. . . .

Tuesday, June 22, 1976

I have been doing some further examination of the Puerto Rico Summit. It seems to be the general impression that the primary concern of the United States' President at the moment is to obtain his party's nomination. This is natural. When the summit takes place, his position will still be uncertain but promising. The discussions will revolve around economic recovery, monetary and financial issues; north and south, energy, trade and investment and east/west relations. The proposed proliferation of international institutions has been dropped from the agenda, but could arise later. . . . I am sure that Trudeau will be prepared to take part in all the issues if necessary. There is an inducement for him to do so: the reluctance of the French to have us there. The work done on the draft communiqué does not seem to have been conclusive. . . . I have learned that when Trudeau saw Ford, the latter told him that Giscard welcomed our participation. We must establish our position firmly, because I am sure that summit meetings will take place frequently from now on. . . .

Wednesday, June 23, 1976

When Trudeau was meeting a few days ago with the Premiers at a federal-provincial conference of first ministers, he frankly observed that if patriation of the constitution was not effected during his term . . . the result would be no patriation for ten or twenty years. . . . Quebec still takes the position that there should be no patriation until there has been a transfer of certain powers, negotiated by the two senior levels of government. I am told that Trudeau took issue with Bourassa's position when he met the provinces the other day. He told Bourassa that he was as entitled to speak for Quebec as the Premier. [Trudeau] is also prepared to fight an election on the issue. Meanwhile, a committee of Quebec members in the federal Liberal caucus has been established to work out an agreed position on the constitution. I wouldn't be surprised to see a public opinion campaign organized as well. In any event, Bourassa will not make a final decision until after the Olympics. This could mean that he may hold out for financial assistance to meet the Olympic deficit. . . . The provincial premiers do not like to see a federal election fought on patriation. It could have a divisive effect. . . . Trudeau suggested that perhaps it wasn't necessary to have all the provinces in agreement. If nine said yes, I suppose, he would consider that a mandate to proceed with patriation. . . .

I went to the Foreign and Commonwealth Office at 5:15 p.m. to sign an exchange of notes with the Minister of State for Foreign Affairs, Roy Hattersley. This brings into effect an arrangement regarding safeguards to be applied to nuclear transfers between Canada and the United Kingdom. The arrangement we signed will stand, until we have a more formal agreement between our two countries or an agreement between Euratom,[7] on behalf of the Community and Canada. I had arranged in 1965 for an informal understanding with

7. Euratom (European Atomic Energy Commission) pooled the resources of the European Community for the development of nuclear energy.

the United Kingdom. I had hoped, as a result of approval given by Arthur[8] that we would have a formal agreement at that time. In any event, the process was begun in 1965. . . . In the meantime and consistent with the stricter safeguards policy announced by Trudeau in December 1974, it became necessary to negotiate a more comprehensive safeguards agreement with the United Kingdom, incorporating the basic elements of the new policy, including application of I.A.E.A.[9] safeguards, with a fall-back to bilateral verification of national safeguards in the absence of I.A.E.A. inspection, an express prohibition on explosive use, and control over re-export of transferred material and technology. . . . It was inevitable that we should mark the occasion with the traditional glass of champagne. This we had in the India Room of the old Indian Office, now part of the foreign office complex. . . .

The Commonwealth Press Union dinner, presided over by Lord Astor of Hever, the President, was a pleasant affair. . . . St. Clair Balfour[10] was given the sixth award of the press union for his work on its behalf. I spoke of his contribution to journalism in Canada. I would like to have gone on and said that the Southam papers were [generally good individually] . . . but that their chain of operations was not really in the national interest. Canada actually has three big chains of newspaper operations, the Thomson papers, F.P. publications, and the Southam newspaper company. Individual newspaper ownership is better for the community it serves. . . .

Thursday, June 24, 1976

Giscard d'Estaing's visit to Britain seems to be going over well indeed. . . . Giscard suggested to Callaghan that they should hold regular annual meetings, beginning this fall. . . . Certainly,

8. Arthur Bottomley, then the secretary of state for Commonwealth affairs.
9. On September 6, 1976 in Vienna, an agreement was signed between the United Kingdom, the International Atomic Energy Agency (I.A.E.A.), and the European Atomic Energy Community (Euratom) which provided for the submission of British non-military nuclear installations to safeguards under I.A.E.A. supervision.
10. St Clair Balfour was chairman of Southam Inc. from 1975 to 1985 and holds an honorary life membership in the Commonwealth Press Union.

if this visit brings about an improvement in Anglo-French relations, it will be all to the good. It may break down some of the French stiffness and tortuous snobbery. If so, this will be good for France, for England and the rest of us. . . . The attitude of public men can have a bearing in international relations. If I were Trudeau, I would make a special effort with Giscard. In many ways they are the same type. One can hardly say that Giscard and Jim Callaghan are of the same ilk. . . .

Friday, June 25, 1976

It will be interesting to follow Trudeau's tactics with Giscard in Puerto Rico this weekend. The advice given by our man in Paris[11] struck me as wise. We should not remonstrate face-to-face. Our contribution at the conference, however, should be solid and, where necessary, active. We should give Giscard the opportunity to explain why we were not at Rambouillet and the reasons for his reserve about us at the preparatory meeting in Washington. Only after Giscard had taken the initiative, should we take a firmer position. . . .

Sunday, June 27, 1976

René Lévesque's Parti Québécois is the alternative to Bourassa's Liberal party. Lévesque asserts people are leaning his way. This I doubt, but elections are an "unknown quantity." If he does not do well in the next election, he will likely resign, or he may be eased out. . . . What would follow if Lévesque became Quebec's premier? He advocates political independence . . . [and] Lévesque says he will try to negotiate a deal to achieve his objective. He now says there would have to be a referendum. The idea of a referendum is a new ploy. . . . Quebec of course, has a unique and certain identity. Trudeau is a protagonist of this fact, as I have always been. Quebec is the *foyer* of French-speaking people in Canada. But there are about two million of these people in other parts of Canada. I am one. . . . I believe in the Laurier model of a Canadian mosaic, with continuing Quebec participation. . . .

11. Gérard Pelletier

The bilingual fact is acknowledged on an increasing scale. Quebec's separation would be tragic. . . . We would in some respects, like the former Pakistan, be divided. It will not happen. The people of Quebec are so much part of what we are, that its people will not be lulled into acceptance of Lévesque's programme of partition. . . .

Monday, June 28, 1976

Trudeau was delayed in leaving for the summit meeting in Puerto Rico because of an emergency cabinet meeting over the Air Canada strike.[12] It would have been ironic, after all our frustrations over non-participation at Rambouillet and the French attitude about our being in Puerto Rico, if he had been prevented from attending the summit. The Prime Minister continues to say that the involvement of bilingualism in the air controllers' attitude and the consequential pilots' resistance creates the most serious problem for national unity since the Second World War. . . .

I put down on paper this morning some of the questions which I must resolve for the Queen's dinner. Do I rise and toast only the Queen — what about Prince Philip? How does one address a marquess — is it "My Lord?" — and how does one address a Marchioness — is it "My Lady?" At what point does Nell invite the Queen and the ladies to have coffee upstairs in the large drawing room? How long do the men sit at the table and when do I say to Prince Philip "Shall we go upstairs?" How do I pronounce the name Abergavenny? Has everyone been told, other than the royal couple, when

12. The Canadian Air Line Pilots Association took the firm position that English should be the language of air traffic control communications throughout Canada. The federal government, however, identified a demand for the use of French in Quebec. The pilots refused to accept French until the question of air safety was resolved. There were wildcat walkouts of air traffic controllers on June 20 and 21, and the airline pilots association instructed its members not to fly until they felt that the skies were safe. The issue split the country between those who wanted an increased use of French and those who felt that English was all that was required. The strike ended on June 28, but the bitter feelings left a bad taste in the federal Liberal caucus and provided popular support in Quebec for René Lévesque's Parti Québécois.

they are to be at 12 Upper Brook Street? . . . Now that there are to be many photographers and not just two — where are they to be stationed — in the library? Are there to be any outside? When does the Queen sign the book? I cannot find it this morning — I must speak to Price about it later today. Do we invite the Queen and Prince Philip to use the elevator? Do we meet the Queen as she alights from her car or do we await her entrance in the hallway? . . .

Tuesday, June 29, 1976

At 11:00 o'clock the Lieutenant-Governor of Alberta and Mrs. Steinhauer and [Herbert] Pickering, the Agent General of Alberta, went with me in my car to Buckingham Palace to meet the Queen and [a visiting delegation of Canadian] Indian chiefs with their wives. . . . The television boys had a field day with the Indian chiefs in full regalia. As they sauntered about Trafalgar Square, even the pigeons looked on in awe, displaying great interest in these fine representatives of Canada's native population. . . .

The Queen and the Duke of Edinburgh came to dinner at 12 Upper Brook Street on the "eve" of their trip to the United States and Canada. They leave Saturday morning. Price and the staff had the residence looking at its best . . . [and] had duly laid the red carpet for the royal couple. . . . From the time of arrival the Queen was in good humour, with an infectious and lovable smile, making everyone feel . . . equally happy. Prince Philip had been to a reception at the English-speaking Union before dinner. He arrived five minutes ahead of the Queen. . . . I got a kick during the evening watching Mary Anne and Mike Bellamy deeply engaged, for a long time, in talk with the Duke of Edinburgh and, later, Mary Anne, again sitting on the floor and this time Nell too, talking to the Queen. . . .

IX

July – August 1976

*O*UR MISSION IN LONDON *heard echoes of the dispute over bilingualism in air traffic control which led to Jean Marchand's resignation from the government. We also provided advice to Allan MacEachen regarding Taiwan's refusal to participate in the Montreal Olympics under any banner but that of the Republic of China. Then, the African countries decided to withdraw from the games because New Zealand would be there. The African governments objected to New Zealand's continuing to maintain organized sports contacts with South Africa. At the end of July, I left for home and holidays.*

Thursday, July 1, 1976

[At] the Canada Club Dinner tonight at the Savoy . . . Roy[1] made a good speech, reviewing British/Canadian history and relations in an expanding world. . . . During the course of dinner, he told me that he had made up his mind, after the loss of the [Labour] leadership, to take on the E.E.C. Commission. This will give him an opportunity for further public service. He could always return to politics later on. . . .

I asked him why he did not persist in the race for the leadership. It was clear, he replied, that he would not get many more votes, although he did have a substantial following. He could see no purpose in prolonging the agony. . . . Denis Healey was built of different material. It was his nature to carry on the battle. From what Roy told me, it is clear that he would like to be Foreign Minister. This ap-

1. Roy Jenkins, the home secretary.

parently has been reserved for Denis at the opportune moment. Crosland will then likely become Chancellor. . . .

Nevertheless, Roy is fascinated by the prospect of working for the Community. . . .

Friday, July 2, 1976

Jean Marchand has resigned from the government. He gave as his reason his disagreement with the terms of the interim settlement of the air traffic controllers' strike. Apparently in the Liberal caucus on Wednesday, violent disagreement was registered by Quebec members against the settlement for an enquiry. One is tempted to think Marchand's resignation is a convenient way to get out. It has been clear, however, that Marchand could not stay long in the cabinet. He has been tired and unwell and attacked on so many fronts. I feel sorry for him, because some of the matters for which he is being criticized are unfair and untrue. Jean, however, has always been a doubtful long-term political figure. . . . From the first day I saw Jean Marchand in cabinet, I did not think he would last. . . .

Jeanne Sauvé* called me from Ottawa [and] . . . I asked her about Jean Marchand's resignation. She had hoped he would not have left the government over the air pilots' strike and the resulting attacks on bilingualism, which has gripped the Quebec and the parliamentary scene. If the inquiry commission recommends bilingual air traffic control at Quebec airports, particularly in Montreal, the president of the air pilots' association affirmed that the pilots might resume the strike. Otto Lang[2] mystifies [me] somewhat by saying that the inquiry could take two years, the final report being available before the next election. . . . The Quebec pilots say they will not co-operate with the inquiry. "English Canada is driving Quebec out of Confederation," a union leader declared. . . .

Saturday, July 3, 1976

I went to the airport to say farewell to the Queen, who was on her way to North America for the United States' bicentennial celebrations and to open the Olympic Games in Montreal.

2. The minister of transport.

Ron Spiers, who had returned from Washington this morning, after two weeks' absence, returned to town from Heathrow in my car. He told me that Kissinger does not get along as well with Crosland as he did with Callaghan. Crosland is inclined to regard foreign affairs people as "cake pushers." . . . Crosland should begin making more contacts with heads of mission. I have no complaint and I admire his style. He could be an able foreign minister. Perhaps he realizes he is only filling in for Denis Healey. Ron says that Healey does not intend to take over for another year. This is too long "a lame duck period." . . .

Monday, July 5, 1976

The Liberals in the United Kingdom will pick a new leader this week. It looks like David Steel. What is the future of the Liberal party in England?—this the great party of Gladstone and Asquith. So much of the statesmanship of the last hundred years in this great country has been rooted in the liberalism of these and other men. . . . Is there a place now for liberalism in the House of Commons? . . . Has liberalism been absorbed by the socialists? Could it be that socialism is running its course and that there will be a return to a recognition that freedom can be maintained only if limitation is self-imposed? The Liberal party's prospects do not look good. Certainly in the short run they are non-existent. . . .

Tuesday, July 6, 1976

Today, our relations with Britain and the European Community will be put on a new basis, as a result of the commercial and economic co-operation agreement being signed in Ottawa. This is the culmination of over a year of negotiation. When I became High Commissioner, Trudeau told me that he had doubts about Britain's support for our contractual objective with the Common Market. Indeed, this was apparent during Trudeau's discussions here in March, 1975, when we met with Wilson, Callaghan, and other United Kingdom ministers. Both Wilson and Callaghan expressed the view that a declaration would be easier to support than a specific agreement. An agreement, however, will be signed later this day. In a sense, part of my mission has been achieved. The agreement will be the first to be concluded between the Community and a major industrial power. It will prove a contractual framework within which the Common Market countries and Canadian industrialists may promote joint ventures within their own territory and in third countries. . . .

Wednesday, July 7, 1976

The publisher of *The Globe and Mail*, Dick Malone, was my guest at lunch today. Others who came were Sir John Hunt, secretary of the cabinet, [and] Lord Thorneycroft. . . .[3] John Hunt said that the Puerto Rico Conference, in spite of its political motivation, was useful. He agreed with me, however, that summit meetings ought not to become a bore. In any event, they should be well prepared. . . . John could not tell me with any firmness that the future status of Canada at summit meetings has now been established. His private view, of course, is that there can be no justification for excluding us from these deliberations. I suspect that, in the future, we will not be excluded, France or no France. . . .

When I returned to the residence, there was a call waiting from Allan MacEachen in Paris. He wanted my views on the position he had taken, regarding the Taiwan delegation to the Olympic Games [in Montreal]. His position is that they cannot participate as the Republic of China. Taiwan should participate in Montreal as it did in Rome in 1960. Allan was not aware that Lord Killanin[4] wants to see him within the next few days. The president of the Olympics and others are concerned about the introduction of political questions at the Olympics. If that is done now, I suggested to Allan, he would have to think what will be the situation at the next Olympics in Moscow.

We discussed the pilots' strike. The terms of agreement made by Otto Lang with the air controllers had not been before the cabinet. He thought it was a great mistake that Otto should have agreed to give the House of Commons a free vote on the Commission's report. The French members

3. Former chancellor of the exchequer and new president of the Conservative party.
4. President of the International Olympic Committee.

had been put in a bad way. It was inevitable that they should remonstrate against the interim settlement, which went right to the heart of the bilingual issue. Trudeau is now hard put. The interim arrangement is now a fact. His defence of it puts him in an invidious position vis-à-vis Marchand and the Quebec members. There is no doubt that Allan is disturbed by developments in Ottawa. . . .

Thursday, July 8, 1976

I am leaving for Scotland—Aberdeen and the highland games at Tomintoul, Banffshire. Nell is leaving for Canada on Saturday and so we say our goodbyes this morning. . . . We have grown so much together in thick and thin that, even a month's separation is hard to take. What a wonderful person she has been and how deeply in love we are. . . .

On our way from Aberdeen to Tomintoul, we stopped to visit Balmoral Castle, where the Queen normally spends a good part of the summer, particularly in August. Balmoral is a fine, but not large, castle with splendid grounds. One reaches it by approach across the river Dee. . . . Queen Victoria wrote: "I seldom walk less than four hours a day and when I come in I feel as though I want to go out again." We walked too, going in one way and out another along a fine, natural path with the same magnificent trees on both sides of the river Dee flowing by. . . .

Monday, July 12, 1976

Dick Malone had dinner with me tonight. . . . [Malone] thinks Trudeau is in great trouble. He sees nobody and maintains no contacts with people like himself. Malone takes strong issue with Keith Davey* but has confidence in Jim Coutts,* who is perhaps as close to the Prime Minister as anyone. Trudeau will certainly have to take stock. He should cultivate the media, particularly at the Dick Malone level. I will tell him so. The feeling in Western Canada against Quebec is stronger now than ever, the publisher of *The Globe* says. That may be but the problem of French Canada has got to be faced. This, Dick does not fully appreciate. . . . I assured Dick that Trudeau was not a wild-eyed star-gazer, that he was pragmatic and had as good a concept of the Canadian Confederation as anyone. Notwithstanding this assurance, Dick said that *The Globe* and other papers would oppose Trudeau in the next election, although he concurred that Joe Clark was a disappointment and admittedly not in Trudeau's class. Nevertheless, Trudeau had better get busy. . . .

Tuesday, July 13, 1976

Ivan Head was on to me by telephone. The Taiwan issue in Canada continues to be disturbing, more so than perhaps I realized. The cabinet was in session as we spoke. The Prime Minister had asked him to get in touch with me. What did I think?—and also to make sure that I was fully aware of Canada's position. I said I was. Canada is getting quite a pounding on the Taiwan issue throughout the United States. "How is it in the United Kingdom?" I was asked. The same —although I pointed out that a London Canadian Press story notes that British press reaction to the Olympic controversy over Taiwan is just about a draw, with equal blame on the Canadian government and Lord Killanin. I asked if it had been wise for Allan to attack the president. I was told that this was a big mistake. The president had not interfered as was suggested by Allan. This I thought might have been the case but one is at the mercy of the news media. Our position on the Taiwan matter is logical. . . . I will send a message tomorrow, giving a synthesis of what the British press has been saying about the Taiwan issue and the Olympic Games. As a matter of fact, we should have done this earlier. Sometimes, I think, at the mission, in spite of the many people we have, we do not originate sufficiently, oftentimes acting only on request. . . .

Friday, July 16, 1976

As hinted to me by Ivan Head late yesterday, the government, following the cabinet meeting, is likely to modify its position on Taiwan. The Canadian government will agree that Taiwan can take part in the Olympic Games under its own flag and play their national anthem. The Taiwan team, however, will not be allowed to call itself the Republic of China. I was a little surprised that the government made any concession. Our position seemed logical and our course of conduct correct. We had acted a long time ago—the delay was on the part of the Olympic Committee. I hope that the concession which Trudeau has now made, dropping two of the three conditions, will settle the matter. . . .

The New Zealand High Commissioner called me early after 8:00 a.m. to tell of his interview with the High Commissioner for Tanzania. That country is not going to retract its announcement of withdrawal from the Games. He advises, sixteen African countries have indicated their intention not to participate. If this is carried out, the result may be more serious than the question of Taiwan. . . .

Saturday, July 17, 1976

Taiwan will not take part. Trudeau's proposal of a compromise has been rejected. Taiwan insisted on using "Republic of China" as her designation. In a sense, "A Comedy of Errors." . . . In retrospect, this will all look quite silly. Trudeau, in a story from Montreal, is called the "first villain of the piece." A month ago, it is argued, Killanin and his committee "could have brought Trudeau into line." Killanin instead caved in. Trudeau did also. The whole affair is truly regrettable. . . .

Monday, July 19, 1976

Over the weekend Grenier of Joe Clark's office came to see me at the residence . . . [about] the Leader of the Opposition's September visit to London. Everything seems to be in order. . . . He gave me some interesting sidelights on the Conservative convention. Paul Hellyer might well have won, had he shown more restraint and less confidence in his own judgment. When I told Grenier that Diefenbaker was for Paul, he expressed some surprise. Grenier, I don't think, was for [Claude] Wagner. The latter's law-and-order stance was against him in Quebec. For instance, Claude Ryan* of *Le Devoir* was a supporter of Mulroney. . . . Human beings are sometimes an odd lot. I would have thought he would have supported Wagner, because of his law-and-order attitude, so full of goodness is Claude Ryan. From what Grenier said, I conclude that Joe Clark's election, desirable as it may be, was somewhat of a fluke. Nevertheless, Joe is not losing any advantage, as his visit to Ford and Kissinger indicates. . . .

Kurt Waldheim* and Sonny Ramphal have urged the African countries to stay in the Games. I suspect that Sonny Ramphal had something to do with prompting the United Nations Secretary General to urge the African and Arab countries not to boycott the Olympics, in their protest against New Zealand's participation, because of that country's sports links with South Africa. Guyana is the first Caribbean country to withdraw from the Games. This would not please Sonny Ramphal.[5] Gestures of this kind, I suspect, he would regard as somewhat childish. . . .

Wednesday, July 21, 1976

I sent a message to Ottawa reporting that the concentration [of news on] the Olympics is centred on confusion over the walk-out of some countries. There is a London-based story that a protest group, known as San-roc, a South African non-racial open committee for Olympic sports, is behind the walk-out. My information is that this group was formed in South Africa in 1962 to campaign against apartheid in sport. Canada is not implicated in the stories on the walk-outs. . . . Talking to MacEachen on the telephone late today, he believes that his press conference in Montreal on Friday cleared the air as far as Canada is concerned. . . .

Thursday, July 22, 1976

This has been a full morning. It began with a call on me by the Rev. Ian Paisley. . . . He wanted to know if there was any difficulty in his being admitted to Canada. There was only one reply. . . . The question was asked because of recent demands, asking that he be barred from coming. The Minister of Immigration[6] had advised us, of course, that there was no way by which he could be prohibited. This I knew beforehand, but it was helpful to have official confirmation from the Minister of Immigration. . . . I confined my remarks pretty well to generalities at this state of my contacts with Paisley. There were many matters I would have liked to discuss. I will do so later. . . .

5. He is a Guyanese.
6. Robert Andras

Later that day, I went to Cambridge for a meeting with some eminent British legal scholars. This initial encounter set in motion the organization of what was to become the Canadian Institute for Advanced Legal Studies. I consider the founding of the Institute to be one of the most important achievements of my High Commissionership.

I dined with Basil Markesinis, Jack Hamson, the Master of Queen's College (Dr. Bowett), a distinguished professor of international law and David Williams, an authority on constitutional and administrative law and senior tutor at Emmanuel College. Each summer, students and lawyers from the continent and the United States come to Cambridge for courses in various aspects of the law. Why not do the same for Canadians? We were agreed in principle that we should. Our discussion ranged over how this could and should be achieved. The four are to present me with a plan. We will meet in London in September and review the matter. It is a worthy objective. I hope it may be possible to assist in the implementation of what we decide should be attempted. How happy I would be to have had a hand in bringing about this arrangement for Canadians. They would come to Cambridge and partake in its rich history, tradition and knowledge. . . .

Monday, July 26, 1976

I have been thinking over Dick Malone's article on Canada and the E.E.C. in *The Globe*. Yesterday, I expressed surprise that he should have taken the line he did, after our long talk two weeks ago. . . . His view of the contractual link as an erosion of private enterprise is startling and invalid. . . . That there is a place for public enterprise does not mean that private enterprise will be abandoned. Dick Malone values, as I do, our economic relationship with the United States. He has no reason, however, to believe that the contractual link will be . . . discriminatory against United States/Canadian trade. The fact that the Community has been in a state of some disarray does not mean that its prospects are not good. . . .

I proceeded at 11:00 a.m. to Heathrow to meet the Queen, who arrived from Canada sharp at noon. . . .

Tuesday, July 27, 1976

The Labour government here technically is now in a minority position. Two Scottish MPs have announced that they are resigning the whips, because of the cuts in public expenditure announced a few days ago by the Chancellor. . . . They were dissatisfied with the government's devolution proposals. They formed their own Scottish Labour party. . . . The government is not in immediate danger. It can count on support on particular issues from outside its own party. I doubt if anyone really wants an election at the present time. Callaghan, Healey, and the Labour leaders are sticking firm in their decision to reduce government expenditures. . . . Callaghan['s] . . . moderate approach is making an impression on the country. His firm hand shows his capacity for leadership, although George-Brown told me the other day that Jim was too old. . . .

[At the Royal garden party] the Queen chatted mostly about her impressions of the Olympic Games, expressing admiration for a Canadian young woman swimmer. The organization of the Olympics had been amazingly efficient. It was apparent that she had greatly enjoyed the Games, and was encouraged by the warmth of the reception she received.

The Prime Minister and I had a good chat. Later, I met his wife, who said how much she was looking forward to her trip to Canada, particularly the Western portion. . . . Jim told me he hoped that the Western portion would be his holiday. He looked forward to the train ride through the mountains which, I assured him, he would long remember. I told him that I would be at the Ottawa talks. He wondered whether I would be going on to Halifax and Quebec. My reply was: "That will depend on MacEachen and what he says." Does MacEachen speak French, asked the Prime Minister? I said, "No, but he speaks Gaelic."

How did I think he was doing? he surprisingly asked me. I suppose he felt that this was a natural question. . . . I told him I thought he was doing well, which is the case. The forthrightness of his responses and the firmness of his positions are making him a highly acceptable leader. The impression he is making on the country likewise, I think, is good. In Parliament, he handles Mrs. Thatcher with skill and did so again yesterday. He has his troubles in his own party with the extreme leftists but he is handling them wisely.

"My, but I have to see a lot of groups," he noted. "I spend so much time with delegations." I mentioned it seemed to me that every day he attended a trade union meeting. . . . Did Trudeau "spend as much time seeing delegations as I seem to do?" "No, he did not," I replied. He had so organized his programme that, apart from four or five national delegations, such meetings were usually with individual ministers. I asked him if he would object to my saying that it was necessary for a Prime Minister to be as free as he possibly could. It was inevitable that there would be certain people he would have to see, such as the Canadian High Commissioner, which provoked a happy laugh from him. . . .

Wednesday, July 28, 1976

Ottawa telephoned to advise me that Jack Johnston, the British High Commissioner, had handed the Secretary of State for External Affairs a message from the United Kingdom government, advising that it has broken off relations with Uganda. I was not surprised by the news, but I was taken aback a little by learning of the British government's policy from Ottawa. After all, I had talked to Callaghan only yesterday. He said nothing about Uganda. Crosland certainly would have discussed this matter with him. . . . The Australians telephoned me, to find out if we had been advised directly here by the Foreign Office. They learned of the British decision from the news media in London. I think, however, it is normal for a government, in formulating a new policy of this dimension, to have its ambassadors advise the governments concerned. On reflection, I recall this practice, which we ourselves normally observe. . . .

Friday, July 30 – Sunday, August 29, 1976

On my holiday in Windsor, I spent my days visiting old friends, although work intruded from time to time. Because Jim Callaghan was planning a September visit to Canada, I helped to iron out some problems with that. And, of course, I got caught up on the Canadian political situation. After Herb Gray called on August 14, I noted that:

Liberal leadership is sunk in gloom and cynicism. That the polls are bad is clear. Trudeau has two years to go [before he has to call an election]. His share of weaknesses and mistakes are not to be ignored. Clark does not appear to be a Jimmy Carter* [and] . . . has not Trudeau's potential strength. . . .

[Pierre's] capacity for debate and "demagoguery" is notable. . . . When these qualities are turned on, they have proven to be effective. . . .

Trudeau's position was not helped by the failure to reach an agreement on the constitution. At a first ministers' meeting late in August, Alberta's premier, Peter Lougheed, insisted that all provinces should have a veto over amendments to a patriated British North America Act. Given that the provinces were not likely to agree, I felt that "Trudeau should proceed forthwith . . . preferably with provincial blessing, but, if not, unilaterally. This is what the Canadian people want. . . ."

We left for London on August 29 and I was back at work at the High Commission two days later.

X

September – October 1976

A few days after I returned to my desk, the leader of the opposition, Joe Clark, came to London on a visit. He impressed me. At the same time, I was increasingly concerned about the comments of prominent Liberals that Trudeau should give up the leadership of the Liberal party.

On the international front, I followed the efforts of Henry Kissinger, the U.S. secretary of state, to resolve the Rhodesian conundrum but did not like his failure to involve the Commonwealth in his efforts.

In mid-September, I left for Canada for a few days to be in Ottawa for the talks between Trudeau and Jim Callaghan, who was visiting. While I was there, Trudeau shuffled his cabinet and I found myself with a new boss, Don Jamieson, who took over External Affairs from Allan MacEachen. Canadian politics took on an uncertain air on October 27, when Premier Bourassa called a provincial election in Quebec.

In Britain, the economic troubles of the government grew increasingly urgent. Although Callaghan appeared to be able to keep the lid on things, there were rumblings in the Labour party and in cabinet about possible tax increases.

Friday, September 3, 1976

In CAN-1, we had a good drive to Cambridge, where I went to participate in a panel of the fourth Annual World Congress of the English-speaking Union. The meetings were held at Churchill College, where I was a guest of the Master, Sir William Hawthorne. . . . During the dinner I had much talk with Roy Hattersley's wife. One learns a good deal on occasion from the wives of important men. I mentioned how well I thought Jim Callaghan was doing. This she acknowledged. She did not think, however, that he would be in office long, hinting at some kind of interim arrangement, perhaps five years. She hinted that the Foreign Office people were not altogether enthusiastic about Crosland as Foreign Secretary. Healey could not be expected to stay at the Exchequer forever, although he was doing a brilliant job there, she thought. She implied that Denis was likely the next leader and that he must be around in the appropriate post for the succession. . . .

Monday, September 6, 1976

I left early for Gatwick to meet Joe Clark . . . [who] is on his way to Europe, accompanied by Claude Wagner and two members of Parliament, Messrs. Fraser and Balfour.[1] We had a good chat in the VIP lounge at Gatwick, reviewing the programme we have arranged for Clark when he comes here on the seventeenth. . . . I was asked what I thought of the proposal of Joe Morris and the Labour Congress regarding labour's participation in the policy-making process of government. I replied by outlining the British Labour government's position. Harold Wilson and Jim Callaghan both made it clear to the Labour party conference and to trade union leaders that a distinction had to be made between the Labour party as such and the government. Only the government could make policy. The Labour party and indeed other parties and groups in the country had the right to make suggestions. . . . Joe was obviously pleased that I had gone to the airport to welcome him. . . .

After I returned from Gatwick airport this morning, I saw a predecessor and former colleague of mine in government, Lionel Chevrier.*[2] . . . Lionel shocked me by saying that Trudeau had to go as leader. I didn't agree and told him so. Why does he feel this way? He says, because there is such a blacklash on bilingualism of every kind, that there is no other

1. John Fraser, MP for Vancouver South, and R. J. Balfour, MP for Regina East.
2. We had joined the cabinet on the same day in 1945 and he had served as High Commissioner in London in the 1960s.

course open. I countered by saying this is all the more reason why Trudeau must stay. I reminded Lionel that the Liberal party had been strong in the past, because it treated its leaders loyally and recognized that they must be given the fullest support. The Conservative party had mistreated some of its leaders in the past, with negative political results. The Liberal party in Canada must not make the same mistake. . . .

Tuesday, September 7, 1976

Western policy regarding the extension of export credits towards South Africa is now being reviewed. We are going to find out if our policy of export credits, investment insurance and foreign investment guarantees are in line with those of other Western countries. Our policy has been to examine requests from Canadian exporters to South Africa for loans on their individual and economic merits. In view of the current importance of developments in Africa, Ottawa is anxious to know whether there are any changes in the policies of other administrations. . . .

It is interesting to note the emphasis Kissinger gives to Britain's role in mediation in South-West Africa. The United States and the British are working very closely together. Both are secretive about what is going on, although in Ottawa Callaghan, I am sure, will open up. The British have been wise to stick as close as they have to the United States. In unity there is strength. The real fact is, however, that the British had come to the end of their rope and needed the help of the United States. . . .

When I awoke this morning, I thought of what Lionel Chevrier had said about Trudeau. This disturbs me more and more. Lionel, sincere as he undoubtedly is, is wrong. Quebec would be up in arms if Trudeau were forced to vacate the leadership. This would resolve nothing. It would create disunity in the party's ranks. I wish I could get Trudeau to change certain characteristics, but he is a strong leader and must be supported. This is a requirement for party unity more particularly, it is essential for Canadian unity. The big-business people likely reflect what Lionel said. This does not mean that they understand the situation or are providing the right diagnosis. Meanwhile, the Prime Minister is criticized for having gone off with the Aga Khan on his yacht and visiting King Hussein in Jordan. . . .

Wednesday, September 8, 1976

Ted Heath will not be coming to my luncheon for Joe Clark. He has asked if I would arrange for him to call on Joe privately. This has been arranged. I have invited two other former leaders of the Conservative party and Prime Ministers, Harold Macmillan and Alec Home to the luncheon. I have not asked Ted, as Mrs. Thatcher is away. It seemed wiser not to do so but I think, if Alec Home and Macmillan come, I could see no problem in asking Ted to the lunch. One dislikes to be constrained in this way but what else can one do in the circumstances? The Canadian High Commissioner would not want to be accused of preferring Ted Heath to Mrs. Thatcher. . . .

Thursday, September 9, 1976

There is more discussion of schemes to assist white Rhodesians with compensation provided for by willing countries. From what I was told in the Foreign Office . . . there is nothing concrete being put forward, except in terms of general principle. As I told Sir Antony Duff,*[3] it is wrong that the countries who are expected to contribute to such schemes, and involved otherwise in the problems of Africa, should not be immediately informed, as are the British, French and the Germans, of what Kissinger is doing. . . .

A complication arose today over the seamen's strike, which could have a stranglehold on Britain's economy. No. 10 Downing Street was in touch with me advising that, because of the strike, the cabinet felt, as did the Prime Minister himself, that he should not be away from Britain at this time. There is a glimmer of hope that the strike might be settled between now and Sunday. Callaghan has, therefore, decided not to leave for Vancouver as scheduled this morning. He will look at the picture sometime on Sunday and will then decide whether he

3. Duff, the deputy under-secretary in the Foreign Office, had just returned from a visit to South Africa.

should go to Ottawa and, presumably, later on to Quebec and Nova Scotia. . . .

Bryce Mackasey, the Minister of Consumer Affairs, and Premier [Gerald] Regan,* on his way to Mauritius for the Commonwealth Parliamentary Association, came to 12 Upper Brook Street around tea-time. It was inevitable that we should discuss the political situation at home. Bryce thinks that, if an election were held today, the Liberals would lose fifteen seats in Quebec. Bryce's characterization of the Ottawa scene is disturbing. He pictures the cabinet in disarray and blames much of the present confusion on the arrangements made by Otto Lang over the air traffic controllers' strike and the reaction to the bilingual policy. Bryce would like to be Minister of Transport and Regan would like to see him assume the portfolio. Gerry thinks Otto's policy, insofar as the Atlantic Provinces are concerned, amounts to a disaster. . . .

Friday, September 10, 1976

I had lunch today for Bryce Mackasey and Martin O'Connell. Others present were Arthur Portelance, MP, parliamentary secretary to the Minister of Manpower and Immigration, and Joe Morris, president, Canadian Congress of Labour. . . . If some of the members of the cabinet could have meetings like this, they might be able to break down the resistance they are now encountering from the trade unions. Joe Morris complains bitterly of the lack of communication between the government and labour. Bryce Mackasey is adept in such situations. Joe Morris has confidence in Mackasey which, I am afraid, he lacks in John Munro,* who has perhaps spoken out too strongly of late. . . . Martin O'Connell, no longer in cabinet, succeeded Mackasey as Minister of Labour and, I thought, he was a good one. It seems sad that, with such personalities in the top level of the parliamentary Liberal party, the government's relations with labour are so inadequate. . . .

Saturday, September 11, 1976

The seamen's strike is now off for at least fifteen days, following all-night discussions with Len Murray of the T.U.C. at Brighton. I will await word from Downing Street to learn what Prime Minister Callaghan has decided to do about the visit to Canada. The western part of the trip is off, because there is not time, unless his stay were to be extended. . . .

While Callaghan has been waiting to see what the seamen were up to, he has been making some changes in his cabinet. He is sending Merlyn Rees to the Home Office and Shirley Williams to Education. Good appointments of two good people. . . . I will go to Northern Ireland under Roy Mason's auspices. He leaves Defence to take over Merlyn's post. Paisley says no one will miss Rees. . . . Roy Hattersley moves from the Foreign Office to Prices and Consumer Protection, succeeding Shirley Williams. . . . There is much applause for Shirley's promotion. She is spoken of as a potential woman leader to face Mrs. Thatcher at some point. I will miss Hattersley at the Foreign Office, where he showed special competence. I don't know David Owen,* who replaces Hattersley. . . . Certainly on the ministerial side, there is a weaker team at the Foreign Office. . . .

I was at the royal airport at Heathrow tonight to bid bon voyage to Jim Callaghan and his wife, now on their way to Calgary. Both are looking forward to their Canadian journey. . . .

Monday, September 13, 1976

We left Heathrow around 3:15 p.m. London time, reaching Toronto after an uneventful trip, seven and a half hours later. I went directly to the Hyatt Regency Hotel on Avenue Road. Arriving there, I read the surprising news that Mitchell Sharp has resigned from the cabinet. He will not run in the next election, but apparently will stay on until then. . . . Bud Drury is planning to follow suit. Trudeau, faced with a major drop in public support, will now work to repair the ship. . . . Unless I misjudge the Prime Minister, he will not quit but go on fighting as a good leader should. Trudeau can recover. He has two years ahead of him. In that time he can do what he did in 1972. Then his fortunes and those of the Liberal party were low. . . .

It was not easy to rest this morning. . . . All kinds of people wanted to tell me what they knew, or thought they knew, and to ascertain what I knew or what I thought might be happening. Most think Trudeau will announce his cabinet changes today. I think this likely tomorrow. Thursday he will be busy with the British Prime Minister. . . .

Wednesday, September 15, 1976

The cabinet changes took over the front page. Otherwise it would have gone to the British Prime Minister. Sharp, Drury and Mackasey have resigned. Allan MacEachen goes back as House Leader and is replaced by Don Jamieson, my new minister. . . . Mackasey gave no indication to me that he would definitely leave. He told me that he was seriously considering doing so. Consumer Affairs did not interest him. If Trudeau had put him in Transport, he would have stayed. In many ways, Bryce was the most popular member of the cabinet. He could have helped Trudeau in the present difficult situation. I have always liked Don Jamieson. He is completely new to foreign affairs, but will adapt himself. Trudeau has an uphill job on his hands. Will his cabinet shuffle help? What is most important for him to do is to to establish a close rapport with the people. . . .

Reading the *Globe and Mail* and *The Toronto Sun*, I found only one story on the Callaghan visit, a short story on his speech in *The Globe* — nothing in *The Sun*. There were excerpts of his speech on television and radio. Looking back, I recall the attention given . . . former British Prime Ministers. . . . Have British-Canadian relations changed that much? After all, a British Prime Minister is one of the world's major figures. His staff, of course, did not undertake "a selling job" as is done these days by most heads of government. When Trudeau went to London a year and a half ago, there had been great preparations for contacts with the media. . . . Jim, on the other hand, had turned down several requests for interviews, television and otherwise, before he left London. Maybe Canadians look at Britain differently now. Is it because we have become more important and Britain less so? I doubt this is the complete answer. After all, the British Prime Minister had a packed hall last night. . . .

I have urged Trudeau to pry open what is going on between Kissinger and Callaghan over South-West Africa. They are being very secretive. They will come to us later for money to help. We should be told what is happening in Rhodesia, Namibia, and South Africa. I believe Kissinger had some problems with Nyerere. We have some influence there. I hope tomorrow we may get more out of Callaghan.

I had a long talk with some of the ministers in Trudeau's government. Jean Chrétien was very frank. Trudeau has a long and heavy road ahead. He will have to bend every effort to hold on and, later, to run ahead. Jean will be a candidate for the leadership, when that takes place. I hope Trudeau manages to hold on. It is vital for national unity that he should not be thrown to the wolves. . . . Allan MacEachen is in hiding. I am told he wanted to see me—well, here I am.

Thursday, September 16, 1976

Many are saying that the new cabinet is the Prime Minister's last hope. It is never wise to generalize with assurance in political matters but there is, at the moment, much pessimism. . . .

John Roberts' appointment to the cabinet is well-received. As Secretary of State, he will be expected to speak out on bilingualism. He should do well. His views are sound. John was helpful to me in the 1968 leadership race. My speech at the convention dealt with the question of national unity. He collaborated with me in the production of a text. It was a good one but not good enough. Tony Abbott* is a good addition to the cabinet. He has the kind of personality which makes people want to work with him. Doug, his father, could cause a stone to smile. He was a good finance minister.[4]

The newspapers, *The Globe*, *The Gazette* and *Le Devoir* don't have a word this morning on the Callaghan visit. Yesterday at lunch, Jim, in response to a question by Nell, said he carried no press with him on this trip. He avoided the press as much as possible. In this way, he minimized their danger. Trudeau observed that when he journeyed, they applied to come along. It was difficult to refuse them. It will be interesting to read how the British press treated Callaghan's Canadian visit. . . .

[In Ottawa] I joined the two Prime Ministers in a ceremony of dedication of the new Callaghan Trail in Newfound-

4. He served in that capacity as a colleague from 1946 to 1954.

land. . . . I met some former cabinet colleagues, all a little stunned with some of the cabinet changes. Allan is certainly not happy. Two conditions of his becoming House Leader were that he would be responsible for CIDA[5] and continue as Co-President of CIEC. Jim Coutts believes both conditions will be fulfilled [but] MacEachen was in no conciliatory mood. When I drove back from lunch at Rideau Gate[6] with Trudeau, he mentioned that it was unkind to move Allan. There was, however, no alternative [because] he was needed in the Commons.

The lunch at Rideau Gate was a working engagement. The two Prime Ministers discussed their respective economic problems, including the refusal of Japan to increase her imports. The working partnership between the unions and the government in Britain was thoroughly discussed. Callaghan is very proud of the social contract and the co-operation he receives from the trade union leaders. I pointed out that such collaboration existed primarily because the Labour leaders and the unions were members of the same political party. Trudeau said my work as High Commissioner was "impressive." His use of the adjective made me feel good. I told him of my lunch last Friday with Joe Morris, Mackasey and Martin O'Connell. He should see Morris. It was not too late to do so. He promised that he would. . . .

Friday, September 17, 1976

[Callaghan] told me quite firmly this morning, when we were saying au revoir, that there are no firm details on Kissinger's manoeuvres in Africa. Whatever is firm is only in Kissinger's mind. Kaunda has repeated to Kissinger what he has said before. There is not time to waste. "If you fail, we shall reach a point of no return. God help your mission." I wish we were more involved in this situation. Our credit with Nyerere and Kaunda is high. The British have taken a secondary position, pretty well in keeping with Jim Callaghan's style and tendency to play things down. . . .

5. The Canadian International Development Agency looks after economic assistance to lesser developed countries.
6. The official government guest house where foreign dignitaries may stay while visiting Ottawa.

Sunday, September 19, 1976

There are many Canadians in London waiting to see me. . . . In addition, the pile of papers is a little staggering. It will all be sorted out in God's good time. I have just had a chat on the phone with the Leader of the Opposition. He was pleased with his welcome on Friday and said he "looked forward to seeing me tomorrow." Gérard Pelletier gave me an account of Clark's visit in Paris, when I phoned him at noon. The visit went off well. Pelletier did not take a "note-taker" with him. Joe might be less embarrassed if we followed this practice in London. . . .

Monday, September 20, 1976

Kissinger had a busy African tour. He spent eight hours with Ian Smith yesterday and is optimistic as to results. One of the conditions of his seeing Smith was that the latter would agree to majority rule within two years. . . . The plan seems to be that there will shortly be held a constitutional conference in Britain [to] . . . set up the necessary machinery to bring about majority rule and independence. . . .

In the kind of negotiation which Kissinger was conducting, should he have taken countries like Canada into his confidence or should he have confided his discussions and reports to the black presidents, the British government and Vorster? Had he consulted a country like Canada, how would that have interfered with his negotiations? Canada has a long association with Rhodesia, with Nyerere and Kaunda. Since in all probability we will be expected later on to put up money to help Rhodesia, are we justified in complaining about not having been kept in the picture? . . .

At 10:00 o'clock, I welcomed . . . Joe Clark and his party. . . . Afterwards I introduced him to the Canada-based staff in the cafeteria room of Macdonald House. Diefenbaker always thought the public service was against him, particularly External Affairs. I used to tell him how incorrect this judgment was. It was apparent to me today, as I introduced our personnel to Joe Clark, that it is a mistake to assume that the public servants are partisans one way or another. Clark had a lot of supporters among those who work under my direction here in the High Commission. The fact that I have their support and loyalty doesn't mean that they give support to the political party from which I spring. . . .

Tuesday, September 21, 1976

Looking back on all that we did yesterday, I have formed a favourable impression of Joe. Politically, he is not to be discounted. He is more mature than his years indicate. He speaks well and is careful. He is most considerate and generous and, I suspect, will be a formidable political opponent.

Our call on Roy Jenkins was useful and interesting. On all our calls today, John Fraser was with us and Balfour came with the Leader of the Opposition and me when we saw Denis Healey. . . . Joe was interested in the British attitude towards the Common Market. Did Britain support the tendency, which Clark detected, for an outward E.E.C. or did Britain support a nationalist position? Jenkins, now Chairman-to-be of the Commission, is a strong internationalist and is European minded. He favours a Community developing along these lines and said so. . . .

We were later to find out during the day that this was anything but the view of the Prime Minister and the Chancellor of the Exchequer. . . . The Prime Minister was generous with his time, when we called on him. . . . He spoke warmly of his visit to Canada. He told me that he was greatly impressed with Bourassa's private hide-out and the beauty of the country around Quebec City. . . . Joe asked Callaghan about his relations with the trade union leaders. Callaghan, in reply, said that it was essential in Britain for the government to get along with labour. Admittedly, this was easier to do when a Labour government was in office. . . . Generally, industry represented, in political terms, the adversary. . . .

Jim gave a pretty good illustration of his agnosticism on the Common Market. . . . He said that there are many pious declarations about the Europeanization of the Common Market by some of its state members, but most of this is talk, not backed up by realities when put to the test. Joe Clark told him frankly that his discussions at the Common Market revealed a different tendency and emphasis. . . . Jim was relaxed, frank and philosophical but on the Common Market, as Joe later reflected, he was anything but the typical socialist leader. . . .

On the way out, I spoke to Jim privately—"What about Africa?" With a smile on his lips, he said: "Ah, the hell with Africa." "What does this mean?" I asked. "Oh, I have so many problems here, Paul." I could not help but wonder what the internationalists in the N.D.P. party at home would say. Jim is the old type of Labour party member—strong in his affiliation with the unions and pretty well influenced by their narrowness and national-mindedness.

Denis Healey, the Chancellor of the Exchequer, reflected the same mood. The members of the E.E.C. were not anxious to concede bits of their sovereignty. This was not the direction the E.E.C. would take. This, coming from Denis Healey, is a little surprising. He and I have been involved for many years through the Institute of International Affairs and its counterparts in foreign policy discussions—as protagonists of world collective security. Denis spoke this afternoon like an old-fashioned British trade unionist. . . .

Nell and I had a large reception tonight for the Clarks. . . . One of our guests, an old time Liberal senator, said to me as he was being received: "Paul, what the hell are you doing entertaining the Leader of the Tories?" He was quite serious in his question, as I learned later. I explained to him that, as High Comissioner, my duty was to treat all political figures alike and this I would do in the full discharge of my responsibilities. . . .

Wednesday, September 22, 1976

Joe said to me yesterday at lunch: "You know, things have greatly changed in Canada. Here I am, a Catholic and a westerner, and no one took exception to these affiliations when I was running for the leadership of the party." I rejoined by saying [that when] I had been in the House of Commons ten years, there was doubt that a Catholic and a Frenchman like me from Ontario would ever be taken into a Liberal cabinet and when it did happen, many wondered what the political consequences for the party would be. "A Catholic and Frenchman from Ontario in the seats of the mighty!" Happily, times have changed.

Jim Callaghan didn't reveal anything yesterday about the situation in Africa. At our reception last night I said to Sykes:[7]

7. Richard Sykes, the deputy under-secretary in the Foreign Office.

"You know, the Foreign Office has been careful not to reveal what is going on in Rhodesia, Namibia and South Africa." He made a humorous reply by saying "The Foreign Office always reads *The Times* every morning." It could be that Callaghan and Crosland don't know as much of the detail of the Kissinger shuffle as one would think. Kissinger is to be here tomorrow night and will discuss the matter with Callaghan and report to him, but it does look as though a breakthrough has been achieved. . . .

I presided at the press conference given by the Leader of the Opposition in my office in Canada House this morning. It lasted about an hour and was wide-ranging. Joe handled himself well. His answers were lucid and responsive. The more I see of him, the more I realize that, young as he may be, he has sophistication, knowledge and competence. . . .

Crosland did not seem to mind that Joe had an unusually large contingent with him. . . . I asked Joe afterwards—what was his impression of the Secretary of State? He found him, I think, diffident and removed. I don't exactly feel that way about Crosland. . . . There are criticisms of him but they don't lie, it seems to me, in his style and manner of speech. He doesn't speak idly and is careful in his assessments. He does give the impression, however, of not being overly interested in foreign affairs. . . .

Joe asked questions, which he has been putting about the British view on the Common Market and its development as a community, with consequential encroachment on national sovereignty. Crosland's response was much less negative than those given by the Prime Minister and the Chancellor of the Exchequer. . . .

I accompanied Joe Clark and his wife from Selfridge's Hotel to the airport, seeing them off to Canada. . . . Every event revealed a plus for Clark. He made a good impression and was well received by the Prime Minister and other ministers and by the High Commission staff. . . . He thanked me personally at the airport for what he thought was a generous welcome by me. I replied that I simply did my job as I would myself, in reverse circumstances, have expected.

Thursday, September 23, 1976

When Trudeau was in Prince Edward Island and New Brunswick, there were strong anti-bilingual reactions. . . . It is going to take wise and effective leadership by Trudeau, his colleagues and others to put the national mood on this question in proper perspective. Political leaders in all groups will have to take a greater hand in support of bilingualism. Then, too, its implementation should proceed more cautiously. . . . I sincerely hope that nothing serious will happen to Trudeau's leadership. Absolute reaction to his leadership could cause trouble in Quebec. I talked this over with Joe Clark. He agrees and assured me that he did not intend to be irresponsible in so delicate a matter. . . .

Monday, September 27, 1976

About 2:15 p.m. I left Heathrow for Blackpool and the annual Labour Party Conference. I don't recall diplomats attending similar functions in Canada. Some twenty heads of mission will be in Blackpool. The Prime Minister will give a reception for them. It is always well to let him know that we are on the "Queen's business." If Crosland is there, I may raise the Rhodesian issue again. . . .

Thursday, September 30, 1976

The Prime Minister showed dismay yesterday at the Labour party conference when, by an overwhelming majority, it rejected direct elections to the European Parliament. The anti-E.E.C. feeling in the Labour party is strong. Notwithstanding the vote, the Foreign Secretary said that the government regarded its commitment to direct elections as binding. . . . One wonders how long the government can carry on with such dissension in its party ranks. . . .

Friday, October 1, 1976

At the Lord Chancellor's reception on the occasion of the opening of the Michaelmas sittings [of the courts], I ran into John Hunt, secretary to the cabinet. He was interested in my reaction to the Labour party meeting in Blackpool. . . . His view is that Callaghan is not wedded to the job and will carry on only as long as he can, but is not prepared to compromise [with the Labour party radicals] on policies which he feels are necessary to sustain Britain at this time. This sums up Callaghan's attitude well, I think, and certainly in the Labour party, there is no one now who could command a consensus in a coalition government. Sir John made the interesting and perhaps valid point: . . . A coalition by itself cannot resolve issues. This can be achieved by sound policy only. . . .

Saturday, October 2, 1976

Shirley Williams was undoubtedly the oratorical star at the Labour party conference. . . . Not only is she a good speaker but as well a good economist and a person of such common sense. When John Hunt and I were talking about her . . . he pointed out, however, that in cabinet discussions, she is quiet and does not intervene much. This surprised me but it does not lessen my admiration for her. I have seen many come and go in Canadian cabinets. The greatest talkers were not always the most constructive and productive colleagues. . . .

Monday, October 4, 1976

Apparently, the cabinet is divided over the likelihood that the International Monetary Fund will attach stiff conditions to the loan requested by Britain. Any attempt by Jim Callaghan and Denis Healey to accept other than the normal conditions will create strong divisions in the party and in the cabinet. The left wing will be more vocal than ever. . . . Contemplating Callaghan's present troubles, it is almost unbelievable that, when Trudeau and I talked with him in Ottawa the other day, Trudeau felt beleaguered, looking to Callaghan as an adviser to resolve Canadian problems. Trudeau's trials continue, but Jim today is not the unmolested leader he appeared to be, when we talked at Rideau Gate. . . .

Tonight Nell and I dined with the American Ambassador, Anne Armstrong, . . . at a dinner in honour of the Vice President of the United States, Nelson Rockefeller. . . . I had not seen Nelson Rockefeller since the funeral of Jack Kennedy. I always remember his predicament in the men's room at the . . . Washington airport. He did not have a dime to put in the slot and had to borrow ten cents from a nice black attendant, who told Rockefeller that he did not have to pay him back. . . .

Friday, October 8, 1976

Mrs. Thatcher made the closing speech at the Conservative party conference [in Brighton]. It was not a great speech but it sounded the theme of the next election. She launched a crusade against a "Marxist future for Britain." She believes the social contract is an arrangement permitting selected trade unionists to dictate to the government what it should spend, on what it should tax and what it should nationalize. . . .

Monday, October 11, 1976

The British are adopting more and more the American and Canadian practice of using special advisers to serve ministers. Trudeau has resorted to this on a vast scale. What effect this has on the public service is not clear. That there is need for specialists is evident. One of the dangers, however, is the erosion of political power. Much depends on how the specialists are used. The able public servant, e.g. Gordon Robertson, is as able as any specialist but Gordon is responsible for so many of the specialists engaged in the Privy Council office. . . .

Tuesday, October 12, 1976

Martin Charteris, the Queen's secretary, dropped in. He and I had a chat about the economic and political situation in contemporary Britain. He wanted my views, which I gave to him discreetly. The monarch's secretary has to have eyes and ears. He receives much information from all quarters and, as he is a discreet and experienced person, one does not hesitate to speak to him confidentially. We were agreed that Britain has her back against the wall. An election now would not really resolve much. Margaret Thatcher is able and a good speaker but could she be put over? Would a coalition government be able to do things not open to party government? Perhaps the difficulty lies in that there is no one dominant political figure who can reach out acceptably to a parliamentary majority. . . . Britain will not be able to endure continuing economic crises. At this stage, it is difficult to know what is likely to emerge.

Wednesday, October 13, 1976

I called on the Secretary of the Commonwealth Organization at Marlborough House this afternoon. I had seventy-five minutes with him. First, we discussed the Commonwealth Games in Edmonton and the refusal of many of the black countries to participate in [them], because of New Zealand's collaboration in athletic competitions with South Africa. If the majority of Commonwealth countries do not participate, the Games are bound to be a failure. . . . He recited the circumstances of the visit of the representative of the Games Division of the Organization of African Unity. He had gone to New Zealand to see the Prime Minister to discuss the matter but was denied an audience with the head of the government. . . .

Were we as much out of the line of communication on Rhodesia and the Kissinger African shuffle as he [Ramphal] was. . . . I had to acknowledge that the United States and the British had kept the nature of their negotiations with Vorster and others very close to the chest [and] I had previously indicated my own frustration in this regard. . . . I agreed fully with Ramphal that in respect of a matter involving the Commonwealth, it is very hard to justify why the British did not fully involve the Commonwealth Organization Secretary. In any event, Sonny was kept fully informed by Kaunda and Nyerere. He could be very helpful at the meeting in Geneva and in respect of other matters involving the Commonwealth. I told Ramphal that Jamieson, only a few hours before, had denied that Canada has committed itself to paying into any Rhodesian trust fund. Moreover, he said, we were not committed to Rhodesian immigrants. . . . A footnote to all this, is that Trudeau went pretty far in his talk with Callaghan and may have committed us in principle. . . . Certainly we have not agreed, unless the Prime Minister's observations are construed otherwise, to a pool of capital assistance, estimated at between one and five billion dollars for Rhodesian compensation. . . .

Sunday, October 17, 1976

I have been reading Harold Wilson's new book.[8] . . . At one point, he observes that the successful operation of cabinet depends in the first place on good documentation. I agree.

8. Harold Wilson, *The Governance of Britain* (London 1976).

The trouble now is that there is too much documentation. So much, that it is not read by most ministers for want of time. Only a prime minister, who has no department to administer, is likely to have read most documents. Moreover, the secretary to the cabinet provides him with notes. This I well know from the many times I have been acting prime minister. Wilson says that he has seen much improvement in the quality of documents. Maybe so . . . .

I agree that there is more informality in cabinet proceedings than is assumed by the political science professors. . . . Wilson allowed smoking as did St. Laurent and Pearson. King did not. Trudeau objected if the smoker sat near him. As I was on his right, there was no problem. When Mitchell Sharp wanted to smoke a cigar, he would change his place at the table. Trudeau did not like the smell of a cigar. Mitchell's brand was generally of the eighteen-cent type. At Wilson's first meeting in 1974, he lit his pipe and said, "Smoking is not compulsory." . . .

Bourassa has announced that there will be provincial elections [in Quebec] on November 15th. He should succeed with a reduced majority. This could be René Lévesque's last chance to get into the Legislative Assembly. . . .

Wednesday, October 27, 1976

At lunch today, Gaby Léger, the wife of the Governor-General, was the guest of honour. . . . She will be leaving for Paris on Friday, several hours after I will have left for Canada for a quick trip, which will see me back in London on Monday. Greater love hath no man than this, than the High Commissioner who goes to Kitchener to put an honorary degree on the shoulders of Allan MacEachen. . . .

Thursday, October 28, 1976

My second caller was Claude Sirois, attached to Government House . . . as executive assistant to the Governor-General. . . . We got on to the question of patriation [of the constitution]. . . . Without expressing his view on the maintenance of the monarchy in Canada, he suggested that . . . would there not be the psychological encouragement for taking the final step [and eliminating the monarchy] with the constitution patriated? I think this is an important point which had not occurred to me before. . . .

Friday, October 29, 1976

There is much talk about the possibilities of an election here. The question is now being asked, can the government possibly withstand the growing pressure. This is more likely, if it is thought that the Chancellor is not prepared for a further round of cuts in public expenditure and I believe this is the case. The cabinet yesterday, I am advised, resisted more cuts. . . . The Chancellor may now prepare to increase indirect taxation by raising the level of value-added tax. This will not be well-received. . . .

Later that day, I flew to Ottawa and then went on to Sir Wilfrid Laurier University in Waterloo. As Chancellor, I presided over the academic and social festivities at the university's convocation and then headed back to London on October 31.

XI

November – December 1976

THE VICTORY OF THE PARTI QUÉBÉCOIS on November 15 was, of course, the event that agitated me most during these two months. From then on, the existence of a government dedicated to breaking up Canada was never far from my thoughts. Once the dust began to settle, I began to feel that the PQ election victory might benefit Pierre Trudeau and the federal Liberal party. Jean Chrétien, president of the Treasury Board, came to London to pick my brains about a response to the PQ challenge. The defeated Liberal premier, Robert Bourassa, made the trek to London to enlist my help in getting him a job.

While the separatist question absorbed Canadians, I found it rather ironic that the British government was considering giving up some of Westminster's powers and establishing separate legislative assemblies in Scotland and Wales. But this was a contentious issue which divided Callaghan's government, already just scraping through several close votes in the House of Commons.

Tuesday, November 2, 1976

The sun is out this morning at 8:25 a.m. as I look from my office window. The American eagle stands in its ugly pouncing mood over the Embassy, looking down into the charming Grosvenor Square. . . . The city of London pulsates. . . .

Don Jamieson, returning from Moscow, said he believes the Soviet Union would like to see Canada act as an intermediary in international affairs. I hope Don was not taken in by this request. Gromyko said the same thing to me in 1965 and Khrushchev* had said it earlier to Pearson in 1955. We had urged a role of mediation for the Soviet Union in Hanoi in 1965. They were not too anxious to use their power for such a purpose then. . . . It is inevitable that Don, a novice, be fresh and enthusiastic. . . . No new ground was covered in Don Jamieson's talks with Gromyko, nor were any results achieved. . . .

Wednesday, November 3, 1976

I got no sleep whatsoever last night or from midnight on, listening to the radio election returns [from the United States]. A close election and, as of 7:00 today, it is clear that Carter[1] will be the next President. The jetlag of only two days ago, however, and this all night marathon . . . means that I am so sleepy there is not much point in going to the office. . . .

Sunday, November 7, 1976

There is another side of the bilingual issue in Canada, other than the federal Languages Act. In the current Quebec elections, the non-French minority is angry at Bourassa over Bill 22 [which] in 1974 made French the official language of Quebec. . . . The problem, of course, is not that simple. The English minority will not lose its language rights, but immigrant children of non-English parentage are being treated as French under Bill 22. If Quebec wishes to stay strong as a French-speaking province, I can understand why Quebec wants to maximize its French-speaking population. . . . [When he was in London] I told François Cloutier, the minister in charge of Bill 22, that his objective was good but he had gone too far and had not taken into account human reaction and the good of Canada as a whole. Meanwhile René Lévesque blasts Bourassa. This time, he seems to be playing down the issue of separatism and a possible referendum on it. First, he wants to win.

Tuesday, November 9, 1976

I was surprised to see that Sonny Ramphal said in Ottawa the other day that he was discussing the possible creation of a Commonwealth presence in Rhodesia in case negotiations in

1. Jimmy Carter, the Democratic nominee, defeated Gerald Ford.

Geneva warranted such a force. It was heartening, however, to hear the Commonwealth Secretary General say that Canada had done useful work in keeping the Conference on International and Economic Co-operation going, although the news today is that there is bound to be a confrontation between the developed and developing world. I hope that we do not give much support to the idea of a Commonwealth force in Rhodesia. . . .

I note that Don Jamieson has told the Secretary General that he should not count on Canada joining a peace-keeping force designed to help Rhodesia on a black majority rule. He says that "I would be just as happy if we weren't asked to take part, if it is to act as a buffer between black and white." In any event, whatever outside action might be contemplated should come through the United Nations rather than the Commonwealth. . . .

Wednesday, November 10, 1976

I recalled my conversation last evening with Walter Blackburn, the publisher of *The London Free Press*. Walter and I have known one another for twenty-five years. I was able on at least one occasion to persuade him to rally behind the Liberal party in a general election. He says that the next time the Liberals will be defeated and that the feeling against Trudeau is strong, as I noted when I was home ten days ago. Social welfare expenditures have reached unsatisfactory levels, Walter says. As he put it, Quebec has pushed its language ambition too far. I tried to make him see that it wasn't Quebec but the federal government which was pushing bilingualism to avoid extreme action in Quebec. It is discouraging to find a responsible man like Walter Blackburn not fully understanding the nature of the problem in Canada. . . .

The government suffered heavy defeat in the House of Commons on the Dock Workers' Regulation Bill. Only the Speaker's vote saved the government from another defeat. Callaghan is not going to be deterred by this reverse and responded by warning the House of Lords [to pass the bill], as so often has been done. Joe Gormley, the President of the National Union of Mine Workers, says the government's position is untenable. Perhaps an election was advisable. I wonder why he said this, when Labour's prospects are so dim? . . .

Sunday, November 14, 1976

Nell and I were at the Home Office, off Whitehall, about 10:30 this morning for the Armistice service. We foregathered with the Prime Minister, members of the cabinet, Mrs. Thatcher, Ted Heath, top military officers and the Bishop of London. There was time for some chit-chat. Mrs. Thatcher . . . indicated that she felt she had Callaghan and company on the ropes. I am sure she is waiting for the kill. Looking at me, she observed that I would understand her mood. . . .

The activities concluded with a reception at the Foreign Office by the Secretary of State for Foreign Affairs, with whom I had a few words. I feel sorry for Crosland. His bag is so full and his duties take him away from London so much. Undoubtedly, he dislikes the criticisms he is receiving from so many quarters. It is not his fault that he has not been able to see more of many heads of mission. He is anxious to do something about his heavily charged programme and this he must do. Countries represented in London have a duty and right to see him. He mentioned that he is doing all he can to receive Jamieson when he comes early in December. . . . Don did not give us much notice.

Monday, November 15, 1976

I left the residence early this morning for Heathrow and Northern Ireland, specifically Belfast, reaching there at 9:10 a.m. Al Troy, our Consul, met us on arrival. I went directly to the office of the Canadian Consulate, Canada House—22 North Street—and met all members of the staff. It was evident, even on the street where our office is, that there had been bombing and destruction. Members of the staff related incidents showing what a sad place Belfast is. . . . There are as many proposed solutions for Belfast's present troubles as there are persons involved. . . .

I had a meeting with officials at the Northern Ireland Office at Stormont Castle . . . [whose] appraisal . . . was as balanced as any I received from any source and, in the hands of competent people like those I met at that office, one should not despair of an ultimate long-term solution. This was a point which Roy Mason, the Secretary of State for Northern Ireland, made with me when we lunched together at the White Wing of The Old Inn in Belfast. . . . Roy impressed on me that the policy of detention without trial had been abandoned and now each accusation is followed by a trial. . . .

Northern Ireland officials . . . took me on a tour of the city, an experience never to be forgotten. We went through check-points in the heart of the downtown district, being searched like anyone for weapons, unable to proceed from one block to another unless this procedure was observed. As I walked with my security, I was shown many buildings where fires had been set and bombs had been exploded, with resulting death. Christian killing Christian—maiming young and old—one could not help but feel the weakness of the Christian faith in this place and among these people, in the presence of such violence. . . .

Tuesday, November 16, 1976

I feared the worst and it has happened. My radio told me at 6:00 a.m. this morning that Lévesque and the Parti Québécois had won the elections in Quebec. The actual defeat of Bourassa is not the occasion for my disappointment. Lévesque's victory is. It means the beginning of a process in Quebec to seek to separate from Canada. The process may not succeed. We must do everything we can to see that it does not but it may now begin. My first act, before 8:00 o'clock, was to go to Quebec House to pay my respects to the Agent General, Jean Fournier. Understandably, he had not yet reached his office. I wanted him to know that he was very much in my mind. . . . The ramifications are many. . . . As Nell reminded me this morning, at least for a while, the reaction in English-speaking Canada could be "Oh, we've had enough—let them go." . . .

Barney Danson, the new Minister of National Defence, came in to see me this morning. . . . We are all of course somewhat stunned by the results in Quebec. I ventured to suggest that Trudeau would be strengthened in the rest of Canada. It would be realized outside Quebec that a Quebec Prime Minister was more likely to succeed in persuading

Quebecers to resist separation. On the other hand, our Ambassador in France, Gérard Pelletier, is inclined to the view that as the sinews of war are now in the hands of Lévesque, this gives him the upper hand. My colleagues in the mission and outsiders were eager to get my reaction to developments and few other subjects were canvassed during the day. . . .

Wednesday, November 17, 1976

To answer any British queries on the Quebec election, Don Jamieson cabled instructions from Ottawa.

He points out that all parties in the provincial elections, other than the Parti Québécois, were running on a federal platform. The forty per cent vote received by the Parti Québécois should not be taken as a vote for separation [because] Quebecers were not voting on constitutional but on administrative and economic issues. Lévesque himself had said during the election that a referendum would be held before any question of separation arose. . . . Clearly, the elections do not change anything in the constitutional structure or in federal-provincial relations. Trudeau will be writing Lévesque that the legitimacy of his government within the strict terms of the constitution is accepted. . . .

Thursday, November 18, 1976

Dick Roberts* phoned, before I had a swim this afternoon, to say that the Queen would speak to me tonight at Buckingham Palace about her hope that the R.C.M.P. might provide part of the accompanying escort in the procession from the Palace to St. Paul's, on the occasion of the twenty-fifth anniversary of her accession to the throne. I was surprised to get this news. When we dined with Sir Martin Charteris, private secretary to the Queen, at St. James's Palace tonight, . . . he also expressed doubts that the Queen would raise the matter again herself. I have a suspicion that it is her Master of the Horse who is putting on a legitimate form of pressure. . . .

The Queen's diplomatic reception began around 9:30 p.m. We assembled in the Blue Room with some thirty or so members of the Canadian High Commission and other diplomatic missions, mainly from the Commonwealth. . . . Behind [me] was the largest diplomatic contingent in the room—that from Canada. The Queen laughingly said she regretted that her house was not big enough to accommodate all at the Canadian High Commission. When Ogilvy[2] came my way he said: "You are having quite a time with elections in Canada." I replied: "Not any more than you are having trouble with the Scots in Scotland." The Queen Mother is a remarkable person. She mentioned that she was looking forward to dining with us some time during the course of the winter. She has a remarkable personality which never varies. It is understandable why she is so popular and beloved. Nell and I well recall her from the visit she and her husband made to Canada in 1939. She was radiant and regal then and no less so today. Princess Alexandra is an interesting person. She irritates me, however, every time we meet—"Now when did we last see one another?" I suspect that this is a formula she uses with everyone. Nothing wrong with the formula, but I find it irritating. I wish she would find a new disc. . . .

Friday, November 19, 1976

It is good to read in . . . the papers this morning, which have just come from Canada . . . that there is a realization of the fear of over-reaction . . . to less of what Lévesque may do, says one, than the reaction of English-speaking Canada to him. . . . I detect already that those writers . . . who have been so critical of Trudeau will now come to appreciate his almost indispensable role. . . .

The poor High Commissioner! Just as I was about to review some telegrams I am sending to Ottawa, an American friend, en route home from Rome, called asking me to get him a room in an hotel. I had to hold my temper but I will do my best. . . .

Saturday, November 20, 1976

The separatist Parti Québécois takes over Thursday next. Trudeau is receiving suggestions about what he should do. . . . A national referendum reflecting the national and sectional judgment has been on my mind for some time. Ted Heath

2. Angus Ogilvy is married to Princess Alexandra.

discussed this procedure for Scotland with me some months ago. I know that Trudeau is aware of the idea. The thought behind the proposal for a federal election soon is also being canvassed. It is too early for that now. I am satisfied that in some form a vigorous federal challenge to Lévesque will become, before the two-year period — a desirable course. Trudeau is the one to lead that challenge, because he is Prime Minister and a Québécois himself. . . .

Monday, November 22, 1976

My day started off well as I stopped to talk to the nice Irish lady who every morning at this hour is bent over, washing the exterior steps at the Italian Embassy next door to my Macdonald House office. I suggested to her that, if she used a mop, it would be easier on her back. . . . How old was she, I asked — just over sixty. "How old am I?" I asked — "I would say about the same," said she. . . . I left her cheerful and full of jaunt. Not only is she a hard-working woman but she is discerning! . . .

Tuesday, November 23, 1976

The Gaullists should mind their own business. In Paris, the Gaullist party executive believes that political autonomy alone will guarantee the survival of the French language and culture in Quebec. An irreversible process is under way, said Marc Lauriol, national secretary of the Union of Democrats for the Republic. . . . It is interesting to note that before the election active Gaullists, along with some socialists, signed a manifesto drawing attention to the Quebec elections and their importance. Among the signatories . . . was Philippe Rossillon, who followed me around in some parts of Canada and in Africa in 1968 when I went to Niger. He was expelled from Canada in 1968. We regarded him as a secret agent in the office of the Prime Minister of France. There were good reasons for believing that Rossillon had been sent by de Gaulle in 1968 to make contacts with French-speaking separatists in Canada. He was in Quebec during the [1976] elections. . . .

Wednesday, November 24, 1976

I will attend the Opening of Parliament by the Queen. . . . With the butler's help this morning, I donned my white tie and hard shirt, well before 8:00 o'clock, and walked down Brook

Street, past Grosvenor Square, wearing my silk hat and feeling not a little unlike Lloyd George and Winston Churchill, as they wore this kind of head-gear day by day on their way to the House of Commons. When I entered Macdonald House this morning, as I well knew they would, the security men looked in wonderment, perhaps thinking that I was just coming from an all night party and decided not to have any sleep before I began this day's work. . . .

When Don Jamieson, our foreign minister, comes here on the sixth [of December] . . . he will see Crosland. I must say, however, that the telegram of instructions from Ottawa is rather amusing. I was told to arrange for Don to see Crosland for not less than two hours. I am not acting on this instruction. An hour will be sufficient. . . . I have been very lucky in being able to speak to Crosland almost at will. Yesterday . . . the Dutch Ambassador complained bitterly to me that he was not able to see Crosland at all. This, of course, is a general complaint, which I know worries . . . top officials in the Foreign Office. . . .

I received a telephone call this afternoon from Robert Bourassa, the defeated Premier of the Quebec elections on Monday night. He had been speaking to Prime Minister Trudeau and Marc Lalonde about . . . spending a year or so at the Common Market. . . . Naturally, I told Bourassa how sorry I was that he had suffered defeat and offered my sympathy. . . . He is anxious to be away from Canada for the next period and this I fully understand. He is a good economist and likely would be of some service to the Market, if this can be arranged. What Roy Jenkins' reaction to an appointment will be, or what he feels he can do [for Bourassa] . . . is another matter. . . .

I had a talk with Marc Lalonde on the telephone after returning from the reception. Bourassa had in fact been in touch with him. . . . There were two problems as I saw it. Canada was not a member of the Community and would this not make it difficult to employ Canadian personnel and further, Jenkins was not yet installed in office. . . .

Friday, November 26, 1976

I talked to Marcel Cadieux* about the Bourassa matter. He had indeed talked to Bourassa in Canada the other day. Marcel is in Ottawa and will talk to Gordon Robertson. . . . He will not press the Bourassa claim before the Commission but sees no objection to my asking Roy Jenkins to see Bourassa. . . . I am quite sure that if Bourassa meets Roy, the latter will say he has no authority in the matter at the moment. . . .

The word I have is that the present French government had no difficulty in dealing with the Bourassa administration. My French source says that the relations between France and Quebec under Lévesque could prove to be more difficult rather than easier. Lévesque is not regarded particularly as a francophile. . . .

Sunday, November 28, 1976

Robert Bourassa had dinner with us at the residence tonight. . . . He had thought that he would win the recent Quebec elections, although once he was on the stump he realized he had a tough battle on his hands. He wanted Marchand and Mackasey as candidates. Marchand, who did not run, would have been a tower of strength to him in the Legislative Assembly. Mackasey [who won the election] would have been of good value as a spokesman for the English-speaking population of Quebec and was of great help in holding a number of English-speaking ridings. We talked of his régime. The Queen's visit pleased him. She was well received by the people of Quebec at the Olympic Games. He thought it was too early to determine if Trudeau would weather the storm. . . .

Wednesday, December 1, 1976

It should not be forgotten that the elections in Quebec, regardless of result, represented a triumph of the democratic process, but it also gave reality and challenge to the rest of Canada in a crisis which cannot be dodged. . . . It is an error for commentators . . . to think that what the federal government is doing is to protect its powers rather than meet provincial concerns. . . . It is wrong to think that the present structure of government in Canada is not a decentralized one. I believe Trudeau is right in thinking that Canada is probably among the more decentralized countries in the world. . . . Perhaps the form of federalism in the future will change. . . . Whatever transformation does take place, the important thing is to make sure that we have a central government with enough power to give meaning to nationhood. . . .

I find it interesting that, while this problem is before us in Canada, Britain is beginning to discuss devolution. . . . The bill on devolution, introduced in the Commons yesterday proposes assemblies in Edinburgh and Cardiff. The Scottish assembly will have wider powers and members of the assembly will be elected directly. Education, except for the Scottish universities and the universities of Wales, will be within the powers of both assemblies [which would] have power over culture, local government, the environment, development and industry, agriculture and housing. . . . Westminster will continue to have constitutional authority over the legislatures in any matter. . . .

Thursday, December 2, 1976

I had a small lunch in honour of Rodney Grey. He is head of our delegation to the Multilateral Trade Negotiations in Geneva. Sir Peter Thornton, the Permanent Secretary of the Department of Trade, thinks that an anti-liberal trading mood prevails among industrial countries. Rod Grey fears the consequences of failure of these negotiations for Canada and is very anxious that they succeed. Acknowledging that there is this rightist tendency currently among countries, as far as Canada is concerned, Rod agreed with me that the strongest evidence of protectionism in Canada has to do with our attitude on export of Canadian resources. . . . Grey indicated quite clearly, by implication, in the discussions today the importance we attach to the M.T.N.[3] . . . [and] believes the British and French are not really interested in a successful outcome. . . .

When I returned to the residence, Senator Jack Austin* called. We gave him a hurriedly prepared meal and he and I spent the evening reviewing the Canadian scene since the Quebec election. He says he sees Trudeau regularly and

3. The Multilateral Trade Negotiations went on for six years under the auspices of the General Agreement on Tariffs and Trade. They were known as the Tokyo Round after the city where they began but the substantive negotiations took place in Geneva in 1977-78.

believes that Trudeau can recoup, as do I. Jack says that Jim Coutts has come in for a lot of criticism in the caucus. He is blamed for many things. Certainly Allan MacEachen thinks that Jim did him wrong when he was moved from External Affairs. In all probability, Jim didn't have the part in this that Allan thinks. A minister's private secretary, particularly the private secretary to the Prime Minister, inevitably is involved in the matter of giving political advice and must accept the consequences. . . .

Saturday, December 4, 1976

We met for two hours in Don's suite. . . .[4] I was pleased with Don's knowledge of foreign affairs issues and the way he handles his staff. They will love him for this and he will grow to appreciate their great qualities. . . . I outlined my talks with Ramphal and the British attitude on a Commonwealth peace force [for Rhodesia]. We have the same views. Don, of course, is anxious that we should not become overly involved in Rhodesia. He is right, up to a point, but it is inevitable that we will become involved, when it comes to contributing to a fund to assist the white population. . . .

I have just had word . . . that Prince Andrew will study at Lakefield, Ontario, for the first two terms of 1977 . . . under a regular exchange programme which already links Lakefield with Gordonstoun in Scotland, where Prince Andrew is at present studying. . . .

The appointment of Cyrus Vance* as [U.S.] Secretary of State has been well received. It is thought that there will be no change in policy [but] the style will be different. . . . An albatross hangs around Vance's neck, however. He was known as one of the strong supporters of the war in Vietnam, as was Dean Rusk.* I would not be surprised if it was Dean who had suggested Vance to Carter. . . .

I accompanied Don Jamieson on his first visit to the Secretary of State for Foreign Affairs. . . . Don invited Crosland to pay a visit to Ottawa. This the latter ought to do at the earliest moment to emphasize the quality of Canadian-United Kingdom relations. Don . . . emphasized the desirabi-

4. Don Jamieson had arrived in London.

lity of a change in New Zealand policy on the Commonwealth Games to be held in Edmonton in 1978. I informed Crosland that the Maoris in New Zealand had announced they would not participate in games with South Africa. This resolves part of the problem but there are other groups in New Zealand who have not taken a similar position. Don urged Crosland to seek to persuade New Zealand to prohibit such participation, otherwise, if the Games were held at all, it would only be with white countries. This would not be in the interests of Canada or of the Commonwealth. Crosland was not too forthcoming. He suggested it might be better if we were to see the Minister of Sport and urge him to exert pressure. I did not remonstrate but the suggestion didn't meet with my favour, nor that of our delegation. After all, the problem is a foreign policy question. . . .

Crosland was interested in learning from Don that . . . hereafter we will not sell nuclear reactors unless there is full compliance with I.A.E.A. safeguards and adherence to the Nuclear Non-Proliferation Treaty. Crosland agreed this was a wise and constructive decision. It will be interesting to see the reaction of his own government. We discussed the question of fishing rights after implementation of the 200-mile fishing zone had been established for the [European] Community as a whole. Don stated that treaty rights with one country and Canada could not be subrogated by the Community, insofar as Canada was concerned. . . . Don, owing to his position in Newfoundland, would be in great danger if we were to give in to the Community on this. He had visions of sighting fleets from all nine countries sailing into Bona Vista Bay.

We emphasized to Crosland the importance we attached to Canadian participation in a new economic summit as suggested by Giscard. To our surprise, the Foreign Secretary said that the British had not been notified of such a possibility. I mentioned that it was all over the press the other day. . . . We urged that, if an economic summit were to be held, Canada should be included. We would hope for British support. He simply nodded, without saying enthusiastically, "of course." This attitude, of course, has worried me for some time, not only on his part but on the part of the government as a whole. Canada is the first Commonwealth country after Britain. We should be among their very first considerations. . . .

Tuesday, December 7, 1976

Lévesque has advised Trudeau that he will be able to attend only the first half of the federal-provincial conference of first ministers later in December. He also advises he will not have any time to discuss constitutional arrangements. It may be just as well that constitutional questions be raised later. Don Jamieson and I discussed this problem yesterday. We agreed that Trudeau should not proceed now with patriation of the constitution.

We went to the Prime Minister's office, back of the Speaker's Chair, in the House of Commons, at 4:30 p.m. . . . We had a good meeting with Callaghan. Don presented a map of the Callaghan Trail in Newfoundland and an album of the Prime Minister's visit. These gifts pleased Jim. Don asked Callaghan about the future [Economic] Summit meeting. We got from the Prime Minister the same replies which we received from Crosland. . . . Putting together what all said, I have the strong judgment that there was some mention made by Giscard of a Summit meeting and that there was more than a mere mention of it by him to the Nine at the recent meeting of first ministers of the E.E.C. at The Hague. Callaghan said at first he didn't know anything about a summit meeting—then drifted into an acknowledgment that there had been some kind of discussion at The Hague, ending up with the surprising observation that the meeting would be called by him as head of the E.E.C. . . . I don't fully accept the British statements that there is nothing more to all this. In any event, Callaghan ought to have said, knowing our interest in the Summit meeting, that this time Canada must be present.

The Prime Minister acknowledged he had ahead of him a difficult, almost insoluble, problem but there was a modicum of comfort in the realization that other countries also had their share of problems. Inflation was up in Britain and so was unemployment. The prospects were gloomy. . . .

Wednesday, December 8, 1976

At the opening of yesterday's federal-provincial finance ministers' meeting, the new Quebec Treasurer, Parizeau,* said that Quebec would collaborate now but separate in due time. . . . I have been thinking a good bit during the last several weeks what I should do about all this. Am I prepared to leave the formulation of policy on the federal side to some of the very weak hands now in control? I am beginning to have my doubts. I am certainly unhappy about the revival of separatist tendencies in other parts of the country. Lougheed's statement the other day about Ottawa's preoccupation with Quebec might mean that important matters affecting other parts of Canada would be overlooked. Then follows the unwise statement that it would be only as a last resort to protect Alberta interests that the ultimate in Western alienation would follow. This is idle talk. Whatever decision I do reach, however, will not be immediate. We ought to treat Quebec in a normal way at the present time. We should not be excessive in what we do. I don't believe that bribery will help us in any way. One concession would only be followed with further demands. . . .

Friday, December 10, 1976

I left Heathrow for Brussels before 3:00 p.m. . . . Marcel Cadieux, our E.E.C. Ambassador, is installed in his new and elaborate residence. He gave a large reception in honour of Don Jamieson for Canadian heads of European missions, who had come to confer. . . .

After dinner, Jamieson outlined the Canada-Quebec problem. Heretofore, I have described this as the Quebec problem. . . . Don accepted the situation as outlined several weeks ago by Trudeau. Separation will not happen; we will not negotiate on Quebec independence. We will deal with Lévesque and his government as with any other province and within the terms of our constitution. . . . I expressed the view that Trudeau's acceptance by the people would grow in English Canada. His position in Quebec will remain strong. It would be foolhardy, with Quebec separation an objective, to remove him, a Quebecer who was also Prime Minister. Some did not agree. Don did. . . . Gérard Pelletier is unhappy with developments in his native province. He is concerned that he is not there to take part in the early stages of the dialogue. I hope the events will not convert what is now a debate into more violent action. I can envisage this happening in a later period, particularly if Lévesque's referendum did not go his way.

Saturday, December 11, 1976

Lucien[5] and I talked of many things, in particular events in Quebec. He is more pessimistic than I. The young people in Quebec are on the side of separation. This he sees in his own children, one of whom practises medicine in Ottawa. Trudeau, he thinks, has lost irrevocably with the electorate. If we depend on him to stem the separatist tide, we will be disappointed. I am, of course, optimistic on this point. . . .

Monday, December 13, 1976

Thinking over Don Jamieson's visit, one of the important subjects was his reaction to the contractual link with the E.E.C. He had told Crosland that Canada looked for results in 1977 from the contractual link. . . . He agreed that success in the M.T.N. discussions might be as valuable as any agreement with the Community [but] at the [Brussels] heads of post meeting, he asked, "What does the contractual link really do?" If business is to come to Canada, it will come from individual countries operating in the private sector. . . . John Halstead, our Ambassador to Bonn, saw the contractual link as a long-term benefit, giving us a special place in relationship to the Community. It was a promotion for international collaboration, out of which would flow inevitable benefit. Our agreement with the E.E.C. would make our relationship with the Community easier. It would create a healthier climate for Canadian business. . . .

Tuesday, December 14, 1976

Yesterday, at the opening of the first ministers' meeting, Lévesque said he does not aim at the destruction of Canada but wishes to adjust its political institutions to Quebec and Canadian realities. . . . I do agree with Trudeau when he says the politics of federalism are the politics of accommodation. Lév-

5. Lucien Lamoureux, the Canadian ambassador to Belgium and a former speaker of the House of Commons.

esque denounced the confrontations which have been recurrent in Canada between federal and provincial levels of government. I tried to tell Pearson at one point that we ought to find some better method than the annual confrontation with the provinces. . . .[6]

Meanwhile, Britain is discussing in Parliament the nature of its "federalism." They are moving toward a referendum. Whether one should be held on Scottish and Welsh devolution will shortly be announced by the government and whatever decision the government takes will be open to debate. At present, as Callaghan told me the other day, the cabinet is now studying the logistics of a referendum which is likely to to take place. . . .

Wednesday, December 15, 1976

The Rhodesian Conference has adjourned and will resume on the seventeenth of January.[7] Meanwhile, its chairman, Ivor Richard, will travel to Africa after Christmas for talks with the five front-line African presidents. He will also visit South Africa as well as Rhodesia. . . .

I received a message today from the Prime Minister asking me to deliver a communication from him to Prime Minister Callaghan. This was done around dinner time tonight. Trudeau assured Callaghan of our concern and interest in the Rhodesian problem, reminding him of our collaboration to date and expressing our willingness to have a Canadian on an advisory group, which may be accepted as part of the ultimate solution. . . .

Thursday, December 16, 1976

There are many odd assignments in my job. The most successful public funeral in Canada in my memory, was that of Mackenzie King . . . [who] apparently had planned a good bit

6. I was referring to the first ministers' meetings.
7. On October 26, 1976, a conference at Geneva began to work on a solution to the Rhodesian problem. It was attended by Ian Smith as well as black Rhodesian leaders and chaired by British diplomat, Ivor Richard. Guerrilla action against the Smith régime and white Rhodesian raids on bases in Mozambique took place while the conference was in session. Needless to say, the conference failed to reach an agreement.

of his own funeral. No wonder it was such a success. Harold Macmillan told me a few months ago that he was one of a committee which had worked along with Winston Churchill himself on the latter's funeral arrangements. One of the reasons why the service was held in St. Paul's was that this would make the funeral procession longer than if it were held in Westminster Abbey. This pleased Winston. . . . And so, this process of contingency planning goes on. I sent a message to Ottawa only a short time ago about the royal funeral for Earl Mountbatten. The earl is in excellent health but contingency planning, with the earl's participation, is underway for his state funeral. I am asked if I would enquire if Canadian Forces would be prepared to send a contingent. . . . I have taken up the matter with National Defence Headquarters. . . .

Friday, December 17, 1976

I left early for the airport to meet Jean Chrétien and his wife. . . . It was good to see Jean. He is a pillar in Trudeau's cabinet and a man who might well become Prime Minister. I had urged him eight years ago to seek the Liberal leadership in Quebec after Lesage left. He would have got it. Perhaps he is the most successful of all Trudeau's ministers. . . .

Jean Chrétien says the political situation at home is precarious. He is optimistic on the Canada-Quebec problem. If Trudeau's administration could avoid making mistakes, it could survive. Jean asked me what I thought. We had a frank chat. Trudeau must stay, but his style must change and so must his understanding of others. He is too insensitive and cocksure but he is the best of the pack. . . .

Saturday, December 18, 1976

Jean gave me Donald Creighton's *The Forked Road*.[8] This is an account of the 1938-57 period, but it is a biased account, written by a bitter Tory scholar, who has not gone beyond his

8. Donald Creighton, *The Forked Road: Canada 1939-1957* (Toronto 1976). Creighton's book continued his personal diatribe against the Liberal party which he claimed had handed the country over to domination by the United States.

achievement of writing a good book on Canada's first Prime Minister. Nothing about health and welfare and yet Creighton writes of the period when Claxton and I laid the foundations for social welfare programmes.[9] It is the period when health insurance was started. There is little about the United Nations and foreign policy. This is the book of a grumpy old man. . . .

Jean and I lunched at the Reform Club in the shadows of Gladstone and Asquith. Jean was thrilled. He is full of the political life and aspires, as he should, to go to the top. Did I think one francophone could succeed another? In the present circumstances anything could happen. Or should he succeed Bourassa as provincial leader in a year's time? We will think this one over. Perhaps tomorrow something of value may emerge as good advice. In any event, Jean will play an important role on the Canadian scene. He says that at one point Trudeau thought he should quit. That period is over. He will fight the next election. Trudeau really likes the job. He is not likely to give up the torch. . . .

Sunday, December 19, 1976

After dinner, Jean and I, our wives with us, did some more speculating. What about an election in the spring? A Liberal victory in Quebec and in the country would erode the referendum idea. After all, the present administration in Ottawa and the federal Quebec members represent more of Quebec than Lévesque's party. To leave the referendum to Lévesque was dangerous. He would have exclusive control of the wording of the referendum. He might ask, "Do you favour separation, with a common market arrangement with the rest of Canada?" This kind of formula would be easier to support. There might well be other variations, beguiling and dangerous. John Robarts had told Jean the rest of Canada must not let Quebec separate. If necessary, force should be employed. At this stage, given an unambiguous referendum question and a majority Quebec vote for separation, force is out. Canada is not the Congo. Quebec is not Katanga. . . .[10]

9. Brooke Claxton was the minister of national health and welfare from 1944 to 1946 when I succeeded him in the job.
10. Katanga, a province in the former Belgian Congo, seceded when the country gained its independence in 1960. The civil war that followed ended in 1963 when United Nations forces came in to restore order.

Monday, December 20, 1976

Jean and I discussed many important matters affecting the welfare of our country. Final decisions and strategies cannot be decided oftentimes on the spur of the moment. What is important is to ascertain the options. . . . One good reason for not taking final decisions at this time lies in the developing economic situation in Quebec. Already the capital markets of New York have turned down one municipality's application for a loan. Unemployment will roll on. The Olympic and provincial debts will hang lustily around Lévesque's neck. The processes of government will drive him to the wall. His untried and inexperienced colleagues will develop tensions. Disagreements among them will follow. The consequences of the circumstances could, in a fairly short time, alter the situation. There will be a moment of decision but that has not yet arrived. . . .

Jean Chrétien came to the office this morning to say goodbye. I introduced him to some members of the staff whom he had not already met. He was pleased with his visit and thought we had had a good preliminary canter in our examination of the Canada-Quebec problem. His last words were: "You must come and help us at the appropriate moment." I told him that there was no more important issue in my life than that of national unity. . . . Now was not the time to come. There would be a time. I would not have to be invited. . . .

Tuesday, December 21, 1976

A message from Ottawa mentions a front-page article in Canada in which someone in the High Commission has intimated that in the event of a peace force in Rhodesia, the participants would come from Canada, Nigeria, and India. The article states that the Commonwealth Organization has conducted paper exercises on the plan. Ottawa's message to us says such articles are obviously unhelpful. They stimulate questions in Parliament. Ottawa suggests a leak from some official source in London. I mentioned this to some of our officers this morning and, rightly, they pointed out that the minister himself, Don Jamieson, in his press conference in Canada House at the end of his visit last week said that Canada had a role to play in Rhodesia. . . .

Thursday, December 23 – Friday, December 31, 1976

Nell and I spent Christmas at the Budock Vean Hotel near Falmouth in South Cornwall. I spent my days walking about with the occasional visit to the local pub. When the waiter there kept calling me "Excellency," I threatened to refer to him as "Field Marshal." For New Year's, we moved on to a hotel in Torquay where, among hundreds of revellers with paper hats and hooters, we saw the old year out and bid a proper welcome to the new.

XII

January – February 1977

*A*S THE NEW YEAR BEGAN, *both Canada and Britain were suffering from a crisis in leadership. The triumph of the separatists in Quebec had led to renewed criticism of Pierre Trudeau. To test the political waters, Trudeau called five by-elections in Quebec and this was interpreted as a mini-referendum on his leadership. At the same time, Jim Callaghan's hold on office grew increasingly precarious as a result of assaults on his government by both the Conservative opposition and the labour unions.*

Monday, January 3, 1977

I picked up John Munro, the Canadian Minister of Labour, at the Savoy. . . . John has been in London for four or five days and stayed on an extra day especially to see me. . . . John is unhappy about the political situation in Canada. This is, of course, an old story. He is not so sure that an improvement has really taken place since the Quebec elections, nor is he sure that Lévesque's victory will assist Trudeau in making a political comeback. I suspect John is over-influenced by what must be the political situation in Hamilton [his hometown]. Moreover, in that city, the sympathy and tolerance towards French Canada is minimal. John does not agree that Gallup polls are a reliable measure. I disagree. The most recent Gallup poll shows Trudeau's stock up and it was taken before the Quebec elections. I am sure Munro is sympathetic to the government's policy on bilingualism but his concern is not so much about national unity and our relations with French Canada as with the political situation itself. He thinks it will deteriorate further, unless he and some others in the cabinet undertake to speak frankly to the Prime Minister. . . . Some recent Senate appointments do not carry political advantage, Munro thinks. I suggested to him that it would be good for the country and for Parliament, if a substantial number of present vacancies in the Senate were filled by individuals who are not necessarily Liberal partisans. . . .

We talked about cabinet problems. John was interested in little else. Trudeau's way of conducting cabinet business did not make stars of members of the cabinet. The public concentration is on the Prime Minister. He might sit back more often and push his ministers ahead, making them national figures as well. This had been the technique of Mackenzie King, St. Laurent and, to a lesser extent, Pearson. I told John that no leader was free of disability. The fact, however, was that Trudeau was an able leader; in the present Canadian context no one could lead the nation as effectively—no one could address English and French Canada with the same authority. What mattered most of all now was the maintenance of Canadian unity. The political problems should be resolved in relation to what is best for Canada in present circumstances.

Sunday, January 9, 1977

In my leisure moments I have been reading Jim Callaghan's life by Messrs. Kellner and Hitchens. . . .[1] The authors are not on his side. They do not think he has the wrong vision, rather they say he has no vision at all. My judgment on Callaghan is that he is a strong political animal, with good judgment of people and of situations. He knows his limitations, which are on the intellectual side. He wishes to keep the Labour party together and the country together. He is stronger in the public esteem at the moment than is his party. . . .

Monday, January 10, 1977

At the executive committee meeting this morning, we reviewed the issues to be discussed at the Canada/United Kingdom Continuing Committee meeting at the end of the month.

1. Peter Kellner and Christopher Hitchens, *Callaghan: The Road to Number Ten* (London 1976).

Once again, I continue to be irritated with the lack of preparation for this meeting by the Canadian side in Ottawa. This is not the first time I have noticed how inadequately prepared Trade and Commerce oftentimes is. . . . Unless we get word today, I will call Jean Chrétien in Ottawa and ask him to see what is wrong. . . .

Thursday, January 13, 1977

[When] I went to Heathrow this morning . . . to greet Premier William Davis [of Ontario] and his wife, Kathy . . . I met Mark Chona, the special assistant to President Kenneth Kaunda of Zambia. I had not seen him since my visit to Lusaka three and a half years ago. I have known Mark Chona and his brother, a minister in President Kaunda's government, for a number of years. Mark told me that there was no reason at any time to doubt that, once transitional government was established in Rhodesia, there would be a discontinuance of guerrilla warfare. There is no hope that emerging nationalist groups will be given access to the Geneva Conference when it resumes. The emerging groups are no more than defections, chiefly from Bishop Muzorewa*'s party. There is no doubt that Nkomo and Mugabe* in their joint leadership[2] are the most viable of the nationalist groups. How long the joint chairmanship of Nkomo and Mugabe will last is problematic [but] it will certainly last until a transitional government is formed. Smith's attitude has delayed progress on transitional government. There are likely to be some defections by the white population but not soon enough to bring about a quick agreement on transitional government. . . . Mark thinks it is too early to say whether a Commonwealth presence, an advisory committee or something similar, will be required. More than likely, there will be a need for a Commonwealth presence of some kind. He is happy to know of Canada's collaboration

2. Robert Mugabe was deputy secretary general of Joshua Nkomo's Zimbabwe African People's Union (ZAPU) in 1961. After detention by Rhodesian authorities in 1962, Mugabe set up the Zimbabwe African National Union (ZANU) from Tanzania. In October 1976, he became joint-leader with Nkomo of the Patriotic Front, leading the Zimbabwe African National Liberation Army in guerrilla tactics against Rhodesian prime minister Ian Smith's white minority rule.

and is particularly grateful for our willingness to participate in the common fund. . . .

Richard Sykes of the Foreign Office and I had an intimate heart-to-heart talk on the conduct of foreign policy. He is one of the best men at the top in the Foreign Office. Like others, he is concerned about continuing attacks on the foreign service. These arise from a misunderstanding of the nature of diplomacy. I believe in professionalism in diplomacy. . . . I have noticed a lowering in the open conduct of foreign policy by the British who, for instance, should not have allowed the great Kissinger to pre-empt their role in Africa. . . . The Foreign Office does need leadership at the present time, although I thought Crosland's speech to the E.E.C. yesterday was statesmanlike and masterly. His problem, I think, is a lack of interest in foreign policy.

Monday, January 17, 1977

I went to the House of Commons this afternoon to listen to tributes [to Anthony Eden, Lord Avon] by the Prime Minister, Mrs. Thatcher [and] the Liberal Leader, David Steel. . . .[3] Ted Heath's tribute, however, had style and was delivered without reliance on a text. It sounded so much better. In any event, all recognized the great qualities of Anthony and what the nation and world owe him. I reflected on my long acquaintance with him, comparing it with what Jim Callaghan said—that he had not known Eden, except in the vague way that junior members know their seniors. . . .

Wednesday, January 19, 1977

Trudeau sent me a copy of his letter to Kaunda in answer to Kenneth's message to him of November 15th. Trudeau's letter, dated January 13th . . . approves of the encouragement given to Zimbabweans to settle their own problems where possible. He thinks the opportunity is at hand for right-minded Rhodesians of all racial origins to co-operate in the establishment of a peaceful transition to majority government. Trudeau mentions that he has been in touch with Callaghan offering co-

3. Anthony Eden died on January 14.

operation. Trudeau told Callaghan that a transitional government under Smith would make impossible a just transfer of power. Consequently, he urged the British to become involved in Rhodesian interim governmental processes. Canada is prepared to contribute in any way that will be thought effective. Progress has been made, legal independence has been agreed on, and the British will play a direct role in the transitional economic assistance. Political factions, however, should be encouraged to close ranks. Kaunda and the front-line leaders value Canada's support, I am sure [and] Trudeau's letter indicates this. . . .

This mission is more than diplomatic in function. It is the largest of our missions. Our reception service in Canada House reports that . . . for 1976, as a whole, there were 99,869 visitors to Canada House, compared with 105,528 in 1975. Who says this is not a busy thoroughfare? . . .

When I returned from my swim at the Grosvenor Hotel, a policeman was on our doorstep. One will be there for an indefinite period as part of the security measures being taken this day. I had previously explained the matter to Nell so that she would not be worried. . . . I had to give up my daily routine programme—when I walked, where I walked and at what hour I swam and so on. I am asked now to vary the programme somewhat and use the car at all times for a while. I hope this doesn't have to last too long. . . .

Thursday, January 20, 1977

[David Owen,] the first Minister of State in rank, is a neurosurgeon by profession and a close friend of Crosland, with whom he has collaborated for so long in Parliament. . . . Obviously, he is a man with a future. I reviewed with him the points on Cyprus.[4] He thinks Carter is likely to attach importance to a solution of the island's problems. . . . He is a protagonist of the E.E.C., although he is not convinced that the economic benefits for Britain are as great as alleged. . . .

Friday, January 21, 1977

Tony Abbott, who spent the night with us, visited with me at the office. I had some of the officers on the third floor in to meet him. We discussed the state of the nation at home. Tony

4. He had just returned from there.

makes a very important point. Assuming that the present Prime Minister in the next federal election won a substantial majority in Quebec and did badly in the rest of Canada, what would be the consequences for national unity? Would this not be regarded as repudiation of Quebec? Would it not encourage Liberal Quebec-elected members in the House of Commons to become lukewarm about Canada and for Quebecers to be lukewarm about the rest of Canada? What would be the effect a Quebec Liberal majority would have alongside a Conservative win in English Canada?

Tuesday, January 25, 1977

The news from Rhodesia is bad. Smith has turned down Britain's plans for majority rule. Smith refuses to surrender. He said, "if we give way now, it would not be majority rule, it would be to a Marxist indoctrinated minority." . . . Smith will now attempt some *modus vivendi* with the moderate blacks. Crosland sees little hope for a peaceful settlement [because] Smith has opened the way to war. What Vorster will do now will not be known until Friday. Some United States action is inevitable. It may not be too late for Carter to act decisively. . . .

I now learn that Trudeau has written to the provinces asking for concurrence in a new version for patriation of the constitution. He will not proceed unilaterally. I am awaiting the full text of Trudeau's letter. I understand that two provinces, Alberta and Quebec, have refused the latest proposal. . . .

Wednesday, January 26, 1977

Meanwhile, Lévesque said on Saturday that he is preparing the basic . . . act for a referendum, which will be held on an equitable basis. This means that the referendum must be prepared honestly, be easily understood, and that there be sufficient time to enable a full discussion. A footnote is *The Toronto Star*'s report that Robert Bourassa called his election on November 15th after he had had a chat with Callaghan in September. This was when I had gone to Canada to be with Callaghan. Callaghan is supposed to have told Bourassa when he saw him on September 17th that the government of the United Kingdom would not oppose unilateral action by the federal government to patriate the constitution. Bourassa knew that no British government could oppose such a federal decision. Bourassa was concerned that unilateral action by Ottawa would create a serious constitutional crisis. This I greatly doubt. . . .

When Bourassa came to see me a week after the election, I am satisfied that he understood the constitutional position, as far as the British Parliament was concerned, acting on a request of the government of Canada and its Parliament. Bourassa did not want to be Quebec Premier when the constitution was brought back against Quebec's will, he now says. How could he be regarded as a traitor to his people in agreeing to patriation? I am not impressed with his argument that unilateral patriation would help the separatists. The reason Bourassa held the elections was because, as he told me a week after, he thought he had a chance of just scraping through. The longer he waited, the more difficult it would be. . . .

Monday, January 31, 1977

I attended a reception tonight, given by the chairman of the committee of the political council of the Junior Carlton Club to meet the Leader of the Conservative party, Margaret Thatcher, and members of her shadow cabinet. . . . It was kind of them to ask me, although I felt a little out of place when I realized that I would be the only head of mission present. . . . Lord Carrington[5] said, jokingly, "imagine you here, with all your years of opposing the Conservative party." . . . On this job, and certainly in this country, there is no need to show one's political colour and, of course, as long as I am High Commissioner, I don't have one. . . .

I thought Margaret Thatcher looked tired. Well might she be. The task of leading a political party is endless and full of burdens. Few can understand how demanding leadership is. "Happy to see you here," she said, "the political council showed good judgment." I told her I was honoured to have been asked to come and foregather with her colleagues. I compli-

5. The Conservative leader in the House of Lords.

mented her on her tribute to Eden the other day in the Commons. Forthwith she said how annoyed she had been with the Prime Minister on that occasion. His reference to Suez in his tribute caused her to strike from her text reference to Jim's "warm and generous comments." It is not surprising that those unfamiliar with party warfare do not understand the adversary quality acquired by those engaged in continuous political combat. . . .

Tuesday, February 1, 1977

A battle royal between Lévesque and Trudeau has seriously begun. There are five by-elections in federal Quebec ridings. The Parti Québécois will not take an official position in them, but Lévesque says his party members may support certain candidates. Trudeau has said the by-elections are a "mini referendum." Trudeau says all the changes Lévesque wants, short of independence, can be achieved within confederation. . . . If Trudeau wins the by-elections, he will be strengthened and so will Canada. I am told the Conservatives will not campaign in the by-elections on the issue of separation. They want to put Trudeau and not Lévesque on trial. They will not accept the by-elections as a mini-referendum on separation. I think the Conservatives are making a tactical mistake, if one's main interest at this time is the unity of the country. If the Liberals lose, will this not be taken as a triumph, primarily for Lévesque? Clark says he is prepared to negotiate with Lévesque. Surely not on independence and separatism? On this there can be no compromise or negotiation. . . .

Thursday, February 3, 1977

The Leader of the Opposition, speaking in Halifax, says that Trudeau and his colleagues are exhausted and discredited after ten years in office. Good phrasing but slightly inaccurate, I should think. He would extend greater authority to the provinces to use their own resources. . . . In immigration, communications, and urban affairs, he would work out adjustments. "Canada's constitution did not require drastic or wholesale change"—I agree but this is exactly what some are now advocating, including John Robarts, but even this is not what Lévesque wants. He wants independence. Now the Quebec Prime Minister says he will hold the referendum in about two years. . . .

Gerry Regan thinks that Lévesque will not take part in constitutional discussions until he has had his "go" at separation. Gerry would like to see a national debate, with everyone participating, on proposed constitutional changes. Lévesque would not accept constitutional changes which were less than the objectives he has postulated. With this I agree.

Last night Nell and I were honoured guests at the fiftieth anniversary dinner—Waitangi Day of the New Zealand Society in the Royal Lancaster Hotel. The dinner was graced by the presence of Princess Anne and Mark Phillips. . . . Nell sat on Captain Phillips' right. From her pleasant loud laugh I could tell they were engaged in useful and happy conversation. "What did you talk about?" I asked. "Well, you know, I treated him as a young man. After all, he is younger than Paul." How were they getting along in their new mansion, which the Queen had bought for them? Apparently they are going to live in three rooms until such time as they can buy more furniture, presumably with the Queen's help. They intend to plant corn, wheat and barley on their 700 acres, but the income will certainly not be sufficient to maintain the place. The Captain seemed concerned about running expenses, just like any other couple starting out. . . .

I happened to mention that I was meeting the head of the Commonwealth Games this morning, Sir Alexander Ross, and would impress on him the serious state of the Games at this juncture. The Supreme Council for Sports in Africa has not taken a firm decision to lift the boycott on sporting contacts with New Zealand. . . .[6] If all the African countries stayed away from the Commonwealth Games, I replied, it would not be good for the Commonwealth. The Captain then said, "Oh, the politicians always interfere." I tried to explain that the situation was not that simple. I did not justify the attitude of the African countries, but underlying their position are understandable political attitudes. I have noticed how royalty or near-royalty speak of government and of politicians

6. As a result, African countries were threatening to boycott the games if New Zealand participated.

in a condescending way sometimes. This may be natural but not justifiable. I noticed this many years ago, when I first met Prince Philip. He said, "Oh, you are one of those (politicians)." . . .

Friday, February 4, 1977

The Foreign Secretary [Anthony Crosland] continues to run into criticism . . . [and] his manner oftentimes conveys the impression that he has not acted or has to be compelled to act. He should not have allowed Henry Kissinger to pre-empt the stage in his recent discussions with Ian Smith. Henry carried the ball. Now Crosland has to carry the ball by himself, when it might have been better if he had done so at the outset. I find myself defending Crosland, even against some of his close advisers, as I did with one last night at the New Zealand dinner. . . .

I met with Sir Alexander Ross, President of the Commonwealth Games Federation. I read out to Ross Prime Minister Muldoon's recent letter. The Prime Minister says he will not refuse New Zealand sportsmen visas for their games with South African teams. The consequence is clear, I submitted. The O.A.U. will not regard Muldoon's letter as sufficient to avoid an African boycott of the Games in Edmonton. Ross agreed with me that, allowing for Muldoon's domestic political situation, he should be able to persuade New Zealanders of the importance of not putting obstacles in the way of a successful meet in Edmonton. To do otherwise will be harmful to the Commonwealth and to Canada. . . .

Saturday, February 5, 1977

I was distressed to learn that George Ferguson of *The Winnipeg Free Press* and *Montreal Star* had passed away.[7] On one occasion, George and Bill Mackintosh[8] spent some time with Alice and Vincent Massey in London. It was a visit in pursuit of

7. George Ferguson had succeeded J. W. Dafoe as editor of the *Winnipeg Free Press* in 1944.
8. W. A. Mackintosh, an eminent economist who helped to work out Canada's wartime economic policies, later became principal of Queen's University in Kingston.

culture—particularly painting—up to their ears. They needed a respite, some fun and drink. This they had in Paris and in excess—so much so that they were driven to contrition. In retribution, they went to the Louvre to see its treasures. Their Parisian jaunt made them tired, and so they lay down on the floor exhausted, when suddenly there appeared in the doorway their London hosts, the Masseys. Quick-wittedly, George said to the startled Vincent and Alice, "if you wish to see these paintings at their best, lie as we are doing." The Masseys followed suit. All four agreed that there was no better way to view the treasures of the Louvre. . . .

Tuesday, February 8, 1976

Esmond Butler, secretary to the Governor-General, lunched with Nell and me at the residence. The incident at the performing Arts Centre in Ottawa, where it was reported the Governor-General had been received with boos, was exaggerated. There were some hostile noises but, for the most part, the Governor-General was well received. . . . The Prime Minister is strong for the Crown, says Esmond, and if now and then in Quebec his words about the Crown are open to question, it should not be forgotten that, when he says we don't need the Crown, he says and the Pope too. Not that he means that either one is irrelevant. . . .

Wednesday, February 9, 1977

The Queen leaves today for her Jubilee trip to Australia. I note the hour of departure is 10:25 p.m. At that hour, the Queen Mother will be at 12 Upper Brook dining with us. When I left the residence this morning the butler, Barry, Thérèsa, Margaret, Howard *et al.* were busy setting up the long dining room table. The rugs had been cleaned [and] adjustments made in the library, where the photographs will be taken. Some changes in furniture in the main salon had been made. The canopy will be put up at the front door sometime during the morning and the flag will be unfurled. . . .

When the royal guest arrived . . . [she] had just come from saying goodbye to the Queen. . . . She had heard, only the night before, from Prince Andrew at school near Peterborough, telling about his liking for the school and Canada generally. . . . Nell and I endeavoured to see that all had a few words with this gracious woman, who would have been impressive in any circumstances, queen or no queen. . . .

Thursday, February 10, 1977

I cannot say that I had a long sleep, because I went to bed late and was up early to meet our Minister of Communications, Jeanne Sauvé, and her husband Maurice,* at Heathrow. . . . Both also expressed the view that René Lévesque is bound to become a victim of his tensions, as his responsibilities accumulate. This, more than anything else, may help in the right disposition of the Canada-Quebec problem. . . .

At noon, I was host to some film industry people at Canada House where former Prime Minister Harold Wilson was guest speaker.

I thought Harold was in good form, in spite of his innocuous speech. . . . It was interesting to hear the comments and speculations of a prime minister out of office. He has little use for Roy Hattersley and Ennals, the Minister of Health. I had expressed the view that these were two good potentials. Crosland has a good mind but his manner suggests a state of perpetual inactivity and, from a political point of view, this is not good. It was true that Jim had intended to give the Foreign Office to Healey after an interval of a few months. Wilson thinks that Crosland will move over eventually to the Treasury and become Chancellor of the Exchequer and that the technically qualified Denis Healey will take over at the Foreign Office. . . .

The Sauvés dined with us. We had a good discussion during and after dinner on the Quebec-Canada problem. Maurice is . . . organizing public sentiment throughout the country against separatism [and] is also interested in . . . renegotiation with the provinces, regardless of the outcome or happening of a referendum. He and his wife acknowledge that programmes of social security, health programmes and the like, all devised in the 1945 period, were desirable for Canada at the time [but] we now have a satisfactory level of social and health legislation, to which were attached national standards. [Now] the process of decentralization in these areas has taken place. Other areas of decentralization must now be pursued to enable the provinces to administer in fields where they can function best. The federal government should now seek to divest itself of those powers not essential for the integrity of the nation as a whole.

My only comment was . . . that, while this emphasis was desirable, the welfare of the nation must not be prejudiced by ill-considered transfers of authority to the provinces. I told Maurice that the press had been calling me during the course of the day [to ask,] "Was it true that he was calling on people to discuss how the . . . Common Market referendum had been undertaken?" I denied knowing anything about what he was doing here and in fact did not. Maurice later confirmed that he had seen a number of people . . . who had been active in the Common Market plebiscite.

Monday, February 14, 1977

Several hundred Canadian ex-prisoners of war will be coming here in the early spring. I have complained to Ottawa that I was amazed to learn that some bureaucrats thought the prisoners should contribute to the cost of a reception which I might give. I have told them in no uncertain manner that the former prisoners of war should be entertained here when they come, and that this should be part of the government's representational responsibilities. . . . I will undertake myself to have the reception covered from funds for hospitality at this Commission, although we regard this as an activity worthy of supplemental support at least from Ottawa. . . .

Tuesday, February 15, 1977

I have been looking over the report of Vice-President Mondale's telephone message to Trudeau early in the month. . . . I believe that our participation in the [Economic] Summit was not raised as such during the course of the Mondale trip.[9] Mondale had said that the United States would favour E.E.C. representation [at the Summit]. The decision was one for the

9. U.S. Vice-President Walter Mondale was on a pre-summit trip to Europe and Japan.

Community itself. The Dutch and Belgians wanted Community representation; the French are opposed. . . . I have been told that Carter would prefer a free-wheeling, broad-based discussion session and one not restricted to economic issues. North-South dialogue should be included as well as East-West trade and political questions—nuclear non-proliferation certainly . . . expansionary economic programmes, E.E.C. balances, and the multilateral trading negotiations. Schmidt would like a preliminary meeting of finance ministers. A further indication that we are in, as far as the Americans are concerned, is seen in the State Department official's briefing to us, when it was said: "a common North American/European position could be put forward to the Japanese in respect of a possible location for the Summit." . . .

There is much regret over Anthony Crosland's illness. He has been under the gun for some months, working hard at the Foreign Office and as Chairman of the E.E.C. meeting in Brussels. He is dangerously ill in the Radcliffe Hospital at Oxford. . . . Dr. Owen, an able but junior man, will carry on for the time being [but] it is not likely that, as deputy, he could carry on in the Council of Ministers as Chairman. It is unlikely that Crosland will return to the Foreign Office, maybe not to Parliament at all [and] there will have to be a cabinet shuffle. With Rhodesian discussions under way and Britain's responsibility as President of the E.E.C., it is not easy to operate without a full-time Secretary of State for Foreign Affairs. . . . A transfer to the Foreign Office of Denis Healey . . . will be difficult to achieve, because of the important discussions underway over pay restraint, which come within the Chancellor of the Exchequer's responsibilities. . . .

Nell and I were guests of Barbara Ward (Lady Jackson) at the House of Lords. . . .[10] Barbara Ward will certainly be one of the most useful and impressive members of the House of Lords. I only hope that her health holds up; she has been ill for some time. She now has a permanent forum to project her views on international development problems, the environment, and other issues of fundamental importance. . . .

10. Barbara Ward, president of the Institute for Environment and Development and a prominent writer on the economic development of the Third World, had just been made a life peer.

There were few more important and influential voices in the world, apart from governments, than that of Barbara. I did not actually see her sworn in as I had to leave for Cambridge. I saw her, however, in her peeress's robes and she looked every bit the part. . . .

My lecture to the seminar of law students at Cambridge took place in the rooms of Professor Markesinis. . . . I pointed out that, unlike the American Bill of Rights, our legislation does not form part of our constitution [and] applies only to matters within federal competence. . . . It may be that the promotion of equality in private relationships is better administered by agencies like the human rights commissions. . . . The discussion with the students was interesting. . . . We seemed to agree that on the whole there was some danger in a consolidation such as is provided by a statute, admitting that a Bill of Rights in statutory form highlights the importance we attach to human rights and fundamental freedoms. There is the fact that these rights have long existed and are capable of protection under the law. . . .

Wednesday, February 16, 1977

After a few quick calls to the office . . . I caught up on some work before our luncheon for Anne Armstrong . . . a very interesting and charismatic United States Ambassador.[11] Good-looking and an excellent speaker, she has been widely accepted in this country. We have become very good friends, although we do not see one another as often as one would think. . . . On the representational side, Anne has done a particularly good job. The luncheon was designed to show that she had and to say goodbye. . . .

Thursday, February 17, 1977

I lunched at the Bank of Nova Scotia at 122 Belgrave Square. The chairman of the bank, Ritchie,[12] . . . has little use for those in the public service at home who have to do with banking policy. He says they know nothing about banks. I

11. As a Republican, she had resigned following the election of Democratic president, Jimmy Carter.
12. Cedric Ritchie

suggested to him mildly that perhaps his criticism was a little too sweeping. What did he think of Bouey,[13] the Governor of the Bank of Canada? Bouey knew little about banking and interfered too much in its processes. Ritchie doesn't think too much of the government's paper on proposed banking legislation. I felt like saying, I presume you are in favour of the present monopoly of the five or six banks which, of course, includes the Bank of Nova Scotia. . . .

Friday, February 18, 1977

It looks as though Canada and the E.E.C., minus France, are near agreement on nuclear safeguards. In that event, we will resume our nuclear sales to Europe. The agreement will include stronger safeguards against nuclear explosion. This we have been demanding since the wrongful use by India of material supplied by Canada to her. The device exploded in 1974 caused us a good deal of heart-searching. We had to have an agreement covering the E.E.C., because, once our uranium reached one country among the Nine, it could freely move to the other eight. . . .

The Secretary of State for Foreign Affairs, Anthony Crosland, died about two hours ago. He did not regain consciousness from a stroke of last Sunday. . . . Now the scamble begins. Who will replace him? Healey, Shirley Williams, Rees, Edmund Dell? Who knows? The Minister of State, Dr. Owen, is able but young. . . .

Sunday, February 20, 1977

The papers have been kinder to Anthony Crosland since his death than during the last few months as Secretary of State. Tribute was paid to him as a man of "passionate concern for liberty, democracy and the rule of law." . . .

Dr. David Owen [has] been named Foreign Secretary. In my prognostications, I had thought he might be regarded as too inexperienced; . . . he is the youngest Foreign Secretary since Anthony Eden. The way is paved for a notable career, which could end up in the prime ministership. I had hoped

13. Gerald Bouey

for Denis Healey, the most technically qualified man in the cabinet for [the] Foreign Office. Tied down to heavy tasks as Chancellor of the Exchequer, it would have been difficult to appoint him before agreement was reached on the third run in the social contract and before the budget. From all accounts, Owen's appointment is not as an interim Foreign Minister. . . .

Tuesday, February 22, 1977

An unfortunate story relating to Jake Warren and his wish to leave his post in order to take up pension rights developed last week, just before [Trudeau's] visit.[14] It became necessary for Trudeau to vigorously deny that the government had asked for Jake Warren to leave. . . . Jamieson said that plans had been laid before Christmas for Jake's term to end sometime in June. . . . The story put before me is that Warren's departure had to do with clashes with Trudeau over how Canada should conduct its affairs in the United States. It is said that last week Warren complained that the Prime Minister's office, meaning Ivan Head, had overlooked the Canadian Embassy in the arrangements made for Trudeau's visit. . . .

It is too bad that this kind of story arose but, in this day of intensive news warfare, what can one expect? I saw a story that Sharp was coming here and that I would be returning to Canada. . . . Sharp would be good as my successor [but] he would also be good in Washington. Is it likely that a seat [in the House] would be opened [by his resignation], however, to facilitate this arrangement? I doubt it. . . .

Ivan Head is a good man. The External Affairs Minister, whoever he is, must take into account the obligations of a Prime Minister, his office and his interest in foreign affairs. In any event, the whole matter is an unfortunate combination of circumstances and greatly exaggerated, I am sure. . . .

Charles Ritchie, in London for his usual two months' winter stay, lunched with me today. . . . We discussed Jake Warren's situation and regretted how the combination of circumstances should have developed to have embarrassed him so. Don Jamieson was unknowingly the cause of the

14. Warren was our ambassador in Washington.

misunderstanding. I am sure no one regrets it more than Don. Perhaps what brought the matter to a head as well was an understandable impatience in our Embassy in Washington with the interventions of the P.C.O. I can very well understand that an embassy might not be able to arrange for a prime minister to speak to the Congress, without the direct intervention of the Prime Minister's Office. The Ambassador and his staff, of course, in such a situation should be in full consultation with Ottawa in the matter. I have not had any trouble in this regard with Ivan Head. He had come here at least on one occasion to do a job I might well have been asked to do, although the information was more readily at his disposal than ours. I made up my mind not to regard his coming as an interference but as a consultative arrangement. This worked well for Ivan and helped us here considerably. . . .

Wednesday, February 23, 1977

The government suffered a major defeat in the House of Commons on the guillotine motion which proposed a limit on the Devolution Bill debate. . . . The vote last night was not a "no confidence" vote. Nevertheless, it is a major defeat and will be so regarded. . . . The government faces formidable opposition in its own party on this bill, as it does on devolution. Callaghan said that some Labour back-benchers would regret the result of last night's vote. I have a strong impression that Harold Wilson would have manoeuvred this parliamentary situation more skilfully than did Michael Foot, and perhaps, Jim. . . .

After going over the night's telegrams and getting a good report on Trudeau's speech to the [U.S.] Congress, Nell and I with Chuck at the wheel, drove to Oxford. . . . Tonight we dined at All Souls, the guests of Father McConica, C.S.B., who is deeply involved in the University of Toronto project for the reprinting of the works of Erasmus, well over a hundred volumes. The first three are now in my treasured possession. . . .

Thursday, February 24, 1977

At noon, the new Ambassador of the Republic of South Africa[15] called. . . . He had served as deputy in London in the sixties and was at the United Nations as Ambassador. . . . [Although] only South Africa has the leverage to force Smith to change his policies, Vorster says he will do no more than give advice and this the Ambassador confirmed. . . . [Botha thought that] the recently revived Vorster détente policy may have brought an end to the riots in Soweto. I suggested to the Ambassador that South Africa is more isolated than ever as black consciousness grows. This will continue, although the Ambassador did not agree, until the apartheid policy has been modified. . . . The Ambassador indicated that . . . there were some important elements in the white business community who were beginning to doubt that apartheid serves South Africa's best economic interests. . . . It is too bad that Vorster has had the additional problem of Rhodesia and Angola, otherwise progress toward liberalization would have been more apparent, said Botha. Muller, the Foreign Minister, who will retire in June, was much more liberal than generally assumed. . . .

Sunday, February 27, 1977

John Kenneth Galbraith[16] called at noon, suggesting he might drop in at the tea hour. Nell and I had an enjoyable hour with him. He was anxious to say that he wondered how wise it was for Trudeau to talk about the Quebec problem so openly as he did, when he addressed the Congress. Was this not a matter for detailed discussion in Canada? Was it not a display of national weakness for the head of a friendly government to discuss a major problem of his own country in the jurisdiction of even a friendly country? Could Trudeau

15. Matthys Botha
16. Galbraith was born in southwestern Ontario. After a distinguished career teaching economics in American universities, President John Kennedy appointed Galbraith as the U.S. ambassador to India in 1961. From there, he returned to Harvard University where he was an emeritus professor.

not have assumed that the United States wanted Canada to stay united? Frankly, this point had never been considered by me before today. There may be something in it. . . .

Monday, February 28, 1977

There is a big sign opposite Canada House on Trafalgar Square protesting the annual seal hunt off the Newfoundland coast, due to begin this year on March 12th. . . . This is done every year. When I left the house this morning, Nell called my attention to a story in *The Herald Tribune*, saying, "of course, I don't agree with Canadian policy when it comes to the annual seal hunt." . . .

Professor Bill Philips, head of the Department of Economics at the University of Windsor had dinner with Nell and me at the residence. He has just returned from Zambia and is on his way to Windsor. . . . Bill had dinner with Kaunda in Zambia the night before last. Like Nyerere, Kaunda has decided that there is only one way to bring the Rhodesian question to a head, that is by an intensification of guerrilla warfare. A man of peace, he would prefer otherwise. Smith has waited too long. Bill confirmed that the support given by the first-line Presidents for Nkomo and Mugabe is because they have power behind them. Kaunda is of the view that, if Muzorewa were to be given preference, there would be a continuation, after majority rule, of trouble in Rhodesia. The way to end guerrilla activity is to entrust power to those who have the support of their guerrillas, even though they come from outside. I must admit this proposition has its own dangers. . . .

XIII

March – April 1977

DURING A TRIP TO OTTAWA in early March to be present while Prime Minister Callaghan paid a call on Trudeau, some of my gloom regarding separatism evaporated. The Canadian Prime Minister was up in the polls and was rising to the challenge. At the beginning of April, the Parti Québécois government introduced Bill 101 making French the official language of the province.

On his return to London, Jim Callaghan confronted further embarrassing defeats in the House and election talk surfaced. But the Labour government survived a vote of confidence with the support of the Liberal party which agreed to a modus vivendi *to keep the government in office for a few months.*

Sunday, March 6, 1977

I have just been to Heathrow to meet Claude Wagner, MP; his wife; Robert Wenman, MP; and Bill Kempling, MP; [who] are on their way to the Middle East.[1] They are all on the External Affairs House of Commons Committee. Claude told me on the way in that Trudeau has jumped ahead in a [Gallup poll] test with Clark. The polled result on parties is coming out on Wednesday. If it was very much Trudeau's way, there would be an early federal election, perhaps in June. There is to be an April budget. . . . Much will depend on the poll result this week. How the pendulum changes!

Wagner obviously has not composed his differences with Joe [and] Mrs. Wagner was outspoken in her criticism of Joe, who beat Wagner by only some thirty votes for the Conser-

1. These were all Conservative members of the House of Commons.

vative party leadership. Joe should have made Wagner his Quebec leader. . . . It could be that, having been a Liberal,[2] Conservatives in Quebec did not approve Wagner sufficiently to give him that status. Nevertheless, I think Joe made a mistake in not doing so. It certainly does not help him to have Claude obviously unhappy and unco-operative. Mrs. Wagner was frank in noting that Joe was getting nowhere in Quebec. Claude thinks that more people in Quebec support Lévesque and his independence stand, perhaps as much as thirty per cent. The referendum result, however, might not be as high. When Joe is away, there is no leader who deputizes. Is it each man for himself, I asked? Almost, replied Claude. . . .

Monday, March 7, 1977

The Service of Thanksgiving for the Life and Work of The Right Honourable Anthony Crosland, MP, Secretary of State for Foreign and Commonwealth Affairs, was impressive. . . . On the way out from Westminster Abbey, Prime Minister Callaghan stopped for a word. He said, "I hear you are coming to Ottawa and I will be seeing you there after my visit to Washington." I wished him well in his talks with Carter and he replied, "I will tell you all about it when I confer with Prime Minister Trudeau."

Callaghan will point out that [while] Britain's first priority is to bring down inflation at home, [he] is wary of excessive reflation. Callaghan will insist on stability of import and commodity prices. He feels that the United States, Germany and Japan have sufficient strength to take risks with current account balance of payments. Countries like the United Kingdom and Canada, he thinks, have to be careful. Their room for manoeuvre is limited. . . .

It has now been agreed that the London Summit will be held on May 7th-8th. . . . There is to be a preparatory meeting for the Summit on March 12th-13th. The Foreign Secretary has told me that Carter would like the meeting to be described as a "Summit" meeting and not "Economic Summit." The

2. Wagner had been a Liberal member of the Quebec Assembly from 1964 to 1970.

United States will propose three non-economic issues — arms transfers, non-proliferation, and human rights. On the economic side, Carter will want to see discussed world economic management, trade, energy, and North/South economic relations. . . .

Tuesday, March 8, 1977

I called on John Smith, the Minister of State attached to the Lord President of the Council, at his office at 70 Whitehall. John is one of my favourite and coming men in the Labour party. We reviewed the state of the Devolution Bill. He agrees it will not be passed this session. Whether it will be revived in its present form is also questionable. The government will want to re-introduce the bill before the next election, although I suspect it will not be voted on before that. . . .

Recently in Scotland, John had done much speaking and put a lot of questions. His judgment is, now that an effort has been made by the government to enact the devolution bill, more and more people in Scotland are asking is it necessary? . . .

Wednesday, March 9, 1977

About a year ago, the Italian Ambassador complained of noise emanating from our building and heard by him in his study next door, where the Italian Embassy and residence is located. . . . I thought the matter had been attended to. I saw the Ambassador at Anthony Crosland's Memorial Service, when he and his Foreign Minister were entering the Abbey. I asked how things were going and, very sullenly, he said not very good, walking ahead of me without further observation. . . . When I returned to my office, I saw a letter [in which] he says that he has been subjected to all sorts of deafening noise, like drilling, excavations, knocking on the walls and the pavement, etc. Then he adds: "If your building had been a private one, I would have favoured the intervention of the police for objectionable disturbance of the peace, etc. etc." . . .

I saw Prime Minister Callaghan and the Foreign Secretary off for Washington and Canada at Heathrow. . . . The Prime Minister and Mrs. Callaghan greeted me warmly when they arrived, he saying, "I will see you in Ottawa on Saturday" . . . then turned to confront many journalists and cameramen, waiting for him to say something about the United States and the Concorde.[3] Callaghan handles himself well. His direct and unequivocal speech helps him greatly. From what he told me, he is anxious, when talking to Trudeau, to get his view on the proposed exclusion of Amin from the [Commonwealth] heads of government meeting in London in early June. [Because] the conference is a collective arrangement, Britain could not by itself bar Amin. . . .

Thursday, March 10, 1977

Before I left Macdonald House for Heathrow, two ministers from Canada sent messages they would like to come to London on government business. By coincidence, they proposed to come during the Easter holiday. No appointments with ministers here at that time, of course. They will be in their constituences or on holiday—and so will I or, at least, Nell and I, armed with good books, may go to York. . . .

I have just learned that the Gallup poll in Canada shows the Liberals four points ahead of the Conservatives. This will be sweet music for Trudeau. It should counteract his distress over publicity given his wife during the last few days. I would not be surprised to see an early election. . . .

I flew to Canada to be present at the meetings between Callaghan and Trudeau.

Friday, March 11, 1977

I reached the External Affairs building [in Ottawa] in time to take part in discussions for the meeting with Callaghan. . . . I have urged Trudeau to see Callaghan off at the airport Sunday morning. After all, the Concorde is on its first Ottawa stop. The talks may be good tomorrow. I wish the arrangements were better. Don Jamieson cannot stay around tomorrow night. . . .

My growing impression is that the separatist cause is floundering, unless some serious error is committed by those op-

3. He was taking the Concorde to North America to show off this product of Anglo-French technology.

posed to fragmentation. Meanwhile, Trudeau is gathering his second wind. He was well received at a large meeting of Quebec students. His humour and realism captivated the students. At one point, he said, "Is my wife here?" The students understood and roared. I am sure they understand Margaret's plight. . . . Her desire to be herself is quite understandable. This is the way Nell felt and still often feels, when hemmed in by my many engagements and official requirements. . . .

I went directly to Uplands around 10:30 this morning. Don Jamieson and his wife were not long behind. . . . Other than [for] the monarch, I had never seen as many people at the Ottawa airport before. The Concorde brought them out. The British Prime Minister gave them a good wave. . . .

Later, we began our talks at the External Affairs building, with the Prime Minister as host. . . . The Amin affair was thoroughly canvassed. . . . Callaghan's idea of permitting a delegation from Uganda [at the Commonwealth Conference], while excluding Amin, will not work. Closer to the event, a final position will be taken. It would be better for Amin to come, than lose Uganda as a member of the Commonwealth. . . .

Callaghan emphasized that twelve million people were out of work in the Western industrial world. The problem had to be met with Germany, the United States and Japan taking the lead. Trudeau mentioned Mondale's reluctance on M.T.N. at Geneva. . . . Carter is thinking more in Roosevelt's terms than anything else. What other alternative was there? We may be thinking of substantial tax cuts. I did not feel that much new ground was reached. Nevertheless, there is an advantage in such meetings, particularly after the two Prime Ministers had seen the new President.

Trudeau was in good form. Margaret's fling at independence did not worry him. He said, "Nell will fully understand Margaret's dilemma." She does. Most people will, in spite of the irresponsible press treatment given her "doing her own thing." The two Callaghans and Trudeaus had dinner at Harrington Lake. Margaret returned from New York in the late afternoon. . . .

Ivan Head told me that before he had written a word of thanks to President Carter, he had received a hand-written note from the new President, thanking Trudeau for coming to Washington and expressing the hope they would work together in friendship. Carter has the right instincts. These are the little acts that count. . . .

Sunday, March 13, 1977

I called at Rideau Gate to accompany the Callaghans to Uplands. In no time we were aboard the Concorde, I for the first time. Jim wondered how long Carter would be able to sustain his programme of initiatives. Of course, he said, there was always an aspect of euphoria with a new administration. Jim is not so old on the job. What is new with him is a style, more forthright [than] equivocal. . . . Jim thought the visit to Carter was conducted almost in military fashion. Carter likes his programme well-timed, less leisurely than British custom. . . .

The Concorde brought us back to Britain in record time.

Tuesday, March 15, 1977

David Owen, the Foreign Secretary, is not letting the grass grow under his feet. He is going to undertake a familiarization tour of Southern Africa in a few weeks . . . [and] he hopes to see Smith in South Africa and does not intend to go to Salisbury. He, of course, will see Vorster in South Africa. He told me he had decided to make this South African visit after his talks with Vance. He hopes to work with the United States in the search for a settlement, both in Namibia and Rhodesia. . . .

I went to the House of Commons this afternoon . . . to listen to Callaghan's report to Parliament on his first prime ministerial visit last week to Washington and his second to Ottawa. . . . He attached importance to visits in both capitals and treated the visit as a whole with a unity of purpose and content. This, I thought, was a tribute to Canada. . . . Callaghan reiterated the special relationship between America and Britain. As president of the E.E.C. he recognized the importance of relations between the United States and the Community. . . . Both he and Trudeau were agreed on the quality of leadership being given by Carter [and] had emphasized in their discussions with the President economic problems and the prospects for the Summit, to be held early in May. . . . Mrs. Thatcher, to my surprise, had nothing to say about Callaghan's visit to Canada. This was a mistake on her part. I must have a chat with her to ascertain why she did not, and fill her in to the extent that it is desirable for me to do. . . .

Friday, March 18, 1977

Last night, the government by its . . . abstention on a motion by Mrs. Thatcher to adjourn the House, avoided defeat on its policy of retrenchment. The matter will be raised again today. Mrs. Thatcher will demand an explanation from the government [since] the abstention of the government last night is regarded by the Conservatives as a refusal . . . to allow a judgment of its policies by the House. One may well ask how long the government can carry on in this kind of situation. A . . . general election could prove embarrassing to Britain, unless held immediately. The Summit is scheduled for May 7th and the heads of government meeting of the Commonwealth early in June. . . . I believe, if an election were held at this time, Mrs. Thatcher would become Prime Minister. . . .

Saturday, March 19, 1977

Mrs. Thatcher will move no confidence in Jim's government on Wednesday. There could follow an election. The prediction is for a close vote. The Liberals are likely to keep Labour in but Steel will impose conditions. Jim says he will make no deals. He went to his constituency in Cardiff to say this. Win or no win, the political war is on. The government, from now until an election, will move from one crisis to another. . . .

The anti-seal people are booing us with zest and have become hostile toward me as High Commissioner, threatening all sorts of things. . . . The police are back at the residence. . . .

Sunday, March 20, 1977

The fate of the Labour government dominates today's Sunday papers and television. Each member will decide this question in large measure on the calculations of personal interest and fortune. Will I be elected? What are the chances of getting into power? . . . Welsh and Scottish Nationalists are fed up with the government. They hope to gain seats. David Steel is in a difficult position. His Liberal party's prospects are not good. A Conservative victory might dwarf it and him. Does he want to be known as the man who kept Labour in office? He has to get something in return. Callaghan, to receive his support, may have to give direct European elections based on proportional representation. . . . Perhaps a majority will decide to keep the Labour party in office just a while longer?

Monday, March 21, 1977

I am surprised to learn that the head of the Foreign Office North America desk has advised that they are reviewing British policy on patriation of the Canadian constitution following the Quebec election. The official position here has not changed. A petition by the government of Canada for patriation would be followed as in the past by the British government and Parliament. [But] the officials are speculating that the United Kingdom may have to play a more direct role [and] that a situation could arise where there would be some need to amend the constitution, insofar as it affects one or more provinces, if the patriation formula had not been worked out satisfactorily in advance in Canada. . . . This disturbs me. . . . Some British officials are now saying they hope the matter can be resolved as soon as possible in Canada. British officials do not wish to interfere [and] . . . if they did, this would be strongly resented.

They suggest that the matter was discussed in private between Trudeau and Callaghan. This is the first intimation I have had of this. I did not see Trudeau after his private dinner with Callaghan, as I left [Ottawa] early in the morning. This is not one of the matters which Callaghan mentioned on the Concorde on the way back. My officials are of the view that no one here is trying to interfere in our domestic issues. They had better not. What they seek to do is to anticipate eventualities which they think may have to be faced. My view is that they would be wise to drop the matter. Patriation is not going to happen in the immediate future. If it does, the Canadian official request will be acted on. . . .

The Secretary of State for Foreign and Commonwealth Affairs gave his first reception for heads of missions. David said, as I came in with Nell, that he had not yet got over the jet lag from our Concorde flight from Ottawa a week ago. He was amazed that I looked so fresh. Ron Spiers, an old friend of the Owens, told me that, although he has not [yet] sought the concurrence of the [British] government and the Queen, President Brewster of Yale's appointment is definite. He is pleased with Brewster, who would be a worthy successor to Anne Armstrong . . . [who] made such a good impression. Ron mentioned that at the American Embassy, he and other officers met two or three times a week with groups of members of Parliament for an hour's discussion. All sorts of questions are reviewed. At these meetings the United States Ambassador does not take part. Accordingly, the discussion is freer, with a wider participation. I must see if I cannot encourage our officers to undertake similar contacts.

Nell and I dined with Ted Heath tonight at his town house, 17 Wilton Street. . . . Ted is a friendly host and a charming man. We discussed many things. He thinks there is a chance that an election could result from Mrs. Thatcher's motion of confidence, something that he does not want at this time and which he believes is not in the national interest. Margaret Thatcher, David Steel and Jim Callaghan had almost seemingly contrived to fumble into an election. He may be right. My hunch is that Jim will get through on Wednesday night. . . . Ted has a fine "baby grand" in his compact town house. Some French musicians, here playing at a concert with Leonard Bernstein, came in after dinner. . . . Ted Heath, the politician, can be very much a musician and a sailor. It is odd that Ted had difficulty holding his party colleagues with him and lost the leadership. . . .

Tuesday, March 22, 1977

I had an extended chat with Antony Duff, who plays an important role at the Foreign Office. He told me they are all pleased with David Owen, whose capacity for absorbing a brief is quite remarkable. Owen is very much an activist and seems to be ahead of his advisers. . . . Ivor Richard is able, I suggested.[4] The trouble was that at the United Nations people relied on him more and more. This involved Britain in commitments from which she might otherwise shrink. . . .

Wednesday, March 23, 1977

I spent the entire afternoon at the House of Commons, listening to the debate on Mrs. Thatcher's motion of confidence in the Labour government. It was a noisy and tumultuous discussion. . . .

Ted Heath seemed to be a solitary figure and, in my ruminations, I concluded that he was perhaps the greatest of all in the present British House of Commons. He did not seem too happy as Margaret developed her no confidence motion. At no time did he signify approval of the actors in the play. From what I had been told beforehand, it seemed clear that Jim Callaghan and David Steel had had an understanding to ensure a government victory. Mrs. Thatcher's speech was not up to her best performance — Callaghan proved to be more effective and masterly. Mrs. Thatcher's speech was of doubtful humour and generous with clichés. She complained about the evils of socialism and described the Prime Minister as "A sort of Jim of all parties and master of none." She called upon Jim to face the electorate as a statesman.

For his part, the Prime Minister emphasized the difficulties of minority government and the calamity which would flow from its defeat at a time, when vital negotiations on incomes policy were under way and just before a budget. Because the government must carry on at the present time, the Prime Minister indicated that he had agreed with the Liberal party on a *modus vivendi*. . . . The arrangements concluded will last until the end of the parliamentary session.

The support of the Liberals gave the government a victory of twenty-four votes. Callaghan did not really have to concede a great deal, but the requirement of consultation clearly did not satisfy extreme elements in the Labour party. . . .

Thursday, March 24, 1977

I have learned that the cabinet had a very animated discussion yesterday morning on the terms of the agreement between Callaghan and the Liberals. The Secretary of State for Envi-

4. British permanent representative at the United Nations.

ronment, Peter Shore . . . who is a strong anti-marketeer, thought the terms for elections to the European Assembly represented further erosion of British sovereignty. Most of the cabinet, however, agreed that the arrangement between the Liberals and the government . . . was preferable to a right-wing government. . . . This might be the only way for the government to get a majority in a subsequent election and avoid the disappearance of the Liberal party. There is satisfaction, however, in the knowledge that the arrangement made by Jim Callaghan with David Steel will serve Britain's interests during the next few months, during which there will have been the Summit, NATO and a meeting of the heads of government of the Commonwealth during Jubilee Year. I should think an election in the fall is now certain. . . .

I sent a message to Ottawa on the results of yesterday's parliamentary exercise. . . . The arrangement Callaghan concluded with the Liberals, I reported, appears to be more structural than expected. The agreement between the leaders could presage a medium-term United Kingdom political future, given that polls are showing the major parties closer together than previously and raising the prospect of succeeding minority governments. I indicated that the parliamentary situation does not necessarily reflect the mood of the electorate. One commentator noted that it was better to conserve under Labour than to labour under Conservatives. . . .

Friday, March 25, 1977

I called on Ramphal, the Secretary General of the Commonwealth Organization, at Marlborough House late this afternoon. He will be in Quebec City at the end of the month. What should be his attitude with Lévesque? He wishes to be of help at this time. As a matter of principle, he believes that outside the emergence from colonial restriction, no encouragement should be given to independence-minded groups, who make their appeal on the grounds of self-determination. . . . Ramphal believes that an easy romanticism, which equates secessionist movements with self-determination and bases its appeal to the Charter of the United Nations, must be rejected. In fact, any attempt at partial or total disruption of national unity and territorial integrity is contrary to the

Charter of the United Nations. Self-determination in the context of the Charter and its consequential resolutions are within the process of de-colonization. They are not related to the destruction of new states through fragmentation. . . . Ramphal can be counted on to handle Lévesque in a manner totally consistent with his recognition of the dangers of separation in Quebec. . . .

Tuesday, March 29, 1977

Today I was admitted to the Freedom of the City of London at the Guildhall. . . . The ceremony took place in the Chamberlain's Court Room in the presence of the Master, Wardens and Clerks of the Distillers' Company and other guests. . . . After the ceremony, the Chamberlain had us to lunch. He made a memorable speech, extolling my virtues in great generosity, mentioning the names of Canadian Prime Ministers, from Sir Wilfrid Laurier on, who had received the Freedom of the City in the Guildhall as distinct from the High Commissioners who received the Freedom of the City in the Chamberlain's Court. At the end of his speech, to my surprise and pleasure, I was given a helmet No. 99, worn by the London city police. Someone had mentioned that I had three Scotland Yard helmets, which repose in my library and that a fourth one from the City of London, would be of special interest to me. . . .

Having been admitted to this distinguished company, I rushed to the House of Commons to hear Denis Healey deliver his ninth budget in many less years. Denis was in a happy mood as he announced tax cuts of 1 billion 290 million pounds. . . . Mrs. Thatcher, speaking for the Opposition immediately after Denis had taken his seat, made one of her best speeches, so much better than that of ten days ago. She spoke from notes and not from a text. How restricting a text is to any good speaker. She didn't miss many tricks. She welcomed the tax cuts and the manner in which they were distributed to the needy . . . [but] she proclaimed the budget "was not a revival budget for Britain but a survival budget for the Labour movement." . . .

Wednesday, March 30, 1977

Those who attended our off-the-record meeting on Canadian studies accepted my invitation to lunch at the residence. . . . It was a good luncheon — not much business, a lot of talk. . . . Several good stories about Winston Churchill were told. One of the best, after the meal was over, was that Churchill, like all human beings, had to resort to the toilet from time to time. Usually, he took his time on such occasions. An important visitor was waiting to see him and had an appointment. Because of the importance of the visitor, Churchill's secretary went to the toilet door several times, pounding on it, advising the Prime Minister that he was way behind in his appointments and that his visitor did not seem to be too happy. In exasperation, Churchill shouted out, "Can't you see I have time for only one s..t at a time?" . . .

Thursday, March 31, 1977

The new Ambassador of Ireland, Paul Keating, paid his first call this morning. He had been lately Secretary of the Department of External Affairs in Dublin and has a long record of service in foreign affairs. . . . We agreed, of course, that there were no bilateral issues between our two countries and we do share so many common positions. . . . The problem of Northern Ireland, of course, has religious and political dimensions, now indistinguishable. Catholics tend to want union with Eire, which they feel would remove their minority status in Northern Ireland. Protestants there cling to union with the United Kingdom to avoid becoming a minority in a united Ireland. Extremist elements, therefore, have had a field day in keeping alive old animosities. This explains why things are done in the name of religion in Ulster, giving at least a superficial justification. Keating agrees with what Merlyn Rees told me last night, namely, that Paisley was really an evil man and perhaps a sick man. . . .

I called on Sir John Hunt, the secretary of the cabinet, in his Whitehall office at 4:00 o'clock. . . . At the [preparatory] meeting in Washington two weeks ago, the representatives of the countries to participate in the Summit meeting in May work[ed] on the agenda and draft[ed] a communiqué. . . .

The Canadian government wanted me to emphasize that . . . we think that the communiqué should refer to the growing problems of financing payments deficits of developed and developing countries; the importance of oil deficit countries carrying out basic structural adjustments . . . in light of the increases of energy costs; the need for countries to limit their accumulation of external debt [and] . . . their capacity to service it; and the need to make special provisions [for] . . . those poorest countries whose capacity to add to their debt is limited. On development matters, I emphasized that we would welcome . . . the resolve of Summit participants to maintain and, if possible, increase the flow of real resources to developing countries. It might be desirable to invite OPEC members to continue to join in this process; the communiqué should stress the importance of private capital flows in the development process and urge developing countries to adopt policies which would generally encourage such investment. On multilateral trade negotiations we would wish to see the language . . . in particular reaffirming a commitment to a comprehensive, substantial trade negotiation. . . . We should recognize that we cannot realistically expect broad results by the end of 1977. We must avoid new short-term action which could have detrimental effects on international trade and threaten longer-term prospects for liberalization.

Finally, I emphasized to Sir John we were anxious that the communiqué should not in any way inhibit discussion among the participants, who should be free to address themselves informally to the great issues at hand. The Canadian government's view is that the Summit could provide a political impetus to facilitate the achievement of a broader multilateral solution and in the appropriate fora. . . .

Tuesday, April 5, 1977

My country is agitated over bilingualism's demise in Quebec. The [provincial] government['s] white paper intends to make French the everyday language of the province.[5] For two hundred years French and English have enjoyed this privilege.

5. On April 1, René Lévesque's government released the white paper called the Charter of the French Language. It provided that, with a few exceptions, French was to be the official language of the province—the legislature, courts, administration, work, business, and education.

Trudeau has declined to comment immediately . . . but, I suspect, that at some time there will be a challenge to the Quebec language [bill] on the grounds of unconstitutionality. . . . I can very well understand the reason for the latest Quebec proposals, but obviously it goes too far and is a violation of human rights.

I have to speak next week to the Rotary Club of London. I had asked the boys to put down something for a text. It is useful to have something for the press but so rarely is it that something is prepared which really touches the point I have in mind. What has been prepared is good but is so essayist in manner. External does develop such a style of its own. Would I not be better to speak right from the heart and from one's own experience? In the first place, the London Rotary Club will not know much about Quebec and little about the problem of alienation. London has so many things on its platter. A boil on one's nose is hidden from one's chin. . . .

Wednesday, April 6, 1977

Allan MacEachen has just telephoned from the airport. . . . He admires the way Trudeau is carrying on in the face of his family problem, doing so with dignity and not allowing his disturbance to interfere with his official responsibilities. . . .

Ted Heath has come out in favour of direct elections to the European Parliament based on a regional list system of proportional representation. . . .[6] There will ultimately be a

6. The European Community came into being in July 1967 by merging three other organizations. The first of these was the European Coal and Steel Community founded in 1952 (composed of France, West Germany, Italy, and the Benelux countries who agreed to eliminate tariffs on the coal and steel industries). The second was the European Economic Community formed by the Treaty of Rome in 1957 which was to eliminate trade barriers and provided for joint social and financial policies. France, West Germany, Italy, and the Benelux countries were joined by Britain, the Irish Republic, and Denmark. The third component was Euratom (the European Atomic Energy Community founded in March 1957 to co-ordinate nuclear energy policies). The European Community consisted of a Commission (appointed by member governments), a Council of Ministers, the European Parliament (begun in 1952 as part of the ECSC and expanded in 1967), the European Court of Justice, and the European

European Federation, just as at some time in America, Canadian Confederation will play its constitutional part in a wider federation involving the United States. That trend is inexorable. Heath sees this. People like Lévesque, with little blinkers on, have overlooked how events have caught up with them. . . .

Owen is now talking of the idea of a conference to draw up a constitution for an independent Rhodesia. Doing so, without first setting up an interim government, is one of several ideas that have been circulating. . . .

Friday, April 8, 1977

John Grace, the editor of *The Ottawa Journal*, . . . and John Turner are long-time friends. As he says, Turner is not forcing the clock. He would like to be Prime Minister but only if it comes about in the normal way. [John] and Trudeau should never have separated. Indeed, Trudeau may have been adverse to John leaving the cabinet in the first place. This is just my surmise. One has to have been in the mill to understand fully how it runs. But the problem with Margaret [Trudeau] is serious. This I get from several authoritative sources. Trudeau has gone on holiday, leaving her behind—perhaps to think matters over. For every Liberal disadvantage, a Tory one arises. Joe Clark is now threatening to kick Jack Horner[7] out of his ranks. Jack has been flirting with the Liberals. All seems a little absurd. . . .

Sunday, April 10, 1977

We are told that Trudeau and his wife are having a three-month trial separation. Rumour has it that their marriage is in difficulty. We all genuinely want it to work out well. Trudeau went to Berkeley for a speech yesterday; accompanied

Investment Bank. A European Council of heads of government began meeting in December 1974. The 198 members of the European Parliament were originally appointed from members of the legislative bodies of each country, but in 1976 the members of the Community accepted that the Parliament would expand to 410 members elected directly by the voters of the member nations.

7. Horner was a Conservative member of Parliament from Alberta.

only by Ivan. . . . Head phoned from Los Angeles to say that Trudeau's appearance at Berkeley was a triumph, at a convocation of some eight thousand people. His theme was philosophical. . . .

Wednesday, April 13, 1977

I had an attentive audience at the Rotary Club today, emphasizing what is happening in Canada at the present time, from the date of Lévesque's election last November. He had removed the independence feature from his party's policy during the election. Quebecers had been free to vote for him without making any commitment on separation. Whatever he wished to achieve, barring independence of course, could be done by negotiation. Federalism was the only principle for a country like Canada. . . .

Thursday, April 14, 1977

Before dinner, Tony Abbott and I had a further discussion about the Canadian political scene. He thought the report of my speech in *The Times* on the Canada-Quebec problem touched the point. I can see aspects of the developing situation at home which are quite disturbing. At present, the Prime Minister is on top. Most people regard his leadership at present as indispensable. The rumour factory, however, may be at work again—and what it can do when it tries! . . .

Friday, April 15, 1977

Word from Ottawa yesterday is that during the Summit and NATO meetings,[8] Trudeau will have no time off. This will give me an opportunity to get caught up on much that will be lying on my desk. My role will not be lightened by the presence of Don Jamieson and Donald Macdonald. I will, of course, be glad to see all three former colleagues. . . . The murkiness of the Canadian scene warrants [Trudeau's] saying something here about the Quebec-Canada problem. I awoke this morning somewhat disturbed about it, particularly the implications of the new language bill proposed by Lévesque.

8. Both scheduled for the following month in London.

Carried to its conclusion, it will mean the end of bilingualism in Canada. This, in turn, means the end of the duality of the Canadian community. We must not let this happen. . . . I wonder if in the provincial Liberal scene there is anyone strong enough to provide the necessary leadership. Maybe this is where Jean Chrétien ought to come in? Would the provincial Liberals stand in the way of a federal candidate? Surely not, if Chrétien was thought to be the strongest and the one most likely able to resist Lévesque. . . .

Monday, April 18, 1977

It looks bad for a third round of the government's wage-restraint policy, which expires at the end of July. The great protagonist of the social contract has been Jack Jones, the Transport and General Workers Union's General Secretary. He is now calling for a return to free collective bargaining, acknowledging that initial claims must be moderate. . . . This is the first real break between Jack Jones and the Chancellor of the Exchequer. The government is going to have its hands full. . . .

Wednesday, April 20, 1977

The Owen statement [on Rhodesia] in the House receives wide attention today. . . . Criticism is now developing by Mugabe and Nkomo as to the co-ordinate power being given the United States at the constitutional conference. This troubles me. I can well understand why the United States' influence is sought but to endow that influence with co-political authority lowers the prestige of Britain's position. Ron Spiers, the American chargé d'affaires, saw Owen yesterday and discussed the time-table and the next stage with him. I think it is a little galling that the British and the United States should work so openly together ignoring, in the case of the British, their Commonwealth partners. After all, over twelve years ago, long before David Owen was about, Pearson and I had indicated to [the government in Salisbury, Rhodesia] that we would not support a unilateral declaration of independence. Moreover, we will be called upon to contribute to the common fund. . . . In the old days, the British Foreign Secretary would likely have called in the Canadian High Commissioner and others and carried on a form of consultation. The only consultation yesterday consisted of my sitting in the gallery for over an hour listening to my friend, Owen, being acclaimed by an unsuspecting and ill-informed British opposition in Parliament.

One can envisage what Mackenzie King would have done in these circumstances — no consultation, no responsibility. All well and good, but don't pass the hat 'round our way when the time comes. . . . King did not want to be involved in these matters, because he did not want to accept responsibility for outside matters. I do want to be involved. We are members of the Commonwealth and of the United Nations and have consequential obligations. Either we discharge these as adults or we don't seek to discharge them at all. . . .

I met Marc Lalonde and his wife at the airport. On the way in, we had a good discussion of the Canadian scene. So much is happening. This is a good way to get information. The Prime Minister seems to be doing well in the country. The problems facing Quebec are increasing. Marc shares my view that sentiment for separation is limited [and] . . . thinks that the political situation in Canada is satisfactory, but there are problems not wholly political. He thinks Donald Macdonald will be leaving [politics] in the autumn. This would surprise me. I did not ask what Marc thought about Jean Chrétien. They must have become undeclared rivals. Politically, Chrétien is definitely in the ascendancy in Quebec. . . .

Thursday, April 21, 1977

While I was entertaining a group of members of Parliament at the residence, headed by Walter Dinsdale,[9] word came that the western Alberta member, Jack Horner, is to join Trudeau's cabinet. . . . The move will have political undertones and some advantages. It may wreck the leadership of the Conservative party and certainly will be a discouragement to many aspiring eastern cabinet ministers. How much good it will do for the federal Liberal party remains to be seen. Will it not be looked upon as an obvious political ploy, particularly in view of the

9. The MP for Brandon and a former Conservative minister in the Diefenbaker government.

strong record of opposition to the Liberal party by the new minister, Jack Horner? Walter Dinsdale and his party colleagues can talk of nothing else. This is understandable. . . .

Friday, April 22, 1977

Most of my morning was spent in examining all sorts of lately arrived requests for tickets of admission to many of the Jubilee public events. I am expected to do the impossible. A friend cabled just as I left the office. As honorary colonel of a regiment, he hoped at this late date that I could get two tickets for Trooping the Colour. I had to tell him they had all been allocated. . . . It is odd that failure to meet requests of this order from friends does worry me. Why? I suppose it is because I have been meeting demands of this sort most of my public life. . . . With all the others on hand from Ottawa, "there is going to be quite a dance in the old town tonight." . . .

Monday, April 25, 1977

The problems arising out of the Jubilee event, the Summit and the NATO meetings crashed on my desk this afternoon with full force. Esmond Butler, secretary to the Governor-General, phoned from Ottawa to say that the Governor-General, his wife, daughter and a staff of three or four would be in London for the St. Paul's ceremony on June 7th, adding that it was the Governor-General's understanding that the former Governor-General and his wife, Roly and Norah Michener, had been invited by the Queen and would be coming along as well. In addition, the former Prime Minister, John Diefenbaker, will be here. Where all are going to stay will be a problem. I offered our residence at once to the Governor-General. He may prefer to stay at a small hotel where they often go. In that event, what about the Micheners and what about John? Is it possible to put the Micheners in the same house as John? This problem I will have to face when it comes. I am sure that I will never forget this spring and early summer. . . .

Tuesday, April 26, 1977

It was clear last night at dinner [at the Japanese Ambassador's] that David Owen had made a good impression. Not only the Lord Chancellor, but others thought he had not only begun well but showed prospects of leadership. In any event, his stock rose with the prospects that all the parties to the Rhodesian settlement are likely to agree to participate in an Anglo-American constitutional conference later this year. Robert Mugabe and Joshua Nkomo have agreed to attend, following pressure put on them by the leaders in the five African states. When they met a few days ago they endorsed, with some reserve, the idea of a constitutional conference. . . .

Wednesday, April 27, 1977

This morning I attended a memorial service for Lady Tweedsmuir[10] at the Grosvenor Chapel. The Queen was represented by Sir Shuldham Redfern, former Secretary to Lord Tweedsmuir when he was Governor-General. Shuldham and I walked to the first pew together. . . . John Tweedsmuir was deeply moved by my going to the service. I said, "How could I avoid doing so, John?" He said, "But you came to the funeral as well." I said, "The Canadians loved your mother as they did your father, one of our best Governors-General. They would have expected me to be here today."

10. Susan Tweedsmuir was the widow of John Buchan, Baron Tweedsmuir, a former governor general of Canada (1935-40).

XIV

May – June 1977

IN BOTH BRITAIN AND CANADA, domestic concerns were put on hold as a series of international events centred on London during late spring. First of all, the third Economic Summit took place and hard on its heels was a NATO summit meeting. Then there was the Queen's Silver Jubilee with all its attendant ceremony — and visitors from Canada — as well as a Commonwealth Conference. Both the mission and the residence began to seem like a train station, as we held dinner after dinner and reception after reception.

The international economic scene as well as particular issues of concern to the Commonwealth (especially Rhodesia) were thoroughly canvassed at the meetings. One question of particular concern to Trudeau was the threatened boycott of the 1978 Commonwealth Games in Edmonton. On June 12, the Commonwealth prime ministers issued a statement on apartheid in sport which called on Commonwealth countries to discourage sporting contact with South Africa.

By the end of June, however, Britain's domestic political insecurity returned when Callaghan again had to scramble to remain in office. At the same time, Trudeau's position appeared rosier after victories in the by-elections, and he pondered capitalizing on this turn of fortune by calling a general election.

Sunday, May 1, 1977

The stories on Saturday's Summit, which Jim wants everyone to call the Downing Street Summit, have begun. . . . Suggestions of a poised confrontation is journalese exaggeration. This does not mean that there are no differences. Why meet if there is full agreement? . . . The interdependence of the world makes it essential for the leaders to meet . . . [but] there are dangers in the frequency of summit meetings [because] too much is expected from them . . . [and] there is always a danger that the conferees feel compelled to exaggerate what they have done. . . .

When the Downing Street meeting is over, all but the French will stay on for the NATO heads of government meeting. The last time it took place was with Nixon in 1974. . . . Trudeau will return early in June for the Commonwealth meeting. Everyone asks will Amin come? I have learned on good authority that Amin suffers from hypomania. This could be a trend to schizophrenia. Certainly the doctors say he has a combination of hypomania, paranoia, and general paresis of the insane. The brutal murders speak for themselves. . . .

Wednesday, May 4, 1977

Practically the whole of my morning was taken up with the ceremony in Westminster Hall, where there were presentations of addresses by both Houses of Parliament to the Queen on her twenty-fifth anniversary. It was a memorable scene. . . . [After] the Lord Chancellor and the Speaker read the addresses of loyalty and congratulations to the Queen, . . . she added: "I can never forget that I was crowned Queen of the United Kingdom of Great Britain and Northern Ireland." These latter words occasioned dissatisfaction from the Scottish National Party MPs, who thought what she said was ill-advised. This part of the speech, as well as other parts, was well-received generally, but it was quickly noted that the Queen's words had a special significance. They exceeded in a sense the restrictions the monarch places on herself in matters of political controversy. . . .

Thursday, May 5, 1977

Don [Jamieson] told me . . . today [that] the new Ambassador in Washington will be Peter Towe,* succeeding Jake Warren. . . . Apparently, one of the reasons why Mitchell Sharp was not appointed to Washington was because of the reluctance to open up a [House of Commons] seat in problematical Toronto. There will be no election this year. Don feels certain Trudeau has taken this position only this week. It will be interesting to see if this mood alters. The Prime Minister thinks there should be no federal election until the situation in Quebec is clearer. . . .

The High Commissioners met this morning at Marlborough House . . . to decide [if they] should give a dinner for the Queen in Marlborough House in Jubilee Year. . . . I mentioned it was regrettable that High Commissioners did not meet as a group more often to discuss common problems. I did not have in mind the establishment of a formal caucus on the lines of what prevailed before the war but, if the Commonwealth meant what we asserted it was, there should be more action in connnection with the Commonwealth itself and the Commonwealth Organization as well. A number of High Commissioners supported what I had said. I hope something comes out of this. . . .

Friday, May 6, 1977

While Jim Callaghan was greeting President Carter [for the Summit], the Conservatives were capturing Greater London Council seats in a landslide victory. . . . Meanwhile in Germany, there is evidence of Chancellor Schmidt's political difficulties and his very small margin. Politically perhaps, the most secure of all who will be at the Summit meeting is Trudeau who grows stronger as the Opposition leader, Joe Clark, seems to have lost much of his strength. . . .

It is desirable that there be co-operation on the part of those participating at the Summit in particular and others, of course, as well. There are mighty problems facing them all. Unemployment is at an all-time high, inflation is of the greatest concern, and the financial system of the western world has had great strains imposed on it by heavy oil prices. . . . The Summit can help create the necessary climate and bring about a basis for partnership and substantial action by governments. There is need for a strong collective leadership. . . .

I talked with Ramphal early this morning on the telephone. He has received a telegram from Amin, requesting that the Commonwealth heads of government rotate each year, with the Queen taking her turn. . . . Amin reiterates his intention to attend the meeting. He would prefer accommodation at St. Ermin's Hotel. If this hotel is not adequate for his party of two hundred and fifty, he asks to stay at Buckingham Palace. Humorously, Ramphal said the palace may not be pleased to be considered second choice accommodation to St. Ermin's. Ramphal thinks the vast majority of Commonwealth leaders abhor Amin and his actions. They really do not know how to handle him. No one wishes him to come but there is no known constitutional way to prevent his attendance. . . . If the British make any move, it would have to be unilateral. Callaghan understands this, although Owen has reservations. . . .

I spent the morning on last-minute arrangements for Trudeau's arrival. This took the entire morning. At the last minute, the Foreign Office called to say that Owen would say a few words of welcome and would our Prime Minister reply? . . .

Normally, it takes half an hour to get to Heathrow. We decided to leave London an hour and a half ahead of time. John thought, as it was Friday night, the traffic would be heavy. We made Heathrow just in time — the plane was just about to land. . . . Everything turned out well, although I was not impressed with the formalities of welcome. Many a smaller state would have done better. One should not be too critical of the British — they are not used to formal welcomes, except for heads of state.

Trudeau was tired, not only because of the change of hours. . . . I learned more about his marital problem today. He has my full sympathy. He wasn't too pleased with the guest list for tomorrow's dinner. He wants to talk with knowledgeable and interesting people, like Barbara, Dahrendorf, Shore, Len Murray,[1] and others. I rejoindered by reminding him that we had sent . . . his office the proposed list of guests and had received approval. He was quite crusty but calmed down, when he realized that we had done our best and that he had been informed about the dinner plans. I think we said "good night" at the Savoy. He hoped that I had not taken his dissatisfaction in a personal way. I told him not to worry, I had not. . . .

1. Barbara Ward, an eminent authority on the underdeveloped countries; Ralf Dahrendorf, director of the London School of Economics; Peter Shore, secretary of state for the environment; Len Murray, a British union leader.

Saturday, May 7, 1977

What a day! Some of it over the dinner tomorrow night. Ivan [Head] phoned to say that he had seen Ramphal. The result: Sonny and his wife, along with Ivan himself, will not be at our dinner. There will be fewer people and more opportunity for Trudeau to discuss the economic questions with Dahrendorf and four or five others. I have been playing with the seating plan, a thankless job, which I trust will not have to be repeated ever. The next time I arrange a dinner for the Prime Minister, I will insist on his making the selection of guests. In this particular instance I have followed revised instructions without complaint, only because I am sympathetic to Trudeau, because of some of his burdens. Moreover, I much prefer the character of the kind of dinner he prefers. . . .

The Summit is on. Giscard arrived this morning. He is not popular over his failure to accept Callaghan's hospitality last night [for dinner]. Trudeau is not pleased with the French President, who will give him a lunch on Thursday instead of dinner. What angers Trudeau most is that there will be many at the luncheon. Trudeau wanted a tête-à-tête arrangement. In this way, he could argue the Quebec-Canada problem more effectively.

John Noble, who is in charge of the organization for our delegation at the Summit, called to tell me that Don Jamieson pulled the scoop of the day, by giving President Carter a ride from Lancaster House to No. 10 Downing Street this noon. Carter said, "How about giving me a lift?" Don obliged. This will likely make him more popular than anything he might do at the Summit.

Sunday, May 8, 1977

Around 11:00 o'clock I drove to the Air Force Memorial at Runnymede to lay a wreath on behalf of the participating countries of the Commonwealth War Graves Commission. . . . When I returned, word came that Donald Macdonald and his wife would, after all, be at the dinner tonight. We are happy that they will be with us. If the Prime Minister had adhered to the approval given the original list of guests, none of this trouble would have happened. I realize, of course, the strain he has been under. Now we will have to re-arrange the place cards, so as to maintain the fullest exposure of the economists to the Prime Minister at dinner. Trudeau and the rest of us will likely have a good laugh at the complications, the tensions, and, of course, the good fun which in such situations is the end result. . . .

During the dinner, we had a sort of seminar, centring on world economic problems examined at the Summit itself, and afterwards upstairs in the main salon a good discussion on the Quebec problem in Canada, with a wide participation on the discussion. Trudeau was very pleased, saying it was one of the best dinners and the kind he liked.

Monday, May 9, 1977

The general impression of the Summit is that, within its terms of reference and limitations, it was a success. The seven-point plan to correct the principal economic problems has made a good immediate impression. . . . This will stimulate action if followed up. They did agree to establish monitoring and reporting devices to that end. The seven have acknowledged that the most important problem on the industrial front is to create more work, while seeking to reduce inflation. . . . All at the meeting had committed themselves to create more jobs, to maintain economic growth, to improve financial resources on an international scale, and to expand opportunities for trade, while resisting protectionism. They resolved to achieve a satisfactory conclusion of the North-South conference. The European Community's proposals to help developing countries will be supplemented by the United States. It looks as though the nuclear energy matter was the main question on which there were differences of opinion. Giscard d'Estaing said the problem was how to develop nuclear energy at a time when energy resources are limited. . . .

There is always a danger of drawing exaggerated conclusions after summits. Proof that this Summit meeting has been a success . . . will depend on action by the governments in their new collective judgment, from which emerged the seven-point declaration of this Summit. Leadership is important [and] President Carter achieved considerable success. He may be said to have stolen the show. In a few months . . . if the world economy has improved because of the policy of individual governments, the conference will be regarded as having succeeded. . . .

Tuesday, May 10, 1977

No sooner had the Economic Summit ended, than the NATO heads of government meeting began.

In his opening statement, the Secretary General[2] emphasized that defence plans would be affected by economic problems. The headlines in *The Times* suggest that Joseph Luns spoke of disarray and disunity as threatening factors in western unity. I should think that Luns overstated the case as he sometimes does. . . .

The Royal Canadian Mounted Police are in London. . . . Today we had a procession from Canada House to the Mansion House. Commissioner Nadon[3] of the R.C.M.P., Commodore Cogdon, the Queen's Master of Horse, and I were conveyed in a landau in the centre of the R.C.M.P. escort, which started off from Canada House. Trafalgar Square was crowded with people, and all along the route into the city, Canada was generously welcomed by the people of this great metropolitan city. . . .

Wednesday, May 11, 1977

[At the heads of government meeting] President Carter affirmed United States support for NATO. He outlined a long-term defence programme for the 1980s providing for co-operation in the development and production of defence equipment. . . . In the view of Helmut Schmidt, the greatest danger lies in the economic field. The partners of the alliance would have to act together to overcome unemployment, energy, and the problems of world underdevelopment. The pattern of the meeting was not to Trudeau's liking. He proposed that, instead of a series of subjects and long speeches by the participants, it would be better to have an exchange of views. This technique had been established at heads of

2. Joseph Luns
3. Maurice Nadon was head of the Royal Canadian Mounted Police.

government meetings of the Commonwealth. Everyone recognized the advantage of this method of presentation. . . .

I had lunch today at the Reform Club in one of the private rooms—actually one of the five libraries of the Club—with Trudeau, Thorn,[4] David Steel, the United Kingdom Liberal leader, and Jeremy Thorpe. This was one of the best functions since Trudeau's arrival—good discussion, quick repartee and some serious talk about NATO, the summit and European affairs. It was a good mixture as well of political gossip and reminiscing. . . . Thorn was very critical of Roy Jenkins.[5] The smaller E.E.C. countries felt that he did not stand up to the big partners and had not lost his United Kingdom affiliation. I defended Roy, saying that, after all, he had just begun his responsibilities. The French and his own former colleagues would not be easy to handle. No one could deny his dedication to European unity. Both David Steel and Jeremy Thorpe thought that Roy was not a man of decision or of steel. Trudeau mentioned that on a previous visit he had seen Jenkins at his home in the country and was greatly impressed. . . .

Trudeau is hopeful about his own political situation and the Quebec problem, but he sees great dangers in the latter. At one time a few months ago, he had thought of retiring from the leadership. It was at this point that he mentioned how unwise John Turner was to have left the cabinet when he did. Trudeau indicated, however, there was no thought of his going now. When he would have a general election was not clear, I thought, but he was confident about the outcome. . . .

I emphasized to Trudeau that the situation in western Canada must be changing rapidly. My visitor, the Horner of the Alberta cabinet,[6] said that there was now in western Canada and in Alberta particularly a fresh realization of the

4. Gaston Thorn, the prime minister of Luxembourg and president of the Liberal International.
5. The new president of the European Community.
6. Dr. Hugh Horner served as deputy premier and minister of transportation in the Alberta Conservative government of Peter Lougheed. He is a brother of Jack who had just defected from the federal Conservatives to become Trudeau's minister of transport.

dangers of division in Canada. Every step must be taken to avoid a Canadian break-up. Clark could not help in this serious situation. Trudeau, obviously, was the man to take charge. Frankly, said Dr. Horner, "Once again the Conservatives have missed the boat. . . ." Trudeau seemed heartened by my report.

Both Trudeau and Thorn were impressed with the Reform Club. I have rarely seen Trudeau as ecstatic as he glanced at the paintings of the great Liberal figures but, like me, he was astounded to find a bust of Cromwell at the entrance to the big library. . . .

After lunch, I accompanied Trudeau to Heathrow on his way to France. We had a good talk on the way about political science and political philosophy at the present time. I mentioned Laski. He spoke of Laski's *Grammar of Politics* and, I think, was a little surprised that I went on to name four or five other books by their titles written by Laski. "I didn't know you were interested in Laski," said Trudeau. "He had a great influence on me." I rejoined by saying that he had had a great influence on me as well, although I broke with him over his last book—*Faith, Reason and Civilization. . . .*[7]

I returned to the residence before evening had darkened to find three bags with papers awaiting me. Discouraged at the sight, I left them untouched for another and hopefully more relaxed period, if that will ever come.

Thursday, May 12, 1977

The town is a little quieter. The big guns have left, but not the problems which concern them. We will have a few weeks to think about them, then some of the leaders, all the Prime Ministers from the Commonwealth, will descend on London again for a hectic ten-day period. . . . Regarding the participation of Amin, . . . Trudeau dismissed the question as one that would not likely arise—if it did, its disposition would not be cataclysmic. He thinks Amin is a British problem. . . .

7. Harold Laski, *A Grammar of Politics* (London 1934); *Faith, Reason and Civilization: An Essay in Historical Analysis* (London 1944). Harold Laski, born in Britain, had lectured at Yale University before moving to the London School of Economics in 1920 where he was professor of political science. He also chaired the British Labour party (1945-46).

Friday, May 13, 1977

The appointment of Peter Jay* as Ambassador to Washington is widely discussed. Callaghan defended it yesterday. He said, quite frankly, he could not oppose the Foreign Secretary's nomination on the single ground that Jay was his [Callaghan's] son-in-law. There are divisions on the question in the Labour party. . . . Apparently, when in Washington a month ago, David Owen was not impressed with the way the Ambassador[8] was conducting the business of the embassy to meet the requirements of today's demands. A fresh and a more youthful point of view should prevail in the embassy, he says. . . . Owen could have handled this matter a little more graciously and with more subtlety. Jim Callaghan may wish that he had. The Foreign Office itself will be disturbed by Owen's decision, good as it may be. I am inclined to think that there are positive reasons to support it.

Many people think that the responsibilities of an Ambassador are less than heretofore. . . . The work of an Ambassador now has been extended, and particularly here in this extrememly busy High Commission, to embrace not only the Foreign Office but many other departments of government. . . . Increasingly, it is becoming an operative rather than a representational function. The demands on an Ambassador or High Commissioner are now very great, but he will not perform his function unless he at least is the beneficiary of good professional experience. . . .

Most of the morning I spent with Don Jamieson [who] . . . is determined not to give in on our insistence on adherence to the Non-Proliferation Treaty[9] before transferring [our] nuclear material [to other countries]. He feels that agreement with the British on this is assured. This is still open, I believe, until the agreement with the E.E.C. on energy has been settled. That, in turn, is complicated by the attitude of France. . . .

8. Peter Ramsbotham
9. A partial nuclear test ban treaty signed in 1963 was followed in 1968 by a non-proliferation treaty, which regulated the disposition of fissionable materials.

Sunday, May 15, 1977

We spent the day at Windsor Castle with the Queen, her husband, her family, her relatives and those who were at the Royal Windsor Horse Show. . . . There we waited for the return to the Castle of the Queen, who was at church in St. George's Chapel. Actually we met her on the grounds, where Commissioner Nadon presented the Queen with the fine horse, Centennial, a gift of the Royal Canadian Mounted Police. She already has another horse of the same vintage, though smaller, on which she rode at the Trooping the Colour last year, Burmese. That she appreciated the gift was apparent today. She loves horses. We stood around for about fifteen minutes chatting after the presentation, while photographs were taken and then slowly walked back to the Castle.

There we had a pleasant luncheon. . . . Nell sat between Prince Philip and Prince Charles and, as both were to take part in athletic events during the afternoon, Nell had laughingly assured the Queen that she would see to it that their drink was confined to water. As the Duke went to take part in the Royal Windsor Horse Show and the Prince of Wales in a polo match, with the same happy manner, Nell signalled across the table to the Queen that she had successfully performed her mission. Princess Margaret sat on my right. I did not find her an easy person to talk to. . . . Nell thinks she is quite sad and perhaps that is the reason. The Queen, on the other hand, was full of gaiety, discussed Canada, how much she loved it and how much she hoped the Quebec problem would be resolved. . . .

Before lunch the Prince of Wales asked me what I thought about his accepting an invitation of *The Times* newspaper to write an article on the Commonwealth. "Why not?" I asked. This does not necessarily involve a political judgment. He seemed pleased with the assurance which I gave him and, I am sure, fully intends to write the article. . . . The Commonwealth means something to him and his recent tour encouraged this fact. "What holds the Commonwealth together, Mr. Martin?" he asked. Before I had time to reply, he said, "The Queen." . . . Did I believe in the Commonwealth? asked the Prince of Wales. Yes, I do, because it is an orderly arrangement of the largest group of states in the world. Moreover, it really is Britain's ticket-of-admission to the big power club at the present time. Britain must not lose her interest in the Commonwealth. The Common Market is not necessarily a competing organization. They could be complementary to one another.

I asked the Prince of Wales if he had had a good chat with Trudeau. He said he found Trudeau difficult. I said, "You mean difficult to talk to?" "Yes, perhaps that is what I mean." I said, "Maybe he is a little shy. You know, sometimes royalty does have that effect on me and on many others." He laughingly replied, "Prime Ministers, too, do have this effect on royalty perhaps." . . .

After lunch, we went to the Royal Windsor Horse Show, the Queen arriving in a small landau, accompanied by the Royal Canadian Mounted Police Ride. It was quite a sight. This Royal Windsor Horse Show is not like others. This was really a family affair. The Queen sat immediately in front of me within easy reach of conversation, with her children and those of Princess Margaret on each side, other members of the royal family nearby, including the ninety-four year old Princess Alice, who seemed to enjoy what was a family outing in which we were able to participate. . . . Among the British competitors was Prince Philip who performed well and won second prize. Now and then, the Queen generously explained the points in judging to us. This was one of the most pleasant days we have had since I have been here as High Commissioner. We saw the Queen as she has often been portrayed in books and articles, happy and fully comfortable in her own home at Windsor Castle. No apparent security — her Windsor subjects around her participating in the annual event. . . .

Tuesday, May 17, 1977

I recalled this morning that the Queen, at lunch at Windsor Castle, mentioned there were some criticisms of her speech to the joint Houses of Parliament the other day. She had said: "I number Kings and Queens of England and of Scotland and Princes of Wales among my ancestors and so I can readily understand these aspirations, the problems of progress, the complexities of modern administrations, the feeling that metropolitan government is too remote from the lives of ordinary men and women. These, among other things, have helped to revive the awareness of historic national identities in these islands," adding, "I can never forget that I was crowned Queen of the United Kingdom of Great Britain and Northern Ireland." She told me that she was not expressing opinion but a fact. This illustrates the difficult path trod by a constitutional monarch. I suggested to her that the warm reception given by most members of Parliament of all parties showed that she had not transgressed constitutional practice. I wondered indeed if there were not occasions when the head of state, by judicious language, might on vital occasions draw the attention of governments and people to special dangers. . . .

Last night, I had an interesting time at the House of Commons, when I spoke to the United and Cecil Club, one of the oldest parliamentary dining clubs at Westminster. It is a Conservative party club. . . . I spoke for about twenty minutes on the Canada-Quebec problem and my impressions on devolution in the United Kingdom. From the reaction, this seems to have been one of my most successful speeches. After I had spoken, the questions were many and the discussion animated. I was surprised to find out that one or two thought the solution for our problem was to let Quebec go its way. I quickly pointed out that this would be disastrous for both Quebec and Canada, implying that underlying the question was a lack of understanding of the nature of the Canadian scene, let alone its geography. . . .

Friday, May 20, 1977

I have been told that Callaghan has decided against allowing Amin to come to Britain for the Commonwealth Conference. It is hoped that Amin will not try to come but, if he does the government will take preventative measures, perhaps closer to the event. Yesterday in the Commons, the Prime Minister . . . said, "Any decision that is taken is not one in which I wish to involve other members of the Commonwealth — it will be for the government to reach a conclusion." This puts a new gloss on the picture. . . .

Sunday, May 22, 1977

It is noteworthy that yesterday and likely today, we have had and will have the full rays of the healthy sun for most of the day. Is this unique? Our climate all winter has been dull, disagreeable, sullen, coldish, dampish — downright miserable. What has it given? Colds, depression and a London shorn of charm and uniqueness. We are the victims of our climate? Grosvenor Square is proof. Yesterday, there the children played in the sun. The older folk walked about or sat in the sun on the benches. Friendliness was in the air. The birds were sociable. The eagle on the American Embassy lost its ferocity. . . .

Monday, May 23, 1977

My talk at noon with Sir John Hunt, secretary to the cabinet, was, as most of my exchanges with him have been, productive and useful. . . . John thought the Economic Summit was a good one. True, the prepared communiqué was not accepted in the form presented but what did ensue embodied the same basic material. In any event, Sir John thinks the work that goes into the preparation of a communiqué is valuable, even if not fully used. I emphasized our Prime Minister's concern about undue expectations from such a meeting, adding my own reaction to the history of the summits. To this, Sir John said there was a difference between a summit involving leading western nations and the Soviet Union and summits among western industrial powers. This is a distinction which I had not made in my own assessments. It is, of course, important at the present time, when the fact of interdependence drives on at an accelerated pace, that the leaders should know one another and, from their discussions, learn about the thinking of the others. That in itself was a useful result of the summit. . . .

Wednesday, May 25, 1977

I have just learned that Trudeau has won the by-elections[10] in four of the five Quebec seats and has taken away the seat in Prince Edward Island from the Conservatives. . . . These results will strengthen the Prime Minister in the Canada-Quebec problem. Had he lost in Quebec, this would have

10. There were six by-elections in all: five in Quebec and one in Prince Edward Island.

been damaging to his leadership and authority. When he arrives here next week, I may have an opportunity to review his latest thinking but, I suspect, it will not have changed. What does this mean to Joe Clark? It is inevitable that a suggestion will be made for a new convocation of the Conservative party. One will not likely be held. Action on accountability, however, can be taken at the annual meeting of the Conservative party, which will take place in Quebec in November. Part of Trudeau's political calculation might be — perhaps I had better go ahead before the Conservatives select a stronger man than Joe. My judgment is that it does not matter at this stage who the Tories have as their leader. Trudeau's electoral strength lies in the fact that, because of the Quebec problem, it is not desirable to dislodge . . . him. This has been my view since the beginning, following the November 15th [Quebec provincial] election. . . .

Before retiring after a long and somewhat tedious day, I dropped in to a reception Christian Hardy and his wife had for their many friends. . . . I was glad to see Sonny Ramphal's wife. Ever since I asked Sonny to the Trudeau dinner at the residence and was compelled to suggest to Sonny that Trudeau preferred a different group, I have felt very self-conscious. . . .

Tuesday, May 31, 1977

I called on Premier Lougheed at his hotel early this morning. We went directly to Canada House for a chat, after which Mrs. Thatcher, Leader of the Conservative party, called to meet him. It was the first time I had received Mrs. Thatcher in Canada House. Before she arrived, Lougheed told me that he had had a satisfactory talk yesterday with Wedgwood Benn on British oil policy. The North Sea flow will have great significance for oil-producing countries. Lougheed felt it was useful to have an appreciation of British policy directly from the minister responsible. He believes his visit to Saudi Arabia and Iran next month will likewise assist his government in the determination of future oil policy. He admitted it is difficult to forecast oil prices through OPEC. . . . Lougheed wants to raise the domestic price of oil and gas to the levels dictated by OPEC.

Mrs. Thatcher met with the Premier and me for over an hour. We had a useful discussion on the general political situation in Britain, in respect of which she maintains strong optimism for the future. . . . Her knowledge of our constitutional arrangements reflected interest and study. She acknowledged that Canada was already a decentralized country. Lougheed pointed out that there were some further matters that might well be renegotiated. . . .

Trudeau thinks Lévesque is ambivalent in his policies. The next move is up to Lévesque in the constitutional debate. Don Thorson, the Deputy Minister of Justice, one of our leading constitutional advisers, is moving over to the Federal-Provincial Relations Office in the Privy Council to work on constitutional change. Trudeau is not moving toward special status for Quebec. Basically, the present division of powers is sound, but he is prepared to consider new proposals. There will be new proposals on language training and a cut-back of the programmes for training federal civil servants in the second language. The Parti Québécois, Trudeau thinks, is not concerned enough with the problems of French-Canadians outside Quebec. He is ready to resume talks with Quebec but on condition that Lévesque will discuss power-sharing and not separation. As Lougheed said this morning, there is room for negotiation. This could take place this autumn. I don't know how this would fit in with Trudeau's time-table, although he made it clear, when I talked to him ten days ago, that he is not planning an autumn election. Pressure on him to do so is strong. . . .

Wednesday, June 1, 1977

We in this mission are unhappy over the lack of final decisions on many matters connected with the [Commonwealth] Conference. Trudeau is giving a reception at the residence on Tuesday night. We have no idea who are coming. We will be expected to issue invitations and, unless we have them by today, it is practically impossible to get the invitations to the parties concerned. . . .

Saturday, June 4, 1977

The interest in this country for the next four days will be the Queen's Jubilee and thereafter for two weeks, the Commonwealth heads of government take over. I have more pages of instructions [and] cards of admission related to these events than one could imagine. My own six-page programme of action is comprehensive but frightening. Would that I could get a swim before each event. Certainly my first open-air swim at Hurlingham was a great joy yesterday at noon. . . .

Trudeau told the press on Friday that his wife was being exploited by them. He let them know that his estrangement would not affect his career. "I am just one of many single parents who have to work." . . .

Sunday, June 5, 1977

Carter, my New Zealand colleague, was on the phone early today. He hopes that Muldoon, his Prime Minister, will take a helpful attitude on the Edmonton [Commonwealth] Games. Trudeau hopes so, too. Sonny Ramphal may have to push a little harder. All the same, Trudeau should not have struck him from our dinner list when he was here for the summit. . . .

Sam and Mrs. Henderson of Windsor . . . had brunch with us. . . . After brunch, Sam sitting in my chair in the library, noticed Gustaf Aulèn's book on Jesus.[11] I told him how difficult I found it to pray. Perhaps reading such a book is a prayer. Sam was incredulous, I think. . . .

Monday, June 6, 1977

I was at Heathrow early this morning to greet the Governor-General (Jules and his wife), the former Governor-General (the Micheners, Roly and Norah), and John Diefenbaker. At the last moment, the Prime Minister asked John Diefenbaker to join him on his plane so, when welcoming Trudeau, I warmly welcomed John D. Trudeau and I rode to the Savoy together. He is pleased with the by-election results, particularly the obvious interpretation given to the results in Quebec. . . .

11. Gustaf Aulèn, *Christus Victor: An Historical Study of the Three Main Types of the Ideal of Atonement*, tr. A. G. Hebert (London 1970).

Tuesday, June 7, 1977

This is the twenty-fifth anniversary of the Queen's Coronation. God bless her. . . . The Queen lit a bonfire last night at Windsor Castle. It began a network of fires extending throughout Britain. Meanwhile, long before the event, people have taken up their positions in front of St. Paul's, Buckingham Palace and elsewhere to see the Queen as she passes by on her way to the cathedral at 10:00 o'clock this morning. She will pass by Canada House, decorated with many Canadian flags and Jubilee bunting. . . .

When we set out for St. Paul's . . . the streets were packed with people. Trafalgar Square, Canada House looking resplendent, was a mass of eager faces. The Strand, before and beyond the Savoy, was likewise. St. Paul's was surrounded tightly by thousands of happy people waiting for the Queen. We were seated in St. Paul's an hour and a half before her arrival. Nell and I had main aisle seats, numbers one and two, not far from where the Queen and the Duke were to be placed facing the altar, just outside the chancel. Trudeau arrived shortly after and gave us a hearty handshake. The Governor-General, the Micheners, and John Diefenbaker came in by the left aisle. It seemed that everyone in the United Kingdom and Commonwealth was present. . . .

The arrival of the Queen, preceded by members of the royal family was picturesque and historic. . . . The Archbishop of Canterbury gave the address. It must have pleased the Queen. I thought he spoke so much better than the Bishop of London at the London service in Westminster Abbey on Sunday. Today there was understatement, moderation, substance, and meaningful rhetoric. The boys choir's rendering of the Te Deum was exquisite. On the way out to greet her people, we bowed to the Queen, who gave us a heart-warming smile. . . .

Wednesday, June 8, 1977

The Commonwealth Conference was opened this morning at Lancaster House with a speech by . . . Jim Callaghan. He pointed out that the Commonwealth, with its thirty-six sovereign states, represents a population of over one billion people. This institution, since my first post in government, has almost quadrupled its membership. Significantly enough, as I looked over the table, none of the thirty-six prime ministers were there when I entered Mackenzie King's cabinet in 1945. Jim Callaghan wasn't a member of Parliament. . . .

The new Prime Minister of India[12] whom I had not seen for eighteen years — at a time when I know he hoped that he would be Prime Minister — now at the age of eighty, spoke of the Commonwealth's importance. Later, at a reception given at noon by the Secretary General, Morarji Desai had a warm greeting for me. I was surprised that he remembered me. . . . He had not yet met Trudeau and was anxious to do so. He wished to resume cordial relations which prevailed between India and Canada in Nehru's day. . . .

Trudeau lunched today with Kaunda. One of the matters they will certainly discuss is the suggestion that countries like Canada might supply military advisers to Zambia in its present troubles with Rhodesia. This we discussed at our delegation meeting this morning before going to Marlborough House. There is not much sympathy for the idea, although Trudeau gave the impression of at least examining it carefully. . . .

The Queen gave a dinner last night at Buckingham Palace and held a reception afterwards for those attached to the various delegations. Nell thought that the Queen and the Duke of Edinburgh were extremely warm in the way they received us and noted especially how cheerful she was. At the reception, Archbishop Makarios . . . recalled our meeting in Cyprus[13] and was kind enough to make reference to my part in the establishment of the United Nations peace force. . . . I expressed the hope that a solution would not be too long delayed so that our troops, who have been there a long time, could return. . . .

We had a good chat with the Queen Mother, who obviously was greatly moved with Nell's enthusiasm for the events of yesterday. . . . The Queen Mother reiterated her concept of the spiritual quality of the commitment made at the Coronation by her daughter twenty-five years ago . . . to serve and reign. The Queen Mother is a strong, friendly personality,

12. Morarji Desai
13. In 1965.

whose goodness and bonhomie pervades so widely. Then we met Prince Andrew, while we were talking to Trudeau. . . . He told Trudeau that he was very much looking forward to the long summer canoe trip over a water trail that Trudeau himself had taken fifteen years ago. Prince Andrew said, "I only hope that Mother doesn't stop me from going." Trudeau replied, "I will put in a good word." . . .

Thursday, June 9, 1977

At the conference yesterday, both Callaghan and David Owen had a tough time defending their policy for a negotiated settlement in Rhodesia. . . . Most of the African leaders are sceptical about the prospects for negotiation. It cannot really take place until Ian Smith fully accepts black majority rule. Unless progress were made in Southern Africa, said Kaunda, there would be an uprising that would put the French revolution in a smaller context. Commonwealth history revealed, he argued, that the racial conflict had been ignored and played down. . . . Smith's powers were rooted in Europe. The failure to impose complete sanctions was proof. Owen is anxious to test Smith's intentions to the limit [and] . . . said that Britain had to act with the full weight and support of American assistance. . . .

I received the Governor-General this morning at Canada House when he paid an official call. We discussed the desirability of a Canadian External Affairs official serving as Rodney Moore has served in the information section at the Palace. Rodney Moore is leaving . . . to return to External. The Governor-General is greatly concerned that, unless an official is on the staff at the Palace, the Queen will not be as well informed about Canadian affairs as she should. Trudeau does not seem anxious to have a replacement for Rodney. He shares the viewpoint of Mackenzie King, who wished to have the Palace keep out of Canadian affairs. Logic, if not politics, is on the Governor-General's side. The Queen, as Queen of Canada, must be fully informed about Canadian matters. Now she is only generally informed although, while Moore has been there, more papers on Canadian matters have come to her attention. . . . The Governor-General writes to the Queen every month, giving an appreciation of the Canadian scene but this is held to be insufficient. . . . The real fact is that Canadian prime ministers, not all of them, prefer a minimum of intervention by the Palace. My own view is that there can be no harm, but much good, in keeping the Palace fully informed of developing situations in Canada which affect the head of state and the nation itself. . . . The only consequence which will likely flow from the Governor-General's discussions with me this morning will be an endeavour by the mission to see that special articles, newspaper clippings and the like reach the Queen's secretariat. . . .

Friday, June 10, 1977

At the Commonwealth Conference this morning, Trudeau made some telling observations in discussing the economic problem. . . . He submitted that the O.E.C.D. countries had not recovered their long-term rate of growth. Unemployment continued to be high, with some fifteen million unemployed in the Western industrial world. Paradoxically, the deflationary pressure had not been accompanied by any real easing of inflationary pressures. . . . OPEC's imposition of a three-fold increase in oil prices had contributed to price inflation, although today's OPEC prices were actually rising more slowly than inflation in the O.E.C.D. It is true that the external causes of inflation have disappeared, but inflationary pressures continue. . . . The reason is that the populations of the O.E.C.D. countries had never accepted the real cause—increase of grain and oil prices—had made them poor. There was a lack of self-discipline in the industrial democracies unable to adjust to the fact that OPEC price rises had transferred real wealth from them to the OPEC countries. Trudeau saw dangers ahead in spite of personal optimism. There was a danger that fascism, nazism and other totalitarianisms might resurge. . . .

Trudeau believes that the answer to our current difficulties depends on a return to discipline, restraint, and a control of expectations. It was difficult, however, to get this necessary consensus in today's society. Rambouillet and the other Summits showed that there was a realization of the dangers. All were still paying lip-service to the free market system, in spite of interventions in almost every aspect of it. For instance, in

Canada, the government had to impose wage and price controls. When they looked at the energy situation, it was realized that the market could not be relied upon to set an ideal price for oil. . . .

Monday, June 13, 1977

When the Commonwealth Prime Ministers confer this afternoon at Lancaster House, I have been told that Callaghan will continue to resist pressure from the African members [on the subject of Rhodesia]. The Commonwealth countries, it is being urged, should give aid to the guerrillas. The African countries in the Commonwealth are urging as well that the British should cut off communication with [the white government in] Salisbury and as well threaten action against the oil companies. Certainly all the African demands will not be met. I find it difficult to understand how there cannot be a restoration of full sanctions against Rhodesia in order to bring about a peaceful settlement. . . .

Tuesday, June 14, 1977

It seems certain that the question of New Zealand's sporting contacts with South Africa will be resolved. Trudeau said yesterday that the formula which he helped to produce was acceptable to the main parties, requiring only confirmation by the full conference. The Africans hopefully will be pleased with the universal condemnation of apartheid and the encouragement given by all governments, including New Zealand, to their . . . nationals to refrain from [sports] competitions with South Africa. It is important that there be agreement, so that the Games can go on, thus avoiding embarrassment to Canada and the Commonwealth.

The conference [and] . . . the discussion on a New World Economic Order resumes today. The Commonwealth deals with this issue a few days after the partial failure of the eighteen-month [C.I.E.C.] negotiation between the developed and developing nations in Paris. The discussions there concluded with a minimum of agreement. The Third World countries at the conference continue to put pressure for a fundamental change in the existing [economic] order. . . . The developing countries want full endorsement from the developed Commonwealth countries for a common fund to regularize world commodity prices. . . .

While Callaghan was chairing the Commonwealth Conference, the weakness of his government in Parliament was expressed in a disastrous day for the government. It was defeated on a number of measures, including seven amendments to the Finance Bill. . . . How the government can withstand such defeats and continue in such parliamentary uncertainty for long is beyond me. I don't think it can. There will likely be an election in the early autumn as I see the situation now.

We gave a reception last night, and I hope the last for a while, to members of the news media travelling with Prime Minister [Trudeau]. I think it was a good party, ending up with a long talk with Bruce Phillips[14] on the situation in Canada. He is disheartened over the low level, as he called it, in the present Parliament. Trudeau will continue in the saddle beyond the next election. Bruce had a lot of praise for the way in which Trudeau has handled his marital problem and has faced up to his governmental responsibilities in the light thereof. . . .

Wednesday, June 15, 1977

The Commonwealth Conference had a restricted meeting yesterday on what to do about Amin. Most countries, if not all, condemned the situation in Uganda and, in particular, Amin's uncivilized conduct. The purpose of the discussion was to find an agreed formula of condemnation for the final communiqué. . . .

One of the by-products of the Commonwealth Conference is the long and useful talk between Trudeau and Desai. . . . Trudeau was interested in Desai's philosophy of government and his system of values and view of moral principles as applicable to political life. . . . It is possible that as a result there could be a return to the nuclear policy of India as I understood it in the days of Nehru and Shastri. . . .[15] Desai

14. A Canadian reporter.
15. Jawaharlal Nehru (1947-64) and Lal Badahur Shastri (1964-66) were both prime ministers of India who opposed their country's acquiring nuclear weapons.

was very much opposed to the proliferation of nuclear weapons. It remains to be seen what agreement can be reached on the question of safeguards. Trudeau found, as I suggested he would, that Desai was closer to the spirit of Mahatma Gandhi. . . .

Tonight I accompanied the Prime Minister to Jim Callaghan's reception at the Royal Academy. . . . Jim Callaghan told us that he was pleased with the conference and hoped Trudeau was. There seems to be a general impression, as Denis Hamilton, publisher of *The Times*, said, that the conference was a success. Undoubtedly, the condemnation of Amin and Uganda helped greatly to give the conference the quality of achievement. Had the Commonwealth Conference not done so, it is doubtful that everyone would have felt that it had gone off well. . . .

Thursday, June 16, 1977

Last night I met with Jeremy Thorpe. The fate of the government now will depend largely on proportional representation in the bill on direct European elections. If the government does not make this concession to the Liberals, it looks very much as though the latter will not support the dying régime of Callaghan. There may be elections in the fall. What Jeremy told me was later confirmed in a speech by David Steel. . . .

Trudeau and I drove out to Heathrow together. Nell, who is travelling back with him, went out earlier with John to get her bags properly arranged. . . . Even before she lifted her feet off the ground at Heathrow, I began to feel lonesome. I don't think she was too keen to go without me.

Trudeau wondered what I thought his decision on the timing of an election should be. Obviously, the Prime Minister is tempted when the going is good, as it is now. I suggested that, while this was the case . . . a general election could always be a weapon against Lévesque, as indeed were the recent by-elections.

Trudeau wondered why in Ontario, good as they are, his cabinet colleagues did not seem to measure up to those in the St. Laurent-Pearson period, apart from Donald Macdonald, whom he thinks is not going to stay in the cabinet. I was about to suggest to him, but did not, that in the days of King and St. Laurent and somewhat in the time of Pearson, ministers were given the fullest opportunity to become personalities in their own right. Trudeau dominates the news. Ministers spend too much time in cabinet and not enough in their respective departments. This interferes with their giving leadership in particular departments of government. I reminded Trudeau that I had told him about this around 1969.

He was pleased with the conference, particularly with the settlement of the Commonwealth Games issue and his own initiative in obtaining condemnation of Amin. . . . He commented on the wisdom of . . . Ramphal's advice to Lévesque, that Quebec should confer with the federal government over getting a seat with the Canadian delegation on Commonwealth bodies. The rules of the Commonwealth, Trudeau said, allow membership only to sovereign independent governments. When Ramphal visited Quebec, Lévesque had raised the possibility of some kind of associate membership. . . . Provincial representation on federal delegations is open to the provinces at meetings such as those dealing with education. It is up to the federal government to determine the composition of the Canadian delegation.

Friday, June 17, 1977

I forgot to mention yesterday that I had seen Nkomo, the joint leader of the Patriotic Front, at Callaghan's reception the night before last. He is convinced that the settlement reached in Rhodesia will be the product of war and not of peaceful negotiation. Trudeau had seen him the day before. The views expressed by Nkomo and also, I understand, by Dr. Ndabaningi Sithole* to Owen yesterday will be in the background of the consultations at the end of the month. . . . Nkomo, moreover, believes that final talks will take place only after the overthrow of Smith. He says the guerrillas will then be in control of the country. Meanwhile, Nyerere, in an article in *Foreign Affairs*, calls on the United States to recognize the inevitability of force and to participate in it.

The [Labour] government has taken the Liberal leader's hint. Its bill of direct elections to the European Parliament will provide for elections based on proportional representation. . . . The Liberal leader will be satisfied [but] . . . this reflects Callaghan dependence on the Liberal vote. This may save Callaghan for a few days but it looks to me very much like an impossible situation, from which Jim cannot extricate himself and avoid an early fall election. . . .

Saturday, June 18, 1977

Christian [Hardy] and I had lunch at the residence. . . . We discussed the film depicting a female nude which had a one-day run in the Canada House gallery. . . . In some places, this may be art and certainly in some places it passes a such. . . . The many Canadian visitors to Canada House would simply not understand the showing of this film with a nude woman in her many poses. We have taken the decision to close the show. The author and artist complain. . . .[16] How unpleasant for us at the mission it would have been, if the visiting Daughters of the Empire had seen this type of Canadian art in Jubilee week at Canada House. . . !

Tuesday, June 21, 1977

The Guardian newspaper has been making enquiries about the closing of an exhibit in the Canada House gallery. . . . The show consists of an installation containing black and white slides and still photographs. The central part of the show is a 16 mm movie, which was actually shot in Canada House, with the artist's comments. The film is not in any way erotic. It has caused offence to visitors and . . . I have stopped it. I reported to Ottawa that I appreciate that the gallery exists to show facets of Canadian visual arts but, in my opinion, we have an important duty to ensure that public sensibilities are not offended by what we show and how we spend the taxpayers' money. . . .

Sunday, June 26, 1977

At Westminster Cathedral this morning, the Apostolic Delegate celebrated mass to mark the fourteenth anniversary of the election of Paul VI, a fine service with exquisite music by

16. The work in question was called "Room for Self Expression," a multimedia collaboration featuring a three-minute film by Noel Harding.

the boys' choir. The Delegate, Bruno Heim, gave me a nice smile and bow, before and after. . . . I gave the Irish Ambassador a lift home. I had purchased in the Cathedral bookstore William Rees-Mogg's new book *Humbler Heaven*. The first two chapters, I read during the mass. The Ambassador quipped that during a long church service, it was permissible to read a lofty book rather than to pray. . . .

Monday, June 27, 1977

Jim's cabinet met with him at Chequers [the prime minister's country residence] over the weekend. The Prime Minister intends to hold on until 1979, if he can. On this he received the backing of all his ministers. Jim wants to get the benefit in 1979 of North Sea oil and an improvement in the economy. . . .

I am arranging a meeting for Don Jamieson and me with the Secretary of State later in the week. He and Owen met at the O.E.C.D. meeting, when David sought to do some armtwisting on Rhodesia. He revived the possibility of a Commonwealth force for Rhodesia, urging Canadian participation. . . . Jamieson replied that our reluctance to become engaged in a peace-keeping force for Rhodesia is already known. It was not our desire to be placed between blacks and whites. . . .

Wednesday, June 29, 1977

Owen believes that the Smith régime is on its last legs. A disastrous collapse would be a humiliation, he thinks, for Britain and would put more pressure on the British government to undertake a rescue programme. . . . There is, of course, concern for British investments in black Africa. The frontline presidents are concerned about the possibility of widespread disorder. They do not want to be engulfed in a Marxist-dominated continent. . . .

Before going to bed, I dropped in at the residence of the new American Ambassador, [Kingman] Brewster, the former president of Yale. We had not met before. He knew I had been at the Harvard Law School before he began to teach there. He seems like a pleasant fellow. . . .

XV

July – August 1977

AFTER THE "SUMMITRY" of the two previous months, various meetings had to put the leaders' policies into place. One of my particular concerns was Canada's involvement in any Rhodesian settlement, particularly in any peace force for the area.

In both the U.K. and Canada, the two prime ministers considered their futures. Trudeau debated the merits of calling an election while Callaghan scraped through another tight vote in the House of Commons.

Friday, July 1, 1977

I accompanied Don to the Foreign Office for an hour's exchange with the Secretary of State. Frank Judd,* a Minister of State in the Foreign Office, was present. . . . Don was particularly effective on the Commonwealth force proposal for Rhodesia. More time was spent on the Rhodesian question than on any other. . . . The British, in consultation with the United States, are still trying to put together a package they hope will lead to a settlement. It strikes me as odd that it is now only being discussed with us. . . . The main objective of the Owen plan is to implement a new constitution based on universal suffrage. The Secretary of State reminded us how difficult it was for the whites to accept. There is a precondition to their acceptance and that is a firm commitment by the Zimbabwe government to honour existing Rhodesian obligations, which include pensions and debts. . . . This is the minimum that can be offered to the whites, who will get little from the total settlement. . . .

Owen was pessimistic about the prospects for the transitional period. The Rhodesian Front or the Nationalists will not accept the presence of the other in a caretaker government. . . . Owen, however, is pursuing the idea of a non-political caretaker government for a period of four to six months, under the authority of a United Kingdom– or United Nations–appointed administrator, whose duties would include the maintenance of stability and the conduct of elections in no less than six months. . . . He must have a force at his disposal, one that will exclude the existing Rhodesian forces and those of the National Liberation movements.

We discussed at some length how such a force was to be constituted. . . . As Owen saw it, the only possibility would be a Commonwealth force, with Britain included. The risks of such a force are apparent. The risks without such a force are incalculable . . . [and] the force would have to have black African participation to be credible. . . .

Jamieson said we had been critical of the proposal from the beginning. Owen acknowledged that others were sceptical as well. Owen seemed to be moved by Jamieson's argument for a United Nations force as a better alternative. When Owen was speaking, I had the impression that most of his thinking was "a priori." After all, his experience is very limited, particularly in these matters. . . .

Saturday July 2, 1977

Last January, Jean Chrétien flew over to spend three days with me . . . to discuss the Canada-Quebec problem, particularly in relation to his leadership possibilities after Trudeau or almost at once in Quebec. The opportunity for the latter is more likely. Jamieson and I canvassed this situation during the last few days. We are both "high" on Jean. And now comes news of a Chrétien triumph at a great Canadian rally in the Montreal forum, marking our national birthday. How stupid for those Torontonians last week to boo Roger Doucet, who sang "O, Canada" in French at Maple Leaf Gardens. Montreal and its rally cheered him on lustily, as they did Jean, who said, "Mon pays c'est le Canada," and added, "Quebec independence was a way to get a Quebec ambassador abroad in a Cadillac." Some think Chrétien used the occasion as a springboard for a later announcement that he might seek the Liberal leadership in Quebec. Jamieson mentioned that Trudeau had publicly endorsed the idea. And so do I. Jean is what Quebec needs. He ought, however, to make up his mind quickly. He can't stay in Ottawa and jump into the provincial Liberal hierarchy at the last minute. . . .

Monday, July 4, 1977

When Don Jamieson and I saw David Owen the other day, the most important subject for us was the nuclear agreement with Britain or with Euratom or both. The British are anxious to conclude an agreement with us, even if it is an interim one, in order to ensure that supplies would continue and also because they are concerned about "Community bashing" by going into a bilateral arrangement with the British. Now Owen, instead of advocating an agreement between the United Kingdom and Canada, thinks that the new compromise proposal of Euratom ought to be accepted. . . .

Tuesday, July 5, 1977

I saw Prince Charles off to Calgary and its Stampede, at noon. He will ride, cowboy hat and all, at the head of the parade tomorrow. He had been a little concerned that the horse selected for him might be too venturous. The steed on which he will mount will be more docile. . . .

Sunday, July 10, 1977

If Jim Callaghan can hold off elections this fall, he will have demonstrated one aspect of strong political leadership. This doesn't mean that he has not proved to be a good political manager. He certainly has, but, from many points of view, his is a floundering administration. When his predecessor, Harold Wilson, allowed seven ministers to speak in opposition to government policy on the E.E.C. referendum, he did the unusual. . . . When Jim Callaghan permitted an equal number in the cabinet to vote against second reading on direct elections to the European Parliament, he demonstrated how divided his cabinet is on that fundamental question. Certainly cabinet government cannot tolerate this independence and last long. . . .

Monday, July 11, 1977

On Friday it had been reported that developments in Rhodesia were such that David Owen might postpone his trip to Africa. Now comes word from John Graham* of the Foreign Office that talks with the Rhodesian government were more successful than anticipated. . . . It would appear that Smith will accept a British-controlled transition government [for] . . . three to six months. Smith objected to direct British rule in any form. Who would maintain law and order in the transition period is a stumbling block. Would all the guerrilla groups accept a cease-fire order? . . .

I called Ron Basford* on the phone to try and tie down his visit to me next week. . . . Ron told me, however, that his plans would not be firm until tomorrow. There may be a cabinet meeting in a few hours, when the question of an election would be discussed. I mentioned that Trudeau was reported as having said in Vancouver that he would not have an election until next year. Basford did not think that was a bar. Likewise, he was unaware of a story which appeared in *The Globe and Mail*, that [said] one of the reasons for Trudeau's visit to Vancouver was to convince Basford to run in the next election. Basford said there was no problem in this regard. I would be surprised if there will be an early election. Basford may be trying to force one. . . .

Tuesday, July 12, 1977

Lord Carrington, Conservative leader in the House of Lords, says that the practical way to safeguard basic human rights, threatened by the supremacy of the House of Commons, would be by electing members to the House of Lords on the basis of proportional representation and doing away with the hereditary principle. He would, furthermore, if his election method were adopted, extend to two years the duration of the suspensory veto of the Lords. This suggestion of electing members to the House of Lords interests me. We had discussed this possibility in Canada during the time I was leader . . . in the Senate. Trudeau was opposed [as was I]. He did not want the government to be responsible to the two Houses of Parliament—one was enough. . . .

Friday July 15, 1977

David Owen is having his frustrations. His initiative in Rhodesia is crumbling. . . . The British cabinet does not seem disposed to support a Commonwealth force, and is opposed, I am told, to the idea of a British presence to supervise the transfer of power. David is put in a clumsy position. His policy has been thwarted by his cabinet colleagues and has not won the support of Smith. He is going to Washington next week. Perhaps, after his talks with Vance, a new approach will be developed. . . .

Tuesday, July 19, 1977

The difficulty which lies in the search for a solution of the Rhodesian problem is highlighted by Ian Smith's decision to call an election. He wishes to show Britain and the United States that his is a united country. He will campaign for a settlement internally on the basis of majority rule. Unless he had an election, he saw no possible settlement being worked out by the British. . . . It reveals his resourcefulness and short sightedness. . . .

The garden party at Buckingham Palace this afternoon seemed to be one of the largest. The traffic on the way to the palace was the heaviest I have ever seen. . . . The Queen, I thought, looked tired. Martin Charteris told me she was and how natural this is. She has carried a tremendous load during the past few months. . . .

When I was speaking to the Home Secretary, Merlyn Rees, the Prime Minister and Mrs. Callaghan joined us. Jim asked me, "How do you think I am getting along?" He is, of course, doing well, in spite of his problems — now over pay restraint in particular and the likelihood of his pact with the Liberals breaking down. Nevertheless, he does not think there will be an election this fall. Who knows, he says, we may be able to carry on for two more years. This, however, I would doubt. . . .

Wednesday, July 20, 1977

The day before yesterday, Dick Malone, the publisher of *The Globe and Mail*, told me there was a possibility of a federal election this fall in Canada. Because of what Basford had told me last week, I doubted it. The recent polls, however, have stimulated more speculation. Trudeau said that he is still waiting to make up his mind—"I suppose if I find good enough reasons, I will call an election and if I don't, I won't." His statement represents, I think, a change of position. The Gallup poll shows his support at 51 per cent as against twenty-seven per cent for the Conservatives. . . . Trudeau will have to make up his mind within the next few days. . . . The Queen arrives in Canada on October 14th on her Silver Jubilee visit. Certainly, it would be wrong and inexpedient to have an election while she was in the country. . . . My own view is that Trudeau should wait until almost the last moment. Meanwhile, Quebec may have moved somewhat on its proposed referendum. . . . A strong verdict for Trudeau in a federal election in Quebec might be an effective sanction or warning to Lévesque. . . .

I took the salute tonight at the Royal Tournament at Earls Court. The performance lived up to its reputation and was a thoroughly good show . . . ending in the finale, a royal review, a display of naval ceremonial, backed up by the massed bands of the Royal Marines and a Royal Marine guard. Last night the Queen took the salute. . . .

Thursday, July 21, 1977

Jim Callaghan's government had a majority of thirty at the conclusion of the debate in the House of Commons on the government's inflationary policy yesterday. . . . Mrs. Thatcher attacked with a blistering speech—a rough and tumble effort, rousing her supporters. The Liberals . . . said they would stick to their pact with the government as long as it fought inflation. . . . It looks very much as though Jim is going to survive another six or eight months at any rate. . . .

John Small, who was our Ambassador in China for four years until recently, lunched with me today at the residence. . . . His admiration for Chou En-lai[1] knows no bounds. . . . Trudeau made a good impression when he was there. His wife, then in a state of pregnancy, had climbed the Wall [of China],

1. Chou En-lai (1898-1976) was foreign minister and later premier of China.

something that Chinese pregnant women would not have tried. Chou was so impressed with this that he caused the incident to be noted as an inducement for Chinese women to emulate. . . .

Friday, July 22, 1977

I went to Heathrow early this morning to welcome the Minister of Justice, Ron Basford, and his wife. Ron is on his way to the Commonwealth Bar meeting in Edinburgh. . . . On the way in, he told me that most members were opposed to a federal election now, the caucus having expressed itself firmly on this point. The concern is that, if there was to be a federal election at this time in the absence of an urgent issue, the government could experience the same result given Davis for holding his election in Ontario, when it was not needed. . . .[2]

Monday, July 25, 1977

The new Israeli Ambassador, Mr. Abraham Kidron, who called on me this morning, impressed me as an intelligent man. . . . The background of my conversation with him this morning was provided by the recent elections in Israel, which brought Begin of the Likud party to power.[3] There is concern in many circles about Begin's reportedly uncompromising attitude, particularly with regard to occupied territories and Jewish settlements. This is a central feature of confrontation. Arab countries have reacted with surprising moderation following certain initial noises. Begin seems to be taking things coolly. . . .

Wednesday, July 27, 1977

The highest total number of unemployed since 1948, when records were first kept, is given today at 1,336,700. . . . This caused Mrs. Thatcher in the House of Commons yesterday

2. Premier William Davis of Ontario had lost seats and ended up with a minority government.
3. Menachem Begin, a former minister in various Israeli governments, had led the Likud (Unity) party since 1963. This right-wing party won the Israeli elections in May 1977 and Begin became prime minister on June 21.

to tell the Prime Minister that this was the worst unemployment statistic since the thirties. Jim, nevertheless, said his economic policies were succeeding. He is heartened, I suspect, by reports, which I have heard, that the Liberal members have decided to renew their pact with the government. . . .

Friday, July 29, 1977

Jim Callaghan has won Liberal party support . . . for the next session of Parliament with a single provision, that failure to get union support for the overall limit of ten per cent on wage increases next year may reverse the situation. This means that the government will survive the next session. What this will do to the Liberal party ultimately, is hard to say. . . .

After a full morning at the office and a quick sandwich at the residence, I was on my way to Heathrow and Canada for a vacation at the fishing camp in the Saguenay owned by Canada Steamship Lines. . . .

Sunday, July 31, 1977

When I awoke from my siesta and joined Paul, we had the first swim in Lac Laurin. Cold, but so refreshing. . . . Paul and I fished in the same boat. . . . With his head on a seat cushion, he opened the "old question": Why should he not run in the next election, if he was assured of a cabinet post? He has the bug, I am afraid. I have, of course, suspected this all along —in fact I have known it. He has told me. Likewise, he has confided his desire to Nell. My reply has been, "Wait until you are older." . . . "You are doing so well as a businessman. Become firmly established as a man of commerce. They will come after you, instead of you pursuing them. You will be treated by some prime minister, perhaps Trudeau, as St. Laurent and Trudeau himself was. They were called to the cabinet and became ministers forthwith. . . . When you are forty-five years of age might be a good time to take the plunge. No one, of course, can foresee the future that clearly. In six or seven years you will likely be a tower of a man. You could do then what I failed to do. If you are still bent on politics, you could be where Trudeau is." There are, of course, many imponderables but now is clearly, in my mind, not the time. When Trudeau and I were driving to Heathrow, after the Commonwealth Conference, he mentioned that "Paul was doing well." (I mentioned that you "had the bug.") "My view is that Paul should wait until he is ready. Waiting around as so many do (like me, he was saying) is such a waste." . . .

Tuesday, August 2, 1977

Jim Coutts[4] . . . is going back to Ottawa early in the morning . . . to help bring on an election this autumn. (1) The economy might not be good next year; (2) The Tories may select a new leader this November; (3) Inflation and unemployment will be up; and (4) National unity may not be the prime issue. I still hold that the election should not take place until close to the end of Trudeau's term. It may give him a trump card when the nation needs him most.

On August 7, Nell and I went home to Windsor for the rest of our vacation.

Wednesday, August 10, 1977

Dorothy Armstrong phoned from Ottawa. The High Commission had raised the matter of royal patronage for the Jubilee portrait exhibition and the showing of the Olympic film. . . . Not much point in complaining that the office follows me. I suppose, if it did not, I would do the complaining. . . .

Friday, August 12, 1977

Jim Coutts had told me . . . that Gordon Fairweather, the Conservative member from New Brunswick, would be appointed Chief Commissioner of the recently established Human Rights Commission. The appointment was announced today. Gordon emphasized that his acceptance of the post did not reflect dissatisfaction with Joe Clark's leadership. Fairweather has long been interested in civil rights. Clark is having difficulties. Trudeau is taking advantage of his strength over the Conservative leader. There are a number of ways to erode political leadership and party position. Trudeau has learned

4. Coutts visited me at Paul's fishing camp.

an additional way to wound his opposition, give someone in Opposition a major appointment. . . .

For the rest of the month, I spent most of my time catching up on my reading and reminiscing with old friends from Windsor. During a fishing trip with them to Lake St. Clair, we chuckled over some amusing incidents from the past. One such story I recalled on August 16:

At the annual church picnic in Pointe-aux-Roches, a young lad surprised me by saying that I knew him and his name and that I had known his father, whom I had often visited. Not to be outdone, I managed to convey to my young friend that, of course, I knew him and his father. Understandably, my young acquaintance was startled when I asked him, "How is your father?" only to be told, "Mr. Martin, my father is dead." I got out of that not too clumsily. After some hours, during which I had met hundreds of my constituents and, somewhat fatigued, I bent my steps out of the picnic grounds, and failed to recognize the . . . young boy. . . . "And how is your father, son?" I asked. Not without reason, the young fellow seemed surprised and responded, "He is still dead." . . .

On August 30, Nell and I left for London with a stopover in Montreal.

Thursday, September 1, 1977

Today Paul had Lionel Chevrier and me to lunch. [Chevrier] believes the people of his province will not support separation. Speaking to Mayor Drapeau,* who came over to greet me, I got the same assurance. I don't agree with Blakeney[5] that the federalist forces in Quebec cannot be led by Trudeau. The ultimate decision will be taken by those with a right to vote in Quebec. But the voice of Canada will be heard in the debate. The Prime Minister of Canada must be heard. He has only begun his participation, when he spoke to the Congress of the United States. To argue that Canada as a whole should be without voice in the matter, is to misread the nature of the problem.

5. Allan Blakeney,* premier of Saskatchewan.

XVI

September – October 1977

The month of September had few "bumps" in it. The major question that I had to deal with was the High Commission's role when ministers from the separatist Parti Québécois government visited London. I was determined that the High Commission would not encourage separatism by appearing to sanction the province's attempt to establish independent foreign relations. Then, the following month, I was involved in organizing the Queen's trip to Canada. As usual, this meant giving a reception for her before her departure, saying farewell at the airport, monitoring the progress of the visit, and welcoming her back to Britain.

Saturday, September 3, 1977

We arrived at Heathrow around 10:00 a.m. . . . In the VIP Lounge, the United States Ambassador at the United Nations, Andrew Young, awaited a plane for Washington. Our first meeting. I found him younger looking than in his press pictures. He and David Owen had had their meetings with Ian Smith[1] [who] has been urged by Owen and Young to study the United Kingdom-United States package, some of whose terms, the Rhodesian said, were "silly" and "insane." Certainly, he is not likely to agree to leave the administration, after his strong election. The proposals put forward were well-balanced. . . . The suggestion of a United Nations force is not readily supported by Smith. Nkomo is not satisfied on all points. Sithole apparently has rejected the whole package. . . .

1. Smith had just won his elections in Rhodesia with the required two-thirds majority in favour of constitutional amendment.

If the plan did not succeed, Young told me, there would be bloodshed and war for a decade.

Monday, September 5, 1977

On my first day at the office, a little late, I am greeted by the usual display of British and world problems. . . . The matters which seem to agitate Canadians are so different from those confronting the British. The front page of *The Times* is different from the *Herald Tribune*. *The Globe and Mail* is different still. Part of the adjustment following a holiday is to get one's perspective right and . . . that will be my essential task today. . . .

Tuesday, September 6, 1977

I was amused to see Don Jamieson addressed as "Dear Donnie" by David Owen in his outline of proposals for Rhodesia.[2] David says that Field-Marshal Carver,[3] as resident commissioner-designate, will be the key figure in the negotiations, hopefully, with the future United Nations commander, eventually the Patriotic Front commander and the Rhodesian military forces. Owen thinks that the key to negotiations hinges on the role of Smith's Rhodesian Army, as it is called by the Africans. David hopes that the front-line presidents will agree to a compromise on disbandment of the Rhodesian force from the time of the cease-fire, and will accept integration with the guerrilla units. The result would be that, on independence, there would be a new Zimbabwe National Army based on Liberation forces and elements from the Rhodesian defence forces. The African governments do not want Smith's army to continue. They suspect British motives. Owen rec-

2. These plans to solve the Rhodesian situation were known as the Anglo-American settlement proposals and were presented to Ian Smith in Salisbury on September 1 and were also given to the United Nations Security Council. The plan included the appointment of a British resident high commissioner to take over authority from the Rhodesian government during the transition.
3. Sir Michael Carver had just retired as chief of the British Defence Staff (1973-76) and had experience in peace-keeping as the deputy commander of the United Nations force in Cyprus in 1964.

ognizes that negotiated safeguards are essential to ensure fair elections during the transition and to preserve the position of a new president such as Muzorewa or Sithole. As soon as the national election reveals the identity of the new president, he will be able to make decisions on the final shape of the Zimbabwe National Army. At that point, the United Nations mandate would remain for an agreed period after independence. David thinks that, if Nyerere supports this scenario, it will receive international acceptance. . . .

Last night, Malcolm and Audrey MacDonald dined with us. They are leaving this week for Asia, Singapore in particular, where Malcolm will do research on his memoirs. . . . It was inevitable that Malcolm and I would have a good talk about David Marquand's book on his father.[4] Malcolm is pleased with it. It puts his father's career in better perspective. Malcolm, who will see Indira [Gandhi] as well as the Prime Minister in Delhi, believes Nehru's daughter is still popular. She might have won if she had not delayed going to the people. Mrs. Pandit's[5] opposition to Indira was not something new. Jealousy was involved between Nehru's sister and his daughter.

Wednesday, September 7, 1977

Donald Macdonald has resigned from the cabinet. For some time this was rumoured. I am sorry Donald is leaving public life. He has been a good Minister of Finance and a strong man in the cabinet. . . . I am a little surprised he has decided to go. I thought he was dedicated to public life and certainly, on the basis of things as they are, would have been a strong candidate to succeed Trudeau when the time comes. . . . He was the best parliamentary secretary I had as foreign minister,[6] doing particularly good work at the United Nations. . . . When the campaign for the [1968] Liberal leadership was

4. Marquand's book, *Ramsay MacDonald*, was published in London in 1977.
5. Vijaya Lakshmi Pandit, sister of Jawaharlal Nehru, was president of the U.N. General Assembly in 1953-54 and served in numerous other diplomatic and political positions.
6. In 1966.

underway, he thought he had better resign, as he was going to support Trudeau. I told him I knew he preferred Trudeau. I appreciated his frankness but I did not want him to resign. . . .

The new Agent-General for Quebec, Gilles Loiselle, came to see me this morning. We had met before, when he was a correspondent for the CBC in Paris. I met him once in London in that capacity. Latterly, he had been in the Department of Inter-Governmental Affairs in Quebec, and is a close friend of the No. 2 man in the Lévesque government, Claude Morin.* . . . I am sure that the new Agent-General will be satisfactory to get along with. . . . We must take advantage of his presence in London to discuss the problem of separatism with its implications. . . .

He said the cabinet liaison in Ottawa with Quebec is not, from that province's point of view, as it might be. He says that Marc Lalonde and André Ouellet are not good contacts. Jean Chrétien might have been, but some of his recent public criticisms of the Quebec government have not helped to make him a good intermediary. It is important that there be someone in the federal cabinet who could be a sort of unofficial contact. I will let Ottawa know what he said. It is too much to expect that Gilles Loiselle is not a separatist himself, although one can never tell. He did say that valuable federal cabinet contact could perhaps direct the development of policy accommodation which would be in the interests of Quebec and Canada as a whole. What this means precisely, at this stage, I do not know but will find out. . . .

Thursday, September 8, 1977

When Nell and I awoke this morning, before 6:00 a.m., we congratulated one another on our fortieth wedding anniversary. I had earlier given her a gift of a very fine brooch. Knowing my interest in books, she presented me with three. . . .

Saturday, September 10, 1977

Tony Abbott dropped in for a drink. As Minister for Consumer Affairs, he and his deputy, Sylvia Ostry, are on a departmental mission. Tony tells me his brother, Lou, on a sabbatical from the University of Guelph, has taken a house in Marlow on the Thames.[7] Lou is a boyhood contemporary of Paul's. When we lived at 448 Daly, next to the Irish Ambassador, Lou and Paul shot at John Hearne's window on the front door and later pelted stones at the Soviet Embassy. It took the then Minister of Finance and the Minister of National Health and Welfare to patch up matters. . . .

While Tony was here, Cindy Nicholas, the new conquerer of the English Channel,[8] her parents, and the official observer of the swim came to dinner. . . . She is studying biology at the University of Toronto. [I found her] a refined person with dutiful parents. . . . I took Cindy to the kitchen, where she met the staff. They were thrilled. Howard, the chef, took pictures. . . . I arranged for CAN-1 and John to take Cindy and her party from Folkestone to Gatwick [on] Monday morning. The heroine and Canada's "pride of the day" will then be on her way to Toronto's ticker-tape welcome.

Wednesday, September 14, 1977

I missed my swim today because I had so much to catch up on, as I worked in the library at home until the reception at Canada House. There I opened the exhibition entitled "The Queen and Canada," the purpose being to inform United Kingdom citizens of the continuous connection the monarch has with Canada. . . . The wife of the new Agent-General for British Columbia[9] bitterly complained, as she was going out, that there were no photographs of the Queen in British Columbia. She may have a point, although I think other provinces were not included in the exhibition, which was prepared not here but in Ottawa. . . .

Friday, September 16, 1977

I have just learned of the changes in the Trudeau cabinet. As strongly rumoured, Jean Chrétien succeeds Don Macdonald in Finance — the first francophone from Quebec to become

7. Their father, Doug, was a colleague of mine in the St Laurent government.
8. This young woman from Scarborough, Ontario, set a world record two days before for the fastest non-stop two-way swim of the English Channel.
9. Mrs Laurie Wallace

Minister of Finance. He will be well received. This means that, he is not likely to go after the Liberal leadership in Quebec. . . . Trudeau has shuffled twelve departments. To some it will be regarded as a major shifting. It can hardly be so regarded when only one addition is made to the cabinet. I have always thought that Trudeau makes a mistake in having so many changes. [Mackenzie] King made few shifts. Ministers were given the opportunity to share the limelight and become known. I gave my view on this aspect of cabinet-making to Trudeau several times. He didn't agree. . . .

Saturday, September 17, 1977

Would like to have slept in this morning. The force of habit and routine is not easily challenged. There was work on my desk awaiting my attention. Later on this cooler day, I visited three of my book haunts—Hatchard's, Foyle's and the Cathedral book shop. Some bargains at Foyle's. At Hatchard's, it is so evident that prices are accelerating. A new book on British foreign policy up to 1918 is priced at over $50. Too much even for me. . . .

Sunday, September 18, 1977

David Owen, the youngest foreign minister in Britain since Eden, has been at the Foreign Office for seven months. . . . He says he appointed Peter Jay to Washington "to project a more optimistic and confident image of Britain." He wanted to have someone "speak for his generation." "Balls," I say. . . .

Monday, September 19, 1977

On my way to the office this morning I stopped to talk to a school boy carrying a heavily loaded bag of school books. I had noticed him before. Today I asked him what was in the bag?—What school did he attend? A cheerful and bright reply indicated he was at the Brompton Oratory School. That, I said, is a fine school. Do you know who John Henry Newman is? He knew enough to say that he had founded a branch of the Oratorians. . . . Do you know how important a man Newman was? I asked my young friend. He nodded his head.

He understood that Newman was a very singular person.[10] . . . As I walked through Grosvenor Square, it occurred to me that in this ecumenical period, particularly when discussions are so penetrating between Anglicans and Catholics in this country, not much mention is made of Newman by either side. . . .

Ottawa has sent a copy of a letter which Peter Towe in Washington has transmitted to Henry Owen, the United States Aid Co-ordinator, for the follow-up activities of the Downing Street Summit. This I have today passed on to Sir John Hunt. In our note, we point out the unsatisfactory evolution of the international economic situation since the Summit. Clearly, targets are not going to be met. Unemployment in Canada has deteriorated. Youth unemployment was 12.5 per cent in early 1976. It has risen to 14.5 per cent in July of this year. These and other points show how important international co-operation will be. . . .

Tuesday, September 20, 1977

It is possible that we may have a visit from Quebec Minister, Robert Burns.* Loiselle has so informed the Foreign Office. It has been indicated that information of this kind should be passed on by the High Commissioner. No dates are given. Meanwhile we have offered the Quebec Agent-General full co-operation. The offer has been neither rejected nor accepted. We will follow established practice. . . . British authorities must be careful what is said to the Quebec spokesmen. The Foreign Office must not seem to give Quebec approval of its political objectives. The Foreign Office will act in a correct way. . . . Apparently, Lévesque had intended to come. Now, it is not likely that he will come before the end of the year, perhaps not before the beginning of next year. . . .

10. John Henry Newman won his reputation as a theologian and preacher while he was an Anglican clergyman. After leaving the Anglicans, he was ordained as a Catholic priest in 1847 and shortly afterward founded an oratory (a brotherhood of secular priests). The London branch became known as the Brompton Oratory. Pope Leo XIII made Newman a Cardinal in 1879. Since my student days, I had admired him as a theologian and a writer.

Wednesday, September 21, 1977

Vorster surprised everyone with his decision to have an election, two years ahead of time. He hopes the result will be an effective response to countries "meddling in the affairs of South Africa." This issue may win the election for him but it will not resolve the problem South Africa faces over apartheid. Increasingly, developed countries' sanctions will engulf South Africa's policy of racial discrimination. . . .

Thursday, September 22, 1977

I tried to get Joe Green[11] several times today without luck. I would like to have had him and his wife over. When visiting Canadians come unannounced, it is so difficult to re-arrange my programme. . . . Nell thinks I am too solicitous. The difficulty is that, while a diplomatic mission is set up to do a particular job in relation to a particular country, unless one looks after visiting firemen from home, the impression of what one does in one's job is not fully appreciated by one's compatriots. One is judged by the attention paid by the High Commissioner to Canadians and not by the importance of his job in Britain in relation to the government, the business community, the trade unions, the universities and so on. . . .

I accompanied Alastair Gillespie to a meeting with Tony Wedgwood Benn . . . which lasted almost two hours. Tony may be a controversial figure but I find him stimulating and bright. We examined the likely duration of oil supply and when nuclear power would become necessary as a substitute. . . . Why have such great errors been made in forecasting oil resources? Some beginning must be made on the strategy of conservation, insisted Benn. . . . The British think there is a United Nations role in these forecasts. . . . Tony Benn emphasized that the elements of major economic disaster are present. . . . As the exchange proceeded, I cogitated on the change in the role of diplomacy. No foreign policy problem has engaged my attention as has this issue, apart from Rhodesia. . . . Benn emphasized that the politics of uranium had to be looked at. Is uranium going to become an OPEC [style

11. A former cabinet colleague.

cartel]? . . . [Gillespie] pointed out that the Americans have not made much money out of their reactors—neither, of course, have we. I was interested in knowing that thirteen per cent of British electricity is now supplied through nuclear power. . . .

Saturday, September 24, 1977

Late this afternoon I attended a memorial service for the Rt. Hon. Sir Alexander Bustamente, Jamaica's first Prime Minister, at Westminster Abbey. . . . The other day I recorded that one heard little of Newman in the United Kingdom. I wrote too soon. There was a prayer composed by John Henry, Cardinal Newman: "O, Lord, support us all the day long of this troublous life, until the shades lengthen, and the evening comes, and the busy world is hushed, the fever of life is over and our work is done. Then, Lord, in thy mercy, grant us safe lodging, a holy rest, and peace at the last: through Jesus Christ our Lord, Amen." . . . Sitting on my left in the stalls at the Abbey was a young woman, the new Ambassador for Zambia.[12] "How young are you?" I said. She replied, "Zambia is a young country." We whispered about Rhodesia. We will talk further—the Abbey is no place to do extensive business. . . .

Sunday, September 25, 1977

I don't know if Ladbrokes [betting house] has opened its book to betting on the next Pope. They did prior to Cardinal Hume's selection as Archbishop of Westminster. . . . Now they are talking about prospects to succeed Paul VI. He will be eighty tomorrow. Who is papabili? Many are mentioned. One list varies from another. . . . My "Canadian" friend, now my own age of seventy-four, Cardinal Sebastiano Baggio and prefect of the Congregation of Bishops, is suggested. We knew him [as apostolic delegate] in Ottawa. I had some correspondence with him a year ago and we lunched together in Rome about four years ago. He is not regarded as a major theolo-

12. Lombe Phyllis Chibesakunda (born 1944), former solicitor-general of Zambia, served as Zambian high commissioner to London 1977-81.

gian, according to American gossip. My closest friend among the Italian cardinals is Sergio Pignedoli, head of the Secretariat for Non-Christian Religions. When I was foreign minister, he was Apostolic Delegate in Ottawa. We worked out together his two trips to Vietnam. . . .

Monday, September 26, 1977

Jamieson says we would be prepared to accept our Cyprus peace-keeping role in a new United Nations group in Rhodesia. . . . Smith has not accepted a United Nations force [but] it is interesting the way Jamieson, and in this I have done my share, persuaded Owen to abandon a Commonwealth force and accept a United Nations body. . . .

Tuesday, September 27, 1977

We have begun a good relationship with Loiselle, the Quebec Agent-General. If Burns comes, I am not overly pessimistic about the result. There may, however, be problems. . . . We thought all along that Burns and those with him would be essentially technical people, but the request contained information that in the party would be those anxious to discuss the E.E.C. referendum. Loiselle told the Foreign Office they would want to see at least four persons of senior cabinet minister level: Michael Foot, Peter Shore, Shirley Williams, and Tony Benn. The four United Kingdom ministers had taken a negative position in the 1975 [Common Market] referendum. It won't be easy for the Foreign Office to secure appointments with ministers on short notice and Loiselle may have anticipated this. We will tell Quebec House that, pursuant to normal practice, a High Commission representative will accompany the provincial visitors on all calls. . . . We had told Loiselle earlier that, if Quebec ministers or senior officers at any level call at the Foreign Office, the practice is for the appropriate High Commission officer to attend. This is the course we follow with other provinces. . . . When we speak to Loiselle again, he may not be overly pleased. We could have repercussions, if Burns makes too much of the issue of a High Commission presence. We will insist on it. The British certainly favour a federal presence. I have asked Ottawa if they expect me to be more flexible. . . .

When I was External Affairs Minister, I had to spend much time sitting next to the same person at every luncheon and every dinner, because most of one's social life was confined to the diplomatic corps. In London, most parties are made up of a sprinkling of the cabinet, representatives of the diplomatic corps, citizens in general, trade unionists and businessmen and, on this account, [are] more interesting. When we have a luncheon or a dinner, I always try to get a minister, senior or junior, someone from the diplomatic corps — not too many — and others from the wider community — professors, clergymen, actors, newspaper people, top labour leaders, businessmen, students and so on. This is as it should be. How can a representative of a country understand the country to which he is accredited, if he ties himself to one group?

Thursday, September 29, 1977

I had a long chat with the new Ambassador for Zambia, whom I had met Saturday last at Westminster Abbey. My reports indicate that Kaunda may have trouble in next year's elections. Because of Rhodesia and the sanctions, Zambia's economic plight is serious. The front-line presidents are not about to impose their will on Rhodesia's successor to Smith. The Ambassador assured me that the choice rests with Rhodesia. Why cannot more pressure be brought to bear on Vorster and on Smith? I assured her there was an almost universal desire to see the one-person-one-vote principle become a fact, as well as Smith's replacement. Cannot more be done, she asked? I told her that everything short of war was now in play. Confidence in the United Kingdom-United States package was developing. Owen was doing his best at the United Nations. I think, when the young lady Ambassador entered her Daimler, she had more confidence in the outcome. . . .

Friday, September 30, 1977

After breakfast, Nell and I embarked from Heathrow for Glasgow and a three-day visit to Scotland and the distilleries owned by Hiram Walker's. . . .

Saturday, October 1, 1977

I had talked so much about St. Andrew's [Scotland] and was so pleased to visit it again with Nell. . . . [Because] the Queen Mother was in town, the streets were lined with uniformed girl students. Dominated by St. Andrew's University, where I had lunched . . . last year, the community of stone buildings was a picture to behold. The baldish golf course, at the head of that game's hierarchy, was as I observed last year—less picturesque than the Essex or the Royal Ottawa. . . .

Sunday, October 2, 1977

We went to mass at Pluscarden Abbey, near Elgin and Moray. This is now a Benedictine Abbey of the twentieth century. It was a thirteenth-century monastery. The high mass in the ancient chapel was sung in Latin and English. It made one wonder why we have dropped the Latin, so beautiful to one trained in the Latin chant. . . . How inferior the vernacular is! The monk who welcomed us . . . gratefully accepted two twelve-year-old bottles of Ballantine Scotch. Like Nell's aunt, who had been a Good Shepherd cloistered nun for sixty-five years, the liquor was taken as a possible "keep warm" stimulant. When Nell would visit her aunt at the Sisters of the Good Shepherd in Toronto, she always took along a bottle of rye to help Sister Mary of St. Martin meet the chill blasts of cold winter. . . .

After mass, we drove on to the Milton Duff Distillery, another Hiram Walker component. . . . Ishbel MacDonald[13] joined us at a buffet lunch within the distillery precincts. . . . Shortly, she expects to be televised in the Lossiemouth house Ramsay had built for her mother. Ishbel lives in it. . . . She had visited Canada with her father many times . . . [and] she remembered when Mackenzie King had said "which would you like to be named after you, a lake or a mountain?" . . .

We returned from Scotland the following day.

13. Daughter of Ramsay MacDonald and Malcolm's sister.

Tuesday, October 4, 1977

Nell and I attended a reception at the home of the Agent-General for Quebec at 6 Ilchester. Loiselle had officers of the Imperial Life Insurance Company of Canada as guests. The chairman of the board of this company, Mr. Castonguay,[14] [is] the former Minister of Health in the government of Bourassa. . . . The last time I saw Castonguay was at the Victoria Constitutional Conference in 1971 [when] I thought he looked so dour . . . [but] tonight he was all smiles and extremely agreeable. I mentioned how inflexible I had found Bourassa and him to be at that time. His reply was that the position they had taken regarding patriation of the constitution and entrenchment of language rights was the only position the Quebec government could take in the light of Lévesque's growing ascendancy. This could be the case, but I doubt it. Castonguay was hopeful that the separatists will not succeed. The possibility that Claude Ryan may become Liberal leader is not distasteful to him. . . .

Wednesday, October 5, 1977

The Secretary-General of the United Nations has named an Indian general to constitute the United Nations presence in Rhodesia. It was an Indian general who succeeded Tommy Burns[15] as head of the United Nations force in the Middle East in the fifties. Tommy said the other day we should not join a peace-keeping force in Rhodesia. He wants someone else to take this on next time. . . . He thinks our soldiers would be unacceptable, because they are white. Also, our soldiers would be regarded as enemies by the white Rhodesians. How valid is this argument? Most countries have been against Smith and his Rhodesian policy. Certainly we could not join the United Nations force in Rhodesia, if it were established without the approval of African countries. . . .

Christopher Young and Nick Hills of Southam newspapers lunched with me at the residence. Young had just returned from Rhodesia and gave me his impressions. He thinks the

14. Claude Castonguay
15. The Canadian general.

white Rhodesians would not be happy with Canadian inclusion in a United Nations peace force. . . .

Friday, October 7, 1977

The American Ambassador in Ottawa, Tom Enders, who has been doing a great deal of speaking in Canada, proposed yesterday that there should be a common market arrangement between Canada and the United States. This must represent the wishes of Carter and is likely part of the continental energy objective of the United States. As soon as I saw a report of what Enders said, I thought of George Ball's book. He said it was inevitable that Canada would become integrated, in its own interest, with the United States.[16] This, of course, would be a mistake and is not in the cards. President Eisenhower asked Lionel Chevrier once when we were "coming in." What would be the effect of a common market arrangement? I doubt if such an arrangement with the United States alone is in Canadian interests. Freer trade, yes — more ad hoc arrangements like the Canada-United States Auto Pact.[17] It will be interesting to see what attitude the government takes on the Enders' speech, if any. . . .

Saturday, October 8, 1977

Late today, I talked to Warren Allmand.* He thinks the decision taken on Bill 101[18] and the federal government's attitude of [not] testing its constitutional validity was sound. To have proceeded by way of a constitutional reference under the Supreme Court Act was fraught with dangers. If the Supreme Court of Canada had found the bill to be *ultra vires* in essential parts, Lévesque would have responded by asserting the Court, made up essentially of English-speaking judges

16. George Ball had served as the American under-secretary of state from 1961 to 1966 and U.S. permanent representative to the United Nations in 1968. His view of Canadian-American relations can be found in R. H. Wasenburg, ed., *Canadian-American Interdependence: How Much? Proceedings of the 10th Annual University of Windsor Seminar on Canadian-American Relations* (Windsor 1970), pp. 27-34.
17. Signed in January 1965.
18. Quebec legislation which promoted the primacy of the French language in Quebec.

from outside Quebec, was biased. Another reason for Quebec to become an independent state would have been the cry. . . .

My Nell does nobly. Many of the so-called experienced socialite wives in the cabinet and elsewhere thought she would find our present life a bore. The fact is she does her job infinitely better than most of her contemporaries. She has humour and character—qualities often lacking in the woman "born to the trade." Anne Armstrong, the former United States Ambassador, [once said] . . . that Nell was the perfect wife for our present assignment. I think so too. But, how can we tire and be bored? I often retire into my private thoughts, when confronted by certain people and on certain social occasions. Even the best race-horse has his off day. A good team, of course, helps. . . .

Sunday, October 9, 1977

Denis Healey, the Chancellor of the Exchequer, will preside at the NEDDY Council[19] tomorrow. . . . I wish we had this arrangement in Canada. If Walter Gordon had listened,[20] we could have. When he brought in the proposal for an Economic Council, I pushed for a NEDDY structure, involving the Minister of Finance, as well as representatives of labour and management. Walter thought otherwise. In Diefenbaker's time, I had urged on Donald Fleming the NEDDY concept. Trudeau, who has had difficulties in getting tripartite meetings, would have been freed from this failure. Joe Morris would automatically have been available for the three-way discussion [with management and government]. . . . It works well here. . . .

Monday, October 10, 1977

Jake Warren, my predecessor, now in charge of our trade negotiations,[21] arrives this morning. I will be with him to meet Edmund Dell, the Minister of Trade and Industry, and senior

19. NEDDY or NED, the National Economic Development Council, was established in 1961 to advise the British government on the planning of the economy and was comprised of representatives of business, industry, and government.
20. When he was minister of finance from 1963 to 1965.
21. As co-ordinator.

officials. In the background of trade policy is the M.T.N. in Geneva [which] we are anxious to see succeed. . . . Canada seeks improved access to export markets [and] want[s] to get an agreement which will improve prospects for overall reciprocity. A plan to give reciprocity between the United States, the E.E.C. and Japan would help Canada. Sectoral agreements could provide substantial help for us. We propose the elimination of duties five per cent and less (with exceptions) and that the E.E.C. accept the sector arrangement for access to markets and security of supply for forest products and non-ferrous metals. . . . If the E.E.C. does not accept this, we will be obliged to expand the list of exceptions and oppose any effort to build into the GATT additional rights and obligations. . . . The British do not see an agreement in the offing on tariff cutting, on the basis of this time-table. They think the United States is moving away from a radical linear cut. . . .

Robert Burns of the Quebec cabinet, Loiselle (the Agent-General) and two Quebec deputy ministers came to see me at 6:00 p.m. They had been interviewing officials and others on the workings of the E.E.C. referendum of two years ago, which settled the United Kingdom relationship with that body. Burns and company saw Michael Foot, the only minister interviewed. He told them that if he were in Canada, he would be against separation and Quebec independence. He pointed to differences in the Quebec referendum arrangements with those used in the United Kingdom. The latter were less restrictive on the permitted participation in debate and financial contribution. Foot emphasized the importance of all-party consultation. The Quebec referendum would lose significance, if not structured on integrity and openness.

Burns and I had a friendly chat. I said he was proceeding on the wrong lines in maintaining that Lévesque wanted a sovereignty-association arrangement. He did not adequately define these terms. We will never separate, I argued. Mildly, Burns replied, "Not if we can work out a relationship which comprehends a sovereignty-association." It seems to me that, if Lévesque and his colleagues are handled in a friendly manner, we can pass this crisis. Burns said Quebec's contact with the federal cabinet was not good. He volunteered, as a good contact, [Francis] Fox, the Solicitor-General, now in

London on security matters. Burns does not seem to get along with Marc Lalonde. The right contact is important. I must think about this.

Tuesday, October 11, 1977

The meeting Jake [Warren] and I had with the Secretary of State for Trade, Edmund Dell, was good. It was forthright. I emphasized that all parties to the GATT negotiations must bear in mind decisions [in favour of freer trade] taken by the Seven at the Economic Summit. . . . Dell observed that Canada has a highly protected industry and the question is how to fit it in with GATT. Our problem was unique. . . . At some point, we must decide to call whatever is achieved a success. Otherwise, we will close the door on the world trading system. . . .

Wednesday, October 12, 1977

The Canadian media like to bring up embarrassing questions to Trudeau on the monarchy. A reporter had said the Queen was not popular among Quebecers. Trudeau responded by saying that the Queen had been well-received by Quebecers at the opening of the Olympic Games. Moreover, the Quebec Premier would attend a dinner for the Queen during her Ottawa visit. These matters do not disturb the Queen as I learned yesterday and as I know from an earlier experience. Meanwhile, we are getting the residence ready for her visit tomorrow night, at what I suppose will be the largest purely Canadian party for the Queen — certainly since I have been here. Alison Ignatieff spent yesterday learning her duties as the Queen's Canadian lady-in-waiting. . . . To accommodate the one hundred and fifty Canadians who have been invited, we will use the dining room downstairs as well as the two salons upstairs. This is a good arrangement. . . .

We had a dry-run this morning at the residence for the Queen's reception tomorrow at 12 Upper Brook. . . . We went through the anticipated scenario beginning with Nell and me greeting the Queen at the front door. For the purpose, Miss Gadd was the Queen, the Deputy High Commissioner — the Duke of Edinburgh, Lorne Green — the Lord Chamberlain. . . . I have learned from the British, who know how to mix in a little humour. . . . It is natural that there should be some butterflies about. . . .

Thursday, October 13, 1977

The security people at Buckingham Palace were in early today at the residence, surveying the situation for tonight, as was the Queen's secretary and public relations officer. Nothing is missed when the Queen moves from one event to another. When I left the residence this morning, I kidded the butler, asking how many times today would he try on his white tie, before the arrival of Her Majesty, the Queen. I was not a little annoyed, when early this morning I received a telephone call from one of the guests who wanted to know, should his wife curtsey to the Queen. Surely the question could have been put later in the day—surely it wasn't necessary to call me. . . .

The Queen and Prince Philip honoured Nell and me . . . when they came for a reception prior to Her Majesty's departure tomorrow for Canada. It was a successful evening in every way, the Queen staying half an hour over the indicated time. She was in good form, happy and relaxed. . . .

Friday, October 14, 1977

I saw the Queen and her husband off for Canada at Heathrow at 12:30 today. . . . The Queen told me how much she enjoyed our party last night. It was a happy affair, she said, and well organized. She particularly liked meeting so many Canadians who represented a wide spectrum of Canadians in London. "I like talking to people," said the Queen. . . .

For the first time in many years, Martin Charteris, her secretary, was not with her as she boarded the Canadian Armed Forces Boeing 707, as it soared over the runway. Martin and Lady Charteris were at the reception last night. He was filled with emotion on his last day of service. . . .[22]

As the royal couple left the enclosure at the special departure section, I said to Prince Philip, please say hello for me to my Prime Minister. He looked my way and gave me an

22. He became provost of Eton College in 1978 and retains the title of permanent lord-in-waiting to the Queen.

understanding look, a meaningful one. I understood what he was thinking. . . .

Saturday, October 15, 1977

The Times story on the welcome to the Queen in Ottawa irritated me somewhat. The mood and problems of the nation are regarded as dampening the occasion. Ninety per cent of Ottawa have been polled in favour of the monarchy. That is the real story. . . . Trudeau's off-the-cuff remarks on the monarchy reach the royal ears, as they have others. His flippancy is not against the Queen, but it sounds that way. He is not the only Prime Minister to have sounded off, at least privately. King was not above a complaint, although in 1939 he organized the most extended of all crown visits. At no time were his public comments indiscreet, as I am afraid Pierre's have been, on occasion. . . . Trudeau's problems with Quebec were in his mind, when he wanted a limited visit this time. His restraint is understandable. The Duke should understand the delicate operation of the Prime Minister at this particular time. I am sure he does. What likely irritates the Queen's husband is the Prime Minister's style of appraising the monarchy in relation to Canada. . . .

Monday, October 17, 1977

The Queen spoke on television last night in Canada. No reference was made to Quebec's desire to secede. Lévesque had expressed the hope that the Queen would not make an appeal for unity. What else could she do? She is the head of state and acts on the advice of her ministers. Are they not to appeal for unity? The Queen could be helpful in the effort to achieve national unity at this crucial hour, just as she is a bulwark at present against American domination and a reminder of national identity. . . . Lévesque recognizes the Queen as a respected and gracious woman, who should not be used as a symbol for political purpose. Nonsense, that is what the Queen is for. . . .

Just as I anticipated, after last week's discussions when Jake Warren was here, we have a speech from Walter Gordon. He said on Wednesday that "sharp tariff cuts would be devastating to Canada's secondary manufacturing industry." He was speaking at York University. He was, of course, aware that Canadian officials were conducting tariff negotiations in Geneva. His ears must have been burning when he thinks of the discussions Jake and I had with the Minister of Trade and Industry and his officials. Walter went on to say that a lack of consensus between government and others in Canada was one reason for our declining prosperity. . . .

Winston Churchill, MP, and the late Prime Minister's grandson, called me again about his Ottawa visit. . . . Trudeau is more difficult to see than the Pope on occasion. The fact that the visitor is a grandson of the world's great World War II champion doesn't fizz Trudeau a bit. . . .

Tuesday, October 18, 1977

Lord Amory thought we had a good meeting of the board of the Foundation for Canadian Studies. . . . In accordance with my custom, the members of the board lunched with me at 12 Upper Brook. The Deputy High Commissioner was present as well. We had a good exchange on books. . . . Lord Amory thinks that novel reading is a waste of time. Certainly I am not a novel reader. In my case, it is largely because I don't have the time. I read much, but mostly philosophy, history, and biography, all of which I find more useful and more interesting. . . .

Wedneday, October 19, 1977

The Queen opened [Canada's] Parliament yesterday and repeated her call for unity. She wants all Canadians to rededicate themselves to the well-being of all, as she herself dedicates herself, as head of state, to Canada. . . .

Thursday, October 20, 1977

The tabloids in London, this time the *Daily Express*, have put out some evil stories. One on Lévesque begins: "The Queen's visit to Canada is certainly fetching the worms out of their wood." It is said we are putting over a rotten image to the rest of the world. Apparently, the Queen and the Duke of Edinburgh turned a wheel-of-fortune when they were on a tour of the museum. To the Queen, it said she was to die in a ship's fire and that Philip was to be assassinated. How ridiculous can one get! The organizers of the wheel-of-fortune might well have shown better judgment—the wheel might well have been rigged beforehand to avoid embarrassment. Lévesque's dress is criticized as is his smoking in the presence of the Queen. This is rubbish. . . .

Friday, October 21, 1977

After reading telegrams and dictating my daily record, Jack Clyne[23] . . . and I proceeded to Cambridge . . . to form an Anglo-Canadian Institute for Legal Studies at Cambridge. . . .

At the opening of the discussion, the President of Queen's College, Dr. Bowett, explained why we had foregathered and emphasized that the proposal of an institute had come from me. I explained the idea arose out of my experience as a student in law, doing graduate work, at Cambridge in 1928-29. I wanted other Canadian lawyers to profit by a similar experience. . . . I had always felt that Cambridge and what it stands for would emerge as the compelling argument. This, I think, is what happened.

We were taken to Evensong at King's. Its great and ancient chapel was an inspiration and a wonder to all. The boys' choir, of course, is well-known. Walking back to Trinity to dress for dinner with Estey[24] and Evans,[25] the former said, "the Cambridge side is underselling itself. What a splendid idea Cambridge inspired the High Commissioner to propose." . . .

Saturday, October 22, 1977

Offered breakfast in our rooms, Estey, Evans, and I preferred the dining hall with the students, with whom we talked and exchanged views on the Cambridge and Trinity of today and yesterday. No time for newspapers and news of yesterday. . . .

23. J. V. Clyne, former chairman of MacMillan Bloedel from 1957 to 1973 and former justice of the Supreme Court of British Columbia. He became the president of the Canadian Institute for Advanced Legal Studies.
24. W. Z. (Bud) Estey was the former chief justice of Ontario who had just been appointed to the Supreme Court of Canada.
25. Gregory Evans, chief justice, High Court of Ontario.

The Canadians at the meeting, after reviewing the entire package in a private session, reported to the Cambridge professors that plans would proceed in Canada to organize attendance at the first Institute course in 1979. . . . I am very pleased with the results of all our efforts [which] . . . will give Canadian lawyers, judges, [and] government and lawyer officials a valuable association with one of the great universities of the world. . . . This may prove to be one of my major contributions as Canadian High Commissioner. . . .

Monday, October 24, 1977

It was generally assumed six months ago that South Africa's dilemma would hold until the end of the century. I have expressed the view that it would mature in half that time. Now it looks as though it is almost in full bloom, because of American active interest in the recent crackdown on a free press and free expression in South Africa. South Africa will face the Security Council tomorrow. . . . The demand is put forward for a mandatory arms embargo. . . . This is the first time sanctions have moved from the threat stage to real possibility. . . .

I asked Stan Carlson [of the High Commission], who is following the Rhodesian matter for me, to join in a discussion on the peace-keeping role for Canada in Rhodesia. Falls[26] thinks Don Jamieson's statement that we would participate only if we could be relieved of our obligation in Cyprus, was a device intended to bring pressure on Cyprus for a solution. The Admiral thinks that we could put in a fighting battalion in Rhodesia, if called on to do so. . . . I expressed my well-known view that we did not suffer by willingly participating in peace-keeping. This did not mean that we should not put forward conditions for participation. I don't agree with Stan Carlson that David Owen had been brushed off over Jamieson's unwillingness to participate in a Commonwealth Rhodesian Force. I, myself, when I first saw Owen, had pointed out the inadequacy of such a peace-keeping operation. My view was that Jamieson had convinced Owen that a United Nations force would be more acceptable and less dangerous. . . .

26. Admiral A. H. Falls, chief of the defence staff.

Friday, October 28, 1977

Loiselle has made contact with Canadian francophone students at the University of London. This information has been related to me by the president of the Canadian student body. Loiselle may try to create a separatist cell. I don't think I have any authority to intervene. . . . What he could do in Canada, he is free to do here. Free discussion is more effective in the long run. . . .

I had a chat with John Turner, who has been here for the Crown Life Association's company meeting. John told me the circumstances of his resignation from the government and the problems he had, from his point of view, with Trudeau. I mentioned how surprised I was that he resigned. I could understand his frustration but wondered if the course he had taken was, from his political point of view, a wise one. He had no doubt about the wisdom of the course he chose. . . .

Monday, October 31, 1977

The new American Ambassador, Kingman Brewster, formerly President at Yale, made his first call this morning. . . . Brewster had a dinner recently when Kissinger was the guest of honour, presumably on his way back from Bonn, where he had gone to see Chancellor Schmidt. He thought Kissinger had lost a lot of weight and some of his halo. I never found Kissinger with a halo. I suggested that the people who knew him well in office, during the period of adulation, may have seen an assertion of importance, less apparent to those who saw him, like me, only from time to time. He agreed, however, that Kissinger was an outstanding Secretary of State. . . .

XVII

November – December 1977

THE SEPARATIST ISSUE CONTINUED to bother me, particularly when René Lévesque paid a visit to Paris and the French government received him as a head of state. Later, I had a visit from Jacques Parizeau, the finance minister in Lévesque's government.

During the first week of November, I went to Eire to visit my colleague, Ed Ritchie, the Canadian ambassador in Dublin. The intractability of the Irish problem impressed me again.

The year ended with a Christmas visit by my son and his family and the happy news that Mary Anne, my daughter, was expecting her second child.

Wednesday, November 2, 1977

Sonny [Ramphal] is not happy with his liaison at the Foreign Office. He told me that he found Owen not as generous with his time and collaboration. This is regrettable [and] it is not the first time Sonny has complained. As Secretary General, he holds an important office, representing as he does the countries of the Commonwealth. The liaison with him should not be less than the collaboration with the State Department. Moreover, Sonny could be of great help in the Rhodesian negotiations. . . .

Thursday, November 3, 1977

René Lévesque was received at Orly Airport yesterday by the Prime Minister of France. The ceremonial went the limit. . . . In Lévesque's speech before the Chamber of Deputies, he said, "a new country will soon appear democratically on the map somewhere, where up to now a federal state has been willing to see only a province among others." The generality of these words lends itself to more than one interpretation. . . . It will be interesting to read what Loiselle says when he appears before the Royal Institute of International Affairs tomorrow. He will say no less than Lévesque but perhaps he will have more muffled words. He will likely use the phrase "sovereignty-association," which is the language of confusion, intrigue and obfuscation. Thank goodness, I will be in Dublin. . . .

I attended the Opening of Parliament this morning. The Queen, after her long trip home yesterday, I thought, looked tired this morning. One, however, admires her devotion to duty. . . .

The British waste no time in starting parliamentary proceedings. After the Queen's speech, they went into immediate debate. The Prime Minister appealed to all in the land for necessary support on pay restraint. He obviously had the miners in mind.[1] . . . Jim had a lot of fun dangling before members the date of an election — spring, fall, or even next year. . . .

Friday, November 4, 1977

Nell and I took a short flight from London to Dublin to visit our ambassador, A. E. Ritchie.

Gwen Ritchie gave us a warm welcome to this magnificent house. Neither of us had seen it before. It lies by the Irish Sea, brightened tonight by the lights of buildings along its shore. The house, once owned by the brother of a former Prime Minister of Ulster, is our finest mission property. . . . We contrasted 12 Upper Brook with this spacious house. No envy, merely a recognition of the fact. . . . The library is a gem, fully comparable to Vincent Massey's at Batterwood [near Port Hope]. . . .

At the dinner table, we reviewed many problems. Ed was interested in Loiselle's talk today at noon to the Royal Institute of International Affairs. [Loiselle] . . . at least implied that

1. The day before, the miners had voted to reject the government's incomes policy.

Quebec did not want to "leave" Canada. As a sovereign nation it would work out practical economic and financial arrangements, which would at least give constructive unity. . . . The Quebec Agent-General was milder than Lévesque in Paris. Loiselle had fumbled questions at the end of his presentation. . . .

Saturday, November 5, 1977

Nell and I went into Dublin with Ed's chauffeur at the wheel. . . . We visited the chapel at Blackrock College and talked to the boys who had gathered around Ed's car. Blackrock — a name I had known so well in my student days at St. Alexander's [College].[2] . . .

Monday, November 7, 1977

What is clear in Eire at present . . . [is that] unity of the island remains the wish. It is a long way off. Dublin would not wish to be saddled with the North's conflict. Many want the British to leave and let the northerners resolve their problem. Power-sharing remains a goal. The North's majority wants continued provincial status with the United Kingdom. Roy Mason and Jim Callaghan would prefer a peaceful agreement among the northerners, which would permit British forces to withdraw. The circle persists in being vicious. Time, however, is inexorably patient and solution-giving. . . .

Tuesday, November 8, 1977

I called on Lord Carrington in his office at the House of Lords this afternoon. It is ironic that the Leader of the Opposition in the Lords has a better office than the Leader of the Conservative party in the House of Commons. Lord Peart's office must be grander than Jim Callaghan's office in the Commons. Jim, however, has a lot of space at No. 10. . . . [Carrington] was in South Africa recently and saw Vorster. For Britain to agree to wide economic sanctions would not only paralyse South Africa but Britain as well, and many

2. St Alexander's was a *collège classique* run by the Fathers of the Holy Ghost who also ran Blackrock College.

countries in the industrial West. David Owen acknowledges this.

What seems to trouble Carrington is the fervour of American policy on human rights. I pointed out that that policy represented growing opinion all over. . . . White and black in the United States and in most countries think the time has come when differences in colour should matter no longer. Nothing would stop the continuing emancipation of blacks. . . .

Thursday, November 10, 1977

I doubt if Trudeau will make any representations to France over the Lévesque visit. After the de Gaulle visit,[3] I took the position that France-Canada relations were normal. My statement was partially designed to ensure that very thing. It was not, however, well received by Trudeau or Marchand at the time. It looks, however, that Trudeau is now doing exactly what I did ten years ago. He may be right, as I am sure I was when I took this course following the de Gaulle speech of "Vive Le Québec Libre" in Montreal. . . . Trudeau is reflecting, I believe, the judgment of External Affairs, that we should not make a diplomatic incident of the Lévesque visit to Paris. Don Jamieson, nevertheless, has said that we will seek clarification of Giscard d'Estaing's reference of support by France for Quebec [and] . . . about the proposed exchange of annual meetings between Lévesque and [Raymond] Barre, the French Prime Minister.

Gérard Pelletier, our main man in Paris, has reported that the honours paid Lévesque were not the equivalent of what would have been extended to a head of state. Nevertheless, I don't think we can deny that the Lévesque visit has introduced a new phase in French-Canada relations. We, at any rate, have every reason to doubt the integrity of France in her relations with us. . . .

Sunday, November 13, 1977

For the third time, I took part in the cenotaph service on Whitehall at the stroke of Big Ben's signal of the hour of 11:00 a.m. The Queen, members of the royal family, the

3. In 1967.

Prime Minister, members of the cabinet and High Commissioners laid wreaths. . . .

Afterwards we were invited to a reception by the Secretary of State and Mrs. Owen. Present also were the Agents-General [of the provinces], whom I presented to Owen [and] it interested me to see how eager Loiselle was to meet the foreign minister. One imagined what may have been in the Agent-General's mind. David mentioned his gratitude for Trudeau's letter, wishing him well on the Rhodesian initiative. How regrettable was the reception the French had given Lévesque. He wondered if there was anything I thought the United Kingdom should do to express its displeasure. I did not think so. It was good of him to offer. . . .

Monday, November 14, 1977

Mark MacGuigan has come to stay for a few days . . . and lunched with me at the residence. Politics is a queer business. This I had confirmed from the account of the parliamentary situation in Canada, given me by Mark. Jean Chrétien, well-accepted as a Minister of Finance, may have problems with the impression he creates on television. Jean is folksy, but one wonders what impression he makes on the business community via television. My impression, of course, is that, important as that section may be, the question is what does John Doe think. There are problems in the cabinet as, of course, there always are. . . .

Tuesday, November 15, 1977

Word has come that Nyerere believes the Anglo-American initiative in Rhodesia must be supported . . . [and] is concerned with information that the British plan may be rejected by the Liberation Front leaders or some of them and by Smith. This will play into Smith's hands. . . . Nyerere wants us to see Dr. Owen and get Ottawa to support the United Kingdom-United States package. In effect, I suppose, Trudeau's letter to Owen goes a long way to meet his wish. Nyerere is prepared to take Russian connivance with Nkomo to the Security Council. He could neutralize Smith on this point. . . .

Wednesday, November 16, 1977

In answer to my query to the department yesterday, Ottawa says it is reluctant to become embroiled in debates between Nyerere and other front-line presidents and Owen. We will, therefore, not become involved in a covert effort to strengthen Owen's hand in the debate. We are further advised that the analysis offered by Nyerere has disturbing implications in spite of its plausibility. We will, in the meantime, enquire of the British whether Nyerere's views accord with their own perceptions. . . .

Monday, November 21, 1977

The Canada Club dinner in the River Room at the Savoy Hotel, with Lord Mountbatten as guest of honour, was a great success. It was the largest meeting since I have been High Commissioner. In introducing Mountbatten, I asserted that he was a great Englishman, recognized throughout the world, particularly by those who served under him in naval forces and combined operations. . . . When I sat down, after introducing Mountbatten, he said to me, quite genuinely I am sure, he did not realize before how highly regarded he was in Canada, where, after all, his associations, apart from the Quebec Conference during the war, . . . were peripheral. [In his speech] he overlooked his part in the Dieppe Raid, but stoutly defended it as a necessary reconnaissance exercise. . . .

Tuesday, November 22, 1977

Our Ambassador in Paris, Gérard Pelletier, called on the Secretary General of the French foreign office and left with him a mémoire asking for clarification of certain aspects of Lévesque's visit to France. We will want to have an explanation of what the French meant when they agreed to annual visits by the heads of government of France and Quebec, and also what Giscard d'Estaing meant by the pledged support of France for Quebec in present circumstances. . . .

Paul Tellier[4] . . . lunched with . . . me at the residence. [He] had come from a meeting with Michael Foot, the Lord

4. Deputy secretary to the cabinet, particularly charged with formulating a response to the separatist challenge in Quebec.

Privy Seal, to discuss procedures used by the British in the referendum on the E.E.C. Tellier assured me a bill would be introduced to provide for enabling referendum legislation in Canada. It is still possible that there might be a national referendum. A number of options are under study. One would involve a federal election in the spring or autumn. It might be followed by a national referendum. A strong Trudeau majority in Quebec would have considerable influence on Lévesque and his separatists. One of Trudeau's election issues will involve a programme for constitutional change. It is remotely possible that Jean Chrétien might seek the provincial Liberal leadership. Tellier thought this would mean a loss to the federal Liberal party. No other strong provincial leader has emerged as yet. Quebec must be given an alternative to Lévesque. . . .

Wednesday, November 23, 1977

Our drive into East Anglia was interesting. Cambridge, of course, is now thought of as East Anglian. Around noon, we signed the register at Maid's Head Hotel, Tombland, Norwich. The Lord Mayor, wearing chain and all, greeted me at the hotel and drove me to the Royal Hotel in his Daimler for my Rotary Club engagement. . . . Apparently, the speaker originally billed for the Rotary luncheon was a Commissioner of the Boy Scouts. The gentleman who thanked me for my speech was not aware that the actual speaker was to be the *Canadian* High Commissioner. . . .

Friday, November 25, 1977

I [went] to Heathrow to welcome Canada's Secretary of State, John Roberts. On the way in, John and I discussed the problems of bilingualism, very much his concern as Secretary of State. He is of the view that we should now report achievement in the bilingual field and reduce the pace, encouraged certainly to do so by Lévesque's indifference. There remains, of course, the problem of furthering French culture and teaching in provinces other than Quebec. . . .

John was one of those who wanted an early election this September. He hopes that economic conditions in Canada will not have deteriorated to the point of weakening Trudeau's chances in the next federal election. On the separation issue, John is of the view, as I am, that it will not succeed. After a referendum or Lévesque's defeat, there will, of course, be a hard core of separatists. Their activities may be of a more dangerous and disturbing type.

Ian Smith may have pulled the rug from under David Owen and the British government. In any event, he has invited the African nationalist groups in Rhodesia to confer with him on a constitutional settlement. Now he accepts the principle of one-man-one-vote, on condition that there will be safeguards for the whites. Smith said he hoped to begin discussions in Salisbury next week with Sithole and other tribal and nationalist leaders. . . .

John and Mrs. Roberts lunched with us. As he told me yesterday on arrival, he had come for a few days to "collect his thoughts." Now he learns he may have to return for a cabinet meeting on Tuesday [because] Trudeau wants to discuss the programme which Tellier outlined to me last Tuesday. It had to do with federal proposals for constitutional reform. . . . But what is important is to determine how far it is desirable to go on [the] division of powers.[5] Senate reform, including the suspensory veto, entrenchment of language rights, changes in the Supreme Court of Canada and such matters are relatively easy changes to accept.

John tells me that some of his cabinet colleagues attend only when matters in which they are concerned are on the agenda. The reason for this lies in the fact that most matters are previously discussed in the cabinet committee on priorities. This looseness existed in a mild form when I was in Trudeau's cabinet. It is a dangerous development which the Prime Minister should stop. John thinks the elections could come in April. A better time would be in June [when] people are happy. . . . He has apprehensions about his own seat. I gave him assurances on the score. Trudeau will not be turned down as long as the Quebec challenge persists. . . .

Monday, November 28, 1977

Lévesque's Agent-General in London is losing no time in popularizing his provincial government. On Saturday night he had all the chauffeurs in for a drink. I was returning from

5. Between the federal government and the provinces.

a swim at the Grosvenor when my man, John Rowan, and his wife were on their way to the separatist drink at Quebec House. I kidded John and, of course, he kidded me. This morning John told me that it was a good party. They had presented Loiselle with flowers and Loiselle had spoken of me in high terms. . . .

Derek Amory has written to say how much he enjoyed the Canada Club Dinner the other night. He writes: "Mountbatten was courageous to recall Dieppe — head on — as it were. Military historians will agree, I expect, that a reconnaissance in force before the invasion of the continent was justified. Whether that one was as well planned as it might have been is another question. But Mountbatten was brave to acknowledge that he was responsible, and he was a great war leader." Mountbatten wasted no words when he spoke to the Canada Club a week ago. Dieppe, he said, was essential to a successful invasion. . . .

I lunched with [my deputy] Christian Hardy, who had as his guest D'Iberville Fortier, our Ambassador in Rome. . . . D'Iberville is not happy, nor is Christian, about [Jean-Pierre] Goyer as Don Jamieson's French/African ministerial associate. It would be better to create a new minister of state for foreign or external relations and assigned to francophone questions under Jamieson. We had a long discussion on what reforms in the constitution could be anticipated at home. They see no problem in the distribution of powers. Like Trudeau, I see great difficulty and danger of erosion of the taxing powers of the federal government. I don't want to enhance the powers of the provinces at the expense of Canadian nationhood. . . .

Wednesday, November 30, 1977

It looks as though there will be agreement on the resumption of shipments of Canadian uranium to the E.E.C. The holdup has arisen over disagreement with our insistence on stronger safeguards. Don Jamieson and Alastair Gillespie have been engaged in negotiating the new safeguards with the Energy Commission of the E.E.C. in Ottawa. It may be necessary for Don Jamieson to resume top-level talks, when he visits Brussels next week. I will see him there. Meanwhile, Trudeau maintains that we will insist on safeguards, even though this means a loss of business. Gillespie thinks that we could get agreement with Japan as well before the end of the year. Don had to do some foot-work in explaining away Jack Horner's remarks about the difficulty of making nuclear sales with our insistence on stricter safeguards. Don concluded, however, that there was no change in our nuclear sales policy and safeguards. . . .

Thursday, December 1, 1977

Walter Gordon has written to acknowledge my letter on his book.[6] He is critical about what he calls Trudeau's rigid attitude about Quebec and "his government's handling of the economy." I don't agree that Trudeau's attitude is too rigid. . . . He adds: "While nothing is to be gained by looking over one's shoulder, I do wonder sometimes what would have happened if Marchand and I had decided in the fall of 1967 to get behind you for the leadership and stay in your government. I am sure you would have been much more conciliatory with Quebec's understandable aspirations. And I cannot believe the three of us would have done such a bad job with the economy. . . ." Trudeau, I think, insofar as Quebec is concerned, is handling the situation well. Someday perhaps people will read what I said about the Quebec problem, when we were contesting for the leadership. . . .

Monday, December 5, 1977

[There is] a new Emperor in Africa. When I saw Bokassa in Central Africa five years ago, I knew he was a bombastic ass! This has been confirmed by designating himself as Emperor of the Central African Empire yesterday, crowning himself, as did Napoleon, with all the impedimenta of true monarchy. This is the man who presides over two million people, whom he disciplines by cutting off an ear, a finger, or even a leg. . . . Other African leaders, like Kaunda and Nyerere, must be embarrassed by Bokassa and Amin. . . .

6. Walter L. Gordon, *A Political Memoir* (Toronto 1977).

Tuesday, December 6, 1977

John and I were at Heathrow early this morning to meet Don Jamieson, here for a day on his way to the NATO meeting in Brussels and our heads-of-post exchange on Friday. Since I last saw him he lost over forty pounds, looking better than I have ever seen him. He told me Goyer's francophone commonwealth had likely run its course.[7] We would not hear much from it, particularly when our relations with France over the Lévesque visit are not all we would like them to be. Apparently, the reply given by the French government to our queries about the Lévesque visit is as equivocal as some of the statements of President Giscard d'Estaing and the Speaker of the Chamber of Deputies, M. Faure. I reminded Jamieson of David Owen's query concerning what he could do to help us vis-à-vis the French. He thought my advice to the Secretary of State to let matters rest was wise. This was the advice he himself had given to Trudeau and others when the full text of the French reply had been examined. Don told me he had a talk the other day with Trudeau, who acknowledged he had been unfair to Allan in removing him from External Affairs a year ago; Don added, however, that Allan's presence in the Commons, as Leader of the House, made a big difference to the morale of Liberal members and the despatch of public business. . . .

I had a visit from representatives of the Rev. Sithole, Austin Chakaodza (chief representative of the Zimbabwe National Union, which is led by Sithole) and Noel Gabriel Mukono (secretary for foreign affairs of ZANU led by Robert Mugabe). They were assured of our sympathetic understanding and concern for the principle of one-man-one-vote. Mukono indicated they were not certain of the use of the phrase "general suffrage"—how this modified the principle. They prefer to adhere to the United Kingdom-United States pack-

7. Jean-Pierre Goyer, the minister of supply and services, had been appointed on May 5 as an adviser to Jamieson on francophone affairs. Then Goyer travelled to francophone countries raising the idea of a summit meeting of the heads of government of francophone states. He denied that the idea was to undercut René Lévesque, who approved if Quebec were a full-fledged member.

age arrangement.[8] They feel that a careful screening process will assist in the integration of the Patriotic Front and Rhodesian Forces. They have some minor views on the constitution. These have been discussed with Owen and relate to special provisions for the whites. Sithole is anxious to have involved the front-line presidents and external nationalist leaders in the settlement process. Both Sithole's spokesmen told me they are satisfied Smith wants to leave the government and, if a Council is established to work with Field Marshal Carver, his withdrawal after elections will be assured. There could be a marrying process of some elements of what Smith has in mind and what the United Kingdom-United States proposal provides. It is clear Sithole wishes to proceed on the basis of the joint package. . . .

Ottawa is anticipating a visit sometime to London by Lévesque. We would regard such a visit, not as the French have done, but as we regard every visit to London of provincial premiers. The British have told us they would not want to give Lévesque an opportunity to make political capital out of a visit to London. Moreover, Lévesque's visit would have to be organized in consultation with the High Commissioner and the Quebec Agent-General. . . .

The Finance Minister in Lévesque's government, Jacques Parizeau, came to see me last night at 5:00 o'clock, accompanied by the Agent-General. He is on his way to Edinburgh tomorrow to speak. I hope his visit has not been arranged by the Centre for Canadian Studies. . . . If so, I should have thought prudence and discretion would have suggested that Parizeau would be asked not to make a separatist speech by the Centre. . . . The Centre, I suppose, has a right to ask anyone to speak on Canadian affairs, but how wise it is to invite Parizeau is another matter. . . .

He agreed with me we were not going to settle the Canada-Quebec problem on strictly legal interpretations or economic arguments. I suggested separatism would be avoided and that goodwill and good judgment in so fundamental a

8. In March 1976, the British outlined suggestions for a transition to black majority rule. Then in September, Henry Kissinger proposed a transitional régime with a consultative council (fifty per cent black) but with a white chairman and a black executive.

matter would prevail. Trudeau's meeting with Lévesque alone could not but be helpful. This was the technique required. Parizeau feels we have gone beyond the stage when separatism can be avoided. The crisis point was at the Confederation [for Tomorrow] Conference called by John Robarts a few years ago in 1967, in the time of Daniel Johnson, then Premier of Quebec. Parizeau's definition of economic association involves customs and monetary union. The catch is, the association would be predicated on a sovereign Quebec. This, Canada could not accept. . . . The matter was so important that the greatest care and consultation must be pursued, to avoid a break-up. I kept repeating this. It is the kind of argument which in the final analysis may be more productive than simple exhortation suggests. When he left, he said, "You feel very strongly about this matter." "I have spent my whole life in vain, if my point of view does not prevail," I responded. . . .

Wednesday, December 7, 1977

Our Ambassador in Paris some days ago, had passed on to the Quai d'Orsay a request for clarification of some elements of the official visit made by the Premier of Quebec a few weeks ago. We have now received [a copy of] the French government's reply [which attempts] . . . to give assurance that there is no change whatsoever. . . . The French indicated that they did not intend to intervene in the Canadian problem. It is under this condition that the fraternal relations with Quebec are affirmed. One could draw the conclusion that the French were saying they were not encouraging French secession from Canadian federation. Our Ambassador, Pelletier, is of the opinion that the French reply is as favourable as we could have hoped, bearing in mind the political situation in France. [Jamieson] . . . thinks that we could say that we have been assured that French policy remains as it was before the Quebec visit. . . .

Don Jamieson came to Macdonald House [and] we reviewed the state of play in our nuclear policy on safeguards. It is now clear that we will make a slight modification to satisfy the E.E.C. We are not likely to insist on the French signing the Nuclear Non-Proliferation Treaty.[9] It looks as though our safeguards will generally apply after a period of testing has taken place. [Although] the Europeans do not want this to apply to uranium supplies now in the mill, we will insist that the safeguards will apply to supplies in the system as well as to future deliveries. . . .

Don agrees that Pelletier's recommendation should be accepted. Hereafter, we will say that the Lévesque visit has not altered the relations prevailing between France and Canada prior to the visit. . . . He mentioned he would like to denounce or have abrogated the French commercial treaty with Canada. . . . I suggested to Don that he might want to take a second look before giving notice of intention to cancel out. After all, we have just had another confrontation with the French over Quebec. Was this the propitious moment to denounce the commercial treaty with France? I am sure this is the view he will take. . . .

At the Ends of the Earth Dinner for the Prince of Wales [last night], I sat on his right. The chairman, Sir Frank Roberts, was on his left. . . . Frank and I monopolized Prince Charles. . . . Why had the Prince on his recent United States visit not gone to see President Carter? "I had not been asked," he replied. There had been some preliminary exploration but Carter did not bite. Perhaps he was too preoccupied with energy problems and Congress. . . . He found the United States people warm and interested in the monarchy and the United Kingdom with its problems. They seemed sincere in their toast to the Queen. . . . It was impossible not to observe the division of opinion when the toast to the President of the United States was offered. . . .

Friday, December 9, 1977

By 10:00 a.m., I was on my way to Brussels and our heads-of-post meeting there. [Because] it was a clear day, sprawling London was clearly in evidence. The dividing line between

9. The treaty of 1968 committed the nuclear powers not to give nuclear weapons to other countries. Other signatories to the treaty renounced the future acquisition of nuclear weapons. France refused to sign the treaty.

the Continent and Britain rolled by inexorably. In less than an hour, our plane descended on Belgium's capital. The beaming . . . Canadian Ambassador, Lucien Lamoureux, awaited me at the terminal. In no time we reached the residence on Franklin Roosevelt Avenue. . . .

By 7:00 p.m., Don Jamieson arrived from the NATO Foreign Ministers' meeting, as did Canada's ambassadors from our posts in Europe. It was good to see them all. Lucien Lamoureux, our host, provided a splendid dinner. . . . Afterwards we gathered in Lucien's large reception room. Much of tonight's exchange dealt with the Canada-Quebec problem. [Jamieson] and Gérard Pelletier emphasized the importance of carrying on as though the problem was well in hand. I believe it is. We should show confidence in the outcome. We should proceed along [the] lines so clearly outlined in Trudeau's statements. It was not desirable at this stage that we should present a structural and strategic response. Most governments sympathized with the federal position and understood the fallacy of Lévesque's position. The battle had to be won in Canada, particularly in Quebec. . . .

Saturday, December 10, 1977

[Jamieson] . . . invited me to comment on the contractual link with the E.E.C. and progress from it. I replied that we were in the position of a year ago . . . [with] no flesh on the skeleton.[10] John Halstead did not agree. The exercise would take time. It would make Canadians better known in the Community. Businessmen would acquire a greater familiarity with commercial Europeanization. Jamieson took the same line I had pursued. The general silence indicated this was the viewpoint of our colleagues. . . .

After the meeting, I returned to London.

10. Early in 1975, after three years of negotiation, Canada and the European Community had agreed in principle to establish a formal agreement to promote closer economic ties. On July 6, 1976, the contractual link "Framework Agreement for Commercial and Economic Co-operation Between Canada and the European Communities" was signed. It came into force on October 1, 1976.

Sunday, December 11, 1977

I often kid Louis Paquette, our substitute chauffeur, for being "a Catholic *manqué*." He drove me to Farm Street for mass. I was startled at collection time to observe Louis passing the plate. He did it proficiently . . . and I am sure he has not been in the habit of being where he could be asked to take up the collection on Sunday. We both had a good chuckle about his surprising new role. . . .

Thursday, December 15, 1977

The day before, the British House of Commons defeated a motion to support proportional representation in the proposed European Parliament. This had been promoted by the Liberal party and its defeat put in doubt whether the Liberals would continue to keep the Labour government in office.

The Liberals will not break their pact with Labour at present. . . . They decided to maintain the arrangement, in spite of earlier claims that the proportional representation vote the night before might jeopardize it. David Steel said Callaghan had lived up to his agreement. . . . David, nevertheless, thinks it may be difficult to keep the agreement going into a more extended future. He would prefer that it did. . . .

Donna McDonald's article in the *[Canadian] Forum* is entitled "Cultural Diplomacy and Art—The Canada House Gallery." It carries a cartoon of me in the nude, not too flattering, a maple leaf covering the vital parts, and so on. . . . The article acknowledges that the film of the nude was shot in the [Canada House] Gallery. This is the first time that this has appeared in print and may require some explanation to satisfy a curious Parliament, although I suspect the matter will not go that far at this stage. It would certainly have caused some comment if it had been earlier known that the questionable film had been executed [by the artist] in Canada House itself. . . .

Friday, December 16, 1977

At my meeting this morning with the French Ambassador, [Jean-Victor] Sauvagnargues, I bore in mind our discussions at the heads-of-post meeting in Brussels [and] ignored . . .

Lévesque's visit to the French government. . . . From what he told me on another occasion, he realizes how important Canadian unity is. He did not approve the interventionist policy of some of his colleagues [when he was minister of foreign affairs from 1974 to last year]. . . .

I like the French Ambassador. It is worthwhile for me to cultivate him [and perhaps] have a direct benefit on the major question, Canada and Quebec. . . .

Sunday, December 18, 1977

I have finished the reading of Mazlish's *Kissinger*.[11] It is a presumptuous book. A professor of history is not fulfilling his role, when he dwells on human foibles and the sex life of a contemporary human being. . . . Kissinger is said by [Mazlish] the historian at M.I.T. to have been a "bottom pincher with his secretaries." I was not shocked by this. There have been many "bottom pinchers" who have had useful and distinguished careers. One of our best chief justices had developed the art to an impressive degree. . . .

I liked Nixon's Secretary of State Rogers.[12] The author said, "Kissinger undermined him." He "became in reality the President for Foreign Affairs." This is fair comment. The head of a government must be served efficiently. The stakes are high. I have heard all sorts of stories about Kissinger and Rogers. The United States system lends itself to this kind of problem. We have it in a lesser way. Trudeau shows an interest in foreign policy. At the outset, he wanted Mitchell Sharp to run the show. Ivan Head, an able Trudeau adviser, was in between the Prime Minister and the Secretary of State for External Affairs. The department often found itself playing a secondary role. Sharp handled the situation more skilfully than Allan MacEachen, who deeply resented the initiatives taken by the able Ivan. Don Jamieson does even better. Ivan, of course, had no personal ambitions to become . . . [Secretary of State for External Affairs]. He wanted to see the Prime Minister head a government with a good foreign policy. Our

11. Bruce Mazlish, *Kissinger: The European Mind in American Policy* (New York 1976).
12. William Rogers, U.S. secretary of state, 1969-73.

system, unlike the United States, has some built-in protections, such as the cabinet and its committee system, Parliament and the relation of the prime minister to his ministers. . . .

Monday, December 19, 1977

I was told this morning that the British did not have much information on Rhodesian negotiations in Salisbury. Smith has clearly agreed to one-man-one-vote. . . . He wants safeguards, not unlike those in the United Kingdom-United States settlement proposals, along with a bill of rights, entrenched judiciary, independent civil service commission, and guaranteed pensions. He wants a third of the representation in the Assembly for white voters and has not given up the idea of a blocking vote. His hope is to wind up the negotiations with elections before the end of 1978. The British would like Smith to make concrete commitments on the constitution. Smith does not want resumption of direct British rule as implicit in the United Kingdom-United States proposals. It was intended by the British to have United Kingdom rule reimposed for the interim period. As I know, Kaunda wants to delay elections to boost Nkomo's chances. Machel in Mozambique wants a settlement which will end raids. . . .

Wednesday, December 21, 1977

We had expected Paul, Sheila, and the three boys early this morning [but] . . . the plane is not due now until much later in the day. . . . Later I was at the airport at 4:30 p.m. to greet them. I expected that they would all look and act tired. They had been at Mirabel since 1:00 o'clock in the morning. All of a sudden, however, David [my youngest grandson] shouted out "Grandpa!" then all five were at me. . . .

Friday, December 23, 1977

The day before Christmas in my office is frustrating. As a cabinet minister, it was a day of hectic activity. In a diplomatic mission, it is more of a holding operation. The staff soon wander off. One officer would not wait to take an important message to Buckingham Palace. . . .

Saturday, December 24, 1977

I have conveyed several communications to the Queen's secretary from the Prime Minister this week, regarding the transfer to the Governor-General of the functions of the Sovereign. The changes are based on the Letters Patent of 1947. They authorize the Governor-General "to exercise all powers and authorities" belonging to the sovereign in respect of Canada. As a matter of practice, only a few formal functions continue to be discharged by the Queen, such as signing letters accrediting and recalling Canadian representatives abroad. . . . It is important to note that the Queen's constitutional position is as Queen of Canada. . . .

XVIII

January – February 1978

MY FOURTH YEAR IN LONDON began with the mission's continuing efforts to work out solutions to concerns that had cropped up earlier. One of them was the question of the international role of Canadian provinces abroad when provincial ministers came calling.

At one point, it was suggested that I might take on an active role in helping to mediate between the black African states and Britain over a Rhodesian settlement, but nothing came of the idea.

Sunday, January 1, 1978

New Year's Day 1978. What will it be like? A repetition of 1977. Nothing on the horizon suggests otherwise. . . . Paul and I went to a high Latin-sung mass at Brompton Oratory. The music was exquisite. Paul sought to sing but some of the Latin escaped him. A chap sitting in the front was disturbed by our relatively loud exchange of approval and comment on the service. . . .

Paul and his family left the following day.

Wednesday, January 4, 1978

Before this day is over, Carter and Sadat will meet at Aswan [Egypt]. There are indications that Sadat will be more flexible on the Palestinian issue [and] . . . will not ask for the immediate establishment of a Palestinian state. . . . Sadat had sent a personal message to Trudeau after the New Year, describing in a comprehensive way his talks with Begin. Trudeau had written Sadat on November 22nd supporting Sadat's peace initiative. In his letter, Sadat says the Palestinian question is the crux and heart of the conflict. Begin maintained that the way to solve the problem of the West Bank was to set aside for the time being the question of sovereignty. Israel would grant self-rule to the West Bank inhabitants [but] its military presence would continue unrestricted. Israelis would be allowed to settle on the West Bank. . . . Sadat said the self-rule formula was inadequate. Begin is adamant in his position. . . . Trudeau is urged to persuade Begin to be more flexible. . . .

Tonight was my first visit to the Gladstone Club[1] on Whitehall Place. Up to now, I have felt that it was wise for me not to be identified with British political party affairs. I think perhaps I was too strict with myself. . . . My enthusiasm for liberalism and Liberal parties has not diminished, but I have subordinated my interest to my job, which must be apolitical. . . . During the question period [following my speech], most people thought our most important problem was the economy issue, unemployment, and the like [not the separatist question]. This reaction is natural. It reflects the lack of full understanding of the nature of Canada. One woman, a strong advocate of proportional representation, suggested that the French had too great an influence in Canada. What a misconception this is of the nature of the problem which faces us. I assured my hearers that Canadian unity would be preserved, notwithstanding Lévesque. . . .

Saturday, January 7, 1978

What is the practice observed by other federal states abroad? When the Governor of Georgia visits London and calls on the Minister of Trade, I presume he is accompanied by the American Ambassador. There are no officers of the individual states comparable to our Agents-General. . . . I have assumed since I came to the High Commission that a visiting provincial minister, calling on a minister in the government in London, should be attended by an officer of the High Commission. In this way, we emphasize the role of the federal government in foreign relationships. Ottawa reminded us twice yesterday that

1. A Liberal political club.

the normal practice for the High Commission to observe is to accompany a provincial minister on his ministerial calls here. . . . When a Quebec minister, Burns, was here last autumn to discuss British experience in the referendum . . . he saw Michael Foot with one of my officers. At first, Loiselle, the Quebec Agent-General, objected, saying the Quebec government would not like this arrangement [but] I insisted that one of our officers should be present. . . .

We were not notified by Ontario of a proposed meeting between the Provincial Treasurer[2] and a Minister of the Treasury here. From Ottawa we were given this information and the date of the appointment. . . . Last night I asked the [Ontario] Agent-General[3] if he could come to the residence for a drink. This he agreed to do with alacrity. In a friendly way, I reminded him of the practice involved in ministerial visits. . . . He said it galled him to note how grasping Ottawa was in its pursuit of power. This was the reason for so much trouble and confusion in Canada. I reminded Ward of the Canada-Quebec problem and the visit of the Quebec minister, Burns. . . . He would understand, I said, I could not treat Quebec one way and other provinces differently. . . . I could see that the Agent-General was unhappy. . . . He left me in an amiable mood but with no expression of concurrence. As he said, the Treasurer is not the obstacle—"I am the one who objects." I thought it best to push the matter no further at this time. We will see how the situation evolves.

Monday, January 9, 1978

Charlie Lynch[4] and his wife have arrived to stay for a few days. They dined with us tonight. Charlie and I sat up until the early hours discussing matters which have transpired since we last met, almost three years ago. . . .

Charlie Lynch finds Trudeau an enigma. He admires him all the same and regards him as indispensable in the present context. He shares fully my view that Lévesque would be given a trump card if Trudeau were to be rejected by the

2. The Ontario provincial treasurer was Darcy McKeough.
3. Ward Cornell
4. A journalist from Canada.

Canadian people at this time. A Quebec leader like Trudeau is best suited to meet the Lévesque challenge. Charlie thinks it would have been better for Trudeau to have had his election last fall. I told him I was not of that view, certainly at the time. Unemployment and economic difficulties were combining to make Trudeau's lot a difficult one at present. There was always the danger, Lynch thinks, of [voters] tiring of the Quebec situation and grasping the weaknesses in economic policy as a reason to repudiate Trudeau's federal government. . . .

Wednesday, January 11, 1978

Claude Ryan, the editor of *Le Devoir*, will contest the leadership of the Liberal party in Quebec. Charlie Lynch wonders if this is his métier. Monique Bégin* regards Claude as the best man to carry the argument which, she says, has ascended to an intellectual level. She will find the debate will descend to a level the people understand. Will Claude be able to compete with Lévesque on this level? That is the question. He does not strike me as being able to do a "Trudeau." The Prime Minister enjoys an intellectual confrontation, but he can also be like Mirabeau.[5]

Thursday, January 12, 1978

At the large reception Gerry Hughes[6] had for trade people in Macdonald House tonight, a number of Canadian bankers stoutly defended the action of Sun Life in moving their headquarters from Montreal to Toronto. I suggested that corporations had no less an obligation in the present difficult situation in Quebec than individuals. How helpful, I asked, was it for a corporation at this time to move out? The action has provoked more discussions about the Canada-Quebec problem than at any time since Lévesque's election victory a year ago. . . .

The following week, Trudeau persuaded Sun Life to postpone its move.

5. Mirabeau was the revolutionary who established his power during the French Revolution by virtue of his oratory and personality.
6. A trade officer at the High Commission.

Greeting a local woman on a visit to Chester, 1977.
(*Liverpool Daily Post & Echo*/National Archives of Canada/PA-164890)

In the midst of a group of school children, Chester, 1977.
(*Liverpool Daily Post & Echo*/National Archives of Canada/PA-164891)

"When I awoke from my siesta and joined Paul, we had the first swim in Lac Laurin." *July 31, 1977.* On holiday in the Saguenay.

"We were presented to Princess Margaret. . . ." *August 6, 1977.* At the gala for the National Ballet of Canada at Covent Garden.

(National Archives of Canada/PA-164942)

"The Queen told me how much she enjoyed our party. . . ." *October 14, 1977*. Elizabeth II signing the guestbook in the library at 12 Upper Brook. (Associated Press Ltd/National Archives of Canada/PA-164959)

"I never found Kissinger with a halo." *October 31, 1977*. At a dinner in Ottawa in 1975.

"This mission is more than diplomatic in function. . . . Who says this is not a busy thoroughfare?" *March 10, 1977.* Having fun with the Gadabouts from Kingston, July 1975.
(Fox Photos Ltd/National Archives of Canada/PA-164927)

Greeting the Canadian Olympic soccer team at the residence, April 13, 1976. (Keystone Press Agency Ltd/National Archives of Canada/PA-164963)

In the salon at 12 Upper Brook Street with Canadian holders of the Victoria Cross.

"An unpleasant dark and wettish day did not add to an otherwise pleasant motor run to Cardiff. . . ." *March 2, 1978. Left to right:* Sir Cernydd Traherne, Mrs W. H. Carling, myself, Lord Parry, Councillor W. H. Carling, Lady Traherne, Councillor Richard Evans, Lady Parry. (National Archives of Canada/PA-164929)

© Bern Schwartz
For our dear friend Paul Martin
with high esteem and sincere regard
Tom Denning 25 Oct

"Lord Denning, perhaps Britain's greatest judge, . . . was guest of honour. He kindly autographed his most recent book for me." *March 15, 1978*. A portrait of Denning in his robes as master of the rolls.

"In a jiffy he was off to Windsor Castle nearby. . . ." *May 20, 1978.* Prince Charles and I arriving back at Heathrow from the funeral of Sir Robert Menzies in Australia.

. . . arriving as almost the first visitor at Quebec House, I wished my hosts a happy St. Jean Baptiste Day. . . ." *June 24, 1978*. Paul Martin shakes hands with Jacques Léonard, the PQ ministre d'état, in the presence of Gilles Loiselle, Quebec agent-general.

(National Archives of Canada/PA-164943)

"Her Majesty had Prince Andrew with her. He made a great hit." *July 17, 1978*. A reception at the residence.

"The Schreyers had a memorable visit. . . ." *January 10, 1979*. "Bobby" Martin with the governor general designate and his children.

". . . he loved to spring surprises on people. . . ." *January 31, 1979*. With Pierre Trudeau after the London period.

"Poppa's girls," my granddaughters Catherine and Julia, 1979.

"I trotted out of the residence before 8:00 o'clock this morning and welcomed the dry, coldish air. . . ." *January 18, 1979.*

"We have just learned that Mary Anne has had a new baby girl. Nell is overjoyed. . . ." *July 26, 1978*. My daughter and granddaughter Julia.

Santa with his deputy high commissioner, Christian Hardy.

"Dear Paul — In recognition of a friendship lasting ever since our first meeting in Bermuda about 20 years ago, this absurd image is respectfully and affectionately dedicated." Inscription by Quintin Hogg, Baron Hailsham of St Marylebone, the Lord Chancellor, 1979.

"... Jim was more effective because he made personal relations part of his foreign policy...." *January 24, 1979.* In a private chat with James Callaghan.

"The first meeting of the Canadian Institute for Advanced Legal Studies is the fulfilment of a dream." *July 9, 1979. Left to right:* Roy McMurtry, Paul Martin, Mr Justice Carruthers, Mr Justice Morand.

"Most of the staff . . . congregated in the reception area at Macdonald House to say goodbye. . . . I wanted the staff to know I valued them all." *October 24, 1979.* With officers of the High Commission prior to leaving London. (Keystone Press Agency Ltd/National Archives of Canada/PA-164948)

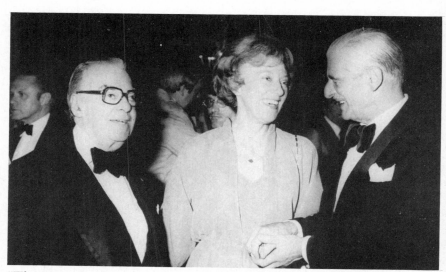

"The presence of the Secretary of State for External Affairs was the evening's extra highlight. She radiates charm. . . ." *August 11, 1979.* With Flora MacDonald and Desmond Smith at Covent Garden.
(Desmond O'Neill/National Archives of Canada/PA-164952)

One of my last engagements as high commissioner: a conference on Commonwealth affairs at the University of Leeds. *Left to right:* David N. Dilks, unidentified man, John Holmes, myself, Gordon Robertson, Allan Gotlieb.

Receiving an honourary degree from Cambridge with Simone Veil, president of the European Parliament.

Home again! Windsor, 1980.

Friday, January 13, 1978

Yesterday at Marlborough House, Antony Duff of the Foreign Office told me [that Ian] Smith had likely lost the chance for a favourable solution in the internal settlement discussions, although Duff did not give the basis for this view. Now it is reported that agreement has been reached on the matter of white representation under black majority rule. This is what Smith wanted. Others matters have yet to be resolved. . . . I believe that, if Smith can "pull it off," the question of international acceptance will lose its relevance. . . . How difficult it would be to go against a settlement made by those who were party to the Salisbury talks and which were open also to Nkomo and Robert Mugabe. I find the position of David Owen in the present situation very difficult to understand. The Australian High Commissioner[7] thinks Owen went too far and was pulled back by his cabinet colleagues. He is now awaiting a good opening. . . .

More than ever since I have been here as High Commissioner, I have felt alienated from Canada. In a sense, this may be due to not having direct participation in the unfolding of events. I keep asking myself, however, what could I do now any different from what I am doing. What is important is to join in the fray at a useful moment. . . .

I was upset today when a message sent to Ottawa on how this mission proposed to deal with the Canada-Quebec problem had not been shown to a number of my officers, whose input is important. Failure to do so arose over one colleague's desire to get the message out before the Christmas holiday. Among those to whom the proposed message had not been shown was the High Commissioner. . . .

Sunday, January 15, 1978

The zest for doing things has taken temporary leave only, I hope. Usually I am full of go—on all fronts. The last few weeks I have been listless and hard to navigate. The weather—who knows? Perhaps not enough swimming and that, because the will to swim had gone off on furlough. . . . Perhaps a

7. Gordon Freeth

mission working at a fully efficient level would be inspiring and prodding. I don't have that at the moment. . . .

Monday, January 16, 1978

I have been studying the fifth General Conference of L'Agence de co-opération culturelle et technique. At the meeting, Claude Morin affirmed that the sovereignty or autonomy of Quebec was an internal matter, to be discussed and agreed on by Canadians and Quebecers, without outside interference. This is not the position which Morin and Lévesque took when the latter was recently in France. It is noteworthy that the proposal for a commonwealth of francophone countries received negative support from France. France would not be associated with any meeting of francophone heads of state and governments to which Quebec was not invited [separately from Canada]. This, of course, is intervention by France in Canadian affairs. . . .

Talking to Ottawa this afternoon, I learned that what I had understood before regarding Basford's electoral intentions will eventuate. When the Minister of Justice was here, I told him it was rumoured that he was not going to run in the next federal election. He assured me that was not the case. Now, he announces that he will not be a candidate . . . [and] his loss will be felt in British Columbia. Bit by bit, the Trudeau cabinet is losing its experienced members [and] . . . is not too strong. In Ontario, there are few outstanding cabinet leaders and figures. The resignation of Donald Macdonald [last year] removed the last of the more credible figures. As I have mentioned before, Trudeau was concerned about the loss of senior personalities in Ontario. In many respects, he is responsible. He has not deliberately downgraded his men but his own ascendancy, style, and manner has not encouraged the development of ministerial personalities, enjoying wide recognition and support. . . .

Tuesday, January 17, 1978

The E.E.C. agreed yesterday with Canada about the establishment of new safeguard arrangements for the supply of Canadian nuclear material and equipment. We had discussed the nature of this agreement with Jamieson at our heads-of-post meeting in Brussels [last year]. To get the agreement, we had to move slightly from our absolute position of a year ago. Before we imposed our total ban a year ago, Canada supplied thirty to thirty-five per cent of the Community's uranium requirements. The difficult discussions culminated in an agreement on re-processing, enriching, or storing of Canadian uranium . . . based upon prior approval and consent. The E.E.C. would not accept this. Instead, a compromise was reached. It provided for notification and consultation. Will this satisfy the Canadian Parliament? Under the new arrangement, the E.E.C. will have to advise Canada before enriching uranium beyond twenty per cent or re-processing used uranium fuel in the case of material supplied after December 1974. France has not yet accepted inspection by the [International] Atomic Energy Agency. Until it does, our material will not be used in French reactors. . . .[8]

Wednesday, January 18, 1978

Trudeau said in Quebec over the weekend that there might not be federal elections in Canada until 1979, close to the date of a Quebec referendum. Last summer, Trudeau told me that he did not want elections in 1977. He would prefer them at a time when the elections could have maximum effect on public opinion in Quebec. Assuming a strong federal victory, it would impress the citizens of Quebec with the desirability of registering opposition to separatism. . . . I am sure that a federal election would result in an overwhelming vote in Quebec for Trudeau. If, perchance, the vote in English-speaking Canada was not as convincing, that would be regrettable. . . .

Sunday, January 22, 1978

I was interested to learn from [Yehudi] Menuhin's autobiography[9] this morning how well he knew Willa Cather. Her *Shadows on the Rock* and *Death Comes for the Archbishop* were

8. On January 16, Canada and the European Atomic Energy Community signed a pact and Canada resumed shipments of uranium to the Community which were cut off a year earlier.
9. Yehudi Menuhin, *Unfinished Journey* (London 1978).

popular and almost supreme in the thirties.[10] It gave me such a thrill to meet her on a boat en route to America at that time. I understand what Menuhin means when he writes that "Aunt" Willa's characters were indigenous to their environment—the Middle West, New Mexico or Quebec. I remember her enthusiasm as we sailed up the St. Lawrence and her exclamation—"There is my dear Quebec!" . . .

Monday, January 23, 1978

Man's world never ends as it searches for agreement and concord. No wonder we yearn for a heaven above. Now, on the economic side, the nations in the Tokyo Round[11] are entering a final phase in Geneva today. Real bargaining starts now, after four years of talks. It is hoped that agreement can be reached soon on a major liberalization of world trade. Ninety-seven nations are attending the discussions. The essential agreement will be with three states, the main trading powers—the United States, the E.E.C., and Japan. They have agreed to an average cut of about forty per cent in industrial tariffs, spread over eight to ten years. . . .

Canada has a big stake in all this. It is too early to speak of the success of the Tokyo Round. . . . Individual governments are imposing new import restrictions. . . . It is difficult for a government to make major public commitments to trade liberalization in such a climate. Markets must remain open, if the investment required to tackle the recession is to become available. . . .

Monday, February 6, 1978

I want to make sure that some in Ottawa will not see a parallel between European integration and Quebec's notion of sovereignty-association. What is at issue in Europe is the establishment of a closer federation or confederation out of a group of sovereign and, often, historically hostile nations for the

10. Willa Cather, an American novelist who won a Pulitzer Prize in 1913.
11. The Tokyo Round of Multilateral Trade Negotiations had begun almost five years before under the auspices of the General Agreement on Tariffs and Trade. Throughout those years, the negotiations moved from city to city.

purpose of promoting the well-being of all. I pointed out [in a message to Ottawa] that, at the beginning, the European movement strove for political union. Economic integration was only an interim step. I emphasized that what has happened in Europe is an arrangement of sovereign countries and not an establishment of a new sovereign entity out of an existing sovereign nation. I suppose it is true to say that some in the United Kingdom favoured British entry into the E.E.C. for somewhat similar reasons to those prompting Quebec's maintenance of economic ties with Canada. In both cases, the hope appears to be that benefits of membership in the wider economic association could be enjoyed, while sovereignty in other areas could be protected and even promoted. As matters have turned out, however, that is not the case. It is increasingly clear that the present and future community structures will be threatened, if there is not an increasing policy of alignment, not only in core economic issues but in the interconnecting web of other areas. To maintain the unity which the E.E.C. now has, it will be important for member states to think of Europe first.

This is what Britain finds difficult to do as a sovereign power, anxious to hold on to her institutions of independence. In the United Kingdom, the acceptance of specific measures has often depended on the extent to which these areas conflict in the public mind with national and community sovereignty. This is accounted for by political factors in Britain. Among these is nationalism—"Little England" at work. Another reason is the nationalism of the Labour left wing. Paradoxically, as it seems, the true socialists are opposed to economic or political integration, because of the belief that the E.E.C. is founded on free enterprise and is incompatible with Labour's objective of building socialism in Britain. The true socialists look upon the European Parliament and direct elections as a further curtailment of Westminster as a sovereign Parliament. . . .

Tuesday, February 7, 1978

I had the six Agents-General for lunch today. . . . As I anticipated, there was raised, though not forcefully, the question of their own status. It is not unnatural that Agents-General should sometimes feel that their subordinate role is not an easy one. Certainly they are here, not as accredited representatives of the government of Canada, but as officers performing a useful function for their provinces in London. . . .

One Agent-General thought it would be nice if he could have a parchment signed by the Queen showing his relationship to her. I countered by suggesting that why could not each provincial government give to the Agent-General a certificate indicating his appointment to London as Agent-General for province "X." . . .

I was in touch this afternoon with Jean Chrétien, the Minister of Finance. He definitely will not contest the provincial Liberal leadership in Quebec. He thinks that Ryan will get the leadership [but] it might be close. He hoped Ryan would be able to defeat Lévesque in an election. On the question of separation and the result of a referendum in Quebec, Jean is optimistic that the people will not support Lévesque's position. He feels, moreover, that federal prospects in Quebec are good [and] . . . expects an election sometime in May, or possibly June. I was surprised that he was so definite on this point. Undoubtedly, preparations are under way. I have, however, seen situations like this before. Notwithstanding Whelan's assurance,[12] I still believe that the elections may not eventuate until the fall and possibly even later. I would describe the situation by saying that it is intended to hold an election not later than June but that long-term considerations in the Prime Minister's mind could alter this decision.

Saturday, February 11, 1978

In Rhodesia, the result of the Salisbury talks are at hand. All now depends on the United African National Council, Muzorewa's party. It will decide or reject . . . agreement which was reached yesterday. The contentious point has to do with the principle of twenty-eight white seats out of one hundred in the future Parliament, and the election of these from a separate roll of voters. Muzorewa has not accepted this arrangement [which] . . . maintains a form of apartheid. I don't think his party will agree. . . .

12. Eugene Whelan, the minister of agriculture, was visiting London the week before.

No country produces so many books and writers as does contemporary Britain. In Hatchard's the day before yesterday, I examined Abba Eban's biography.[13] I found it not strongly bound, with a badly organized index. The experienced lady at Hatchard's bitterly complains about the badly indexed books currently on sale. Eban's index has reference to me but I could not find the page covered by the index. The price of the book is high. This fact and failure to identify what Abba had to say about me, caused me not to purchase the autobiography. . . .

The billboard facing the rear of Canada House and near the National Gallery has been leased again to the anti-seal hunt group. The imminent arrival of Premier Moores[14] to London makes the situation embarrassing. We will have a hectic few weeks over the anti-seal hunt campaign while he is here. . . .

I had intended tonight to go and see a preview of paintings . . . [but] I was thwarted in my desire to do so because of a pressing engagement with a friend from the Foreign Office, with whom I wanted to discuss David Owen's invitation for a meeting with all of the High Commissioners. . . . I had told him [Owen], as well as Antony Duff, some time ago that he should meet with the High Commissioners, if for no other purpose than to emphasize Commonwealth interests. . . . Such meetings with him would not mean his directing any discussion, but participating in it as an equal member of the Commonwealth. This may not be the precise intention, but it is what I suggested tonight to my friend. . . .

Wednesday, February 15, 1978

I had a unique experience yesterday in the House of Commons at Westminster. I have not been in the House of Commons in Canada since I left it [but] . . . yesterday, however, as I sat in the diplomat's gallery listening to the exchanges of the Prime Minister and the Leader of the Opposition, I had a strong nostalgic feeling, momentarily wanting to get back

13. Abba Eban, foreign minister of Israel from 1966 to 1974, published *Abba Eban: An Autobiography* in London in 1978.
14. Premier Frank Moores of Newfoundland.

and cross swords, as I did for so many years. The feeling continued all day, even as I put my head on the pillow for the night. I, of course, will never go back. It is too late and I really do not want to—enough is enough. . . .

From what I learned yesterday, Trudeau has committed himself to elections this year, but not when. I was surprised he went so far. He generally leaves his options open. The pressure for elections on him is strong. I have seen him resist before. . . .

Sir Philip Moore, the Queen's secretary, lunched with me at the residence today. . . . The Queen was not anxious to be divested of the powers transferred pursuant to the Letters Patent of 1947 and arranged at the end of 1977. These remaining powers continued with the Queen. George VI and Mackenzie King both felt strongly that the monarch should sign ambassadorial appointments. I think it is too bad that these functions did not continue with the Queen. The transfer involved in no way any alteration in her status as head of state and in no way altered the constitution. The Queen is a politely determined woman who doesn't easily conform against her views as to what should be done—more power to her. That is what one expects of a person so eminently placed. I insisted that there could be no doubt about our Prime Minister's regard for the Queen as a person. I gather that the Queen fully understands this. . . .

Michel Gauvin has relinquished his responsibilities as director of the royal tours. . . . Michel thought jurisdiction should rest with the office of the Privy Council and not with the Prime Minister's Office. I gather that some of the political boys in the Prime Minister's Office clashed with Michel and perhaps Government House. . . .

Thursday, February 16, 1978

The Devolution Bill was thrown into further doubt after two major defeats last night in the Commons. The attempt to remove the forty per cent electoral requirement in the Scottish referendum was defeated, as was a compromise proposal. . . .

The Salisbury talks led to agreement on ten points yesterday. The heads of the four delegations, in joint declarations, acknowledged they had reached an agreement. Bishop Muzorewa said that a transitional government was close at hand. . . . Nkomo, of course, rejected the settlement and affirmed that the guerrilla war would continue. . . . The whites will have a voice in the legislature but not . . . [be] able to frustrate the will of the majority. The agreement gives a new black régime the choice to use European talent. Majority rule will not be prejudiced or become unreal as a result. . . .

I have just welcomed the Premier of Newfoundland to London for his big press conference on Monday, when he will respond to the anti-sealers and be my guest at a reception at the residence that night. Frank was pleased with the conference of first ministers and spoke highly of Trudeau's handling of it. He termed the conference the most successful federal-provincial meeting he ever attended. Trudeau apparently [was his overnight guest] a few months ago. This pleased Moores very much and made him almost a political partisan of the Prime Minister. He did not appear to be overly enthusiastic about Joe Clark. . . .

Friday, February 17, 1978

Frank Moores did not tell me anything about Lévesque's outburst [at the first ministers' meeting] in Ottawa. Lévesque would not sign the communiqué issued at the end of the federal-provincial conference. He said Trudeau had staged the meeting as a prelude to the federal election. . . .[15]

I bought George F. Kennan's latest book at Hatchard's this morning. *The Cloud of Danger*[16] deals with some current problems of American foreign policy. . . . Kennan has a curious dedication to his wife, Annelise. He says she had no enthusiasm for this or any other excursion of his "into the realm of public affairs." Nevertheless, she had always been loyal to his endeavours. I think this was a rather clumsy way of indicating that his wife had no interest in what he was doing. Surely it cannot be that bad. My wife has never been interested in

15. Trudeau called a first ministers' conference on the economy which met February 13-15. Quebec used the conference to attack the economics of the federal system and Lévesque walked out.
16. George F. Kennan, *The Cloud of Danger: Current Realities of American Foreign Policy* (Boston 1977).

politics . . . but I could never say Nell lacked enthusiasm for what I was doing. It would have been better, I think, for Kennan to have simply thanked his wife for her loyalty or merely to have dedicated the book and said nothing. . . .

Sunday, February 19, 1978

After Rab Butler gave the 1967 Romanes Lecture at Oxford, he wrote his memoirs, *The Art of the Possible*. . . .[17] Biography is a different art to autobiography. . . . Am I so busy with life, doing things, that I hesitate to take up so much time in writing about them? Not many have worked so long. There is always the thought that if my life has been active and constructive, someone will think it useful to write about some of the things I was privileged to try and do—but I am not Napoleon. . . .

Tempus fugit. Trudeau will mark his tenth year as Prime Minister in April. . . . When he was elected leader, it was written he would "catapult the country into the brilliant sunshine of the late twentieth century from the stagnant swamp of traditionalism and mediocrity in which Canadian politics had been bogged down for years." No man could have done that, and this I well knew. . . . Ethnic differences continue. The constitution has not been amended. Inflation and unemployment is twice what it was ten years ago. Our balance of payments deficit is up. Have our civil liberties expanded and are they better protected? The powers of the state have grown. Regrettably the police have found it necessary to open private mail. . . . Is our society a "just society?" . . .

Some will say Trudeau has not lived up to promises. I don't agree. Trudeau promised more than I did. I kept to the record. His charisma and more youthful status carried him along. The problems he faced would have faced me. The world has not changed because he is No. 1. But who can say that it might not have been worse? I think Trudeau has been a good Prime Minister. . . .

17. R. A. Butler, *The Difficult Art of Autobiography: The Romanes Lecture, 1967* (Oxford 1960); *The Art of the Possible: Memoirs of Lord Butler* (London 1971).

Robert Mugabe calls the Rhodesian Internal Settlement deal a treacherous act.[18] It brought Muzorewa "into the enemy camp." . . . I agree with Owen the Rhodesian settlement establishes a fundamental move towards black majority rule. The involvement of the Patriotic Front is a condition precedent to a cease-fire. That is why Mugabe's rejection of the settlement is unfortunate. What will happen when a black government takes over? If the guerrillas keep fighting a black Rhodesian administration, there will be civil war. This will likely bring outside participation. . . . This would create a confrontation between Britain and black Africa. The U.S.S.R. would be pleased. The political balance in Africa would be thus affected. Owen is moving in the right direction and, for these reasons, is doing so cautiously and wisely. Owen wants to bridge the Salisbury group with the Patriotic Front. . . .

Monday, February 20, 1978

I called on the Zambian High Commissioner[19] who has just returned from Zambia. She was not happy with the Salisbury agreement. Unaware that Kaunda [her president] has denounced it, she acknowledged that Nyerere had done so. . . . The young High Commissioner believes that the agreement will not last. War is inevitable and only by it will the blacks in Rhodesia get their desserts. I told her that Nkomo and Mugabe should join in the settlement and take their chances in the elections. She had a note-taker with her and I assume Kenneth Kaunda will soon know my views. . . .

There were conflicting reports on Premier Moores' press conference this morning at the Savoy. The Premier said the publicity from the [seal hunt] protesters had hurt not only Newfoundland's economy but its people's image. The protesters were guilty of half-truths and spectacular stunts. He had with him marine scientists and a veterinary surgeon, who

18. This was an agreement reached by black leaders Bishop Muzorewa, Chief Jeremiah Chirau, and the Reverend Ndabaningi Sithole with Ian Smith and the white Rhodesian government. The Internal Settlement provided for the principle of universal adult suffrage under certain conditions and also stipulated a transition to black majority rule by the end of 1978.
19. Phyllis Chibesakunda

contends that the annual killing of seals was carried out in a humane way. . . .

A side-light on the Premier's visit was the reluctance of the French to have Moores do there what he was doing in London. . . . Some days ago, France had threatened to prohibit the Premier from muddying the current election surface with his defence of the seal hunt. Three per cent of the French electorate could vote adversely to Giscard, it is contended, if the French government were seen to give a rostrum to the defender of the seal hunt. A few days ago, Don Jamieson said the French had decided against a ban on Moores' visit. Now, Giscard was upset over Jamieson's statement. The French foreign office had expressed to Pelletier its dissatisfaction and, if Moores came, threatened to restrain him from speaking. The French policy is unbelievable but, as Pelletier told me over the phone late this afternoon, there it is. I discussed the matter with Moores and his Minister of Industry, [John] Lundrigan. Moores agreed that in the circumstances he could not go to France. We so advised Pelletier. He was much relieved. Trudeau will likewise be relieved. He had called Moores on Sunday, urging Frank not to go to the land of "liberté." . . .

He likely felt comforted by the warmth of the reception we gave him at the residence. Some 120 Britishers came to meet him and showed some sympathy for his problem. Most of the guests were members of Parliament from all sides. He spoke generously of the co-operation of the mission and was pleased at the presence of so many MPs. . . .

Wednesday, February 22, 1978

I was up early this morning and thumbed through Furbank's E. M. Forster's life. . . .[20] I must say, however, that as I read the book the thought struck me, as it has often done before in reading about particular writers, how uncrowded their lives often are. This seems true in the case of Forster. . . . My life is certainly not that way. My hours are long and my day is

20. P. N. Furbank, *E. M. Forster: A Life* (London 1978). Forster contrasted the passion of the Mediterranean neutrality with the conventional English life.

full of things requiring hours of attention. I have little spare time. . . . I know it will be said that a writer has to have time to read and extend his acquaintance with the world, about which, if he is going to be a good writer, he must know something. To that, I respond I read a lot too and have always done so. I have taken into account that writing books involves a lot of preparation and calls for a great deal of effort. It can easily be argued that the measure of achievement is not the time spent in bringing it about. Early in the morning, I am entitled to exaggerate. . . .

Pelletier reports that following the visit [to Paris] of Lundrigan yesterday, the press would be told that Moores, Premier of Newfoundland, cancelled his visit to Paris because he believed it would not achieve the intended purpose in the present circumstances. . . . I don't see how the French could have refused to allow Moores to hold a press conference to answer the anti-sealers. The Quai D'Orsay [the French foreign ministry] now says their objective in discouraging the visit was simply to draw our attention to the problem it would cause. The French will say, however, if they are asked, that they did not say they would cancel Moores' visit. Sometimes diplomacy is removed from reality. . . .

Nell and I attended tonight at the flat of Ray Culverhouse at 33 Chester Square. The dinner was in honour of the Apostolic Delegate, Bruno Heim. We had met Culverhouse about two years ago at the Papal Delegate's for dinner. The guest of honour on that occasion was the Duke of Kent, a nice but rather unimaginative prince. [Among] other guests tonight, in addition to the Apostolic Delegate, was Lady Diana Cooper. . . . Mr. Culverhouse did not forget his earlier offer to buy me a derby. He trotted one out for me to try. It was too big but didn't look bad; he likely will carry out his threat to present me with one. . . .

Lady Diana Cooper, the pin-up girl of the first war generation, is truly a remarkable woman. At the age of eighty-five, she carries herself with such dignity, not fully hiding her former beauty. A pleasant person to meet, with a good memory and much more. I knew, of course, that she was a great friend of Charles Ritchie. This was almost her first utterance. . . . She told me tonight she did not like Eden, because he had apparently done something to her husband, Duff Cooper. . . .

Monday, February 27, 1978

The Zambian High Commissioner called on me this morning. Obviously she was troubled. Recently, I have been explaining to her that she and her President, Kenneth Kaunda, may have been under-rating the [Rhodesian] internal solution negotiations. These could be close to finality. Would it not be better for Nkomo to join the talks, avoiding thereby the consequences of intense guerrilla action? Today she enquired how could this be done, adding somewhat reluctantly "in order to save face." Can it be, I thought, that Kaunda is in a more difficult position than one assumed? . . . I said I would like to consider this and would be in touch with her later.

My problem is that I have no instructions from Ottawa to undertake this role. Do I have to have instructions, as at first some of my officers thought I did? I finally decided otherwise and discussed the matter in the afternoon with John Graham, an Assistant Under-Secretary of State, perhaps closer to this problem than anyone but David Owen himself. John outlined the situation as he saw it. I told him of the Zambian Ambassador's several visits and particularly the one with her this morning. . . . How could Nkomo get into the internal solution now without losing face? As Graham saw it, he would have to join the talks and seek to participate in the interim council. Smith would likely insist on a pre-condition that force would not be used by the guerrillas. This, I rejoined, would not be saving face for Nkomo. It would be capitulation. Graham added that there was the danger of Cuban participation. He was not certain of this, but it could not be discounted. Cuba, of course, means Soviet involvement.

Sonny Ramphal came to see me at the residence around 5:00 o'clock, after I had seen Graham. He has been a strong proponent of the United Kingdom-United States initiative, now likely overtaken by events. I suggested to Ramphal that one could not now overlook the progress made by Sithole, Muzorewa and Smith. When I told him that I suspected Kaunda might be looking for a way out for Nkomo, he did not seem altogether surprised, but was not able to offer any satisfactory solution to meet Zambia's request made to me through the High Commissioner. Sonny will be seeing Owen tomorrow. In the meantime, we will all be thinking about the problem. . . .

Sonny wanted to talk about Canada's relations with the Commonwealth Organization. He had a feeling that we felt less keenly toward it. I assured him that was not the case. It had been suspected that because Trudeau could not see him on his last visit, this rubbed him the wrong way, helping to confirm his judgment that the love-match was not as intense. I assured him we felt no less interested in the Commonwealth than heretofore. He had no doubts, he said, that this was true of Trudeau and me, but what about External Affairs, minister and all? . . .

XIX

March – April 1978

MY INTEREST FOCUSED ON THE CONTEST for the leadership of the provincial Liberal party in Quebec. Whoever filled that job would automatically join the front ranks in opposition to separatism. When the Quebec Liberals selected Claude Ryan, the editor of the Montreal newspaper Le Devoir, *I had some doubts because Ryan had earlier espoused a theory of decentralized federalism that I found disturbing.*

In mid-April, I served as the Canadian delegate to a meeting of Commonwealth trade ministers—shades of the past and my many international conferences. As it turned out, I helped to draft a communiqué which smoothed over serious differences between the developed and the developing countries over the approach to stabilizing the prices of primary products.

Wednesday, March 1, 1978

Mr. Speaker[1] invited me to drinks in his State Rooms along with many others on the occasion of St. David's Day. . . .

I had a good chat with the Prime Minister's chief secretary,[2] who commented on the vagaries of public opinion toward government. Everything had been going well on the economic front, he said, when all of a sudden unemployment staggers in stronger than ever, the dollar dips, the monetary system becomes strained. Britain sells less of her exports and the climate of confidence as a result is greatly lowered and, with it, the fortunes of the government itself. . . . This will

1. The Welsh MP, George Thomas.
2. Kenneth Stowe

likely be indicated in the by-election results tomorrow in Ilford; if Mrs. Thatcher cannot pull off a big victory there, she cannot pull it off anywhere.

Thursday, March 2, 1978

An unpleasant dark and wettish day did not add to an otherwise pleasant motor run to Cardiff. It took John about two and a half hours, slightly longer than the train journey I had been thinking about. . . .

My lecture to the law students at University College seems to have gone off well. . . . I began by indicating that the courts have had much to do with the constitutional powers of the two senior governments in Canada. The Judicial Committee of the Privy Council[3] . . . had wrongly affected the distribution of constitutional powers . . . contrary to the intention of the nation's fathers. It was ironic that, in its failure to observe the intentions of the founders of the United States, the Supreme Court in Washington had thwarted their wishes. . . . Happily . . . Parliament's powers could not be abridged by the Scotland bill. I mentioned how concerned at one point I was, that the United Kingdom might inherit the Judicial Committee's error as we had in Canada. . . .

Friday, March 3, 1978

It is now 7:00 a.m. (1) Someone in Switzerland has stolen Charlie Chaplin's body and coffin. The great comedian joins U Thant[4] and a number of others, who were so treated. (2) The Tories win in Ilford. Is the hand-writing on the wall for Jim? It will not be his fault. His leadership has been impressive. . . .

Saturday, March 4, 1978

We reached 12 Upper Brook [from Wales] just before one o'clock. . . . Today's important news has to do with the agreement signed in Salisbury yesterday. Cecil Rhodes in his por-

3. The British judges who functioned as the final court of appeal until the Canadian Supreme Court was given this role in 1949.
4. Former secretary general of the United Nations.

trait above looked down as Bishop Muzorewa, Smith, Chief [Jeremiah] Chirau,* and the Rev. Sithole formally made black rule the "order of the day." White Rhodesia will give way to black Zimbabwe at the end of 1978. Will the guerrillas intensify their resistance or will they begin to see that their cause has been achieved? . . . Owen says the agreement is only a necessary step in the achievement of majority rule. He would hope to bring in the Patriotic Front [Nkomo and Mugabe], who denounce it. . . .

I have been studying Claude Ryan's views on constitutional change; . . . [these] have taken on growing importance as [he is] a candidate for political office. . . . Many Quebecers do not favour the situation as it is and as put forward by Trudeau, nor the sovereignty-association as given by Lévesque. Ryan says they prefer the other way (his position) which calls for two nations or special status. How will Trudeau get around this last one? We have always opposed special status. As for the two nations argument—it always involves the difficulty of language, meaning, etc. . . . How can we give one province special status? Must we not treat all provinces alike? . . .

Ryan says a two-nation thesis is not sufficient. There is no doubt in his mind about Quebec forming a "distinct national unity," but he says it is doubtful that the other nine provinces could be adequately described as a second nation. A solution might be found by dividing Canada into five parts, making each a "constituent state" and so less inclined to look to Ottawa for help. I think this is pure theory. It may be useful to do this, but it would not have the consequences Ryan envisages, nor the purpose he postulates. Setting up five regions doesn't make the rest of Canada "a distinct national unity." . . . He feels a future constitution must be flexible in allowing recourse in certain cases to opting out or opting in, together with an equitable fiscal or financial compensation. . . . He puts forward one idea that would certainly cause him difficulty with the federal Liberals. He insisted that proposals for change must come from Quebec (outside the present government) and that Ottawa should refrain from putting forward constitutional proposals until a consensus has emerged in Quebec among those backing the federalist option. . . . Ryan uses words freely. He will find they can be used too easily. . . .

Wednesday, March 8, 1978

I talked to Trudeau last night on the phone. He is in good form and confident of his political future and of the situation at home. He has not yet decided on an election but is feeling the way. He will wait for another poll before deciding. If it continues as did the last one, the die will be cast. . . .

Friday, March 10, 1978

It is announced by President Carter that Britain and the United States will press for a conference involving all Rhodesian Nationalist leaders. David Owen, who was expected to go to the Security Council after seeing Carter and Vance, hurried back to London. . . . What amazes me is the way Britain is being led in the affair by the United States. There is certainly not much Commonwealth input, apart from Tanzania and Zambia. . . .

Saturday, March 11, 1978

I [will be] on my way to Canada in a few hours for the Canada-United Kingdom Economic Committee meeting. . . . I [saw] . . . the anti-sealers were enthroned on the Canada House steps with their banners and placards, calling on a cruel Canadian government to abandon its uncivilized hunt. Bruce Levett of the Canadian Press called Lorne Green [my assistant] to enquire if Mrs. Martin had spoken out against the seal clubbing. She likely did, but inarticulately, I hope.

Tuesday, March 14, 1978

After arriving in Canada, I spent a few days in Montreal with my son and his family.

Paul and I lunched today with Maurice Sauvé, a Vice-President of Consolidated Bathurst and a former colleague in the Pearson administration. . . . Maurice is head of an organization in Quebec[5] designed to offset Lévesque's effort at independence. It has more members than the Parti Québécois paid-up membership. Lévesque's objective of separation is

5. The Canada-Quebec Movement.

being successfully thwarted, says my former colleague. It is on the wane. The resistance Lévesque faces could mean that a provincial election could precede the referendum. There might well be no referendum at all. Maurice is concerned with the general economic situation in Canada. It is particularly bad in Quebec. Ryan will win the Liberal leadership in Quebec and a provincial election as well. Because of Lévesque's separatist programme, the federal Liberals under Trudeau will carry Quebec in the approaching federal elections. Clark will do better in Ontario but will make inadequate gains elsewhere. Is this too optimistic a picture? . . .

Wednesday, March 15, 1978

The Opposition in the Commons is attacking Trudeau. The unemployment figures are disturbing. . . . I see a danger. If the economic problem persists and the belief grows that separatism is dying, the electorate could concentrate on the federal government's domestic programme. Clark could conceivably advance. Will Trudeau go to the country with a million people out of work? In spite of the favourable polls, his economic problems could topple him. The next few months will tell and so may warmer weather. . . .

After saying goodbye to Paul and his family, I drove to Montebello through the small towns associated with my boyhood. When I arrived at the Seigniory Club, where we were to have our meetings, I dined with the other participants: Jack Johnston, the U.K. High Commissioner to Canada; Sir Leo Pliatzky, the permanent secretary in the Department of Trade; and Gordon Osbaldeston, the Canadian deputy minister in the Department of Industry, Trade, and Commerce.*

Thursday, March 16, 1978

It is so quiet at the Seigniory Club. When I awoke, the sun had penetrated my bedroom. Its reflection on the snow and the river made a true Canadian winter scene. I must manage a swim somehow later in the day. . . .

Our meeting with British Treasury, Trade, and Agriculture spokesmen lasted until after 7:00 p.m. It was thorough and, in many ways, the best meeting since I have been High Commissioner. The British were frank on the M.T.N. They would not object to a mini result. Unless the talks in Geneva cover a wide front, we will be unhappy.

Inflation and unemployment present great difficulties. Leo Pliatzky said the permanence of unemployment called for a new threshold [for a definition of full employment], not the three per cent envisioned in the thirties, but five or six per cent, possibly as many as a million unemployed in the United Kingdom. . . .

Friday, March 17, 1978

It is interesting to hear the bureaucrats discuss their problems and compare their jargon with cabinet ministers. The basis for cabinet decision is so often different. Both preach against protectionism but political facts often stand in the way. The cabinet minister, as I well know, is understandably influenced by the shutting down of a factory in his area. This simple fact is in the background of Britain's take-it-or-leave-it attitude on the M.T.N. It certainly reflects the British view that a wide range of tariff cuts will at the outset be damaging to British manufacturers. Perhaps the dangers of economic isolation will compel a more general statesmanlike posture in Geneva and later by the United States Congress. . . .

Wilf Lavoie [from the High Commission] and Enid Jones, a British official, drove to Mirabel with me. . . . We were taxied to Mirabel for the British Airways flight back to London. Packed like sardines in third class, we were on our way. Our British colleagues [were] comfortably lodged in first class. . . .

Sunday, March 19, 1978

After a day's respite, Nell and I were on our way to Spain for an Easter holiday. We had an inauspicious wait of three hours on the tarmac at Heathrow and we arrived to another disappointment—a hotel pool so cold that I could not swim in it. Nonetheless, I used our week in Spain as a chance to rest and to catch up on my reading. As I commented:

I read about religion. I comment on theology but I am not a religious man. I wish I were. Nell certainly is. . . . The enthusiast sees "at every turn" the evidence of God's will. "God's will will be done, my dear mother would pronounce. The decision belongs to God." . . .

Then on March 29, we flew back to London.

Thursday, March 30, 1978

Britain is living up to its contemporary reputation — no delivery of any papers today, except the *Daily Express* and the *Telegraph*. The others are on strike. . . .

I had a long talk in my Canada House office with the Under-Secretary of State for External Affairs[6] who is in London with Michael Pitfield, secretary of the cabinet. . . . I mentioned to Allan the desirability of Trudeau undertaking more foreign visits. . . . Why should Callaghan and the others exchange views with other leaders and not our own Prime Minister? . . . Callaghan wonders if the United States can be the chief reserve currency by itself. When the industrial seven meet in Bonn [for the Economic Summit] next summer, Callaghan will discuss with Carter the desirability of agreeing on specific proposals in these areas instead of mere declarations. . . . I must say, however, that no one is better at proclamations than my friend Jim. . . . He told the people in Washington that he wasn't a mediator among the leaders of the industrial west. He doesn't altogether shrink, however, from accepting the appearance that this is the case. All well and good. . . .

There is no doubt that Callaghan did emphasize to the President his concern about the economic prospects for the free world this year and next. Inaction would create serious consequences. Carter's leadership was desirable to improve international economic confidence. Callaghan told the President that he feels there is a need for international action in certain key areas of policy. Bonn could become the focus of such a plan. Helmut Schmidt shares Callaghan's concern and encouraged him to take issue with Carter on certain matters such as reflation. The British Prime Minister took no detailed blue print to Washington, nor did he have any proposal for keeping the dollar within target zones. They discussed the pressure for protectionism and the need for international corrective measures. . . . Personal contacts of this sort are good. Callaghan told Carter Trudeau thinks the President is on the right track on the Middle East. . . .

6. Allan Gotlieb

[In conversation with Michael Pitfield] . . . I reiterated the importance of Trudeau's role outside Canada. After the elections he should have more international contacts. Perhaps in the past this had been minimized, Pitfield thought, by the effective supplementary work of Ivan Head. External Affairs, of course, has always suspected Ivan Head's work as pre-emptive of the department's responsibilities in the field of foreign policy. . . .

Friday, March 31, 1978

I spent some time tonight on a new book on Trudeau given me by Michael Pitfield.[7] The author, a newspaperman, George Radwanski, writes of Trudeau's leadership. . . . John Turner in several quotes explains why he left the cabinet. He didn't want to experience my disappointments, the consequence of being on the scene too long. John could have expressed his ambitions more graciously. He will disappear from public gaze. He has already. We will see who will be around longest — that is in public life and service.

[Nell and I] attended the Service of Thanksgiving to commemorate the sixtieth anniversary of the formation of the Royal Air Force at Westminster Abbey this morning. The Queen, her husband, and Princess Margaret were in attendance. The latter was naturally a subject of interest.[8] Recent criticism and defence of her has focused public attention on the Queen's sister. I have sympathy for her. This does not mean that I think she has been circumspect. In some respects, the royal family possesses an indivisibility. . . .

Sunday, April 2, 1978

The President of the United States made an important declaration in Nigeria [that] great power rivalries must not endanger the peace in Africa. The United States would encourage African solutions by Africans [although] the United States wants a Rhodesian settlement based on the Anglo-American proposals. David Owen is slightly at issue on this one. His

7. George Radwanski, *Trudeau* (Toronto 1978).
8. There were rumours, later confirmed, that she and her husband, Lord Snowdon, would divorce.

scheme for marrying the two arrangements makes more sense. From what the Zambian Ambassador told me on Thursday, Nkomo wants . . . to achieve an accommodation with the "moderate" black leaders. . . .

Wednesday, April 5, 1978

Malcolm Muggeridge[9] was here for lunch today. . . . Like Desai [the prime minister of India], he forewarned me that he neither drank liquor nor ate meat but would be happy to join our table. He wished to discuss his [temporary] assignment at the University of Western Ontario and is anxious that immigration requirements will not stand in his way. I was able to assure him that they did not. Muggeridge talks well [and] I found him less strained in speech than I do in his television performances. . . .

Thursday, April 6, 1978

The Princess Margaret problem continues to receive attention. . . . Edinburgh has spoken within the family circles quite strongly. The Queen is said to have urged her sister to modify her private role. . . . Private affairs belong privately. If, however, the public person's private affairs become a matter of public concern, they then form part of the public judgment, whether one likes it or not. . . . I think one may well argue that the monarchy doesn't depend on the virtuous life of every member of the royal family. . . . It seems to me that at this juncture the bishops, the politicians and the gossip-mongers ought to withdraw from the scene, otherwise will they not be something like the Pharisees? . . .

Friday, April 7, 1978

Next week, we will be doing some negotiating at Heathrow, when Canada and the United Kingdom discuss air routes. The British would like us to have Air Canada use Gatwick instead of Heathrow. They wish to relieve pressure on Heathrow. Spain and Portugal are also being put in the same category. To do so, as far as Canada is concerned, would

9. The British journalist and former editor of *Punch* magazine.

affect our investment at Heathrow. It would hurt the Air Canada service [and] . . . it would place us at a disadvantage with other carriers. The British may be using this as a device to get us to agree to allowing them to fly to more points in Canada.

An election is in the air in Canada, with June 12th, 19th and 26th as possible election dates. There has been no decision taken, although the fact that Jean Chrétien will deliver his budget on Monday next would indicate an early date. The Agent-General for Quebec last night said to me Trudeau would win handily. . . .

Sonny Ramphal [gave a luncheon] in honour of the Secretary General of the United Nations[10] . . . [who told me that] the fact that bilateral negotiations often take the place of the United Nations is not disturbing to [him]. He is more interested in results. All the same, he believes the United Nations has demonstrated its usefulness in recent months. It has effectively responded to criticisms by those who assert it to be a mammoth debating centre. Waldheim would be happy if the formality of the United Nations could be transformed into smaller conclaves of informality. The vastness of the Assembly with its torrent of words was not always effective. Nevertheless, it was a good sounding board. . . .

Sunday, April 9, 1978

I was up early and read a considerable part of the new book on Trudeau. Really not good for my morale, particularly as it had to do with the early period when Trudeau was in Justice.[11] . . . What is unsettling is that he altered the course of my life. We were never at loggerheads. [During the leadership contest] his side made it clear that, if he was down at the convention, he would move over to help me, and I know that is what he would have done. He will recall our heart-to-heart talks in the old prime minister's office behind the Speaker's chair. The book, however, in its examination of Pierre's political philosophy is not so wrong as it is exaggerated. This is to be expected. The best part of the book, for

10. Kurt Waldheim
11. Trudeau was minister of justice in 1967 and 1968.

me at any rate, is the description of the cabinet committee system under Trudeau and Pearson. It is not established by the author that Trudeau's more orderly course yielded better results in a governmental sense than Pearson's. Pearson's problem was to win elections. Diefenbaker stopped him. Trudeau was more efficient in winning elections. . . .

Monday, April 10, 1978

The Liberals are wise in the Quebec Legislative Assembly not to block the passage of Quebec's referendum legislation.[12] It is desirable for the vote on independence to be held as soon as possible. Lévesque asserts that the federal referendum law proposed is an insult to the National Assembly, and to the people of Quebec. René doesn't like the federal tactic. . . .

Sealed copies of Jean Chrétien's budget have reached the mission. We, of course, are not allowed to look at the contents. As soon as we have heard that the budget has been delivered, I will give instructions for copies to be released forthwith. . . .

Tuesday, April 11, 1978

[After its release, I assessed] Jean Chrétien's budget [as] a responsible document. In spite of the prospect of an early election, he does not make irresponsible promises. He says that the theme of the budget might well be "responsibility to what Canada deserves." There are no tax cuts, but money for research will be provided to assist in developing industry and to encourage technical innovation.

With the Deputy High Commissioner, I visited Greenwich today . . . and [later] gave [myself] just enough time to get to the House of Commons to hear Denis Healey's budget which, I suspect, on a cursory examination is more political than Jean Chrétien's. Denis provided for tax cuts for lower income groups. . . .

This year, as in other years, I noticed how few from the diplomatic corps attend the Chancellor's presentation, this year perhaps even less so, perhaps because this was the first broadcast budget. . . .

12. This authorized a province-wide vote on the question of independence for the province.

After dinner, I spent most of the time in reviewing material for the ministerial meeting on the Common Fund.[13] There is to be a full-fledged conference of Commonwealth countries, with some twenty ministers in attendance. Canada will not have a minister but will be represented by me as head of the delegation. I suspect that there will not be very many ministers present who have attended as many international gatherings as I have.

Wednesday, April 12, 1978

We have made a commitment in principle to the establishment of a Common Fund. Our position is somewhat like the British. . . . We are agreed that much fluctuation in commodity prices is harmful to producers and consumers. Poor countries, depending on exports of one or a few commodities, suffer harshly from such fluctuations. Some countries can be severely affected by a tendency for sharp increase in commodity prices and they must ensure that consumer and producer interests are properly represented. Instead of a strong central fund, we believe that the autonomy of the individual commodity agreements must be protected against uneconomic price-setting. . . .

Thursday, April 13, 1978

Jean Chrétien phoned me late last night to discuss some features of tomorrow's conference on the Common Fund . . . [because] the wrong economic moves could affect Canada's mineral wealth and resources. Chrétien told me that no de-

13. This was a meeting of ministers (mainly those responsible for trade) from 32 Commonwealth countries who met at Marlborough House to review the state of negotiations on a proposed common fund to stabilize world trade in a number of primary commodities which formed part of the integrated program we outlined at the fourth session of the United Nations Conference on Trade and Development (UNCTAD). The UNCTAD negotiations had broken down in November 1977 and the forthcoming meeting was to try to reach a consensus between developed and developing countries that would allow UNCTAD to resume. The developed countries had reservations about developing countries' proposals for financing the common fund from direct government contributions.

cision had yet been taken on an election date, and one would not be taken before next week. He seemed disturbed about some of our monetary problems, particularly the drop in our dollar. The United States has the same problem. It is face-to-face with responsibilities as the sponsor of the world's major currency. . . .

There are Commonwealth ministers from thirty-six countries meeting on the Common Fund in Marlborough House today and tomorrow. . . . The chairman of the meeting is Edmund Dell, the Minister for Industry and Trade. Britain and Canada emerged, as was fully expected, as the two countries with a more reserved position. I was anxious that the British should speak first. They did. The British are committed to seek new international commodity agreements.

One of the problems, as I see it in this situation, and this was reflected in Dell's statement, is that all heads of government have loudly proclaimed their faith and belief in the New Economic Order [proposals to aid underdeveloped countries]. Statements such as those made by Harold Wilson in Jamaica two and a half years ago and Trudeau at the Guildhall in March 1976 create a problem when it comes to implementing expressions of noble intention. This is particularly true at this meeting. How different what Dell said today from what Wilson said earlier. He said the scheme of a Common Fund is certainly a starting point for discussion but not the last word. He proposed the need for negotiation. He wanted to see a Common Fund of interest to consuming as well as producing countries. . . .

I found it difficult to speak today, because I was aware that our position, like the British, is not satisfactory to the developing countries and doesn't represent the liberal approach we take *a priori* on the problems of the Third World. On the one hand, we have the generalizations of the Prime Ministers and cabinet policy. These are not consistent. . . . I noted that we had welcomed in 1977 at the Commonwealth heads of government meeting the early establishment of a Common Fund. . . . We recognize the need to ensure the financing of buffer stocks but we are not prepared to commit ourselves to the creation of a central source of financing in advance of the establishment of buffer stocks. . . . The reason for this view is that there is little or no evidence that lack of finance has prevented the establishment of an international commodity agreement. This last statement was violently objected to by Lord Campbell of Eskan. . . .[14]

I had to leave the conference [and] . . . while I was away, apparently the chairman, Edmund Dell, took strong issue with Lord Campbell's disagreement with one of my statements and, more particularly, he took umbrage at Lord Campbell's aggressiveness, when it was implied that there was a lack of political will to support direct contributions and make the Common Fund a reality. . . . When I got to the residence . . . I was called to the phone by Sonny Ramphal. He was quite exercised over the turn of events. He thought that Edmund Dell had gone too far and that the meeting was producing unnecessary strains instead of agreement. Edmund is giving the British official dinner tonight . . . [but] we are guests of Loiselle, the Quebec Agent-General [and] I could not cancel this function. . . . I hope that Edmund was able to smooth matters over a little.

I feel very unhappy, not only about this general turn of events but that, where differences take place, there develop such feelings between the "haves" and the "have nots." I suppose I feel this way because of my own personal sympathies which are very much with the under-developed nations. My position is inevitable, constrained by the obligation to carry out government policy. . . . I was not satisfied that the cabinet had carefully considered all the implications of our position. In any event, these positions did not fit in with the high-minded declarations of the Canadian Prime Minister. This is still the situation. . . .

Friday, April 14, 1978

At this morning's meeting at Marlborough House, . . . I emphasized Canada *had* taken a commitment to work for a Common Fund. We adhere to that commitment. I added, we are a member of every commodity agreement in operation, and support a commodity policy which covers due recognition of the needs of developed countries. . . . I won approval when I stated that no one could deny Canada's interest in the need to

14. A director of the Commonwealth Development Corporation.

help the under-developed world. Sonny Ramphal said he could detect the parliamentarian in me as I made this intervention.

A communiqué had been worked on for several hours. On the chief issues, direct contributions to the Common Fund and other measures, the committee could not agree. Nine heads of delegations were asked to take the matter over. Canada was placed in this group, which took an hour and a half to reach agreement. It was an extremely difficult negotiation. Dell did a brilliant job as chairman. Speaking as the United Kingdom delegate, however, he was as firm in not straying from his beliefs as he had been in open session. . . . I was able to persuade him that we should stay and work out some wording on the clauses in the communiqué covering the two main contentions. With some help from Patterson[15] of Jamaica, we got Dell to agree to my suggestion. As a result, without compromising the Canadian or British position, we got an agreed text, which was later accepted by all Commonwealth countries. No mean achievement. . . .

Monday, April 17, 1978

Claude Ryan was elected leader of the Quebec Liberal party last night. . . . It is anticipated that Ryan, with no previous experience in politics, will be a strong opponent against Lévesque. He shares the aspirations of Quebec nationalists but is a firm believer in Confederation. . . . Claude Ryan will be currently acceptable [but] . . . in time he may give Trudeau some trouble. I am sure he will. When Trudeau ran for the Liberal leadership in 1968 . . . Ryan spoke of a particular status for Quebec, which neither Trudeau nor I supported. . . .

Tuesday, April 18, 1978

Just before our [post management] meeting adjourned, we were reminded of the [Joe] Plaskett exhibition in Canada House, which opens tonight. This led us on to a discussion of the quality of the exhibitions. Largely to pull Christian Hardy's leg . . . I asked a number of those at the meeting what they thought of our exhibitions. The classic response,

15. P. J. Patterson, the trade minister of Jamaica.

and more typical than any others, was given by my assistant, Lorne Green. He said some of it "was crap." This provoked much merriment. . . .

Later in the day, I went for a second time to look at the Plaskett paintings, which are superb. . . .

Wednesday, April 19, 1978

The Foreign Secretary reported yesterday on the Rhodesian situation and his weekend talks in Salisbury along with the American Secretary of State.[16] . . . There is room for widening areas of agreement. . . . I think David Owen was unwise to say that Smith's early retirement could help in bringing about a desirable settlement. The truth of the statement is not likely to make Smith more amenable and co-operative. . . .

Don Jamieson has sent me a message, which I am passing on to the Secretary of State. He wishes to thank Owen for his letter of March 21st on Rhodesia. We agree that the best course is to ensure that the Anglo-United States proposals are not abandoned. Jamieson thinks better results could be achieved by this policy. . . .

Thursday, April 20, 1978

Owen was grateful for the help Canada gave at the Security Council debate on Rhodesia.[17] I passed this on to Don. He thinks it important for the five foreign ministers to get together but not to condemn or endorse the [Rhodesian] internal agreement, nor to abandon the Anglo-United States proposals. Owen thinks it will take some time before he can definitely say if Mugabe and Nkomo will meet [with the other Rhodesian leaders] as proposed. The Salisbury signatories are more entrenched. Meanwhile Nkomo and Mugabe are prisoners of those who fund and equip their forces. They clearly want a dominant role for themselves and control over the

16. Cyrus Vance
17. From March 6 to March 14, the UN Security Council debated a resolution rejecting the internal settlement as illegal and condemning the whites for attempting to retain power. (The vote on the resolution was 10 votes to 0 with Canada, France, West Germany, the U.K., and the U.S. abstaining.)

army and police in the transitional period. They want to influence the election. . . . Owen is going to stick to his policy of neither condemning nor endorsing the internal settlement and try to get the parties together. I think this is sound. . . .

Friday, April 21, 1978

I met Don Jamieson at Heathrow in mid-morning. He has come at David Owen's invitation and on short notice for a meeting of the foreign ministers of the five Western countries involved in negotiations on the independence of South-West Africa, Namibia. Their meeting will be on the eve of the special United Nations General Assembly to deal with Namibia. Owen had sent the invitations, as I was advised yesterday, to the foreign ministers of West Germany, France, and Canada who, along with the British and the United States, constitute the United Nations "contact group" with Namibia. They will likely meet only on Sunday. . . .

I returned with Don to the Dorchester. He told me of the preparation for elections which will take place in the early part of July. It looks doubtful that a constitutional package will be put forward, as originally planned. Important as this is, and not being of interest to Lévesque, the division of cabinet opinion indicated that constitutional reform in terms of the package seems to have little electoral value. The matters in contemplation are important and ultimately will have to be acted upon. . . .

Later in the day, I went to Cambridge.

I had tea in the Master's Lodge at Trinity with Molly and Rab Butler. Rab will be leaving as Master of Trinity in June. He is proud of his thirteen years as Master. . . . When I mentioned that I had re-read his *The Art of the Possible* and his Romanes Oxford lecture on autobiography and biography, Rab jumped with interest. He said nothing to me about my plans in this area, although Molly did. Rab has a capacity for self-emphasis. Maybe this is true of all of us as we proceed on life's path. . . .

Saturday, April 22, 1978

Port does not seem to be one of my friends. This may account for too short a sleep and its accompanying restlessness. I was out walking in Great Court well before 7:00 a.m. and visited the chapel at a very early hour. . . . The dining hall would not open for breakfast until 8:15 a.m. At the Boar I had a coffee and read *The Times*. . . .

Sunday, April 23, 1978

I returned to London to meet with Don Jamieson.

Jamieson . . . would like me to come along for the briefing of tonight's meeting of the five foreign ministers. Jamieson will speak for the five at the special session of the United Nations on Namibia's independence, since 1947. (1) Is Namibia to achieve its independence peacefully? The Russians and the Cubans are deeply involved in neighbouring Angola. (2) Will further sanctions be imposed against South Africa? (3) Will the result create greater conflict between South Africa and the West? The question is how to transfer power to the majority in Namibia. The western plan, put forward two weeks ago, would provide a United Nations special representative to co-operate with the Namibian administrator. There would be free elections before independence. A main problem to resolve relates to the status of Walvis Bay[18] . . . claimed by South Africa. . . .

Monday, April 24, 1978

I accompanied Don Jamieson to Heathrow this morning. . . . [At the foreign ministers' meeting] Vance told Jamieson that he had made some progress with Moscow on the SALT talks.[19] Both countries, the Secretary of State observed, are realistic about their problems. Declarations alone will not remove them. It will be necessary to resort to practical measures and make continuous effort. Vance saw Brezhnev[20] the day before yesterday and reviewed with him Soviet/United States relations. Vance said both the United States and the

18. An area incorporated in Namibia.
19. Strategic Arms Limitation Talks between the Americans and Soviets began in 1969 and resulted in a limited treaty (SALT I) in 1972. Talks began again in November 1974 to discuss the reduction in the numbers and types of missiles.
20. Leonid Brezhnev, president and general secretary of the Communist party of the U.S.S.R.

Soviet Union are anxious to conclude an agreement as soon as possible. They want to work toward a general ban on the testing of nuclear weapons. For the past year, Britain, the Soviet Union and the United States have been working on the terms of a treaty to ban nuclear testing. . . .

Thursday, April 27, 1978

My desk was packed high with all kinds of material, memoranda and matters to read. One of my papers had to do with instructions from the Prime Minister in Ottawa, asking me to speak to Prime Minister Callaghan and obtain his assessment of the purpose and possibilities of the NATO summit, shortly to be held in Washington. Our Prime Minister believes that he would profit from a knowledge of the clearly stated objectives of the British and that these would have a bearing on the nature of the meeting and perhaps Canada's approach to it. Trudeau is desirous that the forthcoming NATO Summit should be thorough and yield a productive discussion of problems facing the alliance in the decade ahead. He has written to President Carter, Chancellor Schmidt, and Prime Minister Callaghan making certain suggestions and asking for their views. . . . Our man in Washington[21] will sound out the President, whose reaction to Trudeau's ideas will be of central importance in planning for our Prime Minister's participation. . . .

Friday, April 28, 1978

Jim Callaghan must be a little disturbed this morning. In the two by-elections yesterday, Mrs. Thatcher's party has won both with increased majorities. . . . Jim's position in the Commons continues to be precarious. Only the Liberals' bad showing in these by-elections can influence David Steel to keep Labour in office a little longer. . . .

SWAPO, by a modification in its position, gives hope that it will accept Western settlement proposals for the territory. It will now seek certain qualifications. Up until now, SWAPO had refused to accept the Western package without Walvis

21. Peter Towe, the ambassador.

Bay.[22] This should please the Canadian Secretary of State for External Affairs. On Wednesday, South Africa accepted the plan worked out by the five Western powers last Sunday here in London. SWAPO was wise to accept the proposal outlined by Don Jamieson, in his speech to the Assembly of the United Nations at the beginning of the week. . . . The settlement of the issue depends on direct negotiations between South Africa and an independent Namibia. . . .

I spoke to No. 10 about my desire to see Callaghan re [the] NATO Summit in Washington. As I am to be at a dinner for the Prince of Wales in Cardiff on Thursday, it would be a happy coincidence if I could see him there. I spoke to his foreign affairs secretary about seeing Callaghan, and sent over a copy of a letter I will hand Callaghan on Trudeau's views on the meeting. . . . He would like to avoid over-structuring, and formal speeches. . . . The NATO Summit will interrupt Trudeau's campaigning. The meeting should be a plus for Trudeau and his electoral objective. . . .

22. The South-West African Peoples' Organization (SWAPO), the leading opponent of South Africa rule, insisted that Walvis Bay had to be part of an independent Namibia.

XX

May – June 1978

THESE LATE SPRING MONTHS were busy with our preparations for forthcoming high-level meetings. Early in May, I went to see Jim Callaghan about the NATO Summit later that month. Then, Claude Morin, the minister of intergovernmental affairs in the Quebec government, paid a visit to London. He left me convinced that although René Lévesque's government did not have a united view of the future of Quebec, the Canadian government could create sympathy for the PQ by its heavy-handed instructions regarding treatment of visiting provincial ministers.

An unexpected trip to Australia with the Prince of Wales interrupted the routine for a few days.

In mid-June, the reform of the Canadian constitution became an issue of even greater importance when Trudeau released his constitutional proposal in two stages. The first, a white paper, examined the basis of Confederation. To me, it all sounded a little too theological. Then the minister of justice, Ron Basford, arrived to give the Queen information on the specific proposals which were made public later and introduced in the House of Commons on June 20.

Wednesday, May 3, 1978

Prime Minister [Callaghan] received me in his House of Commons office today at 3:30 p.m. . . . I started off the interview by indicating that Prime Minister Trudeau wanted to get Jim's slant on the NATO Summit meeting, which will be held in Washington at the end of May. I began by querying what should be done at the Summit. . . . I reminded the Prime Minister that at the last NATO Summit meeting, it was agreed to have a study of long-term trends in East-West relations;

the development of a long-term defence programme and initial negotiations toward improved co-operation in defence production and procurement. This gave him the key to what he wanted to tell me. He agreed that the meeting should provide for a comprehensive discussion of broad principles to govern NATO's course into the 1980s. I mentioned that our Prime Minister did not like set speeches [but] preferred a dialogue with the heads of government. Those who wanted to prepare formal speeches could do so and perhaps table them and, in all probability, give them to the press. Moreover, Trudeau would hope that a broad discussion would permit a productive use of the two-day meeting. Conclusions reached from such general discussion could then guide ministers. . . . Callaghan agrees with Trudeau's feelings on the merits of an informal exchange of views. . . .

Callaghan [felt] it was important to understand the United States' position . . . President [Carter's] wish to carry the Congress with him in his support of decisions taken at the NATO Summit. This could well be partly predicated on the realization that shortly thereafter the special session on disarmament would take place. It was important that the objective of that conference be pursued with vigour in the hope that some agreement would follow [and] that progress would be made by the Soviet Union and the United States on strategic arms. Callaghan did not think the President should preside at the meeting. It was not the practice for the host government to take on this responsibility, as is sometimes done in other types of conference, e.g., a Commonwealth Summit meeting or Conference.

On the way out . . . in the long corridor next to the Prime Minister's office, I met . . . Margaret Thatcher, the Leader of the Conservative party. I said to her: "At the end of the month, you know, I am going to spend the night with you at the Castle in Edinburgh." She looked a little amazed. However, I quickly corrected, saying that my wife and I would be guests at the Castle on the same day and night when she would be there, and that the next day we were going to attend the meeting of the Assembly of the Church of Scotland. . . . She said, "Perhaps you will join me in prayer at the Assembly for the conversion of my political enemies." . . .

Thursday, May 4, 1978

There must be considerable speculation in Canada over yesterday's Gallup poll, giving the government and the Conservatives each 41 per cent of the vote. This is a four-point drop for Trudeau . . . [who] should not go to the country right now. I would be surprised if he did. Don Jamieson had told me ten days ago the election would be on July 3rd. . . . The poll shows that only in one province, Quebec, does Trudeau have a majority. Ryan's election will likely stop Lévesque, but it could well be a factor in the lowering of Trudeau's authority and prestige. Somehow or another I feel that in a general election, the Quebec situation and Trudeau's electioneering capacity will carry him through. One can never tell. I suspect some of the public servants around me are amused by the results, as they have every right to be. They are not overly sold on the political leadership of Canada at the moment. Nevertheless, they all discharge their functions to the full and carry out government policy effectively and faithfully. . . .

Nell and I took British Rail [to Wales] today. It was her first journey on a train. We [usually] do our travelling in Britain by car and plane. Today was partly an experimental experience on a fast British train [at] ninety miles an hour. The road bed is frost free and less bumpy than our own trains. . . . For the Welsh Development Corporation dinner with the Prince of Wales as guest of honour, and to which we were invited, our train sped from Paddington station to Cardiff in two hours. . . . Nell and I were greeted by the Lord Mayor. . . . We were taken to a room where top table guests had assembled. The Prince of Wales shook hands with all. He expressed surprise when he saw me. "What are you doing here?" he asked. Nell replied, as I mumbled, because we were asked and wanted to honour you. He smiled. . . .

Friday, May 5, 1978

I was in Macdonald House about 11:15 a.m. The Deputy High Commissioner was first to see me. Loiselle, Quebec's Agent-General, had phoned late yesterday to say that Claude Morin had instructed him that he wished to be free in London on Sunday. The minister appreciated my thoughtfulness in arranging a reception in his honour on Sunday at the residence. . . . He was, however, anxious to call on me. . . . Poor Loiselle is upset. . . . I called Morin in Quebec. If the press made a fuss, he would explain he was sorry he could not keep Sunday's proposed engagements. . . .

Saturday, May 6, 1978

Thanks to the Foreign Office, I had tickets for today's football cup final between Arsenal and Ipswich Town. Threatened rain gave over to the sun and good afternoon weather. Nell preferred to see the finals via television. John Rowan came as my guest. We had perfect centre seats behind the Prime Minister, Mrs. Thatcher, and Princess Alexandra, who wore a rat-like ensemble. . . .

Monday, May 8, 1978

Claude Morin . . . called on me at 9:00 a.m. . . . I had the strong feeling this morning that Morin, not an avowed separatist, certainly at the beginning, has not become any more enthused about pulling out of Confederation. When I used the word "separatist," he took issue. What was sought in Quebec was "sovereignty-association." . . . He has had no contact with Ottawa, beyond a call on an isolated matter over the telephone with Marc Lalonde—so he says. The only contact between the two governments, private or official, has been when Trudeau met Lévesque a few weeks ago. It should be possible for private talks to take place quite unofficially between the two sides to avoid a tragic result. This certainly would be my method. . . .

Tuesday, May 9, 1978

The [British] government was defeated in the House of Commons last night by eight votes. The vote was on an Opposition amendment reducing the standard rate of income tax [although] . . . the defeat was on a clause in the money bill and not the bill itself. The shadow Chancellor, Geoffrey Howe, called for the government's resignation. The government had no intention of treating this defeat as a want of confidence. . . .

There was a time in British parliamentary practice when an event like last night, or ours in 1968,[1] would have involved resignation by the government, followed by a dissolution or giving the Opposition its opportunity on the Treasury benches. In Britain, since a little after the end of the First World War, what constitutes a vote of confidence has pretty well depended on the attitude of the government itself. . . . A defeat of the government's entire budget, of course, would have had to be considered by Callaghan as a want of confidence. . . .

Trudeau has told Carter that he wants the NATO Summit meeting to be fruitful. He thinks the idea of a luncheon at the White House for an informal discussion is wise. Trudeau is right in asserting that foreign policy views should determine collective defence needs. Our proposals are not intended to delay decisions on the long-term defence programme. Chancellor Schmidt shares Trudeau's views in the main. The impression exists that Canada does not agree with the draft declarations the United States has in mind. This is hardly correct. What Trudeau wants to do is to avoid becoming immersed in details [but] . . . Schmidt may not fully agree with this point of view. . . .

I have been thinking about my talk yesterday with the Minister of Inter-Governmental Affairs in Quebec, Claude Morin [who] is going to Paris. It is aggravating that our embassy people there will not have direct opportunity to know what transpires in Morin's talks at the [French] foreign office. Trudeau ought to discuss this matter with Giscard. I think, from what I have been told, the foreign office itself in France regards such a frank discussion as indispensable. A meeting between Trudeau and the President might well clarify the situation between Canada and France. What will be the situation, for instance, if Morin and the French were jointly to announce that the Prime Minister of France is going to visit Quebec? . . . Our man in Paris[2] has told the French that we should not be kept in ignorance of discussions between Morin

1. On February 9, in the middle of the leadership campaign to succeed Pearson, the Liberal government lost a vote in the House of Commons and we refused to resign. (See my *A Very Public Life*, vol II: *So Many Worlds* (Toronto 1985), p. 618 ff.)
2. Gérard Pelletier

and the French government. The French at the top are a difficult lot. Curiously enough, however, I have never had much difficulty in making my point of view known to them. . . .

I have, of course, reported to Ottawa on my talk yesterday with Claude Morin. When he came to see me, he was accompanied by Gilles Loiselle; I was accompanied by Christian Hardy. The conversation lasted for about fifty minutes. Morin defended himself from the charge of being a separatist by saying that the position of the Lévesque government may not have been always clearly annotated. He described sovereignty-association developing simultaneously. This was an important refinement. In other words, sovereignty-association would not develop completely. It would become a simultaneous fact with the realization of association. The Jesuits may have been able to work out this kind of concept. Maybe that is what Morin is! (I hope the Jesuit Fathers will understand I mean no offence.) On the holding of a referendum, he seemed to speak of this as certain for 1979. The question would be intelligent and honest and I had the impression that the form of the question was already settled. (I now learn otherwise.) . . . Morin understood our instructions about the limits of conversations between provincial ministers and their opposite numbers abroad. Having said often in public that the problems between Canada and Quebec would be resolved between these parties without foreign intervention, and having discouraged his colleagues in the Quebec government from looking for support from abroad, Morin seemed to approve what had been arranged for him in London. He was obviously interested in our having selected the moment of his London visit to proclaim rules which tested his good faith. On the question of the francophone summit he would shortly publicly express the desire of his government to participate in it within the Canadian context. Quebec would not act as an independent state in that situation.

He thought Claude Ryan was the best choice to lead the Liberal party from the point of view of his government. According to him, the PQ's [leaders] were afraid that it might be someone who might regard constitutional questions as of secondary importance and consequently would urge the Quebec electorate to concentrate its attention on other questions such as the economy. He thought Ryan would regard the constitution and the referendum as matters of the highest importance and would not be diverted. . . . I have the feeling that Morin is a troubled man at this point.

Thursday, May 11, 1978

I lunched today with Conor Cruise O'Brien, a senator in the Parliament of Ireland and a member of the previous Cosgrave administration [defeated last year]. It is odd that O'Brien and I, in spite of association with the United Nations, did not meet before. He enjoys his new assignment [as editor] at *The Observer*. The going is tough, however, as he has to carry on his senatorial obligations in Dublin as well. . . . As O'Brien has written . . . the union of North and South in present circumstances is not in the cards. The present government, under [Jack] Lynch, talks of unity for political purposes only, knowing full well that the North will not agree to union. Moreover, Lynch, like the previous government of [Liam] Cosgrave, would not want union with Ulster at this time. It would not want to inherit the problems now on Britain's door-step. On the question of security, O'Brien is sure that the government of Ireland is doing its utmost to co-operate. I asked why there were no extraditions from the South to Britain or to the North. For some reason, which he could not explain, O'Brien said that my friend, Declan Costello, as Minister of Justice, had advised the former government that under the Irish constitution the Parliament of Eire could not pass an extradition treaty.

I gave some thought late this afternoon to my talk with Jim Callaghan, the British Prime Minister, last week on the NATO Summit. Trudeau is right in not wanting the NATO Summit, which opens on May 27th, to be a meeting in the traditional NATO manner. It should reflect defence and foreign policy for the next decade or so. I wonder if NATO could not be organized in such a way as to give it more thrust, with possibly some saving in the cost of operation. . . . It seems to me that the greatest political determination should be shown to strengthen NATO's deterrent and defence posture. To this end, we should concentrate on the priorities of measures required . . . to avoid having a mass of recommendations which produce no results. . . .

Friday, May 12, 1978

Trudeau said yesterday there would be no immediate election. The polls undoubtedly were before him when he reached this decision. He gave as his reason the fact that the nation was faced with some problems which the voters wanted solved. . . .

Tonight at the Ivory Coast reception for the Speaker of the National Assembly of the Ivory Coast, M. Philippe Yacé, I was told by an African journalist, Atetey Komey of the African News Services, that the Africans boycotted our national day last year because I did not attend African receptions. As far as I can see, I was the only white head of mission at the reception tonight. Someone from our mission represents me at all these gatherings, if I can't attend. But that Komey should speak in this way shows how important it is to treat the blacks as we wish to be treated. They are understandably sensitive. . . .

Saturday, May 13, 1978

Claude Morin's visit to London has taken place while Ottawa has been examining the rules regarding visits of Canadian provincial ministers to foreign capitals for talks with ministers in these centres. . . .

Recalling Morin's visit last week, I don't think it made, from his point of view, a positive impact. I am, therefore, concerned about the suggested guidelines for provincial visits to members of foreign governments. . . . Accordingly, I have sent a message to Ottawa . . . [pointing out that] if we, the federal government, play too heavy a hand, we run the risk of providing Quebec with a credibility factor it lacks in terms of solutions to Quebec's problem. This is the situation in Britain. We could stimulate sympathy for Quebec separatists as underdogs. We should not appear abroad as a bogeyman. To be otherwise, invalidates our argument that Confederation is sufficiently flexible to deal with the aspirations of all Canadians. I realize that in a few countries there are those prepared to play games inimical to Canadian interests. In those cases we may wish to deal with visits differently than we do here and in most other places. Rather than lay down rules across the board designed to cope with these problem areas, norms should be established on the basis of a lack of credibility of the PQ thesis internationally. Special cases might be treated as exceptional. . . .

Sunday, May 14, 1978

Late last night, I finished Mortimer Adler's remarkable book.[3] Has there ever been a philosopher who organized more systems for the acquisition of knowledge and who taught as many branches of learning? Maritain, Aristotle, Aquinas—these are his particular heroes. . . . No wonder [Jacques] Maritain was his friend and [Étienne] Gilson too. . . . Maritain, says Adler, "shows that Thomism is a continuously unfolding philosophy." Adler trotted out Aristotle and Aquinas into the modern world, treating these two as relevant, more so than Kant and Bradley. . . . I am much stronger for having read Adler's account of his philosophical views and teaching. I made more notes in this book than in most of my recent reading. . . .

Monday, May 15, 1978

I have been thinking over the report of the discussions between Claude Morin and the Minister of State for Foreign Affairs, Frank Judd. Hardy and Loiselle were in attendance. . . . Judd mentioned that at one time he was anti-E.E.C., but he now had accepted the popular judgment. This caused him to observe that he could not understand that Lévesque and Morin would organize another referendum, if the first was not favourable. This did not strike him as a democratic approach. When Morin said he was not a separatist but a supporter of sovereignty-association, Judd defied him to give a precise definition. Morin said Englishmen often used words which did not have the meaning which we give them. The word "sovereignty" does not exactly touch the reality of things. "If we could find a word which would more adequately express what is meant, we would use it with pleasure, but then we would be accused of changing our position, even of going back on it," said Morin. "Consequently, we have

3. Mortimer J. Adler, *Philosopher At Large: An Intellectual Autobiography* (New York 1977).

no other choice but to continue to use the word, even if it doesn't cover exactly our objective." I find this an odd explanation. . . .

Judd said, "taking into account the wide powers enjoyed by the Canadian provinces, greater by far than the proposed powers for Scotland, it surprised him that Quebec wants more power." Morin acknowledged that the province did enjoy wide powers, but these were not sufficient for Quebec's needs and objectives. Accordingly, Quebec wanted to renegotiate a new contract.

Judd pressed why in the elections Lévesque was elected on a mandate of economic and social reform. Using statistics, Morin said that Claude Ryan was in accord with the greater part of the Parti Québécois programme. The majority of Quebecers would, in time, support sovereignty-association. The future referendum must receive the support of about 62 per cent at least. He acknowledged that, at the present, it might not be more than nineteen per cent. . . . Judd closed the interview by expressing British friendship for Canada and the hope that our country would not be fragmented. . . . "You are a witness," [Morin] said to Judd, "that I am not asking Great Britain to support us in our independence effort." He assured Judd that Quebec felt itself closer to Britain than to France. . . . He told me that he could talk more freely with a British minister than with French ministers.

After this interview, Morin returned to the instructions issued by Ottawa on the eve of his European visit. He thought this rule lacked realism. "I told my officials," he said, "to give my agreement to Ottawa, conscious of the fact that once I was abroad I would speak as I wanted." This is exactly what happened between Morin and Judd. It demonstrates how ridiculous the new guidelines are. It is for this reason that I sent the message to Ottawa which I did the other day saying that "it did not serve the purpose of Canada for us to appear abroad as a bogeyman." . . .

Tuesday, May 16, 1978

Why I wake up so early in the morning is hard to understand. This morning it was 3:30 and, while I lay thinking about many things, I obtained little sleep from that moment on.

The day, however, looks promising. The sun is out, the walk from the residence to Macdonald House was more cheery than it has been for many days. . . . What a lovely sight Grosvenor Square is on a day like this, particularly when one has at one's back the hideous American Embassy. . . .

When I got home there was a call from the Prime Minister's Office. I am to go to Australia to represent Canada at Bob Menzies's funeral.[4] I suppose Trudeau acted on the theory that I was the only one left of a generation in Canada who knew Menzies. And so I am off in the morning, if I can hitch a ride with the Prince of Wales, Harold Wilson, Alec Home, Lord Peart, [and Lord Carrington].[5] . . .

Wednesday, May 17, 1978

At Heathrow, Prince Charles greeted the two ex-Prime Ministers, Lord Peart, [Lord Carrington,] the Governor,[6] and me. To me he said, "You do get around." I had seen him a few days ago in Cardiff. [In the plane] the two Prime Ministers are sitting alone. Peart is paired with the Governor of New South Wales. Carrington and I are sitting together. He has been reading Goebbels' diaries. I am reading Hailsham's last book of essays. Alec Home is reading Fitzroy Maclean's book. Lord Peart, *The Train Robbers* by Piers Paul Read. Harold is reading the first volume of his report on city operations. We move about in the plane and talk to one another. We have it to ourselves. H.R.H. has his quarters in front. . . .

Carrington thinks Ted Heath might have been more forthcoming with his successor, Mrs. Thatcher. He is not so sure that Heath will be invited to join a government which she might form. He agrees that Ted is respected and could play a useful role. Perhaps Peter hopes that he might become foreign minister, as I have heard suggested. It was Carrington's ancestor who was Edward VII's great friend. Victoria blamed the Carrington of her day for some of Edward's style

4. Sir Robert Menzies had served as prime minister of Australia from 1939 to 1941 and again from 1949 to 1966.
5. Lord Peart was leader of the House of Lords and Carrington was leader of the Conservative party in the Lords.
6. The governor of New South Wales, Sir Arthur Roden Cutler, who happened to be in London.

of life. Hopefully, Charles would not have to wait endlessly before he wore the crown, said Peter. The Queen was wise and would so act in regard to her son. . . .

Thursday, May 18, 1978

Before we reached Colombo in Sri Lanka, cushions were placed on the floor. Our bed was ready for sleep. Harold Wilson in his shorts toppled in. Alec Home went to bed with his trousers on. The contrast between the two ex-Prime Ministers! . . .

We landed in Perth . . . just after 1:30 p.m. Australian time. People were at the airport to greet the Prince. It reminded me somewhat of Calgary. Although the beginning of winter, the sun was out in full splendour. At Government House . . . we walked about the beautiful grounds. I saw a eucalyptus tree planted by H.R.H. a year ago. The Prince was amused at the suggestion that his tree was not growing as well as one planted by his father. . . .

It is twenty years since I was in Melbourne . . . [but] darkness denied an opportunity to see how much of the city I remembered. . . . There were no special messages from Ottawa and London, and so to bed for ten and a half hours of profound rest and sleep, [after] twenty-six hours in the air. . . .

Friday, May 19 (Australian time), 1978

[Menzies' funeral] service was short and impressive. The homily, given by The Very Rev. James McKay, a friend of Menzies, was not outstanding. There was little of Menzies' domestic leadership and not much of his international statesmanship. . . . The military bands were effective in their requiem numbers. [In all,] a fitting tribute to a great Australian leader, who was said not to be overly enamoured with soldiers, an odd trait in one who possessed his view of Empire.

[When] the guests, like myself, foregathered at Government House . . . the Governor-General[7] and Paul Hasluk[8] assured me that Australia's states were not sovereign. What-

7. Sir Zelman Cowan
8. Foreign minister during the 1960s.

ever may be the practice, they were not constitutionally justified in going directly to Westminster, except through Canberra. The fact is some of them do. One state constitution provides that the Queen is head of state in that particular state. In Canada, of course, the provinces have no direct appeal to Westminster. That is done . . . by the federal government. There is a difference in the status of the Australian governors and our lieutenant-governors. The former are appointed by the Queen, the latter by the government of Canada. There is an argument put forward in Australia that defence and foreign policy reside at the centre, because the "sovereign states" have conveyed powers in these areas. . . .

Time had come to follow H.R.H. to the airport for the journey home, some twenty-six hours or so away. . . .

Saturday, May 20, 1978

After breakfast, Harold Wilson told me how badly he slept. He did better than I with only four hours of sleep. . . . Wilson . . . had reservations regarding David Owen. David had several years ago called on Harold to resign. A month later Harold sent him to a Ministry of State in Health. Who made who? Had Peter Jay appointed Owen, or was it vice versa? Too arrogant, is the former Prime Minister's description of the Secretary of State. . . .

As we near Italy, Peter is getting restless. The Prince of Wales, only a few feet away, is having a long sleep. Alec has just mentioned he will deliver the homily at Selwyn Lloyd's funeral.[9] He knew of my long-time association with Selwyn, who has had all the great offices. Perhaps, as Speaker, he seemed to flourish best. Selwyn did his assignment well, but he was not a man of vision. Heath is not likely to help Margaret until "the bell sounds." Alec hopes that Peter Carrington will become foreign minister. What about you? His reply, "I will be seventy-five in July, a month after the Canadian High Commissioner." Heath could be given a ministry of European affairs. New, but there lies his interest. Heath would not be good, says the former Prime Minister, at the Home Office. . . .

9. Lloyd, who had resigned as speaker of the House of Commons in 1976, had died a few days previously.

Alec thinks Jim [Callaghan] has been tops. Thatcher will win the next election. He believes the Liberals will vote Tory and Labour cannot gain new seats. . . .

The Prince of Wales joined our group for a moment of adieu. He looked fresh. . . . A sleeping pill had given him a good sleep. I thanked him for the lift. In a jiffy he was in his Rolls, off to Windsor Castle nearby. . . .

Sunday, May 21, 1978

Last Tuesday night at the United Nations Dinner, . . . the Senegal Ambassador[10] discussed with me the desire of Quebec to participate in the Franco-African conference in Paris at the end of the month. He agreed that it was a conference of sovereign states and not francophone "under-states" like Quebec. I said hopefully, not another Gabon.[11] He agreed, adding that the Paris meeting would not include all members of L'Agence.[12] In that body, Quebec's participation has been worked out in relation to the objects of L'Agence. I see that Lévesque has been in touch with the heads of African countries. He wants an invitation to the Franco-African meeting. . . . He adds his government is "the only francophone government in North America." He is wrong. The federal government is the only [sovereign] francophone administration in North America. Trudeau's government represents all Canada, including Quebec and its provinces and the francophones in all of Canada's ten provinces. . . .

Tuesday, May 23, 1978

I sent John Hunt, secretary of the cabinet, the text of a letter which will be formally presented to Prime Minister [Callaghan] when it arrives from Ottawa. It is interesting to observe the consistency of contacts between the leaders in the

10. Sulion Diodj Faye
11. In 1968, when I was minister of external affairs, the government of Gabon invited Quebec to send representatives to a conference on francophone education. Canada was not invited. This led to strained relations between Canada and Gabon.
12. L'Agence de co-opération culturelle et technique, an organization of all francophone nations.

West, e.g., our Prime Minister, Callaghan and Helmut Schmidt. The economic problem continues to occupy the attention of the leaders. This will be foremost at the [next Economic] Summit in Bonn. There is always the danger that achievements of the Summit will not live up to anticipation. . . . The area of correction open to governments in the economic, fiscal, and monetary fields is limited [and] even the most concerted action by governments alone cannot correct the world economic situation. . . .

Our Prime Minister hopes that the [Bonn] meeting will be taken up mostly with long-term issues. The agenda should be so formulated as to bring forward the longer term nature of the forces with which government policies must contend. There is the danger of protectionism. How can this be avoided? How can we promote production and trade in the developing world effectively and meet our interest in expanding trade with them without imposing on our own national communities unacceptable strains of adjustment? What are the factors which stand in the way of the task of reaching acceptable levels of employment and economic activity? Are we taking the right steps now to avoid more energy crises? What can we do to bring about public appreciation of the necessary adjustments which have to be undertaken? The leaders must have an opportunity to discuss matters. . . .

Thursday, May 25, 1978

We dined last night at Lincoln's Inn in the Red Building with Lord and Lady Denning. . . . Lord Denning is not averse to political talk, more so than our judges in Canada. Most of the guests seemed agreed that Jim Callaghan was a better Prime Minister than Harold Wilson [and] hoped that Mrs. Thatcher might become Prime Minister, [though] none seemed to like the pitch of her voice. Mr. Justice Denby, the Chancery Judge, had Margaret as one of his students in his law chambers about 1953. He spoke of her as able and energetic. . . .

Friday, May 26, 1978

Election talk here has been encouraged by David Steel's announcement that the [Liberal-Labour] pact will end at the close of the present parliamentary session. Jim is not likely to give any immediate indication and, I suspect, will try to hold off an election until next spring. . . .

B. K. Nehru, the former Indian High Commissioner, good friend and colleague from my first days as High Commissioner, called on me this morning. He has just come from an assignment at the United Nations and is on his way back to India. . . . He thinks Indira Gandhi [the former prime minister] is on her way back. The parliamentary situation is so unstable, the law and order problem is out of hand, he is concerned about India's short-term and, of course, long-term prospects unless matters are taken in hand. The government is a divided council. Only the integrity and good intentions of Desai as Prime Minister give comfort. Indira's son [Sanjay] has caused her considerable embarrassment. She must take strong measures to win full public favour. India's state of confusion, he believes, lends credibility to the authoritarian measures Mrs. Gandhi took two years ago. The parliamentary system and the political party's weaknesses all point to the need for leadership of the kind given by Indira's father.[13] This is not forthcoming and so B. K. thinks restrictive measures are inevitable, if some order is to issue from the present chaotic situation. . . .

Saturday, May 27, 1978

Does the Canada Club in London, which was established in 1810 and before Confederation, come within the meaning of a club as comprehended by a recent Treasury Board directive? It provides that Canadian hospitality should not be extended in clubs or other establishments which practise discrimination by refusing to make their facilities and services available to particular groups of persons. . . . The philosophy behind the directive is one I support. . . . Ottawa says, while we here are in a better position to judge, it appears that since the club excludes female membership, it must be considered as inappropriate for any official Canadian government-financed hospitality or for payment of club fees by the government. It cannot be imagined that a Canadian official "would want to

13. Jawaharlal Nehru

be an officer of such a club." My view is that the Canada Club is not a club in the sense contemplated by the directive. . . . Some months ago, Maggie Carlson [of the High Commission] objected to the discrimination of the Canada Club in not being allowed to attend the dinner at which Gordon Richardson, the Governor of the Bank of England, was the speaker. Tom Murray [the president] was a little sticky, I thought. We could have squeezed Maggie in and no one would have objected. I know of nothing in this dining organization's rule which would have stood in the way. As High Commissioner, following a long-time practice, I preside at the dinners. . . .

Trudeau spoke in the Assembly at the United Nations in the disarmament debate yesterday. Canada will abandon nuclear weapons in its air force. We have already pulled out nuclear weapons in our aircraft in Europe. Conventional weapons will replace them. This makes Canada the first nuclear armed country "to divest itself of nuclear weapons." . . .

I left Heathrow for Montreal around 4:00 p.m. to spend the weekend with Paul. Jamie, my grandson, was to make his first communion the following day. And then it was on to Waterloo to the convocation at Wilfrid Laurier University.

Tuesday, May 30, 1978

An amusing incident developed when I registered here [at the hotel in Toronto] yesterday. Would I produce some identification? I would, but I had none, I replied. "You must know me." The clerk did not, nor did others at the desk. The bell boy did and so I was given a room. . . . Half an hour later, a big basket of fruit was delivered to my room. A peace offering! But it does show that one is soon forgotten. . . .

After my flying visit, I was back in London by the weekend.

Sunday, June 4, 1978

On my way to mass, Upper Brook at the Park end presented a picture of commotion. Was there another demonstration at the United States Embassy, which stands in all its architectural horror, at one end of Grosvenor Square, opposite Macdonald House? . . . A film was being produced depicting the friendship of Eisenhower and his female military chauffeur. . . . It was interesting to watch the filming. Sand bags protect the windows. Old taxis ply up and down, vying with military trucks, men and women in military uniform everywhere. . . .

Tuesday, June 6, 1978

I went to the House of Commons today to listen to the Prime Minister's report on his Washington visit [last week]. He reported on the disarmament [discussions] at the United Nations and the NATO Summit. . . . He was opposed to the Conservative policy of urging the United States to rush headlong into Africa with arms. . . . He criticized Mrs. Thatcher's "instant solutions." Callaghan said there is no intention to have NATO involved in Africa. . . . The line taken by the British Prime Minister corresponds to the position taken by Trudeau. . . . On arms control, the British Prime Minister said, "We are living in a powder keg situation," as he had said to me when I saw him three weeks ago. The Prime Minister insisted, however, that, in seeking to avoid an acceleration of the arms race, he wanted to lower the temperature. As Trudeau had pointed out, it was desirable to live with Russia and not fight her. . . .

Jim was skilful in his presentation and had an advantage at almost every point over Margaret Thatcher, who hits well and hard. She lacks Callaghan's poise, which is strengthened by his good humour. . . .

Thursday, June 8, 1978

The Canadian position on the neutron bomb admittedly is support for a bargaining position in arms talks with the Soviet Union. . . . There is no doubt that we do not like it. We are, however, in an alliance with the United States. . . . It is easy for us to say that the weapon is repugnant. Jamieson does not disagree that our situation is "the neutron bomb, if necessary, but not necessarily the neutron bomb." Some day, some critic of Don Jamieson will say that he has used opaque words. . . . The nature of foreign policy discussion was ever thus and will ever be until we reach the ideal state. . . .

Friday, June 9, 1978

Denis Healey presented his new budgetary proposals yesterday. These included an increased minimum lending rate, restrictions on the amount of money banks can lend and increased . . . [unemployment] insurance contributions. The Conservatives and the business community have criticized them. They were occasioned by the negative vote on the budget by the majority in Parliament [on May 8 and 10]. . . . If the Chancellor had agreed to his party's proposals from the start, said the Leader of the Liberal party, there would not be a lack of confidence in the government. . . .

Sunday, June 11, 1978

I have just received in today's bag [from Ottawa] the white paper of the federal government proposals for the "renewal of the Canadian federation."[14] . . . Renewal, however, is an almost evangelical term. . . . There is to be a new constitution by the end of 1981. The government will employ the plentitude of its authority to achieve this in consultation with the provinces. The latter are urged to co-operate with the federal government to "renew the constitutional provisions which cannot be amended without their co-operation." . . . Canada will continue to be "a genuine federation, a state in which the constitution establishes a federal parliament with *real* powers which apply to all parts of the country, and provincial legislatures with equally *real* power within their respective territories." . . .

I have just had a call from Paul who, incidentally, told me that the constitutional proposals of the government have been leaked. They are in today's [Montreal] *La Presse*. . . . Any public servant guilty of this kind of action should not be kept on a minute. . . .

Monday June 12, 1978

Apart from the Senate and Supreme Court amendments and the language used regarding the distribution of powers, the white paper is not a sensation. . . .

14. *A Time for Action: Toward the Renewal of the Canadian Federation* was a white paper prepared by Paul Tellier of the national unity group.

In the introduction . . . it is said that we are entering "a period of re-appraisal and Canadians feel the time has come to reconsider what we are and to determine what we want to become." I suppose this is true, but I think that we have long ago reached this decision. We want to stay as we are and grow. Not often in a government document does one quote the poets. Rubert Brooke is mentioned for "the soul — or the personality — seems to have definite room to expand." This is a comment on our unfathomable land . . . [but] a soul could expand on *any* size of land. . . .

Is there a will for us to survive as Canada now is? We are told that Canada will survive if there is a collective will. I think there is such a determination and the reaction to the Parti Québécois independence drive has shown this. We are aware of our identity, in spite of all the wasteful writing on that point over the years. . . .

The paper goes on to say, "to affirm our identity, we must first take care of the nation's roots." There is nothing new in this. That is what Macdonald spoke about, as Laurier did. Our identity lies in the fact, as Laurier mentioned, we are a mosaic. . . . I have talked about this for over forty years — how many times in my own constituency and all over Canada! . . .

Looking at the [section] . . . entitled "The Principles of Renewal," I again note my uneasiness . . . [because] it sounds too theological and "charismatic." Here, emphasis is placed on entrenching rights and freedoms in the constitution. That is something we tried at Victoria [in 1971] when Robert Bourassa, Quebec's Premier and his adviser, Claude Morin, now the No. 2 man with Lévesque, would not listen to Trudeau's proposal for entrenching basic rights and freedoms. . . . Entrenching the equality of our two official languages does not mean that all must become bilingual; it does mean the establishment of language equality "within federal institutions" and that "wherever numbers justify, provincial services must be administered to minorities in their official language." This language, which I take from the white paper, is ambiguous, perhaps intentionally so. It cannot mean in all languages. We must not lead ethnic groups generally to misunderstand the nature of the obligation to the two official language groups and other minorities. . . .

One of the really difficult sticking points [arises where] it is noted that "the division of powers between the two [federal and provincial] authorities must be clarified and made more functional. Some of our government practices restrict the internal sovereignty of the two orders of government and must be revised." Clarification could suggest that on the spending power there will be no basic change. Accommodation and consultation may avoid the demand to give the provinces unlimited taxing power. The phrase "internal sovereignty" is a new one in a Canadian constitutional document. We don't often speak of sovereignty of the provinces but it is wise that we do it within the limitation noted in the white paper. . . .

The government feels that to give effect to many needed changes, there must be in the place of the Senate, a House of the Federation. The Supreme Court must be provided for in the constitution [and] the provincial governments should have a voice when appointments to the courts are made by the government of Canada. This emphasizes that the federal government will continue to make appointments, but a method will be provided for provincial participation in the selection of judges. The constitution must be patriated so that it can be amended in Canada [and] an amending procedure will have to be agreed to. . . .

Tuesday, June 13, 1978

I was awakened early by communications advising that the letter from Trudeau to the Queen had arrived with instructions to deliver it this morning. Along with this message was a note to Sir Philip Moore saying that, in accord with arrangements made between the Office of the Privy Council in Canada and the Queen's secretary on Friday last, Basford, and the Prime Minister's constitutional adviser, Don Thorson, would meet with the Queen Thursday afternoon to outline the general proposals contained in the white paper on the new Canadian constitution. . . .

I met Don Jamieson at Heathrow Airport this morning. We had an hour of talk before he took a plane for Paris. . . . I informed Don that the constitutional proposals in the white paper were tabled yesterday in the House of Commons. . . .

Some weeks ago, he had anticipated that the proposals would not be tabled or discussed before a general election. The reported state of public opinion on party performance as indicated in popular polls had caused a shift in the date for presentation of the constitutional changes. Putting off the election made it desirable for the proposals to be brought forward. . . .

Frank Judd, Minister of State for Foreign Affairs, had me to lunch today at the House of Commons. . . . He wanted to know what I thought about his proposed format when he meets with the High Commissioners in a few days. He will seek to encourage Commonwealth representatives in a general discussion on the many issues facing the Commonwealth and . . . hopes to give the meeting an air of informality by holding it in his own office. . . .

Wednesday, June 14, 1978

When the group of MPs, led by Frank Allaun,[15] came to see me at noon, they congratulated Trudeau for his speech on disarmament at the recent special session of the United Nations General Assembly.[16] Mr. Allaun [who] has a special interest in defence and disarmament matters . . . said Trudeau had given a lead to the world. . . . One of the delegation, Mr. A. Latham,[17] intends to move an early day motion in the Commons, urging the government to offer its congratulations to Canada. . . .

Regarding Trudeau's announcement that we were ending our nuclear role, I pointed out that the decision had been taken earlier to run down our nuclear capability; the Prime Minister's statement was a confirmation that the final stage of this process had been reached. . . . [This] decision by the government has no impact necessarily on NATO defence capability since Canada would in any case be covered by the American nuclear umbrella as Europe continues to be.

15. Labour MP for East Salford.
16. The session took place in New York from May 23 to June 30. Trudeau's speech on May 26 emphasized the unilateral renunciation of nuclear weapons by Canadian forces. He proposed a strategy of suffocation to halt the arms race.
17. The Conservative MP for Melton.

I indicated that the Prime Minister's comments . . . were intended to demonstrate that we were not asking of other countries something that we were not prepared to do ourselves. . . .

I highlighted [Trudeau's] . . . proposals to stop the nuclear arms race through a strategy of "suffocation." This strategy has four elements: (1) . . . a comprehensive test ban to impede the further development of nuclear explosive devices; (2) to stop the flight testing of all new strategic delivery vehicles, thus depriving the super powers and others interested in nuclear weapons of a chance to develop yet more new vehicles for delivering them; (3) an agreement to prohibit the production of all fissionable nuclear material for weapons purposes; (4) an agreement to limit and then progressively to reduce military spending on new strategic nuclear weapons systems. While there would be considerable difficulties in verifying that military budgets accurately reflected such a commitment, it is an idea widely espoused, especially by the non-aligned countries. . . .

Thursday, June 15, 1978

I was up early this morning to meet Ron Basford, Minister of Justice, and the Prime Minister's constitutional affairs adviser, Don Thorson, at Gatwick. On our way in, we discussed the visit they will have at noon with the Queen, when the Minister of Justice reviews with her the constitutional proposals to be laid before Parliament, and certain changes in the royal powers as Queen of Canada and the role of the Governor-General. . . . What has been the practice will now be embodied in the new constitution. . . . After he has talked to them, the Queen's secretary would like some time with the Queen before she receives the Minister of Justice and the constitutional adviser. This will be an important ministerial contact on behalf of the Prime Minister with the Queen. I am sure that she will fully understand the need for the new arrangements. I am satisfied they do not alter the present situation. It will, of course, be argued otherwise by some in Canada. . . .

In mid-afternoon, I conferred with the Minister of Justice and Don Thorson. The meeting with the Queen and Sir

Philip Moore was satisfactory, even perhaps beyond expectation. . . . The Queen went through those portions of the bill concerning the Crown in Canada imperturbably. She fully understood what was provided and sought information rather than imposing any impediment in the government's decision to present the bill. As far as the Crown is concerned in Canada, the bill confirms the factual situation. Elizabeth II remains Queen of Canada. The bill provides for the first mention in the constitution of the office of Governor-General and the powers he will exercise, when the Queen is not in Canada. I suspect that the Queen, such a sensible woman, will be relieved that no drastic action is being taken which would affect her role in Canada. . . . The bill does not specifically provide for a characterization of who is head of state [but] the head of state is the Queen. In the explanations of the bill in Canada, I hope this will be made clear. [Diefenbaker] will charge that the government is continuing the process of eroding the Crown's status in Canada. . . .

It interested me greatly to note how Basford and Thorson reacted to their meeting with the Queen. . . . There was an element of understandable reaction to the mystique of the monarchy, without doubt the most powerful in the world. We talked of this. . . . Their impression is that the day was a satisfactory one on the part of all concerned. I can say for myself, I was relieved by the result.

Last night I had a dinner for the Minister of Justice and the Prime Minister's constitutional adviser. My guests were Sam Silkin, the Attorney-General in the government of Britain and John Edwards, a professor of law in Toronto. . . . We reviewed the policy of the government of Britain in respect of a petition to amend the B.N.A. Act, with or without the consent of the provinces. The Attorney-General agreed with my submission, strongly supported by Ron and Thorson, that it was not open to the government of Britain to go beyond the petition formally presented by the government of Canada. . . .

Friday, June 16, 1978

I woke up surprisingly early after only about three and a half hours sleep with a full day ahead of me, but somewhat exhilarated to be involved, even in a minor way, in such an historical situation as confronted us yesterday. When I left the residence at 8:00 o'clock this morning, the Minister of Justice was soundly asleep. . . .

Saturday, June 17, 1978

Thorson and I dined alone tonight. More discussion on the constitutional changes. The bill on the new constitution in effect abolishes the Senate as it is. Ray Perrault[18] is furious and so will other senators be. The House of Federation (what a bad name) will replace it. Thorson says the good senators can get back in as nominees of the House of Commons. Provincial nominations will be made by provincial legislatures. Something had to be done about the Senate. The proposals for Senate reform seven years ago embodied some of the new features but, as a whole, the plan to which we had committed ourselves in the cabinet was not as sweeping as is now the case.

Sunday, June 18, 1978

Basford and Thorson left about 1:00 p.m. for Toronto and Ottawa. They begged me not to interrupt this "day of rest." . . . In this case, the visit was an important one. We had continuous discussion during Basford's stay. He will be leaving the government in three weeks or so. . . .

Monday, June 19, 1978

At our Monday morning meeting, I was advised that one of the Quebec ministers concerned with environmental problems had made an appointment with the [British] parliamentary Under-Secretary in the Department of the Environment. At first we had understood the appointment had been arranged by the Agent-General. We now learn that it was made directly. Ottawa insists, my officers tell me, that Quebec should first of all have asked Ottawa to arrange for the appointments through the High Commission and that, in any event, someone from the High Commission should be present when the Quebec minister sees the parliamentary Under-Secretary. . . . Loiselle

18. The leader of the government in the Senate.

seemed reasonable when Christian Hardy talked with him. I hope, with his [Loiselle's] help, we can resolve this without embarrassment. The important point, however, is, are we to be bound by [these] ridiculous rules? . . .

Wednesday, June 21, 1978

[When] I was talking to Philip Moore late yesterday, he told me the Queen was grateful to Trudeau for the courtesy of sending over his Minister of Justice . . . to discuss the constitutional proposals. The Queen is pleased with the arrangements made in the constitution regarding the Crown. I think this will settle the matter of the Crown in Canada for a long time. Over a hot-line, Trudeau had said of the disposition being made of the Crown in the constitution the following: "The government was not proposing a change in the role of the Queen." The Prime Minister said: "Canada would remain a constitutional monarchy and the Queen of Canada will remain the head of this constitutional monarchy."

This is perhaps the most definitive positive statement Trudeau has made. . . . I am sending a copy of his remarks to Sir Philip. . . .

The bill providing for the wide changes in the constitution was introduced yesterday in the [Canadian] House of Commons. . . . I suspect that when the bill's provisions were outlined in the Liberal caucus yesterday, there was much discussion and, I suspect, heated criticism. There would be a number who would want to eliminate the Senate altogether and many others will object to provincial nominations. The Senate could not go on in its present form [because] it had for a long time lost credibility [and] not all of its members contributed to its work. Potentially, it could serve a great role, not unlike the work which I think the House of Lords in Britain now performs, at least through . . . those members who take their duties seriously. . . .

In the late afternoon, I went to Frank Judd's office, where he had a reception for the High Commissioners. The room was crowded. This gave an atmosphere of informality . . . [and] Frank Judd has an easy and friendly way about him. This is the sort of thing that is useful for someone in the Foreign Office to do. The High Commissioners do not see one another as a group sufficiently. This is one of my criticisms of Sonny Ramphal. There should be more meetings at the Commonwealth Organization of High Commissioners, not merely their officials.

This meeting, however, was not as successful as it should have been. . . . With some thirty-six High Commissioners attending, Frank should have limited his remarks and permitted wider discussion. He drifted on, as did others, on human rights, although it was intended that we should concentrate on economic questions. One High Commissioner almost wrecked the meeting by a loud speech and persistent intervention, challenging the United Kingdom to observe respect for human rights instead of condemning other countries at all times. The Indian High Commissioner made a sensible proposal that the subject matter of further meetings should be limited essentially to one subject and that the participants should each have a limited and reasonable period to make their points. . . .

Thursday, June 22, 1978

[A phone call from Ottawa revealed] as I anticipated, there is much gloom in the corridors of the Senate. . . . The Senate Leader, my successor, Ray Perrault, spoke as though he was going to a funeral of his dearest friend. I did my best to cheer them up, suggesting that there was going to be a Senate and House of Commons committee and from it would flow many of the details—imperfections from their point of view. Perrault blames the mandarins for the bill, laying particular stress on Gordon Robertson and Thorson, as Don told me he had. The appointment of senators by the Commons on the basis of party numbers in the House reduces the [current] senators . . . who could become members of the House of Federation [and] will eliminate a number of senators already appointed. A strong case can be made for a clause protecting those already in the Senate. It will be for many of them a serious matter, particularly in the case of the older ones, if they are relieved of their assignment and its income. I am sure that Ray Perrault's position vis-à-vis his colleagues in the Senate is much more difficult than mine was. . . . Would I see him if he came to London? I would, of course, I said to Ray, but perhaps I could help him just as well on the telephone. I could do no more, however, than to help him clarify what has already been decided and what amendments might be contemplated when the Senate and House of Commons committee meet. . . .

Friday, June 23, 1978

When I came to the office this morning a few minutes before 8:00 a.m., the following telegram was on my desk, a reminder from my colleagues in the High Commission what this day is for me. I appreciated their thoughtfulness:

> "TO LDN/HIGHCOM ONLY — VERY PERSONAL
> REF JUNE 23, 1903
>
> — AS TIME GOES BY
>
> WE HEARD ABOUT SOMEONE TURNING FOUR SCORE LESS FIVE/ WHAT A NICE LONG TIME TO BE YOUNG AND ALIVE/ TO THE PERSON WE KNOW WHO HAS SUFFERED THIS FATE/ WE SEND WARMEST GREETINGS ON THIS FABULOUS DATE. . . ."

Saturday, June 24, 1978

A call from Senator Laird[19] indicated how disturbed the senators are. [Keith told me that] the Prime Minister realizes that this scheme for a House of Federation could result in legislative delays in the Commons. This is what greatly disturbed Allan MacEachen as House Leader. The Prime Minister insists on his proposal, because he wishes to ensure that the regions and provinces are represented in the upper chamber. The Leader of the Opposition in the Senate, Jacques Flynn, is furious with Trudeau's suggestions. Nevertheless, George-Étienne Cartier was the main proponent of a non-elected Senate, to protect provincial and minority rights. The Senate cannot claim that it lived up to this objective. One may examine the new proposal to ascertain if provincial rights will be protected by the new arrangement.

Parliament may legislate regarding the Senate without provincial consent. It cannot do so, however, without concur-

19. Keith Laird had been my law partner in Windsor.

rence by the Senate. [Although] Trudeau wants provincial agreement, he would not withdraw the proposal for a House of Federation, if one or two provinces objected. . . . What is important is that there be support for the proposal by all parties in the House of Commons. Trudeau believes the Conservatives will be in favour [because] they had recently gone further than the government in proposing provincial representation. If [Alberta's Premier] Lougheed is opposed, the Prime Minister will count on Joe Clark to deal with him.

I had an early telephone call from Michel Gauvin, our man in Strasbourg. I have invited him to our reception for the Queen on July 17th. He had been in charge of the royal tours in Canada. . . . When Michel was replaced, . . . the Palace was unhappy. Gauvin was a favourite of the Queen. She liked his bluntness and frankness. . . .

I attended a reception at Quebec House this evening. . . . [The invitation read] "*Le Délégué Général du Québec et Madame Gilles Loiselle vous prient de leur faire l'honneur de venir célébrer la Fête Nationale des Québécois.*" Now, it is not *La Fête Nationale des Québécois*, it is the feast of St. Jean Baptiste, observed by French Canadians all over Canada. I have observed this feast for many years. I was baptized in *l'Eglise St. Jean Baptiste* on Empress Avenue in Ottawa. All this I told the Quebec Agent-General. He understood, as did his wise little wife. With tongue in cheek, arriving as almost the first visitor at Quebec House, I wished my hosts a happy St. Jean Baptiste day and to Quebec, my warmest greetings and admiration for its indispensable qualities to Canadian nationhood. It was a good party. To many of the younger people present, I extended an invitation to attend our Canada Day reception next week. . . .

Sunday, June 25, 1978

Today is the anniversary of Paul VI as Pope—fifteen years. The Diplomatic Corps, at least the papists in it, were invited to high mass at Westminster Cathedral. I went. Not too many heads of mission were there. I wonder what some of them do. Some never show up. . . . The Irish Ambassador and I responded lustily to the Latin of the mass. He knew the "*Orate Fratres*" and I knew the "*ex hoc nunc et usque in seculum*" faultlessly. I couldn't hear the Italian Ambassador. He likely had some complaint. . . .

Monday, June 26, 1978

At our Monday morning meeting we discussed preparations for the Bonn [Summit] meeting. . . . I sent to Ottawa this morning a report of our relations with the United Kingdom [which] mentioned our cultural and social links and emphasized the sympathy shown in the United Kingdom for our national unity problem. . . . The only possible area of difficulty could be in the renegotiation of the Canada-United Kingdom bilateral air agreement. Britain wants access to western gateways. The United Kingdom wants us to move from Heathrow to Gatwick. . . .

Callaghan's first objective is to win the next election, rendered certain this fall by the collapse of the Liberal-Labour pact. A close result is expected. Callaghan will appear as statesman and mediator in international economic affairs. His second objective is to prevent the British economy from going into further recession. . . .

At the suggestion of the Ambassador for Cyprus, I called on its President, Kyprianou, in his suite at the Grosvenor Hotel, just after I had had a swim in the pool there. I had not seen Kyprianou since 1965.[20] Then, I had gone to see Archbishop Makarios and members of his government. The President told me he had left the office of Makarios just as it was after [his] death. My picture faces him every day, he said. Apparently, I had given one to Makarios. . . .

In the background of today's discussion [with Kyprianou] was my own knowledge of the talks Don Jamieson had in Cyprus a few days ago. Don found the situation bizarre and sad. There is little prospect that those on the island have a real expectation for settlement. The pressure must come from outside. Kyprianou told me that, if the two communities were left alone, they could resolve the matter, but he went on to say [the government of Turkey in] Ankara held the key to settlement. He wants to meet Ecevit, who was bent on

20. Spyros Kyprianou had served as foreign minister then.

partition.[21] This, Kyprianou said, he could not and would not accept. There is no doubt that mutual trust does not exist in Cyprus. The Turks see Kyprianou as intransigent. My host sees himself as the aggrieved victim of aggression. The Greek Cypriots feared partition and argue that the Cypriot government is the single sovereign authority. The Turkish Cypriots are afraid of domination, and exploit the control of northern Cyprus by the Turkish army [which had occupied that part of the island in 1974]. . . . When the Greeks speak of a strong federal republic, the Turks read into this domination. . . .

I said to Kyprianou that we had been on the island a long time.[22] No one had a greater stake in the prestige of the force than I, its author, but the cause of peace-keeping was not served by an indefinite stay. . . . We were anxious to see progress toward a settlement. . . . My impression is that nothing will happen until the United States' decision is taken finally on [whether to lift the arms embargo on Turkey]. The United States will have to exert pressure and force a settlement. As I was leaving him, Kyprianou said, you must come and see me in Cyprus. I told him that I had been planning to do so. . . .

Tuesday, June 27, 1978

Looking over Canadian papers, I am somewhat startled by the criticism of Trudeau's constitutional proposals. Dissatisfaction over the references in the new constitution to the Governor-General, which the *Globe and Mail* interprets as making him head of state, is strongly expressed in many quarters. . . . The strongest proponent may be the Leader of the Opposition, who regards some of the formulations as his own. The Senate is in a fury. I expect much opposition will develop. What the proposals may look like in a year's time is problematical. Would Trudeau have been wise to withhold them until after the election? This, of course, was the view I expressed several months ago to Don Jamieson. We were both

21. Bulent Ecevit, the prime minister of Turkey, wanted the island divided into Greek and Turkish states.
22. Canada had sent a contingent in 1964 there as a member of the United Nations peace-keeping force.

agreed that, on the eve of an election, constitutional revision was not the most exciting issue, although important, to put before the electorate. . . . It isn't easy to satisfy everyone. In the long run, in two years' time or so, everything will settle down. The changes will be found workable. . . .

Friday, June 30, 1978

I note Marc Lalonde, Minister of Federal-Provincial Relations, affirms that the government will not allow opposition from a minority of provinces to hold up the first phase of the constitutional reforms. There will be consultation, of course. Lougheed and Blakeney say the consultations should have taken place before the white paper was tabled and the bill introduced. Constitutionally, their position is wrong. The federal government could not recognize a provincial veto in respect of matters which come under the federal parliament. . . . Lougheed says that the Senate could not be changed without provincial approval. He is prepared to take the matter to court. I think it would have been wiser to consult the provinces, but there was no legal obligation to do so. . . .

Few living have known a saint. . . . Now comes word from Rome that the Pope has decreed that Brother André is venerable. A first step toward his beatification and sainthood. When I was a young boy, a victim of spinal meningitis (some call it polio), my mother took me to see Alfred Bessette at Saint Grégoire d'Iberville, Montreal. We made two visits to his mountain-side church, opposite the institution where he had been a porter. This good and saintly man prayed for my condition. This, together with my dear mother's profound faith, made it possible for me to escape the full handicap of lameness and bodily impairment. . . .[23]

23. Brother André, born Alfred Bessette, became a popular religious figure in Quebec. His miraculous healings were attributed to his interventions with St Joseph. In 1904, he built a small oratory on Mount Royal which was replaced by the existing basilica in 1924-55.

XXI

July – August 1978

THE SUMMER MONTHS passed relatively quietly. The mission in London was on the fringes of the preparations for the Economic Summit, that year held in Bonn, West Germany, in early July. It seemed as though the ever-present election expectations were rising to a fever pitch in both Canada and Britain. At the end of the month, shortly before I was to leave for my holiday in Canada, the government of Nigeria upset the applecart by announcing that athletes from that country would boycott the Commonwealth Games in Edmonton later in the summer.

Tuesday, July 4, 1978

Duncan Edmonds[1] and [Douglas] Roche, MP, were in to see me. They are an advance guard for the Leader of the Opposition; Joe Clark arrives tomorrow morning. . . . Both Roche and Duncan insisted that the important issue in Canada at the moment is the economic question. Ryan is likely to hold Lévesque in check. Separation will not eventuate. . . .

Wednesday, July 5, 1978

I was at Heathrow this morning to welcome . . . Joe Clark. . . . On the way in, Joe and I talked about the situation in Canada. He was not sure when there would be a federal election [and] was surprised that Trudeau had brought forward the constitutional proposals before an election. The reaction to them was critical. He could not see how much political advantage could be derived from them. As a matter of fact, this is my

1. He had been my assistant and then went to work for Joe Clark.

view. . . . [He] told me that the decision to televise the proceedings of the House of Commons had helped his leadership. It also gave the impression that he had behind him a team which could readily be converted into a successful cabinet operation. . . .

The dinner in the Painted Hall at Greenwich[2] was an elaborate and impressive affair. . . . David Owen and the doyen of the Diplomatic Corps spoke at the dinner. David, obviously a little stunned by the plethora of newspaper criticism, affirmed he would maintain strict observance of principle in the formulation of British foreign policy. In the long run, this would win out. There is an under-current of dissatisfaction with David. Arthur Bottomley urged me to tell his protégé what some of this criticism is. Certainly, I don't intend to do that. In the first place, I don't fully share it. . . .

Thursday, July 6, 1978

I joined Joe Clark . . . for lunch at the home of the Commonwealth Secretary General. . . . Sonny and I had a chat about our meeting this afternoon on Belize.[3] The Leader of the Opposition was interested to know that this kind of question came within my jurisdiction as High Commissioner and that there was a discussion of this kind of problem with High Commissioners and the Secretary General. I explained, of course, that [the] discussion . . . was not to formulate policy but to discuss developments in the light of stated positions of the governments we represent.

[At the] meeting of the Belize Committee at Marlborough House, Ted Rowlands, the minister . . . responsible for Belize in the Foreign Office, outlined developments since the new elections in Guatemala. The British have agreed with the parties concerned that the negotiations would begin *de novo*. All previous positions are now abandoned. Rowlands is of the view that there has been some movement on the part of Guatemala. . . . Belize does not want a small forum. The greatest pressure she can exert on Guatemala would come through the United Nations, where her support is substantial. . . . Row-

2. The dinner was for the diplomatic corps.
3. Guatemala claimed part of Belize.

lands made it clear Britain did not intend to give any military guarantee for Belize independence. . . .

As I gradually dozed off, I said to myself: "Well, would I not be unhappy if I was just able to look into the open space in my rocking chair, completely oblivious of what makes the world tick?" . . .

Saturday, July 8, 1978

I saw Joe [Clark] and his wife off at Heathrow at noon, for France and a holiday. He said we had been kind to him. Joe thinks he has good candidates. Crombie, he is sure, will beat Evans.[4] Several good economists will run, one in Vancouver, the other in Ottawa Centre.[5] He would have liked to see Bob Stanfield run. Maybe he will urge him to become Governor-General. This is in Joe's mind. If Joe does not win, he is concerned that western alienation will grow. . . . Would Mark MacGuigan make the cabinet? Joe doubts it. There are stories that Gene Whelan might leave. I don't think so. . . .

Thursday, July 13, 1978

Don [Jamieson] and his wife arrived from New York in the Concorde. . . . We had a general discussion about developments in Namibia. Don, who spoke for the five countries before the United Nations Security Council, is pleased with the acceptance by SWAPO of the Western proposals for independence. The disputed territory will now be in a position to make a peaceful transition by the end of the year. Guerrilla war will draw to a close. The plan will go before the United Nations Security Council for approval, in spite of Soviet and Eastern bloc reservations. The package which Don and his four colleagues worked out calls for United Nations' supervision of elections and a reduction in the number of South African forces.

Don was interested in an account of Ron Basford's discussions with the Queen on the constitutional proposals. Much

4. David Crombie, former mayor of Toronto, was the Conservative candidate in a by-election in Toronto Rosedale running against the Liberal candidate, John Evans, the president of the University of Toronto and the Liberal candidate.
5. Patricia Carney and Robert de Cotret.

to my surprise, he seems to think that the proposals themselves will make more headway than he had at first thought would be the case. . . .

[Don] thinks that the political situation [in Canada] has considerably improved. . . . The sampling from a private poll indicates a likely increase in government support. Don is particularly surprised at the extent of trade union support, much higher, for instance, than the support given to the N.D.P. From what he said, I judge that we are likely to have an election in October. I would look for an announcement sometime about the middle of August. MacEachen feels that to wait until next spring would create an impossible parliamentary situation. He is strongly advocating that the government "pull the plug" for an election not later than the end of October. . . .

Friday, July 14, 1978

[At the meeting today] the exchanges between Jamieson and Owen were relaxed and candid, and lasted for well over an hour. . . . Owen responded enthusiastically to an invitation to attend the Commonwealth Games and later to accompany the Secretary of State for External Affairs on a railway trip though the Rockies. Jamieson expressed satisfaction over support by Britain of our national unity problem. He explained the constitutional proposals and the reaction of the Queen to them. He emphasized that the changes were practical and would not diminish the symbolic importance of the Queen as Canada's sovereign. Owen said there had never been any question where Britain stood on Canadian unity and recalled his conversation with me in that regard. Callaghan and Trudeau had great respect for one another and for Canada. There would be changes in our bilateral relations as they evolved, but they would be based on mature understanding and respect. . . .

The Secretary of State for External Affairs mentioned a recent Economic Council study of Canada's relations with developing countries and asked some questions on the philosophy of development assistance. He and Owen agreed on the need for greater uniformity in practices of the developed world on linking aid and political considerations, e.g., human rights. Both were sceptical about the extent to which countries could continue to assist industries in the developing world which, when developed, would strike at most vulnerable elements of their own economy. I privately have some reservations about the relevance of this at the present time. Jamieson expressed some cynicism about the extent to which countries like Canada could cash in on credit notes extended, for instance, to Africa. Owen thought we would benefit from such programmes and that we had particular influence over Namibia. On the Common Fund, Owen had frustrations. He said the developed world knew the structure they could live with but were afraid to put it on the table, because it would be taken as the first level of bargaining. Instead, we were left with longer and unproductive discussion. Owen thought the time had come for a stronger initiative on this issue. . . .

Jamieson mentioned that Canada had suspended its aid programme to Cuba. We had been urged to go further. Owen said we would get no marks from Africa by condemning Cuba. He agreed that Cuba should be condemned from time to time, but he thought it was important we maintain our bilateral relations with Cuba. . . .

Saturday, July 15, 1978

The main question at the Bonn Summit tomorrow will be how to get West Germany and Japan to expand their economies and reduce their heavy trade surpluses. Schmidt is not anxious to disturb his low rate of inflation. Germany requires more exports, which call for a stronger dollar, he insists. A stronger United States dollar calls for a balanced United States trade. The United States must reduce its oil imports. To meet this, the British offer a "package deal." Germany and Japan should reduce taxes and increase government spending. . . . Britain, France, and Japan should agree to reverse the protectionist trend and thereby promote a liberal trade agreement. All countries should seek to help the developing countries. . . .

I spent several hours with Jamieson and his staff members at the Dorchester this morning. Trudeau, now on his way to Bonn for the Summit, has decided to make the statement on the Russian trial sentences.[6] Don had commented on the trials themselves some days ago. We reviewed our meeting with Owen. I expressed my astonishment at Owen's views on external aid. Am I to believe that the government of Canada is changing its objective treatment of this vital matter? It could be that Jamieson brings a businessman's view to a problem with which he has not been in close contact over the years. Nevertheless, the External Affairs minister is in charge. Owen's dislike of the widespread criticism of Russian violation of human rights, so different from his public condemnation, is something I will find hard to forget. I told Don of my strong feelings. . . .

Sunday, July 16, 1978

Talk persists over an October election in the United Kingdom, as it does in Canada. Shirley Williams prefers that it should come next February. I woudn't be surprised if both Jim and Trudeau went next year. Don Jamieson wants it in October, as does MacEachen. In the old days, prime ministers decided such events, now the pollsters have taken over. . . .

Monday, July 17, 1978

The papers are full of yesterday's Bonn talks, mainly a rehash. The public must get a wrong impression of these summit meetings, when, after only a day's meeting, mention is made of a communiqué almost complete. . . . One of the more significant results of the Summit could be the position taken on the need to stimulate growth and reduce oil consumption. This presupposes a composing of some differences between Schmidt and Carter. . . .

I attended the "Service of Thanksgiving for the Life and Work of the Right Honorable Sir Robert Menzies, former Prime Minister of Australia" at Westminster Abbey at noon. The Prince of Wales represented the Queen. Something kept him from being on time. As a result, the service was delayed

6. Anatoly Scharansky went on trial with other Soviet human rights activists: Alexander Ginsburg, Viktoras Piatkus, Levko Lukyanenko, Alexander Podrabinek. They were all given harsh sentences of several years in labour camps.

fifteen minutes. He looked resplendent when he reached his place . . . not far from where I sat in my stall, next to the Australian High Commissioner. We all derived amusement, if this is permissible at a memorial service, from the fact that the Prince of Wales read from the wrong lesson. . . .

The reception for the Queen tonight at the residence went off well. We had about forty more people than last year and could not have had any more. Her Majesty had Prince Andrew with her. He made a great hit. I introduced the Queen to everyone and Nell presented Prince Andrew. At one point the Queen looked over at her son and said to me, "What in the world is he doing?" The Prince was on his knees, deeply engaged in conversation with Colonel Maynard, a ninety-six-year-old former soldier and the oldest living graduate of the Royal Military College. In some ways this was the most interesting of the Queen's three visits to the residence during our time in London. On arrival, I took the Queen into the library, where some pictures were taken, and we had a few words. I said to her . . . "We welcome you here . . . the head of our constitutional monarchy." The last words, referring to the monarchy, had been used by Trudeau in a radio broadcast when he explained the position of the crown in the constitutional proposals. . . . The Queen got the significance of what I had said and smiled as she looked at me. . . . She mentioned how satisfactory the visit of Basford and Thorson had been and said, "I know you had something to do with all this." . . .

Tuesday, July 18, 1978

The Bonn Summit is over. It is reported that West Germany gave firm commitments to stimulate economic growth and the United States undertook to curb oil imports and fight inflation. . . . I have never seen as little press attention to Canada and Trudeau. I have not seen a picture of him, although on yesterday's front page of *The Telegraph*, Jean Chrétien boyishly marched ahead with Callaghan, Carter, and Schmidt. . . .

It is clear from the GATT talks at the M.T.N. that few important objectives have been reached as far as Canada is concerned. MacEachen put it this way — "very important Canadian objectives are still to be achieved in the negotiations."

Canada has been pushing for lower tariffs on agricultural products, fish, and processed non-ferrous metals and various products. We enjoy an international advantage in these products. If we could process more of our natural resources instead of sending them abroad in their raw form, more jobs would be created. . . . The talks will continue after Bonn.

I notice in today's press summary from Ottawa reference to a story in *The Globe* which suggests that "a fighter tries to regain External's lost stature." The "fighter," of course, is Allan Gotlieb. The suggestion is made that External Affairs slipped badly in the late 1960s and 1970s under a Prime Minister who let it be known that he and his staff were calling the shots. . . . I know that Allan Gotlieb felt dubious about the role played by Ivan as Trudeau's foreign affairs adviser. All the same, Ivan made a notable contribution. . . . Allan, I know, is also trying to regain influence in the P.M.O. When he and Michael Pitfield spent an evening with me three months ago, we debated this very matter [and] Allan put his point well. . . .

Wednesday, July 19, 1978

David Owen has instructed the British embassies in Russia and in Eastern Europe to make regular reports on activities in violation of human rights. . . . He stated there were further cases of distinguished Soviet citizens being deprived of their citizenship while travelling abroad. I find it a little distasteful in view of what David said to Jamieson and me the other day [when he] had criticized the attack on the Soviet Union, particularly by the United States for violation of human rights. In a matter of such importance, I don't think David does himself justice with this double-talk attitude. One of these days I may tell him so. A young foreign minister with limited experience needs a jacking-up on occasion just as well as we oldsters. . . .

Thursday, July 20, 1978

I went to hear John Davies, the shadow foreign minister in Mrs. Thatcher's party, who spoke to the Royal Institute of International Affairs at Chatham House. . . . He has just returned from Rhodesia [and] . . . says there has been no progress in removing discrimination since the establishment of

[the] interim government.[7] He is concerned about the proposed election at the end of the year and wonders how it can be achieved. The war has accelerated in Rhodesia, as has terrorism. . . . It is significant that the Conservative spokesman on foreign affairs believes only the Patriotic Front[8] can bring about a cease-fire. He told me that an all-party conference, as originally proposed by Owen, will not help. A more private arrangement is needed. The economy of Rhodesia is not in a state of collapse but is bad. . . . John Davies . . . [said] it was clear that Soviet military equipment had been used by Mugabe's forces. Davies's assessment impressed all of us. It was factual and did not reflect a British political party label. . . .

When I returned to the residence, there was a message from the Foreign Office asking that I convey a message to Don Jamieson, now in Scotland. There is to be a Security Council meeting on Namibia on July 25th. . . .

I found that Owen had been ahead of me, but it was good for me to have passed on the message for, in so doing, I obtained a good picture of what transpired at the Summit meeting in Bonn. Trudeau apparently had been effective on the question of concerted action by the seven against hijackers and terrorists. I was asked what was the press reaction in Britain. While there had been much Bonn Summit news, no emphasis was placed on the Canadian role. . . .

Friday, July 21, 1978

We drove to Raspit Hill, Ivy Hatch, near Sevenoaks in Kent for lunch with Audrey and Malcolm MacDonald. . . . Our host spoke enthusiastically of the reception we gave for the Queen on Monday. He has known Elizabeth II since the war years. Malcolm attended the King often at Balmoral and elsewhere. George VI loved to play guessing games with Malcolm and other guests. He was not daunted by his speech impedi-

7. This was provided for in the Internal Settlement and established in March and April of 1978. The government was led by an executive council consisting of Ian Smith, Jeremiah Chirau, Ndabaningi Sithole and Abel Muzorewa. The Patriotic Front led by Robert Mugabe and Joshua Nkomo denounced the new government as illegal and continued their guerrilla war against it.
8. Led by Robert Mugabe and Joshua Nkomo.

ment. . . . When it became certain that George VI knew he was to sit on the throne, he had no experience whatsoever in government. He beseeched Malcolm to explain the structure and the operative part of special concern to the monarch. Malcolm assured the King that in six months all would become familar. At the end of the half year, the King surprised Malcolm with a phone call. He said: "You were right. It takes six months." . . .

Sunday, July 23, 1978

There is election fever in the United Kingdom. It looks as though the vote on the government's five per cent pay limit on Thursday will be the barometer. Jim is marshalling his forces. . . . About the middle of August, we may have decided to go to the people in Canada. I will be surrounded with electoral contests and not be part of them. If one is on when I am at home in Windsor, it will be odd to sit on the sidelines. But that is the way I want it, and the way it has to be. . . .

Monday, July 24, 1978

When Trudeau came to Europe in 1975, he had hopes of gaining access to the protective markets of the E.E.C. That was the purpose of the contractual link. Too much was expected of it. Business with the E.E.C. depends primarily on the private sector. . . . We are not as accustomed to Europe as we are to the United States. Our business people have got to learn more about Europe, its business methods and how to get business from the Market. It is there. . . .

I had a useful call on Sir John Hunt, secretary to the cabinet, to discuss British reaction to the Summit. [The] British were quite pleased. They thought that it was a realistic Summit, characterized by commitments that could be reasonably delivered. They realized, however, that the Summit addressed itself only to short-term and immediate problems; in their view the next Summit should be taking a longer view. In making this global assessment of the Summit . . . Hunt . . . stressed to me he did not himself see the Summit as an economic success but primarily as a useful instrument to help governments to resist pressures for more protectionism. Sir John refuted those in the British press who displayed much scepticism . . . and did not hesitate to say that the Bonn Summit was in many respects more successful than the Downing Street's. . . .

In this context, the political will demonstrated by all participants to conclude the M.T.N. successfully was another practical and useful step in the right direction. . . . It was again clear that the British definition of a successful round of negotiations was quite different from ours and they are afraid of too much liberalization which might destabilize their economy.

On North-South issues [concerning the development of the Third World], he admitted that, true to their fears during the preparatory meetings, not much was said about this during meetings. . . . He suggested that the next Summit should address itself to the North-South issues as an important point on the agenda and do better. . . .

I attended a tea and reception on the Terrace at the House of Lords, given to heads of missions and others by Peter Carrington. . . . After the reception, with other heads of mission, I went to the Grand Committee Room in the House of Commons to hear Carrington speak on British foreign policy. I did not see Ted Heath in the audience, although I had noticed him on the Terrace. What could have been in his mind? Was this a play by Peter to become Foreign Secretary in Mrs. Thatcher's government? . . . Peter is an attractive man with a good sense of humour. He referred to himself as a former Ambassador [and] High Commissioner who "ate and drank for the Motherland." . . .

Tuesday, July 25, 1978

The government was defeated on the dock labour arrangement last night in the House of Commons. . . . I went to the House of Commons this afternoon and listened to what could well be the last major debate between the Prime Minister and the Leader of the Opposition before a possible general election. Jim spoke first [and] in the final vote, the government was sustained. . . .

Wednesday, July 26, 1978

We have just learned that [our daughter] Mary Anne has had a new baby girl. Nell is overjoyed and relieved, as I am. Two girls in Mary Anne's family and three boys in Paul's. . . .

We had a large reception for Nova Scotian teachers, High Commissioners whose countries will be participating in the Commonwealth Games in Edmonton, and an athletic group, who participated in the baton ceremony at Buckingham Palace and Heathrow today. While I was at the reception, I received word from our man in Lagos that the Permanent Under-Secretary at the Foreign Office in Nigeria, Ukegbu, had summoned him to say that it was his painful duty to communicate to him the Nigerian government's decision not to participate in the Edmonton Commonwealth Games, on the ground that New Zealand has not complied with the Gleneagles Declaration.[9] This was bad news indeed. It was made clear in Lagos that the government found it difficult to reach this decision because of its high regard for Canada and its leadership in the Commonwealth under Trudeau. Our High Commissioner to Nigeria, [Leonard] Legault, . . . pointed out that the Commonwealth Secretary General had said all countries had implemented the Gleneagles Declaration. Sonny must have known something was in the offing, because the [Nigerian] Permanent Under-Secretary said Ramphal had made real efforts to resolve the issue. Would other countries be involved? he was asked. The reply was he did not know. Legault pointed out that the decision was presaged in a leading editorial in the *Lagos Daily Times*. He thinks Ukegbu was unhappy and embarrassed by his assignment. Legault was right in saying that the incident would damage Nigerian-Canadian relations. Legault does not think an appeal for reconsideration will get far, but it is worth making. There seems to be a split in the Nigerian government on participation in the Games. The hawks have won the day.

Ottawa has informed me that the acting Prime Minister, Jean Chrétien, was phoning Lagos. I got the New Zealand High Commissioner, who was at the reception, aside, told him what had happened and showed him Legault's message. He knew of no justification for Nigeria's action. Other High Commissioners were disturbed, notably Tanzania, Botswana

9. This was the statement condemning apartheid in sport issued at the Commonwealth Conference on July 8-15, 1977, after a meeting at the Gleneagles Hotel in Scotland.

and Ghana . . . all at the reception. I tried to get the High Commissioner for Nigeria on the phone, without success.

On July 27, Nell and I flew to Canada to begin our holiday. In what had become a regular feature, we started off at the Canada Steamship Lines' fishing camp in the Saguenay. After a week there, we headed to Windsor to spend some time with my daughter Mary Anne and her family, including my new granddaughter.

Nell was radiantly happy to have the family under her apron strings again after almost a year.

Tuesday, August 8, 1978

Trudeau may be in a quandary today. The Tories are down three points in today's Gallup. The N.D.P. is up three points. With forty-two percent, Trudeau has an eight-point lead. A week ago he said Canadians should not have an election "at this time." Some of his colleagues will press him to go to the country. . . .

Otto Lang was named acting Minister of Justice yesterday. Some think this presages an early federal election. Why should it? Trudeau could appear to be made indecisive, if within a week he changes his mind. He may have an election in November. Who knows? Otto has confused the provinces. No sooner had he been appointed Minister of Justice, did he speak of the use of the referendum in the process of achieving a patriation of the constitution. In those provinces where the consent of the government was not given, the federal government could ask what the people in the particular provinces thought. This use of the referendum was not well received by the Premiers. Otto should not have been so precipitious in suggesting a device envisaged in the proposed constitutional changes. . . .

Wednesday, August 16, 1978

The unanimous position of the provinces [opposing] Trudeau's constitutional proposals[10] must worry the Prime Minister. The House of Commons-Senate Committee in its meet-

10. They took their stand at the annual meeting of premiers in Regina the week before.

ing yesterday was unusually critical. Marc Lalonde, the Federal-Provincial Relations Minister, said the government will not budge from its plan, regardless of provincial disagreement. This is not the kind of language that will help. . . . Lalonde insisted, and rightly, that the changes suggested for the new constitution did not alter the status of the Crown. It becomes increasingly evident to me that Trudeau erred in bringing [in] the constitutional changes before an election. Don Jamieson and I were agreed on this point, when he met with me in London two months ago. We both assumed there would be an early election in July. Constitutional changes are needed. If the election does not take place until spring, it is desirable to proceed with changes in the constitution.

Friday, August 18, 1978

The blast by [Liberal] Senators, notably Dan Lang and George van Roggen, [against] . . . Trudeau's constitutional proposals gives the impression of a divided political party, not a good image if there is to be an election. Dan Lang, not always an easy Senator to get along with, says Trudeau's proposals leave no effective checks on the cabinet. Per contra, Lalonde thinks the House of Federation could act as a check on the government. On the monarchy, the government insists that there is no change from the actual situation. Diefenbaker maintains discussions between the Queen and Prime Minister are privileged. It is contended that the Queen, in accepting the new arrangement, had no alternative but to act on her minister's advice. . . . That impression is erroneous. The intention is not to alter the present situation. It is not, in fact, altered—but argument will go on. What has happened, as compared with what could have resulted, is that the Crown is more secure in Canada, and for some time, than I thought a few years ago would be the case. . . .

Wednesday, August 30, 1978

One can be on holiday too long. . . . Yesterday, I felt that I should be back on the job. . . . Not much world news in today's media. Carter on a horse, and a slow moving one at that, looked as uncomfortable as he does sometimes in speaking about foreign policy. . . . Preparations are under way for the enthronement of the new Pope,[11] who does not wish to be crowned with the traditional papal headgear. He prefers the mitre. Nor does he wish to be carried. Consistent with his love for the bicycle, he will walk to the altar in St. Peter's Square. . . .

11. Pope John Paul I had been elected on August 26.

XXII

September – October 1978

MY HOLIDAY WAS OVER and I headed back to London. Rumours of elections in Canada were laid to rest in September when Trudeau scheduled fifteen by-elections for mid-October and, about the same time, Jim Callaghan decided against a British election. Instead, Trudeau decided to press ahead with his proposals for constitutional reform. As seen from abroad, the image of the Canadian government was that of a chaotic administration which was coming unglued. Despite his troubles with the labour unions, Callaghan's political leadership impressed me and overall he appeared to be in control of the situation. In contrast Trudeau's situation appeared increasingly precarious.

Friday, September 1, 1978

I have maintained in exchanges with Pearson and Trudeau that any attempt, at the present period of our history, to dislodge the monarchy would be divisive. The debate yesterday in Halifax at the Canadian Bar Association meeting is positive proof. Mike had told the Queen that the monarchy would likely have to go. He didn't say when. The incidents in Quebec, when the Queen was received by Jean Lesage, the Quebec Premier, had caused Pearson to express his frank opinion.[1] I told him at the time he was wrong. Early in Trudeau's régime, I cautioned him likewise. Some of our colleagues, experiencing the euphoria of electoral success, were all for doing away with the monarchy. Mitchell Sharp, in particular. Certainly at present and perhaps for a long

1. On this occasion in 1964, the Queen was booed by the crowd.

time, any displacement of the Crown in Canada would provoke great divisions. . . . Over a year ago, Prince Charles seemed concerned about the role of the monarchy in Canada. In a way, I thought he showed too much concern. The Queen has a capacity for relaxation in these matters. Perhaps the Prince of Wales reflects his father's eagerness. . . .

Monday, September 4, 1978

Trudeau has scheduled seven more by-elections for October 16th, on top of the eight others already announced for that date. It is thought that the latest announcement is an indication there will be no autumn election. . . . Don Jamieson [on a visit to London] is not sure what will happen. The decision to have the further by-elections was taken during his absence and much to his surprise. He would prefer general elections now. I doubt there will be an election before spring. . . .

I was advised over the phone this morning that the probabilities for a [British] election this fall are good. The Prime Minister will be going to Balmoral to see the Queen this weekend. If an election is to be held, she would be the first to know. . . .

We crowd much into our daily lives these days. Any one of these events would cover weeks and months in another day. Now conflicts, international crises, cataclysmic events, international and national pageantry duplicate and follow one another in rapid succession. All day Friday, I was at home in the hot sunshine of Canada's summer—bare feet, no shirt, in shorts. Now I am imprisoned, only two days later, in Macdonald House—with shirt, tie and suit and the restraining influence of shoes and heavy engagements from early morning until the late hours of the night. . . .

I welcomed the Minister of Justice, Otto Lang, at Heathrow tonight. . . . My judgment about the likelihood of the next election date was confirmed. All along, I have felt that Trudeau should have the next election at the closest possible date to the holding of the Quebec referendum. That is obviously what is in the mind of the Prime Minister, as it was a year ago. There will be many surprises in Canada on all sides. I think in the long run this will have proven to be the best decision in the interest of the country and its unity. . . .

Wednesday, September 6, 1978

Jim Callaghan is certainly working up to an election. His speech to the T.U.C. yesterday indicated he is likely to go on October 5th. He would "do a Trudeau" if he did not go on at or about that time. The polls show the Conservatives ahead two points. The election is likely, therefore, to be a cliff-hanger. . . .

[During our] reception at the residence at six o'clock to honour the members of the British Commonwealth Press Association . . . I learned, as did Lang, that the latest polls in Canada showed the government had reached 45 per cent as opposed to the Conservatives 35 per cent, but the N.D.P. dropped five per cent. This places the government in a dominant position. Trudeau was certainly about to indicate there would be no election this fall and this I noted in my record of yesterday. As Otto said, the hawks in the cabinet will be active at today's . . . meeting and will likely want an election. Incidentally, Otto told me today for the first time that all along he had been urging the election, because of the promising picture in Saskatchewan. Already the Prime Minister has said there would be no election at this time. . . . Now, with the results given today, what will he do? What would I do, if I were in his circumstances? Admittedly not an easy decision. . . . Given my view that an election would be an effective weapon against Lévesque's referendum, if I were Prime Minister, I would stick to my guns. The certain defeat of Lévesque's objective is more important to Canada than anything else.

Thursday, September 7, 1978

The general expectancy is that Callaghan will announce the election date today. The cabinet meets in a few hours. The . . . thinking has been that the election would be on October 5th. I would not be surprised if Callaghan advanced the date. If he announces the date later today, it must be presumed that he saw the Queen earlier. Although he was given a triumphant welcome at the T.U.C., with its assurance for support in the coming elections, that body overwhelmingly decided yesterday, once again, to reject the [government's] five per cent guideline on pay rises. . . .

Later in the day, the Prime Minister announced that the government would carry on and that there was no election immediately in prospect. . . .

Ivan Head dined with me at the residence and will be staying for a day or so. He is in London for a conference on development problems, called by Judith Hart, the Minister for Development. Ivan told me that, as Hopper's successor[2] at the International Development Research Centre on . . . development problems [in the Third World], he is pursuing a more open policy and does not hesitate to let Canadians and others know what the Centre is doing. . . . When Ivan was appointed to his assignment at the Centre, Trudeau had hoped that he would not take it on forthwith but would wait until after the elections. Ivan thought this would prejudice his role vis-à-vis other countries and preferred to assume the role forthwith, although he was reluctant to leave the Prime Minister's entourage.

Friday, September 8, 1978

Otto Lang left early this morning. . . . He mentioned he had talked to the Prime Minister. Parliament will be called in the usual manner. It is clear there will be no immediate election. . . .

I talked to Marc Lalonde early this morning, advising him of Otto Lang's telephone exchange with the Prime Minister on the continuance of the government's mandate without any immediate election. . . .

Marc and I had a later discussion on the constitutional proposals. I suggested to him that he should be more accommodating to the provinces. The emphasis with them should be on consultation. The word consent should be avoided. After all, the objective is the maintenance of unity. . . .

Saturday, September 9, 1978

Marc Lalonde, now on his way to Paris, had breakfast early this morning with me. He will see President Senghor of Senegal in the French capital. Senghor has been promoting

2. Ivan Head had succeeded Wilbert Hopper as the president of the International Development Research Centre in March.

the idea of a French commonwealth. Giscard is not too anxious to see the idea flourish. Nor are we. Trudeau told the French President he is not overly anxious either. After all, we do have the *Agence*.[3] It would not please Canada to have Quebec as a full member of such a commonwealth. Its participation in global French cultural matters should be through participation in the Canadian delegation of *L'Agence*. Trudeau plans to have a visit this autumn with the French President. Both heads of government discussed such a visit when they met in Bonn during the summer. . . .

Thursday, September 14, 1978

Denis stayed on a long time with his officers.[4] He told me that Callaghan was never for an early election. Early in July, he had given an indication of what his intentions were. . . . He thinks Jim Callaghan is the best Prime Minister Britain has had in a long time. I have no doubt that Denis would like to be foreign minister in a new Callaghan administration after the elections. This is not an impossibility. Unashamedly, he said that when we first met he was a card-carrying member of the Communist party. I had heard him make this admission on television several years ago. . . .

I sent on a message to Ottawa about our wide-ranging discussion with the Chancellor of the Exchequer, who made clear that the [forthcoming] meeting in Montreal of Finance Ministers of the Commonwealth would largely concentrate on North-South issues, with little likelihood that developed countries could say or do much to comfort their Third World fellow members. . . . He believes that Jean Chrétien could charm any group into an acceptance of his suggestions and looks forward to meeting the Minister of Finance next week. . . . The Chancellor of the Exchequer says that the United States administration is having difficulties in developing and pursuing policies, because of the breakdown with the Congress. He spoke critically of American public life, some aspects of congressional conduct and the seniority committee system, which was paralleled by a highly intelligent President. Healey said,

3. L'Agence de co-opération culturelle et technique.
4. Denis Healey was lunching at the residence.

"Carter was the most brilliant President of this generation but he does not understand the United States' political system." . . .

Friday, September 15, 1978

Later in the morning, I called on the South African Ambassador, Botha,[5] whom I had known in Ottawa and who is leaving his post. The South African Ambassador in most capitals has an unenviable role these days. One should not fully load on to the person of the South African representative the criticisms that one holds against South Africa itself. I told Botha I was sorry to see him go. I sympathised with him in his difficult role, but I did add strongly that only the intransigence of South Africa's official policy was responsible for the situation. He thinks Vorster is making some necessary reforms and is hopeful that in the final analysis his country will not experience the fate which awaits Rhodesia. I told him I hoped that this was so, but I am not so sure. Everything largely depends now on the flexibility and understanding by Vorster and his colleagues of the inevitable facts in the modern world. Included is the recognition that colour cannot be justifiably accepted as a bar to human advancement at this stage in man's history. . . .

Saturday, September 16, 1978

It is now official. Trudeau said yesterday there will be no elections until the spring. The private polls indicated an early election would have shown him down, except in Quebec. The mid-October by-elections will be watched closely. The results could be disastrous. So many by-elections at one time hardly fit into the pattern of good management. There has not been too much of that in Canada for some time, I am sorry to say. . . .

Otto Lang gave no indication that a Supreme Court of Canada ruling will be sought on federal power to abolish the Senate. . . . Wisely, the question of the monarchy will not be submitted for judicial examination. No change in its status

5. Matthys Botha

has been proposed. I am afraid the government is getting itself into increasing difficulty on its constitutional proposals. . . . I am worried about the next ten months. . . .

Tuesday, September 19, 1978

I met Nell at the airport this morning. . . . It was nice seeing my wife. Her absence created a loneliness which really made me very unhappy. . . .

Wednesday, September 20, 1978

Admiral Piers, the Agent-General for Nova Scotia, has just telephoned to say that Gerry Regan's [Liberal] forces have been routed in Nova Scotia, almost two-to-one. Buchanan, the Leader of the Conservative party,[6] will become Premier. The result is surprising although I did hear rumblings. This defeat could be symptomatic. Many in Ottawa will wonder if these results are portentous. . . .

Friday, September 22, 1978

One of my heroes and most eminent professors, Etienne Gilson, passed away on September 20th. He was ninety-four. I studied under him at St. Michael's. . . . Among my most treasured books is *The Philosopher*, his autobiography and a truly great book. . . .[7] The last time I saw Gilson was at a dinner at Government House given by the Governor-General. It must have been ten years ago. . . . He was easily one of the more important influences in my life.

Callaghan and his Foreign Minister, David Owen, will be in Nigeria today for talks with Kenneth Kaunda. It is thought one of the purposes of the visit will be to dissuade the latter from proposing economic actions against South Africa. Kaunda has indicated his deep disappointment at the revelations in the . . . report over Rhodesian oil sanctions violations [by Britain]. . . . Callaghan and Kaunda are friends. It will take a lot of friendship to quieten Kaunda's anger over recent revelations of successive British governments on the violations of oil sanctions. . . .

6. John Buchanan
7. Etienne Gilson, *The Philosopher and Theology* (New York 1962).

Sunday, September 24, 1978

Jim Callaghan is not only a good political leader, he knows when to comment and when to avoid saying anything. So many public figures feel they must answer all questions put to them. I suspect this was Harold Wilson's weakness, among others. In my active political and public career, I knew others who did not know when to avoid comment. Kenneth Kaunda had some strong things to say about Britain last week. He reported that Jim Callaghan had assured him, some months ago, that anyone who violated the oil sanctions against Rhodesia would be dealt with severely. Did Jim know that Wilson, Home, and perhaps Heath would be implicated [in violating these sanctions]? . . . When Jim returned to Heathrow, he would make no comment. The trip to Nigeria to see Kaunda and the absence of unnecessary comment has created a picture of common purpose. Jim and Kaunda are portrayed as working hand in hand. Last week, it looked as though the British government, as presently and formerly constituted, was in trouble over oil sanctions. Jim, by an economy of words, has created a new perspective. That is leadership. . . .

Thursday, September 28, 1978

This morning I met Alastair Gillespie, who had just flown in from Calgary and Ottawa for a quick meeting with Wedgwood Benn. . . .

Alastair and I sat up late discussing the Canadian scene. The prospects in the by-elections, he says, are not good. The best the government can hope for is to hold as many seats in [the] by-elections as we now have by gains in Newfoundland and in Quebec; Alastair says the Toronto picture is grim. This applies to many other parts of Ontario as well. He, himself, had thoughts of getting out of Parliament and not running again. I believe his own prospects are not the most promising. The suggestion is that the Prime Minister is no longer acceptable. Much of this [feeling] arises over the backlash toward Quebec. . . . I suggested that this would be regrettable, tactless and unachieving. Surely the people of Canada recognize the danger in disunity and separation and will rally to the cry of the Prime Minister. To this came the response, desirable as that may be, it is now felt that Quebec's separatism has no chance to succeed. In any event, it is challenged by an effective provincial leadership in the person of Ryan. Given this situation, the economic problem stands foremost. The monarchy issue is regrettable and politically harmful. . . .

The coming session of Parliament will be noisy and chaotic. The Minister of Finance, charming and popular as he is, has lost the confidence—certainly of the business people—and so I went to bed with this panorama of discord and dissatisfaction to dream about. I suggested that, black as the picture is, time offers its remedies. A year ago, the Prime Minister stood high and so did his party's fortunes. In the next twelve months, unexpected events might give a more hopeful picture.

I have no doubt that much of the pessimism during the past while arose over the recognition that what Gillespie said is likely fairly accurate. Is it still not too late to speculate that Trudeau, a son of French Canada, may yet be able to rise out of the din and roar and direct the minds of the Canadian people to Canada's positive advantages and that there will develop the realization of the true values of Canada. Political leadership should emphasize now that there is a Canadian identity, marked by attributes which are common to all parts of Canada. . . . Legalisms are not easily understood by a preoccupied electorate. A national vision could be, if only someone could put the spirit of Laurier back into play and we could escape from our present divisions and uncertainties.

Monday, October 2, 1978

Callaghan is faced with his biggest political crisis over his pay policy and the unions' reaction to it. One could say that he threatened to resign if his pay policy was not sustained. The danger is not over. In any event, the dispute with the unions will not help his case. Jim said: "I am not going to be in the business of presiding over the affairs of the country if we are committed to a policy which would increase inflation again." Some placating words may be found to bridge the difference, but I suspect the damage is done. The Labour [party] conference [at Blackpool] does not want wage curbs. That is clear. The only hope is that the conference might realize that pitting itself against the government means that Labour's immediate future as a government is in jeopardy. . . .

Tuesday, October 3, 1978

This morning I called on the Secretary of State for Trade[8] to emphasize the government's concern that Air Canada receive fair and equal treatment in the United Kingdom, and to seek the Secretary of State's assurance that United Kingdom officials will give serious consideration to Air Canada's objection to moving from Heathrow to Gatwick.

I pointed out that Air Canada . . . has served London and Canada from Heathrow for thirty-two years. The London/Canada route is a major source of Air Canada's overall revenue as well as a major link in British bilateral relations. . . . The transfer of Air Canada's operations will deprive Air Canada of the chance to keep and win maintenance contracts from carriers, especially Middle Eastern ones, flying into Heathrow. The loss or failure in such cases will mean fewer jobs in Quebec. . . . We were unable for a long time to obtain a rationale from the British authorities why they wanted Air Canada to move as opposed to other airlines. . . .

The Secretary of State gave me a good hearing. He had five of his officials with him. He said the decision to ask Canada to move had been taken. He would, however, examine what I had said. . . . I told him that when he went to Ottawa, he would hear more of this problem [because] the proposal was one that Canada simply could not accept. . . .

Friday, October 6, 1978

The political situation in Canada worsens according to the latest poll. It shows the government behind in all but one province: Quebec. The run on the Canadian dollar, I am sure, is a feature in the continuing deterioration.

Last night, I went to the Apostolic Delegate's residence to express Canada's sympathy over the death of Pope John Paul I.[9] A nice Irish nun greeted . . . me, insisting that she would let Archbishop Bruno Heim know I was on the premises. I had a pleasant visit with him. He mentioned he was in Switzerland recently, where he received the news on the late Pope's sudden

8. Edmund Dell
9. He was elected pope earlier this year after the death of Pope Paul VI and he died unexpectedly after a reign of only 33 days.

death. Bruno showed us the first copy of his new book on the papal and episcopal coat-of-arms. . . .

Sunday, October 8, 1978

I awoke this morning from a near nightmare. My long-time colleague and friend, Paul Hellyer, had become Prime Minister. This came as a shock. It was to develop into a disappointment, when he made me a mere Clerk of the House of Commons! . . .

Wednesday, October 11, 1978

I lunched today with Prime Minister Callaghan's secretary, Kenneth Stowe, at the Athenaeum. The British Prime Minister's visit a few days ago to Nigeria, when he conferred with Kenneth Kaunda, was at the latter's urgent request. The Zambian Prime Minister has serious economic, military, and political problems to face. The British are going to help considerably. Already, they have sent a high military officer to advise. The opening of the Rhodesian border was a must, concurred in by Nkomo. Kaunda's outburst over the weekend about the British oil sanctions was more of a tactic than a complaint; a tactic conceived on the eve of the Security Council Meeting at the United Nations. . . .

We talked about Callaghan's leadership, which is highly impressive. It is not likely that the government will be defeated on the motion on the Queen's Address. Afterwards, in view of the particular legislation to be introduced, the government should survive with possibly a majority of over twenty. Subject to this, of course, there will be no election until the spring. This is what Callaghan wants and has intended all along. Like Churchill, he says the government's first duty is to Parliament. That means staying in until near the allotted time.

Callaghan will not give in [to the unions] on his present policy of five per cent pay limit. Mrs. Thatcher may talk of flexibility and increases based on higher productivity. Callaghan likely could do the same but will not talk about it, preferring to maintain a single figure level of inflation rather than talk of compromise and giving in. . . .

Thursday, October 12, 1978

Don Jamieson will fly with David Owen on Saturday in a R.A.F. jet to Windhoek, Namibia. They will be joined in Pretoria the next day by Cyrus Vance, the United States Secretary of State; Genscher,[10] the West German Foreign Minister; and Stirn,[11] the Secretary of State for Foreign Affairs in France. In Windhoek, Owen and Jamieson will have talks with the four main political parties and the heads of the main churches. It is hoped to get the reaction of local leaders to the plan for independence [for Namibia] drawn up by Dr. Waldheim. They will also want the reaction to the South African government's decision to go ahead with elections [in Namibia] in December, without the involvement of the United Nations. . . . In many ways, this is a unique initiative of the foreign ministers. Normally, officials would be sent for this purpose. The importance of Namibia, however, lends an urgency which may also be a first in foreign ministry diplomacy. . . .

Jamieson must be the most widely travelled of all of our External Affairs ministers. Certainly he does more travelling than I did when I was foreign minister. There is something to be said, however, for a foreign minister being in charge of his department and that he cannot successfully do, if he is always on the road. This does not mean to say that the Namibian venture is not a good one. I think Jamieson, Owen and the others are employing a good technique in this situation. . . .

Friday, October 13, 1978

Last night, I called Allan Gotlieb's attention to my message on talks I had with Callaghan's top aide and private secretary. I urged that Trudeau should write to Callaghan re. the Summit and consider a short visit to Callaghan. Both are still Prime Ministers. Gotlieb will discuss my recommendation with Michael Pitfield. I will hear from them next week. . . .

10. Hans-Dietrich Genscher
11. Alexandre Stirn

Tuesday, October 17, 1978

The big news today is the selection of the Archbishop of Cracow, Poland, Cardinal Karol Wojtyla as Pope. He is the first non-Italian in four hundred and fifty years to become the head of the Catholic Church . . . an imaginative appointment, if ever there was one. . . .

Word has just come of the fifteen by-elections in Canada. The Liberals have done badly, as was so widely indicated. The results are: Liberal, two; Conservatives, ten; N.D.P., two; and Social Credit, one. If Trudeau had held five seats, that would have been regarded as satisfactory. It would have shown that he maintained his present strength. . . . The clamour to remove Trudeau will grow. It must not be allowed to succeed. A government and a party leader must show his strength and defiance in this kind of situation. That is a requirement, if Trudeau wants to hold on. . . .

Wednesday, October 18, 1978

There has been some strong media comment on the consequences for Trudeau of the by-elections results. . . . The by-elections are seen as the forerunner of government defeat in the next federal election. *The Times* this morning takes a similar line, adding, however, that Trudeau's political concerns are relevant to Canadian national unity. Certainly, I have been thinking what a national defeat for Trudeau in present circumstances would mean to the issue of unity. If the rest of Canada repudiated Trudeau, a French-Canadian Prime Minister, the result would be detrimental to the resistance of federalists against Lévesque. . . . We have before us a period of twelve months fraught with the greatest peril to our nation. . . .

Thursday, October 19, 1978

I welcomed Don Jamieson at Heathrow . . . [who] felt that the mission to South Africa of the five-power foreign ministers was worthwhile. They did not succeed in getting an agreement [with South Africa] to postpone the December Namibian elections in favour of the Security Council decision to provide for elections during the first half of next year. On the way in, Don spoke of the tough attitude taken by Botha[12] and his colleagues—hard-hearted Teutonic men, unaware of inevitable changes, forced by the policy of apartheid. . . .

Jamieson believes that the talks in Pretoria will have a significant result on Southern Africa's future. If a date is fixed for United Nations-supervised elections next year, the elections prompted by South Africa in December will not receive international recognition. Don did not say so to the conference but, in their private meetings in Pretoria, the South Africans did not show concern or fear over the possibility of United Nations sanctions. One had the impression that the journalists looked on the results of the Pretoria meeting as not only complicated but inexplicable.

Jamieson dined with us. Our dinner and post-dinner conversation touched on the Canadian political scene. I went to bed with the same concern encouraged by my long talk a few weeks ago with Alastair Gillespie, another member of the Trudeau cabinet. This time, there was before us the result of Monday's by-elections, disastrous in every way, portending much trouble ahead in Parliament and in the country. Don does not see much hope. I cautioned against dumping Trudeau. That was not the way to maintain the integrity and strength of a political party. . . . The clamour for John Turner must not be [encouraged]. . . . Don is anxious to support Trudeau to the hilt but there was the obvious implication that he could not win next time, so strong is the feeling against him. This is one of the very worrying aspects of the situation. If Trudeau were turned out, I insisted, Quebec would not forget. The Liberal party might never recover. Only the fact that so many stuck to Laurier in 1917 was a subsequent Liberal victory made possible by Mackenzie King in 1921. . . .

Our discussion tonight shows how serious the situation is and how difficult it is going to be to come out on top. Don says Trudeau is in the hands of the bureaucrats, instead of being his own man under the influence of political colleagues. I observed that this was one of Trudeau's main weaknesses. . . . The cabinet, of course, is weak and has few giants, apart from himself and MacEachen. Don had spoken to Tru-

12. Pik Botha*

deau during the day. The Prime Minister, with *The Toronto Star* and other papers calling for his resignation, said: "We are being pounded at." . . .

Friday, October 20, 1978

I don't see any reference in today's papers about . . . [Namibia and] what Don Jamieson said at his two-pronged press conference in Canada House and Macdonald House. . . . Frankly, it is not easy to determine what the foreign ministers achieved. This is often the way with complicated international situations. To achieve, one sometimes has to move very slowly. That is what happened in Pretoria. I felt a little sorry for Don at his press conference yesterday. He made the best of a complicated result. . . .

A minister's life is never easy—well do I know. . . . If he had more time before the next election, Jamieson would undertake certain important reforms in External. He believes that in the government service generally these days the bureaucracy is too strong [and the] wishes and decisions of the government are not always observed. . . .

Sunday, October 22, 1978

An important question in my mind during the past while has been—is it Trudeau's policies which are resented in Canada or is the resentment against himself as a French-Canadian? If the latter, then the problem of unity is more serious than one originally assumed. The Liberals are now in power in only one province, tiny Prince Edward Island. A federal election at present would see only Quebec supporting Trudeau. This would help Lévesque, not Canada. Trudeau will have to take corrective action. Don Jamieson says there is resentment over the fact that senior portfolios are in Quebec hands. The Governor-General is from Quebec. There will be a change here. Léger will not be succeeded by George Ignatieff. My guess is the next Governor-General will be Stanfield. There will be a new English-speaking Minister of Finance. . . .

Wednesday, October 25, 1978

I sent a message to Ottawa regarding the [meeting of the] Commonwealth Committee on South Africa dealing with the [British] evasion of oil sanctions. It takes place on Friday. The documentation . . . is directed toward an oil embargo to prevent the supply of oil to Rhodesia. . . . The British goverment maintained the fiction of oil sanctions, [knowing] they could not be effective, because they would not work. I have suggested that our intervention at the meeting could involve an expression of regret that the international community was not informed when it was recognized that oil sanctions would be ineffective. . . .

I think the emphasis at the meeting will not be on defending measures for past actions, but what effective measures should now be resorted to bring down the illegal Smith régime. Recent events in South Africa, of course, will influence what is proposed . . . including an oil embargo. . . .

There will certainly be a parliamentary enquiry [into the oil question]. Regarding sanctions violation, the United Kingdom was anxious to avoid economic confrontation with South Africa. There is no evidence to suggest that the British government colluded in sanctions evasion. The mischief lay in the fact that the British government continued to act outwardly as though it believed sanctions could be effective. I want Ottawa's instruction as to whether we should intervene. We can say it is regrettable that the British did not openly inform the international community when it reached conclusions that oil sanctions against Rhodesia would not be effective. . . .

Thursday, October 26, 1978

Gilles Loiselle, Agent-General for Quebec, said that I had trod on dangerous ground when [in a recent speech] I spoke of Ryan, the new Quebec Liberal leader, as a man who ultimately would defeat Lévesque. I must admit that, if I did make that kind of a remark, I should not have done so as Canadian High Commissioner. I have asked him to show me the particular report of what I am purported to have said. It is not improbable that I did say this. It is certainly what I felt and believe, but it is not what I should proclaim, except in the context of opposing the separatists. . . .

I have been advised by the Prime Minister that he plans an "unofficial" visit to Britain and a "private" visit to France in early December. The use of the adjectives "unofficial" and "private" is interesting. "Unofficial" is understandable in the case of his coming to Britain. "Private" is used, I suppose, to avoid any refusal by the French to receive Trudeau with all the ceremony attending Lévesque's visit last year. The Prime Minister hopes to meet Callaghan and Giscard to discuss multilateral and bilateral subjects of current importance and a follow-up of the Bonn Summit. I am asked to investigate the possibility of arranging the visit, which would see Trudeau arrive on the evening of December 6, meet with the Queen, dine with Callaghan December 7, and depart for Paris December 8.

When Trudeau did arrive, it was on December 7 and he spent only twenty-four hours in Britain.

The Prime Minister says he would not expect arrangements to be on the same scale as for an "official" visit "nor to give rise to high priority media attention." If Callaghan offers dinner, such an arrangement would not need to be entirely private. Depending on Callaghan's wishes, the Prime Minister would be happy to meet a reasonably large crowd of about twenty-four people. There would be a separate meeting with the British Prime Minister. I was amused to see that there is an initiative taken on the Callaghan dinner and an indication of how many Ottawa would like to see included. . . .

Friday, October 27, 1978

Callaghan won two by-elections yesterday. . . . Maybe Trudeau will be able to get an inspiration from Jim on how to win by-elections. Certainly Trudeau's behaviour in the House of Commons the day before yesterday is not calculated to raise his prestige. He had been provoked by the Opposition, so much so, that he told an honourable member, "I'll kick his ass." I am sure the Prime Minister was sorry that he let himself go in this way. . . . Normally, he is so gentlemanly. I just do not know what provokes him into these antics; I am sure they do him no good. . . .

Saturday, October 28, 1978

Fred Martin, a friend from Ottawa, came for lunch. He had been in Rome. Although not a Catholic, the new Pope's enthronement captivated him, as did John Paul II. Fred had lunch with our mutual friend, Cardinal Pignedoli.[13] The latter did not want to succeed Paul VI, whose friend he was. Moreover, Pignedoli thought the time had come to have a non-Italian. He voted for a black Cardinal himself. . . .

Sunday, October 29, 1978

I have been officially informed that in the drive to reduce expenditures in this mission, as generally, the consulates in Belfast and Manchester will be closed. An intimation of this came to me last August. At first, all our consulates in the United Kingdom were to go. They are not consulates in the full sense, but immigration offices. British immigration to Canada is two-thirds less than normal. Nevertheless, the decision makes me unhappy. . . . Why no close-down in France and only one in the United States? . . .

13. A former apostolic delegate in Ottawa.

XXIII

November – December 1978

*M*UCH OF WHAT I ACCOMPLISHED *during these months was fairly routine. The question of maintaining sanctions on Rhodesia took up some of my time. Then there were preparations for a brief visit by Pierre Trudeau at the beginning of December. When he arrived, he reiterated his decision to stay on as leader and told me that he had chosen Ed Schreyer as the next governor general. As usual, the year ended with a social whirl and then a relaxing holiday in Israel at Eilat on the Red Sea.*

Wednesday, November 1, 1978

Nell and I attended the state opening of Parliament this morning. . . . I had a chat with . . . the Archbishop of Canterbury.[1] He told me how greatly impressed he had been with the enthronement of John Paul the Second, with whom he had an opportunity to exchange views. . . .

I am told that Trudeau surprised the federal-provincial conference of premiers yesterday. . . .[2] He made concessions to the provinces in the matter of power sharing. . . . Trudeau said he agreed in principle with the notion of giving the provinces, subject to certain fundamental reservations, power to impose indirect as well as direct taxes. This bald statement implies a fundamental change. What it means in practice, I have yet to determine. Traditionally, federal governments have maintained that there can be no erosion of the exclusive taxing power of the federal government. Trudeau is reported

1. Donald Coggan
2. The conference was called for October 30 to discuss the constitution.

as offering a clarification of federal and provincial power on the control of natural resources and inter-provincial and international trade. . . . I suspect this is an effort to meet Alberta and Saskatchewan on the question of resource control. Under the B.N.A. Act, the ownership of the resource rests with the province; jurisdiction on outside trade, including resources such as western oil, rests with the federal authority. I want to study the actual proposal before making a final judgment. If the concession on taxing power is related only to a share in the taxes on a province's resource, I see no great danger. If it is a general power of unlimited taxation given to the province, then I see the greatest danger. . . .

At last night's dinner of the Canada Club there was a greater attendance than I thought likely. . . . Gerald Regan, the former Premier of Nova Scotia, was the speaker. . . .[3] I reminded Gerry of George Bernard Shaw's wise words: "There are two tragedies in life. One is not to get your heart's desire. The other is to get it." . . .

He spoke on Canada's constitutional problems and the challenge of separation. He thought Lévesque had a chance. On this I did not agree. Gerry's speech was not as good as I hoped it might be. He stated the case well enough but marred it, I believe, by the introduction of an element of political partisanship, referring to a press report in which Joe Clark said he would negotiate with Lévesque, if a Quebec referendum showed 60 per cent of the people favoured his point of view. Trudeau has said in no circumstances would he negotiate for separation. Tactically, that is the wise position. Gerry could have attacked this recent statement of Clark without being so pointed. . . .

Thursday, November 2, 1978

Trudeau's proposal to give the provinces the right of indirect taxation of natural resources has run into a barrage of criticism by the premiers. The provinces do not want distribution of taxing powers to be delayed until after the patriation of the constitution. Looking at the situation from this end, it is regrettable that the constitutional proposals were put forward

3. Regan had recently lost an election.

at all at this time. No pleading to the provinces can escape the political advantage some of them see in Trudeau's dilemma. . . .

Friday, November 3, 1978

Yesterday, at the meeting of the Sanctions Committee [of Commonwealth High Commissioners], there was a discussion of the situation in Namibia . . . and the evasion of oil sanctions. I intervened on the oil sanctions item to say Canada considers effective enforcement of sanctions against Rhodesia as an element in bringing the full weight of international pressures to bear on the illegal régime. Canada was concerned at the sanctions evasion . . . which has helped to make it possible for the Salisbury régime to defy the international community for so long. I took note that the appropriate British authorities are now examining evidence [regarding the breaking of sanctions] . . . with a view to deciding what legal action might be appropriate. . . . I assured the Committee that Canada would carefully examine suggestions for tightening oil sanctions against Rhodesia.

On the question of Namibia, I said our objectives in going to Pretoria were . . . to commit South Africa to a full acceptance of the United Nations Secretary-General's report . . . [and] to cancel the elections [that South Africa] had scheduled for December 4th-8th [in Namibia]. In three days of difficult talks, we made significant progress on some points. The South Africans formally acknowledged that their concerns . . . had been substantially resolved by the Secretary-General's clarifications.

The South Africans maintained that it was politically impossible to cancel the December elections, since they were publicly committed to them. The five foreign ministers made it absolutely clear, however, that these elections would be regarded as null and void. . . .

Tuesday, November 7, 1978

When the Prime Minister sees the Queen at lunch on December 7th, the role of the monarchy will be discussed. Trudeau will confirm Canadian support for retention of the constitutional monarchy. . . . The question of the monarchy was discussed briefly at the end of last week's federal-provincial meeting. All were in favour of the monarchy. . . . Trudeau pointed out that the federal government did not make public the constitutional reform proposals until the Queen had seen them. It will be well for the Palace to have this information. I am amazed at the inadequate supply of information from Rideau Hall to Buckingham Palace. . . .

Friday, November 10, 1978

I read in today's *Times* that Sonny Ramphal, the Commonwealth Secretary General, said yesterday that additional equipment, in addition to that supplied by Britain, was required by Zambia to withstand Rhodesian attacks. . . . A week ago, the Commonwealth Secretary General told me Kaunda had called him and asked him to come to see him in Lusaka. I reported to Ottawa yesterday that he found Kaunda in a depressed mood; that [the outlook] in Dar-es-Salaam [when Callaghan was there] was more healthy and militant. In both Lusaka and Dar-es-Salaam, the feeling exists that South Africa may now have decided to fight its battles on northern borders, in Namibia and Rhodesia. Ramphal told me he was considering sending a message to Commonwealth heads of government asking for support and assistance for Zambia. Moreover, he might propose an informal meeting of Commonwealth Foreign Ministers to consider the situation in Southern Africa. . . . I suggested to Ottawa that, if such a meeting would not be thought to be helpful at present, it would be better to let Ramphal know immediately, before he becomes over-committed to the idea. Perhaps Ottawa would prefer to leave the British to pass judgment on the idea. . . .

We had expected Maurice Strong[4] to stay with us this weekend. He phoned, however, to say that he would have to return to Canada forthwith. It looks like a cabinet shuffle in the making. Did I think he should go to the Senate to permit his entry into the cabinet? I thought he should. He could do a Wally McCutcheon[5] role. Later in the elections, he could, as

4. The chairman of Petro-Canada.
5. Wallace McCutcheon was one of John Diefenbaker's ministers who entered the government and was simultaneously appointed to the Senate in 1962.

Wally did, try for a Commons seat. The cases are not identical. Maurice has been nominated for a seat, to be contested in an election. Unless a by-election was declared, he will have to wait until June or thereabouts. What would the riding people say if he went to the Senate to qualify for the cabinet now? I think the fuss would be minimal. He would strengthen Trudeau's team at present. I would be surprised, however, if the Prime Minister would give a senator an active portfolio. He has always refused heretofore. The provocation may be greater since the fifteen by-elections. Maurice may be floating an idea, or perhaps it is Jim Coutts's kite which is being flown?

Monday, November 13, 1978

Few men get into a cabinet with such praise as that given John Smith, and few leave a cabinet with such praise as that given Edmund.[6] Callaghan has not taken the opportunity to re-shuffle his cabinet. I wish Trudeau would copy his technique in this regard. Our man is always changing his cabinet. . . . Callaghan has been very careful about making changes. He made them only when forced to — for instance, when Roy Jenkins went to the European Commission. . . . It is gimmicky the way Trudeau has done so in Canada. I told him this on more than one occasion. The result is, his ministers are not known, they do not have pedestals of their own, apart from one or two. . . .

Nell and I attended the Lord Mayor's Banquet at the Guildhall tonight. . . . We were unprepared for all the fuss and feathers. When we entered the large receiving chamber, some four to five hundred people were seated as the Lord Mayor greeted us. After our names had been called, the applause for Canada was really very touching and loud. . . . To our surprise, we were at the head table. On my right was the wife of the Bishop of London and, on Nell's left, the Lord Chief Justice of England. At one point my wife said, after the Lord Chief Justice had put on his wig, "I bet that makes your head itchy." Only Nell could get away with that. . . .

6. John Smith had just been appointed trade secretary and his predecessor, Edmund Dell, had resigned from the cabinet.

Tuesday, November 14, 1978

Nell and I were invited by the Queen to the state banquet in honour of the President of the Portuguese Republic[7] at Buckingham Palace. There were not many heads of mission invited. . . .

Before dinner, Denis Healey told me how disappointed he was with the T.U.C.'s failure to accept his pay restraints. . . . He said he would try again for agreement, once the dust had settled, but it would take a little time. Peter Carrington mentioned he plans going to Canada next February and would like to consult with me about particular visits and calls. . . . Peter was critical about David Owen, whose credibility in the Rhodesian situation, he thought, was close to exhaustion. Occasions like the state banquet give one an opportunity to discharge a number of responsibilities. . . .

Thursday, November 16, 1978

Some days proceed as though Canada was not about. What is happening in Parliament? Is Trudeau going to make changes in his cabinet? When Larry O'Toole of the Treasury Board was here yesterday, he indicated he would not be surprised if Bob Andras moved on to Finance. Jean Chrétien would come to External Affairs and Don Jamieson would return to Transport, where a job remains to be done. It would be rather good fun to have Jean Chrétien as my chief, although I am not disappointed with Don Jamieson. Will Maurice Strong join the cabinet by way of the Senate? What about Mark MacGuigan? I would like to see him join the inner circle. He is much abler than so many others who are there now. . . .

I had a note from John Turner, thanking me for sending some liquor to his old uncle. This I was happy to do. Old people in England certainly need something to keep them warm on occasion. In his personal note, John does not say "Dear Paul." He simply says "Paul" as though he were writing a memorandum. John operates sometimes like an American real estate agent. His endings are always more personal. I told him about this lacuna in his make-up one day. It was the

7. General Ramalho Eanes

kind of thing that Pearson, one of his admirers, thought lacking in John. . . .

Monday, November 20, 1978

I called on the Secretary for Trade this morning and turned over to him formally MacEachen's letter urging action in the Multilateral Trade Negotiations in Geneva [and] . . . I drew his attention to . . . .

— The importance to Canada of a negotiation which will provide the international environment required for the adjustment of the Canadian economy to meet changing world circumstances;

— The possibility that the importance of the M.T.N. to Canada's industrial [structure] may not be fully appreciated in the E.E.C. and that the scope of a possible agreement with the E.E.C. may be accordingly unnecessarily limited;

— The importance of our forestry, mining, agriculture and fisheries sectors in our effective participation in worldwide structural change . . .

— The inevitability that such adverse effects would weigh upon Canada's relations with the Community and its member states, a result which all would wish to avoid. . . .

The proposed Commonwealth foreign ministers' meeting on Southern Africa suggested by Sonny Ramphal is not thought to be a good idea by Ottawa in present circumstances. It could even pose certain hazards. I am inclined to agree. . . . I will tell Sonny later this week that, in our view, nothing should be done which might appear to be taking an initiative on Rhodesia from the United Kingdom and the United States. As far as the Namibian issue is concerned, it falls entirely within the scope of the United Nations. Ottawa is opposed to a political involvement of the Commonwealth Committee or the Secretariat to review the Southern Africa situation. The suggested action in the Namibian situation by the Commonwealth at this critical juncture might undermine efforts of the principal participants. Ottawa believes, moreover, it would tend to set up an adverse situation between African Commonwealth representatives on the one hand and the United Kingdom and Canada on the other on such difficult issues as United Nations sanctions. . . .

We have advised Ottawa that at the official British level, the reaction is like our own. David Owen's personal view, however, is not yet known. The Foreign Office is preparing a reply for use by Callaghan. I wouldn't be surprised if Callaghan's letter would make encouraging noises about Ramphal's appeal for further Commonwealth assistance. . . .

For the next two days, I made a trip to Birmingham and then to Worcester. I was back in London on Thursday.

Thursday, November 23, 1978

Now I see there is a book about the [Jeremy] Thorpe case by Messrs. Penrose and Courtiour.[8] How the boys like to get at the corpse, wrangle its flesh, and let it be submitted to the continuous rays of the hot sun! Man is not necessarily a lovely animal. . . .

Friday, November 24, 1978

Ottawa advised me this morning to hold myself in readiness to advise the appropriate minister in the [British] government, that a decision had been taken regarding the purchase of British military equipment, long since urged on us by the British, French, and Germans. Later, I received a flash advising me not to act until further instructions were given. There seems to be some uncertainty at the Ottawa end. . . .

Late this afternoon, I called on Wellbeloved[9] to advise him that the cabinet has decided not to buy the British (European) plane [for our airforce]. Instead it will buy either the General Dynamics F-16 or the McDonnell Douglas F-18. This suits our purse and needs. It will now be argued that this is a blow to our "special relationship." I had urged that we should buy the British plane.

Sunday, November 26, 1978

In yesterday's cabinet changes, three new Ministers were appointed: Pierre de Bané, John Reid, and Martin O'Connell.[10] Marc Lalonde goes to Justice. Perhaps Reid will be more

8. Barrie Penrose and Roger Courtiour, *The Pencourt File* (London 1978).
9. Parliamentary under-secretary for defence, James Wellbeloved.
10. De Bané became minister of supply and services; Reid, minister of state for federal-provincial relations; and O'Connell, minister of labour.

sensitive to the Quebec challenge. A little sugar goes a long way. . . . I had hoped Mark MacGuigan might have been given the nod. Pitfield said there would be another shift in February or thereabouts. . . .

What has been the effect of the Lévesque challenge in London since 1976? The general effect in Britain after two years is favourable to the federal government. London's business community looks on Canada's economic problems as more pressing. It would be too much to say that in a country which speaks of devolution, there were not minority interests who were not attentive to the separatists' thesis. We have no reason to fear that British opinion is not in favour of Canadian federalism. Millions of Britishers have direct family links in Canada. . . .

In official Britain, there is full support for the federal position. The Foreign Office is helpful in the support it gives us. The Quebec Agency General has created no problem for me or the High Commission. Our relations are friendly and cordial. Sometimes the British press, following quick Canadian visits, over- or understate, but not seriously. Canada, in their eyes, is an affluent country . . . [and] continues to be attractive to the British investor. They don't, of course, like our high taxes compared with the United States. They note our high wage levels and the level of our productivity, but are satisfied with Canada in the long term. Federal-provincial controversy is somewhat new to the British press. . . .

Monday, November 27, 1978

I am glad to note that there are some in [External Affairs] who agree with my view that in an "eventual" drawing apart of the two sides of the Atlantic, Canada must consider seriously the involvement of Australia and New Zealand in our relations with Europe. A bloc approach would be unwise. Nevertheless, it must be remembered that, while Canadian and Australian interests in Europe are not identical, the three countries have many of the same problems. It isn't a question of ganging up on the nine, but letting it be known that the problem has ramifications "beyond simple bilateralism." One of my colleagues points out that informal consultations depend often on personalities. A formalized mechanism creates an obligation, a contractual link. The "buddy" system was used at the beginning. At that time, Canada relied on the United Kingdom for information about what was going on among the nine. . . . More recently, the nine have got closer together and are virtually "in perpetual consultation." . . .

Tuesday, November 28, 1978

We had a long executive meeting and reviewed the recommendations of a committee set up to determine what cuts in personnel should be made. I had to take a strong hand to protect the positions of long-service employees and this I did successfully. It was interesting to see the bureaucratic mind at work. It is one which I don't altogether disrespect but it lacks often an imaginative and a compassionate turn of mind. . . .

I went to the American Embassy to listen to a lecture on Churchill by one who knew him, Averell Harriman. Averell is a remarkable man. . . . My first meeting with Harriman was in 1932, when he came to participate in the Liberal Summer School organized at Port Hope by Vincent Massey. . . . Harriman revealed that from the first, he was given the fullest opportunity, including attendance at the war council, to follow the policy of Her Majesty's government in the hour of its greatest conflict. Harriman and Beaverbrook were the first on our side to establish satisfactory contact with Stalin. . . .[11] As Harriman went from point to point, showing remarkable memory and speaking without notes, I formed the impression that I had never heard him speak so well. . . . He had reservations about the historians. The best participants of history were the actors. Harold Macmillan thanked Harriman for his lecture. . . . He wanted to know if the present generation would have the will to resist the evils of the world. I thought, as I heard Macmillan, that we had listened tonight to the last actors in a great period in the world's history. . . .

Thursday, November 30, 1978

This morning . . . I reminded John Smith, the new Secretary of State for Trade, that I had seen his predecessor, Edmund

11. Harriman had served in the first years of the war as F. D. Roosevelt's special representative to the U.S.S.R. and later became U.S. ambassador.

Dell, over the British request that Air Canada should move from Heathrow to Gatwick. . . . I urged him to bring to an end the unseemly "haggling" over technical details . . . between his officials and Air Canada by recommending the reversal of the British government's decision to transfer Air Canada to Gatwick, on political grounds. . . . The Canadian government cannot afford to be seen . . . accepting second-class treatment from a country with whom it is supposed . . . to have a special relationship. . . .

I received the new Polish Ambassador, Jan Bisztyga, this morning. . . . Ambassador Bisztyga was himself born and educated in the historic city of Cracow [and] . . . told me of a very interesting incident in connection with the new Pope. The Ambassador of Cuba had wanted to see the Primate of Poland, Cardinal Wyszyński. As in my case, when I went to Poland in 1965, this visit was not sanctioned. The Cuban Ambassador was resourceful. He got to know the Archbishop of Cracow, the present Pope. He said nothing to the officials about his new acquaintance. The Cuban Ambassador told Mr. Bisztyga that not only did he get to know the present Pope, but also got to see him often at dinner in the home of the head of the Communist party in Cracow. If anything could be revealing about the new Pope, it is this incident. He will go out to seek the friendship and the understanding of all groups in the world. That is what a good religious leader really should do. . . .

Saturday, December 2, 1978

Don Jamieson [who was on a visit to London] and I chatted at noon-time about Namibia and Rhodesia. I agree that he should project himself on Rhodesia. He is concerned about pressures to impose sanctions on South Africa over Namibia. There is the restraint of Britain's close friends. Particular sanctions, not fully or directly economic, might be easier to support. The United States is looking at these. We might follow, leaving the British outside, a dangerous thing to do. . . .

Sunday, December 3, 1978

I have suspected it for several months, and lacked the courage to ascertain the fact, that I have put on weight—eight pounds. My wife, butler, and Lorne Green all said otherwise. The battle cry is raised—onwards to [lose] seventeen pounds. . . . Jim Callaghan has my problem. Looking at him in today's *Observer*, he seems to have slimmed slightly. . . .

Monday, December 4, 1978

When Roly Michener, the former Governor-General, phoned last night, asking that I rearrange my reception for the delegation from Canada, who will be here under the auspices of the Canadian Institute of International Affairs, he noted that Trudeau would be here on Thursday. Roly said, "I suppose he will discuss with the Queen proposals for the next Governor-General." I was equivocal in my reponse. I am sure, however, that, if Trudeau has decided on whom he wishes to succeed Léger, he will raise the matter with the Queen. This would be a unique way for the Canadian Prime Minister to let his views be known to the monarch. Usually, the Prime Minister communicates directly to the Queen suggested names in order of preference. . . . I still think Trudeau will recommend Bob Stanfield, although Don Jamieson thinks otherwise. . . .

Tuesday, December 5, 1978

I transacted most of my business this morning on the telephone. Michael Pitfield suggested I should talk to Trudeau on the importance of his holding on and not giving in. Margaret, his wife, has a book coming out very shortly. This apparently is troubling the Prime Minister. . . .

Mitchell Sharp called this morning and understood how difficult it would be for me to see him. We had a long talk on the telephone. He confirms the stories one hears about Trudeau's position vis-à-vis the electorate. He sees no chance of Trudeau winning the election. On the other hand, he would take no opportunity to force him out. I emphasized how foolish, from the party's point of view, that would be. . . . Mitchell does not wish to become Governor-General, he says. . . .

The second day of our meeting with . . . [Canada's] western European ambassadors opened at noon when my colleagues, headed by the Secretary of State for External Affairs and Gotlieb, came for lunch at the residence. . . . After the luncheon, we proceeded upstairs to the large lounge for our afternoon meeting. Jamieson spoke well [and] . . . was particularly good on trade and economic matters; he emphasized how important it had been to restore economic primacy in the Department of External Affairs. . . .

Wednesday, December 6, 1978

Allan Gotlieb tells me his wife [Sondra] has written a first-rate novel. I promised to check with the British publisher, who is also publishing Margaret Trudeau's book, which Pitfield told me yesterday disturbs Trudeau. Gotlieb thought it should not worry Trudeau, as it is just a continuation of the same thing. I am sorry for Trudeau. His wife's estrangement has caused him great anguish. It has many by-products. Apparently, when the provincial premiers were recently at 24 Sussex, and later when Cyrus Vance was there, Margaret came back, ostensibly to see the children. As someone observed, she does come back at the most inappropriate moments. Very tough on Trudeau and I do feel for him. How fortunate a man is when married to a sensible spouse. Where would I be without Nell? . . .

I accompanied Don Jamieson and Allan Gotlieb . . . [for] their call on David Owen. . . . We had an hour and a half's meeting with him. . . . Jamieson asked Owen how Canada could assist the British on Rhodesia. He directed Owen's attention to Trudeau's contacts with Kenneth Kaunda and Julius Nyerere. Owen thought the most effective help we could give would be aid to Zambia. Zambia was a difficult problem. Kenneth Kaunda was not well. Any short-term aid or any gesture, which he termed "ego massage," would be important in having Kaunda continue to support British attempts to find a solution. The United Kingdom has given some military assistance. Kaunda is not satisfied with it, although no one else, not even the United States, has given anything. It is likely that Zambia will look to the Soviet Union for military assistance. A message should be sent to Kaunda, velvet-gloved and iron-fisted. . . .

Mugabe is emerging as a more important force in Rhodesia. Muzorewa's support is going to him and his forces are better trained in guerrilla warfare than those of Nkomo. . . .

Both foreign ministers agreed that a decision to invoke sanctions [on South Africa] would be serious and would not be a mere cosmetic solution. While the talk was under way, Andrew Young phoned Owen, who reported his consultations in Southern Africa. He confirmed support for the solution offered by the five countries. . . . Owen thinks a solution in Namibia is the key to one in Rhodesia. Owen believes, as does Vance, that Canada should continue in the contact group, even if our time on the Security Council finishes at the end of the year. . . .

Thursday, December 7, 1978

Prime Minister Trudeau and his party of seven arrived at Heathrow this morning. I thought he looked tired as one would expect from his all-night journey and the heavy load which he carries. . . .

Trudeau [told me that he] will not give up the leadership, unless he is asked. Stories about visits of Marchand, who is supposed to have called for his resignation, and Gérard Pelletier, our man in France, have no validity in fact, the Prime Minister told me. I reminded him of the resistance Laurier and King had given to demands that they resign from the leadership of the party. They did not give in to the demand. This attitude is vital to the Liberal party's future. Trudeau does not intend to give any press interviews and unceremoniously cut off the CBC man at Claridges when we arrived. There, we were greeted by an endless number of photographers. . . .

I insisted that Trudeau should get some immediate rest. He acknowledged that it would have been wise to have come here a day ahead and fully rest for his talks with Callaghan and on Friday with the President of France. Admittedly, he would have had only two hours before he saw the Queen but this would have been helpful.

He proposes to appoint Ed Schreyer, the former Manitoba Premier and presently Leader of the Opposition in the Manitoba Legislature, as the next Governor-General. This puts to rest the forecasts about George Ignatieff, Stanfield . . . and others. Schreyer's selection is imaginative. Western Canada should be pleased, as will be the ethnic groups in the country, notably the Ukrainians. . . . He is now only forty-two years of age and a well-balanced fellow. Ed was respected in the House of Commons and acted sensibly when he was Manitoba's Premier. . . . I made arrangements for advice to Ottawa, once the Queen had concurred in the Prime Minister's recommendation. . . .

The Prime Minister had a good discussion with the Queen in the presence of Prince Philip, emphasizing that the proposals his government had put forward on the monarchy were the first enshrinement in a statute of the role, status, and the fact of the monarchy in Canada. The description of the Governor-General as "Head of State" was a pure descriptive term. Clearly, the governing words were that the monarch was the Queen of Canada and sovereign. As Trudeau had said, when he submitted the constitutional proposals, the Queen was head of our constitutional monarchy. . . .

Kenneth Stowe, the Prime Minister's private secretary, had called me early in the afternoon to say that the day's parliamentary sitting was fraught with political danger. A vote could ensue which might well topple the government on the question of sanctions against the Ford Motor Company for violation of the government's pay restraint [policy] of five percent [wage increases]. Because of this, the hour of Trudeau's private meeting with Callaghan would have to be delayed as might the dinner. The latter event might even be interrupted by the requirement of the Prime Minister and ministers in the House of Commons for a 10:00 o'clock vote, a situation not unfamiliar to me and certainly not now unfamiliar to Trudeau. As matters turned out, the parliamentary situation was resolved by the House considering other matters. . . .

Our discussions opened up with a review by Callaghan, at Trudeau's suggestion, of the current situation in Iran. Callaghan does not think the Shah can survive [the challenge by Moslem fundamentalists]. On the Canada-Quebec problem and Trudeau's visit to the President of France tomorrow, he outlined what Lévesque's success could mean to Canada and Western countries generally. He hoped to persuade Giscard how important it was for . . . France to observe the practices which should prevail between friendly powers. Continuing intervention in Canadian affairs by France would not be effective in preventing fragmentation in Canada. . . . I raised the bilateral issue of the proposed Air Canada move to Gatwick. I took issue with Callaghan, who objected to my description of Gatwick as a second-class airport. I emphasized that, as Heathrow's oldest tenant, it was unfair and discriminatory to ask Air Canada to move. The unfairness was highlighted by the reluctance of the Scandinavian airlines to stay at Heathrow and the British effort at persuading them that they should. . . .

I found Trudeau tired. . . . He would soon be on his way to France, a country whose leaders have now, for ten years, stood in our shadow. He would see Giscard d'Estaing, who only that day had invited the United States, Britain, and Germany to meet with him for discussions in early January in the sunny climate of Guadeloupe.

On my way to the hotel, I opened up on Giscard. How arrogant the men in the government of France had become! Their elitism did not represent the convictions of the French people. How arrogant for Giscard to call this conference together on the eve of seeing Trudeau. Canada had participated in the other meetings, all except that at Rambouillet. We should not forget, I added, that the British had not helped us too well either. When I raised this matter three years ago, Harold Wilson and Jim Callaghan assured me they would support our participation at the Summit. I replied, "We want more than support. We want you to initiate the matter." We must not forget, I told Trudeau, that it was Kissinger of the United States who had publicly insisted on Canadian participation at the second Summit. While I talked in this vein, I could not tell whether Trudeau applauded or scorned what I said. When I concluded, however, he said, "You are right, their arrogance is something unique." I looked at him in a friendly way and said, "You know, the arrogance that we complain of is something which you yourself have not been altogether free from." This was a good point at which to say good night. . . .

Friday, December 8, 1978

I accompanied Trudeau to Heathrow. He took off in a small military plane from the special section, which the Queen and Prime Minister use on official flights. On the way from Claridges, Trudeau told me he had discussed the future of the monarchy last August with the Queen. There was and is no question in his mind about her indispensability as monarch and on purely personal grounds. What the future will be for her successor is a matter for serious consideration and even speculation. The Queen had performed her functions with such distinction and her personal qualities were projected so strongly that she was a source for stability in her various kingdoms and as head of the Commonwealth. . . .

The Queen did not raise with Trudeau the only possible ambiguity in the outline of the status of the monarchy in the proposed new constitution, where the responsibilities of the Governor-General are articulated. The Queen is described as "Queen of Canada and Sovereign of Canada." These are comprehensive designations. The functions exercised by the Governor-General are occasioned by the absence from Canada of the Sovereign. The designation of the Governor-General within its limited text as "Head of State" creates the ambiguity, but does not establish a constitutional fact. What amazed me in the discussion on the way in the car was that Trudeau himself did not recall the use of the words "Head of State" as applied to the Governor-General in the limited circumstances which I have mentioned. . . . We both agreed that, in any event, in his talk with the Queen yesterday, she showed wisdom in not raising this point. She fully concurred in Trudeau's statement to her that it was ironic he should be accused of eroding the role of the monarch, when it was under his prime-ministership that steps were taken to enshrine in a statute, for the first time, the monarchy itself. . . .

Monday, December 11, 1978

The vagaries of politics! A month after Claude Ryan was selected Liberal leader, the polls in Quebec showed him ahead of Trudeau. Now, less than a year later, stories are written querying Ryan's leadership. He now trails Lévesque in the polls. As far as Quebec is concerned, Trudeau is the man, although it may be otherwise in English-speaking Canada. Ryan doesn't attach much importance to polls. He has spent so much of his life generalizing advice that, like many other journalists serving in the government, he is surprised at the nature of government responsibility day by day. . . .

Tuesday, December 12, 1978

I noticed in the Canadian Press story of Trudeau's visit on Thursday the following: "A small group of reporters waited outside Claridges for Trudeau's arrival. He brushed by the reporters and declined to pose for photographs." I noticed this too. The Prime Minister, of course, was tired. . . . The London visit was my idea and for a purpose. The visit could have been so much more productive for Trudeau and Canada, had he made himself more available to the press. Another story in the Canadian Press said: "Aside from scant details, the only sign of a welcome from Great Britain was a Canadian flag flying over Claridges Hotel luxury accommodation, dismissed by United States President Jimmy Carter as too expensive." This, of course, is ridiculous. The visit was not an official one. . . . I would have preferred Trudeau to stay with us. We could not, however, have accommodated all his staff. He prefers, understandably, to be close to his working personnel. . . . I am not altogether impressed with the Prime Minister's staff, good and able, I agree, but not fully experienced. . . .

The inadequate publicity for Trudeau's visit here and in Paris is due entirely to his own attitude or, at least, the attitude taken by his advisers. Pelletier said the journalists had placed too much importance on the Prime Minister's visit to Giscard. "The visit was only one step up on a phone call." Nevertheless, Pelletier seemed to be pleased with the results of the visit. Trudeau, after his lunch with Giscard, said it was a congenial and fruitful meeting. . . . Some embassy official in Paris was unwise enough to tell the Canadian Press, "it would have been wiser to keep their bureau open for more important news than sending reporters to cover the Prime Minister." It seems that in Ottawa, Trudeau's office sought to discourage news coverage of the trip, although it included a visit to the Queen and a meeting with Callaghan, followed by the Paris visit. I now learn that the newspaper people in London were not told by Trudeau about Schreyer. . . .

Wednesday, December 13, 1978

I attended a Christmas luncheon given by Lord Maclean, the Lord Chamberlain, and the Australian Agents-General in the Cholmondeley Room at the House of Lords. This was a friendly luncheon with the Agents-General of Canada and Australia vying with one another in good humour. The High Commissioner for New Zealand and I were guests. I twitted the Quebec Agent-General. It is well known that the states of Australia regard themselves as sovereign, altogether apart from reality. They refer to the "sovereign states." In Quebec, the P.Q. objective is sovereignty. Lévesque was taking the long route to achieve this status. The Australians had shown the way — a mere declaration of status. Could the Quebec Agent-General not take the hint? He could just as well pronounce sovereignty as seek to achieve it by the Lévesque method. Perhaps after all, I suggested, with tongue in cheek, neither Lévesque nor the Agent-General were serious or perhaps, better still, they should not be taken seriously. . . .

Thursday, December 14, 1978

The events anticipated for last Thursday occurred yesterday, when Callaghan suffered two defeats [in the House of Commons]. . . . As a result, Jim is laying it on the line today. He will seek a vote of confidence, and, if he loses, there will be an election forthwith. I suspect he will skate through. Today's Gallup shows Margaret is up five per cent over Jim. . . .

Friday, December 15, 1978

Jim has pulled it off again, [and] . . . succeeded in getting the House of Commons to give a vote of confidence. . . .[12] Mrs. Thatcher said the government "was one of dying men in a dying Parliament." Undoubtedly, an election cannot be too far off. . . .

What a picture of disunity Isabelle [Quenneville] paints of the Liberals at home. Isabelle is a loyal party official. Never too strong for Trudeau, she does not think he can make it this time. Television, she believes, has altered party politics. Long-term leadership, such as that of King, Gladstone and Laurier, will not recur. Television had made the stars less relevant. People now become so used to the image and personality of public figures that confidence in them wanes. The

12. He won by ten votes.

populace tire of their leaders and look for new faces. This, she thinks, is part of Trudeau's problem. This is what happened to me in 1968.

Monday, December 18, 1978

I have a new book on my desk, *History and Christian Philosophies in the Middle Ages*, by my great teacher, who was a great philospher and historian, Etienne Gilson. . . .[13] There was a time when I was familiar with Aristides and Quadratus, Basil the Great, Augustine, Boethius, Peter Abelard, Albert the Great, Thomas Aquinas, *et al.* One would have to ask now, "Does memory hold the door?" . . . The last sentence in this history by Gilson is a quotation from Aquinas: "The highest felicity of man consists in the speculation through which he is seeking a knowledge of truth." . . .

Wednesday, December 20, 1978

One's patience is somewhat tried by the number of Christmas parties held in this mission, as in other organizations. This, the High Commissioner feels, I suppose more than anyone else, because he has to go to them all if he wishes to satisfy those who loyally support him in the work of the Commission. . . .

Thursday, December 21, 1978

I hope the government and Air Canada have not openly admitted that the United Kingdom card in the proposed move to Gatwick is the British want of access to Western Canada. As early as August 1973, the British government granted British Airways the rights to serve cities in western Canada from points in the United Kingdom. This was done without any consultation with Canada. Air Canada takes the position that the designation of B.A. to additional cities in Canada is not provided for under the existing bilateral air agreement. The government of Canada must ensure that we do not surrender more in valuable operating rights than is won from the other side. . . .

13. Etienne Gilson, *History of Christian Philosphy in the Middle Ages*, 2nd ed. (London 1978).

We have invited the Governor-General, Jules Léger, who will have left his office on January 2nd, to stay with us or, at any rate, to partake of our hospitality. Jules and Gaby will spend the night before leaving England, early in February, with H.M. the Queen. The new Governor-General, Ed Schreyer, and his wife will be in London in early January. I have sent a message to him saying we would be happy to have him stay with us at the residence. . . . If they bring their three children, we will have to fit them in somehow. . . . We will be a crowded household. I feel strongly, however, that an ambassador's residence is for such a purpose. . . .

Friday, December 22, 1978 – Tuesday, January 2, 1979

Nell and I went to Israel for a winter holiday at Eilat on the Red Sea. It was a time to read and relax. On Boxing Day, by chance, we met Mrs. Jacob Herzog, wife of a former Israeli ambassador to Ottawa. As I wrote on December 26, seeing her again reminded me of an amusing incident involving her husband and his conscientious despatch of duty:

I saw him often as foreign minister in Ottawa. At noontime, he called to say he must see me again. There was something further on his mind, which he wished to impart. "Jacob, you can see me at my 'swimming hole' on the Rideau River." . . . He came too. Jacob could not swim. This I did not know, as I saw his white skin in what looked like a new bathing suit. Into the water he came. At that point, the depth of the Rideau was only several feet. As he unfolded what he insisted I must be told, I kept on swimming. Suddenly, I realized he was not with me. He was over his depth and in trouble. A bystander noticed the situation and took corrective action. Whenever I think of Jacob Hertzog, I recall the able Ambassador, who was prepared to go under for his country.

XXIV

January – February 1979

AT THE BEGINNING OF THE YEAR, I was most concerned about a possible revolt by some members of the Liberal party against the leadership of Pierre Trudeau. In Britain, strikes by truck drivers and others crippled the country and led to a vote of no confidence in Parliament which the government survived. But the strikes did not abate, and criticism about the misuse of trade union power gave increased public support to Conservative leader Margaret Thatcher. I continued my crusade against the attempts to force Air Canada to move from Heathrow to Gatwick.

Talk of an election in Canada remained a current topic of interest and this paralleled similar political gossip in the U.K. Trudeau, however, appeared inclined to pursue constitutional reform through a series of meetings of first ministers.

Wednesday, January 3, 1979

A sign of the times were notices on my desk about these troubled times of bombings. We are urged to be on our guard against the unusual and the unexpected. Security guards constantly patrol the building and look for anything out of the ordinary. . . . The chauffeurs are urged to lock all doors when the car is unattended, to keep all doors locked during a journey. Windows must be closed to deter a missile being pushed into the vehicle. The driver of a car is urged not to touch a suspicious object under the car but report it. . . .

Thursday, January 4, 1979

I have been thinking a good bit the last while about developments in Canada. Trudeau must stay on and fight to the end. It is too late to change leaders. To force him out now would be unheroic. . . . Why have we got into this situation? is the question which persists in my mind. Trudeau has had a long tenure in office. One cannot say he has not been successful. . . . He is not condescending enough. He may be grateful but he does not know how to express his thanks and appreciation. He has let his cabinet become depleted, instead of holding on to good men. Those who remain do not seem to have even subordinate leadership talent. Trudeau has been able in elections to show himself a tribune of the people but, after the contest, he returns to his seminar [leader's] posture and his studies of national issues. . . . Meanwhile, [he forgets] that he is a political leader, who must constantly be in touch with the people, who must like him for his intimacy and who will not like him only because he is charismatic. I am afraid the situation is even worse than I thought. There may not be a palace revolution in being, but the quiet talk at certain high levels is disturbing. . . . The cabinet must rally behind Trudeau.

Friday, January 5, 1979

I had a further talk today about the situation in Canada. The view is strongly held that, unless an expected Gallup poll shows an improvement in the government's position with the electorate, the Prime Minister may want to relinquish his party and governmental responsibilities, allowing time for someone else to take over. Some expressed the opinion that, if that were done and Turner was the man selected, the government would be sustained. I regard this as a highly dangerous course. . . .

There will be no agenda for the Guadeloupe Summit.[1] I am trying to ascertain what will be discussed. . . . Political subjects will be at the forefront; economic subjects, of course, will be relevant. Others bound to be mentioned are Southern Africa, the Middle East, China and the NATO southern flank. Turkish economic problems and the general situations there will certainly be on President [Carter's] mind. There is likely to be a discussion on the future of Western democracies. One

1. This was an informal meeting held at the initiative of President Giscard. Canada was excluded from the meeting.

wonders how a subject like this can be on the agenda without other major partner democracies being included in the discussion. . . .

Saturday, January 6, 1979

When I was at Gatwick yesterday morning to welcome the Schreyers, I learned that an accident held up air traffic on the one and only runway. This should help us in our resistance . . . to move Air Canada from Heathrow. An interruption of traffic would be a serious matter for the Air Canada flights to and from Canada. Maybe my determination will yield results. . . .

After dinner tonight, Schreyer and I talked in my library. He was concerned with his speech, when he is sworn in as Governor-General on the 21st of the month. We talked of the theme he should pursue. It was natural for us to talk about the state of our nation. Of this, he wants to say something. He was impressed by what I said about Laurier and national unity. . . . Canada's new first lady and her three children have come in early. The "Nutcracker Suite" was good, but fatigue stood in the way. They abandoned the theatre for a deserved early sleep. . . .

Monday, January 8, 1979

Britain's main concern today is the continued lorrymen's strike and the petrol drivers who threaten to cut off oil and gas to British car users, with serious indirect consequences affecting food and industry—all because the lorry drivers want more pay. . . . Mrs. Thatcher has called for the declaration of a state of emergency. The government over which she would preside would curb union power. . . .

I attended a memorial meeting for Golda Meir, Israel's former Prime Minister . . . Francis Pym, the shadow foreign minister in Mrs. Thatcher's party, told me on the way in, he thought Callaghan had not played his cards well in trying to get a Camp David type of meeting on Rhodesia. Pym would like to have involved the Commonwealth members in the effort. Pym is an attractive man, who speaks well. . . . I would not be surprised to see Francis Pym become leader of the

Conservative party. He did not want to come up to the front of the hall. He said in an aside, "That's for Margaret." . . .

Tuesday, January 9, 1979

I am a little annoyed with Sir Martin Gilliat, secretary to the Queen Mother. I could also be annoyed with her but perhaps I should withhold my steam. I had arranged for Trudeau to see the Queen Mother [in December] in the hope that her desire to visit Canada, mainly in the Toronto district, would be acceptable to the Canadian government. In this objective I succeeded. I know the Queen Mother was grateful as was her fussy secretary. It was, therefore, with surprise that I received a communication from Sir Martin a few days ago, saying that the Queen Mother would not be able to alter her programme for the Canadian visit. I so reported, although I felt the Queen Mother was ill advised not to accept the suggestion made by the Prime Minister to go to Nova Scotia. At no time did I ever suggest that the Queen Mother should go to Windsor, Ontario. The only intimation of this came from Sir Martin himself, after the Prime Minister had met the Queen Mother, following his luncheon with the Queen. . . .

It was, therefore, with some amazement today that I learned from the Agent-General from Nova Scotia, Debbie Piers, that he had just heard from Sir Martin to the effect that the Queen Mother would go to Nova Scotia. No such intimation came to this office. Only this morning I had talked to Lord Elgin, who was anxious that we put additional pressure on the Queen Mother to have her participate in the World Clan meeting in Nova Scotia. . . . I was surprised yesterday afternoon to get a call from the Canadian Press in Toronto. "Was I annoyed that the Queen Mother was not going to Windsor?" I said that there was never any likely prospect that she would be going to Windsor. What I cannot understand is how Canada knew, almost as quickly as we did in this mission, that there had been a change in plans. . . .

Wednesday, January 10, 1979

Roberto Ducci, the Italian Ambassador . . . has written a little book entitled *Twenty Four Hours at 4 Grosvenor Square*. It is rather well done. Anxious to know privately the Italian reaction to not being included at the Guadeloupe Summit, I thought I would call on my colleague at 4 Grosvenor Square and tell him what a wonderful little book he wrote. Trudeau and Ottawa are not anxious that we should officially indicate our displeasure at not having been invited to Guadeloupe. I told Roberto that the Canadian government had taken no official position on not being invited to join Giscard, Carter, Callaghan and Schmidt in the Caribbean, but that did not preclude one from having a view about the impropriety of the restricted meeting. What did he, Roberto, think? He not only told me what he thought but how annoyed his government was. . . . The Italian Prime Minister let Giscard and the others know how they felt as, I understand, the Netherlands did as well. . . . How is it possible to maintain firm partnerships, alliances, [or] special relationships, if contrary action is taken by those who regard themselves as more eminent? . . . In the days of Napoleon, Castlereagh, Metternich and Talleyrand,[2] those assumed to be the most powerful divided Europe or sought to do so without outside assistance. It is anachronistic for the modern French Talleyrand, the modern Castlereagh, the modern Prince Bismarck, and the modern President Jackson to hold salon gatherings, open only to men of their status, grandeur and experience. . . .

The Schreyers had a memorable visit with the Queen at Sandringham [on Sunday and Monday]. The occasion will not be forgotten by the children. I think Ed, with his farmer's background, was intrigued by his visit to the Sandringham stables. On his return . . . he received some pheasants which had been shot at Sandringham. . . .

Air Canada passed on word this morning that . . . the Trade Department, in charge of air negotiations, was about to issue a release to the effect that, following yesterday's conversations with Air Canada, the government of the United Kingdom had decided finally that Air Canada should move to Gatwick. It seemed to me, in view of the fact that the last

2. Castlereagh, Talleyrand, and Metternich, the foreign ministers of Britain, France, and Austria, following the defeat of Napoleon, set up a European system based on the balance of power at the Congress of Vienna in 1814.

meeting occurred only yesterday, it was unfair and unusual for such peremptory action to be taken. . . . I spoke to the Assistant Under-Secretary, Mr. Steel, who assured me it was not contemplated to issue such a release. I have advised Ottawa of the situation. . . .

Sunday, January 14, 1979

Almost overlooked in the current spate of crippling strikes is the consequence of rising inflation. . . . The mania from wage agreements over the five per cent limit threatens the present inflation level, now under ten per cent. If the oil truckers, the lorrymen and the railway workers get out of hand this week, prices will rise. An election could take place earlier than Jim intends. He is thinking of one in June. He could be forced into one much sooner. . . . Jim does not want to give the picture of a complacent Prime Minister. This will be much on his mind on Tuesday's House of Commons debate. The belief is that he will get a majority on a motion of censure. The Prime Minister is counting on Welsh and Scots Nationalist support. . . .

Tuesday, January 16, 1979

Recent clippings on the cancellation of the Queen Mother's visit to Hamilton and Windsor came as a surprise to me. Apparently, there was more of a polemic in the matter between Premier Davis[3] and Trudeau than I had known. If Rideau Hall had only told us what it was doing, instead of monopolizing the channels with Buckingham Palace, we might have been able to set the situation right. Apparently, Pauline McGibbon, the Lieutenant-Governor, got into the act last July. When she saw me here in September, she didn't say anything about a possible visit of the Queen Mother to Hamilton and Windsor. . . . I would certainly have been pleased to see the Queen Mother go to Windsor for the 125th anniversary of the city. Bert Weeks[4] should have got in touch with me — not a word from him or anyone in the city. Davis has seen me

3. William Davis, premier of Ontario.
4. The mayor of Windsor.

several times and never mentioned the matter. Had I known about it in time, I could have fixed it up. . . .

I went this afternoon to the House of Commons. More ambassadors than usual were in the gallery. The House of Lords section overflowed. . . . No vote of confidence will follow today's debate. It will, however, provide the Opposition with an opportunity to put the whole issue of industrial unrest more effectively before the people. . . . Mrs. Thatcher had a captive audience. She made good use of her time and was the star of the debate. . . . At the end of the day the House defeated, by a majority of twenty-four, the Conservative procedural motion for adjournment. . . .

Wednesday, January 17, 1979

I am advised that Air Canada has succeeded in impressing the Department of Transport with the need for strong action to resist the proposed move to Gatwick. We may expect publicity from Air Canada, now that public relations people will go to work for the company in Britain, to supplement efforts here in the High Commission. . . . I hope we will deliver a protest and that I will be instructed to do so. Perhaps the preliminary step should involve a call by Jamieson to Owen, to say that we will make a protest. . . .

Thursday, January 18, 1979

I trotted out of the residence before 8:00 o'clock this morning and welcomed the dry, coldish air of London much more than I did the work on Upper Brook by Westminster's Department of Public Works. I can hardly recall a month when Upper Brook Street was not torn up for one reason or another. This morning, close to the entrance of the American Embassy, they were at it again. . . . As a matter of fact, the Borough of Westminster now and then reflects, not only a lack of planning, but downright stupidity, such as placing four telephone booths directly in front of Canada House, one of the three fine buildings which hug Trafalgar Square, helping to form the pre-eminence of this part of London, and hiding the entrance to Canada House. . . . Happily, by cajolery, denunciation, and abuse almost, we were able to get Westminster to remove the damn boxes. . . .

The report Callaghan gave on the Cledwyn Hughes' Rhodesian mission is, in the final analysis, a reflection of Britain's present impotence.[5] If the United Kingdom-United States package is not acceptable, what would be the result if Britain were to support, even at this late date, the Internal Solution arrangement? . . . External would prefer to keep out of the Rhodesian situation. I am not sure that this is right. Sonny Ramphal had hoped to persuade Owen this would be a good thing to do. David Owen told Sonny Ramphal he did not favour widening the list of possible conference participants to include other Commonwealth countries. A little like Giscard?

As I dictate, I have received a message from Ottawa instructing me to deliver a first-person note to the Secretary of State for Foreign and Commonwealth Affairs on an "urgent" basis. . . . Ottawa wants me to deliver the note before the Air Canada campaign goes public [next Monday]. . . . The note will not be classified so that it can be released publicly in the future. . . .

I called on the Minister of State for Foreign Affairs, Frank Judd, and personally handled him a copy of my letter to the Foreign Secretary. . . . The "note" asked permission for Air Canada to carry on at Heathrow. David has much on his mind and on his calendar. If the situation had been reversed and I was in his place, I would have wanted to receive the letter directly from the High Commissioner. David, able as he is, has a lot to learn yet. . . . I was constrained to tell Judd that he was not up on the facts, that the denial to Canada would be a major blow for Canada and a serious matter in our relations. Frank Judd is a sensitive man and understood this. . . .

I have been thinking about this matter since rising early this morning, I am not so sure that our letter to the Foreign Secretary was a wise one. We asked for permission to stay at

5. Callaghan announced in the House of Commons on November 23 that he and President Carter had agreed to send Cledwyn Hughes, chairman of the parliamentary Labour party and a former minister to Rhodesia, as Callaghan's private emissary. Hughes was to attempt to bring the various parties in Rhodesia to a conference in Britain in 1979. Hughes reported back that any conference would fail and make a bad situation worse.

Heathrow. . . . Should we not have taken a more definite position, saying that we would expect a re-examination of the entire question and that, if the British persisted in their view to have us out, we would have to consider effective retaliatory action? . . .

Friday, January 19, 1979

As I come to the end of this day, I have to conclude that it has been perhaps the most frustrating day since I have been here. It all began with a long and tortuous ride in over-crowded London streets to the Polish embassy for a return call on the Polish Ambassador. The protocol officer was surprised to see the Canadian High Commissioner. The Polish Ambassador had gone to Poland. Had I not been informed by my office? . . . Once again, John and I drove through crowded streets along circuitous routes one must take . . . through this metropolis.

Situations of this order piled up all day. The little irritating frustrations continued. During a reception around 6:00 o'clock, for the Arts Council of Canada and the British Council, a man called to say he must see me at once. When I told him I was engaged he "blew his top" to tell me he was more important than our guests. . . . He was suing the United States and, as a Canadian citizen, he wanted to discuss the matter with the High Commissioner of Canada. I finally persuaded him to come to the office early Monday morning. Not too happy, he agreed. I now find at that time I will be on my way to Gatwick to greet the retiring Governor-General. This will make the man furious. Hopefully, my secretary will be able to compose the gentleman's irrepressibility. All in a day.

Saturday, January 20, 1979

Ivan and Anne Head have arrived to stay for the weekend. They leave Monday for Cairo. . . . Ivan . . . is still very close to Trudeau. There is no danger that the latter will not run. The Prime Minister greatly values Don Macdonald's loyalty and is unhappy about John Turner's posture. . . .[6]

6. Both had left the government.

Monday, January 22, 1979

My friend, the Master of the Rolls, Lord Denning, celebrates his eightieth birthday tomorrow. A new book will be published on his birthday, a sort of legal autobiography. A great judicial law-maker regrets there is no way of providing for those who suffer from the abuses or misuses of trade union power. The Master of the Rolls acknowledges that in the past thirty years the courts have protected members of trade unions against injustice [and] he has led in this constructive work. . . . The Master of the Rolls . . . once told the Lord Chancellor amusingly that he was not of a "retiring" nature. Denning will go down as the greatest judge since Mansfield.[7] Sometimes he gives the impression of being against the common law theory of precedent and has resisted too rigid an application of it. . . . I must get in touch with Denning to offer congratulations on his birthday. He has been a good friend. . . .

I was up early this morning, unnecessarily, because Governor-General Léger's plane is late. . . . When Jules arrives at Gatwick, he will still be Governor-General; by bedtime he will be plain Mr. Léger. . . .

He and Gaby were surprised at Schreyer's nomination. They had counted on George and Alison.[8] Indeed, I am sure that when the Queen chose Alison two years ago as her Canadian lady-in-waiting, the Légers had made the suggestion. I noted that, just as the Légers were surprised by the appointment, so were the Micheners. Norah mentioned to me how disappointed they were for the Ignatieffs. Roly's realism had not left him. Norah, a neophyte in these matters, said Trudeau had a political motive in mind when he recommended Schreyer. Looking at Norah, I said, "Did he?" Jules

7. Lord Chief Justice William Murray, the first Earl of Mansfield (1705-95), converted English mercantile law from chaos into order and improved the law of evidence and court procedure. He gave "Mansfield's judgment" (1772) where he stated that slavery was not allowed or approved by English law.
8. George Ignatieff was a former colleague of Jules in External Affairs. He had served as our permanent representative to NATO (1963) and our ambassador to the UN (1966-68) and then as ambassador at the Geneva disarmament talks. When he left the department in 1972, he became the provost of Trinity College at the University of Toronto and chairman of the board of the National Museums of Canada.

and Gaby have come for a three-week holiday, during which they will see the Queen. . . .

Roly Michener and Norah came to the residence ahead of time for our reception for the C.I.I.A.[9] and its British counterpart. Roly and I thought it would be a good idea to discuss arrangements for the Duke of Edinburgh, who was to be one of our honoured guests, among 170 others. I took His Royal Highness to meet members of the C.I.I.A.; they had assembled in the dining room (with all the furniture removed). . . . His Royal Highness is quick and jovial, but sometimes . . . is provocative. There were several occasions tonight when I felt like giving him a good parliamentary reply and jab. The Queen is much more imperturbable. At one point, Edinburgh said to a member of the Institute, "Well, what do you do discussing these international problems?" I remember, on another occasion many years ago in Ottawa, when he said to a colleague of mine in Parliament, "and what do you do in Parliament, talking all the time?" That particular member was able to give him a very effective reply. I have learned on several occasions that Edinburgh hasn't fully learned his lesson, but he is a charming, bright man. . . .

Tuesday, January 23, 1979

Although the government had a majority of twenty-four in the House of Commons yesterday, after the emergency debate on Britain's industrial crisis, that does not seem to have improved the situation. The negotiations with the lorry-drivers got nowhere last night. One million five hundred thousand public employees on strike yesterday will continue a selective programme of industrial resistance. They staged a mammoth parade through London yesterday, ending with meetings with members of the House of Commons. The trainmen are on strike today and will do so again on Thursday.

The Prime Minister . . . said the nation had not reached the point of national crisis. . . . When Jim spoke on television last night, both Nell and I thought he had more emotion in his presentation as he pleaded for an avoidance of panic and realism. . . .

9. The Canadian Institute of International Affairs.

After dinner, I went to Central Hall, Westminster, to attend a meeting marking the International Anti-Apartheid Year. . . . There were not more than two or three High Commissioners in attendance. Particularly noticeable by their absence were the High Commissioners from Africa and Asia. . . .

David [Owen] is an able fellow but his personality does not lend itself to assisting him in his job. Laughingly, I told him I was surprised he knew the High Commissioner for Zambia by sight. He just laughed in acknowledgment. . . .

Wednesday, January 24, 1979

Lord Hailsham[10] and Louis Heren of *The Times* were this morning's speakers at the C.I.I.A. meeting. . . . I thought I had better show appreciation to Hailsham in particular and also to Louis Heren by being present. . . . [Louis] acknowledged Britain was not doing well; as he saw it, the big problem is to get Britain underway. Britain, he thinks, has not recovered from its loss of status as a great power. Louis said he was a socialist in his youth. Why should we say that there is something wrong with a young person who is not a socialist before thirty? Louis expressed the common view.

It was amusing to see Hailsham sitting at the table, playing with his briefcase and making a lot of noise with it, dropping it several times, while Louis was speaking. Heren looked at him and in a friendly way said, "Am I bothering you?" . . .

Don Jamieson has asked me to convey his congratulations to David [Owen] on the birth of his baby. I am willing to bet anything that this will not really interest Owen. Nor do I think he was overly moved by my note of congratulations to him last Thursday. David suffers from lack of the quality Jim Callaghan has in abundance. In many ways, David is a better foreign minister than Jim was, although he does not portray an image which helps him. Jim was more effective because he made personal relations part of his foreign policy. . . .

Thursday, January 25, 1979

Christian Hardy had a reception tonight, with many interesting Britishers and Canadians present. . . . I told Leo Pliatzky his department's proposal for Air Canada to move to Gatwick

10. He was lord chancellor from 1970 to 1974.

was . . . one of the most serious issues in a long time between Britain and Canada . . . [and] it involved putting to the test our special relationship. . . . Leo made a somewhat hopeful remark — "I did not realize," he said, "Canada took this matter so seriously." "I will certainly look into it." I believe he will. He is that kind of man. . . .

Friday, January 26, 1979

The Unity Task Report has been issued.[11] I want to give this the fullest possible study. I am nevertheless disturbed by a quick analysis in today's *Telegraph* which suggests the task force recommends that, if the residents of French-speaking Quebec vote to separate, Quebec should be allowed to do so. This will disturb Trudeau. All along, he has insisted that he would not negotiate separation, even if Quebec residents voted for independence in a referendum. Trudeau said he had no mandate to negotiate separation. On the surface, the task force recommendation gives support to Lévesque's claim for separation. I had some concern at the outset about this task force and the wisdom of setting it up. Too many cooks spoil the soup. . . .

I was interested in seeing the final text of the Governor-General's address on January 22nd, when he was installed. The speech is basically as we discussed it at the residence during Schreyer's visit. I derived some satisfaction from the quotation I gave him from Laurier. It is interesting that the final sentence, "out of these elements I would build a nation great among the nations of the world," was repeated in German and Ukrainian. Laurier gets more mention in this speech than any other Canadian statesman. I am so glad, because he has been forgotten in Canada, even by Trudeau. . . .

Sunday, January 28, 1979

There is every reason to believe we will have an early election in Canada, from what I now learn. I had not thought one would come before May or June. The narrowing in the polls

11. Jean-Luc Pepin, a former minister in the Pearson and Trudeau governments, and John P. Robarts, a former premier of Ontario, were members in 1977 of a Task Force on Canadian Unity. It was part of Trudeau's response to the separatist threat.

is likely to continue. The political barometer can be as changeable as the weather. The reaction to Joe's travels may have helped to clear the way for Trudeau. He will not wait long.

The press made much of the fact that Clark's party lost their baggage and drew an analogy between this lack of organization and the Tories' capacity to govern.

In Britain, it will take much determination for Callaghan to continue the battle against inflation. . . . Jim must now hold off from an early election. He needs a period of calm and an absence of national turbulence, if he is to do well when he faces the people. . . . Jim will not want an election to be fought against the background of further industrial upheaval. When we dined at No. 10 on December 7th, Jim was seemingly in a strong position. Five weeks later, Trudeau's position and prospects may be brighter. . . .

Monday, January 29, 1979

Recalling Roly Michener's two-day visit with us, it interested me to think again about what Roly told me of the control exercise by Buckingham Palace over Governors-General. He had been tripped up several times by the Queen's secretary for not being able to supply information about troops to be reviewed by the Queen. This, I suppose, goes back to the days when the monarch selected the Governor-General. She continues, if her secretaries are being properly judged, as exercising a continuous authority over the Governors-General. Queen Elizabeth is never put in a position where she seems to be intervening. . . .

Tuesday, January 30, 1979

The lorry-drivers' strike is just about over. In the south-west they were awarded sixty-four pounds for a forty-hour week —way over the five per cent limit. . . . If Callaghan gets an agreement [with the rest of the unions], some think this will mean an early election in March or April. My view is he will wait until October. Some of his ministers fear a delay in bringing [on] an election will see a rise in inflation to double figures. . . .

Chancellor Schmidt has informed Trudeau he believes the Summit of the four [in Guadeloupe] was useful. The Chancellor raised with the other three the suggestion that Trudeau had made . . . namely, the possibility of having regional attendance at Economic Summits. This would have taken care of Australia's wishes to be at Tokyo.[12] The Chancellor said there was no disposition by the Guadeloupe Summit participants to enlarge the participation. . . .

Trudeau said he would be happy to campaign on the basis of the Pepin-Robarts general approach to Canadian unity and the constitution. This was the thought which came to me when I learned we are closer to an election than many think. Trudeau, of course, does not agree with the report's reference to language minorities. He thinks Pepin and Robarts are dead wrong, not in their goals, but in their proposed solutions, namely, to leave language minority questions to the provinces, on the assumption that they will protect linguistic minorities, following which there will be entrenchment of language rights. Trudeau thinks that such optimism is misplaced. . . .

Wednesday, January 31, 1979

When I was walking across Grosvenor Square this morning with John Rowan, he mentioned that Barbara Streisand had written in her biography that she was on the point at one period of marrying Trudeau. I remember the period. It always struck me that this friendship was odd. At the time I felt, as I met Miss Streisand . . . with Trudeau, that he loved to spring surprises on people — to suddenly exhibit his friendship, or whatever it was. . . . I thought it was a sensational way of attracting attention to himself. Trudeau, of course, is not alone in this. . . .

Saturday, February 3, 1979

I was speaking to Alison Ignatieff this morning. She and George are at their place in France. . . . The Schreyer appointment stands on its own feet, but one cannot be too understanding of the way George and Alison must feel. They would

12. Japan was to host the next Economic Summit.

have been good at Rideau Hall. The trouble about their position is that they assumed, and with some justification, that they would succeed the Micheners. They and many others are now saying that the Schreyers were selected by Trudeau for political reasons. Since when did politics not influence in some way decisions of this sort? Most of our Governors-General appointments, from Lord Monck[13] on, had a political flavour of some sort. I am sure that Trudeau genuinely wanted to recognize Western Canada and the other ethnic groups. George would have been helpful in the latter regard. What worried me a little was that Jim Coutts had indicated he strongly favoured George. From this, the publicity built up and encouraged George to believe he would become Governor-General. . . .

Monday, February 5, 1979

Callaghan's relaxation of the public sector pay limits may bring a quick end to the current industrial crisis. Apparently, Jim eased the restraints for local authority workers over the weekend. . . . This is the first time the Prime Minister has given in publicly. I give him good marks and Denis Healey, too, for steadfastly clinging to their pay restraint policy. What could the Prime Minister do in the light of the demands being made by so many workers? . . .

Tuesday, February 6, 1979

As I reflect on today's condition in Britain, it is impossible to ignore the criticism of trade union power. The theoretician of the Conservative party, Sir Keith Joseph, complains of it. One hears from the man of the street that the unions have gone wild. Members of the Labour party, including the Prime Minister, criticize irresponsible trade union manoeuvres. The Master of the Rolls says there is little restraint on union power. Will this lead to bringing the unions under the law, as in other countries, including Canada? . . . The trade union movement is such an integral part of one of the two major

13. He was the first post-Confederation holder of the office.

political parties that curbing trade union power by parliamentary action has not been found easy since 1926.[14] . . .

Wednesday, February 7, 1979

I think I sometimes forget, when I record my daily activities, the many obligations Nell has. This morning, for instance, she had a coffee party. . . . Last week, she had two large gatherings, one of 120 and the other some 80 people. This type of social obligation she performs continually, quietly, and effectively. I don't know what I would do without her. I always remember, when I agreed to come to London, one woman saying, "But will your wife like it?" implying not only that question but "would she fit in?" I was a little annoyed at the time—"Would she fit in?" There has never been a wife of a Canadian diplomat who has endeared herself to so many people any place as has my wife—no side, no pretension—always herself. . . .

Thursday, February 8, 1979

In Canada, the first ministers conferred on February 5-6 and did not reach an agreement on constitutional issues.

The latest Gallup poll in Canada shows Conservatives, 40 per cent; Liberals, 39 per cent; N.D.P., 17 per cent; undecided, 29 per cent (equally divided among Conservatives and Liberals). Trudeau says now the cabinet has two options which it will study today—either an election or another constitutional conference. There would be a further conference only after the cabinet felt that enough progress had been made at the latest conference. It looks as though Trudeau feels progress was made.

He said the federal government went a long way to meet regional alienation. On the question of language, he had gone some considerable distance to remove the fears which lan-

14. 1926 was the year of the British general strike. The strike began as a reaction by the miners' unions against mine-owners' demands for wage cuts and longer hours. The Trades Union Congress called out workers in other major industries for nine days in sympathetic support.

guage policy seems to have occasioned. Five provinces at least want to see basic linguistic rights entrenched in the constitution. On the question of limitation of federal power . . . the federal government would limit the declaratory power and the spending power; there would be recognition of joint jurisdiction in the off-shore and agreement to limit the trade and commerce power to protect the resources of the provinces from federal interference. . . .

On the question of patriation of the constitution, there were difficult discussions between Quebec and Ottawa. . . . Quebec was opposed to any form of patriation before the question of distribution of powers was settled. . . .

On the question of individual rights, the federal government proposed two charters, one dealing with rights generally, the other with linguistic rights, both to be entrenched in the constitution, with a possible formula for opting out. The majority of the provinces supported entrenchment of civil rights . . . but, on linguistic rights, there was a considerable division of opinion, although perhaps more support than last November. . . .

We had an interesting dinner tonight at 12 Upper Brook in honour of Jules and Gaby Léger to mark his retirement as Governor-General of Canada. . . . I had a very good chat with Harold Wilson. . . . He told me at the outset that the present industrial crisis was as bad as the incidents of 1940. I suggested this was somewhat of an exaggeration. Later . . . that evening, he thought perhaps it was an over-statement. The present crisis, however, was more serious than the general strike [of 1926]. In the earlier situation, the government had not lost control. He was afraid that in the present instance it had. . . . Harold begins a new newspaper column next Monday. I am afraid, from what he said, there will be criticism of his successor and his administration.

I did not find Harold particularly helpful in his judgment of Jim and this crisis. I should have thought there was a sort of duty on the part of the former Prime Minister to speak more in support of the present administration, so closely allied to his own. . . . Certainly, when I left Trudeau's government, I didn't feel it incumbent on me to openly criticize his administration. As the years wore on, I allowed myself the luxury of criticism somewhat more generously. In Wilson's case, he has a responsibility. What is happening is, in a sense, related to his own administration. In any event, he feels strongly that the unions have exceeded their authority, and that they should be brought within greater control by the law and rules which provide for the general good.

Harold has little use for David Owen and says so without restraint. Mary, his wife, told me the same, when we talked of possible successors to Jim Callaghan. . . . When Callaghan goes, Harold thinks, as does his wife, that Denis Healey should be the leader.

Harold told me he liked Ted Heath and thought that, if he did not become foreign minister in a Thatcher government, Margaret would do well to send him to Washington. It would be the first time a [former] British Prime Minister had gone to Washington as Ambassador. . . . Wilson would like to see Heath as foreign minister. In that event, perhaps Lord Carrington would be sent to Washington. . . .

Friday, February 9, 1979

Trudeau told me last night, when I was in touch with him, that he was pleased with the progress on constitutional change. He feels free to move unilaterally in bringing about certain changes. I cautioned against doing so before an election. There undoubtedly has been a change in the mood of some of the premiers since last autumn. [At the recent conference] they were more co-operative. This time they did not all side with Lévesque. The unhappiest of their number was Lougheed, who saw no political will by the first ministers to change the underlying law. . . .

Monday, February 12, 1979

Nell and I left by car for Canterbury to attend Burgon Bickersteth's funeral service, which was held in the undercroft of the Cathedral. The Archbishop of Canterbury officiated and spoke of Burgon's exemplary and religious life, together with his devotion to the Church. I read the lesson, I Corinthians. . . . During the service, I thought of my friendship with Burgon, his many kindnesses to me in my early days as a student, of the days I spent visiting his father and mother at

Meister Omers, where they lived, within the precincts at Canterbury. . . .

Wednesday, February 14, 1979

At the moment, the British government is occupied with issues other than Gatwick. It is difficult to think that it wants to add to its problems a major diplomatic row with us over Gatwick. I think we have until an election in the summer or fall of 1979 before the Labour government would be in a position to issue an order to move. The election of a Conservative government would cause delay. A new minister would want to review the whole question. I should have thought the British government would attach greater importance to British Airways' potential loss because of the transfer . . . twice as great as would be Air Canada's. I am not so sure that the Conservatives would be less sympathetic than the present government to Canada's claim for special consideration.

I advised Ottawa today that Owen's speech of January 23rd does not represent a change in policy on apartheid. . . . I think Britain will avoid a choice between its major commercial economic interests and the application of sanctions. . . . Britain's domestic and international interests demand something of a balancing act. On the night of January 23rd, Owen's remarks may have moved to one side [because] he was speaking along with the Zambian High Commissioner and the Commonwealth Secretary General. Foreign ministers regard double talk on occasion as a convenient weapon. The Labour party requires this traditional stance. Whenever sanctions are spoken of by the United Kingdom government, in reference to Southern Africa particularly, they are generally dealt with in the abstract or heavily hedged in by conditions. Owen made it clear that he was referring to the theoretical usefulness of sanctions. . . .

The protection of the United Kingdom's enormous economic interests in South Africa is understandably a major element in its policy towards Southern Africa. United Kingdom exports to Southern Africa are around £580 million per annum; its imports are £880 million per annum. The total British investment in Southern Africa is valued at over £5,000 million United Kingdom earnings, including invisibles of around

£2,000 million annually. The estimate of the initial effect of the imposition of full economic sanctions on Southern Africa would result in the loss of 70,000 jobs in the United Kingdom with subsequent loss of a further 180,000 jobs. . . .

United Kingdom moves are directed to reduce the causes for criticism of British companies in Southern Africa rather than encouraging disinvestment. The government, I believe, has rejected any idea of publicly discouraging investment or trade with Southern Africa. The farthest the government has gone is Owen's encouragement to trade unionists and students to have their institutions as shareholders demand accountability on [the] use of investments along lines of recent developments in the United States. . . . Major United Kingdom companies do not need to be told which way the wind is blowing . . . [and] are running down their investments in Southern Africa. United Kingdom policy is directed to protecting investment already there by reducing the most objectionable features. . . . In the speech Owen made on January 23rd, he pointed out how investment in Southern Africa should be seen and used as a positive instrument of change and as a method to exert pressure inside Southern Africa. . . .

Thursday, February 15, 1979

I called on Tony Benn, the Minister of Energy, this afternoon at Alastair Gillespie's request. Ottawa wanted to acquaint Benn with subjects which he felt should be discussed at the next OPEC/non-OPEC oil producers meeting, scheduled for March 3-4. . . . Gillespie's wishes could well have been placed [by] his officials. When Benn heard that someone would be coming to his department, he asked that I come. I suspected one of his reasons for his doing so was his desire to have a general chat. We had not seen one another for some time. My suspicion was correct. We rapidly despatched the official business and proceeded to a forty-minute discussion on the general political and world situation. He is a good conversationalist. In spite of the fact that so many have reservations about him, I find Tony an extremely interesting and able person; not because I am in full agreement, but because I think he has an active mind, is courageous, if not always discreet. . . .

Benn took issue with me when I said that Harold Laski had written in his book, *Faith, Reason and Civilization*, that, once the socialist state had been established, it would not be open for a parliamentary effort to change the basis of the state. I am sure that I am right in attributing this to Laski. I must look up the reference and send it to Benn. . . .

Friday, February 16, 1979

The big news this morning were Britain's blizzards. Off and on all week it has been snowing. As I dictate, I look out into Grosvenor Square . . . covered with snow. . . .

My second diplomatic exchange this morning was with the Polish Ambassador.[15] It is definite that John Paul II will go to Poland in May. He will fly to the shrine of the Virgin Mary, call on the head of state in Warsaw, say mass in his cathedral in Cracow, and spend a few days in his home village. My Polish and communist fellow diplomat seemed happy with the formula agreed [to]. . . . The relations between Cardinal Wyszyński[16] and the Polish government have not always been easy. . . . The Ambassador wanted me in on a "secret." A long corridor separates the office of the Foreign Minister and the Prime Minister. He had been in to see the former. On his way out, two figures emerged from the office of the latter. They were arm-in-arm, amicably engaged in conversation as they walked along. Who were these two persons? — Cardinal Wyszynski and the Prime Minister. The Ambassador seemed to imply that, if this particular intimacy (even occasional) were widely known, it might come as a shock, to one's comrades and to one's flock. An amusing story; the Ambassador delighted in what he might think was a thaw in relations of church and state. . . .

Monday, February 19, 1979

Allan Gotlieb spoke in Toronto the other day. He said that External Affairs had been reorganized so that it could play an effective, influential, and dominant role as a central agency in government . . . like the Treasury Board, P.C.O., and the Finance Department. . . . This was done at the Prime Minis-

15. Jan Bisztyga
16. Primate of the Catholic Church in Poland.

ter's request. These matters Gotlieb discussed with me when he assumed the Under-Secretaryship. . . . I agree with Gotlieb's stance. Matters of foreign policy must be channelled through External Affairs. I insisted on this arrangement when I was minister. At first, there were problems. Some departments, notably Trade and Commerce, would carry on negotiations with Washington, oftentimes on economic questions, without the Department of External Affairs being informed or often sometimes aware. I soon learned that it was essential to strengthen the economic division of External Affairs. When this was done, the problem of inter-departmental consultation and the primacy of External Affairs in foreign policy matters was restored. . . .

For the last week in February, I went to St Lucia to attend the Independence ceremonies on this Caribbean island. Despite protests against the government of Premier John Compton, the ceremonies went ahead. Nell and I arrived back in London on February 27.

XXV

March – April 1979

*A*T THE BEGINNING *of the month, the long-awaited referenda on devolution took place in Scotland and Wales. But far from clearing the air, their indecisive results posed problems for Jim Callaghan who faced a divided party. Some Labour MPs called for devolution or defeat while others could vote against him if he moved to establish the regional assemblies. At the same time, I was expecting Trudeau to call a general election at any moment.*

The suspense in both countries ended. Trudeau asked for a dissolution of Parliament on March 26 and the following day, Callaghan lost a vote in the House of Commons. For the next few weeks, I was absorbed by comparing the two election campaigns and prognosticating about the possible results. Although the Canadian campaign appeared to be a cliff-hanger from the start, I treated Margaret Thatcher's victory in Britain as almost a foregone conclusion.

Thursday, March 1, 1979

Trudeau will see Carter this weekend in New York. They will go to the theatre. I understand that a visit by Carter to Canada has been postponed until after the [Canadian] elections. This looks more promising for Trudeau according to a CTV poll, which gives him the lead. At this stage and from this point, the election date looks uncertain. Is it to be April or June? Mark MacGuigan has written to say it is certainly imminent. He has been assured by Trudeau of the first [available] cabinet appointment. . . . I cannot conceive that Trudeau would keep Eugene Whelan and bring in Herb [Gray] and Mark.[1] Leaders

1. They were all MPs from Essex County.

have to think ahead. Trudeau might well say to himself, if I have a minority situation, I could have all three Essex County members in at the same time. After all, that is the situation which prevailed for almost six years when Gray, Whelan and I, all three from the same county, were in government. . . .[2]

I sent a message to Ottawa on the referendum on devolution. The voting takes place today. There are two devolution referenda to take place — in Scotland and Wales. The referendum [in Scotland] is of far greater importance because of the extent of powers being proposed for the Scottish Assembly and because of virtual certainty now that the Welsh electorate will reject devolution. Polls in Scotland this past week show a high level of uncertainty. The vote is bound to be close. The basic issue being presented to the Scottish electorate is whether they want a directly elected Assembly with no taxing powers, limited powers to legislate, and to oversee public administration in certain areas. A clause in the Scotland Act requires that forty per cent of the electorate must vote in favour of devolution, failing which Parliament may withdraw the bill. . . .

It is the government's hope on the one hand that, if the referendum succeeds, the bulk of the Scottish electorate will continue to support Labour and that S.N.P.[3] strength will continue to wither. Alternatively, if the referendum fails, the hope is that the government's show of good faith will bear electoral reward. The Labour party is divided on measures proposed. The main objection seems to come from the machine which controls existing levels of local government in Scotland, i.e., local and regional councils. . . . The Tories rally behind the banner of devolution but not in its present form. They oppose the assembly on the grounds that it is too complicated, too bureaucratic, too expensive, and that lack of definition of its powers will inevitably lead to conflicts with the central government and to demands for further independence for Scotland. . . .

Before going to bed tonight, I had a call from Ray Perrault, Leader of the Government in the Senate in Ottawa. I

2. Herb Gray became minister without portfolio in October 1969 and served in cabinet posts to August 1974. Throughout this time, Eugene Whelan was minister of agriculture and I was leader of the government in the Senate.
3. The Scottish National Party.

gathered that the announcement of an election is imminent. Jacques Flynn, [the Conservative] Leader of the Opposition in the Senate, would not agree to the early discharge of certain House of Commons measures. Had he done so, an election announcement could well have been made yesterday. Now, one is expected for next week, with elections to take place about May 11th. This is not the first time I have prognosticated about the elections. Whenever I have done so, it has been on the basis of information given me by a minister. . . .

[Perrault] is happier now with proposals for Senate reform. He says the provinces do not want to disturb the Senate as it is. They would leave the main structure unchanged. There would, of course, have to be provision for a suspensory veto.[4] It looks very much like a move to patriate the constitution, with or without the consent of the provinces. In spite of indications of an early election, I still would not be surprised if Trudeau made an effort before calling an election to get provincial consent, proceed with a petition to patriate, and use this as a colourful argument for endorsing the government at the polls.

Saturday, March 3, 1979

Unquestionably, today's important news involves the vote yesterday in the devolution referenda in Scotland and Wales. The vote for a Scottish Assembly was 32.87 per cent "yes" and "no," 30.78 per cent. . . . The government will have to decide what it should ask Parliament to do. . . . The results are bad for Jim Callaghan, who urged a "yes" vote in Scotland and Wales. Callaghan all along has insisted that the referenda were advisory. I agree. His political problems are compounded by the stunning Conservative victories in yesterday's two by-elections. I believe it will be difficult for the Prime Minister to avoid an early election. . . .

4. As an appointed body, the Senate had not used its powers to kill legislation but by instituting a delaying mechanism such as a suspensory veto like that of the House of Lords, the Senate might become a more effective legislative body.

Sunday, March 4, 1979

One branch of the Labour party calls for devolution or defeat. Another 40 Labour party rebels could vote against Jim Callaghan if he seeks to get accepted an order to establish the Scottish Assembly. The government will not act quickly . . . but the fat is in the fire. . . .

Monday, March 5, 1979

Alarm systems likely vary in their effectiveness. Latterly, I have been swimming . . . one door down on Upper Brook Street. All I have to do is go out of my back door into my neighbour's garage, down a few steps of stairs and I am in a magnificent indoor pool, which has helped to keep me fit. . . . A new alarm system, however, has been put in. . . . Nothing is more annoying than to hear these alarm bells ring. We hear a number of them around 12 Upper Brook. Yesterday, I was about to open the door leading to the lower hallway near the pool when the bell started, through no fault of mine. I had the butler call the police to explain that the place was not being raided. . . . My morning beef. . . .

Wednesday, March 7, 1979

When I saw him at tea at his country estate near Chester yesterday afternoon and at dinner last night, the . . . popular Duke of Westminster did not reveal his concern over press comment about his wealth, following the [recent] death of his father. Gerald had received 8,500 letters of sympathy from "ordinary people who had written to express their sorrow." The media, he said, had an "hysterical preoccupation" with his family's fortune. . . . [5] He complained that no one had commented on his father's parliamentary and other achievements. I did not know that Gerald's father had been Selwyn Lloyd's minister of state at the time of Suez.[6] The duke told me that he paid 98p. on the pound income tax [but] he did not propose to become a tax exile. . . .

5. It was estimated to be the largest in Britain.
6. Actually, he had been the parliamentary private secretary to the foreign secretary (Selwyn Lloyd) from 1957 to 1959.

I went to the residence, once again to be inundated with paper and messages, one from the CBC who wondered how long I would stay on as High Commissioner. When I decided to return to Canada was not even on my mind. When I knew, I would let everyone know. . . .

Thursday, March 8, 1979

I was interested in learning from a correspondent in Ottawa that, when Jamieson was asked questions [in the House of Commons] the other day on the Heathrow-Gatwick matter, the members laughed when he said my advice was that the House of Commons should not pass a resolution at this stage in condemnation of the proposal. My correspondent said:

> I found their laughter extremely revealing, for it was the laughter of men suddenly recalling your making a statement, qualifying that statement, and somehow coming up with a final statement that seemed to meet the requirements of the moment; it was a laugh full of respect and affection and possibly for a man a great deal more cognizant of any issue abroad today than any Minister. . . .

Saturday, March 10, 1979

When Norman Robertson, then High Commissioner for Canada in London, opened the new radiotherapy centre at Mount Vernon Hospital, in Northwood, London, which houses Europe's first cobalt unit,[7] he could not know . . . that twenty-five years later, I would participate in a ceremony to turn the unit over to the British Museum after valiant years of service. This, I did at noon, at a luncheon and reception where the unit has been in operation. The guest of honour was Professor Sir Brian Windeyer.[8] He and Stanford Cade, an eminent cancer surgeon, came to see me when I was Minister of National Health and Welfare. They wanted to know if we

7. In 1954.
8. Sir Brian Windeyer, a professor of radiology of the Radiotherapy Department at Mount Vernon Hospital, had later become the vice-chancellor of the University of London.

could make it possible for a cobalt 60 beam therapy bomb to be given Britain. This, I was able to get for them. . . .

Sunday, March 11, 1979

On again, off again—it looks like an election before June 18th. Why did Don tell me the announcement would come in February? . . .

Monday, March 12, 1979

Hundreds of calls [concerning the Newfoundland seal hunt which began today] came in to Macdonald and Canada House over the weekend, I was told by the security officer on duty at Macdonald House this morning. One of the callers said he would "skin the High Commissioner alive. . . ." The British do not like the way we dispose of the seals. They *shoot* their own. . . .

Later, talking to the Chancellor of the Exchequer, I was told that there could be an election in June. The situation in the House was difficult. A vote of confidence could develop at any time and could result in a government defeat. This is the first strong note of concern I have heard in recent weeks from a member of the government. . . . Chips[9] and Elizabeth Maclean mentioned how amused they were in Westminster Abbey [for the Commonwealth Day service] this afternoon when, on her way out passing by them, Nell tipped her hat in a manner that I know so well. . . .

On January 29th, I received a communication from one Prince Adetokunboh Odufunade . . . "on an issue of grave universal significance." This is related to unidentified flying objects in the atmosphere of the earth. Because of the friendship which he has with Canada, he selected our country to handle this delicate and vital issue of our time. . . .

Tuesday, March 13, 1979

Ralph Stewart, whom I have known for many years, as a Liberal and latterly as an MP,[10] has left the Liberal party, crossing the floor to join Joe Clark. . . . Looking back, there

9. He was lord chamberlain.
10. He was the MP for Cochrane.

have not been in my thirty-nine years in Parliament many members who have crossed the floor on either side. The only one who did so and who achieved ministerial rank was Jack Horner. Immortality will hardly be Jack's claim to fame. . . .

Thursday, March 15, 1979

In a press conference yesterday, the Air Canada president[11] is reported as saying that, if Air Canada was forced to transfer to Gatwick, action would be taken to deny British Airways the right to use the Toronto airport. . . . This is the first time in print the suggestion has been made that, if forced to move to Gatwick, we would retaliate by denying the British access to Toronto. It will be interesting to see the reaction to the use of this option by Air Canada. . . . Would it have been better to have used this weapon in the bilateral discussions and by the government of Canada itself and not Air Canada? . . .

[Tonight's affair at the residence] was—apart from the functions attended by the Queen—perhaps our most memorable dinner. . . . Lord Denning, perhaps Britain's greatest judge since Lord Mansfield, was guest of honour. He kindly autographed his most recent book for me in generous terms. The occasion was strengthened by the presence of two ministers, the Home Secretary Merlyn Rees and Sam Silkin, both of whom think Jim will weather the storm. Sam, as Attorney-General, has had some victories in the courts at the expense of the Master of the Rolls, who does not, I am sure, suffer victors enthusiastically. . . .

Friday, March 16, 1979

The anti-sealers are going too far, [and] . . . have called to threaten bomb attacks on our mission. Late this afternoon, Lorne Green reports that I am threatened with being kidnapped. . . . A special police guard will watch the residence and me over the weekend. It is difficult to credit that an event of this kind could take place. There are cranks in many situations. It only takes one to do the job. The anti-sealers are surprisingly aggressive. . . .

11. Claude Taylor

Monday, March 19, 1979

When I came out of the residence this morning, two motorcycle policemen on their machines were waiting, part of the security arrangements over the threats of the anti-sealers in Britain against the Canadian High Commissioner. It seems to me unnecessary, but John thought it would not be advisable to ignore the arrangement in view of police instructions. Accordingly, I drove in CAN-1 with a motorcycle officer on his machine in front and one at the rear. The police know their business and who am I to question it, but it is absurd all the same, that in this free country arrangements of this kind are considered necessary. . . .

Tonight was starless and a misty time to drive to Aylesbury for the exhibition "Canada at Aylesbury" . . . at the Civic Centre of this fine town, not far away from Oxford. . . . [On] arrival, a motorcycle escort directed us on the way and particularly to look on with other policemen as thirty anti-seal picketers greeted me at the entrance to the centre. It had been suggested that perhaps I should enter by the back door. This I refused to do and met the anti-sealers head on. I found them restrained and polite. They presented me with a thousand signatures, which I will pass on to Ottawa forthwith as I said I would. I talked to most of the pickets, avoiding argument which I think, in the circumstances, gets one nowhere. . . .

Tuesday, March 20, 1979

Today a message came in from New York, where Don Jamieson . . . and Owen discussed the Heathrow-Gatwick matter. Owen proposed a joint communiqué saying that Edmund Dell had announced a year ago the United Kingdom government's decision that Air Canada should move to Gatwick. The two governments were now engaged in considering financial aspects of the move. . . . It has upset me. I sent back a message at once to the Secretary of State for External Affairs advising he should regard the proposed communiqué as completely unacceptable. To suggest that all that remained was a financial assessment of the move, as far as Canada was concerned, was contrary to Owen's reply to me of some weeks ago, a denial of Callaghan's statement to Smith[12] that "Canada should not be discriminated against," and inconsistent with Smith's statement in the House of Commons that the matter was still under negotiation. . . . We must stand up to the British on this question. . . .

Thursday, March 22, 1979

After the receipt of my telex in answer to Don Jamieson's on the day before yesterday, the Secretary of State for External Affairs told David Owen the communiqué was unacceptable. . . . When it was first offered by David, I understand he mentioned that the United Kingdom might have to protest the seal hunt. A weak argument. . . . With an election in the offing, the government may not feel able to withstand the pressure as easily as in other years. . . .

Friday, March 23, 1979

The murder of Richard Sykes, the British Ambassador in Holland, and his Dutch footman made the headlines today. Although no real evidence exists, the I.R.A. are natural suspects as well as the Baader-Meinhof gang,[13] the Palestinians, and the Iraqis. The police called early this morning wanting to know if I was going to the office and suggested I should leave about a quarter after eight. The uncertainty in situations like this is a little difficult to understand, certainly for a Canadian. Some people feel so strongly about the seals that the police don't want any chances taken. . . .

Monday, March 26, 1979

At lunch today, I had a good chat with Kurt Waldheim and his wife at Chatham House, 10 St. James's Square, preceding his talk to the Royal Institute. He spoke of the United Nations; aspirations and realities. . . . It interested me to have him note that the more members in the United Nations, the more were the problems. In 1955, when I pushed the new members

12. The secretary of state for trade.
13. A German terrorist group.

package deal, Waldheim was the Austrian Observer at the United Nations, pushing for membership of that country in the organization.[14] The Secretary General gave a gloomy picture of the world. The great powers are fearful of each other. The middle powers are so divided as to be unable to provide an effective middle force in world affairs. He did not think there would be a world war, because of nuclear danger. The fact was, however, that since the end of the Second World War, not one regional conflict had been solved. The United Nations is not used by governments. . . . The Secretary General prefers quiet and private diplomacy. . . .

Tuesday, March 27, 1979

Not much news from Canada on elections. Could it be because of the still poor showing revealed in the polls in the Toronto area? It is interesting to note that Trudeau has gone further into the fifth year of office than any other Prime Minister in peace-time since R. B. Bennett in 1935. The withdrawal of [Maurice] Strong and John Evans as Liberal candidates in Toronto has been unsettling. In Quebec, some are concerned about the impact of Fabien Roy, the Social Credit leader. I believe the swing is Trudeau's way. He cannot wait much longer. . . .

When I read my morning telegrams, I was not aware from anything contained therein that the Prime Minister had indicated a dissolution of the 30th Parliament. This I realized only about 10:00 o'clock this morning. Parliament was dissolved with an announcement by Allan MacEachen last night. The Commons had just finished discussing the government's spending plans and had received parliamentary approval of two pieces of legislation. The election will take place . . . on May 22nd. . . .

Wednesday, March 28, 1979

Trudeau said yesterday the campaign would be about ensuring our unity, creating a decade of economic development, improving the quantity and quality of Canadian life on the

14. See my book, *A Very Public Life*, vol. II: *So Many Worlds* (Toronto 1986), pp. 178-218.

job and in retirement, reducing deficits to fight inflation, and guaranteeing an energy supply. The election was announced on Monday night. *The Telegraph* today (two days later) has a story on the dissolution of Parliament. *The Financial Times* thinks the elections in Canada could go either way, with Clark or Trudeau forming a minority government as Trudeau did in 1972. . . .

The prognostications this morning suggest Callaghan will be defeated in today's vote. Mrs. Thatcher may have a majority of two. The papers protect their prophetic powers by adding that the vote will be close and it might go either way. . . .

A little tired and not altogether free from my cold, I decided, instead of going directly to the House of Commons Chamber, that I would listen to the debate via radio. Mrs. Thatcher's motion of confidence speech was not the most effective she has delivered. She said the government had failed the nation, that it had lost credibility, and that "it is time for it to go." The Prime Minister was in great form — a real fighting speech — during which he outlined a programme of social security improvements which would be in a budget, if it was not denied by tonight's vote.

During dinner, we received word of the vote in the Commons. Jim lost by one vote, marking the downfall of his government. . . .

This was the first time, since Ramsay MacDonald lost a vote in 1924, that a vote in the Commons forced an election. Such defeats are more common in Canada which has had several minority governments. The last election called after a defeat in the House was in 1974.

Robert Fellowes, the Queen's assistant secretary, was seated near me at dinner and acknowledged that Buckingham Palace would be a busy place tomorrow. . . . Personally, I have a great deal of affection and admiration for the Prime Minister who, I think, has handled himself well, but the result was as I had anticipated. . . . I maintained a conscious imperturbability, when the results were announced and received so jubilantly by all present, except Fellowes and me.

Thursday, March 29, 1979

The first thought that occurred to me this morning was the announcement that a Conservative victory in Britain might have a psychological effect in Canada, not necessarily unhelpful to Joe Clark.[15] Nevertheless, I think Trudeau should win and, I think, will. . . .

Peter Carrington, Leader of the Opposition in the House of Lords, had me there to lunch today. . . . As we were lunching after Callaghan's defeat in the House of Commons, I said to Peter, "Who knows, I might now be speaking to the man who will be Secretary of State for Foreign Affairs in a few weeks." I suspect Francis Pym, a member of the House of Commons, is a more likely choice. . . .

I told Peter about our problem over Heathrow and Gatwick. I thought I had better get in a plug early. I had a suspicion that, while he sympathized with our case, he was not going to be fully responsive for fear that he might have something to do with the problem later. He did say there was great congestion at Heathrow, "But why pick on Canada? Why not pick on some of the smaller airlines operating at Heathrow?" which, of course, is one of our main contentions.

I asked Carrington what he thought of the Canadian political situation. He repeated what one hears continually: how unpopular the Prime Minister is and how incompetent and inexperienced is the Leader of the Opposition. He was inclined to think, however, that on the whole, from what he heard, Trudeau would be returned on the 22nd. . . .

Friday, March 30, 1979

The political parties in the May 3rd election will press for a better deal in the E.E.C. I have advised Ottawa that certain powerful ministers are ideologically opposed to the E.E.C. The Tories, with wide disparities of enthusiasm, have embraced Europe and cannot back away from identification with it. Nevertheless, irrespective of which party wins, Britain will continue to press for a sharp cut [in her share of the budget of the Community]. . . .

The Telegraph this morning speaks of Joe Clark as the underdog and Trudeau as a man of charm. Clark is charged with a vagueness of speech and a disposition to talk in generalities. Trudeau affirmed that, if Canadian voters do not see national unity as an important issue, "then I can only

15. The British election would occur on May 3 before the Canadian one.

wring my hands." Walter Gordon told me yesterday on the phone he thought Trudeau would squeak through, but with a minority government. He also stated, if he were in the United Kingdom, he would be behind Jim Callaghan and Labour. . . .

On the way to 12 Upper Brook, I realized the delight of not having to depend on my motorcycle police escort in the immediate future. I thought too of my friend, Richard Sykes, who was assassinated in The Hague last week. I had no sooner opened the front door, when John Rowan hurried to tell me that Airey Neave, the Ulster MP, had been killed by a bomb placed under the floor of his Vauxhall in the Palace Yard at Westminster. Neave was certainly a potential Thatcher minister. His regrettable assassination could carry major implications for Ireland and British-Ulster relations. . . .

Monday, April 2, 1979

This morning, I was confronted with one of those journals, a strict observer of ethical practice, *The Daily Express*, picturing Margaret Trudeau on the front page, with the first episode in her serialized biography[16] strewn throughout the magazine. As I read about Morocco, her father (Jimmy Sinclair, a former cabinet colleague),[17] how she met Trudeau and her innocence (perhaps it *is* innocence rather than guile), I felt sad for her husband, our Prime Minister. I recalled when Nell and I, Pierre and Margaret walked within the walls of Dubrovnik after dinner on the deck of Pierre's chartered boat with Michael Pitfield and his charming wife. Alas, all has come loose. Margaret is going to tell her story as the Prime Minister begins his national election campaign. She will make a lot of money but what will all this do to her husband? Most people think he has reacted with such dignity in the matter and, as the custodian of his three boys, so well, that sympathy is all on his side. I hope this is so. The book should not be serialized simultaneously with the election, if the young lady had respect and admiration for her husband. . . . What would have hap-

16. Margaret Trudeau, *Beyond Reason* (Toronto 1979).
17. James Sinclair had served as minister of fisheries, 1952 to 1957, in Louis St Laurent's government.

pened twenty years ago to a politician in these circumstances is self-evident. I wonder what its effect will be now. . . .

An hour after I had been asleep, the Prime Minister's secretary, Jim Coutts, called from Montreal. . . . In a Toronto speech over the weekend, Trudeau had declared he was not going to dismantle "the work that Paul Martin had achieved in the provision of health care. . . ."[18] He says the election will be tight. Everyone else says the same. I still have trouble in believing that Trudeau's troubles are so formidable.

Saturday, April 7, 1979

Jim Callaghan seems to have had his way in the election platform issued by the Labour party. Tony Benn and Eric Heffer[19] came out second-best. In the section "Democracy at Westminster," it is maintained that "no one can defend on any democratic grounds the House of Lords and the power and influence it exercises in our constitution." The Labour party proposes to abolish the delaying power and veto [in the Lords]. In Canada, we cannot long delay imposing on the Senate a suspensory veto. Certainly, when the constitution is patriated, this will have to be undertaken. The Senate will be strengthened as a result.

Paul telephoned to say he had gone to Trudeau's nomination meeting in Montreal. Not as well attended as before. Trudeau did not speak well, said my son, who was with Coutts at the time. I have the impression that the start of the campaign has not been brilliant. The blunder by the Prime Minister about the shortcomings of the farmers, and Royce Frith's[20] prognostication of the defeat of three cabinet ministers in the Toronto area were clumsy declarations. Hopefully, from now on, such ineptness will not reappear. . . .

Monday, April 9, 1979

I am in receipt of a letter from the Lord Great Chamberlain . . . inviting Nell and me to attend the ceremony of the State Opening of Parliament. My guess is that there will be a woman Prime Minister. . . .

18. During my time as minister of national health and welfare, the government approved a national hospital insurance plan.
19. A left-wing Labour MP.
20. A Liberal senator and campaign strategist.

Thursday, April 12, 1979

Some are criticizing Clark for saying little in the election. From the point of view of democratic practice, the criticism may be valid. From the point of view of electoral success, there is another consideration. Mackenzie King won a good many elections without over-committing himself. Trudeau is accused of crossing the country insulting one group of Canadians after another—the farmers in Quebec, the unemployed in New Brunswick, and the postal workers in British Columbia. It could be that there is method in his madness. The farmers in Western Canada are not going to support Trudeau in any event, the postal workers are not popular in Canada, and . . . he may have touched a point of strong agreement with the Canadian people as a whole. More difficult to understand is taking issue with the unemployed in New Brunswick. My general impression is that Trudeau's campaign thus far has not gone as well as many would like to see it develop. . . .

My attention is directed to positions taken by the Commonwealth Secretary General in matters clearly within the jurisdiction of governments in the Commonwealth and not of the Secretary General. The problem, of course, is not easy for him and it is not new. Some Commonwealth governments seem to need directions; others are capable of making their own decisions and resent being dragooned. The tenure of Sonny Ramphal expires in 1980. I should think that if he wishes a second term it ought to be accorded him, as it was Arnold Smith. . . . The government of India has let it be known that, when the present tenure of the Secretary General expires and if a consensus emerges, a nominee from India might be considered. This does not mean that Ramphal's leadership is unacceptable. India is simply putting in a caveat. The rotational principle should be kept in mind, if there is to be a fair opportunity for key posts to be distributed equitably. . . . When Sonny hears of this, it may put him on guard as stories of this kind often do. . . .

I called on Premier Compton at the Eastern Caribbean Mission at 10 Kensington Court this morning. John is in London primarily and ostensibly to participate in the official opening of a St. Lucia film on Independence Day celebrations.

More particularly, he was here for important discussions related to Bishop's coup d'état in Grenada.[21] It was regrettable that the constitutionality of the take-over had not been observed in Grenada, followed by elections. To have proceeded constitutionally would have prevented other attempts to take over government by force and unconstitutional means. Bishop's action in Grenada could be followed in other Caribbean countries. It takes little to bring about a coup. Preventative measures are necessary. [Compton said that] a regional force, with adequate training and conforming to a particular plan outlined for me, was essential [as was] . . . Canadian, British, and United States assistance. . . . The United States is undoubtedly aware of the implications in the Grenada situation. John is certain of Marxist influence in the Grenada government, Bishop himself and others even more dedicated. . . . A meeting of the United States, Britain and Canada will take place shortly. . . .

Tonight at the Foreign Affairs Club, Lord Denis Greenhill, a former Permanent Under-Secretary at the Foreign Office, reminded me that, over ten years ago, the United Kingdom anticipated the Cuban-West Indies situation. The British had to relinquish their custodial hold in the Carribbean. For financial reasons, they could no longer bear fully the defence responsibility. The United States and Canada were invited to participate. We did not respond for financial reasons. We were asked to provide a naval presence on a continuing basis. At any rate, Denis agreed that the present situation required the interest of the three countries to avoid Cuban involvement in the Caribbean. . . .

Saturday, April 14, 1979

Today is not only another day; it is one with which, for many months, this country has had no experience. It is a lovely sunny day. London is a new city. The trees have come to life. The daffodils are thick and yellow. The birds chirp lustily. People smile and are happy—all because of the sun. . . . Thank goodness for this beautiful day. My spirits were low. They have now revived and I must return to the full life. . . .

21. Maurice Bishop had led a coup d'état which took over the government of Grenada on March 13.

Tuesday, April 17, 1979

An officer has passed on to me the irritating designation which reads "Ambassade du Québec (Délégation Générale du Gouvernement)" in Paris. There is no such thing as a Quebec Embassy in Paris. We complained about this to the French government — such pretensions! . . .

Thursday, April 19, 1979

I am anxious that the repairs to Canada House . . . will provide justification for more extensive renovation to provide adequate facilities for our cultural and information programmes. . . . Security in Canada House should be minimal [because] the need for ready access . . . by the public is important. . . . We are now having large audiences at the musical, academic and literary functions. I am disturbed by a report that a bullet-proof enclosure is being designed for Canada House and this will require visitors to pass through one by one. I object to this strongly. . . .

The second day of the Rhodesian majority-rule elections[22] has gone off better than anticipated. I hear rumblings that the Commonwealth Secretariat and Sonny Ramphal are concerned over Tory policy on Rhodesia. Ramphal has been opposed to sending observers to monitor [the elections]. If Mrs. Thatcher wins, her attitude will present a problem to the Commonwealth Organization. It had condemned the new situation as racist and its position supports Nkomo and Mugabe. As I previously noted, however, if the elections are successful, the election results cannot be ignored. . . .

Saturday, April 21, 1979

No reference to John Compton appears in today's intimation of United States concern over Cuban communist ties with Grenada. The United States told Bishop, an L.S.E. graduate, of its apprehension over Grenada's ties with Cuba. Bishop insists that Grenada was in "nobody's back yard." Moreover, he resents United States' meddling in Grenada's affairs. What

22. These were organized by Ian Smith, Abel Muzorewa, Joseph Chirau, and Ndabaningi Sithole.

will he say when he learns that the United States, Britain and Canada have been exchanging views? . . .

Maurice Strong, here for two or three days, had lunch with me today. He reports that Trudeau's stock, based on private polls, has improved in the Toronto region. He believes Trudeau will be re-elected. If a minority situation arises, the N.D.P. have not stopped themselves from supporting the Liberals. . . . Maurice does not preclude a majority for Trudeau, but he acknowledges the general view that the result will be close. . . . He has seen Michael Pitfield recently. The Clerk of the Privy Council is not concerned about his personal position over the elections. Clark or Trudeau would find it difficult to dispense with the services of a public servant, on whom so much depends for the conduct of government at the top. . . .

Monday, April 23, 1979

The heavy turn-out in the Rhodesian elections will not bring about an immediate reaction by the British and the United States governments. Indications are that Bishop Muzorewa will become the first black Prime Minister of Rhodesia. He said yesterday the lifting of sanctions and international recognition could no longer be denied. I am inclined to this view. . . .

Barbara Ward and Maurice Strong had dinner with Nell and me tonight. . . .[23] In my present pessimistic mood, which has persisted now for some months, I talked of this gloomy period in history, with its disregard for human life. Barbara was inclined to think, and in this she had the support of Nell and Maurice, that there were pluses as well as minuses now, as in other periods of history. . . .

Tuesday, April 24, 1979

It is interesting to compare the style of elections in Britain and Canada. Basically there is no difference, but sometimes I have the impression that they hit harder here. Yesterday,

23. Barbara Ward was an eminent writer on the problems of development in underdeveloped countries. Maurice Strong, the former director of the United Nations Environment Program, was the chairman of Petro-Canada.

Denis Healey tried to stir up uneasiness among Conservatives by suggesting the rivalries in the Conservative party were great. Are they not equally competitive in the Labour party? One Conservative member said that Denis was at his worst "mud-slinging, smearing, dirt-throwing style. . . ." Denis says he finds great scepticism about Conservative leadership. Nothing under-handed in that. Denis prefers to leave the Conservatives with their private grief and, therefore, will not discuss Mrs. Thatcher's personality any further. This is mild stuff really.

Howard Johnson, a former Conservative MP from British Columbia, was in this morning on his way home from an Inter-Parliamentary Union meeting in Prague. He is confident of a Conservative victory, although he acknowledges Clark would likely form a minority government. Each party holds on to the hope that it will come out on top. . . .

Wednesday, April 25, 1979

A letter awaited me from Jules Léger, written from his new office in the Pearson Building.[24] He thanks Nell and me for hospitality when he and Gaby were in London recently. The highlight of that visit was their lunch with the Queen on February 7th. The experience parallels one which he had at Buckingham Palace in 1948, when he had gone to deliver flowers to the Queen Mother for Mr. King. King wanted to thank the Queen for the visit the royal couple had made to the Dorchester Hotel to see him when he was ill. Jules said, "that visit taught me something." Five minutes before the royal couple arrived, Mr. King had an empty bed removed from the bedroom — in that way an embarrassment would be avoided of having an empty bed in his room next to his own when the Queen Mother arrived. . . .

Thursday, April 26, 1979

The campaigns in Canada and the United Kingdom are getting hot. A poll in Canada will give encouragement to many. Gallup says that the Liberals stand at 43 per cent, giving them a five-point margin over Joe Clark at 38 per cent.

24. After his retirement as governor general, Léger had an office in the Department of External Affairs (the Pearson Building), where he planned to write about his experience.

In Britain, the Liberals seem to making some headway. Their 1974 vote may hold up better than expected. A Tory revival north of the border [with Scotland] is a subdued one. At last night's dinner at the Mansion House, there was not much evidence of Labour support, except perhaps among the diplomats. . . .

I sent a telex to Ottawa on the elections in Britain so far. I pointed out there has been little discussion on foreign policy, mostly indicating a difference in emphasis and tone between the parties. On two questions, differences which could have implications for Britain in the future were Europe and the nature of East-West relations, with little attention paid to them by Labour. Labour has tended to adhere to a somewhat ambiguous policy of defence, East-West relations, and Europe because of opposing factions within the party. Its manifesto puts great weight on disarmament, including SALT,[25] and makes a commitment to further defence cuts. There is no significant discussion of East-West relations.

On Europe, the Labour manifesto reflects some of the negativism of the left wing. It does not question the E.C. nor has Labour proposed new directions for it. Europe is treated largely in domestic dimensions rather than as an opportunity to project Britain's presence in the world. There isn't much evidence of an attempt by Labour to define a coherent overall approach to Britain's role. . . .

Friday, April 27, 1979

I note that our embassy in Paris has had many complaints against the disenfranchisement of Canadians living abroad. When I was at Cambridge the other day, the students expressed regrets that the Elections Act did not give them the right to vote. This should be corrected, just as the extension of the franchise to public servants abroad was found possible to achieve. . . .

25. The Strategic Arms Limitations Talks. Beginning in November 1969, Soviet and U.S. representatives held talks aimed at restraining the arms race and signed a treaty (SALT I) in May 1972. A second agreement (SALT II) would later be concluded by presidents Carter and Brezhnev in June 1979.

I called on the Irish Ambassador this morning at 17 Grosvenor Place. . . . We discussed the general problem confronting Ulster and the remoteness of unity in Ireland. . . . The Ambassador believes the trouble in the North today, resulting in murder and terrorism, is the work of a limited number of people, perhaps four hundred in number, motivated less by political objective than by rowdyism, thievery, and murder. . . .

I am amused by a message from Ottawa on the status of wives of polygamous diplomats. I have been asked to supply information regarding the policy of the government in Britain on official recognition of the wives of polygamous diplomats. I am asked, "Are all wives provided identity documents to identify them as the wife of a diplomat? Are full privileges and immunities, such as tax exemption cards to complimentary driver's licence, etc. accorded?" . . .

Saturday, April 28, 1979

Harold Wilson told me a month ago that he was going to write a weekly column. In a newspaper report in today's press, he says his wife may vote for Margaret Thatcher, whose talents he eulogizes. His former colleagues are understandably upset. There is a time for everything. An election period is not the time for Harold Wilson, former Prime Minister and Leader of the Labour party, to praise Jim Callaghan's chief rival. Harold has issued an explanation, the kind of device which, often in the past, compunded his indiscretions. Harold's characterization of David Owen as "very pompous" and [statement] that Ennals "should go" will hardly sit well with the Foreign Minister and the Minister of Health. Wedgwood Benn may be surprised to learn that his former Prime Minister found him "so boring." . . . Some people have a compulsion to talk. . . .

Monday, April 30, 1979

The following comments represent my present reaction to the United Kingdom elections and my comments on polls: this election may be much closer than Labour had a right to expect when elections were forced on it last month. What Labour has apparently succeeded in doing (with some help from the Tories, who have failed to exploit its weak record) is to shift the contest, to a considerable degree, onto its own strongest ground, the benevolent face of the welfare state. This is a particularly strong drawing card in key marginal constituencies in [the] Midlands and [the] North, areas of high unemployment, heavily dependent on government intervention to sustain jobs in ailing industries. [The] Conservatives' free-enterprise platform, particularly [the] pledge that they would allow unsuccessful companies to go to [the] wall, has not been well received.

Similarly, Labour has had significant success undermining [the] Tory tax and public expenditure cut proposals that were central to Conservative policies for stimulating incentives and productivity. [The] Tories have been insistently challenged to demonstrate how . . . the lower paid would be aided by income tax cuts which would need to be offset in part through increased VAT.[26] Policy has been portrayed as giving wage earners with one hand and taking from consumers (i.e., women) with the other. On the other side of [the] equation, Labour has managed to throw opprobium on Tory public expenditure proposals by painting them as measures that would radically affect [the] present level of basic social services, e.g., health care and education. For good measure, [the] main result of Tory proposals for devaluation of [the] pound has been depicted as raising food prices . . . [higher than the] Tories claim. Thus, without actually proposing significant new policies of their own, Labour appears to be defusing what were major thrusts of [the] Tory campaign and to be forcing [the] Conservatives to launch in new directions. Doing so, especially when momentum has temporarily been lost to them, appears fraught with considerable risks as [the] only major arrows left in [the] Tory quiver are highly emotive gut issues of law and order and [the] power of unions.

It is precisely on these questions that Mrs. Thatcher, whose abrasive personal style has been kept carefully under control while Tories had a comfortable lead, has now chosen to place new emphasis. Unions, whose support for Labour while very real, was much muted until now, have predictably reacted to

26. The Value Added Tax.

her characterization of union leaders as extremists, and her calls for strict and strictly enforced legislation for their control. Whatever rights and wrongs of argument on her side, or of Callaghan's insistence that consensus and voluntary cooperation is [the] only viable means of ensuring Labour peace, this turn of events has tended to play into the hands of Labour which has all along stressed that the Tories would unleash unprecedented and fruitless conflict in the industrial sector. It has also highlighted [the] "Thatcher factor," her personal lack of appeal with the electorate, which now gives Callaghan a full ten per cent lead in its . . . choice for Prime Minister. . . .

There is at least a possibility, especially if the Liberals managed to do well in marginal seats, where they are concentrating their efforts, of [a] very close race and even perhaps narrow Labour victory, something few here thought even conceivable two weeks ago. . . .

I joined Bryce Mackasey, chairman of the Air Canada board, and Claude Taylor, president . . . and others of the board of directors at dinner at the Inn on the Park. . . . I got a mass survey, as it were, of the Canadian political scene. Most of the directors of Air Canada are men with political experience, and most of whom could be expected to be supporters of the present federal administration. The general report I got from them was anything but good for Trudeau's prospects. Even the chairman of the board, Bryce Mackasey, a former colleague of Trudeau's and mine, thinks the election is going to be very close. Bryce does not think that Jean-Luc Pepin[27] will win in Vanier or that the Liberals will recover the seat where he ran hopelessly last fall in the by-election.[28] "Why did you run," I asked him, "when the prospects were so dim?" The reply was that Trudeau was then on the verge of quitting the leadership. His prospects were bleak. He decided to help him by running in the Ottawa seat. It didn't work out. He knew that he could not win but it gave Trudeau a breather. It is apparent from this distance that I don't know all that has been going on.

27. Pepin was trying to re-enter politics.
28. Mackasey had lost Ottawa-Centre.

XXVI

May – June 1979

THE BRITISH ELECTION of May 3 established that the desire for change had triumphed over the status quo. Margaret Thatcher became prime minister and took over the government; my task as high commissioner was to establish good relations with the new régime. When the Canadian election took place almost three weeks later, the situation was not quite as clear-cut. The Conservatives, led by Joe Clark, won more seats than Trudeau's Liberals but not enough to form a majority government. The changes in the governments of Canada and Britain only confirmed my decision to leave my post within the year, and after Clark's victory, I wrote to him advising him of my plans.

On June 4, I had a new boss when Joe Clark took office as prime minister and Flora MacDonald became the minister of external affairs. They created an immediate storm in the Arab world by the decision to move the Canadian embassy from Tel Aviv to Jerusalem, the disputed capital of Israel. In that tempest, my job consisted of pouring oil on troubled waters. Throughout these months, I wanted to make certain that the new Conservative administrations in Ottawa and London established good initial relations.

In terms of policy, we all waited to see how the Thatcher government would deal with the issues inherited from the previous administration. It was obvious that Mrs. Thatcher, for example, was more sympathetic to the Rhodesian government, particularly since the black leader, Bishop Abel Muzorewa, had taken over as prime minister in Salisbury.

Tuesday, May 1, 1979

Too much election fever everywhere around me these days —in Canada and in the United Kingdom. Everywhere, variations from poll to poll. This morning, for the first time,

Labour is given the lead in the national opinion poll of the *Daily Mail*, where Labour has a seven per cent lead. . . . I still think Mrs. Thatcher will win. It is interesting to note the number of peers with former Labour affiliations who are urging her election. . . . Each generation, of course, thinks its statesmanship and personalities are superior.

It seems to me that I have noticed many ill-advised *obiter dicta* in our elections. For example, there is the remark attributed to my friend, John Roberts: " . . . People tend to focus on the Prime Minister. . . . When they talk about him, they cite his arrogance and insensitivity. . . . The Prime Minister, from what I see, hasn't taken off." Now, why would John say this? His remark will be quoted by his opponents. It will not help his own candidature. John is a good friend, and was of great help to me in the national Liberal convention.[1] Why should he allow his frankness to run over at a time when discretion is his best hand-maid? Equally maladroit is John Roberts' opponent, Ron Atkey,[2] who, . . . to the question, "which issue is causing you the greatest problem?" answers, "Joe Clark," Atkey's own leader. . . . Why would Atkey belittle his own witness? The new trend in politics, I am sure, has exposed itself and to its own loss. . . .

Thursday, May 3, 1979

When I walked through Grosvenor Square two butlers, whom I see from time to time walking their dogs, had not yet voted. Jokingly, I said that I had been approached by Mrs. Thatcher to solicit their support and to urge them to vote early. . . . *The Telegraph* gives Mrs. Thatcher a majority of thirty. I think it will be greater. I have a bet of 10p with someone that she will get a majority of 60. She has conducted an able campaign. So has Jim. . . . Whatever happens, Jim Callaghan is an able political leader. [But] the merit of an argument is not necessarily the determining factor in election results. . . .

I went to bed early, in the hope that I might become so absorbed in sleep as not to be tempted to listen to the election returns. Practice and habit, however, had other plans for me.

1. In 1968.
2. They were running against each other in St Paul's riding, Toronto.

For several hours after 2:00 o'clock, I lay in bed learning of Maggie's mounting victory, and of my own good guessing on the range of her majority. [Her majority was 43.]

Friday, May 4, 1979

One admires the British despatch in effecting a change of government. We generally take a few weeks. Here, they take no more than a few days. Mrs. Thatcher will see the Queen late today, once the final returns are in. It is more than likely she will see her again next week and earlier with the names of her new cabinet, although I suspect she has a good many of these in mind already. . . .

Saturday, May 5, 1979

The new Prime Minister has just announced her principal ministers. Peter Carrington is in as Foreign Secretary, just as Alec Home said last May. I called Allan Gotlieb and told him about Carrington and Francis Pym, who goes to Defence. (Our communications are not working this week.) I wanted messages of good wishes to go to these two ministers forthwith. . . . Ted Heath is not included. . . .

Sunday, May 6, 1979

Ted Heath apparently wanted the Foreign Office. . . . Willie Whitelaw, the new Home Secretary, had acted as intermediary between the present and former Prime Ministers. The strength of Thatcher's majority may have convinced her it would be burdensome to have her former leader in her cabinet. . . . In any event, the Prime Minister's decision was passed on by letter and not in a face-to-face meeting. . . .

Peter Carrington's appointment is welcomed. He is described as the most experienced of the ministers, having first served as a minister with Churchill in 1951. A "brisk, unpompous, and rich" man, he is modest and dislikes bureaucracy. A good politician, Peter could well have become leader, if he had been in the Commons. We are good friends but even this could not encourage me to stay here beyond November 1st. My time has come and I want to go. Other matters await me. . . . John Nott goes to Industry and Trade. I will have to deal with him on the Heathrow-Gatwick matter, about which, some weeks ago, I had a word or two with Peter Carrington. . . .

George Haynal[3] worked with me on a message to Ottawa on the new cabinet. Holiday or not, a wide-awake mission keeps the home office fully advised on major developments, and what is more important than a new ministry of a new government in the country where one is accredited. . . . At first, the suggestion was made that other missions would not be overly active on this holiday weekend. On the contrary, when our letters were delivered to the Foreign Office, about twenty other missions were active in doing the same thing, as evidenced by the presence in the Foreign Office courtyard of mission cars. I would have been humiliated, if we had not shown the kind of initiative which marks an active post. . . .

Tuesday, May 8, 1979

Mrs. Thatcher's election on Thursday has conveyed a wide impression of a return to the right. . . . Talking to Canada, I have heard people there say that Mrs. Thatcher's success will stimulate more moderate action in governments of many nations. For a while this may be the trend. Unfortunately, problems do not stand still. It is too much to expect that even a right-wing Conservative government can ignore the inexorable movement of new situations. . . .

Wednesday, May 9, 1979

Peter Jay has announced he will resign as Britain's Ambassador in Washington. . . . Peter Carrington told me Jay had done a good job in Washington and left the impression that, as far as he was concerned, Jay could stay on. Mrs. Thatcher, however, has had other views apparently. It is reported today, she would like both Jay and the British Ambassador at the United Nations, Ivor Richard, to be replaced. Different governments pursue different courses. When I became foreign minister, I kept George Drew on for well over a year.[4] I was disappointed when, at the end of that time, he insisted on retiring. . . .

3. A member of the High Commission staff.
4. He was our high commissioner and a former leader of the Conservative party.

Friday, May 11, 1979

Looking over some of my papers today, the impression strengthens that pressures in Mrs. Thatcher's party are likely to build up rapidly in support of recognition and lifting of sanctions in Rhodesia. It may be difficult for Peter Carrington to resist these pressures. It is suggested we might wish to advise the British government of our views on a Commonwealth handling of this question. . . .

Saturday, May 12, 1979

We left [London] early for Southampton on our way to Exbury to lunch with Edmund de Rothschild and his wife at their impressive estate, with its several houses and world-famous gardens. It was a large party of interesting people. . . . Edmund I have known for over fifteen years. . . .

I had a good chat with Mrs. Steinberg, the daughter of Lord Wolfson. What an intelligent and wide-awake woman, who delights in visiting the two Wolfson colleges and learning from its scholars. She told me many interesting things about Isaiah Berlin who, she says, speaks better than he writes.[5] This I find curious. True, his writing is not in the contemporary style but its long sentences convey much more than the puny formulations of a Hemingway. . . . Jack Colville[6] gave me an interesting account of how he had collected funds from individuals and Commonwealth governments to establish Churchill College at Cambridge. In spite of George Drew's efforts, John Diefenbaker, allegedly an enthusiastic admirer of Churchill, would not join his government with others in tribute to Winston. Canada, if not its government, through H. R. MacMillan,[7] supplied precious British Columbia timber for the College Hall. Jack had not seen Rab Butler for some time. Because the Master of Trinity had become so enamoured with his many achievements, Colville found it more congenial to avoid hearing directly of Rab's indispensable role. . . .

5. His better known works include *Karl Marx: His Life and Environment* (London 1939), *The Hedgehog and the Fox: An Essay on Tolstoy's View of History* (London 1953), and *Historical Inevitability* (London 1959).
6. Winston Churchill's former private secretary.
7. President of MacMillan Bloedell.

On our return we were heartened to hear that Michael Bellamy had received an appointment at St. Thomas' College in Minnesota with tenure and a substantial raise in salary. Nell observed jokingly to our daughter and her husband, that their theological theories had been overlooked by the grace Nell acquired following her visit to Lourdes last week. . . .

Monday, May 14, 1979

I had to leave . . . for . . . the first reception given to heads of mission by the new Secretary of State for Foreign and Commonwealth Affairs. . . . It was a good occasion to add personally a word of congratulation on Peter's appointment. . . . There was a full attendance of High Commissioners and certain other heads of mission. Peter was wise in having this reception early in his ministry. His predecessor waited almost a year to do so, in spite of several urgings of mine. Peter made a witty speech, intimating that, as a former High Commissioner in Australia, he knew of our difficulties and problems. He has a good sense of humour, a friendly manner, and good intelligence. These qualities will take him a long way. Peter says the Anglo-United States initiative on Rhodesia has been overtaken by events. This is not presently the Canadian official position, nor is it that of the United States, but I suspect Carrington is right. Britain, under him, will honour its manifesto pledges on Rhodesia. He, however, wisely speaks in generalities at this stage, when he speaks to the press.

Wednesday, May 16, 1979

Mrs. Thatcher gets high marks this morning for the Queen's Speech, a business-like document, lucid, and not too long, so often the case in speeches from the Throne in Canada. . . . The Prime Minister offers a middle ground and that is what the people want, she affirms. Jim thinks the programme is negative and divisive. There are to be tax cuts, legislation to limit picketing, assistance for the victims of the closed shop, and provision for secret trade union ballots. . . .

At the end of yesterday's . . . [opening of Parliament] in he House of Lords, I signalled to one of the attendants to come and talk to me. I wanted to compliment him on the way he bolstered up one of the Queen's four pages who was about to faint, just a minute or so before the Queen left her Throne to depart from the Lords. The attendant, garbed in his black uniform with white tie and wing collar, whispered to the little boy to stand on his toes. . . . As the Queen left, the attendant gradually released the boy's back and the boy walked out alert, carrying his portion of the Queen's train along with the three other pages. . . . At this point I made my bow to the Master of the Rolls and the Lord Chief Justice, who still sat on the woolsack. It was this scene which our superb maid, Theresa, said she saw on the television. . . .

I attended the Memorial Service at St. Martin's-in-the-Field for the late Airey Neave . . . who was blown up within the precincts of Westminster by the Provisional I.R.A. some weeks ago. . . . I had not seen Jim Callaghan in person since the elections. We exchanged a few remarks about the last few weeks. He wondered how Pierre was getting along? . . .

Thursday, May 17, 1979

When I saw Sonny Ramphal early this morning at Marlborough House, we were both aware that Lord Boyd[8] had reported to Prime Minister Thatcher last night [that] the recent elections in Rhodesia were free and fair. The report is likely to increase support in Parliament for lifting sanctions. I suggested to Ramphal that Mrs. Thatcher would not likely make a decision until after Lusaka in August. . . .[9] Ramphal is concerned over the decision of the United States Senate for removal of sanctions, particularly in the light of the recent Security Council decision, which denies the validity of the recent elections.

My meeting with Ramphal was a useful one. It gave me an opportunity to go over a problem which has changed perceptibly since the Rhodesian elections. . . . There is no doubt that Mrs. Thatcher and some of her cabinet colleagues are

8. Boyd had gone to Rhodesia as an observer of the elections in which the Muzorewa faction had gained a majority. I felt that his report might bolster the strong Conservative sentiments to recognize the new régime as a conciliatory gesture.
9. The Commonwealth prime ministers were to meet in Lusaka, Zambia.

sympathetic to the new [Muzorewa] government in Salisbury.[10] Hostile reaction from Commonwealth members will prevent an early decision being taken. . . .

I sent a telegram to Ottawa yesterday outlining the points just covered, suggesting that we should prepare for a modification in our position in the light of positions being taken by President [Carter] and the new administration here. I emphasized that whatever was done ought to be done with an eye to our relations with the African countries. An outright recognition of Muzorewa now would anger Kaunda and Nyerere. . . . It would be regrettable if every effort were not made to avoid a conflict between those opposed to the present arrangement in Rhodesia and those who support the Patriotic Leaders. . . .[11]

Friday, May 18, 1979

Our meeting at Marlborough House this morning, when almost all the High Commissioners were present, reminded me of the heads of government meeting in the same place, two years ago. We had come to discuss British government policy in Rhodesia. The African, Asian, and Caribbean Commonwealth is not happy with indications of British Rhodesian policy. Peter Carrington's declaration that "events in Rhodesia have caught up with the Anglo-American initiative" came under fire, as did Mrs. Thatcher's assertion that the Anglo-American plan was dead. What is clearly at stake is the unity of the Commonwealth. A blow-up in Lusaka at the heads of government meeting in August must be avoided.

I pointed out that the Canadian position had been restated by Jamieson on April 24th. He made it clear that the Canadian government has no plans to recognize the new government in Rhodesia. He insisted there will have to be

10. The Rhodesian elections held on April 20 resulted in an elected black government under Bishop Abel Muzorewa who took over on June 1. Many African governments, however, refused to condone the lifting of economic sanctions against Rhodesia because they believed Muzorewa was a puppet of Ian Smith and the white minority. Muzorewa had guaranteed white control of the public service, judiciary, police, and the military.
11. Robert Mugabe and Joshua Nkomo.

further negotiations, further initiatives, to resolve the Rhodesian situation in a manner satisfactory to the world community. I said this remains the position of the government.

A proposal that a committee of High Commissioners of the Commonwealth call on the Foreign Secretary to advise him of Commonwealth feeling was accepted. I was named to the committee, along with Australia, Ghana and Guyana. Some wanted the call to be made on the Prime Minister. I suggested we should first call on Carrington. This was agreed. Hopefully, we will see Peter before he meets with Vance. . . .

Saturday, May 19, 1979

John Robarts, Ontario's former Premier, was in to see me at the residence at noon. I had seen him last night at a reception at the home of one of his London colleagues. . . . From John Aird,[12] I knew that John was interested, in the event of a Clark victory, to come to London as High Commissioner. He has good precedents. Two former High Commissioners, Howard Ferguson and George Drew, both Ontario Premiers at one time, became head of this mission.[13] . . .

Robarts would like to come to London. One can only presume he will endeavour to do so. I have no reason to believe he has any assurances or has put forward a claim. If perchance, Clark was elected and wanted the former Premier, John told me it would suit him fine to have me leave by November 1st or, depending on my arrangements, about the time I have been suggesting and working out in my own mind. This ratiocination involves a number of situations, including farewells, seeing the Queen, particular ministers and, of course, the Prime Minister, but so much depends on what happens on May 22nd. Pierre may still be Prime Minister. The latest polls show him at 37½ per cent, Clark 37½ per cent, and the N.D.P. around 24 per cent. Trudeau could get stronger. I suspect he may. One sure thing, I will not sit up Tuesday night and early Wednesday morning to find out. . . .

12. A former Liberal senator and a Toronto businessman.
13. Howard Ferguson, premier from 1923 to 1930, served as high commissioner from 1930 to 1935. George Drew, premier of Ontario from 1943 to 1948, was in London from 1957 to 1965. Both were Conservatives.

Within the last few hours, I have had a further talk with Ramphal. We are agreed every effort must be made to build on the fact that Muzorewa is in place. Changes in the constitution, to put power in the right hands, are inevitable. How to bring Mugabe and Nkomo into the picture is the question. The African Commonwealth states have much to offer in this regard. . . . When Cyrus Vance sees Peter Carrington, he will urge no recognition of the Muzorewa régime at present. This is our policy. I am sure that Carrington is not bent on precipitous action. . . .

Monday, May 21, 1979

The Secretary of State, Cyrus Vance, is here for two days of talks with Lord Carrington. Rhodesia will be on the agenda. The Senate resolution calling for withdrawal of sanctions [against Rhodesia] has given Vance and the President a problem. . . .[14] My information is that, notwithstanding the Senate vote, the President will hang tough on sanctions, for a while at any rate. Before the Senate vote, the administration had intended to remain firm on retention of sanctions. The State Department maintained that Rhodesia's elections were comparable with those organized by the colonial powers for purposes of granting independence. Such elections were more democratic and more freely contested than in Rhodesia [and] . . . were the standard against which Rhodesia's elections should be measured. . . . For some American conservatives, Rhodesia gives an opportunity to show black Americans that they should not go too far in the United States. The United States is not likely to recognize the new régime early and may resist pressures to provide aid, particularly military aid. . . . The United States will not act in opposition to Britain. . . .

Lévesque says, when the federal election is over, he will announce the time-table for Quebec's referendum about June 21st. If he had announced this earlier, Canadians might have appreciated Trudeau's importance more.

14. It showed the Senate's discontent with President Carter's African policy which it regarded as support for so-called guerrilla régimes.

Tuesday, May 22, 1979

When the March 3rd, 1978 agreement, establishing the so-called [Rhodesian] transitional government, was signed, there was some optimism in the West that this would lead to black majority rule. The number of concessions made in the draft of the constitution has led many people to decide that the constitution does not really leave the majority in a position to rule. The specially entrenched provisions, which can be amended only with the affirmative votes of some of the twenty-eight white members, cover appointments to the judiciary, the public service commission, the commissioner of police, and command of the armed forces. There will be a government of national unity, under which the whites will have between a quarter and a third of the ministries. There are barriers in the path of land reform. . . .

Bill Barnetson's[15] annual luncheon on behalf of the directors of United Newspapers Limited at the Savoy Hotel was a pleasant engagement. Bill placed me at his right and I felt specially honoured. Harold Wilson, the former Prime Minister, was on my right. . . . Harold . . . is almost a compulsive talker, always friendly with me. He is finishing volume two of his record. . . . Harold is proud of his writing and fell for Lord Barnetson's blandishments over *The Governance of Britain*.[16] That book was not as good as Harold was told by our host. The former Prime Minister speaks of it as though it was a rival to Bagehot, which it is not. . . .[17]

I was amazed to learn how much he detested Denis Healey, who had been his Chancellor of the Exchequer. But why should he talk so frankly, even to an old time acquaintance like me about his colleagues? As for Michael Foot, the former Prime Minister regards him as a sorrowful figure. . . .

Later in the afternoon,

I hurried to Marlborough House for a meeting of those members of the subcommittee of High Commissioners who

15. Bill Barnetson, Baron Barnetson of Crowborough, was the chairman and managing director of United Newspapers and chairman of Reuters news agency from 1968.
16. Harold Wilson, *The Governance of Britain* (London 1978).
17. Walter Bagehot wrote the classic book on the form of British government (*The English Constitution*).

are to meet with [Lord Carrington] . . . early tomorrow. I suggested [that] at our meeting with the Foreign Secretary, we should not confront him as an opponent. We should explain that we had come in pursuance of his desire to consult with the Commonwealth, as he had done with the E.C. and with Vance. We should say we were satisfied it was not the British government's intention to recognize the Muzorewa administration now. I am sure the African countries will not be happy unless Peter acknowledges sooner or later the fact that the constitution has to be revised to permit a transfer of power from the whites to the blacks. . . .

Wednesday, May 23, 1979

The results of the Canadian elections of the day before had come in.

Trudeau has acknowledged defeat. At least thirteen of his ministers have lost. The slaughter of the ministers was in the Toronto area. Joe Clark will form a minority government. The N.D.P. improved their parliamentary position and will hold the balance of power along with a small group of Social Crediters from Quebec. Joe Clark has had an indecisive but remarkable victory. He will do his utmost, I am sure, to see that national unity is preserved. I am afraid, however, he is going to have real problems with Quebec and Lévesque. People may come to see that this, after all, is the major Canadian issue. The standing in the elections at 6:00 o'clock this morning was Progressive Conservatives, 136; Liberals, 114; N.D.P., 26; Social Credit, 6. . . .

At our meeting with Lord Carrington, the Lord Privy Seal, Sir Ian Gilmour, was in attendance. The subcommittee spokesman emphasized the purpose of the interview with Carrington was to discuss in a spirit of friendly co-operation the situation in Rhodesia. Lord Carrington said, in formulating British policy, the new Conservative government took into account its commitments in the election, the state of opinion in the Conservative party and the fact that the elections in Rhodesia had been successful and widely participated in. I urged the Foreign Secretary to consider that there was another consideration which we would want to bear in mind, the reaction to the Rhodesian situation by the Commonwealth countries in Africa, Asia, and elsewhere. Lord Carrington had spoken of the Muzorewa régime and the need for it to receive international recognition. That would depend on meeting the objections of the African and other countries. I don't believe this point has yet registered fully with Peter. . . . The Secretary General told me afterwards he shared my concern. . . .

After lunch, I saw Richard Luce[18] who underlined that the position of these [African and Asian] countries was very important, [and] that . . . they had serious problems about the nature of the constitution. Luce said that Carrington fully understood that aspect and that the problem was not with him but with Margaret Thatcher, who has not followed the details of Rhodesian developments closely so far. Luce said that this was an extremely important factor at the present stage. . . .

Thursday, May 24, 1979

I welcomed Premier [Sterling] Lyon of Manitoba at Heathrow early this morning. He brought greetings from Joe Clark, to whom he had spoken on the telephone yesterday, likely discussing prospects for the former's cabinet. . . . Meanwhile, Joe says he has no intention of making any immediate changes in public service personnel. His advisers have suggested that Joe may take two weeks before taking over. Premier Lyon had given me the impression it would be some time next week. Clark said Parliament will not be recalled before September or October next. . . .

Friday, May 25, 1979

[I had] a visit with the new Lord Chancellor, Hailsham. Quintin is the second Lord Chancellor to return to the woolsack, after already having served as Lord Chancellor.[19] The other

18. He was a Conservative MP and parliamentary under-secretary of state.
19. Quintin Hogg, Viscount Hailsham, had served as lord chancellor (speaker of the House of Lords) from 1970 to 1974 in Ted Heath's government and was reappointed to that position by Margaret Thatcher.

person with a corresponding achievement was Quintin's father.[20] As he descended from the steps of the Throne at Parliament's opening, I told the Lord Chancellor I watched him with pride and delight. . . .

Sunday, May 27, 1979

Nell and I spent the weekend in Devon with Derick Amory and his sister-in-law.

A quick look at the front page of the papers gave . . . good news: the appointment of Jack Kennedy's friend, Lord Harlech, as Britain's man to discuss a Rhodesian settlement with African governments, with no formal accreditation.[21] He will seek to narrow the differences with Muzorewa and the Patriotic Front. An international settlement of the conflict will be the major objective. He will talk to Mugabe and Nkomo. Will they talk to him? . . .

Monday, May 28, 1979

Barney Danson telephoned from Ottawa. His defeat has not dampened his resolve and spirits. He was caught in a typhoon and was helpless to resist. Joe Clark takes over on [next] Monday. Barney surprised me with Don Jamieson's plans. Don is on his way to Newfoundland to take over the leadership of the Liberal party. This means that sooner or later he will become Premier of Newfoundland. His counsel will be missed in Ottawa. . . .

I believe, from my long-distance contacts today, that Trudeau will stay as leader until the Quebec referendum has taken place. The polarization of election results in Canada, with Quebec on one side and English Canada on the other, is taken as a plus for Lévesque. He said, "It is English-Canada

20. Sir Douglas Hogg (died 1950), a prominent Conservative attorney general between the wars, served as lord chancellor 1928 to 1929 and 1935 to 1938.
21. William David Ormsby-Gore had served as British ambassador to Washington from 1961 to 1965 and became a good friend of President John Kennedy.

and us." Others think the federal elections give the nationalists some encouragement. In the coming months, Trudeau may play a decisive role in Quebec. His own province supported him resolutely. . . .

Tuesday, May 29, 1979

Jim Callaghan sent me the following letter on the May 24th:

> My Dear Paul,
>
> Would you please get this note to Pierre for me. It is very personal and I do not want anyone to open it except him. You know how much I admired him, and how sorry I am.
>
> And sorry too, that this will mean your term of office will draw to a close. I shall have a chance in the coming week to meet you. I hope to say personally how grateful I am for all your kindness whilst you have been in London.

I sent this letter to Trudeau at once. I will not be able to tell him precisely of my plans but I can of my intentions. . . .

I sent the following letter to the Prime Minister-designate this morning. It sets out present intentions about when I leave this post:

> My Dear Prime Minister,
>
> As you assume your heavy responsibilities I offer you my best wishes.
>
> Some weeks ago I informed . . . the Department of External Affairs that it was my wish to vacate the post of High Commissioner in London this year. . . . If, however, it would be of any assistance in arranging for my replacement, I could help and accommodate you by staying on for a limited period, hopefully not later than November 1. . . .
>
> Nell joins me in wishing Maureen and you every happiness in the discharge of your heavy obligations. . . .

Allan Gotlieb thought the action I was taking was wise, adding [that] . . . it would take the government some time to make up its mind who should succeed me. The two names which have come to my attention are John Robarts, the former Premier of Ontario, and George Hees. The latter has been elected to Parliament. It would seem odd for him to have undertaken the inconvenience of going through a two-month election and giving up his seat hurriedly to replace me. John Robarts, I know, is interested. Allan had no firm idea who would be our minister. I wouldn't be surprised if Clark carried on in External Affairs until after the [Economic] Summit meetings, possibly naming Roche to external aid and as acting minister, until such time as Joe was in a position to make a final decision. An alternative plan might be to appoint Flora MacDonald, David MacDonald, or the Toronto MP, [Sinclair] Stevens.[22] Another idea which occurs to me is that Joe might want to give a senior ministry to someone from Quebec. He likely has in mind a Minister of Finance from Ontario. . . .

Wednesday, May 30, 1979

Chief Linklater, who is here in connection with a proposed visit of the Indian chiefs, was in to see us this morning. . . . The chiefs are hoping to see the Queen regarding their treaty complaints [with Ottawa]. The Trudeau government, however, through Rideau Hall, has advised the Queen it would be preferable for her not to give this delegation any encouragement until after the fall meeting, when the government will be meeting on Indian claims with the provincial governments.

After lunch . . . I reviewed matters . . . on the [forthcoming] Tokyo [Economic] Summit. It is interesting to note that Callaghan usually went to the summits, certainly the last one, with only one official, the Secretary to the Cabinet, John himself.[23] When Mrs. Thatcher goes to Tokyo, I understand Hunt will be along, as well as Michael Palliser, the Permanent Under-Secretary at the Foreign Office, and, of course, Peter Carrington, the foreign minister. . . . It is hoped there will be an avoidance of bilateral meetings. There will be no time.

22. Douglas Roche was a prominent Conservative MP as were the others.
23. Sir John Hunt.

[President Jimmy] Carter feels he should see Mrs. Thatcher. He should see Clark as well. . . .

Thursday, May 31, 1979

The Egyptians are not happy over Clark's declared intention to move the Canadian Embassy to Jerusalem. This message has been conveyed to us forcefully within the last few hours. . . .

Monday, June 4, 1979

The Nigerian government has said it will regard moves toward recognition of Muzorewa's administration as a wanton disregard for African opinion. British companies have been warned that their tenders for contracts will not be considered during the period of uncertainty over British policy. Britain's exports to Nigeria are its largest in Africa. In Nairobi, the Foreign Ministers of Tanzania, Mozambique, Angola, Zambia, and Botswana have said recognition would "seriously jeopardize Britain's relations with African countries." Nkomo and Mugabe, meeting in Tanzania, have created a joint military command to intensify the war against Rhodesia. President Carter has to consider what he does about lifting sanctions by June 15th. He has sent an emissary to discuss the matter with Muzorewa. . . .

Tuesday, June 5, 1979

We sent on late last night a report on the United Kingdom position for the Tokyo Summit as given me by the secretary of the cabinet. . . . He told me Mrs. Thatcher is approaching the Summit with an open mind, but is not too convinced of the importance of summits. Hunt says she is a direct person, not enthusiastic about discussions on generalities or platitudinous expressions. After Bonn, she had criticized Jim Callaghan for giving an unrealistic account, as she saw it, of the Summit's attempt to manage the world economy. She saw no point in setting world economy growth targets, nor in putting pressure on the economies of any one of the seven countries. She preferred a shorter term view and a higher selective discussion.

Her main interests in Tokyo will be inflation, energy, and its impact on the world economy. She would pay special attention to nuclear energy. . . . The United Kingdom shares the reaction of European countries to the United States action on subsidies on energy. I could not get John Hunt to indicate any difference of view by Mrs. Thatcher because of North Sea oil. She will want from the Summit a strong message that nuclear energy was essential and hopes to avoid [an] . . . international enquiry on safety. . . . As for the communiqué, Mrs. Thatcher would want a short, less analytic, and more action-oriented document. . . .

Prime Minister Clark was sworn in yesterday. For the first time in Canada, the . . . ceremony was carried on television. Jacques Flynn, former leader of the opposition in the Senate when I was government leader, is named Minister of Justice and Attorney General. Martial Asselin, also in the Senate, is named Minister of State for CIDA. Flora MacDonald becomes my boss and Secretary of State for External Affairs. . . . All ministers are to be members of full cabinet. Clark will have an inner cabinet committee, with five policy subcommittees as the main policy-making framework of the government. The inner cabinet, to be chaired by the Prime Minister, will be responsible for overall priorities of the government and major policy decisions. . . .

I was distressed to learn that Joe has dispensed with Pitfield's services as Clerk of Canada's Privy Council. Michael was close to Trudeau, perhaps a little too much. Diefenbaker, however, kept Bob Bryce when he became Prime Minister.[24] Joe cannot have overlooked that Pitfield came into the service under Davie Fulton's patronage.[25] The Pitfield family was notoriously Conservative in party affiliation.

Wednesday, June 6, 1979

Flora MacDonald, our new Secretary of State for External Affairs, said yesterday in Ottawa that the Clark government will move [our embassy in Israel] to Jerusalem, as Clark stated

24. Robert Bryce was the clerk in 1957 when Diefenbaker formed a minority government after twenty-two years of Liberal rule.
25. Fulton was a former Conservative minister.

during the campaign. The decision to do so is highlighted as a spurning by Canada of Carter's advice. The President had intimated that such an act could disturb delicate negotiations in the Middle East. Flora did not say when the move would take place. I was glad to see her announcement that we would not decide on recognition of Zimbabwe-Rhodesia until after the Commonwealth Prime Ministers' Conference in Lusaka in August. . . .

Ramsay Melhuish of the Foreign Office and in charge of the American desk, including Canada, was Christian Hardy's guest at luncheon today at noon. . . . I learned from Melhuish that there would be no change in British policy on Rhodesia until after the heads of government meeting in Lusaka. I was anxious to send this word at once, because of Ottawa's query. . . .

In anticipation of the Commonwealth heads of government meeting in Lusaka in August, I considered the draft report of the Commonwealth Committee on Southern Africa, which I saw for the first time tonight. . . . I support the recommendation already made to Ottawa that we must ask for more time to examine the report. In the first place, it is prepared by the Secretariat. A meeting of High Commissioners or their representatives has no authority to commit governments to the conclusions in the report. The British government wants considerable revisions. . . .

Thursday, June 7, 1979

We spent some time this morning getting ready for the Queen Mother's luncheon at 12 Upper Brook on the 13th. . . .

A High Commissioner has to deal with many odd questions. The Queen Mother, accompanied by Viscountess Hambleden, will wear a hat. . . . What do the others do, particularly the younger ladies present? I thought it best to call Martin Gilliatt, the Queen Mother's secretary, who assured me that Nell, as hostess, would not be expected to wear a hat nor should the others be concerned about doing so. . . . The Queen Mother likes wearing a hat at such functions. . . .

I have just received instructions on the position to be taken on Rhodesia and Namibia at the meeting to be held Friday afternoon on the draft report to Commonwealth heads of government. Specifically, events since May 3rd have made the report controversial. . . . Ottawa points out that they have not been able to focus on the Rhodesian question since the changeover [in government]. We will not participate, therefore, in the discussions on substantive issues at the meeting. . . . The new Secretary of State for External Affairs instructs me to take the view, which I have already assumed, that Rhodesia should not be a divisive issue in the Commonwealth, and that I should do what I can to encourage the British and Africans to find a maximum common ground, certainly not to paint themselves into a corner prior to Lusaka and before the British consultation process gets into high gear. . . .

[When] I saw the Commonwealth Secretary General this afternoon, [he] gave me a detailed account of his recent visit to Southern Africa. . . . There are signs among the front line states of a possible change in attitude to Muzorewa if the necessary disposition for constructive negotiations can be provided. I suspect that Kaunda will be prepared to take a constructive position regarding the Patriotic Front if Commonwealth countries stand firm and if the British government does not take action which puts it in opposition to them. . . . The British are dependent on Nigerian trade and will want to act carefully before pursuing a course which would not be supported by most Commonwealth countries. . . .

Friday, June 8, 1979

Joe Clark's decision to recognize Jerusalem as Israel's capital was re-affirmed yesterday. The Arab world is up in arms, with threats to break off diplomatic relations and impose trade sanctions against Canada. . . . The Arab countries, through their ambassadors in Ottawa, issued a joint statement calling on the government not to recognize Jerusalem. This would profoundly affect Arab-Canadian relations. Some Canadian officials fear the policy could lead to the loss of about a billion dollars' worth of business. I think Joe has a problem on his hands with this one. I doubt if it got him as many votes as he thought it might. . . .

Saturday, June 9, 1979

Among . . . matters I will take up with the Secretary of State is Clark's desire to discuss Rhodesia with Mrs. Thatcher. It is important that the two Commonwealth Prime Ministers should get to know one another. Clark is understandably concerned about Commonwealth ramifications over Rhodesia. I will tell Peter I think the British government is proceeding wisely on Rhodesia. Commonwealth countries are concerned about prolonging minority rule in Rhodesia. After Lusaka, "we hope that full and substantial negotiations will continue." I will ask Peter to explain what he meant [in a speech] at The Hague about "action, earlier than Lusaka, on Rhodesia." . . .

Sunday, June 10, 1979

Mark MacGuigan, who was returned in Windsor-Walkerville for the third time in the recent elections . . . has been here for two or three days at a conference on the problems of democratic government along with some American legislators. He dined with us and the Ritchies,[26] following which we had a long discussion about who should be in certain posts in Canada's diplomatic service. Ed took the position that it was a discouragement to the permanent service for the Canadian government to appoint other than career men to any post, including London, Washington, or Paris. He made an exception in my case, because I had been a foreign minister. . . . I understand Ed's point and to a great extent I share it. I believe, however, that it is good for our foreign service to have some infiltration from outside. London, perhaps, is the post which lends itself best to this purpose. We have had good career men in London and some good outsiders. The case for having an outsider in Washington and in Paris is more difficult to justify, but justifiable all the same in particular situations. . . .

I am sure that, when I came to London, even Ed, a good friend, and others in the service thought it was a slap at that service for a former cabinet minister . . . to be appointed to

26. Ed Ritchie, the Canadian ambassador to Ireland, and his wife were visiting us.

London. I am told that my work here has been of an order that early feelings no longer exist. . . . What Ed had particularly in mind was that my successor should come from the service itself. He would, therefore, not look kindly on Stanfield, Robarts, or George Hees coming here. He would not quarrel if George Ignatieff[27] were appointed but would prefer to see his successor, the former Under-Secretary, Basil Robinson, instead.

When I retired, I felt I had earned a good rest. A telephone call from Paul in Montreal kept me awake for a little while. Off and on, Paul talks about getting into public life. This I have discouraged. . . . It always seemed to me wrong for him to interfere with his business career at this stage. Prompted as I was by my own experience as an early participant in public life, I sought to advise him that he should not go into politics until perhaps around the age of forty-five. Last night he said, "Dad, I want to have a talk with you soon. Now is the time for me to get my feet wet." He even went further and said, "Now is the time for me to begin to become a candidate for the prime ministership." Shades of the father! . . . I added further that now was not a propitious time with the Liberals in opposition. What he is thinking about is the likelihood of an early election because of Clark's minority situation in Parliament. What he overlooks is that, if there was an early election, say within a year, Clark would likely repeat Diefenbaker's 1958 performance and return to office with a bigger majority. . . .

Monday, June 11, 1979

My interview with the Secretary of State at 5:30 p.m. lasted for almost fifty minutes. . . . He wanted further particulars on the new Secretary of State for External Affairs. I was pleased to strongly commend her. . . . Peter then asked, "What about you, Paul? Are you going to stay here or are you going because of the change in government?" I reminded him that, before he had taken office, I had mentioned I had told Ottawa of my desire to leave this post not later than November 1st. After Clark's election, I told Peter I had written to the Prime

27. Ignatieff was a career diplomat.

Minister confirming this intention. . . . It was at this point Peter said, "It would be nice if you were here during my Secretaryship. Do you want me to speak to Clark to urge him to keep you?" This, I know, was a friendly gesture on Peter's part. It is not, however, what I want. . . .

[Our] meeting was relaxed and friendly. The particular items discussed were Rhodesia and prospects for the Clark/Thatcher and MacDonald/Carrington meetings. Mrs. Thatcher is anxious to meet and talk with Clark. Carrington had been a luncheon guest of Clark's when he was in Ottawa two months ago, an arrangement which I had suggested. . . .

I mentioned there was great concern in Canada over Rhodesia. On the question of timing of possible British moves on Rhodesia, the central feature of my call was set out in an Ottawa telegram of an impression received by the Under-Secretary at the recent Hague NATO meeting. Carrington said, if he seemed reluctant in The Hague over outright assurances, this was because he did not want to commit himself on timing [of lifting sanctions against Rhodesia]. This did not depend on him or British policy but on circumstances. For example, if the United States Senate and the House of Representatives decided to lift sanctions tomorrow, it would be politically impossible for the United Kingdom not to follow suit. British policy was to get a settlement in Rhodesia. . . .

On the Commonwealth, the Foreign Secretary said we should be in no doubt about the great importance the United Kingdom attached to the Commonwealth relationship. It would be misleading, however, not to recognize that the relationship must be two-way. . . . Peter was at great pains to emphasize he was speaking of the "new" Commonwealth, not Australia, New Zealand, and Canada [alone]. He said, if Lusaka turns into an anti-British baiting exercise, as had happened before, particularly at Singapore, such a development would inevitably affect public opinion in the United Kingdom. . . .

Wednesday, June 13, 1979

When the Australian Ambassador called on the Kuwaiti Minister of Foreign Affairs, most of the conversation centred on Canada and the announced policy [of moving our embassy to Jerusalem]. The Foreign Minister said steps would be taken against Canada. They would not be related to oil. An example of Canada would be made to the rest of the world. "We can buy Canadian goods elsewhere," he said. Ironically, I am told, the Foreign Minister is in the process of assembling the first two Canadian pre-engineered homes, which were manufactured in Alberta. . . . It is interesting to recall that when I saw Peter Carrington the day before yesterday, he was not over-excited one way or another about the proposed move to Jerusalem. This does not mean that he approved it, but he received it with characteristic British sangfroid. . . .

The Queen Mother lunched today at the residence to mark her visit to Ontario and Nova Scotia in a few days. . . . She seemed pleased to see so many young Canadians in attendance. As I have previously recorded, her enthusiasm for the visit to Canada knows no bounds. The Queen Mother spoke to each person at the luncheon before we sat down at the table. Afterwards during coffee she was generous in repeating the same routine. . . . I asked the guests to join in a toast "to one of the most beloved women in the world, Her Majesty Queen Elizabeth." I had learned a year ago that she greatly appreciated being so characterized. . . .

Thursday, June 14, 1979

Tonight I attended a dinner given by the Royal Bank of Canada at the Savoy Hotel. The president of the bank, R. C. Frazee, spoke briefly. . . . Bank presidents in Canada have often put their foot into it. . . . I thought Frazee did it tonight when, after explaining the bank's initiative, he spoke of the Canadian political scene. I thought that naive and improper. There are occasions when bank presidents should be as apolitical as High Commissioners. I don't think his remarks about Quebec, not the separatist movement but Quebec, were too helpful either. . . .

Friday, June 15, 1979

Yesterday I had an exchange with Philip Moore, the Queen's private secretary. . . . We talked of the former Prime Minister [Trudeau], his strengths and some of his inadequacies. A speech he made to the Oxford students a year and a half ago had caused wonderment, not only in our High Commission, but in Buckingham Palace. Trudeau's Ottawa office was badly manned in Philip's view, insofar as Buckingham Palace was concerned and involved. The fault did not lie [with the Clerk of the Privy Council] . . . but more in the secretariat of the Prime Minister's Office itself. The Prime Minister did not give much time or notice about the last Governor-General appointment [of Ed Schreyer]. My only comment was that it was done at the last moment and few ministers knew about it much ahead of time. Jules Léger, always helpful, continues to write to the Palace and this is appreciated. . . .

I emphasized in my exchange with Philip that there were many things Trudeau did which were unsatisfactory but, on the position of the Crown in Canada, he had gone to further lengths in providing for its durability than any previous Prime Minister. This should not be forgotten and Philip agreed. . . .

In Joe's new cabinet, there are no former ministers from the Commons. George Hees, Alvin Hamilton and Walter Dinsdale[28] were left out. Mackenzie King generally took the view that experienced people were more important than new faces. One of Trudeau's mistakes in his eleven years of brilliant leadership was the weakness of his cabinet, due largely to too many new and fresh faces. . . .

Saturday, June 16, 1979

We attended today's annual ceremony of Trooping the Colour, always a military ceremony of great interest. Its liturgy is rich in symbolism. It touches the British tradition and history at many points. . . . Nell and I were seated immediately behind the Prime Minister and her husband. We sat with Sir Ian Gilmour, the Lord Privy Seal, and his wife—a charming couple. . . . He told us he had taken part in the Trooping in 1946 with a Guards unit, of which he was the commanding officer. Nell was amused when Ian told her the officer commanding was a "good fellow" but he couldn't ride. That, of course, wasn't apparent to us. . . .

At the reception after the Trooping, I had a chat with Mrs. Thatcher who said she looked forward to meeting Clark in Tokyo and Lusaka. I mentioned how important it was for

28. They all had been ministers in John Diefenbaker's government.

the Canadian and British Prime Ministers to be known as close colleagues. She agreed. I noted it would be useful for visits to be exchanged as soon as possible. . . . Without commitment, I said it might be worthwhile for my Prime Minister to stop off in London for a day or so before or after Lusaka. She agreed that this should be looked into. . . . Mrs. Thatcher asked would I be staying on. I explained what I wanted to do. "You should not go now — you have done so well in London." I thanked her, adding that I immodestly felt I hadn't done so badly in Ottawa. She laughed in an appropriate way. . . .

Sunday, June 17, 1979

I took Jack Pickersgill[29] next door for a 7:00 a.m. swim. It cheered us up. To next door's new Cairo cook, I sent a warm "Salaam," which seemed to impress my former colleague, who later said he had learned for the first time what "salaam" meant. At first he thought it was a fruit. . . .

I hear that the cabinet here is beginning to feel that Ian Smith is an obstacle to the lifting of sanctions and international recognition of the new Rhodesia. Growing acknowledgment of white control of defence, security, and major economic offices as further obstacles are more evident now than two weeks ago. These points were impressed on Mrs. Thatcher by President Moi of Kenya on Wednesday and Thursday. She was pleased to note that the Kenyan spoke of a "new situation" having emerged after the election of Bishop Muzorewa. Continued white supremacy was an insuperable obstacle, which stood in the way of compromise. Transfer of power from the whites to blacks will be essential to avoid a Commonwealth crisis at Lusaka. . . .

Monday, June 18, 1979

Nell was very upset this morning over the plight of the Vietnamese refugees. . . . For the Malaysians to accept eighty-thousand Vietnamese is to change the balance in that country

29. Pickersgill*, a colleague from the St Laurent and Pearson governments, was our guest for a few days.

between Malays and Chinese. The same problem faces Singapore and, for that reason, its Prime Minister [Lee Kwan Yew] is now in London to see Mrs. Thatcher, who is urging international action. Peter Carrington talked to me about this a week ago today. My Ottawa principals had instructed me to say there was a danger in international organization of this problem. I wonder how accurate Ottawa is in this regard. Some civil service types often start with a reluctance to do anything. I think Mrs. Thatcher is on the right track; I told Allan Gotlieb so on the telephone last night. . . .

Tuesday, June 19, 1979

Lord Carrington, the Secretary of State for Foreign and Commonwealth Affairs, hosted his first diplomatic corps dinner at the Mansion House. He proposed three toasts with a minimum of verbal effort: The Queen, Sovereigns and Heads of States here represented, the Lord Mayor, the Corporation of London and the Sheriffs. . . . To the second toast, the Doyen of the Diplomatic Corps, the High Commissioner for Mauritius,[30] replied. The Doyen is a nice man but a bad speaker, who always asks me at the end of each function, "Did I speak well tonight, Paul?" I never discourage him. . . .

Joe Clark, our new Prime Minister, called from Ottawa this afternoon. He had received my letter indicating my desire to return home. He began by saying, "You know I am in no hurry for you to leave. It would help me a little if you would stay on at least until October." This I agreed. I was touched by what Joe said about my public life and my work here. No one could have been kinder in this regard than he was. He mentioned how fate played its games. He was Prime Minister of Canada at the age of thirty-nine, a fledgling in the House of Commons. No one in high authority has ever spoken to me as generously as did the present Prime Minister. I will always be grateful for what he said. . . .

I dropped in at Hatchard's before going to the Reform Club and bought two books: *Against the Current* by Isaiah Berlin and Mary Soames' life of her mother, *Clementine*.[31]

30. Sir Leckraz Teelock
31. Isaiah Berlin, *Against the Current: Essays in the History of Ideas* (London 1979), and Mary Soames, *Clementine Churchill* (London 1979).

Isaiah Berlin was standing near the Reform Club talking to some unknown gentleman. I intervened and told him I had just bought his most recent book. This pleased him. I now have a dedication in the book by him. . . .

Thursday, June 21, 1979

I am told that Mrs. Thatcher finds time to dine with the back-benchers of her party in the Commons dining room. She has learned a lesson which Ted Heath did not appreciate. Of the four Prime Ministers I served under, the only one who dined frequently with the members was St. Laurent. I don't think I ever saw Mackenzie King in the parliamentary restaurant. . . .

Barney Danson is in town. On the telephone, he informed me he doubted there was much political advantage in the election pledge by the present government to move the Canadian Embassy to Jerusalem. . . . The idea, he said, had first been proposed by a Jewish organization in Canada. There could be no quarrel with their recommendation. He thought most of his fellow Jews had not been misled by the promise. Barney, in good spirits, was naturally disappointed in not having won his seat. . . .

I am amused by assurances that the Liberals will not move to defeat Joe Clark's government. It is wise, of course, for the Leader of the Opposition to maintain a low profile at the beginning of a new government take-over. It is reported that MacEachen and Lalonde are in an accepting mood. MacEachen says Trudeau will not leave the political scene. All this reminds me of the mood after the [Liberal defeats in the] elections of 1957 and 1958. The fact is that, if it had not been for Pickersgill, Chevrier, and myself, Pearson would not have become Prime Minister as early as he did.[32] Political warfare, essential for the proper functioning of the democratic parliamentary [system] . . . calls for vigilance from the beginning. . . .

Friday, June 22, 1979

At the reception hour, Barney Danson [and] his wife . . . were in for a refreshment and talk with us. . . . He does not think Trudeau will stay long as leader. Turner is in the wings. In

32. The press called us the Four Horsemen.

spite of his criticisms of former colleagues, Barney thinks John is the likely successor.

Saturday, June 23, 1979

Jeremy Thorpe and the three others accused with him were acquitted of plotting to kill Norman Scott, who had alleged a homosexual relationship with the former Liberal Leader. Thorpe denied the relationship. Jeremy was also found not guilty of the charge of incitement to kill Scott. The former Liberal leader showed relief from the burden, which he has carried since the first barrage of publicity covering rumours long before the trial. We will hear of this trial for years to come. . . .

Sunday, June 24, 1979

I returned to Kissinger, as interpreted by Peter Dickson.[33] . . . Kissinger was wrong, I believe, in thinking that "cool calculation of power and national interest encourages restraint." This view of politics can create fears "out of all proportion to the actual significance of the change in power." It can result in a "spasmodic policy." What guarantee is there that pragmatic-minded leaders will avoid the dangers of miscalculation better than statesmen who are "blinded by religious, moral or idealogical concerns?" Not even a master diplomat can avoid miscalculation.

Monday, June 25, 1979

Clark has made a partial retreat on . . . [his] move to Jerusalem. He has established a special mission under Bob Stanfield, his predecessor in the Conservative party leadership, to look into our relations with the Middle East. Joe told the Arab Ambassadors in Ottawa, over the weekend, Canada will not move from Tel Aviv before the commission has completed its work and only after consultation with Arab countries. . . . One Arab Ambassador said after the meeting that he was personally quite satisfied with Clark's explanation. Joe has taken the right course. . . .

33. Peter W. Dickson, *Kissinger and the Meaning of History* (London 1978).

Our proposal for a campaign to promote trade between Britain and Canada ... is not making much headway.... Personalities apart, there are different views on how this should be undertaken. I think we should go out after trade more than we do, just as I think the private sector could show more aggressiveness in its sales efforts in Britain and on the Continent. We rely too much on our proximity with the United States for quick and readier sales....

I called on Sir Ian Gilmour, the Lord Privy Seal, at the Foreign and Commonwealth Office.... Sir Ian said, as he welcomed me, "You must know this office." I was able to recall it as that formerly occupied by Frank Judd....

I raised with Gilmour Britain's participation in the Commonwealth. I had been asked recently by a number of Commonwealth African countries what would Britain do in Lusaka, if there was a final show-down on Rhodesia. Would she opt for the Commonwealth or for her own position on Rhodesia? Ian thought this was somewhat of a hypothetical question, but it served to draw out his view that the Commonwealth had a primacy of position. He gave me the same strong assurance that Callaghan had given two years ago....

Tuesday, June 26, 1979

I admire some of our Middle East diplomats who have not been afraid to tell Ottawa to stay quiet on the Jerusalem issue.... It is surely the right and the duty of a head of mission to speak frankly.... The government may have to act boldly and withdraw its announced policy of ultimate location in Jerusalem....

Thursday, June 28, 1979

We could have some problems next week over the visit to London of the Canadian Indian chiefs. They will be here to protest the patriation of the Canadian constitution.... The Indian chiefs, who represent the National Indian Brotherhood, want the Queen to intervene. This, of course, is constitutionally impossible. This is a matter involving the Parliament of Britain and the government of Canada. The Indians contend their treaties with the British Crown pre-date the constitution. The Indians also allege, once the constitution is patriated to Canada, we will downgrade the role of the monarchy. The Indians say that this is what Trudeau did. They are, of course, mistaken. . . .

I have had some discussion, of course, with the Queen's private secretary. It is likely that I will have more dealings with him before this matter has been satisfactorily disposed. The chiefs want to see Mrs. Thatcher. The Indians would like to see the Queen, as they did two years ago, to reaffirm the sacred nature of the treaties with the monarch, who symbolizes the sanctity of the treaties along the lines indicated by the Indian chiefs.

We discussed this matter here in the Commission yesterday. We will point out to Chief Starblanket[34] that the High Commission acts on instructions from the federal government. The policies are not made by us but by our masters. All the same, it will require some careful diplomacy. I have already seen several of the Indian chiefs and their public relations man. . . .

I wonder how much consideration Crosbie, the new Minister of Finance, has given to the implications of absolute free trade by Canada with the United States? Crosbie said this is one of the options we will have to examine and rightly said, if we are going to be dominated by anyone, [he] would prefer it to be the Americans. He added, the third option — more trade links with Europe and Japan — simply [has] not worked out. Should he not have added "yet?" . . .

34. Noel Starblanket was the chiefs' spokesman.

XXVII

July – August 1979

At the beginning of July, the leaders of the Western nations were at the Economic Summit meeting in Tokyo, and then the mission had to help with preparations for the Commonwealth heads of government meeting in Lusaka, Zambia, from August 1 to 7. The rest of the Commonwealth remained concerned that the Thatcher government might end economic sanctions against Rhodesia, despite the opposition of the African states, and split the Commonwealth.

Important as these questions were, they receded — in my mind at least — when the first Canadian Institute for Advanced Legal Studies opened at Cambridge. Preparations to set up the institute had begun two years earlier. I had consulted with eminent legal scholars and judges from Canada and Britain and the organizing committee had assembled an impressive roster of speakers and participants from both countries. Establishing this institute, for Canadian judges and lawyers, had been one of my dreams since I assumed the high commissionership.

After the Commonwealth Conference ended, I played host to my new minister, Flora MacDonald, and then it was off to Canada for a holiday. But this sojourn was interrupted by the assassination of Lord Louis Mountbatten.

Monday, July 2, 1979

Important as an agreement on oil importation is, and this was reached in Tokyo,[1] one cannot deny that . . . the Summits of the Western powers . . . should be used more sparingly. Giscard thinks they are a waste of time. . . .

1. At the Economic Summit.

Tuesday, July 3, 1979

The Queen insists on going to Zambia to open the Commonwealth heads of government meeting. This was announced at the Palace yesterday. Mrs. Thatcher, speaking in Australia, had expressed concern over the Queen's safety, in view of recent bombing of Nkomo's guerrillas in Zambia. The Queen will visit Malawi, Tanzania, Botswana, as well as Zambia. These are countries opposed to the Muzorewa administration as presently constituted. I would think that Muzorewa and Nkomo would be unlikely to encourage any threat to the Queen's safety. . . .

Southern African problems will be the most contentious. When Mrs. Thatcher saw Fraser[2] in Canberra, disagreement was expressed over the Zimbabwe-Rhodesia situation. Fraser is solidly behind United States sanctions and is opposed to recognition. . . . Fraser told Mrs. Thatcher under the [new] Rhodesian constitution, real power resides with the whites. He maintains no effective transfer of power has taken place. That is my view. . . .

I presided tonight at the Canada Club dinner to mark Canada Day. . . . I did not intend to mention when I was likely to leave London. I thought, however, I would forewarn the Club, when I said I did not expect to be present for the next meeting. Tom Murray[3] took this as a signal and spoke generously of my time in London and my role as chairman at the Canada Club dinners. I was moved when the large audience stood and, by its applause, seemed to concur in what Tom said. It would be funny if I were still High Commissioner at the next meeting. Hopefully, I will not be. . . .

Wednesday, July 4, 1979

I sent a message to Ottawa late yesterday on the Queen's visit to Lusaka, recalling what Mrs. Thatcher had said in Tokyo about her responsibilities for the Queen's safety. . . . I pointed out to Ottawa that the responsibility is one which Mrs. Thatcher shares with the heads of other Commonwealth governments,

2. Malcolm Fraser, the prime minister of Australia.
3. The honorary secretary of the club.

notably those where the Queen is head of state, as in Canada, Britain, Australia, and New Zealand. . . . She is not a free agent and must act in response to the advice she receives from her constitutional advisers, as I am sure she will. Nevertheless, I am confident that the Queen will not be weak in the matter. She has shown strength on other occasions. She would prefer to face the music rather than to have it said she was afraid to move among her people. . . . The sensible course would be for Prime Minister Clark to tell Mrs. Thatcher how he feels directly on the telephone or, as was done in the abdication, through the High Commissioner.

I have greatly admired how the Queen goes about when she visits her people. When she came to the residence on three occasions since we have been here, she arrived in her own car with a sole inspector. All the impedimenta which follows heads of government in particular countries is not her style. . . .

When Lord Carrington returns to London today, he will be questioned on Mrs. Thatcher's indications that her government would not continue sanctions after November. This is Peter's view but he has been wily enough not to say so. Mrs. Thatcher has spoken out of turn. Peter prefers the effectiveness of quiet diplomacy. Mrs. Thatcher will learn in time that this is the wisest course in foreign policy. . . .

Thursday, July 5, 1979

Earlier, I received a call from Messrs. Hannen and Spowers of Christie's.[4] They came to see me regarding Ken Thomson's call of last Friday. They are undertaking to sell for some fourteen million dollars one of the most valuable libraries of English books, dating way back. It is thought this library might be of interest to Canada or Australia. The Bodleian would only be interested in portions of the library, as they have many other sections of it in individual form. The owners of the library, a foundation or trust, will not sell the library piece-meal. I was shown three heavy volumes containing a list of the books. The list itself is very impressive. . . .

Late in the afternoon . . . I went over some material in preparation for my talk with the Chancellor of the

4. The auction house.

Exchequer.[5] . . . There is no doubt that our intention to have a [Canadian] national economic development conference in the fall gives us the opportunity to confront the very problems facing the Thatcher government—two Conservative governments facing almost identically the same situation: inflation, high unemployment, the need to discover a proper vehicle for dialogue, and to decide who should be participants in the dialogue. It may be that I will be able to get some useful reactions from the Chancellor to pass on to Crosbie and the Prime Minister.

Friday, July 6, 1979

Joe was wise when he said, the other day in Toronto, his decision to move the Canadian Embassy in Israel from Tel Aviv to Jerusalem was a mistake. I had not had a chance to be briefed on all the nuances. It was a mistake of tone. . . . Joe showed a lot of wisdom in the mea culpa. . . .

In my talk with the Chancellor of the Exchequer, we discussed four areas: political management of the United Kingdom economy after June 12th, when he presented his chancy budget; public expenditure reductions; European monetary system; and the Tokyo Summit. . . . The problem of reducing the public's economic expectations had to be faced. In the past, in Britain, attempts to create a public forum wherein consensus on the economy might be developed had failed because, in the main, the unions had dissociated themselves whenever they thought pay restraint was a hidden motive. . . .

Re: public expenditure reductions, a whole range of options are being examined. The aim is to put as much decision-making as possible at the level where cost benefit analysis of economies could really best be made. The Chancellor recalled Shirley Williams' comment when [she was] in the Labour cabinet, that the further away from cabinet these decisions are taken, the better. . . .

The Chancellor thought the Tokyo Summit was useful. It enabled the oil-consuming countries to develop a collective response to OPEC. He noted particularly in Tokyo a sense of

5. Sir Geoffrey Howe

the E.E.C. acting as a community and believed the outcome of the meeting was different as a result. The Chancellor of the Exchequer remarked on the excellence of Prime Minister Clark's performance at Tokyo.

Howe is a clever, conscientious man, who will work hard to manage the United Kingdom economy. His references in our conversation to lessons of past experience suggest a somewhat more pragmatic approach to the economy than the press believes. . . .

Sunday, July 8, 1979

After lunch, John [Rowan] and I were on our way to Cambridge. It was hard to believe that the Institute was on the rails and about to function. Tonight at dinner, the Queen's College dining hall was filled with judges, barristers, and their wives from Canada. I had some difficulty in controlling my emotions. . . .

Monday, July 9, 1979

It was good to wake up in Great Court. An early riser passed by my window happily whistling away. I looked forward to the day. . . . The Canadian Institute of Advanced Legal Studies got off to a good start at 10:15 a.m. Mr. Justice Carruthers,[6] the President of the C.I.A.L.S., opened the session [and] . . . pointed out that the Institute was established for . . . advancement of the administration of justice in Canada to foster, encourage, and promote education in law, in legal science, and in law reform. . . . [He was] kind in references to my part in helping to launch the centre two years ago. . . .

After this, I gave my own speech.

The first meeting of the Canadian Institute for Advanced Legal Studies is the fulfilment of a dream. In my long life, the periods at university and the law schools were perhaps the most satisfying. The time [I] spent at the University of Toronto, Osgoode Hall, Harvard, and Cambridge were happy years. . . . The pace at Cambridge on the Cam was different.

6. Douglas H. Carruthers of the Supreme Court of Ontario.

The sanctity of and reverence for the past was strong and enduring. . . . This ancient university itself, with its great names down through the centuries and historic buildings with all their revealing tradition, was responsible. . . .

Tuesday, July 10, 1979

The dining hall at Queen's was jammed for Denning.[7] He spoke on "Administrative Law and the Misuse of Power." . . . Referring to the loud-speaker, he recalled the speaker who observed "these 'agnostics' are sometimes terrible." Happily, that was not so tonight. . . .

The law was important, but justice is what was sought [said Denning]. . . . Corruption was as bad as mugging and terrorism. It was the duty of the judge to uphold the sanctity of the law, by maintaining respect for the policeman, now condemned so loosely. All, including the press, have a duty to support and defend those who uphold the law. . . . [When he said that] the courts have the duty to rectify trade union abuse . . . I thought Denning was on dangerous ground. . . .

Wednesday, July 11, 1979

I took Judge Allan Hollingsworth and two other participants to see Trinity College, only part of which they had seen at my reception on Monday night. It is interesting to watch the admiration the visitor has for the colleges of this ancient university. . . .

Thursday, July 12, 1979

William Whitelaw mentioned the other day at the [Queen's] Garden Party that, as Home Secretary, he had to give a lead in the matter of what to do about capital punishment. Long ago he was opposed to abolition. Now his views are firm. He is in favour of abolition. In a few days, Parliament will come back to the question. There is little doubt about what public opinion wants. It is in favour of returning to capital punishment. He doubts that a majority of the members, who will vote freely on the matter next week, want to reverse Parliament's earlier decision. . . .

7. Lord Thomas Denning, the master of the rolls.

Friday, July 13, 1979

Late last night, Chief Justice Nemetz[8] called [to say] . . . that Chief Justice Deschênes's[9] Tuesday lecture was reported in the *Globe and Mail* on Wednesday with a false headline. It suggested the Chief Justice of the Supreme Court of Quebec had made a "Separatist" speech. Nemetz says Deschênes is very disturbed over the unfairness of the headline. I was told he hopes to be appointed to the Supreme Court of Canada, presumably in succession to Mr. Justice Pratt,[10] who recently resigned. Nemetz wondered if I would call the Minister of Justice and point out the headline was in no way justified from the text of the speech. . . . I read the speech carefully before retiring last night. There is no justification for referring to it as a "Separatist" lecture. In his lecture, the Chief Justice examined parallels in Quebec and Scotland. Reading what the Earl of Durham had said in 1837-38, one wonders why Durham's recommendations are not used by the "Separatists" more than they are at present. . . .

During the discussion following the lecture, a Winnipeg lawyer said, under international law, other nations would not be allowed to recognize Quebec independence, if Quebec declared it without the consent of the rest of Canada. This, of course, is not correct. The point has nothing to do with the misinterpretation put on Deschênes's words. The question of recognition is a matter for each sovereign nation to decide. . . .

I have just learned that a number of persons, all anti-whalers, four in number, locked themselves in a Canada House office last evening to protest Canada's policy and that of other countries at the current meeting of governments, called to consider methods to preserve the whale species. My assurances a week ago to some of the leaders of the protesting group must not have been as effective as I thought. How the trespassers got into Canada House is not clear. . . .

Saturday, July 14, 1979

I sent a telex to the Prime Minister and External outlining my views on a policy for Canada at the Commonwealth heads of government meeting in Lusaka. . . . Following Lusaka, the

8. Nathan Nemetz of British Columbia.
9. Jules Deschênes of the Court of Appeal in Montreal.
10. Yves Pratt of Quebec.

British will propose to bring Rhodesia to independence on an acceptable international basis and on terms comparable to other Commonwealth countries. This represents a gain for Carrington and the Foreign and Commonwealth Office against hardliners in the Tory party. November is the deadline.[11] If no progress has been made by then, a more simplistic solution may be sought by Mrs. Thatcher. This could have complications for the Commonwealth. Canada should seek to support the moderate trend of policy pursued by Carrington. This should be put forward in terms of viability of the Commonwealth rather than the intricacies of the Rhodesian situation or moral arguments. . . .

The Prime Minister's more simplistic solutions explain conflicting signals on British Rhodesian policy. . . . It is not impossible that unreasoning opposition in Lusaka could encourage [her] hardline attitude. After Lusaka, Peter will have to show progress. In most ways, Carrington's proposals are not basically different from David Owen's. What is different is Peter's more engaging manner and style and [his] resumption of United Kingdom leadership [on the issue]. . . .

Mrs. Thatcher could apply in foreign affairs her style of leading rather than seeking a consensus. She could seek to do what she conceives to be right, rather than what is attainable. She may believe herself especially qualified to interpret what is right, like the Old Testament prophets, to whom she often compared herself in the last election campaign. Any effort by a head of government in Lusaka to moralize or lecture her would produce a negative reaction and encourage her to move unilaterally. That could sabotage the slim chance for an early and peaceful settlement in Rhodesia. . . . Taking off sanctions by the United Kingdom in November would have a persuasive effect on the United States and other countries in the West. If the moderates of British policy, along with moderates in Africa, reach a compromise and can show good results, there may still be a chance to avoid a discouraging trend in Southern Africa. . . .

Sunday, July 15, 1979

Philip Moore . . . wanted my impression of the state of play in Canada since the elections. . . . Philip (and this is the Queen) was not happy with Trudeau's sudden advice on Léger's

11. This was the date set for the renewal of sanctions.

successor. The appointment of Alison as Canadian lady-in-waiting for two Canadian [tours] was undoubtedly prompted by the likelihood of George going to Rideau Hall. . . .[12] In any event, the Palace was not happy when Trudeau took it unawares. He was, of course, within his constitutional right to give as little notice as he wished. At the time, December 7th, 1978, Trudeau had so much on his mind. Trudeau's recommendation for Governor-General not only took the Queen by surprise. It took his own cabinet by surprise.

I suspect, with Trudeau out of the Prime Minister's seat, Philip felt freer. He brought up some of Trudeau's antics—e.g., dancing after the Queen had moved on at a Palace reception. She had read of his sliding down the banister. What worried the Palace were more [of] Trudeau's ambiguities in a speech to Oxford students two years ago. His references to the Crown suggested its existence had little meaning for him. When this interpretation on his words was made by Philip, I told the Queen's secretary not to confuse some of Trudeau's expressed contradictory views. The fact was that he had recently proposed constitutional changes which would have given legislative [meaning to the Queen's position as head of the Canadian state]. . . . [This I confirmed] when she was at 12 Upper Brook over a year ago. No other Canadian Prime Minister had ever gone as far. . . .

Thursday, July 19, 1979

This afternoon [at the Law Institute], Sir Rupert Cross joined Arthur Maloney, Q.C., of Canada and D. A. Thomas, a well-known author on sentencing, and Lord Justice Waller in an exchange on sentencing policy. . . . Lord Waller makes the important point that the prosecution must have nothing to do with sentencing. This always disturbed me when I practised in the criminal courts. The prosecution in the cases of summary conviction clearly had a hand in this. . . .

The first Institute ended its preliminary two-week session with a closing dinner at Queen's College. The Canadians and the Cambridge people were pleased with the results. . . . They had seriously applied themselves to serious study. They were grateful to those who had conceived the idea and were gen-

12. George and Alison Ignatieff

erous in acknowledging wherein lay the birth of the idea. . . . It was in every way a moment of joy. I suppose my part has been fulfilled. The Institute has been launched. . . .

Friday, July 20, 1979

Flora MacDonald has accepted my invitation to attend the last day of the Canadian ballet at Covent Garden. This means a delay of six days in getting to Canada for my holiday. It would be wrong not to be here when the Secretary of State for External Affairs makes her first London visit. I have invited her to stay at the residence. . . .

Saturday, July 21, 1979

Sonny Ramphal came in for a chat before dinner. He will be going to Lusaka for the heads of government meeting. He has had assurances from Nyerere and Kaunda [that] they will work for a negotiated settlement. Sonny is afraid Mrs. Thatcher may not be as subtle as Carrington. My view is that the foreign minister's views will prevail over Mrs. Thatcher's more pragmatic views.

Where will Canada be, asks the Secretary General? I had to say I did not know. . . . Clark cannot be expected to have a full appreciation of African questions. After all, I have been working on these for many years; as a result, I have a "feel" for them. . . . Flora, too, is new. Australia could steal a march over us. Fraser supports the African position. Sonny likes him but would prefer to see Canada giving the lead. We must not make a mistake in Lusaka. We are highly respected as a Western power in Africa. To go against the majority trend and support a possible position of Mrs. Thatcher's would mean the loss of our role in the Commonwealth among African countries. It is my hope that Joe will see what Trudeau would have done. He will be wise to emulate him in this regard. . . . Sonny suggested Clark would profit if I were with him in Lusaka. Probably. This is out of the question. In any event, I have confidence in Joe's good judgment. Sonny wondered if, as a Conservative leader, Clark would have Mrs. Thatcher's instincts and views. . . .

Monday, July 23, 1979

The Indian Deputy High Commissioner called my office to say that . . . his High Commissioner had seen a group of Canadian Indians on July 6th. The appointment had been made on the mistaken assumption that "Canadian Indians" meant Indian Indians living in Canada. The Indian High Commission beat a hasty retreat. . . .

I called on Peter Blaker, one of the Ministers of State at the Foreign Office—a nice chap whom I first met when he was with the British High Commission in Ottawa, and whom I have seen from time to time in London. He had just returned from Geneva where he attended the refugee conference and had lunch on Saturday with Flora MacDonald, our External Affairs Minister. She had spoken well in outlining Canada's commitment to take more refugees from Vietnam. . . . Blaker told me, when Mrs. Thatcher had seen Kosygin* in Moscow on her way to Tokyo, she had not pulled her punches, urging the Soviet Premier to bring pressure on Vietnam against its refugee policy. Kosygin had replied by telling the British Prime Minister it was up to her to tell the Vietnamese what they should do. That was not Russia's responsibility, nor was his country responsible for the expulsion of Vietnamese who have since become the world's most prominent refugees. All the same, Mrs. Thatcher was impressed with Kosygin's forthrightness and disposition to face the issues. In turn he had reported, through his Ambassador in London, that he found the "iron lady" a strong personality. . . .

Wednesday, July 25, 1979

The Reform Club, of which I have been a member for the last four and a half to five years, is a staid Victorian institution of continuing liberal-minded men. It has long ceased to have a role in party politics. Ladies have a limited participation as guests of the Club, in restricted hours, only to receive hospitality. It is, therefore, a matter of the greatest surprise to learn from *Penthouse Magazine* that a young woman in full nudity was at the Reform Club the other day [in] the famous library. . . . She was not bothered with much covering, except for the *Financial Times*. I wonder what Gladstone, Lord Durham, Lord Brougham, John Bright, Cobden, Asquith, Campbell-Bannerman, *et al.*, would say about the lady's visit. They likely would have got quite a kick! What would Cromwell have said? There is a bust of him at the entrance of the main dining room. I never understood why—was Cromwell a liberal with a big or a small "L"? . . .

I was at the House of Commons this afternoon . . . to hear the debate on the [forthcoming] heads of government meeting in Lusaka. . . . Mrs. Thatcher indicated she will attempt to get agreement of the Patriotic Front leaders to her plans for restoring independence to Rhodesia. Showing a change in emphasis, [she] . . . said the government's plans would be submitted to all parties to the conflict. Like her Foreign Minister, she indicated she was anxious to secure agreement of the two Patriotic Front leaders, Nkomo and Mugabe, to British plans. . . . Mindful of the difficulty she got into . . . she would not be drawn on renewal of sanctions in the autumn. "If we are successful, sanctions will fall." . . .

Thursday, July 26, 1979

I had gone to the House of Commons to listen to a debate on the forthcoming Commonwealth Conference.

The Secretary General of the Commonwealth Organization sat next to me as we listened to the debate. We had been trying to get one another on the phone all day. He wanted me to know he had spoken to our Prime Minister, who had called to say the Secretary General could be assured that the Canadian government would not be a necessary captive to Mrs. Thatcher and Peter Carrington at Lusaka. Ramphal thinks Joe was indicating he would pursue a role not dissimilar to that of Fraser of Australia. This point worries me considerably. Canada has in recent years been regarded as the mediating influence in Commonwealth heads of government meetings. This was true in 1964 at the first meeting which dealt with Rhodesia. It would be embarrassing for the Commonwealth and Canada's position in it, if Britain and Canada found themselves at loggerheads on the Rhodesian issue from the rest of the Commonwealth, including Australia. After listening to Mrs. Thatcher yesterday and knowing Peter Carrington's views, I don't think this will happen. . . .

Friday, July 27, 1979

The Deputy Prime Minister of Zimbabwe-Rhodesia, Mundawarara,[13] has been in London this week. . . . [Today] he gave our officers an outline of the background of the new constitution, [and] . . . maintained his country could not afford to tamper with the constitution. To do so would lead to an exodus of whites, who are presently essential to the economy. He said lifting sanctions would be of major importance for economic and psychological reasons. Those who were fighting against Zimbabwe-Rhodesia were encouraged by every announcement of the continuation of sanctions. Mundawarara directed attention to statements of the Patriotic Front leaders that they were not interested in further consultations. "Muzorewa could do nothing more except surrender." In these circumstances, the continued witholding of recognition and continuation of sanctions by responsible democratic countries would be surprising. He hoped Prime Minister Clark would say this at the Lusaka meeting. Many of the African countries are now waiting to see how more influential countries like Canada, the United Kingdom and United States were going to move before reaching a decision. Even the United Kingdom, he said, would be influenced by the views of others. Someone had to move first. He hoped Canada would show the lead. . . .

The Lord Chief Justice and Mrs. Widgery gave a dinner tonight at Lincoln's Inn . . . [which] was so peaceful this summer night. Among the guests was my former foreign minister friend, the Chief Justice of the Supreme Court of Australia, Garfield Barwick. I had not seen him since 1964. At the United Nations, we both confronted Alec Home, then Britain's foreign minister over Rhodesia. Alec, for whom I have unbounded admiration, was not flexible enough on the question. Much of the present difficulty might have been avoided if a more passionate interest had been taken in the blacks. This criticism, only to a lesser extent, applies to Harold Wilson later. . . .

13. Dr Silas Mundawarara

Sunday, July 29, 1979

I cannot imagine that an all-party conference [on Rhodesia] will not take place some time after Lusaka. . . . Recently, Mugabe said he was not against talks but he wanted to know the agenda. Muzorewa, a reasonable man, will not resist talks. It is not in the cards that a Commonwealth policy will come from the heads of government meeting but the common position will have an exemplary consequence. . . .

Monday, July 30, 1979

Last night I read more of William Shawcross,[14] who writes that Kissinger took a tougher line over Indo-China than did the Secretary of Defence, [Melvin] Laird. He says, in the late sixties, Robert McNamara became disillusioned with the Vietnam War. My recollection of McNamara, when I met him with Rusk at the State Department in 1963, was not that of a disillusioned man. My colleagues and I queried the Vietnam War. McNamara wasn't too pleased with my attitude. "When will the war end?" I asked. His reply was, "if necessary, in a thousand years." . . .

The stage is all set in Lusaka. The front-line states' presidents and the Patriotic Front guerrilla leaders will hold a meeting today. It is presumed they will draw up a common strategy for the Commonwealth Conference. Lord Carrington will play a leading role in directing the timing of British announcements on policy. What I have known for some time is now out. Malcolm Fraser, Australia's Prime Minister, has taken over "Canada's traditional role of honest broker on the Rhodesian issue." This won't sound good back home. When I sent a message to Ottawa ten days ago, I envisaged this and made the message so complete as to suggest that there was a role for us to play. . . .

Tuesday, July 31, 1979

Gerry Regan, the Nova Scotia former Premier and now Leader of the Opposition in the Legislature in Nova Scotia, called on me early this morning. . . . He is biding his time. I think he

14. William Shawcross, *Sideshow: Kissinger, Nixon and the Destruction of Cambodia* (New York 1979).

hoped Trudeau would invite him to join the federal cabinet before the last elections and after his own provincial defeat. What Trudeau will do is not clear in anyone's mind. I told Gerry that it was Bud Estey's view that Trudeau would have to go after the Quebec referendum, because he had no support in Western Canada. Estey, of course, is a strong supporter of John Turner. I told Bud, after King's defeat the same was said; "King must go." Later in the elections of 1935, the Liberal chant was "King or chaos." . . .

Wednesday, August 1, 1979

The Commonwealth heads of government meeting, so much on my mind during the past few months, opens today. . . . On the eve of the Conference, the Nigerian dictatorship has announced British Petroleum oil interests in Nigeria have been nationalized. . . . The action is directed at Mrs. Thatcher with the warning that recognition of Muzorewa could have serious economic repercussions, stimulating like action in other countries. This was what many of us had in mind when, shortly after Mrs. Thatcher's election, we reminded Carrington and the Foreign Office of the state of Commonwealth feeling. . . .

Thursday, August 2, 1979

Peter Carrington showed his mettle in Lusaka yesterday. He told the Nigerian Minister for External Affairs that his country's take-over of B.P. would have a serious effect on Anglo-Nigerian relations. He added that nothing was more likely to be counter-productive. . . .

Kaunda made an odd speech and one not too helpful. He said Africa supports the Patriotic Front. Behind him sat Joshua Nkomo, not far away from Mrs. Thatcher. There was no approach by either. Nkomo had previously turned down an invitation to meet the Queen. He did not like having been called a terrorist by Mrs. Thatcher. She said Britain had pledged to exercise its constitutional responsibility on Rhodesia. Her government was dedicated to "genuine black majority rule . . . on a basis which the Commonwealth and the international community will find acceptable, and which offers peace for the people of Rhodesia and her neighbours." . . .

Carrington, I suspect, will see Nkomo. Some Presidents and Prime Ministers are hopeful that a consensus will emerge. I think the majority of African states will give way somewhat. . . .

I have been thinking about Rhodesia a great deal, almost daily for the last two years. Rhodesia is a symptom of understandably sick Southern Africa. A satisfactory solution to this problem will go a long way to settling others. That is why so much attention is being paid to it and a constructive solution of it. . . .

I called on the Apostolic Delegate at his residence late this afternoon. I was curious about certain aspects of the Pope's visit to Ireland. When I called on Peter Blaker, the Minister of State at the Foreign Office [last month], two or three days after the news of the visit had been announced, I was told the Foreign Office had been taken by surprise. The Delegate, my friend Bruno Heim, had had no previous intimation. The news apparently emanated from New York, likely the United Nations. . . . Bruno, a Swiss, smilingly assured me the Italians were not masters of protocol, but their ceremonials generally turned out well in the end. . . .

Bruno said the visit would not include Armagh in the North, the seat of the Primate of all Ireland. He telephoned the Secretary of State at the Vatican, to complain he should have been advised of the visit before the news media. . . . Bruno said [Jack] Lynch, Ireland's Prime Minister, had known only a half hour before the world had been told. . . .

Saturday, August 4, 1979

Yesterday, the British Prime Minister and President Nyerere were able to change the climate of the meeting [in Lusaka]. The British put forward four basic propositions: Only Britain has the constitutional responsibility to grant legal independence. The aim must be to give independence on the basis of a constitution comparable to other countries. Proposals will be given to the parties. They will be called on to cease hostilities and proceed to a settlement. The British government is wholly committed to genuine black rule. . . .

Nyerere was more moderate than . . . [previously]. In Lusaka, he did not refer to the Patriotic Front "as the sole legitimate representative of the people of Zimbabwe-Rhodesia." . . .

Sunday, August 5, 1979

When I was in Hatchard's yesterday morning, my eye spied Evelyn Waugh's diary. . . .[15] I asked the knowledgeable and agreeably fattish woman, who dominates the first stall, as it were, "Why Waugh?" She looked at me in momentary reaction. Quickly, she recovered. "Yes, why Waugh? Why Waugh?" she repeated. As I closed the door on leaving, "Why Waugh?" she continued and burst into a hearty laugh. We both feel the same about Evelyn. . . .

The second day of the debate on Muzorewa's government will be tomorrow. . . . Mrs. Thatcher captured support and attention when she emphasized: "There could be no legal recognition, if the Commonwealth was opposed." What an achievement these words signify for the Foreign Secretary, Peter Carrington! Early in the piece, I told him in the presence of the committee of High Commissioners . . . [that Conservative] party problems were understandable. What was at stake was the Commonwealth. Every country but Britain wanted to effect a real transfer of power in Rhodesia. It could be Britain against the Commonwealth. Peter at that point looked at me knowingly. And so the guiding hand in Lusaka, when Mrs. Thatcher spoke, was Peter's. He has shown great skill. . . .

Monday, August 6, 1979

Today's big news is from Lusaka. As a result of weekend talks . . . [the Commonwealth leaders] agreed on a new British initiative for an all-party Rhodesian constitutional conference. It was Mrs. Thatcher's Friday speech that did the trick. The agility of Peter Carrington was ever-present. The British Prime Minister and her Foreign Secretary will submit the constitutional proposals at a cabinet meeting in London on Friday. The agreement last night was endorsed at a special session of thirty-nine full members of the Commonwealth. The propos-

15. Evelyn Waugh, *The Diaries of Evelyn Waugh*, ed. M. Davie (London 1979).

als will be put to all parties, following new elections, to be supervised under the authority of the British government and with Commonwealth observers. It is clear that Julius Nyerere was a force behind the British plan. . . .

I was met tonight at the Royal Opera House, Covent Garden for the gala performance of the National Ballet of Canada by Sir Claus and Lady Moser. . . .[16] We were presented to Princess Margaret [and proceeded into our box with her]. . . .

After the first act, at Princess Margaret's suggestion, . . . I took a second row seat, so that she could have with her two unknown persons. Only Princess Margaret could have been so lacking in diplomacy. It didn't really matter to me. I am sure Mr. Reginald Samples, President of the ballet, must have wondered. Princess Margaret is . . . certainly the most irregular of the royals, so unlike her mother and sister, the Queen. No wonder her rating is so low with the British public and, I suspect, the public elsewhere. That she is interested in the ballet and knowledgeable too goes without saying, but one thing she does not have is an understanding of her fellow human beings, as does her mother. She is fat and ever-smoking, with a deep cough and a general bearing not usual in a royal personage. Between the two acts, we had dinner for those in the Royal Box. The two unidentified persons, one of them a designer, dined at a table of their own. . . .

Tuesday, August 7, 1979

I went to Heathrow this morning to meet Premier Lougheed of Alberta and drove him to his hotel, where he joined his wife, a member of the National Ballet of Canada board, whom I had seen at the Gala opening last night. . . .

Lougheed thinks Trudeau will give up the leadership of the party after the referendum. If Trudeau were to hold on, he might find opposition in Western Canada overwhelming. Mackenzie King, leader and Prime Minister for many years, had pockets of continuous opposition as well. He defied such opposition. Could Trudeau not do likewise? . . .

16. Sir Claus Moser was the chairman of the board.

Thursday, August 9, 1979

Mrs. Thatcher arrived home last night after her triumph in Lusaka, which today's *Telegraph* attributes to Peter Carrington and rightly so. . . .

Mugabe and Nkomo have taken a hard line. Nyerere and Kaunda, I am told, are unhappy with the guerrilla leaders' reactions, ignoring the high cost of the war. Mugabe wants the disbandment of the Zimbabwe-Rhodesia Army, to be replaced by the guerrilla forces as a pre-condition for the acceptance of new elections. This may be more crucial than agreement on a new constitution. . . .

Allan Gotlieb, the Under-Secretary of State in External Affairs, telephoned from Dar-es-Salaam. . . . He reports my pre-estimates of Carrington were accurate. The foreign minister distinguished himself by his work at the heads of government meeting. [Gotlieb] is anxious that I should emphasize to the Secretary of State for External Affairs some of the points I recently outlined to the Under-Secretary . . . for attention in the department. He thinks that, coming from me, a common objective for desirable administrative policies might help. Clark apparently did well at the Conference and he finds the Secretary of State for External Affairs interested and full of initiative; an acquisition to External Affairs, he assured me. . . .

Jeanne and Maurice Sauvé were in to see me this morning at my office in Canada House.[17] . . . We discussed the reasons for the Liberal débâcle in the last elections a few weeks ago, noting, however, the good run Trudeau had as Prime Minister. One of the reasons for leadership weakness in Trudeau's case was that he was not fully dedicated to the long-time traditions of the Liberal party in Canada. Only recently, it was suggested, he had begun to speak of Laurier. As a matter of fact, this is my complaint with the modern Liberal party in our country. It has not only forgotten its traditional role, but its heroes. . . . Jeanne is not sure whether she will like opposition or not. . . .

I was amused today to receive [a] . . . letter from the private secretary to Princess Margaret, Countess of Snowdon.

17. Jeanne had retained her seat, Ahuntsic, in the recent elections and was still sitting as a Liberal in the Canadian House of Commons.

Usually, letters of this kind are sent much later after the event. I think I know why the Princess had the letter of thanks written to me forthwith. . . . It amused me to have her say how pleased she was to see me again. I was likewise amused when it was noted "the Princess found many old friends at the reception in the Crush Bar." . . .

Friday, August 10, 1979

I went to the airport early this morning to greet Flora MacDonald, the new Secretary of State for External Affairs, on her way home from Lusaka. . . . She is as enthusiastic about Carrington as I am. Moreover, she is under the spell of Britain's Prime Minister, Mrs. Thatcher. . . .

Flora came to Macdonald House at 3:00 p.m. to meet my officers and staff. . . . Flora has a friendly manner [and] her lucid explanations of policy were well done. With her pleasing personality, she will emerge as a good Canadian foreign minister. Laughingly, I told her of the standard which prevailed between 1963 and 1968. She acknowledged she had read my speeches. I enjoyed that retort.

Later, her strengths were revealed again at a press conference with Canadian and foreign correspondents in my office at Canada House. She spoke highly of the contribution of Mrs. Thatcher at Lusaka. Canada was prepared to help in an observer role, in supervision of the proposed new elections in Rhodesia. A re-examination of foreign policy in Canada is under way. I reminded Flora of the limitations in foreign policy change. Trudeau and Sharp had found that to be true. I agreed it was useful from time to time to examine the postulates of foreign policy. . . .

Saturday, August 11, 1979

The cabinet approved Mrs. Thatcher's policy at Lusaka yesterday. Plans are under way for a conference in London in September. Carrington will preside. Copies of a draft constitution will be circulated. It will follow the pattern of instruments approved for former colonies on reaching independence. Will Smith attend the Conference? I suspect he will be invited. . . .

I did a little quiet work this afternoon and had a reception for Flora and the ballet people, following which I took her to the last performance of the ballet at Covent Garden. . . . The presence of the Secretary of State for External Affairs was the evening's extra highlight. She radiates charm and inspires loyalty. . . .

It has been a long week for me — five ballets, the visit of the Secretary of State for External Affairs, and much work at the office. Now to bed. Tomorrow to Nell, Windsor, and later, Paul and his family on Lac Laurent.

Sunday, August 12, 1979

I am pleased to see that the Secretary of State for External Affairs is department-oriented. Jamieson did not spend enough time in the department. He did not know his people as I did and as Flora will. Don was a good foreign minister, who surprisingly had a liking for David Owen. Flora has much admiration for Larry Smith, one of my top favourites in External. I hope she will be comfortable with Allan Gotlieb. He is purposeful and able. I emphasized his qualities to her. . . .

The press foreshadows my departure from London in October, mentioning I am on leave in Canada. My successors are speculated on. Mentioned are John Robarts, Basil Robinson, and George Hees. Flora was not certain who it will be. Joe is the boss. . . .

Wednesday, August 15, 1979

I had been in Windsor for two days.

Isabelle and Ramona Quenneville called on us last night. These two friends are politically conscious and active. They were part of my Essex East team. The former joined my staff in External. . . . For the past few years, she has been deputy director in the federal Liberal organization in Ontario. . . .

She says there is a strong desire for new federal leadership. John Turner is in the wings. Donald Macdonald is a good man, but is that a valid reason for wanting the job? John does not have it all his own way. Trudeau's immediate problem is the strong feeling in English Canada that he should go. Moreover, there will be an accountability meeting within the year. My present view is that, if Trudeau wants to stay on, he should be permitted to do so. To force him out would not sit well in Quebec, where the basic Liberal party support resides. . . .

Thursday, August 16, 1979

Word has just come of the passing of John Diefenbaker. The CBC television gave me the news by telephone. John had a long and vigorous career. Most of our political lives were in Parliament together. . . . The battles are but a memory. What we had in common is more lasting and memorable. . . .

Monday, August 20, 1979

Nell drove me to the Windsor airport. . . . The next stop for all of us was Bagotville, some sixty miles from St. Simeon, close to our camp, or I should say the Canada Steamship Lines camp [where I was to spend time with my son, Paul]. . . .

Thursday, August 23, 1979

During our fishing on Calabash Lake last night, Paul and I discussed his future. We have known for some time that he had the political bug. Fortunately, he had other interests. He is certainly one of the ablest of Canada's younger businessmen. . . . I have discouraged him from entering Parliament whenever he raised the issue, and primarily for economic reasons. I would say to him, wait until you have made your mark in business. . . . Then, they will hand you the top assignment. The course I followed was otherwise. I went into politics early, sitting in the back benches ten years before King beckoned to join his cabinet. Paul took my advice. Last night, he wondered if he had been wise. Now he thinks he should have run in the last election. In any event, it would be fun to be in opposition. Sometimes a reputation is made on its benches.

It is not impossible that Paul might seek a seat in the next election. If Trudeau decided not to run again in Mount Royal, Paul would like that seat. One problem, at least, presents itself. Among party leaders, that constituency had been reserved for Liberals from the Jewish community. Pearson had intervened in Trudeau's case, because he wanted him in the Cabinet along with Marchand and Pelletier. Lazarus Phillips[18] told Paul it would be difficult to break the Jewish preference arrangement again in Mount Royal. If there was agreement for a second exception, Laz, in view of our close friendship, would help Paul, if he were interested. All this speculation shows how Paul's thinking runs these days. . . .

Who knows what lies ahead? . . . There is, of course, John Turner. Who can tell? . . . I will hereafter try and be less of an obstacle if he points to political life.

He eloquently explained that, "if at the end he had not done something to help his fellow men, let us assume in the underdeveloped world, he would be unhappy." . . .

Sunday, August 26, 1979

I closed Rowse's chapter on "Words and Music"[19] before any sign of human life joined me this morning. As I had noted, drama had an unique place in the Age of Elizabeth. It is an art form involved in "poetry, the dance, drama, and music." . . . The Elizabethans did not reach a pinnacle in painting, . . . though Henry VIII was "the first effective collector among our monarchs," [and] the vogue for collecting began in Elizabeth's reign. The present Elizabeth is a great collector as well. Has there ever been a monarch more often painted? One night when Nell and I stayed at the Castle, I was amused, as the Queen was showing us through Windsor early in the midnight hours, to observe Edinburgh in a dispute with the Queen over the location of one of Holbein's paintings. . . .

Monday, August 27, 1979

We lunched again today on the flat rocks by the falls at the head of Le Petit Saguenay. On our way, we were shocked to learn of the death of Lord Mountbatten. Apparently, a ship carrying him from Northern Ireland was blown up. Two groups of terrorists claim responsibility. . . . When I intro-

18. A prominent Montreal Liberal and senator.
19. A. L. Rowse, *Shakespeare, the Elizabethan* (London 1977).

duced Mountbatten last year at the Canada Club, I referred to him as the most gallant of living Englishmen. A month ago, he told me at the Queen's Garden Party that the Prince of Wales would prove a good President of the Atlantic College. . . .

As a result of Lord Mountbatten's assassination, our holiday had to be cut short. I went to Ottawa to catch a government plane which was carrying a delegation to his funeral.

XXVIII

September – October 1979

*O*N A SCALE OF WORLD EVENTS, *my departure from my London assignment would rank very low. But to me, after almost five years on the job, saying goodbye was a hard task. And along with the difficult farewell speeches, parties, and calls was a taxing period of work. The question which absorbed the bulk of my efforts throughout September was the conference called in London to resolve the Rhodesian dispute. Finally, in mid-October, I won what had become a personal crusade—Air Canada was to remain at Heathrow. At the end of that month, I left for home.*

Monday, September 3, 1979

We disembarked at Heathrow after 9:00 a.m. . . . We were met by representatives of the Queen and the Foreign Office. This, of course, was for the two ex-Governors-General.[1] We discussed how unusual it was for ex-Governors-General to be used in the present arrangement. We were agreed that a Governor-General has no continuing function after he has left the office. Neither has a minister of the Crown. . . . There is no problem in using ex-Governors-General for representational purposes but better that be done by a Governor-General in office. Schreyer wanted to come but his engagements at the Citadel in Quebec stood in the way. I suspect that two ex-Governors-General, roaming about without official responsibilities, are apt to present some problems if the practice of keeping them on the high altar is extended. . . .

1. Jules Léger and Roland Michener were to lead the Canadian delegation to Lord Mountbatten's funeral.

Thursday, September 6, 1979

No nation organizes its great state occasions more efficiently than Britain. This was demonstrated yesterday at the memorable service for one of its greatest sons. Thousands of people lined the streets. Some waited all night on the pavements to see plumed helmets and veterans' medals glitter as the funeral procession moved to muffled drum beats.

Sitting directly in front of me was the Ambassador for Ireland, who played host to his Prime Minister, [Jack] Lynch. After the ceremony, the latter and Mrs. Thatcher had a five-hour session of inconclusive talk on what to do about the situation in Eire and Ulster. . . .

I hope that Harold Macmillan is not too tired this morning after the long ceremony yesterday.[2] I noticed that when we were leaving Westminster Abbey, he had to be seated. Ted Heath solicitiously looked after him. Harold Wilson said to me, "I don't have to worry about my car, because we live so close by." . . .

Friday, September 7, 1979

It occurred to me this morning that the death of Lord Mountbatten marks the close of Britain's Empire history. He was perhaps the greatest of Britain's pro consuls. Although christened in the arms of the Empress Victoria of India, Lord Mountbatten was a twentieth-century man. Earlier than Churchill, he realized that the survival of the British Empire depended on a successful transformation of it into a partnership of independent sovereign nations. . . .

One of the frustrating problems in a mission like mine is arranging who should be invited to dinners and luncheons in honour of Canadian ministers. Who would they like as guests? A minister on official business is entertained as a rule by his opposite number. I try and reciprocate by having that minister in the United Kingdom to a function at the residence. Oftentimes, the Canadian minister suggests friends, who may or may not fit in with guests from the British government. They would like to discuss matters of concern to their governments

2. He was eighty-five years old.

or to both. A mixed list becomes a problem. Sometimes names are suggested to Ottawa. A busy or disinterested minister may leave the Ottawa decision to his young executive assistant, often inexperienced, with the result that the Ottawa reaction becomes impossible or inappropriate. Oftentimes there is no response from Ottawa at all. . . .

I called on Nicholas Ridley, one of the Ministers of State at the Foreign Office. Under Peter, he is responsible for the Americas, North, South and Central, including the Carribbean. . . . Ridley told us of his visit to the English colony on the Falkland Islands and Argentinian pretensions regarding them. . . . We will be kept advised. . . .

Monday, September 10, 1979

Premier Blakeney of Saskatchewan was in to see me at Macdonald House this morning. I gave him a short briefing on the British political scene. . . . I pointed out to Blakeney there was no doubt Mrs. Thatcher's victory last May was a convincing one. Her government is proceeding with the implementation of a comprehensive and quite radical programme to stimulate economic recovery on free-enterprise principles. I indicated this programme may create social and economic difficulties before results are apparent. . . .

The Labour party is in a painful period of re-appraisal. Callaghan is defending a party structure which could probably use a shake-up from an onslaught of . . . reforms. . . . The party is in ideological ferment. Tony Benn and the left wing are anxious to convert the party into a more radical socialist direction. The object will not succeed. . . .

I explained to Blakeney [that] there have been changes in the tone of British foreign policy since Mrs. Thatcher came into office. I don't see much basic change in direction. There will be less reliance on open United States collaboration. Britain will try to be her "own man," as both Maggie and Peter show. The Tories are more committed to a strong defence posture against the European East than was Labour. Defence expenditures are to be increased. Other items are to be pared. . . .

We had a briefing at 5:00 o'clock today from Sir Antony Duff on behalf of the Secretary of State for Foreign Affairs on the first day of the conference on Rhodesia.[3] Duff referred to it as the Rhodesian Constitutional Conference. . . . Carrington, as chairman, proposed he should make the opening statement, then call for an adjournment to give the other participants an opportunity tomorrow to make their opening statements. In this way, Carrington's appeal for a positive approach stood in stronger perspective and by itself. Some objection was registered at the opening of the conference to the seating arrangements. The Patriotic Front objected to gazing at "those criminals sitting right in front of them."[4] It would be preferable to have them placed facing Lord Carrington, who showed firmness when he refused to change the seating arrangements. The result was that Nkomo and Mugabe faced the Muzorewa front row. It included Ian Smith.

Duff said the Foreign Secretary made it clear he was unlikely to be swayed by the Patriotic Front to extend priority to military issues. The conference was a constitutional one, its purpose to decide the basis for the granting of legal independence to Rhodesia. The mere act of having the conference was important in itself. . . . No party, Carrington said, could benefit from failure to reach agreement. "The people in this room have power to end the war." . . .

After the briefing conference, we joined Carrington and other ambassadors at a reception given by the Foreign Secretary. Peter told me how disappointed he was that the Patriotic Front leaders, Nkomo and Mugabe, had written to him in the morning saying they did not intend to attend his reception, because of the presence of their enemies, Bishop Muzorewa and the other members of the Salisbury government. They said they couldn't distinguish the colour of the tea from the blood of the women and children which the puppet régime of Smith and Muzorewa is shedding. I presume that Mugabe and Nkomo did not want to have relayed back pictures of their association with Muzorewa *et al.* when fighting is still under way. . . .

3. This conference, at Lancaster House, was the result of the agreement by the Commonwealth heads of government at Lusaka.
4. This was the delegation led by Abel Muzorewa.

Tuesday, September 11, 1979

Among my callers this morning were Senator and Mrs. Keith Davey. I have not seen them for five years. My last conversation with him was when I left the Trudeau administration in the fall of 1974, prior to my coming to London. Keith had exercised undue power over Trudeau in the formation of his government at that time, and subsequently. His role was organizer of the party. He went beyond that role, with Trudeau's approval apparently, exercising a control which should be reserved for the leader and Prime Minister. Keith may be a good political organizer but knows little about government and parliamentary institutions. I suspect some of Trudeau's troubles arise from this fact. His writ ran beyond his competence. . . .

Wednesday, September 12, 1979

The second meeting of the Rhodesian Conference was not as difficult as one might have assumed. Nkomo said Lord Carrington was avoiding the real issues [but] Nkomo was not particularly specific. . . . Nkomo called the Constitutional Conference a "Peace Conference." Among the essential questions put to Carrington by Nkomo were: Whose army was to defend Zimbabwe and its people? Whose administration and judiciary shall serve the people of Zimbabwe? Who, apart from the British supervisory and Commonwealth observers, would administer fresh elections? The generality of these interrogations suggest that Nkomo was anxious to avoid a head-on confrontation. . . .

Thursday, September 13, 1979

Christian Hardy called last night to say he had learned that an announcement would be made tomorrow of the appointment of my successor, George Hees, a member of the House of Commons for some years and former Minister of Trade and Commerce in the Diefenbaker government. George will make a fine High Commissioner. His experience in trade matters will be of special value. Mibs, his wife, as Nell said this morning, will be helpful to him. I suspect one of the reasons for George's appointment is that it will open a safe seat for Clark and enable him to put Robert de Cotret . . . in the House of Commons rather than in the Senate. I had expected that John Robarts would have succeeded me, but the political requirement of finding a seat in the Commons likely proved a more important consideration to Joe. . . .

Friday, September 14, 1979

Under the constitution proposed by Britain for Rhodesia, there would be white MPs, but their power of veto would be eliminated. The Patriotic Front gave Carrington notice it would present its own constitutional proposals, perhaps this afternoon. Ian Smith is not likely to support some British proposals. He expressed his views at a meeting called by Bishop Muzorewa of the Zimbabwe-Rhodesian government delegation. In Nkomo's proposals, Zimbabwe, without the addition of Rhodesia, would be the given name [of the country]. He would provide a bill of rights with a limited period of five to ten years for white membership in Parliament. Muzorewa said he might leave the conference after the constitution had been agreed to. . . .

Monday, September 17, 1979

Ian Smith was very unhappy with Muzorewa's broadcast to Salisbury over the weekend. Smith says safeguards to protect the minority whites are essential. There is a suggestion that Smith might leave the delegation. This I doubt. In any event, if he did, it would not be fatal. The Patriotic Front is opposed to special privileges for the whites. I agree the whites must not be given a veto.

The real difficulty may arise if and when the conference at Lancaster House discusses transitional arrangements before independence. . . . Nkomo indicated the Patriotic Front will not insist on guerrilla forces in control during the transition. He would prefer a neutral body, such as the United Nations. Muzorewa has repeated his strong reservations about agreeing even to interim arrangements which, he says, are non-starters. Some of this manoeuvring may be tactical. . . .

Tuesday, September 18, 1979

Carrington is running into heavy weather at the Rhodesian Constitutional Conference. Muzorewa wants separate discussions at the bilateral level. . . . The Bishop is taking the position that he came to London to reach an agreement on a constitution. He does not want to discuss new elections and is disturbed by the Patriotic Front's private negotiations on their version of a constitution. This means separate talks. . . . Is there some pressure which could be exerted by some of the Commonwealth countries? Not many are prepared to give primary support to Muzorewa. I don't know of any useful move I could make at the moment. . . .

Wednesday, September 19, 1979

Ian Smith called on Lord Carrington last Friday along with several members of the Salisbury delegation. . . . The Foreign Secretary must have told him that there could be no blocking mechanism [for the white minority] in the new constitution. . . . This does not mean that Carrington did not feel that some safeguards for minority representation should be provided. But these could not be of a dimension to interfere with legislation or constitutional amendments. I understand that Carrington told Smith the British government would provide that minority representation and a bill of rights must not be amended for a set period. That, it seems to me, was a dangerous concession. . . . Carrington recognizes that it would be difficult for the régime in Salisbury to wait until November for sanctions to be withdrawn or fall. Salisbury would make a mistake in thinking that sanctions would necessarily fade away in November. I understand that Smith said that this was news to him. He has been told the situation many times. It could be that Carrington and Mrs. Thatcher might prefer not to try to renew Section II of the Southern Rhodesia Act [providing for sanctions] before November 15th, in this way avoiding a split in the Conservative party and a possible rejection of parliamentary sanctions renewal. . . .

Thursday, September 20, 1979

I called for John Crosbie, the Minister of Finance, at noon at the Savoy. Later we attended a luncheon [with Sir Geoffrey Howe] at No. 11 Downing Street . . . [where] the emphasis was on the domestic economy. Crosbie wanted a chance to learn about new policy directions in the United Kingdom and to meet some senior Treasury economic advisers. He had no particular subjects to raise himself. Before our engagement, I . . . emphasized [that] the new Treasury team is monetarist in philosophy — that is, disinclined to attempt to tune the economy through the manipulation of public expenditure and the ensuring of significant government deficits. The Treasury people are likely more doctrinaire than the new Canadian government. . . .

Friday, September 21, 1979

I sent a message to Ottawa last night expressing optimism for a Muzorewa-British agreement on a new constitution for the independence of Zimbabwe. Ian Smith has taken a more conciliatory line, recognizing that what the British offer in the proposal for twenty white MPs is the best he can get. Rhodesia's foreign minister, Mr. David Makome, promised a major announcement — the Muzorewa government will accept the British proposals for a new constitution. This will mean new elections. . . . Yesterday, Robert Mugabe criticized the proposals to give the whites special seats when they represented only three per cent of Zimbabwe's population. The Patriotic Front will now have to get down to hard negotiations. . . .

Sunday, September 23, 1979

Muzorewa is not going to Rhodesia [as he had planned]. This gives some ground for optimism at the conference in Lancaster House. The Patriotic Front will likely want to begin discussions early on the thorny issue of the transitional period before independence. They may ask to postpone discussions on the new constitution. Nkomo and Mugabe take the view that the Bishop's acceptance of the constitution means his delegation has been absorbed and that Muzorewa's objections to discussions on the transition are no longer relevant. The British will not agree. . . .

Thursday, September 27, 1979

With Premier Davis, I called on . . . the Leader of the House of Lords, Lord Christopher Soames, in the Old Admiralty Building. I had told the Premier he could expect to meet a strong, dynamic personality in the person of Churchill's son-in-law.[5] He was not disappointed. . . . Soames acknowledged the objective of the Thatcher government was to ordain the free enterprise system in Britain. The task was difficult. If successful, he argued the ramifications would be world-wide. . . . He did not think Europe would become a federation or a confederation. The form of union was not as important as to articulate a strong Europe. On this, he thought the Secretary of State, Peter Carrington, was not strong. . . . Soames seemed to be impatient with the African problem. Europe was so much more important.

I had the suspicion that Christopher, with his experience in government, diplomacy as Ambassador in France, and his Commissionership in the E.E.C., hankered to be Foreign Secretary, not out of sheer ambition, but in fulfilment of his training and capacity. . . .

Davis spoke of the desirability in Canada of upholding the present basic constitutional arrangement. It would be a mistake to weaken Canada at the centre. This may not be acceptable at the moment, but this view will be upheld in the future. He was not too happy with the federal government's announcement of giving the provinces ownership of the resources of the sea. One detects an understandable envy by the premier of a land-locked province in this further concession to the provinces. . . .

Saturday, September 29, 1979

I did not know that the secretary of the cabinet, e.g., Sir John Hunt, does not participate in cabinet discussions. He is present but is not expected to make comments, nor are ministers encouraged to look to him to solve their problems in the cabinet room. The secretary of the cabinet in Canada does not participate in the full sense. He briefs the Prime Minister before cabinet meetings, often responds to his queries at cabinet. I myself have often gone to Gordon Robertson as clerk of the Privy Council or Michael Pitfield and asked questions. It is only to this extent in our system that there can be said to be participation. The relationship, however, in

5. Soames was married to Winston Churchill's daughter, Mary.

Canada between the Prime Minister and the clerk of the Privy Council is one of great intimacy, almost to the point of political involvement. I don't see how it can be otherwise. . . .

Sunday, September 30, 1979

Only the Rev. Mr. Paisley seemed out of tune with the Pope after his first triumphant day in Ireland. In Drogheda, he said, "On my knees I beg you to turn away from the paths of violence and return to the ways of peace." . . .

Monday, October 1, 1979

At the Chinese Embassy . . . Ross Stainton, president of British Airways, wondered when I was returning to Canada. I told him I did not intend to leave until I had got a satisfactory reply from the British government on the Heathrow-Gatwick matter. This was an inaccurate statement. I thought it wasn't a bad idea, however, to let the British know that they could not hope to get out of the Heathrow dilemma by having me quietly depart. I suspect they think that my thunder and lightning will be more difficult to resist than that of a new man. . . .

Tuesday, October 2, 1979

At our briefing before dinner at Marlborough House tonight, we were given a blow-by-blow account of the [Zimbabwe-Rhodesian Conference] proceedings of the last four days. I fully expected that someone would raise at the beginning the massive attacks by Salisbury on Mozambique. Negotiations to end war are generally unaccompanied by war itself. The attack made at the end of last week on Mugabe's guerrillas in Mozambique does not seem to have stopped the negotiations. . . . I learned, however, that very strong pressure by Nyerere, Kaunda, and Mozambique had been exercised on Mugabe and Nkomo to continue the negotiations—in itself a good sign. . . .

Wednesday, October 3, 1979

The Provisional I.R.A. in Ulster replied coldly to the Pope's plea for an end to terrorism. The church leaders and the politicians, it was said, were "bankrupt in the lack of solutions to the present social and economic problems suffered by our own people and created by British interference." . . .

Thursday, October 4, 1979

A Canadian will become Lord Mayor of London in a few weeks. The Lord Mayor's show is an annual spectacular event. To give effect to the Canadian aspect of the procession, I am asked to arrange for the use of Her Majesty's two Canadian horses, Burmese and Centennial, by members of the Royal Canadian Mounted Police. . . . The second request I will make, and both are addressed to Lieutenant-Colonel Sir John Millar at the Royal Mews, Buckingham Palace, is to help us find where an Alberta "chuckwagon" may be located. . . .

Friday, October 5, 1979

By-elections have been called in Ottawa in the ridings formerly represented by John Diefenbaker and Don Jamieson. No vacancy was created in George Hees' riding. This means George is not going to be High Commissioner and my successor. . . .

The Prime Minister called from Ottawa in mid-afternoon. He has picked my replacement. Jean Wadds . . . will come here. Was there not another woman High Commissioner? He knew of the Zambian High Commissioner. I have known Jean for many years. Earl Rowe's daughter,[6] she married his friend Clare Casselman, the long-time Conservative whip in our House of Commons. After "Cass" passed away, she married a Mr. Wadds.[7] . . . The Prime Minister asked me to get the conventional acceptance from the British Prime Minister. . . .

Saturday, October 6, 1979

Flora has made some challengeable statements recently. She thinks we have been "international nice guys" too long. Our billions of dollars on aid have been "branded as imperialist."

6. Earl Rowe had been a Conservative member of Parliament and then the lieutenant governor of Ontario.
7. She had succeeded to her husband's seat in the House of Commons and was a member for Grenville-Dundas from 1958 to 1968. In October 1979, she was serving on the Ontario Municipal Board.

She would relate aid to economic and political policy. Our assistance to Pakistan did not prevent that country from attacking us in Havana. Our aid policy is under review, as is our peace-keeping policy. I think Flora has expressed an understandable reaction. I doubt the wisdom of her doing so.

Muzorewa has given formal notice of his acceptance of the British constitutional proposal. He will take part in new elections under British supervision. I believe the Patriotic Front will do likewise before the end of next week, perhaps by Wednesday. My reasoning is pure calculation. . . .

Sunday, October 7, 1979

If corridor gossip is right, the Lancaster House conference "has turned the corner." [Although] Muzorewa asserts the Patriotic Front leaders will accept the new constitution, they did not commit themselves. They will make it contingent on the transitional arrangements. Nkomo and Mugabe would not want to see a separate deal between Muzorewa and the British.

At Lady Camoys' [farewell] luncheon today at Stonor, Bruno, the Apostolic Delegate, wondered about the frequency of the papal ecumenical visits and pronouncements. He seemed to suggest a concern, not with ecumenical doctrine, but with the frequency of utterance and the bluntness of exposition. Others at the luncheon wondered too, but basically there was admiration for the Pope's orthodoxy, courage and communicating power. Perhaps his address to the General Assembly of the United Nations was too long. . . .

Monday, October 8, 1979

Air Canada "wins the fight to stay at Heathrow" is a headline in this morning's *Daily Telegraph*. . . . The story mentions the British agreement to allow China to fly into Heathrow. I raised hell about this when I saw Nott [the trade minister] a few weeks ago. I am sure that our opposition to this discrimination won, or will win, the day for us. . . .

Tuesday, October 9, 1979

General Arnold Brown, head of the Salvation Army, came to the office this morning prior to our call on the Chinese Ambassador. The General is a Canadian who holds the highest office in this great religious army. We discussed what his approach to the Ambassador should be. . . . I suspect the Chinese will extend a welcoming hand to the Salvation Army.

The Ambassador received us warmly. He had known of the Salvation Army when he was a young boy in China many years ago. The General put up a strong plea for admission to the most populous country in the world. The Salvation Army had had a well-established position in China. In the meantime, its properties had been confiscated. The Army would not ask for compensation or restoration of the properties. They had been taken over by a different régime in China. A liberalization is taking place in China's attitude towards organized religious bodies. I would be disappointed and surprised if this request to return to China were denied. . . .

I learned this afternoon with the greatest satisfaction that the Thatcher government will allow Air Canada to stay at Heathrow. . . . This has been a long and tiresome negotiation. In many ways it was one in which this High Commission took the initiative, before we had even received instructions from the Trudeau government. . . .

At our briefing on the Lancaster House negotiations on Rhodesia, we had a most difficult meeting. The African High Commissioners showed impatience with the take-it-or-leave-it attitude of the Foreign Secretary. My friend, the High Commissioner for Zambia,[8] reported that Sir Ian Gilmour, the Lord Privy Seal, had said to her and others, if the Patriotic Front does not wish to accept the British proposals, "they can take-it-and-lump-it." It was agreed, not with my full support, that there should be a meeting tomorrow of the Committee on South-Western Africa at which the Patriotic Front leaders, Mugabe and Nkomo, would state their objections to the British proposals. I intervened to say that we should not panic, a negotiation was under way in Lancaster House, the end had not been reached. . . . Would it not be better, I urged, to wait until the conference was over or close to an end before injecting an outside influence of significant proportion. . . .

If there was to be a meeting [with Commonwealth representatives] as proposed with the Patriotic Front, perhaps it

8. Phyllis Chibesakunda

should be informal and open to all sides. That, however, is not the way matters turned out. Tomorrow, an informal meeting will take place with Mugabe and Nkomo present. A plea to hear Muzorewa got nowhere. The Nigerian High Commissioner said his government did not recognize that administration. It was impossible to sit at the same table with the Bishop. I ridiculed this suggestion. We didn't recognize Muzorewa either, but that was no reason why we couldn't have an informal chat about matters of such importance. . . .

Wednesday, October 10, 1979

Flora's survey of Canadian foreign policy addressed itself to many questions requiring answers. Her speech [last week] to the Empire Club I think was basically an error. It would be a mistake for us to appear nineteenth- and not twentieth-century in our approach. We don't want to appear a scrooge in the world family nor must we be profligate. We must, however, be prepared to render a helping hand to dependent peoples. I certainly don't agree with her question, ". . . do we care about Namibia?" We, of course, do. We are members of the United Nations. We have a world responsibility. If we don't accept it, are many other countries likely to? . . . Flora is right to be pragmatic but there is nothing wrong in statements pointing to ideals. I find it hard to say anything critical of Flora—I like her so much. . . .

Friday, October 12, 1979

Bob Stanfield, on his way back from his Middle East mission to get Joe off his "faux pas" for suggesting Canada might move its Embassy from Tel Aviv to Jerusalem, dropped in to tell me how he got along. Clark could not have picked a better man for that purpose. Displaying his rich sense of humour, he mentioned what an "easy-going" lot the Iraqis are. . . .

John Turner is ill with the 'flu at the Dorchester. We had a word on the telephone. Even John can't transmit a germ over the telephone. Is he waiting in the wings? He is, of course. Hoarsely, he said he does not know when Trudeau will step down. Trudeau must not be forced out. . . .

At the meeting with the Patriotic Front yesterday at Marlborough House, it was made clear that the Patriotic Front will attach reservations to their acceptance of the constitution. . . . The two Patriotic Front leaders expressed concern that acceptance of the constitution could lead to its implementation unilaterally. There is pressure from some Commonwealth countries to convene a Commonwealth committee on Southern Africa to provide for expression of Commonwealth opinion, if the conference in Lancaster House reaches deadlock. . . . It was encouraging that Mugabe said the Patriotic Front would not walk out of the conference. They would insist on proceeding to the second item of the agenda—holding onto its reservation about some aspects of the constitution. Nkomo expects most of these reservations would fall away, once agreement was reached on the interim arrangements. . . .

At last, we have received a press release about Jean's appointment as my successor. My colleagues and the Upper Brook Street staff have been assured what a fine person she will prove to be. In his announcement, Joe mentions the special relationship between the Prime Minister and the High Commissioner in London. He mentions her experience in Parliament and diplomacy. Jean has served at the United Nations, once, I think, in my time as External Affairs Minister. Bob Stanfield had not known of the appointment until he saw me this morning. He hopes John Robarts will not be overlooked by Joe for something else. I share that hope. . . .

Sunday, October 14, 1979

The same political party in both Houses of Parliament in Canada does not always agree. A caller discloses that a move is afoot to make Marchand [the] assistant house leader in the Senate and ultimately leader. The Senate insists on making its own appointments and . . . does not favour the national leader's intervention. All the same, it would be prudent to have a working arrangement among Trudeau, Perrault, and the Liberal Senators. In any event, Marchand would be a disaster. Perrault has done well [as Senate leader]. Is it true that he was closed out of a meeting of the Liberal shadow cabinet? Oh well, I am glad to be out of that kind of situation.

Marchand has had trouble wherever he has moved. It would be a mistake to make him Senate leader. . . .

Tuesday, October 16, 1979

When I was waiting for Bob Stanfield to arrive at the Foreign Office for his meeting yesterday with Blaker, the Minister of State, some of Nkomo's and Mugabe's assistants were in the Foreign Office waiting room. Nkomo and Mugabe were with Lord Carrington. They had been there for some time. Their meeting, I am told, was the most critical in the negotiations at Lancaster House since the conference began. . . .

After we had seen Blaker, I had a chat with Antony Duff who told me at the meeting with the Foreign Secretary, the Patriotic Front leaders were told by Carrington what he proposed to do. They would not be able to participate in talks today on implementing the constitution, unless they accepted the terms agreed to by the Bishop and the British government. What will happen today is not clear. It may be presumed the Front's aim has been to wear out the British, get them to agree to postpone the unresolved issues over the constitution and proceed to a three-way discussion on the transition period before full independence. . . .

We gave the first of our large farewell receptions tonight for some two hundred people. I need not emphasize how glad I was to jump into bed when it was over.

At the end of our reception, the High Commissioners for Ghana and Grenada came to report on the briefing meeting at Marlborough House. Sonny Ramphal received the endorsement of the High Commissioners for the stand he took in criticizing Lord Carrington's unwillingness, "in spite of Lusaka," to recognize the position of the Patriotic Front regarding the proposed constitution. They believe there is a good chance that Mugabe and Nkomo, given certain clarifications, might be able to move towards acceptance of the constitution and participate in the second phase of discussions with the Foreign Secretary. I strongly urged, in view of the progress made towards providing compensation for land in Rhodesia, it would be the grossest folly and tragedy if a solution was not found, thereby bringing an end to the conflict. . . .

Wednesday, October 17, 1979

I went to see the Secretary of State this morning at the Foreign Office at 9:00 o'clock with Bob Stanfield. Peter made casual mention of Ramphal's criticism and expressed the hope that the Patriotic Front would return to the table. Stanfield outlined his tour and got little encouragement from the British Secretary of State for moving our Embassy to Jerusalem from Tel Aviv. . . .

When I saw Peter Carrington this morning at the Foreign Office, he raised with me, as did Michael Palliser, some questions regarding Flora's speech before the Empire Club of Toronto. I am told by my Ottawa masters that . . . the . . . speech must be viewed against the general . . . intention to ensure that foreign policy is seen by Canadians as relevant to identifiable Canadian interests. It was intended as well to encourage domestic participation in the foreign policy process and to stimulate input from Canadians outside the government. . . . Miss MacDonald's reference to Namibia, however, did not imply that we would withdraw from an exercise at a decisive stage in the contact group endeavours. My instructions add:

> It has struck her, as it has a number of her colleagues, that Namibia has involved an expenditure of resources and diplomatic effort which could not by any stretch of imagination be justified on grounds of real Canadian interest or responsibility alone.

My reaction to that is, we certainly cannot formulate foreign policy on that narrow basis and if the government pursues that standard our foreign policy will indeed not merit the name. . . .

The dinner in our honour by Lord Carrington . . . was one that rounds off this period of goodbye gatherings. . . . I will always remember this dinner for a number of reasons, foremost because of Peter's frank comment on the personalities involved in the present Lancaster House discussions. There is universal dissatisfaction with Smith. Nkomo is as jovial a personality, in Carrington's judgment, as any of the other actors. Given an opportunity by Smith years ago, he might have been the best possible leader for Rhodesia under a new constitution with a black majority. I found the Secretary of State pessimistic about the outcome of the talks at Lancaster House, certainly within the time frame of the limits set for economic sanctions against Rhodesia.

On the way home, I remarked the dinner really marked the end of our official life in London, apart from calling on the Queen tomorrow. The Foreign Secretary's dinner epitomizes the nature of a High Commissioner's assignment. With the official goodbye at the Foreign Office, there was not much left but to go. Nell thought that it had been a memorable evening. She was impressed with Carrington and his performance. She thought I discharged my own satisfactorily.

Thursday, October 18, 1979

Nell and I called on the Queen at Buckingham Palace after 12:00 o'clock for our farewell audience. Normally, this would last fifteen minutes. We were with Her Majesty for over thirty-five minutes. I sat in the same chair next to her where I had sat five years ago when she first received us. Nell sitting opposite, looking radiant in a new green dress, seemed precisely as she was when we came at that time.

The Queen was her gracious self, much like a kind friend and neighbour next door. She began "and so you're going, life is that way. I see so many come and go. I am sorry to see both of you depart." She mentioned she had given instructions for her horses, originally given to her by the Mounted Police, to be used in the Lord Mayor's procession. We had a good laugh about what "horse furniture" meant. . . .

"What was my impression of the talks at Lancaster House?" I mentioned the Foreign Secretary's pessimism as to the outcome. "Could that be a tactic on his part?" she asked. I had already anticipated this possibility in my record of yesterday. It interested me to note the Queen had seen this herself, or perhaps she had been told. She spoke of Lusaka and cleverly injected the importance of the Crown in that situation. She didn't minimize her contribution in outlining her conversations with various Prime Ministers at luncheons and similar gatherings. She had talked quite frankly to them. Not that she was involved herself in policy making. . . .

Her last words and ours were like those of friendly neighbours saying goodbye. "I will see you again," said the Queen—

"You are likely to be back this way and I am likely to be in Ottawa. We must keep in touch. I hope you enjoyed being here. We were glad to have you in Britain." The Queen gave Nell a beautifully bound frame of her latest picture and a corresponding one of Prince Philip. She said, "I know you have many pictures of us but you might as well have the latest." . . .

Once more tonight the parade of farewell parties. I was glad that so many of my staff . . . were present. What makes these parties difficult for me is not the party itself but that so many well-meaning friends say, "How sad to see you go." The repetition of that farewell is beginning to get me down. I am beginning to think that it is sad. Am I wrong to go at this time? . . .

Friday, October 19, 1979

Optimism prevailed in another quarter, when Mugabe and Nkomo, the Patriotic Front leaders, indicated they did not want to be left out of the Lancaster House discussions. They would not want Carrington to sew up a deal with Bishop Muzorewa and, in a document handed to the foreign secretary, said, "If we are satisfied beyond doubt about the vital issues of the transitional arrangements, it will not be necessary to revert to discussions on the constitution." Carrington wisely accepted this formula, although it doesn't amount to an official acceptance of the constitution. . . .

I must note that this is the first morning in five years, I think, that I have not been at my desk before 8:00 o'clock. . . .

Saturday, October 20, 1979

This is likely to be my last weekend in my library at 12 Upper Brook. What a fine room it is. It did not seem so when we arrived five years ago. Nell added so many good touches, cheerful and colourful seating arrangements. My many books have not only been my companions, they give life to this lovely room. I will miss it.

At Lancaster House, Peter had problems yesterday. Muzorewa announced his government would not stand down during elections. He asserted the British would not be impartial supervisors of a new election. During the interim, Muzorewa would have to leave office. There would be a dismantling of the armed forces. The British cannot act as supervisors of the elections. Mugabe says, "they have their bias." The battle for the upper hand is on. Carrington will distribute his proposals for the transition over the weekend. He thinks a cease-fire would be in jeopardy if the elections were delayed too long. . . .

Perhaps my visit to Hatchard's this morning was my last before returning home. Hopefully I will come back to this great "source of supply" often in the future. . . . This morning I got Wilson's *Final Term.*[9] . . . When I came here five years ago, I assumed that Wilson would be in the saddle throughout. He resigned as Prime Minister in 1976. And so, I have served as High Commissioner under three Prime Ministers of Britain. . . .

Mrs. Judith Chalones, the friendly American who sells Father Blake's books at Farm Street Church, gave me a parting gift last Thursday, when she and her husband were at our reception at 12 Upper Brook. On one of our many exchanges in the Book Room at Farm Street, I told Judith how difficult I found it to pray. Many years ago, St. Laurent, then Prime Minister, said the same to my Nell, who does and knows how to pray. The gift was a book by a Capuchin friar . . . "a personal journey into prayer." . . .

Monday, October 22, 1979

I visited two floors of Macdonald House this morning, saying goodbye to my staff. I find this a heart-breaking performance. It is not easy to say goodbye to one's personnel after five years of association. . . .

Wednesday, October 24, 1979

The conference at Lancaster House goes on while Zimbabwe-Rhodesian air and ground forces destroyed a heavily fortified camp of Nkomo's guerrilla army. . . . It is amazing to me how the conference carries on while the war continues. . . .

9. Harold Wilson, *Final Term: The Labour Government, 1974-1976* (London 1979).

I paid my farewell call on Mrs. Thatcher this morning. She saw me in one of the drawing rooms at Number 10. The call lasted about twenty-five minutes. . . . She recalled her first meeting with me and the second when I called on her with Trudeau in March 1975. We discussed events during the five years. I was surprised that she had not known of my lengthy parliamentary service. She knew I had been in the Commons for some time, but when I mentioned I had been in Parliament for thirty-nine years, six of which was spent as Leader of the Government in the Senate, and almost twenty-three years as a minister, she gasped. I gave her occasion for a further gasp when I mentioned that I was [perhaps] the Commonwealth cabinet minister with the longest service after Lord Palmerston, Mackenzie King, and [Sir Robert] Walpole. . . .

I mentioned how important it was for the Prime Ministers of Canada and . . . Britain to keep in touch with one another. Churchill during the war had come and spoken to our Parliament four times, as had Eden and Macmillan. No Labour Prime Minister had ever done so, although Harold Wilson never came to America without coming to Canada, and never to Canada without going to Washington. We fully understood that on her December trip [to Washington] it was not possible for Mrs. Thatcher to be away for more than the two days she was taking. We drew some satisfaction from her assurance that she would come to Canada early in 1980. She said, ". . . I do appreciate everything that you say about the continuing contact with the head of the government of Canada." I might have added she would find it mutually advantageous. . . .

When I came out of the meeting it was a little past the time for cabinet. Most of the members of the cabinet were in the lobby. I must say they were kind and thoughtful. I was warmly greeted by [Peter] Walker, the Minister of Agriculture; John Nott, Minister of Trade; my friend, Lord Hailsham; Peter Carrington who said he had found out where [Lord] Durham was buried and had written accordingly; Christopher Soames; Willie Whitelaw, the Attorney-General and Geoffrey Howe. These I do remember vividly and they were all so generous. . . .

Most of the staff at Canada House and Macdonald House congregated in the reception area at Macdonald House to say goodbye. . . . I sought to avoid mentioning names of particular personnel, making an exception inadvertently of John Rowan. I wanted the staff to know I valued them all. I have found these au revoir ceremonies generous but difficult to take. We become too emotionally involved. Afterwards, my office and household staff congregated in John's basement apartment. . . .

Thursday, October 25, 1979

Nell and I had lunch with the Secretary General of the Commonwealth Organization and Mrs. Ramphal at their home. . . . [Sonny] had said what a great man I was — statesman, international affairs authority, and good High Commissioner. This mention of my attributes [contrasted with my situation], I said in derision. . . . This morning, I was greeted with a telegram from Ottawa from the bureaucracy telling me — the great statesman, great international affairs authority, the pride of Canada, the former Secretary of State for External Affairs — that External Affairs would pay for the transfer of my belongings in London to Ottawa but not to Windsor. This caused the merriment and laughter I intended. All had, in some way or another, at one time, experienced the bureaucracy's power and insensitivity. . . . My remarks at least supplied the material for what seemed a humorous speech. Nell thought it was my best. I was so angry that I had to find some way to get it out of my system and I got well rid of it in this way.

Nell and I had tea with Her Majesty, the Queen Mother, at Clarence House. She had generously asked us to lunch, but that hour had been pre-empted earlier. . . . She spoke of her last visit to Canada and expressed gratification for my part in the arrangements. She did not remember all her tours. . . . She would have liked us to stay longer. I explained we had our last reception tonight. . . . But, we must come back again, anytime, when in England. She gave Nell a beautiful snuff-box. . . . As we drove away from Clarence House, the immense personality of this remarkable woman had made its imprint.

Then, we were faced with several hundred people at 12 Upper Brook to say goodbye — the Lord Chief Justice of

England, Ministers of the Crown, former Ministers of the Crown, of whom I recall Tony Benn and Merlyn Rees, many High Commissioners—all to say goodbye.

Friday, October 26, 1979

I noticed . . . the following in yesterday's *Daily Telegraph*:

> Canada's High Commissioner, Paul Martin, said his farewell to Mrs. Thatcher in Downing Street at breakfast time yesterday. . . .

No conclusion should be drawn from the early hour of the Downing Street visit. Both participants are firm believers in the advantage of early birds over worms. . . .

Tuesday, October 30, 1979

I received the following message this morning from Flora MacDonald . . . :

> Your assignment in London . . . provided all of us with an example of the many benefits . . . that can be obtained by pursuing a second or, indeed, a third career. . . . Keep on swimming . . . !

Wednesday, October 31, 1979

I received the following . . . this morning from Prime Minister Joe Clark . . . as I leave this post:

> I appreciated report on your final call on Mrs. Thatcher and sense of tradition it conveyed. I too look forward to seeing her here in 1980 at which time we will undoubtedly reflect on your invaluable personal contribution to Canada-U.K. relations.

List of Characters

This list includes the people most frequently mentioned in the diaries. Many of them are politicians, and for the most part, they are identified by nationality and political party, and by the offices they held during the years 1975-79. Other individuals are identified simply by the positions held at that time or by their particular significance for the author of the diaries. In the text, an asterisk following a name indicates that the person will be listed below.

Abbott, Anthony Canadian, Liberal; minister of consumer and corporate affairs, 1976-77; minister of national revenue, 1978-79.

Allmand, Warren Canadian, Liberal; minister of Indian affairs and northern development, 1976; minister of consumer and corporate affairs, 1977-79.

Amin, Idi President of Uganda from 1971 until overthrown by Tanzanian-led troops in 1979.

Amory, Derick Amory, Viscount British Conservative minister from 1951; chancellor of the exchequer, 1958-60; high commissioner to Canada, 1961-63.

Andras, Robert Canadian, Liberal; minister of manpower and immigration, 1972-76; president of the Treasury Board, 1976; president, Board of Economic Development from 1978.

Armstrong, Anne U.S. ambassador to Britain, 1976-77.

Assad, Hafez al- President of Syria, 1971-

Austin, Jacob (Jack) Canadian, Liberal; principal secretary to Prime Minister Trudeau and deputy minister of energy, mines and resources to 1975; appointed senator in August 1975.

Barnetson, William Barnetson, Baron Chairman, United Newspapers Ltd from 1966; chairman, Reuters Ltd, 1968-79.

Basford, Ron Canadian, Liberal; minister of justice and attorney general from 1975; resigned from House of Commons, February 1979.

Begin, Menachem Prime minister of Israel, 1977-83.

Bégin, Monique Canadian, Liberal; minister of national revenue, 1976-77; minister of national health and welfare, 1977-79.

Benn, Anthony Wedgwood British, Labour; secretary of state for industry, 1974-75; secretary of state for energy, 1975-79.

Bishop, Maurice Led a coup which took over the government of Grenada in March 1979.

Bissonnette, André Canadian deputy high commissioner to London, 1972-75; deputy under-secretary of state for external affairs, 1975-77.

Blakeney, Allan Canadian, New Democrat; premier of Saskatchewan, 1971-82.

Botha, Matthys South Africa's ambassador to Britain, 1977-79.

Botha, Roelof Frederik (Pik) South African minister of foreign affairs, 1977- .

Bottomley, Arthur British, Labour; member of Parliament, 1945-59, 1962-83; cabinet minister, 1964-67.

Bourassa, Robert Canadian, Liberal; premier of Quebec, 1970-76.

Brewster, Kingman U.S. ambassador to Britain, 1977-81.

Brimelow, Thomas Brimelow, Baron Permanent under-secretary of state in the Foreign and Commonwealth Office and head of the diplomatic service, 1973-75; member of the European Parliament, 1977-78.

Burns, Robert Canadian, Parti Québécois; minister of state for parliamentary reform and parliamentary house leader, Quebec National Assembly, 1976-79.

Butler, Esmond Canadian; secretary to the governor general of Canada, 1954-85.

Butler of Saffron Walden, Richard Austen (Rab) Butler, Baron British, Conservative; master of Trinity College, Cambridge, 1965-78.

Cadieux, Marcel Canadian, diplomat; head, Canadian Mission to European Community, Brussels, 1975-80.

Callaghan, James British, Labour; prime minister of Britain, April 1976 until May 1979.

Camp, Dalton Canadian, Progressive Conservative; president of Progressive Conservatives (1964-69), helped to force John Diefenbaker out of the party leadership.

Carrington, Peter Carrington, Baron British, Conservative; leader of the opposition in the House of Lords, 1974-79; secretary of state for foreign and Commonwealth affairs, 1979-82.

Carter, Jimmy Democrat; president of the United States, 1977-81.

Castle, Barbara British, Labour; secretary of state for social services, 1974-76.

Castro, Fidel Prime minister of Cuba, 1959-

Charteris, Sir Martin Private secretary to the Queen, 1972-77; appointed lord-in-waiting and provost of Eton College in 1978.

Chevrier, Lionel Canadian, Liberal; cabinet minister, 1945-54, 1963-64; high commissioner to the U.K., 1964-67.

Chirau, Jeremiah Headed Zimbabwe United Peoples' Organization; member of four-man executive council set up as a result of the Internal Settlement in Rhodesia-Zimbabwe, 1978-79.

Chrétien, Jean Canadian, Liberal; president of the Treasury Board, 1974-77; minister of finance, 1977-79.

Clark, Joe Canadian, Progressive Conservative; leader of the opposition 1976-79; prime minister, 1979-80.

Compton, John Premier of St Lucia, 1967-79, and its first prime minister after independence, February-July 1979.

Cornell, Ward Agent-general for Ontario in London, 1972-78.

Coutts, James Canadian, Liberal; principal secretary to Prime Minister Trudeau, 1975-79.

Couve de Murville, Maurice Prime minister of France, 1968-69; deputy, French National Assembly, 1973- .

Crosbie, John Canadian, Progressive Conservative; minister of finance, 1979-80.

Crosland, Anthony British, Labour; secretary of state for the environment, 1974-76; secretary of state for foreign and Commonwealth affairs, 1976-77.

Cullen, Jack (Bud) Canadian, Liberal; minister of national revenue, 1975-76; minister of employment and immigration, 1976-79.

Danson, Barnett J. (Barney) Canadian, Liberal; minister of state for urban affairs, 1974-76; minister of national defence, 1976-79.

Davey, Keith Canadian, Liberal; senator and party strategist.

de Cotret, Robert Canadian, Progressive Conservative; senator, minister for industry, trade and commerce, and minister of state for economic development, 1979-80.

Dell, Edmund British, Labour; secretary of state for trade, 1976-78.

Denning, Alfred Thompson (Thomas) Denning, Baron British; a judge and master of the rolls, 1962-82.

Diefenbaker, John Canadian, Progressive Conservative; prime minister, 1957-63.

Drapeau, Jean Mayor of Montreal, 1960-86.

Drury, Charles Mills (Bud) Canadian, Liberal; minister of public works and minister of state for science and technology, 1974-76.

Duff, Sir Antony British; diplomatic, deputy under-secretary of state, 1975-80.

Dupuy, Michel Canadian; diplomat.

Ennals, David British, Labour; secretary of state at the Foreign and Commonwealth Office, 1974-76; secretary of state for social services, 1976-79.

Faulkner, Hugh Canadian, Liberal; secretary of state, 1972-76; minister of state for science and technology, 1976-77; minister of Indian affairs and northern development, 1977-79.

Fleming, Donald Canadian, Progressive Conservative; cabinet minister, 1957-63.

Foot, Michael British, Labour; secretary of state for employment, 1974-76; leader of the House of Commons, 1976-79.

Ford, Gerald Republican, president of the United States, 1974-77.

Fournier, Jean Agent-general for Quebec in London, 1971-78.

Fraser, Malcolm Liberal, prime minister of Australia, 1975-83.

Gauvin, Michel Canadian; diplomat, consul general in Strasbourg, France, 1976-78; Canadian secretary to the Queen and co-ordinator of royal visits, 1976-77; ambassador to Morocco, 1978-80.

George-Brown, George Alfred George-Brown, Baron British, Labour; deputy leader of the British Labour party, 1960-70; member of the House of Lords.

Gillespie, Alastair Canadian, Liberal; minister of energy, mines and resources, 1975-79.

Giscard d'Estaing, Valéry President of France, 1974-81.

Gordon, Walter Canadian, Liberal; minister of finance, 1963-65; president of the Privy Council, 1967-68.

Goronwy-Roberts, Owen Goronwy-Roberts, Baron British, Labour; minister of state at the Foreign and Commonwealth Office and deputy leader, House of Lords, 1975-79.

Gotlieb, Allan Canadian; diplomat, under-secretary of state for external affairs, 1977-81.

Graham, John British; diplomat, ambassador to Iraq, 1974-77; deputy under-secretary at the Foreign and Commonwealth Office, 1977-79.

Green, Lorne A career foreign service officer and assistant at the High Commission.

Gromyko, Andrei U.S.S.R. minister of foreign affairs, 1957-85.

Halstead, John Canadian ambassador to West Germany, 1975-80.

Hamson, Jack An old friend from my student days at Cambridge.

Hardy, Christian Canadian; deputy high commissioner to the U.K., 1975-81.

Hart, Dame Judith British, Labour; minister of overseas development, 1977-79.

Hattersley, Roy British, Labour; minister of state in the Foreign and Commonwealth Office, 1974-76; secretary of state for prices and consumer protection, 1976-79.

Head, Ivan Canadian; adviser on foreign policy in the Prime Minister's Office, 1970-78.

Healey, Denis British, Labour; chancellor of the exchequer, 1974-79.

Heath, Edward (Ted) British, Conservative; prime minister, 1970-74; leader of the Conservative party, 1965-75.

Hees, George Canadian, Progressive Conservative; member of John Diefenbaker's cabinet, 1957-63; member of Parliament, 1950-63, 1965-

Hellyer, Paul Canadian, Liberal; a cabinet colleague in the 1960s.

Home of the Hirsel, Alexander (Alec) Douglas-Home, Baron British, Conservative; secretary of state for foreign affairs, 1960-63; prime minister, 1963-64.

Hunt, Sir John British; a civil service officer who served as secretary to the cabinet, 1973-79.

Ignatieff, George Canadian; retired diplomat.

Jamieson, Donald (Don) Canadian, Liberal; minister of industry, trade and commerce, 1975-76; secretary of state for external affairs, 1976-79.

Jay, Peter British; ambassador to the United States, 1977-79.

Jenkins, Roy British, Labour; home secretary, 1974-76; president of the European Commission, 1977-81.

Jones, James (Jack) British; general secretary of the Transport and General Workers' Union, 1969-78.

Judd, Frank British, Labour; minister of state in the Foreign and Commonwealth Office, 1977-79.

Kaunda, Kenneth President of Zambia, 1964-

Khrushchev, Nikita General secretary of the Communist Party and prime minister of the U.S.S.R., 1958-64.

Killanin, Michael Morris, Baron President of the International Olympic Committee, 1972-80.

King, William Lyon Mackenzie Canadian, Liberal; prime minister, 1921-30, 1935-48.

Kissinger, Henry U.S. secretary of state, 1973-77.

Kosygin, Alexsei Chairman of the U.S.S.R. Council of Ministers (prime minister) from October 1964, later sharing leadership with Leonid Brezhnev.

Lalonde, Marc Canadian, Liberal; minister of state for federal-provincial relations, 1977-78; minister of justice and attorney general, 1978-79.

Lang, Otto Canadian, Liberal; minister of justice and attorney general, 1972-75; minister of transport, 1975-79.

Léger, Jules Governor general of Canada, 1974-79.

Lesage, Jean Canadian, Liberal; premier of Quebec, 1960-66.

Lévesque, René Canadian, Parti Québécois; premier of Quebec, 1976-85.

Lloyd, John Selwyn Brooke Lloyd, Baron British, Conservative; former cabinet minister, speaker of the House of Commons, 1971-76.

Lougheed, Peter Canadian, Progressive Conservative; premier of Alberta, 1971-85.

Luns, Joseph Secretary general of NATO, 1971-84.

MacDonald, David Canadian, Progressive Conservative; secretary of state, 1979-80.

Macdonald, Donald Canadian, Liberal; minister of energy, mines and resources, 1972-75, minister of finance, 1975-77; left Parliament in 1977.

MacDonald, Flora Canadian, Progressive Conservative; member of Parliament, 1972- ; minister of external affairs, 1979-80.

MacDonald, Malcolm British, Labour; former politician, diplomat, and an old friend.

MacEachen, Allan Canadian, Liberal; secretary of state for external affairs, 1974-76; president of the Privy Council, 1976-79; deputy prime minister, 1977-79.

MacGuigan, Mark Canadian, Liberal; member of Parliament for Windsor-Walkerville, 1968-79; minister of external affairs, 1980-82.

Machel, Samora President of Mozambique.

Mackasey, Bryce Canadian, Liberal; minister of labour, 1968-72; postmaster general, 1974-76; minister of consumer and corporate affairs, 1976; resigned to run for the Quebec National Assembly.

Maclean, Charles (Chips) Maclean, Baron British; chamberlain of the Queen's household, 1971-84.

Macmillan, Harold British, Conservative; prime minister, 1957-63.

Marchand, Jean Canadian, Liberal; minister of transport, 1972-75; minister without portfolio in 1975; appointed senator, 1976.

Mason, Roy British, Labour; secretary of state for Northern Ireland, 1976-79.

Massey, Vincent Canadian; high commissioner to the U.K., 1935-46; governor general, 1952-59.

Michener, Roland Canadian; governor general, 1967-74.

Moore, Sir Philip Private secretary to the Queen, 1977-86.

Moores, Frank Canadian, Progressive Conservative; premier of Newfoundland, 1972-79.

Morin, Claude Canadian, Parti Québécois; minister of intergovernmental affairs in the Quebec government, 1976-81.

Morris, Joe President of the Canadian Labour Congress, 1974-78.

Mugabe, Robert Co-founder of Zimbabwe African National Union, 1963; joint leader of the Patriotic Front with Joshua Nkomo, 1976-79.

Muldoon, Robert Prime minister of New Zealand, 1975-84.

Muller, Hilgard Minister of foreign affairs for South Africa, 1964-77.

Mulley, Fred British, Labour; minister in the Department of Transport and Department of the Environment, 1974-75; secretary of state for education and science, 1975-76; secretary of state for defence, 1976-79.

Mulroney, Brian Canadian; Progressive Conservative; ran unsuccessfully for the Conservative party leadership in 1976 (and successfully in 1983).

Munro, John Canadian, Liberal; minister of labour, 1972-78.

Muzorewa, Abel Zimbabwean ecclesiastic and member of the transitional executive council of Zimbabwe-Rhodesia, 1978-79; prime minister, June-December 1979.

Nkomo, Joshua Organized the Zimbabwe African People's Union (ZAPU) which amalgamated with others to form the African National Council in 1974; joint leader with Robert Mugabe of the Patriotic Front in 1976-79.

Nyerere, Julius President of Tanzania, 1964-85.

Owen, David British, Labour; minister of state in the Foreign and Commonwealth Office, 1976-77; secretary of state for foreign and commonwealth affairs, 1977-79.

Palliser, Sir Michael British; permanent under-secretary of state at the Foreign and Commonwealth Office, 1975-82.

Parizeau, Jacques Canadian, Parti Québécois; became Quebec minister of finance and minister of revenue in 1976.

Pearson, Lester B. (Mike) Canadian, Liberal; prime minister, 1963-68.

Pelletier, Gérard Canadian, Liberal; ambassador to Paris, 1975-81.

Perrault, Raymond Canadian, Liberal; leader of the government in the Senate, 1974-79.

Pickersgill, John (Jack) A colleague and cabinet minister in the St Laurent and Pearson governments, 1953-67.

Pitfield, Michael Canadian; clerk of the Privy Council and secretary to the cabinet, 1975-79.

Pliatzky, Sir Leo British; a career civil service officer, permanent secretary of trade, 1977-79.

Price The butler at the High Commission in London.

Ramphal, Sir Shridath (Sonny) Minister for foreign affairs and justice of Guyana; secretary general of the Commonwealth, 1975-

Rees, Merlyn British, Labour; secretary of state for Northern Ireland, 1974-76; secretary of state for home affairs, 1976-79.

Regan, Gerald Canadian, Liberal; premier of Nova Scotia, 1970-79.

Richardson, Elliot U.S. ambassador to Britain, 1975-76.

Ritchie, A. E. (Ed) Canadian; diplomat, ambassador to Ireland, 1976-82.

Ritchie, Charles Canadian; diplomat, high commissioner to London, 1967-71. He began publishing his diaries once he retired.

Robarts, John Canadian, Progressive Conservative; premier of Ontario, 1961-71.

Roberts, Dick Canadian; diplomat, officer of the Department of External Affairs.

Roberts, John Canadian, Liberal; secretary of state, 1976-79.

Robertson, R. G. (Gordon) Clerk of the Privy Council and secretary to the cabinet, 1963-75; secretary to the cabinet for federal-provincial relations, 1975-79.

Ross, Sir Alexander Chairman, Commonwealth Games Federation, 1968-82.

Rowan, John Driver at the High Commission.

Rusk, Dean U.S. secretary of state, 1961-69.

Ryan, Claude Canadian, Liberal; publisher of *Le Devoir*, 1964-78; leader of the Quebec Liberal party, 1978-82.

Sadat, Mohammed Anwar El- President of Egypt, 1970-81.

Sauvé, Jeanne Canadian, Liberal; minister of communications, 1975-79.

Sauvé, Maurice Canadian, Liberal; a cabinet colleague in the Pearson government, 1964-68.

Schmidt, Helmut Chancellor of Germany, 1974-82.

Schreyer, Edward Canadian, New Democrat; premier of Manitoba, 1969-77; leader of the opposition in the Manitoba legislature, 1977-78; governor general of Canada, 1979-84.

Sharp, Mitchell Canadian, Liberal; secretary of state for external affairs, 1968-74; president of the Privy Council, 1974-76.

Shore, Peter British, Labour; secretary of state for trade, 1974-76; secretary of state for the environment, 1976-79.

Short, Edward British, Labour; leader of the House of Commons, 1974-76, with responsibility for devolution.

Silkin, Samuel British, Labour; attorney general, 1974-79.

Sithole, Ndabaningi Leader of the Zimbabwe African National Union from 1963.

Smith, Arnold Canadian; diplomat, secretary general of the Commonwealth, 1965-75.

Smith, Ian Prime minister of Rhodesia, 1964-79

Smith, John British, Labour; minister of state, Department of Energy, 1975-76; minister of state, Privy Council Office, 1976-78; secretary of state for trade, 1978-79.

Stanfield, Robert Canadian; leader of the Progressive Conservative party until February 1975.

Steel, David British, Liberal; leader of the Liberal party, 1976-87.

Strong, Maurice Canadian; executive director of the United Nations Environmental Program, 1972-75.

Thatcher, Margaret British, Conservative; leader of the opposition, 1975-79; prime minister, 1979-

Thorneycroft, Peter Thorneycroft, Baron British; chairman of the Conservative party from 1975.

Thornton, Sir Peter British; permanent secretary of trade, 1974-77.

Thorpe, Jeremy British; leader of the Liberal party, 1967-76.

Thorson, Donald Canadian; deputy minister of justice and deputy attorney general, 1973-77; constitutional adviser to the prime minister, 1977-78.

Towe, Peter Canadian; diplomat, assistant under-secretary of state for external affairs, 1975-77; ambassador to Washington from 1977.

Trudeau, Pierre Elliott Canadian, Liberal; prime minister, 1968-79, 1980-84.

Turner, John Canadian, Liberal; minister of finance, 1972-76; resigned in 1976 (and became leader of the Liberal party in 1984).

Vance, Cyrus U.S. secretary of state in the Carter administration since 1977.

Varley, Eric British, Labour; secretary of state for energy, 1974-75; secretary of state for industry, 1975-79.

Vorster, Johannes Prime minister of South Africa, 1977-78.

Wagner, Claude Canadian; a former Quebec cabinet minister who became a judge. He resigned the bench to run federally for the Conservatives and then ran unsuccessfully for the federal party leadership in 1976.

Waldheim, Kurt Austrian; secretary general of the United Nations, 1972-81.

Warren, Jack (Jake) Canadian, diplomat; high commissioner to Britain, 1971-74; ambassador to the United States, 1975-77; Canadian co-ordinator for Multilateral Trade Negotiations, 1977-79.

Whelan, Eugene Canadian, Liberal; minister of agriculture, 1972-79.

Williams, Shirley British, Labour; secretary of state for prices and consumer protection, 1974-76; secretary of state for education and science, 1976-79.

Wilson, Harold British, Labour; prime minister, 1964-70 and 1974-76.

Abbreviations

BA	British Airways
BNA Act	British North America Act
BP	British Petroleum
C.H.	Companion of Honour
C.I.A.L.S.	Canadian Institute for Advanced Legal Studies
CIDA	Canadian International Development Agency
C.I.E.C.	Conference on International Economic Co-operation
C.I.I.A.	Canadian Institute of International Affairs
CLC	Canadian Labour Congress
CNR	Canadian National Railways
C.S.C.E.	Conference on Security and Co-operation in Europe
EEC	European Economic Community
Euratom	European Atomic Energy Commission
FLQ	Front de libération du Québec
GATT	General Agreement on Tariffs and Trade
h.c.	high commissioner
IAEA	International Atomic Energy Agency
I.D.R.C.	International Development Research Agency
IRA	Irish Republican Army
L.S.E.	London School of Economics
M.I.T.	Massachusetts Institute of Technology
MTN	Multilateral Trade Negotiations
NATO	North Atlantic Treaty Organization
NDP	New Democratic Party
NED	National Economic Development Council
NORAD	North American Air Defence Command
OAU	Organization of African Unity
OECD	Organization for Economic Co-operation and Development
OPEC	Organization of Petroleum Exporting Countries
PCO	Privy Council Office
PLO	Palestine Liberation Organization
PMO	Prime Minister's Office
PQ	Parti Québécois
SNP	Scottish National Party
SWAPO	South-West African Peoples' Organization

TUC	Trades Union Congress
UDI	Unilateral Declaration of Independence
UN	United Nations
UNCTAD	United Nations Conference on Trade and Development
VAT	Value Added Tax
ZANU	Zimbabwe African National Union
ZAPU	Zimbabwe African People's Union

Index